Social Foundations of Education

Social Foundations of Education

A Cross-Cultural Approach

COLE S. BREMBECK
Michigan State University

John Wiley and Sons, Inc.
New York · London · Sydney

To the memory of H.S.B. and P.J.B.

master teachers, unawares

Preface

This book is about human beings who live and work together in schools; it is also about human beings outside the schools who are concerned, for a variety of reasons, with what happens on the inside. The book's characters are children, teachers, administrators, parents, and other citizens. Its theme is what every teacher knows, that the school is a social environment. The most important things that happen in the school result from human interaction.

Children, teachers, administrators, parents, and other citizens do not live in isolation, cut off from their fellows. They are whole human beings linked together by social ties. We call the product of this interplay of personalities in schools education, for education is a social process.

The teacher who seeks new insights into his art may well find them in the study of education as a social process. Such inquiry opens wide vistas of understanding. The child who rebels and strikes out, the slow learner, the gifted, the disadvantaged, the advantaged, the adolescent and his peer group, indeed the teacher, principal, and parent can all be better understood as members of their social environment inside and outside of the school. The prospective teacher and the in-service teacher can make no better investment in their professional futures than to study the influence of social environment on students' learning and on their own teaching. The purpose of this book is to help them receive the best return on this investment.

What are the appropriate uses for this book? It is designed as a text for students and in-service teachers in teacher education programs which go by a variety of titles but which have in common a consideration of the social aspects of education. A recent survey of course titles in this subject matter area reveals the following listings: Social

Foundations of Education, Foundations of Education, Educational Sociology, Sociology of Education, Introduction to Education, Foundations of American Education, School and Society, Education in the American Social Order, and The Social and Historical Foundations of Education. The broad scope of this book is intended to make it a useful tool for both students and instructors in the subject matter areas represented by these and similar course titles.

The book is divided into six main parts and twenty-one chapters. I would like briefly to describe the substance of the six parts.

Part I deals with the social aspects of teaching and learning. The first two chapters set the cross-cultural tone of the book by describing four children who are growing up in contrasting social environments, a suburb, a city slum, a small town (all American), and a Pakistani village. Each child brings to school his unique way of life. Chapters 3, 4, and 5 consider the classroom as a little society, the conditions which make for good mental health and learning, and the ways in which a teacher can improve the learning climate of the classroom.

Part II turns from the social environment of the school to that of the student's family and peer group. However, the school is not forgotten. The family and peer group both influence the student's adjustment and achievement in school. The nature of this influence is described and illustrated in Chapters 6 and 7.

Part III analyzes social-class influences on learning. The interest today in the problems of socially disadvantaged students indicates our awareness of how a child's social class influences his progress in school. Chapter 8 describes the attitudes toward education held by people in different social classes. Chapter 9 takes a sympathetic look at students who strive to move up. Chapter 10 is directed at the problem of teaching socially disadvantaged students and at what teachers can do.

Part IV is entitled The Schools. Does a school have a unique cultural style? Chapter 11 describes the cultural values which pervade four types of schools. It describes the human behavior which flows from these values through students, teachers, administrators, parents, and citizens. It gives insight to the teacher who wants to understand the cultural values of a particular school. The remaining three chapters of Part IV analyze the school as a society in which students, teachers, administrators, board of education members, parents, and citizens interact with one another.

Part V focuses on the teachers. What is involved in the decision to teach? What motivates a person to make the decision? What do we know about the characteristics of good teachers? Chapter 15 deals with these questions. Chapter 16 describes the revolution that is taking place in methods of teaching and learning. The new technology of education and new methods for teaching are described and illustrated.

Part VI, Chapters 17 through 21, turns to current social issues in education and will be of special interest to students and instructors who are concerned with the social dimensions of educational problems in our changing society. The struggle for control of the schools, the politics of education, schools and the urban crisis, the Negro child and the schools, and the dropouts are topics which are dealt with sympathetically yet realistically.

The six parts of the book are arranged to be used in the order in which they appear. The reader will notice that Part I moves quickly into the classroom, the center of the school. Parts II and III move outside the school to the educational aspects of the child's environment and the influences of social class upon his learning. The book then returns to the schools in Part IV and to the teachers in Part V. The discussion of crucial issues confronting education in Part VI serves to summarize and sharpen the concepts which have been discussed earlier in the book. The parts of the book are interchangeable, however, and each can stand independently of the others. They may therefore be rearranged to fit the needs of a particular course.

It is appropriate to mention briefly five special features of the book which instructors and students may find useful.

Although the focus of the book is on American schools, there is a strong cross-cultural or comparative flavor. This approach can be attributed to my work from time to time in the schools of distant lands and to the commonsense observation that we are cross-cultural within our own country. That is, we are composed of diverse ethnic, religious, social, and economic backgrounds. These differences are mirrored in our schools. Above all, however, I use comparative materials from home and abroad because in working with my own students I have observed how obscure matters become clear when dissimilar objects are held close together for comparison and contrast. The role of the family in the child's school achievement, for example, becomes suddenly clearer when we study dinner table conversations about the day's events at school among parents and children of a middle-class family and then contrast these conversations with those of a lower-class family. In the former group there is eager concern for the child's progress, a sharing of triumphs and failures, coupled with incentives to do better. In the lower-class family there is frequently no dinner table conversation at all, indeed frequently no dinner. The four children from suburbia, the city slum, small town, and foreign village who periodically appear throughout the book are symbols of this cross-cultural approach. The very differences among them help to illuminate the common themes which run through the social foundations of education.

A person need not have traveled far in order to use the comparative approach to the study of the social aspects of education. Rich comparative materials are as close as the nearest school or library. The author recalls one of his students who found such striking differences in the social-class backgrounds of students in the high school he attended that his report became an eye-opener for the entire class. And the act of comparing is itself a good way to learn through discovery.

The discussion questions and suggested projects, a second feature of the book, are integrated into the text at relevant points. The questions are intended to involve the student as an active participant, as well as to offer possibilities to the instructor for classroom discussion. The projects are within the student's resources to do, and they will help to bring the subject matter to life. I have tested most of the discussion questions and projects with my own students and have found them useful.

The comprehensive reference lists at the end of each chapter, a third feature of the book, cite titles of paperbacks, hardbacks, and periodicals. Because paperbacks now provide a rich selection of reference literature in the social foundations of education, they are given in a separate section. The references to hardback books and periodicals have brief annotations to assist the reader.

Fourth, examples, illustrations, and short case studies are used liberally throughout the book. Wherever there was a choice between the abstract and the concrete, I chose the concrete. My aim is to permit the reader to "see" the idea being discussed and develop his own reactions to it, rather than to short-circuit the thinking process through the use of abstractions and generalizations. Only the reader can evaluate my effort to cast my subject into concrete and living situations.

Finally, the reader will find throughout the book a catalog of current concerns in education and an analysis of their social dimensions. The analysis is an interdisciplinary one, drawing selectively on sociology, social psychology, psychology, anthropology, and education. Here is a representative list of the current topics which are examined for their social significance for the teacher: the ways in which children learn their particular ways of life, the social dynamics of classroom groups, mental health and school achievement, learning climates in the classroom, the selection functions of schools, self-concept and achievement, individual differences, learning by discovery, ability grouping, ungraded classrooms, classroom control, family influences on students' educational aspirations and classroom behavior, peer group influences on school learning, social-class influences on students' educational opportunities, teaching socially disadvantaged students, programs for socially disadvantaged students, cultural differences among schools, the formal and informal social systems of schools, open and closed climates in schools, the influence of teacher-pupil relationships on the climate of the school, teacher-parent relations, the social functions of student activity programs, the influence of childhood models on the decision to teach, student teaching, the career plans of beginning teachers, teaching machines and other new educational technology, team teaching, large- and small-group instruction, teacher–school board negotiations, the impact of the federal government on schools, the impact of urban change on schools, changing suburbs and changing schools, racial integration in the schools, the learning problems of the Negro child, the characteristics of the school dropouts, and what schools are doing for potential dropouts.

These topics and others are described and analyzed from the point of view of their social content and implications. The intent is to help the student see these issues in relation to his own teaching.

Writing a book is a solitary adventure, but it is not an independent one. The extent of one's dependence on others is evident in the simple act of recalling their names. The list is long indeed. It includes university faculty colleagues and students, my fellow board of education members in our local school district, administrators, teachers, and parents, and friends around the world who live and work in schools. Each has contributed to my own understanding of education. Since such a list is far too long to include here, I simply acknowledge my great debt.

Herbert G. Vaughan and John A. Dobson conducted much of the library research which later found its way into the book. Dr. Louis Hofmann took the leadership in preparing the test items in the Instructors Manual. My secretary, Marion Jennette, kept her practiced eye on the dozens of details which comprise the making of a book. The staff at John Wiley and Sons, Joseph F. Jordan, editor, Arthur Hepner, Stella Kupferberg, and Carol Silverstein, were invaluable in their contributions. To them I express deep appreciation.

I wish to thank the following persons and companies for the photographs that appear on the pages indicated: Ken Heyman, Meridian (p. 2); Hanson Carroll, Deerfield Academy (p. 120); Max Tharpe, Monkmeyer (p. 120); Sam Tamashiro (p. 174), Fritz Henle,

Monkmeyer (p. 174); Ken Heyman, Meridian (p. 174); UNATIONS, Government N. Reg. of Nigeria (p. 242), Ken Heyman, Meridian (p. 242); George Zimbel, Monkmeyer (p. 346); and Martha M. Roberts, Monkmeyer (p. 402).

Finally, my heartfelt thanks go to Helen, Beth, and Mark who, in spite of the countless weekends, evenings, and vacations consumed in research and writing, still claimed me as a member of the family when I returned home.

Cole S. Brembeck

East Lansing, Michigan
February, 1966

Contents

Education and Society

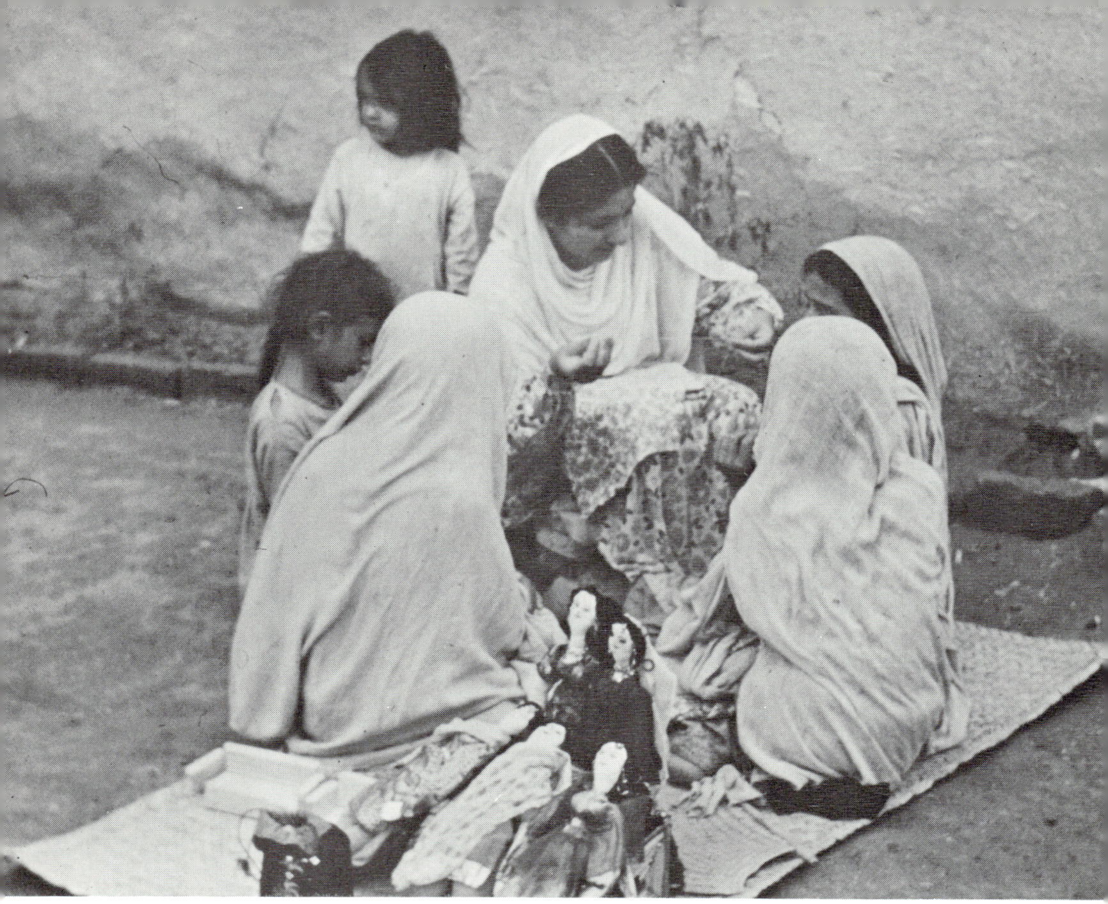

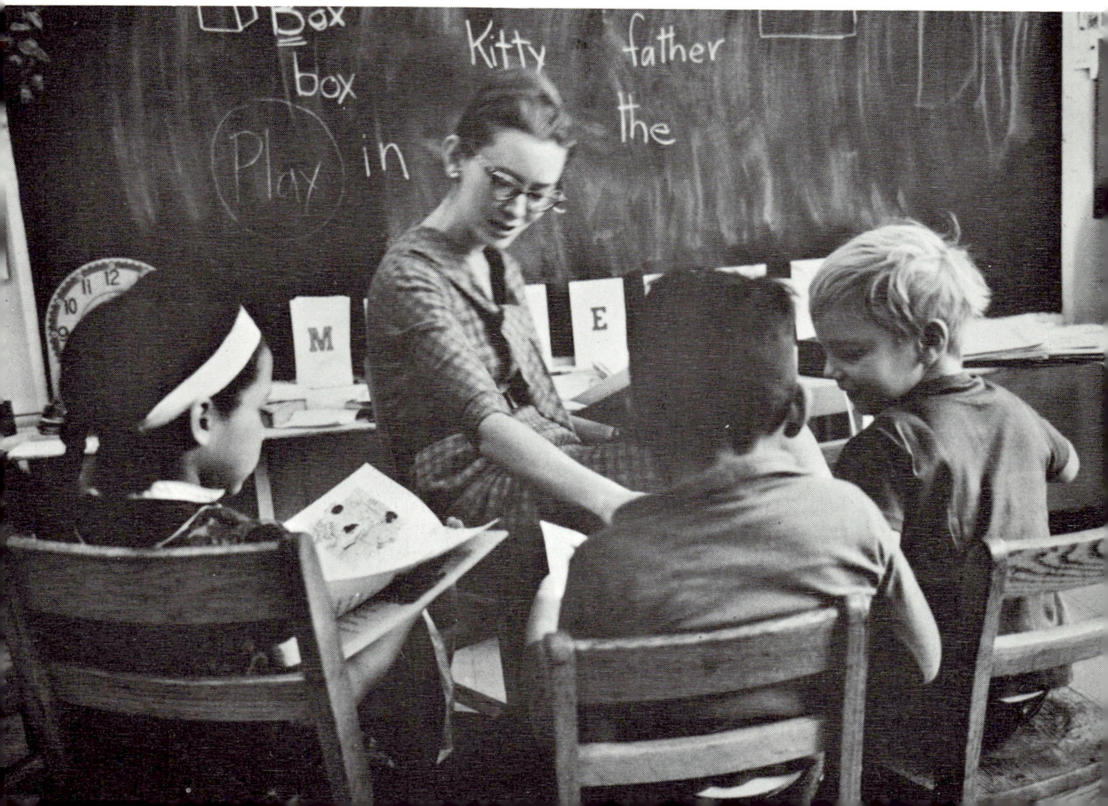
Box
box
Kitty
father
the
Play
in
M
E

I

The Objects
Children Look Upon

"There was a child went forth everyday, and the first object he looked upon that object he became."   WALT WHITMAN

Going to school is a common experience for children around the world. American children tumble from yellow buses in front of their schools. In Hong Kong, children wearing blue and white uniforms, with their shoulder bags bulging with books, pick their way through the crowded streets. In a village in north India, children with tattered readers in hand pad barefoot through the dust. Education is becoming universal, one of the common experiences of children everywhere.

Although the experience of going to school is common, there is much about it around the world and within our own country that is uncommon. The communities in which children go to school, the homes from which they come, the reasons for which they go, the beliefs they carry in their heads, what they learn, and how they learn are all somewhat different.

These common and uncommon experiences in schooling tell us much about education. They tell us, for example, that education is what a society is, a blend of people, time, and place. Children entering American schools look upon objects which have the indelible stamp of our society and culture upon them. The educational objects Chinese children look upon in the airy schools of Hong Kong have written on them the oriental values and the culture of that crossroads of the Far East. The teaching and learning to which Indian village children are exposed are a sure expression of village India today. These children, going forth every day, look upon the objects which the school provides for their education and, as Walt Whitman said, become like them.

The educational environment in which the child becomes like the objects around him is a social one. The most important objects that the child looks upon are other people; it is like them that he will become.[1] Education is everywhere social. Because education is always a human process, one good way to understand it better is to study its social side. That is the purpose of this book.

Periodically we shall encounter in this book four children of school age. Their names are Beth, Julia, Raymond, and Hamid. As children they are real enough, but our interest in them is not in that fact alone. They stand for something important to teachers because they symbolize children who are growing up in very different ways of life. They come from contrasting home environments and attend schools with sharply different cultural styles. Each views the school from a different vantage point, and each is viewed by the school in a different way. In these children we see the influences of society on the education of children, the way they learn, and the way they are taught. These four students tell us much that we need to know about the social aspects of teaching and learning.

Beth lives in a suburb on the rim of the city; Julia lives in a slum of the inner city; Raymond lives in Midwest, a small town. All three are American. Hamid lives in a Pakistani village in the vale of Peshawar in central Asia. As we observe these four children, we shall note that each takes with him to school the way of life he has learned in suburbia, in the slum, in the small town, and in the foreign village. Each child's way of life influences what he learns in school, how he behaves, and what he becomes as he grows up.

The schools these children enter reflect the communities around them. Beth's suburban school is new, with expansive glass and gardens. Julia's slum school is old, as are the tenements and dilapidated storefronts around it. Raymond's small-town school is a substantial two-story structure which reflects the relatively stable community of Main Street and farm. Hamid's Pakistani school has no building at all. It is a tree school, spread under the cool shade of a large banyan tree, where the boys sit on the smooth, packed earth.

In school each child joins with other children from his community. The children within each school are more like their classmates than different from them. They are alike in that they share a common subculture, different in that they come from separate homes and from somewhat different economic and social positions. The teacher brings with him his own style of life. He, too, shares the common subculture

[1] For a discussion of how school environments influence the student's self-concept, see "Quest for Self," *Childhood Education*, Volume XL, No. 1, 1964, entire issue.

of the children, but he brings to his job the unique values and attitudes of the role of teacher in his society.

If we compare and contrast the children and teachers from the four schools in suburbia, slum, town, and foreign village, we observe more striking differences. Each school is set in a different social and cultural environment. The families from which the children come hold different values and beliefs. They share different positions in the social structure and their economic conditions differ. The children who enter the four schools reflect these differences. The teachers also reflect the contrasting environments of suburb, slum, town, and foreign village.

These four children and their teachers, strangely different in some ways and vastly alike in others, are about to engage in an endeavor which is characteristic of almost all schools almost anywhere in the world: They are about to create a little society of their own, a classroom, whose purpose is primarily educational. The kind of little society they create will depend on two matters: What they bring with them to the school from the society into which they were born, and how they build personal relationships among themselves in school. The quality of the teaching and learning which takes place depends in large measure both on what the children and teacher are like as human beings and on how they work together to achieve their purposes.

WHY DO WE STUDY THE SOCIAL ASPECTS OF EDUCATION?

In the first place, teaching and learning are social acts, always carried on within a social setting. Can one possibly imagine teaching and learning taking place in isolation, separated from all human contact? Learning is made possible by human interaction; it flourishes only *among* people.

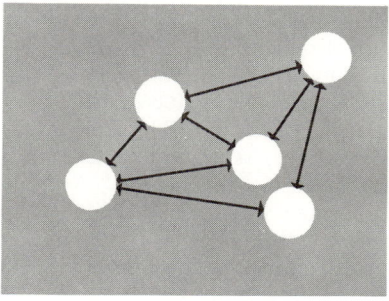

Fig. 1-1 Learning is made possible by human interaction.

Second, we are concerned with the social aspects of education because the classroom itself is a little society whose goal is the education of those within it.[2] Very quickly after the opening of school each classroom develops its own social organization with a network of personal and group relationships. These relationships help to shape the nature of the human interaction carried on within the classroom. More important, they help to determine the quality and extent of the learning acquired by each child. The little society teaches.

Third, the school itself, a collection of classroom societies, is a social institution with a cultural style of its own. Students who have had the experience of going to several different schools comment about how different schools can be. Teachers, too, who have taught in different schools note the uniqueness of schools when they speak about the "personality" of each school. A school is a living social organization with goals, codes of conduct, leaders, and participants. It, too, is a network of human relationships which are the basis for the human interaction which takes place within it. This interaction may positively advance the educational purposes of the school or it may frustrate and negate them. The school as a society also teaches.

Fourth, the school is created by the larger society around it to perform certain educational functions.[3] The school is an instrument of the community, designed to achieve goals which the community finds it difficult otherwise to achieve. The relationship, then, of the school to the larger society becomes a crucial matter. The expectations of society for its schools help to determine what the school will be, what it will teach, and what is learned.

Finally, education itself is a social force which profoundly influences the very society that creates it.[4] In the United States every year over fifty million people engage in some type of formal educational activity. The impact of this aggregate amount of educational activity on American society would indeed be difficult to overestimate.

Why do we study the social aspects of education? Because they bear so directly on teaching and learning in the classroom, and on

[2] Case studies which describe the social dynamics of a classroom and its influence on learning are presented by S. Marshall, *An Experiment in Education,* New York, Cambridge University Press, 1963.

[3] G. F. Kneller states it this way: "Education is the inculturation in each generation of certain knowledge, skills, and attitudes by means of institutions, such as schools, deliberately created for this end." *Anthropology, Culture, Education,* New York, John Wiley and Sons, 1965, p. 11.

[4] J. L. Childs points out that the school must recognize that it has a profound social force on society, and it must consciously assert its moral leadership. *Education and Morals,* New York, Appleton-Century-Crofts, 1950.

what education does in society. Why do teachers and future teachers study the social aspects of education? Because such knowledge is a tool for improved teaching.

WHAT ARE THE OBJECTIVES OF THIS BOOK?

The first and most important objective is a personal one, to help make teaching and learning exciting and rewarding experiences for both teachers and students. Knowledge about education is in itself passive; it springs to life only in the hands of good teachers. Its true test is in the changing behavior of students, the ultimate object of all education.

The study of the social aspects of education takes as its prime subject matter students like the four children mentioned. It observes them in their social milieu, in other words, in their human environment. It examines the impact of the environment on children, especially on their behavior and achievement in school. It studies children as every teacher must study and know them, as products of the large society outside the school and of the little society within it. And it studies children as more than products; they are also the makers of their society. They both act and are acted upon. The study of education and society, then, views the child as the teacher sees him, not as an abstract laboratory object but as a living human being of value who needs to be both understood and taught.

The second objective is to understand the social dynamics of classrooms, how those dynamics influence the learning of each child, and, more important, what a teacher can do about them. The view of this book is that learning does not take place by itself, unaffected by the human situation in which it occurs. It is our view that learning is dependent on the social milieu. The teacher who complains that "Johnny simply won't learn" would be more precise if she were to say "Johnny won't learn *the particular things I want him to learn in this particular situation.*" For Johnny is learning things, among them probably a dislike for what the teacher is attempting to teach him. There are reasons why Johnny does not learn, and a social analysis of the classroom will most likely reveal them. When Johnny *does* learn, some of his reasons for doing so may similarly be found within the social climate of his classroom.

In a sense the social-psychological view of learning is an optimistic one. Based on a belief that intelligence is not a fixed quantity and that learning does not have fixed limits, this view holds that barriers to learning can be removed by enriching the social climate in which it takes place. This approach agrees with the view that ultimately children learn what they *want* to learn and that the art of teaching lies in creating appropriate wants through the right social conditions. This view would agree that Julia, fourth-grade child of the slums, is probably capable of reading material more complex than the first-grade material she reads now. The deprivation is not fixed within Julia, although socially inflicted scars are there. The real deprivation is in the society around Julia. Were that to change for the better, so would Julia. We have called classrooms little societies, and as such they are limited in their influence, in contrast to the larger society. But they do engage the life energy of youth during formative years for considerable lengths of time. They do teach. How to enhance the educational impact of that little society must be understood by all who call themselves teachers.

The third objective of this book is to help teachers see the school as a social institution and as a planned instrument of society for teaching the young. In this institution, the interests of the adults within the school converge with those of parents and citizens outside to sanction a program of learning in which children must engage. The effectiveness of that program always depends, as we have said, on the social inheritance which children and teachers bring from their homes and communities and on the efficiency with which they organize themselves for teaching and learning in school. The problem is to make the school an effective instrument for helping to satisfy society's need to learn and to know. Hamid's tree school in Pakistan is as much an instrument of village society as Beth's school is of suburban society. In both village and suburbia there is a working consensus between the adults in the community and school about what children need to know in order to grow up to be good villagers or suburbanites. We shall focus on the nature of this consensus, its points of stress, and its impact on teaching and learning.

The fourth objective is to increase one's understanding of the educational dimensions of the larger society which encompasses the little society of the classroom and school. Because we live in a teaching society, we need to examine the forces that educate. There are many, but for this book we have selected three: the child's peer group, his family, and his place in the social-class structure. When Hamid leaves his mud-walled home for school in Pakistan he immediately joins other village boys on the way. They constitute his peer group. He spends many hours with them playing, studying in school, and sometimes working on village projects. These boys are effective teachers of one another. In addition to the peer group, we need to examine

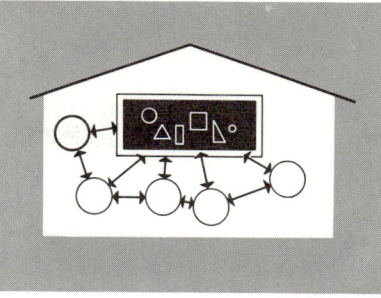

Fig. 1-2 The school is a social institution, a planned instrument of society for teaching the young.

the family as a teaching institution in order to see how what is taught in the home influences what is learned in school. Hamid's family belongs to the landlord class, which owns but does not personally work the land. The family has a high and well-defined place in the social structure of the village. This family position assures Hamid, the individual, a preferred place in the social structure of the village and conditions his attitudes toward what is proper in human relationships. His social position also influences his attitude toward school and his reason for going. Because of his position he views school as important, whereas the children of the landless workers in the village do not take such a view of education. For them, school is not available as a life choice. Social class has powerful impact on education, and we shall examine it from this point of view.

The fifth objective of this book is to help understand how education is meeting several specific challenges in our rapidly changing society, especially in the areas of urbanization, integration, economics, politics, and technology. Increasingly, education is regarded as a way for nations and individuals to shake off economic and political shackles and to assume positions of freedom and dignity. We treat education as a means of helping people to achieve rising expectations. Rapidly changing technology is practically eliminating ordinary manual labor which can be done by a person with little or no education. Those without education are now frequently without jobs. There is now almost "no room at the bottom." In human terms this means that the future of children like Julia is as bleak as the slum in which she lives. Yet her numbers increase. How is education meeting these challenges of our changing society? In a series of chapters we view education's role in the crucial issues of our time.

Finally, our sixth objective is to look at the school of the future. The school as a continuing institution is also changing rapidly. What will the new schools be like? No one can say for sure. We shall not attempt to guess. There are developments, however, which are fundamentally altering schools as places of teaching and learning, and we need to know what they are. The new school architecture, learning systems and technology, television, teaching machines, team teaching, and ungraded classrooms are all altering the future social shape of education. What will it be like?

Children do become like the objects around them. But how? That is the question we raise in Chapter 2.

REFERENCES

Paperbacks

Childhood and Society. Erik H. Erikson. (Rev. Ed.) W. W. Norton and Co., 55 Fifth Ave., New York ($2.95).

Educating the Expert Society. Burton R. Clark. (Orig.) Chandler Publishing Co., 124 Spear St., San Francisco, Calif. ($2.75).

Education in Culture: Anthropological Approaches. George D. Spindler. (Orig.) Holt, Rinehart and Winston, 383 Madison Ave., New York ($4.95).

Education in Western Culture. Robert Ulich. Harcourt, Brace and World, 757 Third Ave., New York ($1.75).

The Schools. Martin Mayer. (A331) Anchor Books and Anchor Science Study Series, Doubleday and Co., 277 Park Ave., New York ($1.45).

Schools, Scholars and Society. Jean D. Grambs. (Orig.) Prentice-Hall, Englewood Cliffs, N. J. ($2.25).

Sociology of Teaching. Willard Waller. Science Editions Paperbacks, John Wiley and Sons, 605 Third Ave., New York ($1.95).

Books

Bartky, John A., *Social Issues in Public Education.* Boston: Houghton Mifflin Co., 1963, 340 pp. Chapter 8, "The School and Culture," discusses different types of cultures to be found within the school.

Brameld, Theodore, *Cultural Foundations of Education, An Interdisciplinary Exploration.* New York: Harper and Brothers, 1957, 330 pp. Brameld's main objective is to help teachers apply a theory of culture in their everyday work.

King, Edmund J., *Other Schools and Ours.* New York: Holt, Rinehart and Winston, 1958. This analysis of schools in six countries shows how the schools both reflect and contribute to the national society.

Marshall, Sybil, *An Experiment in Education.* New York: Cambridge University Press, 1963. A warm and descriptive account of a teacher's experience with Eskimo children in a one-room rural school in Alaska.

Seeley, J. R., R. A. Sims, and E. W. Loosley, *Crestwood Heights: A Study of the Culture of Suburban Life.* New York: John Wiley and Sons, 1963. Chapter 8, "The School: Secondary Socialization," describes the earlier role of education in simple transmission of factual knowledge in contrast to today's schools which are concerned with the socialization of the whole child.

Spindler, George D., *The Transmission of American Culture*. Cambridge, Mass.: Harvard University Press, 1960. An anthropological description is given of the ways in which the teacher imparts social values to his students.

Periodicals

Gladwin, Thomas, "The School, Society and the Child," *Psychology in the Schools*, Vol. I, No. 2, April 1964, pp. 162–173. An analysis of the many roles played by the school in the social development of the child.

Jarolimek, John, "New Orbits in Social Studies," *P.T.A. Magazine*, Vol. 59, No. 2, October 1964, pp. 24–26. This article illustrates a social function of education, namely that of preserving, understanding, and transmitting culture.

Landes, Ruth, "Cultural Factors in Counselling," *Journal of General Education*, Vol. XV, No. 1, April 1963, pp. 55–67. The author describes how the counsellor acts as mediator between the school and the culture.

Mead, Margaret, "A Redefinition of Education," *NEA Journal*, Vol. 48, No. 7, October 1959, pp. 15–17. Education has a new function, that of helping students to adapt to a rapidly changing world.

Wax, Murray L., et al., "Formal Education in an American Indian Community," Supplement to *Social Problems*, Vol. 11, No. 4, Spring 1964. A study of the conflicting influences of national and local values on American Indian children in reservation schools.

2

Education Is
a Social Process

"Education consists of a methodical socialization of the young generation."
ÉMILE DURKHEIM

We begin with a statement which seems simple: *What a human being knows he has learned.* The statement *is* simple in the sense that to learn obviously is to know. Yet the fact that we *must* learn what we know actually discriminates between what is human and what is nonhuman. Because the nonhuman animal can live out his life guided largely by its biological inheritance, its need to learn and to know is relatively small.

The human animal, on the other hand, begins life, like other animals, with a biological inheritance. But how he exists after that depends on his ability to learn. Very quickly he must learn a vast, intricate, often conflicting and confusing way of life which other humans before him have devised. That way of life, the culture, cannot be biologically inherited. It is not included in one's genes but must be learned anew by each human being. Fortunately, we are born into an educating society where it is almost impossible not to learn.

EDUCATION IS SOCIALIZATION

Look now at the process by which this learning takes place. Socialization may be defined as the process by which a person learns the ways of the society into which he was born. It is made possible through social contact, by the daily ebb and flow of human interaction.[1]

[1] R. E. Parks and E. W. Burgess early defined socialization as "a process of interpretation and fusion in which persons or groups acquire the memories, senti-

In the sentence at the head of this chapter, Emile Durkheim comments that "education consists of a *methodical* socialization of the young generation." [2] What does he mean by methodical socialization? Actually, he is making a distinction between the socialization that takes place in and out of school. Human interaction outside the school tends to be *unmethodical* as a learning experience, informal and spontaneous. The family, for example, teaches the child in an informal way through the daily give and take of family living. The family does not organize its teaching or schedule its learning in the sense that the school does. Much that we learn outside of school takes place in this informal manner.

School learning, in contrast, is methodical; it is planned, organized, and scheduled. Teachers are hired to teach specific subjects and students are tested to find out how much they learned. This whole process is socialization; and because it is methodical rather than unmethodical we call it education. The process results in learning, a great deal of which takes place outside of school, some of which takes place in the school.

In this book we are interested in both in-school and out-of-school learning. Why? Because one influences the other. [3] How the child is socialized outside the school influences how well he learns in school. To understand him in school we must understand what we can about him outside of school.

In this chapter we shall see how a student's out-of-school socialization conditions his in-school learning. As examples we shall take the four children we met in Chapter 1 and demonstrate how their growing up determines the attitudes and values which they carry to school.

Each society has its own ways of inducting its young into the adult world. [4] Contrast, for example, the growing-up experiences of two of the four children whom we encountered in Chapter 1. Beth is a child of an American suburb, Hamid a child of a Pakistani village.

---

ments, and attitudes of other persons or groups, and, by sharing their experience, and history, are incorporated with them in a common cultural life." *Introduction to the Science of Sociology*, Chicago, University of Chicago Press, 1924, p. 735.

   [2] Author's italics.

   [3] P. Abrams examined socialization in the out-of-school and in-school setting and found a high degree of correlation. "Notes on the Uses of Ignorance," *Twentieth Century*, Volume CLXXII, No. 1019, 1963, pp. 67–77.

   [4] Margaret Mead, in a classic study of children in both primitive and modern societies, described the differences that exist in the enculturation process. "Our Educational Emphasis in Primitive Perspective," *American Journal of Sociology*, Volume XLVIII, No. 6, May 1943, pp. 633–639.

Hamid's growing up is the responsibility of a large, joint family and extended kin group. This joint family does not really think in terms of "rearing" Hamid at all. He is simply regarded as one of the group who will quite naturally take his place among the others when he is grown. If Hamid does not find his wants fulfilled by one member of his large family, he simply turns to another. An uncle, aunt, grandfather, or grandmother will do quite as well as his own parents. Beth's growing up, on the other hand, is conditioned by her small nuclear family which, borrowing our society's values, takes a more professional attitude toward raising children. Her parents are concerned about the unique needs of girls at her age, are sensitive to what authorities say, and try to keep abreast of developments in child psychology. The adults to whom Beth can turn are limited in number, two parents, a teacher or two, and only periodically other members of the family. The number of adult "models" available to her are few. For Hamid there are many.

The socialization process is different not only for children in different societies but also for children in different subcultures of the same society. Contrast, for example, the growing up of the two other children we met in Chapter 1. Raymond is a child of Midwest, a county seat town. Julia is a child of the urban slum. Raymond's growing up is marked by continuity and stability, Julia's by rejection and frustration. Raymond views the adult world as something dependable upon which he can call in time of need. Julia learned early that her adult world, with the exception of the teacher who befriended her, was unreliable. She had to learn to cope with uncertainty.

One might conclude by looking at the various ways in which children grow up that there is no common element. This is not so. In each of the examples we just mentioned, one thing is apparent: Each group uses the same process for preparing children to live within it, the process of socialization.

THE PRECONDITIONS FOR SOCIALIZATION

Socialization depends on three preconditions: (1) certain biological endowments, (2) an ongoing society, and (3) an opportunity for the person to interact with the society.

The biological inheritance of the child is the beginning.[5] Without it, nothing can proceed. The physical capacity to experience the

[5] A. Scheinfeld describes the delineating factors of biological inheritance in his popularized and readable book on heredity. *You and Heredity* (Revised Edition), Philadelphia, J. B. Lippincott, 1951.

world through seeing, hearing, touching, and talking depends on the child's biological inheritance. But the child needs more than biological inheritance; he needs a social inheritance from those who have preceded him.[6] He is not born into a social vacuum, alone and unattended, but comes into a society. From the moment of birth others care for his physical needs, and before long he is being taught to think and behave as they think he should. His capacity to think and behave depends on the third precondition for socialization, his opportunity to respond to the society around him. In responding, the child in a sense becomes his own teacher, for he is interpreting the world around him. He appraises what his perceptions let him experience. He may reject, accept, or modify what he experiences. Whichever he does in this selective process he becomes an individual. He becomes socialized.

A simple incident in the relationship between a mother and her baby will illustrate an early moment of socialization. It is feeding time and the mother wishes to awaken the baby in order to feed him. Leaning over the crib, she looks for a glimmer of recognition, a fleeting smile, an indication of growing social awareness. The child is normal biologically and he is healthy. He can respond. The mother strokes his face and chucks his chin, speaking mother talk as she does so. She represents the child's society, there before him, probably gone before him, teaching him, and being taught by him. Slowly the baby rouses, stretches, blinks a time or two, focuses his eyes on his mother, and smiles. In this simple act he is responding to the social stimulation of his small world; he is being socialized.

This small world will enlarge rapidly. Whereas now his reaction potential is confined in large measure to such matters as light and dark, heat and cold, hunger and pain, the fear of falling, the child is learning the social dimensions of his small world. The small world soon enlarges to include other members of the household—father, brothers, sisters, and others who come into the home. Later his social learning extends beyond his home to playmates, adult neighbors, and family friends. Then one day comes the biggest single step in his own socialization: he goes to school.

[6] M. L. Hutt and R. G. Gibby accurately point out that "the individual at birth is 'born into' a particular culture, and is largely captive to these influences that he experiences." *The Child: Development and Adjustment,* Boston, Allyn and Bacon, 1959, p. 51.

CHILD OF THE SUBURB

Beth, age ten, awakes in her four-poster bed surrounded by possessions she holds dear, a doll collection, books, a transistor radio, and a phonograph. The four-poster belonged to her mother when she was a girl, who promised Beth that she could have it when she was "old enough." Now she is old enough and she enjoys sleeping in the bed, which was refinished in bone white with a dust ruffle and a canopy from material to match the blue and white wallpaper on three sides of the bedroom. The fourth side of her bedroom has a built-in wall of shelves and storage, also in blue and white, and a desk for studying and writing. The upper shelves on the left-hand side over her desk hold her books. The upper shelves on the right-hand side contain her foreign-doll collection, accumulated through various travels of her family and Beth herself. There is a peasant doll from Greece, a village doll from India, a tribal doll from the northwest frontier of Pakistan, dancing dolls from Thailand and Turkey, a Chinese peasant doll from Hong Kong, and a Japanese doll in formal dress from Tokyo. Beside the bed and near the big pillows where Beth likes to read stands a pole lamp with milk-glass shades.

Beth awakes when her mother, a graduate of an Eastern college for women, comes into her room, closes the window, turns on the desk lamp, and leaves the door open so that Beth can hear music from the downstairs phonograph. Beth gets up, makes her bed unusually well for a ten-year-old, dresses in her plaid skirt and matching sweater, goes downstairs to a breakfast of juice, cereal, and toast, and eats about half as much as her mother thinks she should. Getting up from the table she pulls back the curtains at the kitchen window and looks across the wooded ravine to Cathy's house.

"The light is on in Cathy's room—she must be up," she comments. And in her mind she is making plans for after school.

As Beth is pulling on her coat she is reminded by her mother that "This is Girl Scout day to swim at the 'Y' and I'll take you and the other girls, so don't make any other plans." Beth picks up her violin case in one hand and her school books in the other and heads down the short flight of stairs of the four-level home to the garage where her father, a professional man, has just started the car in order to take her to school on his way to the office. The driveway goes down a slight grade to the blacktop street where there is little traffic at this hour, and Beth and her father have time to look at the homes along the way. Most of them, built within the last ten years, are set well back on green lawns which show obvious and tender care. A number of the

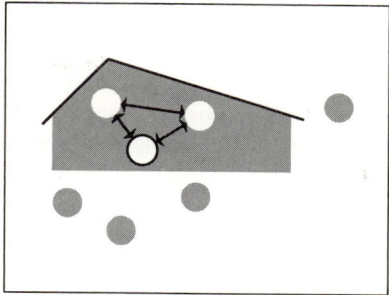

Fig. 2-1   Beth's growing up in the suburbs is conditioned by her small, nuclear family.

homes which back up to the river sell for more money than those across the street.

Woodlawn is representative of many suburbs that ring our major cities.[7] The citizens who live in them belong to the middle class, occupy both professional and entrepreneurial positions, belong to country clubs, help support suburban churches and charitable causes, worry about high taxes, and demand the best education for their children. They are quick to sense threats to their suburban way of life and oppose changes in zoning laws which would permit business and industrial buildings or apartment houses near their homes. They are wary when the highway department wishes to expand a nearby two-lane road into a four-lane for fear that it will change the nature of the subdivision. The homeowners' association is concerned with the general good of the subdivision and is supposed to alert the citizens to problems as they arise.

The sidewalks are filling up now with children walking to school, and on the road a number of children are riding their bicycles. Beth takes going to school pretty much for granted and generally likes it. Relating to her peers, however, does not come easily for her, and when she feels excluded from the group she "despises" school.[8] These moods pass, and her parents have noticed that her interest and achievement in schoolwork increase when things are going well socially.

In the fifth grade Beth has a considerable amount of homework,

[7] For a careful description of upper-middle-class suburban culture which will provide additional insight into this strata of society, see J. R. Seeley, R. A. Sim, and E. W. Loosley, *Crestwood Heights*, New York, John Wiley and Sons, 1963.

[8] Affective factors influencing pupil motivation will be examined in detail in Chapters 6–10.

about which she is developing marked self-discipline, going to her desk after school and frequently after the evening meal. Her teacher commented several times about the good quality of her homework and this apparently has improved Beth's motivation for doing it.

One day when she did not come home from school at the usual hour, her mother went to the school and found her in the library working alone at a table, "getting some things I need for my homework, since I don't have them at home."

Three blocks from Beth's home, her father leaves the subdivision and turns for a short block onto the thoroughfare which dead-ends at the school; a guard is directing traffic with the help of elementary school boys who wear their white safety belts. In front of the school a number of children are scrambling from late model cars driven by fathers and mothers. Other children are parking their bicycles in the racks at the edge of the large playground. The children wrestle and jostle their way into the school to the banging of locker doors and children's talk. Beth takes her violin to the orchestra room, hangs up her coat in the locker, and steps into the bright classroom which still smells of custodian's wax applied the night before. A new day at the Woodlawn school is ready to begin.

1. On the basis of what you know about Beth, what would be your guess about how well she achieves in school?

2. What are the reasons which cause you to speculate as you do? List as many reasons as you can.

CHILD OF THE SLUMS

Beth's style of life is marked by continuities and regularities. She can depend on it being pretty much the same from one day to the next. The adults in her life give her support when she needs it. She has lived most of her life in one neighborhood, one which she is coming to understand and appreciate. The school fits the pattern of continuity and regularity in her life.

Julia's style of life in the slums,[9] sharp in contrasts with that of Beth's, is filled with discontinuities and irregularities, including those of attendance at school. The social heritage she takes to school, when she goes, profoundly influences her contribution to the little society, and the character of that little society in the slum school profoundly influences her learning and growth.[10]

[9] Barbara Cummiskey, *Life*, Volume 52, No. 4, January 26, 1962, p. 61.

[10] Robert J. Havighurst estimates that about 30 percent of the children in our large industrial cities and 15 percent of the total child population may be clas-

"A block-and-a-half from the school, the winter wind cuts through 104th Street, scattering papers along the gutter. At a shattered basement window the wind flaps a flowered curtain left behind by the last tenants. This is where Julia used to live when she and her sisters went to school. Now a small boy looks at the broken window and says, 'Julia gone. They all gone away.'

"Julia is only one of the hundreds of children who leave the school every year—not by graduating but simply by moving away, usually to another slum neighborhood. This huge turnover is one of the great problems of all slum schools. It means that whatever good and stability the school has been able to bring is almost certain to be lost in the upsetting wrench of moving to a new world of strangers.

"When Julia had to move away—to an even worse slum in Brooklyn—she was frightened. She cried at school and begged her teacher to let her stay, for the school was the only safe place she had ever known. As long as she was able to stay at school, Julia managed to keep on believing that some day things would be better for her. Once she drew a picture for the guidance counselor of what she expected her life to be like. The picture showed a big house standing in a field of flowers. A bird flew through the sky and smoke curled from the chimney. 'A family lives here,' Julia said. 'There, on the lawn, that's my sister playing.' Julia's picture of this kind of life could have come only from the school. In the basement apartment on 104th Street she shared a dark, tiny room with two other children. The family lived here because the mother Elena was superintendent for the tenement. When the police discovered she was selling policy tickets, the family was evicted. Julia's father had been out of work for months and Elena, supporting nine children, had needed the extra income to pad out the city welfare checks.

"Julia laughs about her father. 'He is good to us when he is not drunk, but he is a lot of the time very drunk and he is mean then. When he hits us, we run away to the streets and wait for him to go to sleep.'

"The other place Julia ran to was the school. There she lived in the reading book world of Spot, Dick, and Jane, who romp on green lawns under blue skies and eat big meals at grandmother's farm. In that world father is never drunk and mother is always present. 'We try to make school a little bit of heaven for them,' explained Julia's teacher. 'Not for always, but just for now.'

---

sified, like Julia, as socially disadvantaged. "Who Are the Socially Disadvantaged?," *Journal of Negro Education*, Volume XXXIII, No. 3, 1964, pp. 210–217.

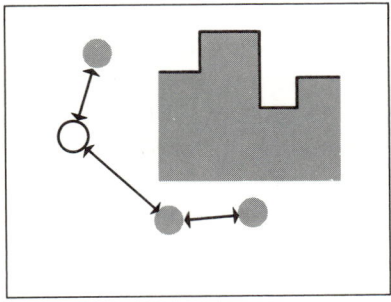

Fig. 2-2   Julia's home life in the slum is marked by rejection and frustration.

"In school things happened for Julia that could not happen anywhere else. When her fourth-grade class planted beans to learn how seeds grow, she hovered over her bent green sprig in awed concern. She watered it carefully every day and stretched on tiptoe to hold it up as close as possible to the sun. Another time she was chosen to be a princess in a play. 'People say I look pretty,' Julia remembers. 'I had a crown and they gave me flowers. The other kids were mad because I won, but they let me be princess anyway.'

"But school was not always wonderful, not for a girl who was ten years old and growing up in the slums. Julia could not concentrate on the difficult business of learning to spell and read. She was always tired, and often when a lesson got too hard, she dropped off to sleep, covering her ears with her hands. Though her I.Q. was average, she could read only a first-grade book. Sometimes she rebelled furiously at the unattainable world of Dick and Jane. It seemed some kind of cruel joke when she read: 'Oh, Dick, no one lives in the new house. Who will come to live in it? It is a big house. Maybe a big family will live in it. Maybe the family will have girls.' Julia could not stand it. 'I do not like this Jane,' she said. 'Dick is dumb.' Another day she tried to make a paper figure in class. She produced a sadly battered creature with wings unlike the vision she held in her mind. Her eyes filled and tears streamed as she crushed the figure of the bird.

"But in spite of the occasional disappointments and failures, Julia believed in the school, and even now she cannot accept the end of her dream. Although she lives far away in Brooklyn, she returns over and over again to the school and to 104th Street, making the long subway trip back to the place where teachers sometimes made her happy.

"When her visit to the school is over, Julia wanders through the old neighborhood. Evening comes down on 104th Street under a cold gray sky. Men huddle together on the tenement steps, as motionless as reptiles. At the windows Julia can see women's shadowed faces and hear their soft voices fluting the familiar call to the passers-by. The women disappear suddenly when the wail of the police car or ambulance announces another call on death, drunkenness or dope addiction, the three ready escapes from 104th Street.

"When the police leave, the car's flashing light creates a red flickering on the cages of the fire escapes. The children chant: 'Calling on car 717. Go find the man with the snow ballie bean, take his dice, shoot him twice, and lock him in jail for the rest of his life.' A snow ballie bean is heroin—Julia knows that."

3. Do you suspect that the school serves quite a different function in Julia's life than in Beth's? Can you explain the difference?

4. We are told that fourth-grader Julia has an average I.Q.; yet she can read only first-grade materials. How do you personally explain this discrepancy between intelligence and achievement?

5. Julia rebels at the middle-class values of Dick and Jane. Would you give her a reader that expressed slum values instead? If so, why? If not, why not?

CHILD OF THE TOWN

Raymond, age seven, lives in Midwest,[11] a county seat town in rural America. His style of life contrasts as much with Julia's as Julia's does with Beth's. Both Beth and Julia live in segments of society which are homogeneous although they are vastly different in character. From morning until night Beth is exposed to the subculture of suburbia and Julia to the subculture of the slum. The social structure of Midwest is different in that it is quite a self-sufficient community whose population represents various social classes, though the variety and range is not great. The social heritage, therefore, that Raymond takes to school with him is markedly different from that of Beth or Julia.[12]

"Midwest is a town of 725 people. It is the seat of an agricultural county in the central part of the United States. It is surrounded by rolling, partly wooded farmlands and pastures that are cut by winding creeks. The farmland in the immediate vicinity of Midwest varies from

[11] Adapted from Roger G. Barker and Herbert F. Wright, *One Boy's Day*, New York, Harper and Brothers, 1951.

[12] J. West's sociological study of rural Missouri further illustrates life in a Midwest town. *Plainville*, by Carl Withers (pseud.), New York, Columbia University Press, 1945, p. 238.

poor to good. Corn, oats, winter wheat, milk, beef cattle, and hogs are the chief agricultural products of the county. . . .

"The town is neither wealthy nor poor. There are no rich families in Midwest. A number of families maintain a living standard which includes a new car on the Buick or Chrysler level once every two or three years, clothes of the latest fashion for the wives and older daughters, a sizable yearly vacation, a modernized home with the latest equipment, an education for the grown-up children in a nearby college or university. At the other extreme, a few aged and infirm persons are receiving public assistance, although not a single employable resident of Midwest is on relief. A few families are without one or more of the available utilities: running water, gas, electricity, telephone. Seventy-two percent, electricity; seventy percent, a telephone . . .

"Raymond Birch is a sturdy boy, slightly shorter and heavier than the average boy of his age. His dark hair is usually slicked down and his brown eyes often light up with a friendly smile. Grown-ups of Midwest remark that he is good looking and impish. At seven years and four months he is the youngest among the fifteen second graders of the Midwest school.

"Raymond is the only child of Jack and Joan Birch. Although he has no other relatives in Midwest, both his maternal and paternal grandparents live on farms in Midwest county, and he is a frequent visitor at their homes.

"Mrs. Birch is in her late twenties. She is a brunette of less than average height and weight and is always well-groomed and attractively dressed. She was born and reared on a farm in Midwest county. . . .

"Mr. Birch is in his early thirties. He is of average height and weight. Although he was born in a neighboring state, some of his ancestors were early settlers in Midwest county. . . . Since 1946, the family has lived in Midwest, where Mr. Birch has been with the Cooper Hardware Company, one of the town's largest business concerns. . . .

"There is, as far as Raymond is concerned, at least, one other member of the Birch family—Honey. Honey is a black-and-white fox terrier. She is old, fat and broad. . . .

"The record starts with Raymond sleeping soundly in his bedroom. His room is at the southwest corner of the house and it has a window in each outside wall. Raymond's bed, a double one, takes up one corner of the room. A dresser, its top cluttered with boyish treasures and toilet articles, shares the east wall with a chair and a door, through which one can enter the living room. A small basketball goal is fixed on the inside of this door. . . .

"Mrs. Birch said with pleasant casualness, 'Raymond, wake up.' With a little more urgency in her voice she spoke again: 'Son, are you going to school today?' . . .

"Mrs. Birch took some clothes from the bureau and laid them on the bed next to Raymond. There were a clean pair of socks, a clean pair of shorts, a white T-shirt, and a striped T-shirt. Raymond's blue-jean pants were on a chair near the bed. Mrs. Birch continued to stand beside the bed. Raymond put on his blue-jean pants as he stood by his bed. . . . His father, who had been reading the morning paper in the living room, came by in the hall on his way to breakfast. He turned into Raymond's room and greeted him in a friendly, jocular way, 'Well, Clam, are you ready to eat?' Raymond promptly and easily replied, 'Sure.' . . .

"The breakfast table is laid in the Birchs' pleasant kitchen. Windows on the south and north let in the morning light. The electric refrigerator and table-top gas stove are conveniently placed in relation to the sink and table, and they are immaculately clean. . . . While Raymond continued to eat quietly, he listened to the conversation of the parents. The father talked about going fishing. He said, 'A day like this makes me want to grab a fishing pole.' . . . Mr. Birch said that he and Raymond had gone fishing a few days before. Raymond had been the only one who caught any fish. Raymond smiled at this reference to him. . . .

"The grassy courthouse square and the office of the County Clerk within it, where Raymond's mother works, are as familiar to Raymond as his own house and yard; for, on school days, while school is out, Raymond's headquarters is usually the 'square.'

"Here Raymond meets the people who work at the courthouse, those who come there on business, and other children who regularly or occasionally play on the square. And he sees many of the adults in a wider context. For example, he knows Mr. Frank Pechter as Raymond Pechter's father, just as Mr. Pechter knows Raymond as his son's classmate and Jack Birch's son. . . .

"Raymond immediately fell into step with his parents as they started down the walk toward the west. The path from the courthouse to school is only two short blocks.

"He walked briskly on. . . . Since the school building serves both town and rural children of all ages from the first grade through high school, Raymond comes in contact with town and country children of all ages on the school ground before and after school.

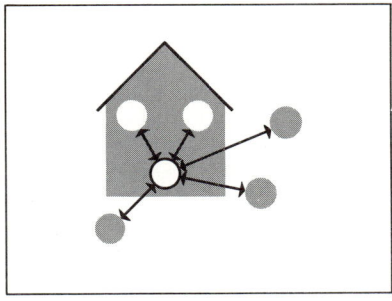

Fig. 2-3   Raymond's life in the small town is characterized by continuity and stability.

"As the time for the beginning of school approached, more and more children arrived on the school ground. At this time the front yard was swarming with children of all ages.

"Mrs. Logan is the first- and second-grade teacher. She was born and raised in Midwest, where she taught prior to her marriage. She returned to teaching here when her son entered high school, but she and her husband live, as they had for some years before, on a farm about six miles from Midwest. Mrs. Logan is well established as a solid citizen, independently of her position as a teacher. The parents of the first and second grade children feel that her motherliness is a real help in the adjustment of bewildered six-year-olds, particularly since there is no kindergarten. It seems to them that she brings to her job an unusual fund of patience, tolerance, and genuine affection for children.

"Anyone who has ever gone to school in a small town would immediately feel on familiar ground in the Midwest Public School. In Raymond's room, word lists and simple sums are printed on the blackboard; gold-starred charts and some pictures, among them Song of the Lark, Friends, and Lincoln, share the wall space. And in the atmosphere there is the fused odor of chalk dust, overshoes, and lunches.

"A pleasant touch is added by the collection of dolls, cowboy hats, and guns which rest on the window sills until their owners claim them at recess. Plants, tended by Mrs. Logan, are also on the south and east window sills. Low tables along the north wall are used mainly by first grade children for spelling and reading. A large closed cupboard at the back of the room contains library books for reading during free periods. Under the bulletin board at the front, there are low cabinet shelves containing various supplies such as paper and paper towels.

A narrow platform runs along the wall under the blackboard at the front of the room, behind the teacher's desk. The school desks vary in size and neatness. The contents of some of the desks are arranged in an orderly fashion on the shelf space beneath the stationary desk top. Other desks are overflowing with papers, pencils, crayons, books, and an assortment of personal belongings.

"When Raymond first enters this classroom . . . many of the children are already milling around freely, chatting in small groups, sitting on desks and swinging their legs or drawing at the blackboard."

6. We are told that Raymond's teacher, Mrs. Logan, is "well established as a solid citizen, independently of her position as teacher." She is no "sociological stranger" to the community as teachers frequently are. Do you think this fact makes any difference in Mrs. Logan's effectiveness as a teacher?

7. At the courthouse square Raymond meets people "in a wider context." Using the limited evidence available, how would you compare and contrast the socialization of Raymond and Julia?

8. Raymond's classroom presents an atmosphere of the "fused odor of chalk dust, overshoes and lunches." How would you evaluate this classroom as a physical setting for learning?

A TREE SCHOOL IN PAKISTAN

Beth, Raymond, and Julia are American children, both alike and different, all sharing a common American culture yet each taking with him to school the unique attitudes, values, and beliefs of that particular segment of society in which he is growing up. Although they are strikingly different as people, Beth, Raymond, and Julia do share common history, traditions, and government.

Now we turn to a child who does not share our common culture, Hamid, a Pakistani boy of ten, who lives within sight of the fabled Khyber Pass on the northwest frontier of Pakistan, near Peshawar. Our choice of Hamid is deliberate, for he lives in a culture strikingly different from our own, in a house and a family strikingly different from that of Beth, Raymond, or Julia.[13] His is a village society, set in the rural culture of a Moslem land. If we can see how the social and economic forces of his society influence Hamid's style of life, we

[13] George D. Spindler's book of readings provides a most useful cross-cultural perspective on the general theme of cultural differences. Part Three contrasts education in a Hopi tribal village with an Israeli kibbutz and a West African "Bush School." Although each culture exhibits dramatic differences they all achieve the same goal of transmitting the culture of their people. *Education and Culture,* New York, Holt, Rinehart and Winston, 1963.

shall, by reflective comparison, be able to see better how these forces influence socialization in our own culture.

Hamid is a Moslem, as are his fellow villagers and most of his fellow countrymen. His home is of mud-wall construction with an open court in front where much of the family living takes place. Hamid's home is located near the white mosque, whose courtyard is shaded from the hot sun by the overarching branches of large trees. Here Hamid watches the villagers come to say their prayers, the faithful praying five times each day. After he has finished his day at the government school, his parents like to have him sit with the religious teacher in the mosque and memorize portions of the Holy Koran. Hamid's parents also expect that the teacher in the government school will reinforce the precepts and values taught in the Holy Koran. Religion is therefore a pervasive influence in Hamid's life.

This Pakistani boy is a member of a large family, a joint family headed by his grandfather and consisting of his own parents and brothers and sisters as well as of three aunts and uncles and their children. Hamid has never differentiated among his own immediate family and those of his aunts and uncles and their children. To him they are one family, with his grandfather as head, and his parents, brothers, and sisters, and aunts, uncles, and cousins as other members. The family ties are strong, fixing deeply in Hamid's behavior what is proper and improper in human relationships. Throughout life he will be influenced by what he has learned in this joint family.

His family owns land outside the village walls. Hamid has observed that the many families who do not own land frequently work for those who do. He has observed that the families of other landowners come to his house to talk socially with his father, whereas the landless

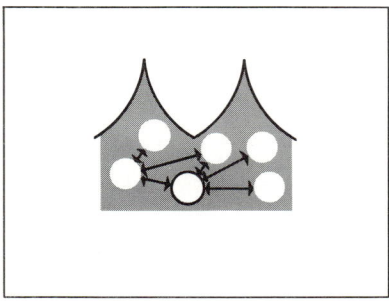

Fig. 2-4 Hamid's growing up in the village is the responsibility of a large, joint family and extended kin group.

ones come only to make requests. Hamid is learning about the social-class structure of his village and how he should behave as a member of the upper part of that structure.

Hamid's village is poor, depending almost entirely on agriculture. For this and other reasons, there are more boys outside of school than in. Most families need the boys in the fields and cannot afford to send them to school. These boys will take up menial tasks for a living and will likely remain poor. The boys in school will have a better chance of getting jobs. Some of the parents of these boys have sent them to school precisely for this reason. Economic conditions have a deep impact on the life chances of Hamid and his boyfriends in the village.

Because Hamid's village and country are overpopulated and underdeveloped, food, clothing, and other goods are scarce and out of reach of many. The people live clustered in mud-walled villages and move out each working day to their fields over narrow footpaths. At night they return to the crowded village, which is the center of their social and family life.

The mass media of newspapers, radio, and movies are only beginning to have their influence in Hamid's village. The word television is not known. Several landowners read native language papers and one an English language paper. The village's one radio is located in the village meeting place, where in the evening the villagers squat on the ground and listen to native music and to speeches by government leaders.

One evening the president tells about a new constitution and the rights and responsibilities of citizens under it. He speaks of a program of basic democracies under which citizens can elect their own local governing councils with powers to act on village problems. Political institutions cannot be ignored in the catalogue of influences which bear on Hamid's growing up.

The impact of science and technology is not strongly felt in Hamid's mud-walled village. The exception is the growing influence of the radio. But when the village radio breaks down, no one knows how to fix it. No one yet understands the technology of a radio or the science of radio wave transmission. But one of the boys who attended the tree school went on to secondary school and became a radio operator in the Pakistani air force. When he returns to the village he is a hero. The boys flock around him and ask him how one gets to be a radio operator and wear an air force uniform.

When Hamid leaves for school each morning, he joins his peers along the way, boys from other parts of the village also heading for school. They have just left houses where parental rule is strict but usually kind. Hamid's father likes to tell the Americans whom he knows that "you bring up your children; we simply live with ours."

Hamid and his friends will enter a school where obedience to the teacher is unquestioned. Between home and school the boys are free. Jostling and joking with one another, they throw clods of dirt into the muddy street that meanders through the center of the village, and try to inveigle a piece of sweet sugar cane from the vendor who sits near the place where the boys hop across the stream on their way to school. These boys constitute a peer group, and within this group they have strong social influences on one another.

Across the stream they run along a narrow path between the edge of the stream and a high mud wall which constitutes one side of their school. Farther down the wall, about fifty good-sized hops for the boys, a weather-beaten wooden door is set in the wall and is standing ajar. The boys swing it all the way open as the rusty hinges protest. They step inside their school, drop the books which they have been carrying bound together in a leather belt, step out of their shoes,

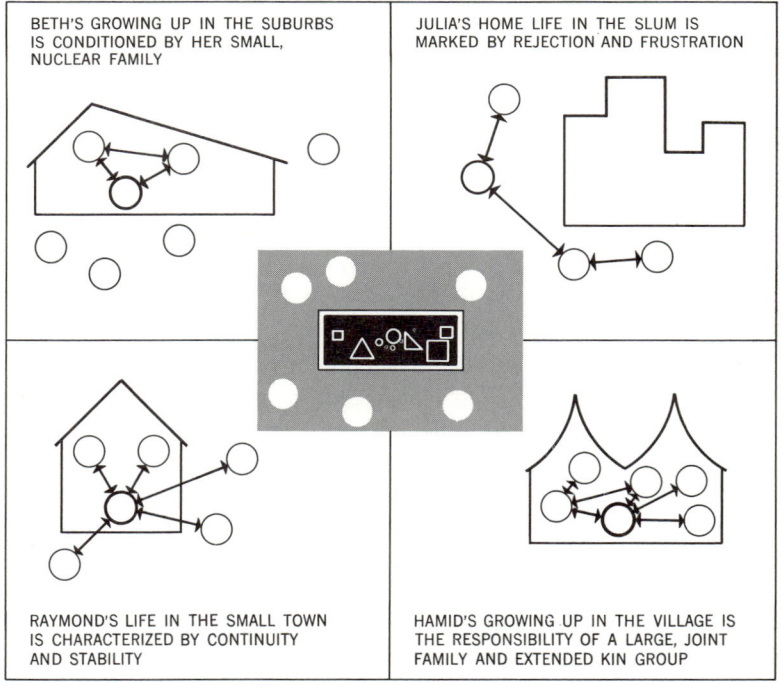

Fig. 2-5 A child's out-of-school socialization conditions his in-school learning.

and place them in a neat row at the inside base of the wall. They look around at an open and spacious courtyard with a tiny stream ambling through the middle, and look beyond to the great spreading tree which provides protection from sun and rain and constitutes a natural classroom of rustic beauty.

9. Comment on Hamid's socialization compared with Beth's, Raymond's, and Julia's. How is the socialization of the four children alike? How is it different?

10. We have only bits of information about Beth's and Hamid's schools. Knowing what you do, however, about their respective communities, could you speculate about how these two schools are both different and alike with respect to the educational functions they serve?

11. We said there were three preconditions for socialization. Do these preconditions differ for the four children? If so, how?

12. It is frequently said that a teacher must understand the individual differences among the children in his classroom and adjust his teaching to them. Individual differences may be of several kinds: physical, psychological, and social. From what you know about Julia, Beth, Raymond, and Hamid, what psychological and social differences might you expect to find among them? Do these differences suggest anything to you about teaching these four children?

In these vignettes we went with four children to the classroom door. In this chapter we were concerned chiefly with the socializing influences that make the child what he is outside of school. We are ready now to step through the door and see the classroom from the inside.

REFERENCES

Paperbacks

Childhood in Contemporary Cultures. Margaret Mead and Martha Wolfenstein, Editors. Phoenix Books, University of Chicago Press, 5750 Ellis Ave., Chicago, Ill. ($2.95).

Children of Sanchez. Oscar Lewis. (V280-Vin) Vintage Books, Random House, 457 Madison Ave., New York ($2.95).

Children of the Kibbutz: A Study in Child Training and Personality. Melford E. Spiro. (SB93-SB) Schocken Books, 67 Park Ave., New York ($2.95).

Coming of Age in Samoa. Margaret Mead. (MP418) Mentor Books, New American Library, 1301 Ave. of the Americas, New York (60¢).

Crestwood Heights: A Study of the Culture of Suburban Life. J. R. Seeley, R. A. Sim, and E. W. Loosley. Science Editions Paperbacks, John Wiley and Sons, 605 Third Ave., New York ($2.45).

Educational Anthropology. G. F. Kneller. (Orig.) John Wiley and Sons, 605 Third Ave., New York ($2.45).

Family in Various Cultures. Stuart Queen, Robert W. Habenstein, and John B. Adams. (Orig.) (P-1) Preceptor Books, J. B. Lippincott Co., East Washington Square, Philadelphia, Pa. ($1.85).

Growing Up in New Guinea. Margaret Mead. (A58) Apollo Editions, 425 Park Ave. South, New York (Imprint of T. Y. Crowell, Dodd Mead, William Morrow, and The Dial Press) ($1.95).

Language and Thought of the Child. Jean Piaget. (M10) Meridian Books, The World Publishing Co., 2231 W. 110 St., Cleveland 2, Ohio ($1.55).

Life in a Turkish Village. Joe E. Pierce. (Orig.) Holt, Rinehart and Winston, 383 Madison Ave., New York ($1.50).

Patterns of Culture. Ruth Benedict. Science Editions Paperbacks, John Wiley and Sons, 605 Third Ave., New York ($1.65).

Small Town in Mass Society: Class, Power and Religion in a Rural Community. Arthur Vidich and Joseph Bensman. (A216) Anchor Books and Anchor Science Study Series, Doubleday and Co., 277 Park Ave., New York ($1.45).

Street Corner Society: The Social Structure of an Italian Slum. William Foot Whyte. (Orig.) University of Chicago Press, 5750 Ellis Ave., Chicago, Ill. ($2.95).

Suburbia: Its People and Their Politics. Robert C. Wood. Houghton Mifflin Co., 2 Park St., Boston, Mass. ($2.75).

Talk in Vandalia: The Life of an American Town. Joseph P. Lyford. (Illus.) (CN/51) Harper College Paperbacks, Harper and Row, 49 E. 33 St., New York ($1.25).

Tepoztlan: Village in Mexico. Oscar Lewis. (Illus.) (Orig.) Holt, Rinehart and Winston, 383 Madison Ave., New York ($1.50).

Yankee City. W. Lloyd Warner, Editor. (Abr., Rev. Ed.) (Y72) Yale University Press, 149 York St., New Haven, Conn. ($2.45).

Books

Ashton-Warner, Sylvia, *Teacher.* New York: Simon and Schuster, 1963, 224 pp. A comparative study of how Maori children of New Zealand learn and interact in the classroom situation.

Barber, Roger G., and Herbert A. Wright, *Midwest and Its Children.* Evanston, Ill.: Row, Peterson and Co., 1956. Barber and Wright present detailed information on the everyday lives and behavior settings of children in a small Midwest town.

Elkin, Frederick, *The Child and Society; the Process of Socialization.* New York: Random House, 1961. Chapter 3, "The Process of Socialization," describes the teacher as a significant model. Teachers as models, at one extreme, serve as sources of simple imitation; at the other, they establish strong emotional ties with the child.

Haan, Aubrey, *Education for the Open Society.* Boston: Allyn and Bacon, 1962. 358 pp. Chapter 4 shows how children bring their families and neighborhoods to the school.

Haskew, Lawrence D., and Jonathon C. McLendon, *This Is Teaching.* Chicago: Scott, Foresman and Co., 1962. Chapter 4, "Here Live the Learners," offers tables and charts illustrating how the social and economic influences in the community influence the learning of the child.

Havighurst, Robert J., et al., *Growing Up in River City*. New York: John Wiley and Sons, 1962. The authors report the findings of a depth study of responses of youth in a Midwestern community to school and other social situations.

Landes, Ruth, *Culture in American Education: Anthropological Approaches to Minority and Dominant Groups in the Schools*. New York: John Wiley and Sons, 1965. Landes' cultural approach stresses mental gifts and social heritages of human groups rather than physical appearances and test scores.

Redl, Fritz, "Group Emotion and Leadership," in *Small Groups, Studies in Social Interactions* by A. Paul Hare, Edgar F. Borgatta, and Robert F. Bales, New York: Alfred A. Knopf, 1955, pp. 71–95. The author discusses ten types of groups found in educational settings.

Spindler, George D., Editor, *Education and Culture*. New York: Holt, Rinehart and Winston, 1963. Chapter 11 by Jules Henry, "Spontaneity, Initiative and Creativity in Suburban Classrooms," deals with education of American middle-class children.

Westby-Gibson, Dorothy, *Social Perspectives on Education: The Society, The Student, The School*. New York: John Wiley and Sons, 1965. Part III describes education as a social process. Socialization occurs through group experiences, inside and outside the family, in organized voluntary groups, and through mass communication.

Periodicals

Benedict, Ruth, "Transmitting Our Democratic Heritage in the Schools," *American Journal of Sociology*, Vol. 48, No. 6, May 1943, pp. 722–727. The transmission of the democratic heritage is most threatened at the transitional point from adolescence to adulthood.

Borke, Helen, "Continuity and Change in the Transmission of Adaptive Patterns Over Two Generations," *Marriage and Family*, Vol. XXV, No. 3, August 1963, pp. 294–299. Parents encourage children to develop patterns similar to those they experienced in their original families.

Lewis, M. M., "How Speech Grows," *P.T.A. Magazine*, Vol. 59, No. 3, November 1964, pp. 8–10. The article brings together the biological infant and its inculturated mother in explaining how a member of society begins the long process of "teaching" the child.

Mekeel, Scudder, "Education, Child-Training, and Culture," *American Journal of Sociology*, Vol. 48, No. 5, May 1943, pp. 676–681. This paper compares the American Indian's own informal "education" with the alien formal one imposed upon his culture, and discusses the pertinence of the findings for action programs in the education of culturally alien people.

Taba, Hidda, "Cultural Deprivation as a Factor in School Learning," *Merrill-Palmer Quarterly of Behavior and Development*, Vol. X, No. 2, February 1964, pp. 147–158. The role of school is shown to be that of bridging the gap between the culture of the home and that of the school.

Ramsharan-Crowley, Pearl, "Creole Culture: Outcast in West Indian Schools," *The School Review*, Vol. 69, No. 4, Winter 1961, pp. 429–436. Past colonial history and educational policy in two West Indian islands have attempted to minimize local Creole culture. The result is a wide difference between formal education and everyday life.

3

The Classroom Is a Little Society

"Let no one be deceived, the important things that happen in the schools result from the interaction of personalities." WILLARD WALLER

The classroom is a social microcosm, a small human society.[1] Its primary purpose, learning, is achieved through human interaction. The human interaction takes place, as we know, between the teacher and the student and between one student and another. The crucial question is: Will the interaction add to or detract from the purpose of learning? The answer depends in part on what has gone before in the lives of both teachers and students, upon the kind of people they are, and upon how teachers and students work together to achieve their intended purpose. There is another kind of interaction in each classroom, between student and subject matter. This interaction is also conditioned by what has gone before in the life of the student and by the way the little society organizes itself in order to learn the subject matter.

In this chapter we are interested in classrooms as learning societies and in the human interaction within them. In Chapter 4 we shall be concerned with the way the human interaction influences mental health and achievement.

Much depends upon the human relationships of the classroom. The little society can inspire the child to want to learn, to embrace

[1] Talcott Parsons classifies the classroom as a "collectivity," that is, a subsystem of a larger social system (the school). The school is itself a subsystem of an even larger social system. The criterion that identifies the classroom "collectivity" is its defined membership and its common task orientation. T. Parsons, E. Shils, K. D. Naegele, and J. R. Pitts (Editors), *Theories of Societies,* New York, The Free Press of Glencoe, 1961.

the learning goals of the classroom, and to extend himself to achieve those goals.[2] The little society can also reject children, cast them to its margins, and make them want to fail.[3] It can stimulate, exhilarate, cast down, and depress. It sorts out the children who are to proceed to higher levels of education and to positions that require more education. It diverts others into terminal channels and to lesser positions that accept lower levels of education. The little society is a selector for the larger society—an important microcosm indeed.

Before we begin our analysis of the classroom we shall figuratively step inside four of these little societies to see what is going on. Our purpose in doing so is to sensitize ourselves to social factors within classrooms that help to determine the quality of learning which takes place. These brief classroom vignettes suggest profitable speculations about how the social climate fosters or detracts from learning. More specifically, they stimulate some of the following questions.

1. How would you describe the interaction between students and teacher, students and students, students and subject matter? Spontaneous? Motivated? Learning directed? Forced? Unmotivated? Distracting?

2. What seem to be the aims of the socialization which is taking place at the moment of observation? To give information? To teach a skill? To transmit a value? To build a group image?

3. How would you describe the social climate of the classroom? Supporting? Threatening? Competitive? Cooperative?

4. How would you describe the role of the teacher? Dominating? Pleading? Prodding? Stimulating? Inviting?

5. How would you describe the participation of the students? Apathetic? Aimless? Reluctant? Casual? Thoughtful? Spontaneous?

In each of the following small scenes we can begin to see how social factors influence what is learned and how well it is learned.

INCIDENTS IN CLASSROOM LEARNING

Mrs. Mullen's First Grade Discovers the Letter "W"

"The first-grade classroom buzzed with excitement. Something wonderful was about to happen, and the six-year-old boys and girls

[2] F. R. Harris, M. M. Wolf, and D. M. Baer concluded from their study of positive and negative reinforcement that the teacher can willfully direct a child's behavior patterns by selective reinforcement. "Effects of Adult Social Reinforcement of Child Behavior," *Young Children*, Volume XX, No. 1, October 1964, pp. 8–17.

[3] R. E. Herriot, in his study of 1489 adolescents, found that a student's peers are a major influence on his motivation. "Some Social Determinants of Educational Aspirations," *Harvard Education Review*, Volume 33, No. 2, Spring 1963, pp. 157–177.

could not wait to find out what it was. They wiggled in their seats, whispered to one another, craned their necks for a peek at the chart that the teacher blocked from view. They could hear her scissors snipping away and knew that the great event was coming closer. Suddenly a tow-headed boy with a missing tooth and flaming red tie jumped up and blurted out, 'I know what it is, Mrs. Mullen!'

"The teacher finished snipping, looked around, then stepped away from the chart. The room exploded with laughter. Some clapped, some did nervous little dances, others just stared at the chart. There, plainly revealed for all to see, was the magnificent letter *W*." [4]

This little society is intriguing for what must have preceded this event. There has been a buildup of interest in letters. Letters in this classroom are not ordinary things but are lively objects of interest. In the masterful hands of Mrs. Mullen, learning about a new letter is a major event filled with suspense. This glimpse does not tell us much about the interaction among students, which seems to be spirited, but it does tell us something about the high interest in the interaction between teacher and students. And it does reveal a great deal about the interaction between students and the subject. Under Mrs. Mullen's skilled direction the students find intrinsic interest in the subject of letters. The motivation of the children to learn about letters does not seem to be trumped up or external to themselves. It is personal and direct.

We gather that emotions are expressed in Mrs. Mullen's classroom. The room "buzzes with excitement" and the children "wiggle in their seats" and "whisper to one another." And the "tow-headed boy with the missing tooth" was not afraid to jump up and blurt out that he knew the answer. The social climate of the classroom seems to be marked by controlled freedom of expression, by good feeling among the students and rapport with the teacher. This little society seems to teach. [5]

Mr. Jeffries' Sixth Grade and the Tortoise

In an American suburban classroom Mr. Jeffries performs the role of a contemporary middle-class father. He is buddy-buddy with the

[4] Normand Poirier, "The Extraordinary Amidon School," *Saturday Evening Post*, December 19–26, 1964, p. 22.

[5] T. Campanelle concludes from his experience with teachers and adolescent students that the teacher who is able to positively demonstrate his high motivation for teaching will find a ready and receptive class that will be likewise stimulated to learn. "Motivational Development of Adolescents," *Education*, Volume 85, No. 5, January 1965, pp. 310–313.

boys and sweetheart to the girls. With the girls he uses endearing terms and with the boys nicknames as he pats them on the head or puts his arm around their shoulders. We have the feeling that his room is much less controlled than Mrs. Mullen's, and that part of the time it is rough and tumble.

"The class is having a reading lesson. Teacher says, 'Galapagos means tortoise. Where are 300-pound turtles found?' A boy says, 'In the zoo,' and teacher says, 'Where are they native in this country?' A girl says, with a grimace of disgust, 'We saw them in Marine Land in Florida. They were slaughtered and used for meat. Ugh!' John has raised his hand and teacher calls on him. 'We saw one in Wisconsin about the size of Bob's head.' Teacher says, 'That's plenty big,' and the class laughs.

"Teacher asks, 'What was Douglas (a boy in the story) doing on the island? Have you ever been scared, John?' 'Yes,' replies John. 'So have I,' says the teacher, and the class laughs. Teacher says, *'That's what I like about buddies.'*

"Teacher says, 'Let's read the story silently,' He says to a girl, 'Do you mind putting your beads away for the rest of the morning instead of tearing them apart?'

"The room is now very quiet. He walks around the aisles as the children read." [6]

Mr. Jeffries' children are spontaneous, and he obviously runs a democratic classroom. He is not an aloof figure but rather does all he can to level the distance between himself and his pupils. He says he is their "buddy" and, like them, can be "scared." Yet he does exercise control when he wants to and can command the class to quiet down, though perhaps not for long. The class seems to enjoy laughing together, not at somebody but with one another. We might question the joke about the size of Bob's head, but there seems to be little question that the students are fond of Mr. Jeffries. Everyone, including the teacher, seems to have a wonderful time.

Mrs. Miller's History Classroom

"Mrs. Henrietta Miller stands in front of a paper-heaped desk in the north wing of Chicago's vast Senn High School. She is a large woman, a trifle ungainly on thin legs. Her friendly eyes fairly snap

[6] Jules Henry, "The Problem of Spontaneity, Initiative and Creativity in Suburban Classrooms," *American Journal of Orthopsychiatry*, Volume XXIX, No. 2, April 1959, p. 271.

with animation as she presides over the apparent anarchy of a truly extraordinary history classroom.

"The topic under discussion—history source books and the importance of keeping file cards on them—would seem conducive to day-dreaming, perhaps even dozing. For a time Mrs. Miller seems not to be teaching at all, merely asking questions as the half-formed thoughts of the students rattle around disjointedly like dice in a shaker. But there is little boredom among the thirty juniors and seniors in Room 249. No one seems aware of the yelps from the gym class in the dusty quadrangle below the classroom windows or the periodic bellow of jet airliners entering and leaving the air traffic pattern of O'Hare International Airport.

"As the class discussion continues, Mrs. Miller moves about the room. Sometimes she sits by her desk (never behind it), stands in the back of the room, even sits in a vacant desk amid the students. Her punctuating questions begin to nudge here, clarify a bit there.

"She is challenging the students. 'Now why are we concerned about our sources of information?' she asks. 'Mark, are you concerned?' . . . 'Any other reasons? We can get more specific.' . . . 'Why worry about the author, the point of view, your reaction to the source?' . . . 'Do you think you could be brainwashed? What's brainwashed?' . . . 'Ah!' . . . 'That's right, make you believe almost anything, everything, that you had believed was untrue.' . . . 'What do you think, Mickey?'

"After 20 minutes of group groping and flailing, Mickey comes up with an answer: 'If you believe everything everybody tells you, you're actually a puppet. If you think things out for yourself and make your own conclusions, then you're an individualist.' Mrs. Miller smiles with delight. A student presenting a sound idea in teen-age terms is, she believes, more eloquent for the class than she can ever be. This is the way she teaches.

"'I hate this class, I positively *hate* it,' mourned a pretty youngster to her friend as they took their seats in Room 249. 'It's too interesting— it makes me work.'

"Another girl says, 'She's always asking "Why?" "Why?" That makes you do the same thing to your fellow students. And Mrs. Miller just stands there beaming while the arguments fly back and forth. She gets so much enjoyment, and you feel kind of maternal toward her. All you can do is try to join in.'

"Henrietta Miller has set herself the goal of teaching young, often indifferent minds the painful process of analytical thinking. She considers her biggest weapon to be freedom—'freedom of inquiry into anything, freedom to discuss their findings, the freedom to make up your own mind as well as the freedom to change your mind.'

"Mrs. Miller refuses to go over the factual 'story,' as she calls it. 'Why should I spend my time giving students what they can get in books?' she asks. 'I always take the position that we are learning together and I must never slip into the role they expect me to play—the superhuman being who can meet all their questions with the truth.' Instead, Mrs. Miller fires back her own questions. . . .

" 'You've just *got* to join in the class discussions,' said one of her students. 'But you can't join in unless you've done your homework— that's the awful part!' " [7]

6. Does this student comment that "You've just got to join in" tell you anything about the relationship between the social climate of the classroom and student achievement?

Mrs. Miller's classroom is quite different as a learning society from that of Mrs. Mullen or Mr. Jeffries. The interchange among students is a much stronger component in the learning process. Mrs. Miller encourages students to question and learn from one another. The students soon learn to pick up her style of questioning and use it on one another. Thus Mrs. Miller has multiplied herself as teacher. Each child is both teacher and learner; the group, as a teaching and learning group, is irresistible even to reluctant participants. As one girl states, "I hate this class . . . It's too interesting—it makes me work." Here is the little society at its best in the act of teaching.

The group pressure moves each participant toward its center, and toward the learning goals.[8] Note Mrs. Miller's social role in this process. "I always take the position," she says, "that we are learning together and I must never slip into the role they expect me to play— the superhuman being who can meet all their questions with truth." Through skillful teaching she has shifted responsibility for learning to the group.

The socialization in Mrs. Miller's classroom pushes students

[7] Richard Meryman, "The Rewards of a Great Teacher," *Life*, Volume 56, No. 11, March 13, 1964, pp. 70–72.

[8] M. R. Goodson points out that for a group of individuals to function as a social system, "there must be some degree of interdependence among its interacting members. This interdependence generates a strong demand for conformity among them, and the demand has to be satisfied to some degree for the preservation of the group." "The 'Person' and the 'Group' in American Culture and Education," *Dynamics of Instructional Groups*, N. S. S. E. Yearbook, 1960, pp. 14–15; *Sociopsychological Aspects of Teaching and Learning*, Nelson B. Henry (Ed.), 59th Yearbook of the N. S. S. E., Part II, pp. 11–29.

toward maturity of judgment and independence of thought. When students flounder she is not concerned at all. She wants students to be a little bewildered, to be uneasy until they can get matters clarified. She asks them to be more mature than they want to be, and the supporting spirit of the little society helps them. It is truly a learning society.

Miss Plapinger and the Porcelain Dog

Whereas the previous examples have been primarily concerned with the interaction between the teacher and the group, the following incident takes place between a teacher and a single student. There is another difference. The previous incidents involved the interplay of students, teachers, and subject matter. This incident involves a stolen porcelain dog and represents a question of values. What should a teacher do when a problem boy of the slums steals a gift for her out of affection? The point of the incident is clear: The little society teaches values as well as subject matter.[9] It must be deeply concerned about the values involved in human relationships and in reinforcing those that the larger society supports. Notice how Miss Plapinger does this.

"George came to my desk. 'Still got the dog I gave you?' 'Of course. I'm taking him home with me today.'

"He was leaning on my desk, looking at the porcelain dog. He stayed for a while. Then, very softly: 'Know where I got 'im? I stole 'im.'

"I heard the rest very clearly, a separate paragraph that became part of my brain. 'I went on the market and I waited till the lady turned around and then I grabbed it and I ran all the way home and at night when I went to sleep I hid it so my mother couldn't see and in the morning I take it in my pocket and bring it here to give you.'

"The words were on my tongue without passing through my mind. Right was right and wrong was wrong, and stealing was wrong. I knew what a teacher must say to a child. I was looking at George's face, very round, and his pale eyes, catching the light from the window, held up toward me.

"I put my hand on George's and, very, very slowly, hoping I was saying the right thing, because I wanted this boy to grow up knowing

---

[9] Rhoda Métraux suggests that the implicit teaching of values is a more significant function of the school than instruction in subject matter. "Implicit and Explicit Values in Education and Teaching as Related to Growth and Development," *The Merrill-Palmer Quarterly of Behavior and Development,* Volume 2, 1955, pp. 27–34.

that life was full of love, I said, 'George, you know that if you take something from that lady and don't pay for it she might not have enough money to buy food for her children. And I know you don't want that to happen, and that you understand now it wasn't a good thing to do.

" 'But I know that you wanted to give me a present very, very much, and I'm so happy to know you thought about me and wanted to give me something—it's a wonderful thing to do. And for that reason I love this dog.

" 'You're going to promise not to take any more things, aren't you? And I'm going to take this beautiful dog home with me and keep it forever and ever.' " [10]

7. If you had been in the teacher's place how would you have responded to George? What would have been your reasons for responding as you did?

In this incident the teacher is confronted with hard choices. She knows the importance of George's affection for her. This boy who has so few love objects has found one in his teacher. While the relationship is tumultuous, it does give security to George's hectic existence. The teacher wants to keep the affections of the child secure. Yet, "right was right and wrong was wrong, and stealing was wrong," and something had to be done. Miss Plapinger elects to treat the problem in concrete human terms rather than in terms of abstract right and wrong. She reminds George that he hurt the lady from whom he stole and extracts a promise that he will not do it again. She then reaffirms her affection for the child by declaring that she will keep the dog "forever and ever."

Here is a simple yet complex example of the socialization of a child within the little classroom society. We do not know its impact. We do know that the little society in this instance performed one of its most important socializing functions: It reinforced one of the important values of the culture.

These four examples indicate something of the range of social functions of the classroom. These functions encompass relationships of students with one another, of teachers with students, and of both with subject matter and social values. Let us now turn to a more analytic look at the cultural and social-psychological functions of classrooms.

[10] Sylvia Plapinger, "The Angels," *Ladies' Home Journal*, Volume LXXXI, No. 4, May 1964, pp. 50–51.

CULTURAL FUNCTIONS OF THE CLASSROOM

The classrooms we just observed are strikingly different. Yet in the cultural purposes which they serve they are very much alike. All four classrooms are agents of American culture. As such they are expected to perform certain social functions. They are expected to help induct the young into the culture, to help the young become adult Americans.[11] To survive, the culture needs an ever-renewing flow of youth which is prepared to perpetuate it, and the classroom is an agency for assuring this flow.

Our accumulated wisdom is possible only because we have devised ways to take what others before us have learned, add to it our own contributions, and then, in turn, pass it along to the next generation. Without this capacity to inherit as well as extend culture, each new generation would have to start afresh. If the contribution of each generation were lost to the next, no great culture could ever be built. Progress is dependent upon continuity: Classrooms help to provide that continuity.

Classrooms, of course, are not the only institutions that lend continuity to culture. The family, religion, social groups, government, mass media, and many other institutions help to give continuity to culture and assure its perpetuation. The school, however, is usually regarded as the *formal* and *planned* agency for inducting the young into the culture. For this purpose the teacher selects appropriate materials that will develop within the young a commitment to the values of the culture and an enthusiasm for extending it. The subject matter of the classroom mirrors the culture. The history, science, language, social studies, and moral values are drawn from the culture and are used to create both an appreciation for it and an adherence to its norms.

But most schools do more than transmit the culture. They also extend and change it. Especially in our own rapidly changing society, they build into youth a propensity for change.[12] In this dual responsibility both to preserve and to change the culture lies one of the sensitive areas of education. Can the schools, agents of the culture and

---

[11] G. F. Kneller calls this process "enculturation," which he defines as the means "by which a growing person is initiated into the way of life of his society." *Educational Anthropology*, New York, John Wiley and Sons, 1965, p. 12.

[12] K. D. Naegele observes that change is inherent in the survival of a social system. He points out that where the "sources of change have been institutionalized" the continuity of society is insured. T. Parsons, E. Shils, K. D. Naegele, and J. R. Pitts (Editors), *Theories of Society*, New York, The Free Press of Glencoe, 1961, p. 1222.

created by it, really change or modify that culture? Many persons raise an even more fundamental question: Should they? Much current controversy in education is at its heart an issue of the role of schools in relation to change. The commitment of schools to preserve, improve, and extend the culture exists and is supported by current practice and custom.

Observe in the aforementioned incidents of the four classrooms how the school transmits and extends culture. Language is a key to cultural survival. In Mrs. Mullen's first-grade classroom the children are learning letters, the essential ingredient of written language. In this simple yet wonderful act Mrs. Mullen is teaching more than a unit in the alphabet. She is enabling children to inherit their culture and to extend it through written language. This little incident is a cultural event of tremendous importance.

Or consider Mrs. Miller's history class. The present and future are always meaningful in terms of the past. How we think about our history gives us an image of our future. The ability to think analytically, as Mrs. Miller is teaching her students to do, is an act of immense cultural significance. Or consider the case of Miss Plapinger, George, and the stolen porcelain dog. Our culture, as we know it, would fly apart without basic honesty in personal dealings. Miss Plapinger was doing more than attempting to dissuade one boy from stealing. She was invoking a cultural necessity.

Culture cannot be inherited like biological traits; it must be taught. That is one of the functions of classrooms.

8. A good way to become aware of the cultural transmission functions of classrooms is to observe them directly with this in mind. Visit a classroom, observe the activities of students and teacher, and make a list of the different ways in which cultural values are being transmitted to children.

THE SOCIAL-PSYCHOLOGICAL ASPECTS OF THE CLASSROOM

In the social-psychological area classrooms serve two main functions. First, they train youth to perform adult roles when they are grown. In other words, they teach basic and applied skills which are useful in later life. Since these skills tend to be those possessed by adult models, we call this the "modeling function" of classrooms. Second, classrooms help to determine which students will perform what roles as adults. They help to select and sort out students for different roles and occupations, and because different roles carry different status they help to determine the eventual social status of students as adults. This we call the "selection functions" of the classroom.

THE MODELING FUNCTION OF CLASSROOMS

We have said that classrooms create within students a commitment to the culture. Another function of the classroom is to create in youth the commitment to perform specific kinds of tasks within the structure of society. Each society has a multitude of tasks to be performed if the work of the society is to get done. These tasks are performed by adults who must, in time, be replaced. The new generations must be both motivated to assume these tasks and skilled to perform them well.

Classrooms perform this function by holding before students "models" of the different roles to be performed in the society. Some of these models are associated with vocational choice: scientist, engineer, teacher, doctor, farmer, white-collar worker, blue-collar worker, and many more. Other models relate to social roles: mother, father, husband, wife, brother, sister, team member, citizen, neighbor, and many others. When Miss Plapinger spoke to George about stealing, she had as a reference a model of citizen and neighbor. In the act of stealing the porcelain dog George had violated the model. When Mrs. Miller helps her juniors and seniors to think analytically for themselves, she has in mind a model of an educated person and his intellectual equipment. She is helping them to become like the model.

Consider the importance of the school as a provider of occupational and social models for children. The school performs this role in

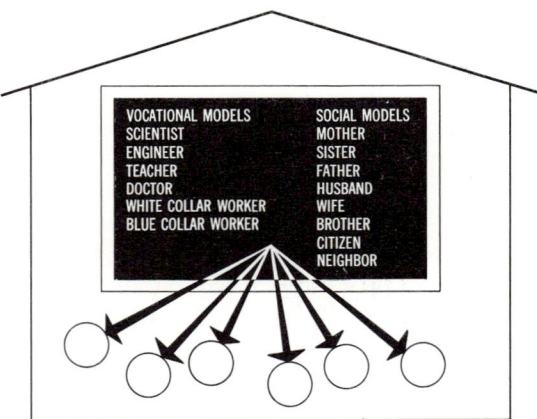

Fig. 3-1 Modern American schools present the child with alternative adult models.

practically all societies. As an institution the school widens the child's choice and points to new prospects beyond his immediate family. Going to school is the child's first major step into the vast world beyond his own home.

From one society to another there is a vast difference in the kind and number of models which the school presents to the child. Schools tend to offer to children the models that are present in the society of which they are a part. If the society is traditional and underdeveloped, the number of models tends to be small and the range of types narrow. If the society is modern and changing, the number of models is large and the range of types wide. The traditional society does not expect its schools to give high priority to this function because the models the children need are present in the immediate neighborhood. The modern society, by contrast, expects its schools to give high priority to providing new models for children. The neighborhood is not sufficient. The child must be upwardly mobile and familiar with new opportunities open to him beyond his community. His survival depends on it.

Consider, for example, two of the children we observed in Chapter 1, Beth of American suburbia and Hamid of the Pakistan village. Notice how the models available to each child differ. At home Hamid is surrounded constantly by the adult members of a joint family and an extended kin group. At home Beth has as adult models two parents of a nuclear family and other adults only periodically.

Hamid's small village is relatively homogeneous with a great deal of socializing among adult members. Children are not segregated from adult activities in the village; they mingle freely. The adults of the village are therefore available to Hamid as models: the mullah who sits in the mosque, the landlords, the shopkeepers, the tax collector, the landless workers. The airman who comes to the village is also a model, but he is an exceptional one. There are not many like him. The teacher in Hamid's school provides a model, but the content of the curriculum does not provide a range of models to the children because the society itself is traditional, and is only now opening up to development. Hamid's "life space" is therefore largely confined to the village, and when he travels to another village he will be presented with no new adult models. The nearby villages are about the same as his own. The adults Hamid sees, therefore, are models of traditional village values and tend to create in him a self-image not greatly different from that of his village elders. The models in Hamid's life do not propel him toward change.

In Beth's suburbia, children mingle some with adults but tend to be much more segregated in their own activities. Peer models are more available and adult models less available in the immediate neighborhood. The range of types of models available to Beth, however, is much greater than to Hamid. Her "life space" is larger. Through radio, television, books, and travel, her number of models multiplies. In fact, some of the popular idols to whom she is exposed are a frequent concern of her parents. They could do with less exposure to certain of them. Hamid's parents do not worry about this—the limited village society automatically restricts their son's contacts.

The major difference between Beth and Hamid in this respect is that Beth lives in a rapidly changing, upwardly mobile society in which children are by design exposed to an ever-widening circle of models. And the school is expected to help widen that circle: The child is expected to move beyond the family and the suburb, and the school's program is planned to help him do it.

The school serves this function in many ways. In its large number of teachers, each with a variety of backgrounds and experiences, the modern American school provides alternative adult models. Just as important, through its instructional, counseling, and guidance programs the schools extend the range of models available to students. Experience with a wide range of models will help Beth make important future decisions about occupational choice and a marriage partner. As she widens her circle of associates her choice of models will reflect her progressing status in society.

One way to judge the importance of the school in this process is to ask: What would happen to the child's choice of models and his attendant aspirations if there were no schools? In the case of Prince Edward County, Virginia, we have such an example. Because of the integration dispute, the public schools of this county were closed for a period of four years, from 1959 to 1963. Fortunately a group of scholars were able to study what happened to those children who did not go to school during the period.[13] Here are the conclusions of the study regarding the models which were available to the out-of-school children.

"Contrary to what was expected regarding the child's choice of models as he grows older, the children in the sample did not draw their models from a progressively widening circle of acquaintances. Throughout the sample, family based figures maintained a high incidence of choice whether the respondent was being considered by age,

[13] R. L. Green, L. Hoffman, et al., *The Educational Status of Children in a District without Public Schools*, East Lansing, Bureau of Educational Research, College of Education, Michigan State University, 1964, pp. 180–181.

sex, or amount of schooling. The data from this study suggest that the normal process of identification and imitation, and the choice of significant others has been severely impeded or interrupted by the public school closure. It is probable that the interruption of the imitation process was affected by the absence of one of the most important socializing instruments: the school as a continuing factor in the environment. When the school does not exist, or exists only partially and sporadically as it did for children sent outside the county, the child's contact with an increasingly wide variety of significant others is restricted and he is thrown back into the family circle. Peers decrease in number; teachers, for many, become nonexistent; and the educational channels (classroom discussion, textbooks, etc.) through which awareness of more abstract, appropriate models could be sharpened, are lacking. Associates become limited to parents, siblings, and other family members whose presence does not depend on the school's existence." [14]

Not only do classrooms present models of the vocational and social roles to be performed in the adult world: They also teach the specific skills required to carry out these roles. In the classroom of the early grades the emphasis is on the basic skills in language, science, and mathematics required of all roles. Just as important, the early grades, through social studies and reading, implant attitudes toward work, the use of time, and human relations that are crucial in performing adult tasks. In the later years of high school and college the emphasis turns to training in the specific vocational skills. Classrooms, then, may be regarded as agencies for generating both commitment to and skills for accomplishing society's work.

9. Make an analysis of the different models which were available in the high school you attended. Include the "live" ones such as teachers, administrators, and fellow students, and also the "silent" ones which were represented in the courses you studied and the books you read. Have any of these had an influence on your own occupational and social aspirations?

THE SELECTION FUNCTION OF CLASSROOMS

Classrooms prepare youth for adult roles and help to determine who will perform particular ones. Modern society has an infinite variety of tasks to be performed. These tasks, in terms of education required to perform them, vary widely. Some may be performed with a

[14] For another study of the Prince Edward County Schools, see B. Smith, *They Closed Their Schools: Prince Edward County, Virginia, 1951–1964,* Durham, University of North Carolina Press, 1965.

grade-school education, some with a high-school education, and some require highly sophisticated higher education. The tasks that can still be performed by those with only a grade school education are diminishing rapidly, almost to the vanishing point in our technological society. On the other hand, those requiring training at higher levels are increasing rapidly.

We also noted that classrooms help to determine the eventual adult status of students.[15] Higher status is usually attached to tasks that require longer periods of formal preparation. Generally speaking, those people with higher levels of education will be found in the higher vocational and professional levels, levels that usually carry with them higher income and status.

How do classrooms operate as agencies for allocating youth to particular tasks and statuses in the structure of society? There are two factors at work that influence this allocation. First, there is the *ascriptive* factor, the socio-economic status of the child's family. The family status is "ascribed" to the child as a part of his social inheritance. He has little or no control over it. Each of the four children discussed in Chapter 1 grew up in suburbia, slum, town, or village and each had a different "ascribed" status. Each was born into a different social and economic condition, and this condition has much to say about where the child starts the school race. For example, it would be assumed that Beth of suburbia would start the race considerably ahead of Julia of the slum.[16] Surrounded by books, in a home in which intellectual interests are frequently discussed, in a community which values education, Beth's school life is a natural extension of her out-of-school life. Such is not the case with Julia for whom the values of the school present a sharp break with those of the slum. The status ascribed to each girl plays a crucial role in what she will become.

The second factor which operates to allocate youth to certain tasks

[15] Ralph Linton early developed the concepts of statuses and roles. He pointed out that most statuses are *ascriptive* in nature—sex, race, and family. He went on to say, however, that the dynamic quality of a society is the result of *achieved* status, and that achieved statuses "are not assigned to individuals from birth but are filled through competition and individual effort." *The Study of Man*, New York, D. Appleton-Century Co., 1936, p. 115.

[16] R. C. Wylie, in her study of self-concept, found that children of lower socio-economic levels make more modest estimates of their educational ability than do children of higher socio-economic levels. This finding would suggest that despite a child's actual educational potential, his perceptions of his ability are closely correlated with his lower class status role. "Children's Estimates of Their School Work Ability, As a Function of Sex, Race, and Socio-Economic Level," *Journal of Personality*, Volume 31, No. 2, June 1963, pp. 203–224.

and statuses is classroom *achievement*. What a child achieves in the classroom depends in large measure upon his own motivation and ability. Even though Beth, Julia, Raymond, and Hamid have different ascribed statuses, each must compile his own record in school. Here individual ability and application count. Both factors, their social inheritance and actual achievement in the classroom, combine to determine the level of education and status they will achieve.

SELECTION IN THE ELEMENTARY SCHOOL

Just how important is the elementary school classroom in this selection process? Parsons suggests that "by far the most important criterion of selection is the record of performance of elementary school. These records are evaluated by teachers and principals, and there are few cases of entering the college preparatory course against their advice. It is, therefore, not stretching the evidence too far to say broadly that the primary selective process occurs through differential school performance in elementary school, and that the 'seal' is put on it in junior high school." [17]

The social inheritance that the child brings to school, his ascribed status, combines with what he does in school, his achievement, to determine what he shall become. Note in the following example from a French sixth-grade classroom how what the student is, the ascriptive factor, combines with his classroom achievement to cause the teacher to predict that the student will go on to the *lycée* (the French status secondary school).

"There are about thirty-five boys in the room, ranged in seven rows facing front. One of them, a handsome boy with well-brushed black hair, is called upon to recite, and to the accompaniment of some ragging from those in his row strides to the front, where he does not slouch. The teacher, a faintly shabby, but highly dignified man in his early forties, ignores the ragging.

"On request, the boy draws the femur of a rabbit on the blackboard. It is assumed in France that all children can draw accurately—and, oddly enough, the assumption seems to be correct. The teacher says to the visitor, in a stage whisper, 'The son of the mayor. He will go to the *lycée*.'

---

[17] Talcott Parsons, "The School as a Social Class System: Some of Its Functions in American Society," in A. H. Halsey, Jean Floced, and C. Arnold Anderson, *Education, Economy and Society*, New York, The Free Press of Glencoe, 1962, p. 436. The author wishes to express his debt to the work of Talcott Parsons in the following analysis of selection in the schools.

" 'Oh.'

"The teacher turns to the child, pleasantly. 'What kind of animal is the rabbit?'

" 'Herbivorous.'

" 'A complete sentence, please.'

" 'The rabbit is a herbivorous animal.'

" 'Why is he a herbivorous animal?'

" 'Because he eats plants.'

" '*Only* plants?'

" 'Only plants.'

" 'Good.' "

This boy, because he is the son of the mayor, has an ascribed status. Because he is also achieving well in the classroom, he will go to the *lycée*, and beyond.[18]

10. Take as a case study a fellow student whom you knew in high school and describe both his ascribed and his achievement status. In this case do the two coincide? Or is one high while the other is low? If so, can you explain the discrepancy?

FEATURES OF THE QUEST FOR ACHIEVEMENT

Let us now turn to some of the features of the social conditions under which children are asked to achieve in the elementary classroom.

First, there is the attempt to assure each child a fair start in the competitive race. The child enters a classroom of age-mates and is not asked to compete with persons older or more experienced than himself. This is especially true of the graded elementary school. The ungraded elementary school presents a somewhat different situation. In the ungraded classroom the child is permitted theoretically to "move at his own speed," in other words, at a speed that is "fair" for him.

Second, American elementary school children tend to come from homogeneous communities around the school and therefore tend to have similar ascribed statuses. The "neighborhood" school is an almost sacred concept in American education. It assures an initial equality in the contest for achievement. In recent years the racial integration struggle has brought the neighborhood school into sharp focus and controversy. The neighborhood school may offer roughly equal educational opportunity within a particular neighborhood, but neighbor-

[18] Martin Mayer, *The Schools*, Garden City, N. Y., Doubleday and Co., 1963, p. 12.

hoods differ, as do their schools. Among neighborhoods, educational opportunity may be, and frequently is, grossly unequal. The plans for "open admission" and for bussing children from one neighborhood to another are supported as ways to equalize the child's initial start in the contest to achieve. Opponents of these plans use the same argument of equality. They argue that these plans may increase the opportunity for one group of children but do so at the expense of another. This, they say, is not the way to achieve true equality. The merits of the arguments aside, there is in the American educational value system strong support for equalizing initial education opportunity.

Third, children are asked to perform a common set of tasks. Third-grade children, for example, are not required to perform tasks appropriate for fourth graders. Individual differences are such that children frequently do perform above or below their grade norms, but there is a common expectation against which all children are measured. Programs of "enrichment" are simply ways of providing for children who are at variance with the grade-level norms.

Fourth, there is a systematic process of evaluation. Children are measured by the same instruments and take similar examinations. In other words, the achievement of each child is measured in the same way. And we are concerned when we suspect such is not the case— for example, when human variables enter into the evaluation of children. The "good" teacher is "fair" with students and "treats (in terms of grading) them all alike." But the teacher who "plays favorites," who uses differential standards in grading, is regarded as a "poor" teacher.

These four features of the quest for achievement tend to equalize the opportunities of children in the early years. The child competes with his age-mates from similar backgrounds in common tasks under the same evaluation. Let us now turn to the content of achievement in the elementary schools.

The Content of Achievement

The act of achieving in the elementary school is illuminated further by characterizing what children are asked to achieve.

First, the content is selected for its appropriateness to the school situation. School learning is circumscribed by many factors: the age and capabilities of children, the school as a physical place for learning, the materials of instruction, the methods of teaching, and the capacities of the teachers. What children learn will always be conditioned by these limiting factors. We assume that in affluent schools where learning resources are great children will achieve more than where learning resources are meager. Both affluent and deprived schools must choose to teach what may be taught within the limitations of schools.

What is taught in schools is determined by both cultural and educational considerations. For example, in Hamid's Moslem culture it is considered appropriate, even mandatory, to teach religion as expressed in the Holy Koran. In Beth's culture, because of court interpretations regarding our historic separation of church and state, the teaching of religion in the schools is inappropriate.

Recent changes in our understanding of children's learning have caused us to alter our ideas about what is educationally appropriate as subject matter in the elementary schools. Children, we are finding out, are capable of learning much more sophisticated subject matter than we previously thought. The limitations, we are now coming to suspect, are not so much in children's ability to learn as in our ability to teach. In his exciting small volume on *The Process of Education*, Jerome S. Bruner includes this quotation from a researcher in the field of child learning: "It seems highly arbitrary and very likely incorrect to delay the teaching of, for example, Euclidian or metric geometry until the end of the primary grades. . . . So too with the teaching of physics, which has much in it that can be profitably taught at an inductive or intuitive level much earlier. Basic notions in these fields are perfectly accessible to children of seven to ten years of age, provided that they are divorced from their mathematical expression and studied through material that the child can handle himself." [19]

Second, the content of achievement reflects the values which the adults of the society regard as important. During the current years the heavy emphasis on mathematics, language, and science, "the fundamentals," may be properly regarded as a value judgment of the American people about the content of achievement in elementary schools.

Third, achievement in elementary schools is cognitive. Children are expected to learn basic facts and skills that are regarded as important in the adult society. The children in Mrs. Mullen's class who were learning the letter "W" were in the process of meeting this requirement for achievement.

Fourth, achievement in the elementary schools also has a moral content. Children are supposed to learn to "work together," "be helpful," "share," be "good citizens." Moral achievement is given high priority in elementary classrooms, and the good student is frequently at

[19] Jerome S. Bruner, *The Process of Education*, Cambridge, Mass., Harvard University Press, 1960, p. 43.

the same time a "good" boy or girl. Cognitive achievement and moral achievement are regarded as interdependent.

Selection in the elementary school is thus determined by both ascriptive and achievement factors. The child's quest for achievement takes place under conditions which make for, but do not necessarily insure, equality of opportunity. The content which is both cognitive and moral is selected for its suitability to the classroom situation and its sanction by the adult society. Selection within secondary schools has many of the same features as that in elementary schools, but we shall note some major changes.

Selection in Secondary School

Selection in the high school is based on a number of changes which take place gradually in the student's transition from elementary school. Most of the changes are in the direction of widening the child's contacts with teachers and peers, exposing him to more heterogeneous models, and stepping up his socialization.[20]

In the elementary school the child typically has one teacher with whom he spends most of the time, though he may have some contact with other special-area teachers in classes in art, music, physical education, and speech. As the child moves toward high school he is exposed to an increasing number of teachers, and he usually takes each course with a different one. The sharp break usually comes in junior high school when students go on a "platoon" system, moving from room to room and from teacher to teacher. Psychologically, the "homeroom" in secondary school is designed to give the student a feeling of belonging somewhere although he is constantly on the move.

The secondary school draws students from a wider geographical area than the elementary school. The elementary school usually serves the neighborhood immediately around it, whereas the high school may serve a vast area. The city high school usually serves a large section of the metropolis, the town high school the entire town, and the consolidated school a vast rural region. The child who moves from elementary to high school is thus exposed to teachers and students with a wider range of statuses. In short, he is exposed to more and differ-

---

[20] J. Piaget outlined the stages of intellectual growth. He pointed out how children in the early elementary grades tend toward egocentric thinking. Then, as they grow older and their thought patterns develop, there is a natural socialization process wherein children extend their perceptions to include multidimensional socialized thought patterns. If Piaget is correct, a major function of education is to build the socialization milieu and teach through it. *The Language and Thought of a Child,* New York, Harcourt, Brace and Co., 1926.

ent models. Such increased exposure usually leads the child to reshuffle the friendships he formed in elementary school.

The high school also offers more extracurricular activities than either the junior high or the elementary school. In athletics, clubs, and school-sponsored social activities, the student finds a widening circle from which to select models and "significant others."

The curricular organization of the secondary school also tends to expose the student more systematically to different kinds of people. The separation of the curriculum into academic and vocational streams throws the student in with new groups. This differentiation also segregates him from others who have statuses different from his own. Most secondary schools offer some elective courses which present yet another opportunity for meeting and socializing with other students and teachers.

How do these changes relate to the process of differentiation and selection in high school? Actually they present the conditions in which differentiation and selection take place. Let us turn to the specific characteristics of differentiation and selection in the secondary school.

Emphasis on Type of Achievement

In the elementary school the emphasis is on the level of capacity to achieve. In secondary schools the emphasis shifts to the type of achievement. The purpose in elementary school is, first, to build into the child a desire to achieve and, second, to evaluate his capacity for achievement. The evaluation differentiates among those with high, average, and low capacities of achievement. The main emphasis is on the level of achievement rather than on the particular type of achievement.

For example, recall Mrs. Mullen's classroom in which the children were learning the letter "W." The enthusiasm of the children would suggest that Mrs. Mullen had indeed built into the children a desire to learn letters. This does not suggest, however, that all the children will learn the letters equally well. When Mrs. Mullen sits with the parents of these children in parent-teacher conferences, her professional judgment of the different levels of achievement will be reflected in the conversation. To the parents of one child she may say: "Kathy is learning her letters well." To the parents of another: "John is having some difficulty with letters." To the parents of a third: "Mary will improve with remedial work." In each case she is saying something about the level of achievement at the time of the conference.

In the secondary school the primary emphasis shifts to the *type* of achievement and where it is likely to lead the student as an adult.

The differentiation is therefore on the type of capacity and the status which the type of capacity carries with it. Let us be more specific. The several curricular "streams" which most American high schools offer students symbolize what we are talking about. The names of the streams differ, but common ones are "academic" (or "college prep"), "commercial," "vocational" (or "trades and industrial"), and "general." These streams differentiate among types of achievement. Each carries its own status. Those with desire and ability to do academic work are pointed toward college and the university. Those with desire and ability to do commercial work are pointed toward business and commerce. Those with desire and ability to do trade and industrial work are pointed toward the shop and factory. The "general" stream in the American high school is frequently a catch-all for those students who do not fit into any other classification. The trade and industrial stream is also frequently the recipient of such students.

If one divides the high school population simply into the "college" and "noncollege" groups, further differentiation of types of abilities is apparent. In the college group there are students with different types of abilities, and these types of abilities help to determine the kinds of colleges and universities they attend and the curricula they select. In the noncollege group are students with a variety of abilities and interests, for example, in technical, vocational, entrepreneurial, or managerial fields. The kind of ability the student has helps to indicate his eventual role and status in the occupational and social structure. Those with technical competence are likely to be found among the skilled tradesmen, those with general vocational ability will be

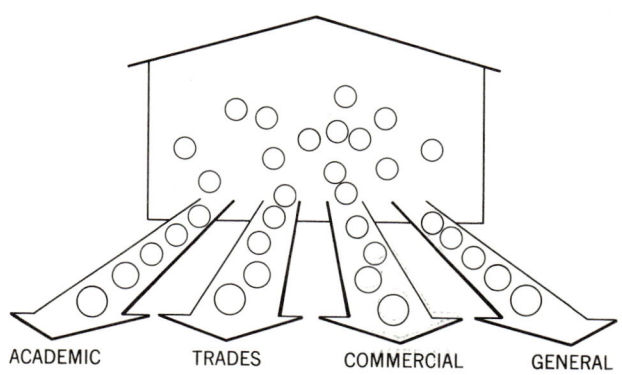

Fig. 3-2 Curricular "streams" differentiate among types of achievement.

among the semiskilled, and those with human-relations orientations may find employment in clerical work and sales, service jobs, and in middle- and lower-level management positions.

Wherever the selection process points the student, there are usually present the two factors mentioned earlier, the level of achievement, which is of special importance in elementary school, and the type of achievement, which assumes significance in secondary school.

Both of these elements were present in Mrs. Miller's history classroom. Mrs. Miller caused her students to think for themselves, to raise questions, to participate actively in their own learning. In this she was concerned with their level of achievement. But she was doing more than this. She was interested in a particular type of achievement. She was spurring her students toward achievement in critical thinking, an achievement which is especially important for those students who are college bound. The type of achievement sought was suited to the aspirations of the students.

Youth Groups and Selection

There is a second way in which high-school selection differs from that in elementary school. Youth culture emerges in the high school and brings with it a new basis for selection beyond that of the level and type of achievement. Youth culture stresses the group and the ability of the individual to achieve status in the group.[21] Achieving membership in the group is itself a valued attainment. In the peer group, snobbery is expressed freely and creates sharp prestige stratification among groups.

What are the qualifications for membership in these groups? We reserve for a later chapter a fuller analysis of peer groups, but can say here that ascribed status is one of the factors. The child's socioeconomic background has an influence in the particular peer groups with which he associates. But we should not forget that there are other factors at work. In elite high-school peer groups we frequently find youth of low-level ascribed status who have achieved membership in high-status peer groups because the school has provided them ways to achieve in other areas. For example, achievement in athletics, extracurricular activities, or student government is frequently the credential of the student with low ascribed status to be admitted to peer groups with high status.

But the central function of the stratification of youth groups which we wish to emphasize here is this: The prestige of the high-

21 "Peer Influences on Adolescent Educational Aspirations and Attainments," *American Sociological Review,* Volume XXIX, No. 4, 1964, pp. 568–575.

status youth group serves to enhance the value of academic achievement. We may view the matter this way: There are two orders of values within the high-status youth group. One is the value of achieving and keeping membership in the group. The other is that of keeping academic achievement sufficiently high to gain admission to the college and university. Within the group these two values tend to reinforce each other. For example, membership in elite groups is usually open (1) to those who are high academic achievers and have satisfactory social relationships, and (2) to those who rate high in social relationship and have satisfactory academic achievement. Acceptance on these two points tends to set the limits for group membership. If a member is in danger of falling below the limits in either social acceptance or academic achievement, group pressure is applied on him to come into line. This type of pressure is salutary in respect to achievement. Notice how group pressure works in the following conversation among high-school girls.

BETTY: In some schools a girl has to play dumb to get boys. But here . . .

HELEN: If you want to go with dumb boys, you play dumb, of course. But around here that probably wouldn't come up. I think it's better to stay home (she hesitated) for a while (she laughed) than to go out with dumb boys!

BARBARA (struggling to get a word in): Well, I'm just not interested in schoolwork. I like other things. (She laughed, then continued with some irony.) Maybe that's why I go out with jerks. Only they're not jerks. They might look like jerks in this school. They don't go to this school, but there are other things besides academic subjects.

I (the interviewer) broke in: Can someone who is poor in his studies get status here if he excels in some other part of school life?

BETTY: Maybe—say in dramatics. But a clunk couldn't get into a play. The deans would take him out so as to keep his time for his work.

BARBARA: That's not fair. Maybe he could really shine in dramatics. That might be the one place where he could reveal what he had on the ball.

HELEN: That might be true. The trouble is, if you're good in dramatics, you're probably good in other things too. You probably wouldn't have a good actor who couldn't write a sentence.

BARBARA: I'm interested in caring for animals. A boy could be interested in mechanics. This school doesn't touch these interests. If you have them, you're lost around here.

HELEN (thinking a minute, then summing up the situation): *It's just that those aren't the interests that are expected to take you places around here.*[22]

[22] David Mallery, *High School Students Speak Out*, New York, Harper and Row, 1962, pp. 33–34.

In this example Betty and Helen are within the limits of the elite group. Barbara is not. Betty and Helen are sensitive to the need to combine social acceptance in the group with academic achievement, whereas Barbara does not feel this pressure.

Barbara's attitude suggests that in low-status groups the pressure might be in exactly the opposite direction—for low academic achievement. In the absence of the motivation provided by college entrance and elite-group approval, the pressure may well be toward academic norms more in keeping with the group's lower order of achievement and aspiration.

Whatever the direction of the pressure from the group in respect to achievement, secondary school groups do exert pressure on their members. That pressure reinforces the selection process in the school. Both the level and type of achievement are influenced by the norms of the peer group.

Boy-Girl Relationships

A third difference in selection between elementary and secondary school is related to the increased cross-sex relations in the school, especially outside the classroom. The school's extracurricular activities, its clubs, groups, and sponsored social events, provide increased opportunity for boys and girls to become acquainted with the opposite sex outside the classroom. This mixing of the sexes in youth performs a valuable function in our society where the selection of mates is based largely on personal choice: It is a time for testing relationships and forming standards of selection. In American schools the boy-girl relations foreshadow marriage and family formation.

Notice how this function of the school disappears in a society where marriages are arranged by families and the personal choice of youth is only a small consideration. For example, in the case of Hamid, the Pakistani boy, his father will at the appropriate time select a marriage partner for him, making sure that the ascribed status of the girl is equal to that of Hamid's. Accordingly, Hamid attends a boys' school. If he goes to high school, that will likely be segregated along sex lines, or the girls will attend separate classes within the same school.

Selection in the secondary school serves, on the one hand, to reinforce the existing statuses of students and, on the other hand, to encourage upward mobility. Existing statuses are reinforced in part by the controlled environment of the school. Recall, for example, the conversation of the three high-school girls, Betty, Helen, and Barbara, when the interviewer asked: "Can someone who is poor in his studies get status here if he excels in some other part of school life?" Helen replies by describing the environment of the school: "It's just that those aren't the interests that are expected to take you places around here."

We should not imply, however, that the secondary school is a closed society, open only to those who have high ascribed statuses which tend to be reinforced in school environments. Elkin gives a fair appraisal of the selectivity of the secondary school when he says: "Those children who do well in school, whatever their family backgrounds, are likely to win awards, be encouraged by their teachers, go on to higher education, and become successful men and women in the community. There is some opportunity for the children of economically poor families to attain positions higher than those of their parents and, conversely, for children of well-to-do families to fail and drop into positions lower than those occupied by their parents."[23]

11. Taking the high school you attended as an example, can you describe the patterns of selection which were found there? How did the selection process work?

Conditions Underlying the Process of Selection

The process of selection which we have observed in both elementary and secondary schools does not exist in isolation. It is dependent upon certain conditions which support and make it possible. To sum up the matter of selection we should look at a few of the conditions which make possible this important function of the school.

First, for achievement and selection based on achievement to be honored in schools, there must be a shared understanding of its value. The adults in the school and in the society around it must share a belief in the value of achievement. Together they must view it as a value they want transmitted to children. American society places high value on achievement, as do the adults who control, administer, and teach in the schools. The school is therefore organized to differentiate students on the basis of achievement.

Second, a system of selection on the basis of achievement must be modified to fit differential rates of achievement among students. American society supports two fundamentally different and even conflicting positions in regard to educating the young. There is the position that the school is a specialized agency for teaching the young to achieve, frequently under conditions of veiled but fierce competition. On the other hand, there is deep concern for the child who cannot

[23] Frederick Elkin, *The Child and Society*, New York, Random House, 1960, p. 58.

achieve and compete. The two positions need some reconciling instrument which will help the schools to serve all children; without such a device the school would simply reject without concern all those who do not achieve at high levels. That instrument is our concept of giving to children at the beginning equality of educational opportunity, of allowing them to begin the race at the same starting line. For those who fall back in the race there must be special provisions. In schools these provisions are embodied in many programs for slow learners and underachievers. For selection on the basis of achievement to operate effectively in our particular society there must be consensus that having programs for nonachievers is just as important as having programs for achievers.

Third, selection is made possible by a selective rewarding of valued performance. When people share a common belief in selective achievement, it follows that good performance in respect to the goals of achievement will be rewarded. Our grading system, awards, scholarships, and college and university admission, are all rewards for valued performance. The value of the rewards diminishes as the value of the achievement diminishes. The rewards are selective. For example, for a boy to receive a college or university scholarship on the basis of performance on the National Merit Scholar Examination is clearly prestigious, because the accomplishment it represents is prestigious. For a boy in the school woodworking shop to receive an award for the best coffee table is noteworthy, but the accomplishment it represents is not regarded as prestigious in our society.

The fourth condition pertains to one of the human results of the system of selection on the basis of achievement. Differentiation among students in the manner which we have been discussing inevitably brings about a status system in the class. Some students are regarded as "better" than others. The basis is therefore laid for a social structure within the classroom which has a profound influence on both the mental health of students and their achievement. For this reason we shall devote Chapter 4 to the social structure of the classroom and how that structure both encourages and discourages good performance.

REFERENCES

Paperbacks

Conflicts in the Classroom: The Diagnosis and Education of Emotionally Disturbed Children. Nicholas J. Long, William C. Morse, and Ruth G. Newman. (Orig.) Wadsworth Publishing Co., Belmont, Calif. ($4.50).

Education and the Development of Nations. John W. Hanson and Cole S. Brembeck. Holt, Rinehart and Winston, 383 Madison Ave., New York ($4.95).

Elementary School Child. Daniel A. Prescott. (Orig.) Educational Services, 1730 Eye St. N. W., Washington, D. C. ($2.75).

Experience and Education. John Dewey. (AS515) Collier Books, 60 Fifth Ave., New York (95¢).

Human Learning in the School: Readings in Educational Psychology. John P. De Cecco. (Orig.) Holt, Rinehart and Winston, 383 Madison Ave., New York ($5.25).

Learning to Understand Pupils. Laban Peachey. (Orig.) Herald Press, Scottdale, Pa. $1.25 (pupil's ed.) 50¢ (teacher's ed.).

Process of Education. Jerome S. Bruner. (V-234) Vintage Books, Random House, 457 Madison Ave., New York ($1.35).

Sociology of Teaching. Willard Waller. Science Editions Paperbacks, John Wiley and Sons, 605 Third Ave., New York ($1.95).

Books

Bany, Mary A., and Lois V. Johnson, *Classroom Group Behavior: Group Dynamics in Education.* New York: Macmillan Co., 1964. Characteristics of classroom groups, factors influencing group behavior in the classroom, and techniques for changing group behavior are discussed.

Bloom, Benjamin S., *Stability and Change in Human Characteristics.* New York: John Wiley and Sons, 1964. This interesting study is concerned with change measurements and how they are related to the significant environmental conditions in which individuals live. The social environment, of which the school is an integral part, is a determiner of the extent and kind of change.

Charters, W. W., and N. L. Gage, Editors, *Readings in the Social Psychology of Education.* Boston: Allyn and Bacon, 1963. Section IV deals with student relationships in the classroom. Sociometric patterns, group dynamics theory, and social structure in the classroom are among the topics discussed.

Dahlke, H. Otto, *Values in Culture and Classroom: A Study in the Sociology of the School.* New York: Harper and Brothers, 1958. Part II, The Social-Cultural Context of Education and the School, and Part IV, The Informal Social Structure and Relations within the School, treat the classroom as a little society.

Flanders, Ned A., "Diagnosing and Utilizing Social Structures in Classroom Learning," in *Dynamics of Instructional Groups, The Fifty-Ninth Yearbook of the National Society for the Study of Education,* Part II, Nelson B. Henry, Editor. Chicago: University of Chicago Press, 1960, pp. 187–219. Maximum individual development calls for flexible social structures in the classroom.

Hodgkinson, Harold L., *Education in Social and Cultural Perspectives.* Englewood Cliffs, N. J.: Prentice-Hall, 1962, 243 pp. Chapter 3 discusses social mobility and education.

Kneller, George F., Editor, *Foundations of Education.* New York: John Wiley and Sons, 1963, 650 pp. Dickerman and Sheats in Chapter 18 discuss concurrent and continuing learning within the school as a social institution.

National Education Association, *Learning and the Teacher,* Yearbook. Washington, D. C.: NEA, 1959. This yearbook presents a description and analysis of learning in actual classroom situations. The emphasis is on the personality and behavior of the teacher.

Periodicals

Brinkman, Erwin H., and Ruth A. Brinkman, "Group Influence on the Individual in the Classroom: A Case Study," *The Merrill-Palmer Quarterly of Behavior and Development*, Vol. 9, No. 3, July 1963, pp. 195–204. A year-long study of a lower elementary school class showed that the peer group was the most powerful influence in classroom learning, even more powerful than the teacher.

Jensen, Gale, "The Sociopsychological Structure of Instructional Groups," *The Dynamics of the Instructional Groups*, National Society for the Study of Education Yearbook, 1960, pp. 83–114. Each classroom group is composed of individuals who bring to the class their unique background and their sociopsychological needs; as a consequence, the educational objectives of the group are molded by the participants.

Lewin, Kurt, Ronald Lippitt, and Ralph K. White, "Patterns of Aggressive Behavior in Experimentally Created 'Social Climates,'" *Journal of Social Psychology*, Vol. 10, No. 2, May 1939, pp. 271–299. This classic study compared two groups of boys under periods of democratic, autocratic, and *laissez-faire* leadership conditions.

Morse, William C., "Self Concept Data," *Bulletin of the National Association of Secondary School Principals*, Vol. XLVIII, No. 293, September 1964, pp. 23–27. An exploratory account on how self-concept feelings develop and how they influence achievement and social behavior in the school setting.

Ripple, Richard, "Affective Factors Influence Classroom Learning," *Education Leadership*, Vol. 22, No. 7, April 1965, pp. 476–480. A review of the research literature and description of the factors involved in affective learning.

Schmuck, Richard, "Sociometric Status and Utilization of Academic Abilities," *Merrill-Palmer Quarterly of Behavior and Development*, Vol. 8, No. 3, 1963, pp. 165–172. This empirical study indicates possible linkage between the informal, interpersonal processes of classroom groups and the formal classroom functioning of individual pupils.

4

The Classroom Group, Mental Health, and Achievement

"Today our children, instead of loving knowledge, become embroiled in the night-mare."
JULES HENRY

Despite the exceptions, for the most part the rule holds: children who achieve well in school tend to do well in life, but those who achieve poorly in school face a difficult time in the larger society beyond the school. Thus the school's selective function is certainly crucial in predicting the future for children and youth. For this reason we must probe further into the classroom conditions that shape children's chances for success or failure in later life.

In this chapter we shall examine two topics which help us to understand the environment of the classroom and how this environment influences the child's mental health and achievement. First, we shall look at the social organization and structure of the classroom; here we view the classroom as a learning group. Second, we examine the relation between the social climate of the classroom and both mental health and academic achievement. In Chapter 5 we shall look at the practical implications of these matters for classroom teaching and the improvement of learning.

Let us set the stage by observing two examples that pose some of the problems with which we shall deal. The examples present two classroom scenes in which we note major differences in the social climate. In the one there is a feeling of warmth and support for achievement;[1] in the other there is a feeling of anxiety about achieve-

---

[1] L. Beals, P. Simmons, and F. Black found, after extensive interviews with HAPS (high academic potential students) dropouts that the lack of teacher support and personal interest were major factors in their school failure. "Administra-

ment.[2] We sense, too, that achievement in the one classroom outdistances achievement in the other. We suspect that the mental health in the one classroom is wholesome and in the other poor. These examples help us understand better the components that make up the classroom group and the factors within it that make for good mental health and achievement.[3] Here are questions we might ask ourselves about these examples:

1. How is the information communicated? We are interested here not so much in the techniques of presentation as in the spirit in which it is communicated, either by the teacher to the students or among students. Does the manner in which the information is communicated stimulate further learning? Or does it tend to block further learning?

2. How does the student participate? What is his attitude toward participation? How does he work in relation to his peers? Does he praise? Does he ridicule? Is he hostile? Is he cooperative?

3. How does the teacher participate? What is his attitude? Is he encouraging? Discouraging? Is he personal? Impersonal? Does he accept the child's spontaneous responses? Reject them? Does he point out only "bad" things in the student's work? Only "good" things?

4. What forms of classroom control are used? Is the control relaxed or tight? Is affection used as a form of classroom control? Are rewards and punishments used as forms of control? Is group sanction used? Fear? Ridicule and threat? Is peer group control encouraged?

5. Are the students learning what the teachers intend that they should learn? It is assumed that if the teacher teaches mathematics, the students are to learn mathematics. However, the nature of the student-teacher relationship is such that the student usually learns many other things besides the formal subject being taught. For example, he may learn to love or to hate mathematics. He may learn to love or to hate the teacher. He may learn that he is inferior or superior to his classmates in mathematics. He may learn that the only way for him to survive the mathematics class is to cheat on examinations. The range of such possible complementary learnings in any classroom is great. Can one detect complementary learnings going on in the two examples which follow? What are they?

6. What kind of self-concepts are created in students? All of us carry in our heads some concept of ourselves. This self-concept is built up from our

tive Implications of a Study of Gifted Students," *The Bulletin,* Volume 49, No. 297, January 1965, pp. 83–91.

[2] I. G. Sarason found a high correlation between a student's level of anxiety and his intellectual performance. "Test Anxiety and Intellectual Performance," *Journal of Abnormal and Social Psychology,* Volume 66, No. 1, January 1963, pp. 73–75.

[3] For a perceptive discussion of these and other factors in social learning, see Jules Henry, "A Cross-Cultural Outline of Education," *Current Anthropology,* Volume I, No. 4, July 1960, pp. 267–305.

earliest years and its formation continues throughout life. Among the factors contributing to our self-concept is the response of other persons to us. For example, if the response of others to us tells us that we are "friendly" and "attractive" as human beings, we are likely to incorporate and live up to our self-concept. On the other hand, if the response of others tells us that we are "unfriendly" and "unattractive" as persons, we tend to carry that concept of ourselves and live down to it. The self-concept which students have is, therefore, important in their mental health and school achievement. What kind of self-concepts are being built up in the following classroom scenes?

These questions, taken together, ask one large question: What does the little society do to the child in his effort to achieve? The child, we said, is under a cultural mandate to achieve in school because the school evaluates him on the basis of his level and type of achievement. The society outside the school opens or closes doors to him on the basis of achievement. In other words, the whole weight of the cultural belief in achievement rushes in upon the child in school. Important matters in his life are being resolved in the whirling struggle for achievement as it is defined in school.

The decisiveness of this matter is seen in yet another way. Some critics, looking at the large number of "dropouts" from the school, and others who drop out mentally but not physically, claim that the school is failing to teach the young. It is quite possible that this alarmingly large number of students testifies not to the failure of the school but to its very success in establishing achievement as a selection device.[4] In other words, the dropout may not be rejecting achievement as a desirable value. He indeed may wish desperately to achieve, but is simply making an honest and realistic appraisal of his own chances to achieve along the lines upon which the school insists.[5] Increasingly high standards of academic achievement simply make his own chances more remote. Thus the very success of the school may be the cause of failure among those students whose disadvantaged backgrounds

[4] J. A. Kahl has shown that the selective process clearly favors the middle class and that lower-class children are least favored. *The American Class Structure*, New York, Rinehart and Co., 1953, p. 283. Educational Testing Service in a more recent survey shows similar patterns of relationships between social class and academic success. *Background Factors Related to College Plans and College Enrollment and High School Students*, Princeton, N. J., E. T. S., 1957.

[5] M. Weiner and W. Murray found in their study of culturally deprived children and their levels of aspiration that they too wish to achieve, but with them it is only a wish; with the middle class it is an expectation. "Another Look at the Culturally Deprived and Their Levels of Aspiration," *Journal of Educational Sociology*, Volume 36, No. 7, 1963, pp. 319–321.

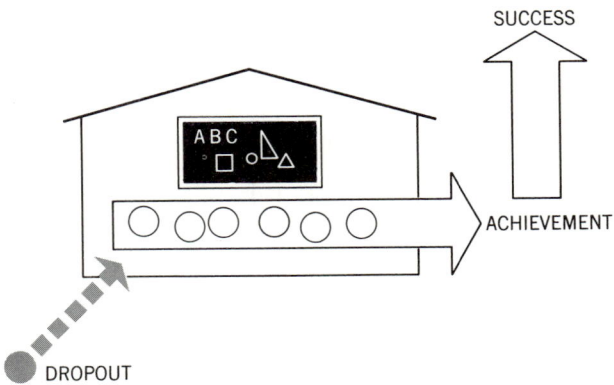

Fig. 4-1 The dropout is not necessarily rejecting academic achievement as a desirable value. He may be making a realistic appraisal of what his chances are for success.

outside of school, or social frustration within it, do not permit them to compete with others who start a step or two ahead in the race. If this reasoning has merit, we may expect that as the achievement standards of the schools continue to rise, the problem of the nonachiever will become even more acute. The only solution is a massive assault on conditions of deprivation which are the source of the problem.

The question we really raise, then, in the following examples and in this chapter, is the question posed by Jules Henry in the sentence at the head of the chapter. Will the classroom be a place where children, in the quest to achieve, learn to love knowledge and its pursuit? Or will it be a place where they learn the "nightmare" of failure and frustration?

Let us turn now to two classroom examples:

"Cyril reads. He stumbles and mispronounces the word con'-tent. After three attempts he pronounces it con-tent'. Teacher says, 'Cyril, do you or don't you know what you are reading?' She emphasizes 'do you' or 'don't you' as she gives Cyril a sharp look. 'Are you making up words to suit yourself?' Cyril looks at the teacher, smiles, then lowers his head, and reads on. He comes across a sentence stating that 'interest is our first important point,' but he reads it, 'Interest is one of our most important point.' The teacher raises her voice as she looks at Cyril directly, and says, 'Don't add words that are not there. All right, Jerry, you read for us.' Jerry reads softly and rapidly, and the teacher says, sternly. 'Open your mouth.' As she says this, she opens her own mouth in order to say each word distinctly. Jerry stumbles over the word cumulatively but pronounces it correctly. . . .

"A boy reads smoothly. He has no trouble in pronouncing the word pinioned. The teacher interrupts him to ask, 'What do we mean when we say pinioned?' The boy says, 'Tied down,' and the teacher asks, 'Are you sure?' The boy shrugs his shoulders and smiles as he slowly writes the word on a piece of paper in a half disinterested manner. The teacher says, 'That's why we don't understand what we read. What's the use of copying the word and looking up the meaning later? It is now that you need the meaning, to give the story some sense.' She looks around the room and calls on Antoinette who had her head down on her open book. 'Antoinette, you tell us all about it, since you know so much (pause) or is it that you are too tired or too old to look?' " [6]

For contrast let us now turn to another classroom scene.

"The teacher says, 'Mike, how is your eye?' and Mike replies, 'Fine today.' The teacher says to the class, 'First I'd like to talk to you about some work in vocabulary that you handed in and on which you made some mistakes.' She goes to the board and writes the words our, are and or. She now says, 'Let's have some sentences, first with are.' She points to a girl at the front of the room, and the girl makes up a sentence, 'Are you going too?' Teacher says, 'Yes. Another.' She points to a boy, who makes up the following sentence, 'Tom and John are going to town or for a ride.' The teacher says, 'How did you say that? Which did you put first?' The child says, 'I or . . . Oh! Jim or I are going to the show.' The teacher says, 'O.K., that's better. You all seem to know how to use them right today.' " [7]

Let us look briefly at these examples in terms of the questions posed at the beginning of the chapter.

How is the information communicated? What is the essential difference between the two classrooms in the way the information is communicated? Does the manner in which it is communicated stimulate or frustrate learning? Does it make any difference as far as achievement is concerned that in the first classroom there is ego deflation and in the second ego inflation?

How does the student participate? In the first example the children participate under conditions which would seem to be painful, in

[6] *Ibid.*, p. 288.
[7] *Ibid.*

the second example under conditions which would seem to be pleasant. Both teachers are seeking to get their students to achieve. Is it possible that one is teaching the "nightmare" and the other the "love of knowledge"?

How does the teacher participate? In the first example the teacher points out the "bad" things in the students' work, in the second the emphasis is on the "good" things. In the first example the teacher is hostile, sarcastic, ridiculing, in the second solicitous, polite, and rewarding of correct responses. Is there perhaps a correlation between these factors and mental health and achievement?

What forms of classroom control are used? In the first classroom ridicule and sarcasm are means of control, whereas in the second a group feeling of accomplishment is an instrument of control. Group sanctions seem to be at work. What factors are important in determining what forms of control should be used in classrooms?

What is the relation between the intent of the learning and the results? Is Cyril, in the first example, learning as the teacher intended? Is he learning complementary things? If so, what? Is Mike, with the sore eye, in the second example, learning complementary things? In the two examples does the complementary learning add or detract from the main business being learned?

Finally, what kind of self-concepts are being built up in students? Self-concepts, we said, are created in part from our perception of how others view us, especially others who are significant to us. How would we describe the self-concepts being formed in these two classrooms? In what way may these self-concepts stimulate or block learning?

These questions can never, of course, be answered in terms of only two examples, or even a hundred. We shall now pose these questions within the larger framework of the social organization and structure of classrooms. In viewing the organization and structure of classrooms we shall consider three matters: (1) characteristics of classrooms as social groups, (2) stages in the development of classroom groups, and (3) status and role in the classroom group.

CHARACTERISTICS OF THE CLASSROOM AS A SOCIAL GROUP

Most social groups have similar characteristics. For example, social groups usually have some *goal or purpose*, some reason for being. They have *membership*, persons who participate in the activities of the group, and *leadership*, individuals or groups within the membership who assume leadership responsibilities. Finally, most social groups have some kind of *relationship to other groups*.

The classroom as a social group shares these characteristics. It has well-defined goals and reasons for being. Its members or participants are the students. Leadership in the formal structure of the classroom is assumed by the teacher. And the classroom has a definite relationship with other classroom groups within the school. The classroom is a unique social group but not because it possesses characteristics not found in other groups. The uniqueness lies in the classroom nature of these elements and in the particular way in which they operate within the little society. Let us look at the unique qualities of these characteristics within the classroom social group.[8]

Classroom Goals

The primary goal of the classroom group is learning. This goal is a "given" of the classroom society, determined not by itself but by the larger society of which it is a part. For example, neither Cyril's teacher herself nor Cyril determined that Cyril should be taught to read. What is to be formally learned in schools is always predetermined by the larger society or by representatives of it, such as boards of education.

Learning in school is *planned* learning,[9] not left to chance or to the choice of those who are to do the learning. A teacher may present to students various choices for their learning, but these are usually within the areas of assigned learning and have more to do with the *how* of learning than with the *what*. A fifth-grade teacher, for example, may permit students to select a project which they will do in social studies, but he does not give them the option of bypassing social studies.

Although learning is the primary goal of the classroom group and is sanctioned by society, we should not infer that this goal is equally shared by all the participants or pursued with equal enthusiasm and success. Sometimes the personality needs of individual participants drive them to put other goals ahead of learning.[10] Experienced teach-

[8] For a perceptive analysis of the social organization and structure of classrooms see Jacob W. Getsels and Herbert A. Thelen, "The Classroom Group as a Unique Social System," *The Dynamics of Instructional Groups*, Chicago, University of Chicago Press, 1960, pp. 53–82.

[9] In Chapter 2 we distinguished between methodical and unmethodical education; "planned learning" is developed here as a part of methodical education.

[10] H. Speare and I. Pivnick, in their study of San Francisco schoolchildren, found that typical disadvantaged children tend to be motivated in directions other than academic achievement and consequently found the learning patterns of the

ers know the diversity of goals which may be found among the students in a single classroom. Herein lie the "individual differences" of children. Teachers also know that sometimes the individual goals must be attained before the primary goal of learning can be achieved. Here is an example of a teacher of underprivileged children who realizes that before her students can learn, their physical needs must be provided for.

"The children seemed to like coming to school; at least here there was steam heat and, for the lucky ones, free lunch. Despite the attractions, however, attendance was poor.

"During snow storms Irving said it was too cold to get out of bed. George was absent for two weeks because his shoes had fallen apart. Cornelia stayed away whenever the temperature dropped; she had no winter coat.

"Because the school was overcrowded, there were three sessions; we were in the 7:40 to 12 group. At 10 o'clock we had a recess for snacks. It was a long stretch, and I, too, welcomed milk and cookies half-way through the morning.

"Soon I became aware of the children who had neither food nor milk but sat quietly at snack time, watching the others. And then one day I looked up from my sipping straw and found several pairs of large eyes focused intently on me. I never again drank milk in the classroom.

"At the first official meeting of the second grade teachers I asked a superior why the city, which gave free lunch to some of the children, did not provide milk for everyone." [11]

This teacher knows, of course, that her primary goal in the classroom is not to secure a lunch pass or milk for hungry children. Yet she sees it as a humane thing to do, as a way of helping her children pursue the primary goal of learning. The test of the little society is its ability to teach what must be learned. In the case of these deprived children, the teacher is worried about a block to learning which has its origin outside the classroom, but she is determined to do what she can about it within the classroom. Cyril and his classmates may not share the learning goals of the teacher because of the tense social climate of the classroom.

classroom more complicated. "How an Urban School System Identifies Its Disadvantaged," *Journal of Negro Education*, Volume XXXIII, No. 3, Summer 1964, pp. 245–253.

[11] Sylvia Plapinger, "The Angels," *Ladies Home Journal,* Volume LXXXI, No. 4, May 1964, p. 47.

Classroom Participants

The classroom is an "accidental" group as far as its participants are concerned. They are brought together by accident of birth, residence, and assignment, rather than by choice. The students of Beth's fifth-grade room in suburbia, mentioned in Chapter 1, are participants in that little society because they all happened to be born about the same year, live in the same area, and were assigned to this particular room. Beth's teacher, too, may not be in this particular fifth grade entirely by choice. Though he may have had the opportunity to choose this group, he was probably assigned to teach in this particular classroom in this particular elementary building of the school system, especially if he is new in the system and without "seniority."

Furthermore, the students have no choice in whether they participate in the little society; they are compelled to attend school. They may argue that the experience is painful, as it can be for some, but they must attend. The larger society orders it. The classroom lacks the qualities that are present in voluntary groups which are held together by free choice of association and by goals mutually arrived at and worked toward. We see the task of the teacher in better perspective when we remember the accidental and mandatory nature of the classroom group.

The problems of students can also be better understood within this framework. The student does not come to the classroom group, as he does to his other social groups, supported by feelings of choice. Indeed, the classroom may contain persons he expressly does not like to associate with. Yet the "givens" of the situation require that he work with them. The student has no recourse but to stay with the group. How he adjusts to this requirement does much to determine the success of the little society in achieving its primary objective of learning.

Classroom Leadership

The control of the classroom is vested in the teacher.[12] His authority is given by both law and custom and it is reinforced by his age, which is greater than that of his pupils. The teacher may choose to exercise his leadership in a variety of ways. For example, he may rule the little society with firm discipline or encourage great individual freedom and initiative. The various methods of exercising leadership

[12] See Willard Waller, *The Sociology of Teaching*, New York, John Wiley and Sons, 1965, p. 189.

should not obscure the teacher's responsibility for leadership and control.

This is not to say that the teacher's leadership is absolute and closed to question. There have been and are, however, some societies where the teacher's word is "law." That in our own early educational history the teacher's word was more authoritative than it is now reflects changing authority patterns throughout our social fabric.

The classroom teacher's leadership is always conditioned by the leadership of other authority figures within the school system. The principal, for example, is usually held responsible for the educational program in his building. His role as principal is far different from that of classroom teacher. Teachers and principals are apt therefore to view classroom problems differently, as in the following case. You will recall the classroom incident in which Miss Plapinger told us of her experience with the boy who stole the porcelain dog. In the portion of her account which follows, notice how the leadership responsibilities of the teacher and principal are expressed differently in terms of the same classroom incident.

"The principal occasionally tiptoed into the room to observe my teaching. One day he found the room in one of those moments of abandon. I really can't blame him for being upset:

"'Miss Plapinger! Just what is going on here? What is that girl doing walking around the back of the room with white gloves on?'

"How can you tell a grown man that every little girl must have something beautiful? It was the coldest day of the year and the first time Lucy had worn gloves to school. They were white cotton, her Sunday School gloves, and she hoped to become the envy of every child in the class." [13]

In this incident the principal regards it as part of his leadership to see that order prevails in the classroom and that formal learning takes place. The teacher, at this moment, expresses her leadership in terms of satisfying a child's need for recognition.

Today teachers assume classroom control within restrictions of written law, the rules of the school system, and the informal sanctions of parents and community. Perhaps the best way to describe the teacher's leadership is to call him a mediator of the culture. He stands between the larger society outside the school and the child in his little society. In making the decisions that are his to make and in transforming these judgments into teaching he assumes his best leadership.

[13] Sylvia Plapinger, "The Angels," *Ladies Home Journal*, Volume LXXXI, No. 4, May 1964, p. 48.

THE RELATIONSHIP OF THE CLASSROOM
TO OTHER GROUPS

Classroom groups bear a variety of relationships to other groups, both within the school and without. Consider first some of the relationships which the classroom participants have with groups outside the school. In Chapter 1 we observed that each student brings to school a social inheritance contributed by the sum of his out-of-school experiences. His family, gangs, clubs, church, and community associations all contribute to his personality. Sometimes his outside associations conflict with the expectations of his classroom. For example, the student may find that in order to keep on good terms with his out-of-school associates he must defy the teacher or perhaps his fellow classmates. More fortunate is the student whose outside associations and experiences reinforce what he is doing in the school.

Within the school the classroom is a part of a network of relationships of the formal structure of the school. Each grade is a step in a sequence through which pupils pass on an annual basis. It is important in the graded school system that students pass smoothly from one level to the next and be prepared to do so.

Further, individual members of each class group have a special set of relationships to the school beyond their particular classroom. Those who play musical instruments associate with the band or orchestra. Athletes have their own associations with members of athletic teams. Those with speech problems associate with groups in speech therapy. Children who work in the library may be in still another group. Each child must build up social tools for meeting the various expectations of each group.

7. Interview an elementary or secondary school student. Make a list of the various groups with which he or she associates during the course of one school week. Include groups both inside and outside the school. Find out what you can about the expectations of each of these groups and how your interviewee responds to these expectations.

The distinctive character of the classroom group lies, as we said, in the distinctive character of schools and of our society. The classroom group is a vortex of our social system. There are few institutions in which converge so many expectations from such a variety of people with such divergent views. This crucial position of the classroom may help to explain why society reserves for it some of its greatest expectations and deepest reservations.

STAGES IN THE DEVELOPMENT OF CLASSROOM GROUPS

Children and teachers coming together for the first time in the classroom do not have, under most circumstances, a predetermined set of personal relationships. Unlike the ascribed status of each child, which is given, the personal relations among the children and with the teachers are not given. They are developed and built within the little society by the process of socialization, and it is this classroom socialization which has so much influence on the students' achievement.

One of the results of socialization is the development of a social structure and organization. In the process of developing such a structure, the group is likely to go through several distinct stages.[14]

Formation

During the first days of the school year students assess both the physical and the human aspects of the new classroom situation. The child looks around the classroom and appraises, perhaps unconsciously, its colors, lighting, and equipment. This is a time for getting first impressions of the other students, the teachers, and the interaction among them. The teacher talks to students about what they shall be doing, begins to associate names with faces, and starts to establish the kind of social climate he would like to see prevail in the classroom.

Exploration

After the formation stage students make exploratory efforts to establish satisfying relationships with one another and with the teacher, if they have not already done so upon the basis of earlier experience. This is a crucial period for most students because it involves the risk of rejection of their overtures of friendship. It also gives the reward of offered friendship returned. Relationships are structured during this period, and the choice of "significant others" takes place. Students begin to assign labels to class members like "leader," "follower," "best liked," "least liked," or "brain." Some of these labels will shift during this period, but some will stick. The particular roles that students will perform in the social structure of the group are beginning to appear. Each student is being assigned a role and status within the social structure of the group.

[14] See Gale Jensen, "The Sociopsychological Structure of the Instructional Groups," *The Dynamics of Instructional Groups,* Chicago, University of Chicago Press, 1960, pp. 83–114.

Building a Group Image

The classroom group, like most groups which socialize together on a continuing basis, soon starts to develop a group image. This is a crucial stage for both teacher and student. The teacher desires that the classroom group hold a positive image of itself, that it regard itself as "the best class in the school," a group that "works together," "shares," a group in which everybody "participates." These are all positive values in American classrooms—ideals perhaps, but positive. The teacher thus attempts to build a group image consistent with his own value system and with the values which he feels the community supports.

The students also contribute toward the group image, not always as the teacher does, but in terms of their own personality needs and desires. The ascribed status of each child has a great deal of influence on his personality needs and how he wishes the group's image to reinforce them. Whatever particular image may emerge during this period, the group is developing a perception of itself that will profoundly affect what is accomplished within the classroom.

The exploration stage is also important in the formation of the child's self-concept in respect to the classroom group. During this period he is beginning to see himself as others in the group see him. If he gains a wholesome image of himself, he will be aided considerably in his efforts to achieve.

Stabilizing the Relationships

Finally the group comes to the stage in which personal relationships are stabilized. The teacher feels he "knows" each student and has some appraisal of how to "handle" each, the unique "needs" of each, what to "expect" of each. He knows the students whom he can count on to do those things that he regards as important, and he also knows the ones he cannot count on. Similarly, the students have stabilized their own personal relationships and have been assigned roles and statuses. At this point it is possible to say that the classroom meets the qualifications of a "little society."

Not all members of the group, of course, are going to be happy with their assignments. Some of those who have been assigned places on the periphery of the group or who are altogether isolated from it may acquiesce, but others will rebel, fight back, or possibly withdraw altogether. We should not assume that once the social structure of the classroom is stabilized it is forever frozen. Some changes will occur, but the basic social patterns are there and tend to remain.

POSITIONS, STATUS, AND ROLE IN THE CLASSROOM

Whenever humans associate together, they organize themselves in some way. That is, their relationships with one another are arranged in a particular order. A family as a little society, for example, arranges its relationships around what is expected of the father, mother, and children. In a sense, the structure of a society is made up of the *positions* which people occupy in it. For example, in a small American school there are positions of principal, teacher, and students. In a large school system there are positions of superintendent, supervisory personnel, coordinators, department heads, classroom teachers, special teachers, students, and a host of others.

Each position in the social structure carries a certain *status,* which is occupied by one or more individuals. In schools, for example, the position of superintendent usually carries more status than that of principal, and principal more than that of teacher. In addition to giving a status, each position defines a *role,* that is, a pattern of expected behavior which is assigned by the society. Teachers, for example, are expected to perform certain roles and to behave in certain ways. Students are expected to perform the role of students and not that of teachers or principals.

The position which an individual holds in a society and the status and role assigned to that position by the culture shape and mold him.[15] His view of life is considerably influenced by his position in the social structure because this position helps to determine his self-concept. Since each position and its status and role is somewhat different, each individual learns about his society from another point of view and therefore has a unique self-concept. We all see things from our particular vantage point in the social structure. It is for this reason that different individuals and groups may see things in such sharply divided ways. The parent's view of the child, for example, is different from the teacher's. The *roles* of parent and teacher are different; so are their views of children. The parent who is also a teacher (for one individual may hold more than one position in the social structure) will tend to view his own children in ways appropriate to a parent, and his students in ways appropriate to a teacher.

Return now to the social structure of a classroom. We said that after a few weeks the classroom takes on the characteristics of other

[15] Linton explained that the behavior of the individual must be studied not simply in terms of the general culture, but in relation to the particular cultural demands which his society makes upon him because of his place in it. R. Linton, *The Study of Man,* New York, Appleton-Century-Crofts, 1964.

societies. It has a structure in which there are positions, and each position has a status and role. First, there are the positions of teacher and students, each carrying with it a status and role expectation.[16] Next, each child has a position within the little society that is assigned to him by the society itself and is labeled in different ways. For example, children may hold positions labeled according to their school achievements: "bright," "average," "dull," or "retarded." Other labeled positions indicate something about the child's group relationships: "best liked," "least liked," or "a loner." We said that an individual's view of life is considerably influenced by his position in the social structure. Similarly, a child's view of his classroom is considerably influenced by his position in the structure of the little society. He tends to live out the expectation or self-concept of the position to which he has been assigned. The social structure and climate of the classroom therefore have a decisive influence on both his mental health and academic achievement.

8. Interview a classroom teacher about the social structure and organization of his classroom. Find out all you can about the various positions which students hold in the classroom and their roles and statuses. Ask the teacher how the social structure of the classroom influences how the children learn. Report your findings to the class.

Let us now see exactly how the social climate of a classroom influences the child's mental health and achievement. We look first at influences on mental health.

THE IMPACT OF CLASSROOM SOCIAL CLIMATE UPON THE STUDENT'S MENTAL HEALTH

The child lives for a large part of each day in the classroom. With the exception of his home, the classroom is the most influential environment in his life. In this environment the child's two most important relationships are with his teacher and with his peers. These relationships tell the child about *his* position and that of *others* in the social structure of the classroom. And his position influences how he answers such important questions as these: Who am I? What am I able to do? What am I unable to do? What is expected of me? Can

---

[16] Here is the way one student succinctly describes his role expectation of the teacher: "The most important thing around here is a teacher's personality—its interplay with ours—his ideas—the way he gets us to think—the way he shows his interest in us. . . ." D. Mallery, *High School Students Speak Out*, New York, Harper and Brothers, 1962, p. 47.

I live up to the expectation? Who likes me? Whom do I like? Do I like the teacher? Does he like me? Who is the "best" in our class? Who is the "poorest"? Who is looked up to? Who is looked down upon?

As the child finds answers to these questions he is discovering the social structure of his classroom and his position within it. This social structure becomes the dominant aspect of his classroom environment because it helps to determine his attitude toward learning. His motivation, even his ability to learn, is influenced by the way the human relationships are organized. In other words the child's position in the social structure of the classroom bears directly upon his personal mental health.[17]

How much consensus is there among classmates about who belongs where in the social structure? Does the social structure of the classroom change during the course of the year? Ronald Lippitt and Martin Gold found that in 39 elementary classrooms which they studied there was remarkable consensus among students about who was liked most and who was liked least. Further, they discovered that once the students make up their minds about the social structure of the classroom they tend to keep them made up. Lippitt and Gold conclude: "The evidence is clear that the interpersonal structure of the classroom forms rapidly and maintains a high degree of stability throughout the school year. The same children remain in positions of low power and isolation or dislike throughout the year, and the same children stay at the top of the totem pole." [18]

What constitutes good mental health in the classroom?

What factors influence a child's mental health in the classroom? Richard Schmuck, Margaret Luszki, and David Epperson list four such factors:

"1. *The pupil's attitudes toward himself.*

The child who feels he is liked, valued, and accepted by his classmates, who describes himself in favorable terms, and who feels that he is a part of the classroom group, may be thought to be in a positive state of mental health.

"2. *The pupil's perception of reality.*

The pupil whose perceptions of the classroom are relatively free

[17] L. Crow and A. Crow present data which clearly implies that a student's academic and social achievement closely relates to his mental health. *Mental Hygiene for Teachers,* New York, Macmillan Co., 1963.

[18] Ronald Lippitt and Martin Gold, "Classroom Social Structure as a Mental Health Problem," *Journal of Social Issues,* Volume XV, No. 1, 1959, p. 40.

from distortion has better mental health than the pupil who distorts reality frequently.

"3. *The pupil's mastery of his environment.*

The child's adequacy in meeting the school's formal learning requirements represents one type of mastery of the environment, while his adequacy in establishing positive relationships with other pupils is another type. Both generally result in a satisfying state of affairs for the pupil and are considered to be indicators of positive mental health.

"4. *The pupil's actualization of his potential.*

A child with academic abilities he does not use is presumed to have poor mental health. In many such cases, energy is being drained off by excessive anxiety, worry, and hostile feelings, so that the pupil is not free to utilize his ability in performing classroom tasks." [19]

These four elements refer to the student's feelings about people and tasks in the classroom environment. Mental health, then, consists of two elements: (1) the student's relationship to his learning environment and (2) the positiveness of his feelings about himself.

The Student's Self-Concept and Significant Others

It is clear that the self-concept the student holds is influenced to a large extent by the significant others in his classroom environment, namely his teacher and classmates. Our conception of ourselves is built up from our perceptions of how other people view us, and we depend on others to give us a "self." The relationships, then, that are established among students help determine their self-concept and mental health.

The student who feels that he is appreciated, valued, and wanted by the significant others around him will tend to regard himself with realistic esteem. On the other hand, the student who is devalued by his teacher and classmates will tend to regard himself as incapable of achievement and of little worth to the group.

Classroom Affection and Mental Health

One aspect of the social structure of the classroom is the way in which affection is distributed among the members of the classroom. This has an important bearing on how the learning objectives of the group are carried out and the degree to which they are attained. The distribution of affection also influences mental health since it determines the classmates' willingness to help and support one another.

[19] Richard A. Schmuck, Margaret B. Luszki, and David C. Epperson, "Interpersonal Relations and Mental Health in the Classroom," *Mental Hygiene,* Volume XLVII, No. 2, 1963, p. 290.

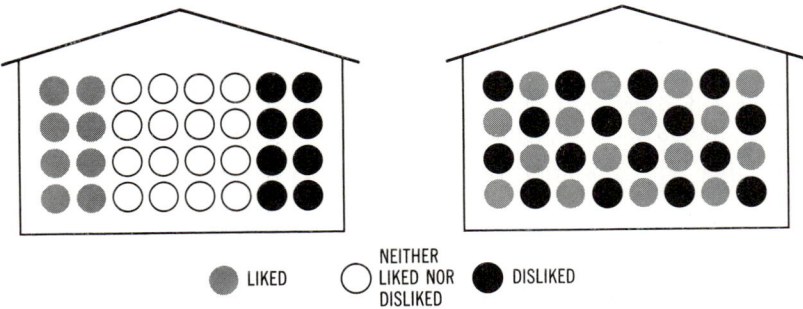

Fig. 4-2 In the classroom at left, there is a narrow focus of affection. In the classroom at right, affection is distributed widely. Which pattern makes for better mental health?

Two kinds of classroom affection patterns can be described.[20] In the first there is a narrow focus of affection. In this pattern a large number of students select a small group of individuals as the ones they "like the most" and a small group of individuals whom they "like the least." As a result of this narrow focus on the small popular and unpopular groups, many members in the middle are neglected and are neither liked nor disliked by anyone.

In the second pattern classroom affection is distributed widely and fairly among both positive and negative choices. Almost everyone is "best liked" or "least liked" by somebody. In these groups there are no subgroups or cliques whose members receive a large proportion of the positive or negative preferences.

Now we may ask, which pattern of affection encourages better mental health in the classroom? Schmuck and his colleagues studied this question and evolved two general propositions about it.[21]

First, *classrooms with a wide focus of affection lead more often to conditions of mental health than do groups with a narrow focus of attention.*

The child who is more disliked than liked by his peers is more painfully aware of that fact when the group has a narrow focus of affection. On the other hand, he is less aware of his "disliked" position in a group that has a wide focus of affection. Further, pupils in a classroom where affection is widely diffused evaluate themselves more highly than pupils in classrooms where affection is narrowly focused.

[20] *Ibid.*, p. 292.
[21] *Ibid.*, pp. 293–299.

Second, *when a student thinks other students do not like him, his mental health is likely to be less positive than when he thinks he is liked*. In testing this proposition the researchers found support for the following hypotheses: (1) Students who are accurate in estimating that they are not well liked make less use of their academic ability than students who are well liked. (2) Students who perceive themselves, not necessarily accurately, as not being well liked make less use of their academic ability than those students who perceive of themselves as being well liked. (3) Pupils who perceive themselves as not being well liked show lower self-esteem than pupils who perceive themselves as being well liked.

These tested hypotheses reaffirm that if a student does not think that others in the class value him, his self-concept as a participant in classroom learning is likely to be negative. Since, as we have said, individuals behave in a manner consistent with their self-concept, it seems to follow that those students who do not perceive themselves as valued members of the classroom group will be less likely to make full use of their academic potentials. Psychological research indicates that the social climate of the classroom indeed has a great deal to do with how students perform academically. We have just observed that the child who perceives that he is not valued tends not to make full use of his academic potential.

This conclusion necessitates an examination of the relationship between classroom social climate and academic achievement.

SOCIAL POSITION AND ACADEMIC ACHIEVEMENT

Let us turn now from the student's utilization of academic ability to a closely related matter, his actual academic achievement. Is there a positive correlation between the student's position in the social structure of the classroom and his academic achievement? Is the academically bright student "twice blessed," with achievement on the one hand and good social position in the classroom on the other? And is the academically poor child "twice cursed," with low achievement on the one hand and poor social position on the other?

Deborah Elkins [22] studied ninety eighth-grade children to determine the relationship between their status in the classroom and their academic achievement. In order to find out the position of students in the social structure, Elkins asked each child: "With whom would you

---

[22] Deborah Elkins, "Some Factors Related to the Choice–Status of Ninety Eighth-Grade Children in a School Society," *Genetic Psychology Monographs*, LVIII, No. 2, 1958, pp. 257–258.

like to sit during homeroom periods?" The choices received by a child were then weighed, three points for the first choice, two for a second, and one for a third. Scores were added and results arranged in rank order to determine each child's position. Interviews were then held with each child in order to give him an opportunity to tell "how you happened to choose. . . ." In order to establish a reason for the interviews that would be logical in the minds of the children, the investigator told them that he was interested in "knowing what things about other people seemed important to teen-agers." In order to determine the achievement of each child, a standard achievement test was administered to all ninety children.

The results of this investigation indicated that the academically bright child tended to be "twice blessed," whereas the academically poor child tended to be "twice cursed." Of the thirty children who enjoyed the highest position in the social structure, 57 percent were in the top level of academic achievers. Only 10 percent of the thirty made very low scores. This is in contrast to the thirty least chosen children of whom only 10 percent made high achievement scores. Fifty-three percent of the least chosen children made very low scores. Academic success, this research indicated, is related to social acceptance.

Conditions of Threat and Academic Achievement

If the social climate of the classroom causes anxiety or fear, academic progress is hindered. If, for example, the student feels threatened in the presence of his teacher or classmates, his personal effectiveness is diminished.

Conditions of threat may take many forms in the classroom. For example, threat may be present in test situations. An experiment by A. W. Coombs and C. Taylor [23] illustrated how even mild degrees of threat reduced the student's achievement in test performance. In this experiment belligerent examiners introduced mild threat into a situation requiring intellectual functioning. The fifty participants in this experiment were asked to translate sentences into a simple code. With only one exception, the students required longer periods to complete the coding and made a greater number of errors in translation when they were working under threatening conditions than when under comparable but nonthreatening situations.

Threat may be present in a classroom situation when students are not permitted to gain some measure of self-esteem and influence with

[23] A. W. Coombs and C. Taylor, "The Effect of the Perception of Mild Degrees of Threat on Performance," *Journal of Abnormal and Social Psychology,* Volume 47, 1952, pp. 420–424.

their peers. E. E. Van Egmond [24] studied 640 elementary school children to link the student's relationship with other pupils and the extent to which students achieved their academic potential. He found that boys who achieved some measure of self-esteem and recognition by being able to influence other boys came closer to using their full academic potential than boys who were not able to gain esteem and recognition through influencing other boys.

Van Egmond found that for girls the threat of being surrounded by other girls who exhibited dislike for them appeared to be disruptive enough to affect their classroom performance significantly. Those girls who were liked by their classmates used their academic ability rather fully, whereas those who were disliked, or liked by very few, used their academic potential less fully.

Conditions of threat may be present in classroom situations where one student's failure makes it possible for another student to succeed, where one child's misery becomes another child's delight. Take, for example, this incident from a fifth-grade arithmetic lesson.[25]

"Boris had trouble reducing $12/16$ to the lowest terms, and could only get as far as $6/8$. The teacher asked him quietly if that was as far as he could reduce it. She suggested he 'think.' Much heaving up and down and waving of hands by the other children, all frantic to correct him. Boris pretty unhappy, probably mentally paralyzed. The teacher, quiet, patient, ignores the others and concentrates with look and voice on Boris. After a minute or two, she turns to the class and says, 'Well, who can tell Boris what the number is?' A forest of hands appears, and the teacher calls on Peggy. Peggy says that four may be divided into the numerator and the denominator."

From Boris' point of view, this incident could only serve to raise his level of anxiety about his ability to perform academically in the classroom and lower his desire to try again.

9. Incidents like this one are so common in American classrooms that we do not regard them in any way as extraordinary. In fact, one may argue that if Boris cannot reduce $12/16$ to its lowest terms he should suffer some social pain. Perhaps the experience will cause him to be better prepared next time. What do you think?

10. Assume that Boris' teacher wanted to spare him the mental paralysis of the situation and thought that he might learn better if he were so spared. How do you think he might have handled the matter?

[24] E. E. Van Egmond, "Social Interrelationship Skills and Effective Utilization of Intelligence in the Classroom," Ann Arbor, University of Michigan (unpublished doctoral dissertation).

[25] Related by Jules Henry, "American Schools: Learning the Nightmare," *Columbia University Forum*, Volume VI, No. 2, 1963, p. 27.

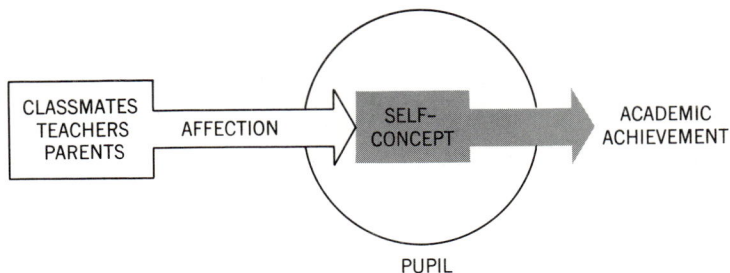

Fig. 4-3   The student tends to learn what his self-concept tells him he can learn.

SELF-CONCEPT OF ABILITY AND ACHIEVEMENT

We said previously that the student tends to learn what his self-concept tells him he is able to learn. This self-concept is acquired from the expectations of the significant others around him, especially from his classmates and teacher.[26] Wilbur Brookover set out to test the relationship between a student's self-concept of his ability and his actual achievement. Specifically he tested these three hypotheses and found them to be valid:

1. The self-concepts of high achievers among junior high-school students with similar levels of intelligence differ significantly from self-concepts of low achievers.

2. Students' self-concepts of ability in specific school subjects vary from one subject to the other and differ from their general self-concepts of ability.

3. The expectations of significant others as perceived by junior high school students are positively correlated with the students' self-concepts as learners.[27]

Since self-concept of ability is associated with achievement, we may profitably raise this question: Can a student's self-concept of ability, and thereby his achievement, be changed? Shailer Thomas [28]

[26] G. Mead early developed the position that an individual's concept of himself is derived from his perception of how other people view him. *Mind, Self, and Society*, C. Morris (Ed.), Chicago, University of Chicago Press, 1934, p. 144.

[27] Wilbur B. Brookover et al., "Self-Concept of Ability and School Achievement," East Lansing, Office of Research and Publications, Michigan State University, 1962.

[28] Shailer Thomas et al., "The Effects of Three Treatment Conditions on Changing Self-Concept and Achievement," a paper presented at the Ohio Valley Sociological Society Meetings, April 30 to May 2, 1964, Columbus, Ohio. (Mimeographed)

reports an experiment designed to test three different attempts to change the self-concept of low-achieving students in the ninth grade. In the first instance parents of the low-achieving students were coached to help their children achieve a higher self-concept. In the second instance a person who was defined as an "expert" worked with the students, and in the third a "counselor" worked with the students. The general aim of each of the three types of persons was to give the child a more positive perception and acceptance of self-abilities, to help him recognize that weaknesses can be improved, and to effect a greater confidence and feeling of responsibility for maximum improvement. The conclusions of this experiment were that the "expert" and the "counselor" both failed to induce significant changes in either self-concept or achievement. The parents, however, did significantly raise the self-concepts of their children. These findings tend to suggest that attempts by persons who are not significant others to change self-concepts will not be as successful as attempts by significant others. The "experts" and the "counselors" were not regarded as significant others by the students, but the parents were. The conclusions of this research are significant because they get at the matter of how to enlarge the child's learning horizons. This study concludes:

"Perhaps the most important implication of this investigation concerns a common assumption of much educational literature and practice. This assumption is that only a limited proportion of the population is able to learn the necessary levels of mathematics, languages, science and other subjects needed for our advanced technological society. The major finding of this study, *that achievement can be improved by self-concept enhancement,* implies that the conception of fixed limits of ability or potential is not valid.

"Although educators are aware of the importance of social factors in learning, frequently educational programs are based on the assumption that each child has a fixed capacity and that this capacity can be identified and measured. Related to this assumption is the idea that students with low intelligence cannot learn at a high level. Often programs are organized to provide the low IQ child with a less difficult curricula. Such programs constitute a self-fulfilling prophecy in that the students in these special programs will not learn the more advanced subjects.

"If, however, schools were oriented to the theory and findings of research such as this, programs would be developed to enhance the abilities of all students to the maximum rather than to limit learning opportunity on the basis of an assumed level of fixed capacity. There would not be attempts at classification of students early in their school career on the basis of an assumed level of innate ability." [29]

How can the child's learning potential be most effectively maximized in the classroom? All that we have said in this chapter raises that question. In Chapter 5 we shall turn to the practical applications in the classroom of the concepts with which we have been dealing in these first four chapters.

REFERENCES

Paperbacks

Constructive Classroom Control. Irwin O. Addicott. (Orig.) (TGB) Chandler Publishing Co., 124 Spear St., San Francisco, Calif. ($1.25).

Critical Incidents in Teaching. Raymond J. Corsini and Daniel D. Howard. (Orig.) Prentice-Hall, Englewood Cliffs, N. J. ($4.25).

Educating for Mental Health: A Book of Readings. Jerome M. Seidman. (Orig.) Thomas Y. Crowell Co., 201 Park Ave. South, New York ($4.50).

Education and Mental Health. Unesco, International Documents Service, Columbia University Press, 2690 Broadway, New York ($2.50).

Helping Children Reach Their Potential. Gladys Gardner Jenkins. (Orig.) (5512) Scott, Foresman and Co., 433 E. Erie St., Chicago, Ill. ($2.75).

Human Learning in the School: Readings in Educational Psychology. John P. De Cecco. (Orig.) Holt, Rinehart and Winston, 383 Madison Ave., New York ($5.25).

Learning to Work in Groups: A Program Guide for Educational Leaders (Studies of Horace Mann-Lincoln Inst. of School Experimentation). Matthew B. Miles. (Orig.) Teachers College Press, 525 West 120 St., New York ($1.50).

Mental Health and Segregation. Martin M. Grossack. (Reissue) (Orig.) Springer Publishing Co., 200 Park Ave. South, New York ($4.00).

Understanding Mental Health. Robert L. Sutherland and Bert Kruger Smith. (Orig.) (29-Insight Books) D. Van Nostrand Co., 120 Alexander St., Princeton, N. J. ($1.95).

Books

Crow, Lester D., and Alice Crow, *Mental Hygiene for Teachers: A Book of Readings.* New York: Macmillan Co., 1963, 580 pp. Chapter 10 presents articles concerning human relations in the classroom. Some of the topics discussed are the emotional climate of the classroom, fostering mental health, and classroom grouping.

Gronlund, Norman E., *Sociometry in the Classroom.* New York: Harper and Brothers, 1959. This book presents the principles and procedures of sociometry that have implications for the classroom teacher.

Haskew, Lawrence D., and Jonathon C. McLendon, *This Is Teaching.* Chicago: Scott, Foresman and Co., 1962. Chapter 3 presents an analysis of the learners in a school situation. The following topics are discussed: What Is Misbe-

[29] *Ibid.,* pp. 27–28.

havior?, What Causes Behavior?, and How Can Teachers Effect Changes in Behavior?

Lippitt, Ronald, and Martin Gold, "Classroom Social Structure as a Mental Health Problem," in *Readings for Educational Psychology*, Second Edition, William A. Fullager, H. G. Lewis, and C. F. Cumbee, Editors. New York: Thomas Y. Crowell Co., 1964, pp. 449–458. This report explores the socio-emotional environment which is marked by stratification of the children.

Redl, Fritz, *Mental Hygiene in Teaching*, Second Edition. New York: Harcourt, Brace and Co., 1959. The author discusses classroom applications of mental hygiene in teaching. Chapter 14 presents some common dilemmas teachers face.

Periodicals

Epperson, David C., "Some Interpersonal and Performance Correlates of Classroom Alienation," *The School Review*, Vol. 71, No. 3, Autumn 1963, pp. 360–376. There exists a strong relationship between peer exclusion and other forms of alienation.

Keislar, Evan R., "Peer Group Ratings of High School Pupils with High and Low School Marks," *Journal of Experimental Education*, Vol. XXIII, No. 4, 1955. This study gives support to the hypothesis that teachers are influenced by personality factors in giving grades.

Lippitt, Ronald, and Martin Gold, "Classroom Social Structure as a Mental Health Problem," *Journal of Social Issues*, Vol. XV, No. 1, 1959, pp. 40–49. This study explores the low status of certain children in the classroom group. The difficulties are created and maintained by a circular process contributed to by the child, his classmates, and teacher.

Phillips, A. S., "Self-Concept in Children," *Educational Research*, Vol. VI, No. 2, 1964, pp. 104–109. The author analyzes the relationship between the pupils' performance in school and their concept of how others perceive them.

"Quest for Self," *Childhood Education*, Vol. XLI, No. 1, January 1964. The entire issue is devoted to various aspects of the self-concept as it relates to school situations.

Schmuck, R., "Sociometric Status and Utilization of Academic Abilities," *Merrill-Palmer Quarterly of Behavior and Development*, Vol. VIII, No. 3, 1962, pp. 165–172. The author correlates social and biological factors with an individual's academic performance.

5

Improving Learning Climate in the Classroom

"Learning is so mixed up with relationship that it becomes part of it. What an unsung creative medium is relationship." SYLVIA ASHTON-WARNER

What causes some classrooms to be filled with the excitement of learning and others with only the boredom of it? Why do some classrooms stir up in students a strong desire to learn and others only a strong desire to escape? In this chapter we examine these questions and suggest how the teacher can organize the classroom group in order to enhance the learning of every individual within it.

The beginning teacher frequently discovers that the class as a group is his biggest concern. He feels reasonably confident in his ability to teach the child as an individual, but the child in the group is a different kind of person. He is himself, plus the reflection of every other person in the room. And it is in the group that the child is to be taught; the group is around him, influencing him, and helping to make him what he is. Through the group the students learn from one another, sometimes more than they do from the teacher.

CLASSROOM BEHAVIOR REFLECTS THE CULTURE

The group behavior of children in classrooms is an expression of the culture in which the classroom is set. In Chapter 1 we said that education was an expression of people, time, and place. So is the group behavior of children in classrooms. One who walks into classrooms in different parts of the world is struck at once by the unique styles of child behavior. Some children are extremely passive before adults, sitting quietly in rows on benches or on the floor, taking instruction without question. In other cultures children are naturally boisterous, aggressive, constantly challenging and pounding one another. They are like fractious young colts which the teacher must first break to halter before he can teach them. Some children are naturally competitive, delighted to take advantage of a fellow classmate's failure to answer a question to demonstrate their superiority. Other children would consider it bad manners to show superiority over a classmate.

What children reflect in classroom behavior, of course, are the norms which they have learned in their culture. Children bring with them through the classroom door a predisposition to behave as they do in groups. What the teacher can do to turn group relationships toward learning is always conditioned by the behavior pattern which children bring to school. The skilled teacher, then, seeks to use the cultural predispositions which the children bring in order to promote learning.[1]

To make the importance of this matter clear let us take three examples of childhood behavior drawn from different cultures. Our purpose is to see how these behavior patterns modify the teacher's handling of the group and how learning is carried on. Hamid's tree school in Pakistan provides an example of children who are obedient in the presence of adults and whose behavior may be described as passive. Sylvia Ashton-Warner, on the other hand, presents us with an example of boisterous, erupting behavior in Maori children, a minority group which she taught in New Zealand. Their behavior may be described as compulsive. Finally, we shall consider middle-class American children whose behavior may be described as spontaneous.

Passive Behavior

Hamid is one of 125 students in the tree school. The school has no rooms and no partitions, but is an open outdoor space surrounded by a high wall and graced by a spreading tree. This space is truly a "multipurpose" room: It is classrooms, playground, lunch room, and study hall, all combined. It is all this for eight separate grades of boys. More amazing, it is all this for one teacher and his single assistant. An American teacher faced with the prospect of teaching 125 boys in only one grade would recoil in shock, let alone 125 boys in eight different grades all in one place at one time.

The Pakistani teacher faces the situation with complete equanimity. It would not occur to his pupils to challenge his authority or that

---

[1] W. Waller describes teaching skill as the ability of the teacher to perceive the personality of the classroom and then draw on its strengths to organize students for learning tasks. *The Sociology of Teaching*, New York, John Wiley and Sons, 1965, p. 162.

of his assistant. They are adults to be respected and obeyed. The teacher could therefore move from group to group, listening to recitations, giving instructions, and making assignments, with no disorder in the ranks. As groups recite they would stand up before the teacher in respectful attention.

In this classroom of 125 boys the dominant relationships are not within the group but rather between the individual student and the teacher. The group relations of the boys are secondary to the relationship of any single one with the teacher. In a sense this Pakistani teacher does not have to deal with his students as a group. He deals, rather, with 125 boys, one by one.

The type of learning which is carried on in the tree school is congenial to this pattern of teacher-pupil relationships. Most learning is by rote memory, to recite multiplication tables, to spell, and to memorize what is read, and then to give the answers when called upon. Question and answer learning seems natural in this teacher-centered classroom.

Compulsive Behavior

Contrast the passive behavior in Hamid's classroom with that of Miss Ashton-Warner's Maori children in New Zealand.[2] She describes her children as "young Maori warriors, full of take, break, fight, and be first" who cause "tribal excitement" to surge through the school. "Sometimes," she adds, "tribal emotion rises up to the level of our eyes," and "we hold our breath and rely on the inner disciplines."

How does Miss Ashton-Warner use this tribal energy in her Maori children for purposes of learning? Notice how she has adapted her learning methods to the group behavior of her children. Here are her words:

"I don't try to describe to others the force of our New Race. Indeed, when I speak of it as 'force of energy' I'm grossly underestimating it. It's more like a volcano in continuous eruption. To stand on it . . . to stand on it with both feet and teach it in quiet orthodoxy would be a matter of murders and madness and spiritual deaths, while to teach it without standing on it is an utter impossibility. The only way I know to deal with it is to let it teach itself. And that's what I've been forced to do. . . . It plays the very devil with orthodox methods. If only they'd stop talking to each other, playing with each other, fighting with each other and loving each other. This unseemly and unlawful communication! In self-defense I've got to use the damn

---

[2] Sylvia Ashton-Warner, *Teacher*, New York, Simon and Schuster, 1963.

thing. So I harness the communication, since I can't control it, and base my method on it. They read in pairs, sentence and sentence about. There's no time for either to get bored. Each checks the other's mistakes and hurries him up if he's too slow, since after all—his own team depends on it. They teach each other all their work in pairs, sitting cross-legged, knee to knee on the mat, or on their tables, arguing with, correcting, abusing, or smiling at each other. And between them all the time is this togetherness, so that learning is so mixed up with relationship that it becomes part of it. What an unsung creative medium is relationship." [3]

The key in Miss Ashton-Warner's teaching is a recognition that there are built-in cultural behaviors in her children and that the genius of teaching lies in using those behaviors to promote learning. She knows better than to fight the basic patterns. She controls them, and sends them in the direction she wants them to go. She uses the culturally determined social behavior of the classroom to teach. Thus in her classroom she is not the only teacher: The group and each child within it also teach.

Spontaneous Behavior

Compare now Hamid's classroom and Miss Ashton-Warner's with that of an American middle-class classroom. Student behavior in American classrooms has undergone great change in recent times, reflecting major changes outside the school.

In today's American homes, for example, children enjoy freedom of expression with only slight deference to the authority of their elders. They are encouraged to be spontaneous, and they carry this spontaneity and freedom into the classroom. Further, among American children there is strong peer-group identification which frequently weakens their relationships with adults. What their peers think is frequently more important to children than what adults think. In American classrooms children are fully as sensitive to group pressure as to adult pressure. By contrast, the boys in Hamid's classroom are far more sensitive to adult pressure than to group pressure.

1. Classroom behavior is the expression not only of the larger culture in which children live but also of the specific subculture in which they live. For this reason children tend to behave differently in rural schools than in urban schools, differently in slum schools than in middle-class suburban schools. Select a classmate whose background is somewhat different from your own and compare notes on the classroom behavior in your respective high schools. Report your observations to the class.

[3] *Ibid.*, p. 105.

The task of the American teacher of middle-class children begins with the recognition that these children are predisposed to express themselves freely and spontaneously and to be influenced strongly by their peers. These are the basic patterns, just as passivity is for the Pakistani and compulsive action is for a Maori child. The American teacher will therefore plan to use the spontaneous behavior rather than try to suppress it, and use the group rather than try to dissolve it. When a teacher is able to harness spontaneous expression and group activity to enhance learning, we may say that his classroom has a good learning climate.[4]

We then ask how such a climate can be achieved in a classroom. To find answers to this question we shall draw upon one American teacher's experience.

STEPS IN IMPROVING THE LEARNING CLIMATE OF CLASSROOMS

In reading the following report by Robert Merriman one might ask oneself these questions:

2. Does the group life in Mr. Merriman's classroom enhance mental health and achievement?

3. What cultural functions are being served in this classroom?

4. What kind of model for behavior does Mr. Merriman provide? What kind of models do the students provide?

5. How does one describe the quest for achievement in this classroom?

Here is Mr. Merriman's description of his own classroom.[5]

"My teaching responsibilities are three freshman classes of General Science, two classes of Senior Forum, and one General Review class for seniors who have had academic difficulties. The total number of students per week is about one hundred and eighty. We have an hour-and-four-minute class period, five periods a day, and all students take five subjects per day with no free periods.

"Let us first consider the freshman General Science group. This group consists of about eighty percent rural students and students coming from parochial schools. The class is required for these students and is elective for those who have come up through our city school

---

[4] L. W. Sontag and J. Kagan have found that students in spontaneous climates more readily develop motives for intellectual achievement than in suppressed settings. "The Emergence of Intellectual Achievement Motives," *American Journal of Orthopsychiatry*, Volume 33, No. 3, April 1963, pp. 532–535.

[5] Herbert J. Klausmeier, *Teaching in the Secondary School*, New York, Harper and Brothers, 1958, pp. 378–380.

system. Obviously, there is a wide variety of abilities, characteristics, interests, and backgrounds represented in this group. . . .

"The first day in class I distribute books, make assignments, and spend about fifteen minutes explaining what I expect so far as class procedure is concerned. The main discussion is about mutual respect, one student for another and my respect for each of them. This acts only as an introduction to the subject but I stress this phase each day as we continue through the year. Only a short time passes before the student realizes the idea of respect and responsibility, and 'discipline problems' do not exist.

"Though we teach a basic background of subject matter, my primary job is to know each student as well as possible. I check cumulative records and make whatever notations I feel important in my class book. Then I spend several weeks trying to learn the characteristics of each student. Usually by the end of the first four weeks I know the special interests of each student. I know how he will respond in class and the type of question he can handle best. I become familiar with the student's home environment and learn who his friends are. By this time I have had an opportunity to meet most of my students informally and have had a chance to talk farming with an interested farm youngster, hunting and trapping with another, shows with some, or sewing, or any of a number of different activities in which they are interested. I want to be interested in their activities and want them to know I am because soon I share their interest and confidence. The net result: the class is not a formal 'sweat session' but is rather informal and becomes fun.

"After becoming acquainted more or less personally with each student, it is an easy matter to 'bend' subject matter toward the interest and ability of the student, and the student responds confidently because he feels that this information applies to him. Soon the 'slow' student feels success and achievement and he is willing to go ahead and try the next assignment. The 'fast' student likewise feels he can master the current subject and there are individual projects and assignments for him in addition.

"Assignments are made in a block form covering a total unit of work. I also propose dates for completion but include with this schedule the statement that these are only probable dates, that discussions, slides, or the students' projects may delay this schedule. My main emphasis is that I do not care how fast we go but I do care how well they do and I want to include all the phases of the subject in which they are interested. So far this approach has worked very well. One of the contributing factors lies in our schedule. During the hour-and-four-minute period there is ample time for study and discussion, demonstration, or activity. Quite often the first part of the hour, about thirty minutes, is used for study and the last part for activities, demonstrations, etc. My thought here is that each student has had a chance to stretch between classes and it is easier to study the first part of the hour. As soon as interest lags, students become uneasy, or tired of reading and individual study, I get them into discussions, moving around in lab work, etc. This program in class is not 'iron-clad' but is changed in accordance with the day. Some days the group is uneasy and not inclined to study. When I sense this I move them into some active participation. Other days it seems they want to continue studying throughout the period so we do just that. With the students in class for study instead of in study hall, the individual help theory becomes practice.

"Differences in abilities and interests are provided for in several ways. Probably the most important adjustment to ability and interest is to avoid a set scale of accomplishment that all students must attain. For some students a grade of 75 would be a high mark and their test scores would average about 65 percent. But the final grade would probably be a 'C' or even higher. If someone wanted to know how a student with an average of 65 got a 'C' I would show him that class participation, interest, effort, extra credit activities, along with tests and daily work, are all incorporated in the final mark.

"My 'discipline' is handled on a mutual respect basis. I have yet to 'bawl out' a student in class, nor do I send him to the office as I feel he has not violated anything in the office. Instead when he leaves class I ask if he would please stop in after school as I feel we had better arrive at an understanding before both of us get into trouble with each other. In eight years of experience no one has failed to appear for that after-school meeting, and no one has left without a satisfactory explanation and readjustment for both of us so that we can each do a better job. I try to make my 'discipline' a matter of mutual agreement instead of my telling the student what I think of him and letting it go at that.

"Seating arrangements in all classes are primarily determined by the students. There are two exceptions. First, if the student has a physical defect, I try to seat him where it will suit him best. The other exception occurs only if the student feels he is headed for trouble if he continues to sit where he is and requests to have his seat changed. In this instance someone else has to be moved as we have no spare seats.

"Generally speaking, an individual or a group of individuals lives up to a reputation that they feel they have or that others have for them. By instilling in the student or the group a feeling of security, mutual respect, and a display of compatibility, I soon have a sound, harmonious learning situation. By earning respect instead of demanding respect and by steering the students instead of commanding them, a good learning situation is readily achieved."

Mr. Merriman's experience suggests some guidelines for improving the learning climate of classrooms. First, there is established a wholesome circular response among the student, the teacher, and the group. In other words, all persons within the classroom reinforce one another in positive rather than negative directions. Second, individual differences are provided for. All children are not held to one rigid standard. Third, the self-concept of students is enhanced. Mr. Merriman knows that students who hold a favorable concept of their ability to achieve are more likely to use their abilities fully. Fourth, the group dynamics of the class are recognized and provided for because Mr. Merriman treats the class both as individuals and as a group. Fifth, group methods of instruction are employed. Sixth, classroom control is based on sound group relationships. Finally, competition is constructively handled.

A Wholesome Circular Response Is Established

I want to be interested in their activities and want them to know I am because soon I share their interest and confidence. The net result: The class is not a formal 'sweat session' but is rather informal and becomes fun.

Where shall we go in a classroom to find the real sources of learning climate, be it good or bad? It seems clear that the learning climate does not reside in any one place or in a single person or condition, but is, rather, a circular social process contributed to by all who live in the classroom. The individual student, the group, and the teacher act upon one another to create a good learning situation.

Observe how this process works. Since it is circular we could begin with either the teacher, the group, or the child. Let us begin with the child, one who holds a positive self-concept. Because he does hold a positive concept he will project this into his relationship with the group. In other words, he will tend to hold the individuals in the group in wholesome regard.

And how about the group? The group will respond to this favorable estimate from the individual student. It will accept him and, more important, will reinforce his already favorable self-concept. His confidence in his ability will continue to grow. At the same time the self-concept of the group has been enhanced.

What is the teacher's contribution to this circular and reinforcing process? In the narrative we saw Mr. Merriman's immediate effort to develop positive personal and group attitudes about human relations.

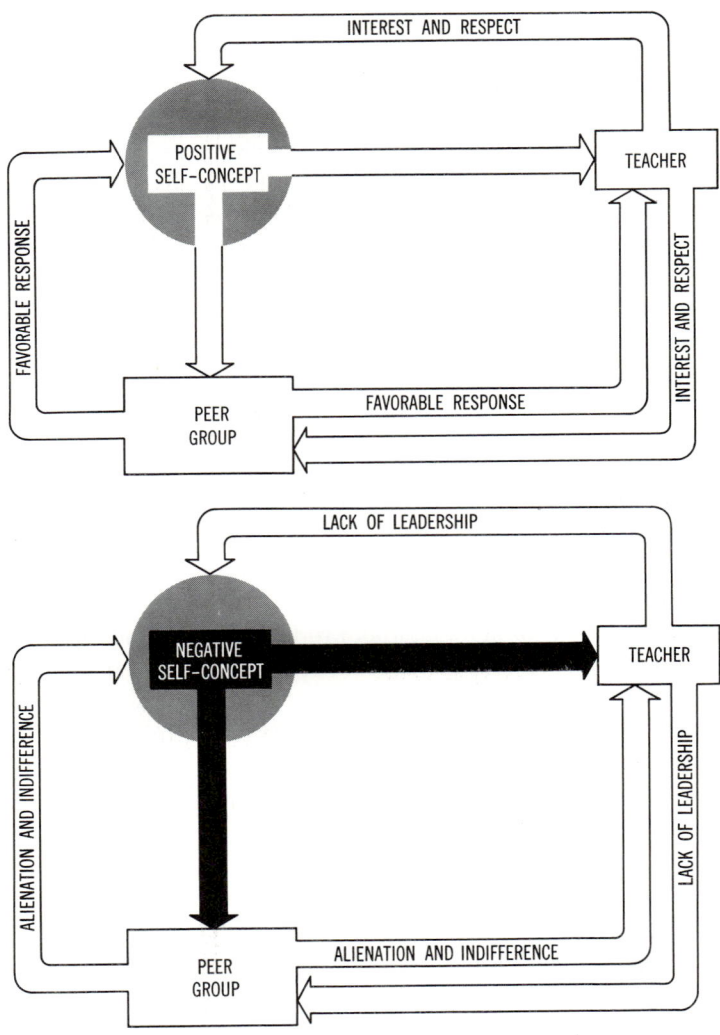

Fig. 5-1   Learning climate in a classroom is a circular social process contributed to by the student, the group, and the teacher, as they act upon one another.

He took this step early in order to get the circular and reinforcing process moving in a positive direction from the very beginning of the class. He did not wait until "bad" attitudes developed, until the circular process started in the wrong direction. He knew that if good relationships were to be established, they needed to be established early. He did not leave matters to chance but started the circular response in the right direction with positive response of his own.

The behavior that develops in the classroom is clearly the result of this circular interaction among the individual, the group, and the teacher. The interaction is also cumulative and, in a sense, self-generating. We see this clearly in Mr. Merriman's classroom. He sensed how important it is to establish the correct attitudes at once. He started with himself, showing a keen interest in the activities of individual students, sharing their interests and confidence. The net result: the class becomes "fun."

In hands less skilled than Mr. Merriman's the same process can work in the opposite direction. Let us say that the individual student begins with a poor self-concept. He transmits this poor self-concept to others in the form of hostility, aggressiveness, or possibly isolation. His classmates feed this self-concept back to him through their attitudes of indifference or possibly alienation and his self-concept is further damaged. As for the rest of the group, they have evaluated him quickly and labeled him in an unattractive way, and they have a strong tendency to maintain this evaluation. The group, furthermore, has very few skills for communicating to this individual the sympathetic guidance he desperately needs if the social cycle is to be reversed. Meanwhile, the teacher may not focus on developing wholesome personal and group attitudes or provide grouping practices in the classroom that will help the individual student and his classmates to reverse the cycle.

Mr. Merriman avoided this situation by beginning immediately to work on constructive group attitudes and by demonstrating that he meant what he taught by exhibiting and practicing those attitudes himself.

6. Observe a classroom in an elementary, junior high, or senior high school in order to watch and describe the circular response among the individual students, the group, and the teacher. Does the circular response enhance or impede learning?

Individual Differences Are Provided For

After becoming acquainted more or less personally with each student, it is an easy matter to 'bend' subject matter toward the in-

terest and ability of the student, and the student responds confidently because he feels that this information applies to him. Soon the 'slow' student feels success and achievement and he is willing to go ahead and try the next assignment. The 'fast' student likewise feels he can master the current subject and there are individual projects and assignments for him in addition.

In describing the circular and reinforcing nature of the social process in the classroom we underscored the importance of the individual. His perception of himself determines in part his attitude toward others. In Mr. Merriman's classroom the students are treated as individuals, each with unique abilities and each capable of making a contribution and achieving a measure of success. Thus Mr. Merriman is starting the circular social process in a positive rather than a negative direction.

Mr. Merriman does not hold each student to the same hard, unyielding standard of achievement. He begins with the assumption that individual differences in the classroom are positive assets for learning and he sets out to make the most of them. He appreciates another important aspect of the teacher-student relationship: How the teacher handles a particular student is usually observed closely by the group and has an impact on the group. Thus, a good way for the teacher to develop a positive attitude in the group is to exhibit a positive attitude toward individual students. The teacher confronts this matter especially in handling discipline problems in the classroom.

How does a teacher's method of handling the misbehavior of one child influence other children who are observers of the event but not themselves targets? The research available on this question indicates that how teachers treat individual students is carefully recorded by the other students and has an influence on their attitudes, behavior, and achievement. J. S. Kounin and P. V. Gump [6] sought to determine the influence of punitive and nonpunitive teachers upon children's attitudes toward misconduct. Three pairs of first-grade teachers were selected for the research. One member of each pair was rated "punitive" (antichild, ready to threaten and inflict harm) by officials and others in the school. The other member of each pair was rated as nonpunitive. Children in the classes of these teachers were interviewed individually during the third month of the school year. The interview consisted of the question "What is the worst thing a child can do at school?" and in answer to the reply a second question "Why is that

[6] J. S. Kounin and P. V. Gump, "The Comparative Influence of Punitive and Non-Punitive Teachers upon Children's Concepts of School Misconduct," *Journal of Educational Psychology*, Volume 32, 1961, pp. 44–49.

so bad?" The types of misconduct that the children talked about were coded for content and for certain other qualities. The following conclusions were drawn from the children's answers to the questions.

1. Children with teachers judged to be punitive showed more preoccupation with aggression. Their misconduct was more serious and their targets suffered more harm. They more frequently cited physical assaults on others as misconduct.

2. Children with punitive-rated teachers had more conflicts and were more unsettled about misbehavior in school.

3. Punitiveness in teachers detracts from children's concern for values which the school is supposed to teach. For example, children with punitive teachers talked more about physical attacks on peers. Children with nonpunitive teachers talked more about learning, achievement losses, and violations of school values and rules. In these experimental classrooms the teacher's handling of individual students did indeed influence group attitudes.

In his concern for individual differences Mr. Merriman was on sound ground both in terms of mental health and achievement. But he was interested in more than individual differences. He cared about the individual worth of each student. In this concern he added to the group's conception of its worth.

7. Educational literature is filled with discussions of problems of individual differences among students. Select three articles or selections which deal with individual differences and compare their observations and points of view.

The Self-Concept of Students Is Enhanced

Generally speaking, an individual or a group of individuals lives up to a reputation that they feel they have or that others have for them.

In Chapter 4 we reviewed research findings on self-concept and its relationship to mental health and achievement. A student's self-concept is the product of many influences, among the most important of which are the "significant others" in his life. The student's parents, peers, and teachers rank high as significant others, and the student takes his cues about himself from them. Mr. Merriman, as a teacher, realizes the importance of self-concept in mental health and achievement. He knows that the individual student and the group will tend to "live up to a reputation that they feel they have or that others have for them."

The teacher can enhance or deflate the student's self-concept in many ways. One point of critical importance in the teacher-student relationship is the manner in which the teacher comments on the student's work. Does it make any difference whether a teacher "praises" or "blames" when he comments on students' work? Here is an investigation which helps to answer the question.

Ellis Batten Page [7] conducted research on these questions: (1) "Do teacher comments cause a significant improvement in student performance? (2) If the comments have an effect, which comments have more than others, and what are the conditions, in students and class, conducive to such effect?"

Seventy-four selected secondary teachers and 2,139 students were involved in the experiment. For the investigation the teachers administered to students whatever objective tests occurred in the usual course of instruction. After scoring and grading test papers in their usual way the teachers randomly assigned the papers to three treatment groups. The first group of papers received no comments beyond the grade. The second group received free comments that the teacher felt were appropriate for the particular students and test concerned. The third group received specified, deliberately encouraging comments that were designated in advance for each letter grade, as follows:

A: Excellent! Keep it up.
B: Good work. Keep at it.
C: Perhaps try to do still better?
D: Let's bring this up.
F: Let's raise this grade!

Then the teachers reported scores achieved on the next objective test given in the class, and the scores became the criterion for measuring the effect that the comments had on the students. This study concluded: "When the average secondary teacher takes time and trouble to write comments believed to be 'encouraging' on student papers, these apparently have a measurable and potent effect upon student effort, or attention, or attitude, or whatever it is which causes learning to improve, and this effect does not appear to be dependent on school building, school year, or student ability. Such a finding would seem very important for studies of classroom learning and teaching method."

[7] Ellis Batten Page, "Teachers' Comments and Student Performance: A Seventy-Four Classroom Experiment in School Motivation," *Journal of Educational Psychology*, Volume 49, 1958, pp. 173–181.

The Group Dynamics of the Class Are Recognized and Provided For

As soon as interest lags, students become uneasy, or tired of reading and individual study, I get them into discussions, moving around in lab work, etc. The program is not 'iron-clad' but is changed in accordance with the day.

Mr. Merriman here expresses a keenly developed sense of the group dynamics of his classroom. He sees his classroom as more than an aggregate of individuals. He understands it as a group in which each member both influences and is influenced by the other members. He sees his class as a social organism which has its changing moods and he is prepared to adjust his learning program to those moods. He has learned to use the group rather than to be used by it.

Mr. Merriman also recognizes the importance of the group to the individual student. The need to be accepted by the classroom group is strongly expressed in the behavior of most children. The result is that they tend to conform to the norms of the group, whatever those norms may be. The pupil who is left out is likely to develop some anxiety about his rejection. Thus the energy which he would normally devote to learning is drained off in anxiety.

Not all pupils, of course, have the same need for group acceptance.[8] Those who have a high need for social approval and a low need for independence are likely to be influenced strongly by what the group does and thinks. On the other hand, those students who have a high need for independence and a low need for social approval are less likely to conform to the norms of the group.

Students who cannot be motivated by the group fall into different classifications and may present particularly difficult problems for the teacher.[9] First there are the individuals who have given up the quest for group relationships. These are the children who once tried to develop meaningful relationships but failed. They believe that no one could like what they do in class, and they may even come to enjoy

---

[8] L. E. Hock advocates a variety of grouping procedures in the classroom in order to provide for the varying needs of the pupils. She points out that often a pupil's group-acceptance needs vary with their moods, the subject matter, or a multiplicity of other factors. "Classroom Grouping for Effective Learning," *Educational Leadership,* Volume 19, April 1961, pp. 424–426.

[9] L. G. Johnson, a sixth-grade teacher in Georgia, developed a "love therapy" approach to difficult children in her classroom. Her case studies illuminate the need for a teacher to continually work with problem children. "Love Therapy," *NEA Journal,* Volume 51, No. 2, February 1962, pp. 18–19.

their loneliness. These children are frequently quiet and may be mis-classified by teachers as "good," and "no trouble at all." Sometimes these alienated children take the opposite route and become aggressive and disruptive in the classroom. The good teacher tries to bring these students, however they react to their rejection, into the mainstream of the group; their learning depends on it.

Another nonsocial group are those children who are essentially egocentric, who follow only their own impulses, do not develop group loyalties, and are frequently self-assertive. The group exercises no pull on them because they lack the ability to share the learning drives of either the teacher or the group.

A third group of nonsocial children are those who are more motivated by adults than by their peers. Sometimes this behavior is an expression of a particular age. Ruth W. Berenda,[10] for example, found that younger school-age children tend to follow the teacher's position, whereas older children and adolescents are more influenced by their peers. Those children who are more motivated by adults than peers find the center of the school relationship and their sole source of encouragement in the teacher. The student, however, who is to be an active learner should learn to use both his peers and the teacher as sources of encouragement and support.

Fourth, there is the group of children who have a high need for social response but not in the classroom. This is a relatively new phenomenon, especially in American classrooms. This group may be responding to the increasingly rich life beyond the classroom and may find their identification outside rather than inside. These students are apt to have no sociometric choices within the classroom group because they choose their friends outside the group. Because they put a low value on social response coming from others in the classroom, the learning climate of the classroom has no special appeal to them.

Finally, there are the students who are honestly inner-directed and who do not need the psychological support of the group in order to be motivated to learn. They have their own inner creative resources, springing probably from sources in the home and other out-of-school contacts. They are likely to be impatient with group learning activity. The teacher must also make provision for these, for the danger is that such children may be labeled as antisocial when they are actually individualistic. From this group of children may come the researchers, the creative thinkers, the challengers of conventional thought with

---

[10] Ruth W. Berenda, "The Influence of the Group on the Judgments of Children," New York, King's Crown Press, Division of Columbia University Press, 1950.

whom a democratic society is frequently impatient, but upon whom it must depend for self-renewal and critical appraisal.

These various nonsocial groups are usually a minority in the classroom. They do, however, cause the good teacher to plan the group life of the classroom in such a way that the learning resources of the group will reinforce the learning of the individuals within it.

Let us turn to specific methods and techniques which are available to teachers for group instruction.

Methods of Group Instruction Are Employed

Some days the group is uneasy and not inclined to study. When I sense this I move them into some active participation.

The good teacher is skilled in the use of group methods and techniques. Mr. Merriman spoke of his use of "discussions," "students' projects," and "active participation." Underlying the use of all group methods and techniques are certain basic understandings about the group process which alter considerably the traditional role of the teacher. Traditionally the teacher was regarded as the answer-man for all questions, drilling his students to memorize the answers and duly record them on examinations. Books, also, were regarded as answer-books. Both teachers and books traditionally represented fountains of knowledge from which unquestioning and obedient students were supposed to drink. The student was in the passive role, a kind of receptacle to be filled by the school. Our new understanding of the group process tells us how much this approach actually hampers good learning because it ignores the learner's need to participate deeply in his own learning.[11]

Let us consider some specific group methods and techniques which are useful in the classroom and which involve the student in his own learning.

Classroom discussion. Recall Mrs. Miller's history classroom at Senn High School which we discussed in Chapter 2. Mrs. Miller gives us an example of one of the most effective forms of classroom discussion. In her class the discussion is no simple question-and-answer affair, the most elementary and possibly the least effective type of class discussion. Mrs. Miller is looking for something more than answers. She is using class discussion as a means of getting her students

[11] J. McV. Hunt found in his studies of I.Q. and the culturally deprived that by involving a deprived child with other children in a learning and developmental process significant intellectual growth is possible. "How Children Develop Intellectually," *Children,* Volume XI, No. 3, 1964, pp. 83–91.

to think for themselves in their own words and to formulate reasonable solutions to problems. Notice how she achieves this effect: [12]

"The topic under discussion—history source books and the importance of keeping file cards on them—would seem to be conducive to day-dreaming, perhaps even dozing. For a time Mrs. Miller seems not to be teaching at all, merely asking questions as the half-formed thoughts of the students rattle around disjointedly like dice in a shaker. But there is little boredom among the thirty juniors and seniors in Room 249.

"As the class discussion continues, Mrs. Miller moves about the room. Sometimes she sits by her desk (never behind it), stands in back of the room, even sits in a vacant desk amid the students. Her punctuating questions begin to nudge here, clarify a bit there.

"She is challenging the students, 'Now why are we concerned about our sources of information?' she asks. 'Mark, are you concerned?' . . . 'Any other reasons? We can get more specific.' . . . 'Why worry about the author, the point of view, your reaction to the source?' . . . 'Do you think you could be brainwashed? What's brainwashed?' . . . 'Oh!' . . . 'That's right, make you believe almost anything, everything, that you had believed was untrue.' . . . 'What do you think, Mickey?' "

Here is classroom discussion at work, stirring students to think, involving them, causing them, sometimes tortuously, to find their own answers.

Where is the focus in Mrs. Miller's classroom? Is it on the teacher? The students? The subject? One of the advantages of a group discussion like this one is that it enables teachers to make the learning group-centered and subject-centered rather than teacher-centered. Notice how Mrs. Miller subtly shifts the learning process from herself to the group. As one student put it: "She's always asking 'Why?' 'Why?' That makes you do the same thing to your fellow students. And Mrs. Miller just stands there beaming while the arguments fly back and forth. She gets so much enjoyment, and you feel kind of maternal toward her. All you can do is try to join in."

What does research say about the relative effectiveness of teacher-centered and group-centered teaching? Richard C. Anderson [13] reviewed 49 pieces of research related to this question and drew the following conclusions. (1) Morale tends to be higher in group-centered

[12] Richard Meryman, "The Rewards of a Great Teacher," *Life*, Volume 56, No. 11, March 13, 1964, p. 71.

[13] Richard C. Anderson, "Learning in Discussions: A Résumé of the Authoritarian-Democratic Studies," in W. W. Charters, Jr. and N. L. Gage, *Readings in the Social Psychology of Education*, Boston, Allyn and Bacon, 1963, pp. 153–162.

classrooms than in teacher-centered classrooms. (2) There tends to be a greater change in behavior of students in the group-centered classroom than in the teacher-centered classroom. (3) Students in group-centered classrooms tend to have more interest in the subject and are more apt to pursue the subject on their own than students in teacher-centered classrooms. (4) There tends to be little or no difference in the *amount* of learning between group-centered and teacher-centered classrooms.

The general conclusion is that good classroom discussions stimulate interest, create good morale among students, and help to change behavior in desirable directions. The amount of learning which takes place is equal to that of the teacher-centered classroom.

Learning by discovery. Another kind of group learning, not unlike the method employed by Mrs. Miller, has been introduced with the teaching of "modern" mathematics, science, and social studies. The system most often used for structuring these learning programs is called the "discovery" process.[14] Sometimes it is called "problem solving" or "critical thinking." Rather than teach a child a set of facts and simply tell him that the facts are true, the teacher sets up problem situations that call for investigation, discussion, demonstration, trial and error, and eventually "discovery."

Of interest in this method of teaching is how it revises the human relationships in the classroom. The teacher's main task is not to give answers but to help the students find answers. The student's relationship both to the subject and the teacher is altered. He now turns to the teacher not for answers but for ways of finding answers. For him the subject consists not of a body of subject matter to be memorized but of a collection of problems to be solved. In this new relationship to the teacher he is not a passive outside observer but is active and deeply involved in his own learning.

Notice how learning by discovery takes place in the following example. The scene is a classroom of second- and third-graders engaged in original inquiry concerning "physical systems, equilibrium, interaction and simple relativity." [15] The teacher starts the lesson by showing the class two drawings. "The first, labeled 'Before,' shows a beaker half-full of colorless fluid, with a small cube resting at the bottom. Bubbles are rising from the cube. The second picture, labeled 'After,'

[14] See J. Bruner for a cogent discussion on the topic of learning through discovery. *The Process of Education*, Cambridge, Mass., Harvard University Press, 1960.

[15] Ronald Gross, "Two-Year-Olds Are Very Smart," *New York Times Magazine*, Volume CXIII, September 6, 1964, pp. 10–11.

shows the beaker, still half-filled with fluid, but minus the cube and bubbles. Question: What has happened?

"The following responses were given by different children in one class:

PUPIL: 'It's sugar. It's a sugar cube. A sugar cube breaks up in water.'
PUPIL: 'It's ice, and the ice melts in water.'
PUPIL: 'It's not ice. Ice would float at the top.'
PUPIL: 'It looks like sugar, it's a sugar cube because it's square.'
TEACHER: 'Could ice be square?'
PUPIL: 'Yes, but not all the time, so it's probably sugar.'
TEACHER: 'Will sugar float at the top?'

"The children say no, sugar will not float at the top, but they do not seem entirely ready to accept this idea.

PUPIL: 'It's a dice.'
PUPIL: 'No, dice doesn't melt!'
PUPIL: 'Somebody might have taken it out of the water.'
PUPIL: 'It's soap, because of the bubbles coming off.'
PUPIL: 'It's not soap, soap takes too long a time to dissolve, and any-how it forms lots of bubbles and lather.'
PUPIL: 'I measured, the height of the water in both is the same—about 16 inches.'

"The teacher writes down on the board all the things the class thought might be in the jar. The next day she places three jars of water before the children and has them try out each of the possibilities. One of the children who thought the object in the jar was ice obtains a piece from the school cafeteria for the experiment. Others bring a cube of sugar and a piece of soap. After observing and discussing the experiments, the class decides for sugar. Apparently the telling clue is the fact that the sugar cube in their own experiment gives off bubbles like those shown in the picture the day before.

"The teacher could, of course, have given the children the relevant facts at the outset. Instead, 30 third-graders spent a considerable time observing, analyzing their observations and using them to defend or modify their conclusions. This type of lesson is sometimes called 'How to Take Half an Hour to Teach What You Could Tell in One Minute.' "

Ability grouping. There has been great interest in recent years in grouping students by ability of achievement levels. Interest in grouping has been accelerated by efforts to help children achieve faster and not be tied to levels of work which they have already mastered while others catch up. It is also claimed that the slower student is more comfortable and will make more progress when he works with others of similar ability. Thus homogeneous grouping practices have emerged in which students with similar abilities are placed together.

Basically two patterns of homogeneous grouping are followed. One is partial homogeneous grouping in which students are separated for certain subjects or for certain times of the day. For the rest of the day the students remain in their heterogeneous group. The second pattern is complete homogeneous grouping in which children are placed permanently with others of similar abilities.

What do we know about the impact of grouping on the mental health and achievement of students? There is a considerable body of literature concerning homogeneous and heterogeneous grouping, especially in such subjects as reading and mathematics. Using scores on reading achievement tests as a basis for homogeneity and heterogeneity, research workers have generally favored homogeneous grouping as a useful device in terms of classroom achievement.

E. Paul Torrance and Kevser Arsan [16] studied the relative effects of homogeneous and heterogeneous grouping on performance of creative scientific tasks. Both measures of creative thinking ability and intelligence quotients were used as a basis for the groupings. The subjects were fourth-, fifth-, and sixth-grade children. This study concludes: "It seems reasonably clear that we may expect greater disruptive social stresses when we divide the classroom groups heterogeneously than when we divide them homogeneously for creative activities. . . . These results should not be interpreted to mean that teachers should always form homogeneous tasks for creative groups. There are signs that some homogeneous groups tend to be dull and uninteresting and unproductive when new ideas are required. There seem to be times when it is advantageous to increase social stress. . . . Then it would seem that a classroom teacher may within limits control the degree of social stress in work groups by choosing varying bases of grouping."

This research notes other tendencies. "One of these is the fairly consistent and frequently dramatic all-out performance of low-ability groups under homogeneous conditions." Moreover, "the findings tend to contradict popular beliefs that homogeneous grouping will make children unhappy, especially the low-ability ones, and that the high-

[16] E. Paul Torrance and Kevser Arsan, "Experimental Studies of Homogeneous and Heterogeneous Groups for Creative Scientific Tasks," in W. W. Charters, Jr. and N. L. Gage, *Readings in the Social Psychology of Education*, Boston, Allyn and Bacon, 1963, pp. 133–140.

ability pupils will become conceited and low-ability ones overwhelmed by their feelings of inferiority." [17]

This last conclusion touches upon the mental health aspects of ability grouping. Not all investigators draw the same conclusions as do Torrance and Arsan. Maxine Mann [18] studied fifth-graders to find out what ability grouping did to their self-concepts. She found that students in the highest and lowest groups were most aware of the level of grouping. When asked why they were assigned to a particular group, all the children in the top section and the second section gave responses which indicated positive self-concepts. The children in the third and fourth groups, however, gave responses which indicated negative and unfavorable self-concepts, such as "we don't know much," "we're too dumb," "we are lazy." Mann concluded that ability grouping was cruel to all but the top students.[19]

Loretta Byers [20] reviewed the research dealing with ability grouping and mental health and came to the following conclusions: Where there is *part-time or partial segregation* of students along ability lines, (1) ability grouping may enhance the emotional security of some bright students; (2) in the cases studied cliques did not develop among the selected capable children nor was intolerance fostered; (3) there was little cross-mingling in personal friendships between ability groups; (4) some children bemoaned the limitation of their contacts with other children and the attitudes they felt teachers held toward children in special classes.

In studies of cases of *total or full segregation* along ability lines Byers indicated that the research justified the following conclusions. (1) A halo effect seemed to accompany assignment to a class for the gifted. (2) Children in gifted classes tended to feel more secure in those classes than in more heterogeneous groups. (3) Children who were not in gifted sections evidenced feelings of worthlessness and sometimes of rejection.

The research evidence on ability grouping poses difficult problems

[17] *Ibid.,* pp. 139–140.

[18] Maxine Mann, "What Does Ability Grouping Do to the Self-Concept?" *Childhood Education,* Volume XXXVI, April 1960, pp. 357–360.

[19] F. R. Deitrich found that children who were grouped homogeneously were more aware of their status ("bright or dull") than were heterogeneous grouped children. "Comparison of Sociometric Patterns of Sixth-Grade Pupils in Two School Systems: Ability Grouping Compared with Heterogeneous Grouping." *Journal of Educational Research,* Madison, Wisconsin, Dunbar Educational Research Services, Volume 57, No. 10, July 1964, pp. 507–513.

[20] Loretta Byers, "Ability Grouping—Help or Hindrance to Social and Emotional Growth," *The School Review,* Volume 69, No. 4, Winter 1961, pp. 449–455.

for the classroom teacher. It calls for the exercise of judgment involving important values. On the one hand, the evidence indicates that ability grouping can enhance academic achievement. On the other hand, the evidence would point toward a hardening of social-class lines in the use of ability grouping. The concept of flexible grouping may provide a sensible approach for the classroom teacher. In flexible grouping the teacher uses neither homogeneous nor heterogeneous grouping exclusively but uses both in a manner best calculated to help achieve the goals of the classroom. A good teacher will sense what can best be achieved by one kind of grouping, what best by another kind of grouping. The skillful mixing of the two will probably bring the best results.

Ability grouping may or may not require a reorganization of school classes. If the ability grouping is grade-wide and if children are divided into separate sections based upon achievement, no single teacher can effect this change without the cooperation of other teachers. Within a self-contained classroom, however, an individual teacher may practice partial grouping without reference to practices in other classrooms.

Ungraded classrooms. One method for achieving flexibility in grouping is through the ungraded classroom. Schools were first organized around grades because there was the assumption that learning was a regular step-by-step process and that a normal child would advance in an orderly way up the steps. The graded school system provides a grade for each step and children are expected to move year by year up the graded system.

Modern knowledge of child development tells us, however, that learning is not an orderly process in which the child predictably moves on the schedule prescribed by the graded school system. Children begin school at different levels of maturity, learn at different rates, and achieve learning objectives at different times.[21] Children learn to read, to use and understand numbers, and to write good sentences at different rates. Further, the rate of an individual child changes from time to time. For some time a child may stumble along in a new learning activity and then may suddenly catch on and spurt ahead. Other children may start off rapidly, only to slow down along the way. Some may move at a steady pace, while some may not get started at all until weeks after the others are well ahead.

[21] A. Anastasi contends that all individuals exhibit, in some manner, individual differences. Indeed, it is these differences that identify the person within the group. *Differential Psychology* (Third Edition), New York, Macmillan Co., 1958.

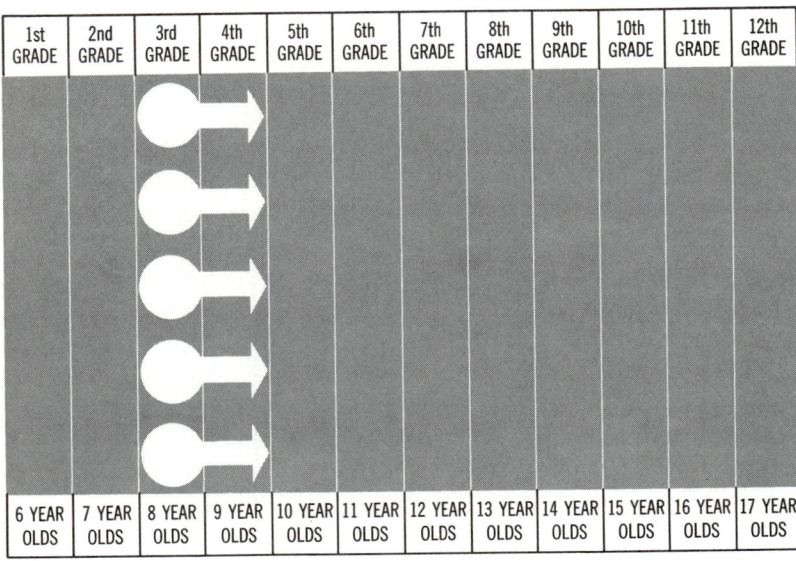

1st GRADE	2nd GRADE	3rd GRADE	4th GRADE	5th GRADE	6th GRADE	7th GRADE	8th GRADE	9th GRADE	10th GRADE	11th GRADE	12th GRADE

6 YEAR OLDS	7 YEAR OLDS	8 YEAR OLDS	9 YEAR OLDS	10 YEAR OLDS	11 YEAR OLDS	12 YEAR OLDS	13 YEAR OLDS	14 YEAR OLDS	15 YEAR OLDS	16 YEAR OLDS	17 YEAR OLDS

Fig. 5-2 In the graded school system the expectation is that all children will move year by year up the graded ladder.

Because of individual differences, children who enter first grade may have a difference of three or four years in their "readiness" to learn. This range may increase as children progress through the elementary grades until the distance between the slowest and fastest learner in a single-graded classroom may be six or eight years. Put another way, after six grades the slow child may be reading at the second-grade level while the fastest child may be reading at the tenth-grade level.

In a genuine sense, then, it may be accurate to say that there is no such thing as a fourth-grade class and a fourth-grade teacher. There are only groups of students in the fourth grade and a teacher of these students, but the range of real achievement among the group of fourth-graders will likely extend from the "primer" stage of reading to a superior mastery of reading skills.

How does the ungraded system attempt to handle this problem? How can "ungrading" the system achieve results which the graded system may not? One school system which uses the ungraded elementary school answered these questions for parents in this fashion.[22]

22 "The Ungraded Elementary School," *The State Journal,* Lansing, Mich., Tuesday, May 26, 1964, Section D, p. D-2.

"Simply stated, the 'ungraded' elementary school is a school without grade designations such as 'first,' 'second,' or 'third.' It is a school where each child progresses under ideal circumstances, from month to month, year to year, at his own rate.

"Perhaps a good illustration which would point up the difference between the 'graded' system and the 'ungraded' system would be a description of four children—two girls and two boys—attempting to climb a rope. Each child would begin to climb, hand over hand, at the same moment. Let's say that the first child was a strong, husky boy who had little trouble in quickly working his way to the top. The second boy is not so strong in the hands and arms. He can make it all the way up the rope, but in a much longer time than his stronger classmate.

"Our third youngster is an active, alert girl, who by using both her arms and legs, could inch her way to the top about as fast as the second boy.

"On the other hand, the fourth youngster is small and shy, and not given to such antics as rope climbing. In time she will be able to climb that rope with a lot of practice and even more encouragement. But not now. She is just not ready to do much more than hoist her feet a yard or so off the floor.

"Now in the ungraded program, each child will climb that rope in his own good time and at his own rate, according to strength, ability, and inclination. For instance, let's say we put a time limit of one minute on the rope climb. Climb as high as you can in 60 seconds. The first boy goes all the way to the top with seconds to spare. The second boy makes it up about three-quarters of the way; the stronger girl about halfway. The smaller girl struggles her usual four or five feet up the rope, then the time is up.

"In the graded elementary school, only the first boy is eligible to 'pass' to the next challenge. The other three children might have to start over next time which is next school year, or spend most of their time competing with children far ahead of them in ability.

"In the ungraded school, all pick up where they have left off, but they don't forfeit what they have achieved simply because time ran out. Neither does the quick-to-learn child wait idly for others to catch up with him."

The ungraded system shares some characteristics with ability grouping. The ungraded system, however, stresses flexibility in grouping, allowing a student to move from group to group, even from teacher to teacher, as his level of achievement changes. If an individual student is ready to move much sooner than his classmates, he moves to

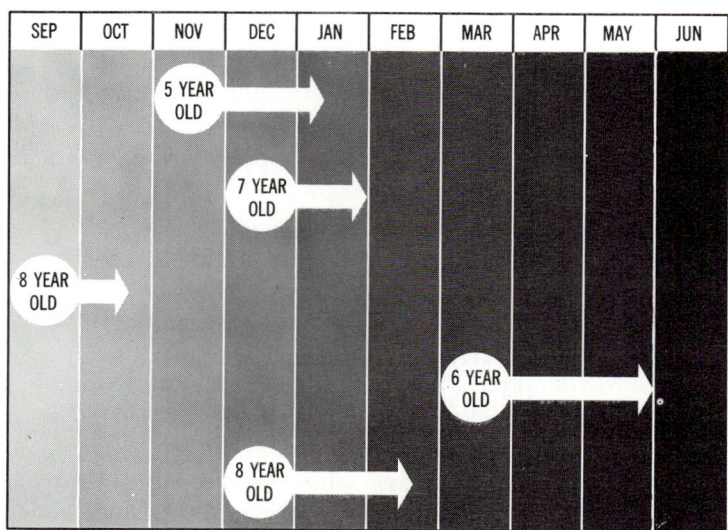

Fig. 5-3   In the ungraded school each child progresses from month to month, year to year, at his own rate.

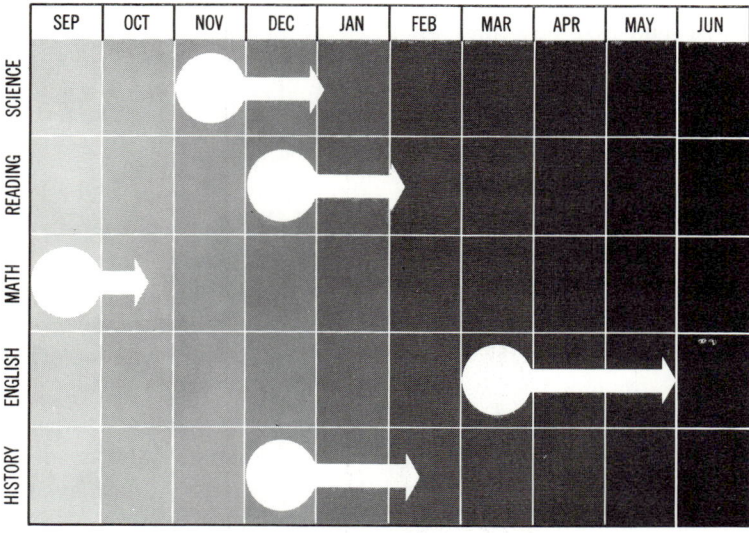

Fig. 5-4   In the ungraded school the same child progresses in different subjects at his own rate.

another learning group where the work being done is the kind he is ready to do.

Other group methods which teachers can use. Thus far we have noted four major methods of classroom learning. Discussion methods are applicable in almost all classroom settings. Learning by discovery is especially applicable to science, mathematics, and social studies, where problem solving is important. Ability groupings may take place within a single classroom or among many classrooms. Ungraded classrooms call for major organizational changes in the school.

In concluding this section we should mention several other methods which teachers find helpful and which can be accomplished within a single classroom. The use of "buzz groups" encourages especially the participation of the student who is reluctant to contribute to large group discussions. There is a tendency for a few students to dominate large group discussions and others to be "left out." In using buzz groups teachers usually divide the total class into small groups, each of which investigates some aspect of the problem under discussion. Each group may choose a chairman and "recorder" and later report its deliberations to the entire class. These buzz groups can provide experience for students in small group deliberation as well as leadership experience for the chairman and recorder.

Panel discussions are a useful method for involving large numbers of students in active learning. Students may choose to serve on a panel of their choice, or they may be assigned to panels by the teacher. There may be five to eight panel groups in one class, with five or six members each. Members of the panel spend several days, perhaps weeks, investigating the topic under discussion. They then organize a panel discussion with each student making a short presentation, followed by panel and class discussion of the topic.

Role playing is the spontaneous enacting of an incident or of a person in action. Usually participants discuss the roles they are to play in order to get the "feel" of the situation and the personality being portrayed, after which they may practice their respective roles.

Role playing may serve many purposes in the classroom. It may develop empathy and insight into personalities and problems. It can help students gain insight into a situation because it dramatizes that situation and makes it come to life. Role playing can also give insight into abstract subject matter. Students who are studying the administrative structure of their city's government can understand the roles of the mayor, councilmen, and department heads if they study and then actually "play" those roles.

Group teaching methods are the teacher's tools for accomplishing the goals of learning. When used wisely and skillfully they help facilitate the learning of every person within the group.

8. This question will give you an opportunity to reflect upon how you learn in school situations. List several methods of classroom discussion to which you have been exposed. Compare them in terms of their learning impact upon you.

Classroom Control Is Based on Sound Group Relationships

By earning respect instead of demanding respect and by steering the students instead of commanding them, a good learning situation is readily achieved.

Mr. Merriman had no discipline problems because, as he said, students were handled on a "mutual respect" basis. He realized that good discipline springs from the social relationships established within the classroom. The relationships, both within the group and between individual students and the teacher, are the important factors in classroom control. These *are* the relationships which control the discipline of the class. If they are based on mutual respect for the others in the group, the control is positive. Such control does not depend solely on the authority of the teacher because it rests where it should, within the group's own concept of what is right.

Competition Is Constructively Handled

By instilling in the student or the group a feeling of security, mutual respect, and a display of compatibility, I soon have a sound, harmonious learning situation.

Competition is a very important part of our society, and before children come to school they have already learned a great deal about how to compete, for example, with their brothers and sisters. The classroom, therefore, cannot and probably should not escape competition. Indeed a heavy burden falls upon the teacher to help children learn to compete well. That burden is seen in better perspective when we add that students must also learn the opposite of competition, cooperation. Our modern business, industrial, and professional enterprises require people who can cooperate with large numbers of other people in order to advance the goals of the organization. Modern society mixes these apparently conflicting ingredients in different ways, and students must learn the complicated business of handling well both competition and cooperation.[23]

[23] J. Samler examines the problem of teaching economic and social values and the consequent mental health complication. He concludes that teachers must

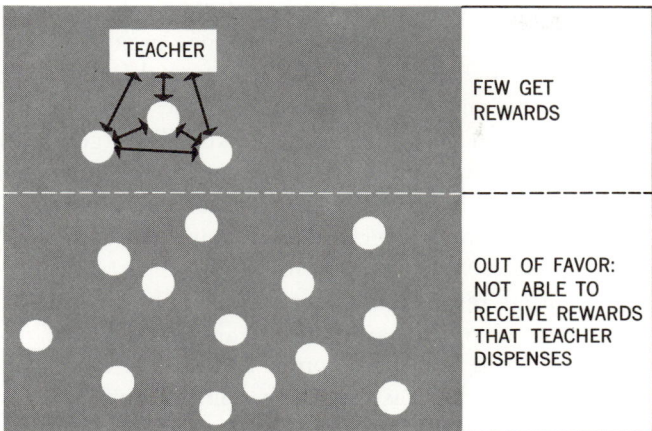

Fig. 5-5   In a highly competitive classroom only a few students can be at the top. Children who cannot be at the top are made to feel inferior.

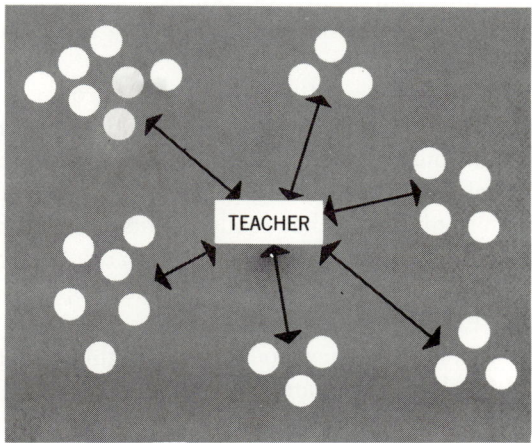

Fig. 5-6   In a noncompetitive classroom all the children have a chance to excel in some way.

Perhaps the crucial matter lies in the way the teacher organizes the emotions of the classroom. They may be organized toward either disruptive or constructive ends. The skill in teaching lies in the ability of the teacher to channel the emotions away from disruptive behavior and into constructive relations. One teacher may organize the emotions of the classroom in such a way that children turn their hostility toward one another and the success of one child can be achieved only at the failure of another. Another teacher may skillfully organize the emotions of the classroom around the achievement of specific learning goals. Organized in this way, the emotions of the classroom will not lead to the destruction of peers but will reinforce common learning goals. For this reason Mr. Merriman instilled in his students a "feeling of security, mutual respect, and the display of compatibility," and thereby achieved "a sound, harmonious learning situation."

The teacher faces few more complex problems than that of handling competition in the classroom. As pointed out earlier, there is tremendous pressure on the student to achieve and to be "selected" for future opportunity which ensues from advanced preparation. Although the classroom cannot escape competition if it wishes, it need not stress competition to the detriment of either learning achievement or students. Learning in our modern world calls for people who have developed skills of cooperation and who know how to work together for common goals. Indeed a good case can be made for saying that the skills of cooperation are far more important to successful living than skills in competition.

Overemphasis on competition in the classroom can frequently result in unfortunate comparisons among children. In a highly competitive classroom only a few students can be at the top and the rest are made to feel inferior. The highly competitive classroom teaches children that the only thing that really counts is to be first. Learning for its own sake is discounted, for learning in an intensely competitive classroom is only a means for climbing to the top. What is learned is subordinated to the competitive impulse.

In conclusion, let us review some of the highlights of this chapter.

The good teacher understands that children are culturally predisposed to behave as they do in classroom groups. What the teacher may interpret as bad or indifferent behavior on the part of children may simply be the expression of cultural behavior patterns learned

---

understand the nature of conflicts in order effectively to teach these values to pupils. "The School and Self Understanding," *Harvard Education Review,* Volume 35, No. 1, Winter 1965, pp. 55–70.

in the early years at home and in the community. These behavior patterns differ among subgroups of the same culture—children from suburb, slum, town, and village will all tend to behave differently in classrooms. The good teacher learns to use these behavior patterns for learning purposes, as Sylvia Ashton-Warner used the volcanic energy of her Maori children to promote their own learning.

In order to channel the classroom behavior of children into constructive learning the good teacher understands the circular nature of classroom relationships. Good teachers begin at once to respond to the class positively, thus setting in motion a wholesome circular response. The good teacher provides for individual differences and enhances the student's self-concept. He understands the group dynamics of his classroom and uses group methods of instruction. He develops within the group wholesome relationships which serve to control behavior. Finally, he handles competition in such a way that students learn also the value of cooperation.

In the five chapters of this first part we have concerned ourselves primarily with learning which takes place in the classroom. In speaking of socialization, we said that classroom learning is actually only a small part of a child's learning. The learning influences that pour in upon him outside the classroom are large and incessant. We need to look at these. In Part II we shall examine two of the child's most powerful teachers outside the classroom, his family, and his peers to see how these influences bear on his life in school.

REFERENCES

Paperbacks

Change and Innovation in Elementary School Organization. Maurie Hillison and Ramona Karlson. Holt, Rinehart and Winston, 383 Madison Ave., New York ($3.95).

Critical Incidents in Teaching. Raymond J. Corsini and Daniel D. Howard. (Orig.) Prentice-Hall, Englewood Cliffs, N. J. ($4.50).

Educating for Mental Health: A Book of Readings. Jerome M. Seidman. (Orig.) Thomas Y. Crowell Co., 201 Park Ave. South, New York ($4.50).

Encounter with Early Teens. Mary Elizabeth Wycoff. (Orig.) (20-0599) The Westminster Press, Witherspoon Building, Philadelphia, Pa. ($1.25).

Enriching Social Studies. Murray Polner. (Orig.) Teachers Practical Press, 47 Frank St., Valley Stream, N. Y. (Distributed by Prentice-Hall, Englewood Cliffs, N. J.) ($1.95).

Enriching the Curriculum with Current Events. Lillian C. Howitt. (Orig.) Teachers Practical Press, 47 Frank St., Valley Stream, N. Y. (Distributed by Prentice-Hall, Englewood Cliffs, N. J.) ($1.95).

How to Use Role Playing Effectively. Alan F. Klein. (1394-LL) Association Press, 291 Broadway, New York ($1.00).

Learning to Work in Groups: A Program Guide for Educational Leaders (Studies of Horace Mann-Lincoln Inst. of School Experimentation). Matthew B. Miles. (Orig.) Teachers College Press, 525 West 120 St., New York ($1.50).

Revolution in Teaching. Alfred de Grazia and David Sohn, Editors. (Orig.) (NM1006) Bantam Books, 271 Madison Ave., New York (95¢).

Understanding Your Pupils. J. Vernon Jacobs. (Orig.) (9912P) Zondervan Publishing House, 1415 Lake Drive S. E., Grand Rapids, Mich. ($1.00).

Books

Association for Supervision and Curriculum Development, *Learning and the Teacher,* 1959 Yearbook. Washington, D. C.: The Association, 1959. This yearbook presents chapters which discuss the knowledge we have about how learning processes influence teachers in the classroom.

The Dynamics of Instructional Groups, National Society for the Study of Education, 59th Yearbook. Chicago: University of Chicago Press, 1960. Sections I and II present articles on the sociopsychological characteristics of instructional groups.

Grambs, Jean D., and L. Morris McClure, *Foundations of Teaching: An Introduction to Modern Education.* New York: Holt, Rinehart and Winston, 1964. Chapter 3 presents a description of teacher behavior in the classroom and the classroom social climate needed for good teaching.

Lindgren, Henry Clay, *Educational Psychology in the Classroom.* New York: John Wiley and Sons, 1956. This textbook presents different approaches to learning and emphasizes learning through group methods.

Lucio, William H., Editor, *Readings in American Education.* Chicago: Scott, Foresman and Co., 1963. Readings are presented on the problem of project and group discussion methods of instruction.

National Education Association, *Schools for the Sixties.* New York: McGraw-Hill Book Co., 1963. Chapter 3 presents an interesting discussion on planning and organizing for teaching, with emphasis on curriculum in the classroom.

Taba, Hilda, and Deborah Elkins, *With Focus on Human Relations.* Washington, D. C.: American Council on Education, 1950. An excellent description of how a teacher worked with an eighth-grade class to know the interpersonal relationships of her students.

Wilson, W. Cody, and George W. Goethals, "A Field Study," in *The Role of Schools in Mental Health,* Monograph Series, No. 7. New York: Basic Books, 1962, pp. 175–280. The field study reveals the problem of shifting and conflicting expectations faced by teachers. The first half of the monograph is a survey of the literature pertaining to mental health and education.

Periodicals

Campanelle, Thomas, "Motivational Development of Adolescents," *Education,* Vol. 85, No. 5, January 1965, pp. 310–313. The author presents an overview of motivational factors which influence adolescents, pointing out that the teacher's opportunity is great for being of significant aid to the developing teen-ager.

Ebel, Robert L., "The Social Consequences of Educational Testing," *School and Society*, Vol. 92, No. 2249, November 14, 1964, pp. 331–334. The author highlights the positive and negative social consequences of tests for making educational assessments.

Hoyt, Kenneth B., "Guidance and School Dropouts," *Education*, Vol. 85, No. 4, December 1964, pp. 228–233. The author suggests that it is time for teachers to reorient their thinking and practices in order that the nonachiever will have a place within the school setting.

Jensen, Gale, and Thomas Parsons, "The Structure and Dynamics of Classroom Groups and Educational Systems," Chapter 3, *Review of Educational Research*, Vol. XXIX, No. 4, 1959, pp. 344–356. The authors present a model for conceptualizing the group phenomena in the classroom.

Preston, Malcolm G., and Roy K. Heintz, "Effects of Participatory vs. Supervisory Leadership on Group Judgment," *Journal of Abnormal and Social Psychology*, Vol. 44, No. 3, July 1949, pp. 345–355. This study suggests that participatory leadership is more effective than supervisory leadership as a technique for effecting changes in attitudes.

Raths, James, "The Dignity of Man in the Classroom," *Childhood Education*, Vol. 40, No. 7, March 1964, pp. 339–340. Teacher-student relationships should stress empathy, not just methodology and curriculum.

II

The Student and His Environment

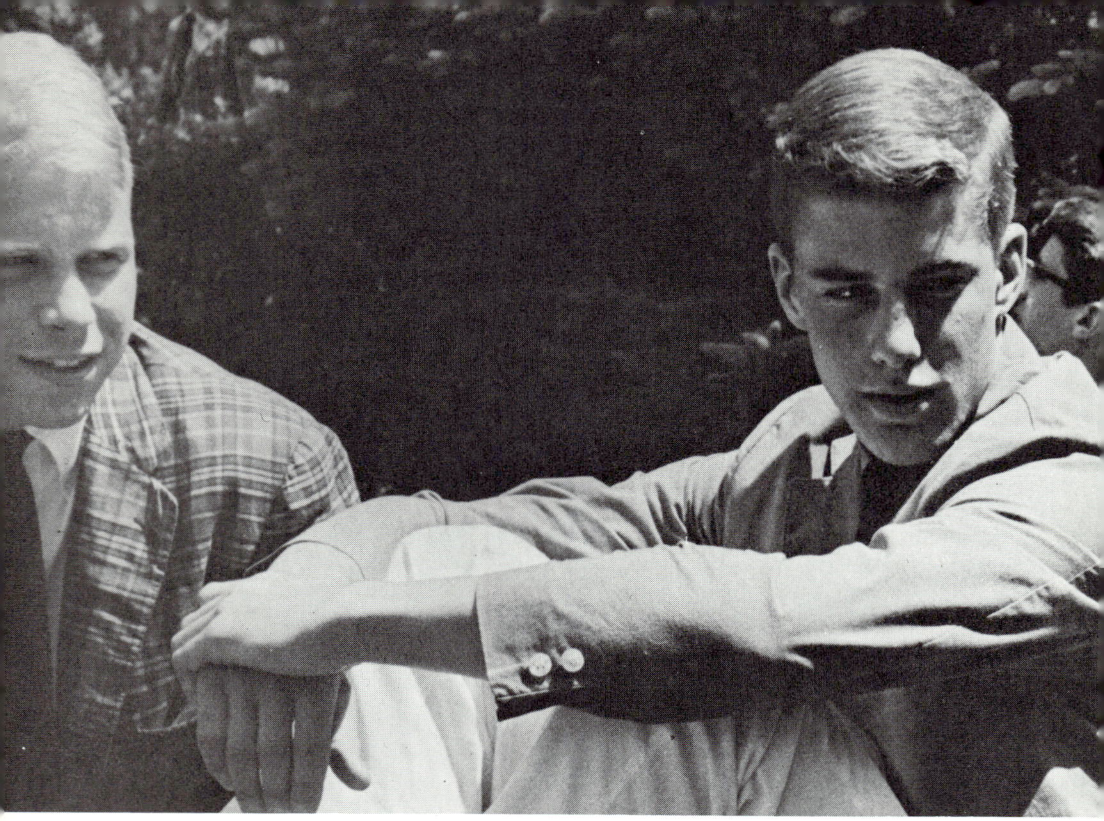

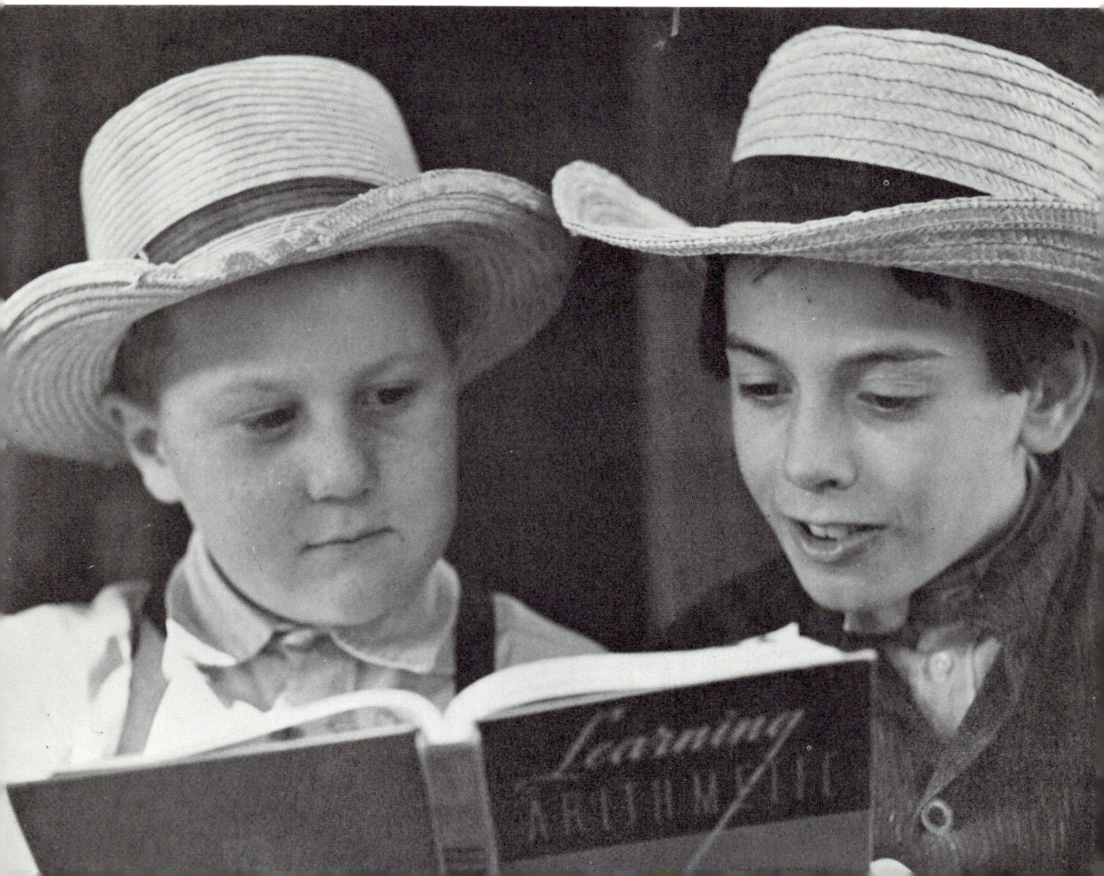
Learning

6

The Student and His Family

"If we begin by assuming that what educates deeply is the immediate experience of a child, then the family is what educates the most and the soonest."

HAROLD TAYLOR

The child is born into a family, his first socializing group. The family not only is the first group to which he is exposed, but also is in many ways the most influential. Generally the child, until he goes to school, spends all his time in the family. After he enters school and until adolescence, he spends roughly half his time in the family, and after adolescence a quarter of his time. Further, after he leaves his parental home, marries, and starts a home of his own, he continues with the family, this time in the role of husband or wife and likely parent. The human family, because it shapes the lives of all of us, is one of society's most influential teachers.

In Part I of this book we considered the social dimensions of classroom learning. Now we turn to the educational dimensions of society itself and to the informal education which takes place for the most part outside the classroom. It is in the world beyond the classroom that the child encounters his first teachers, frequently the most influential teachers in his life. Even after he enters school these teachers-outside-of-school continue to educate and influence him. When school days are over they still act upon him, and he upon them.

For Part II we have selected two of the most important out-of-school influences in the life of the child, his family, and his peers. To each we shall devote a chapter. These chapters pose serious questions about how social forces outside of school influence what does or should happen in school.

Our purpose in discussing the family and peer groups is not to treat these subjects for their own sakes, interesting though this would be. Rather, it is to focus on the particular aspects of these topics that teachers and future teachers need to understand. We direct our attention to the way in which the family and the peer group influence how children learn and behave in school. In other words, we are primarily concerned with the relationship of the family to the school, the manner in which peer groups influence child and youth behavior, and how both bear upon the child's learning in school. The emphasis is on how these teachers of the larger society influence what teachers of the little society can and should do.

WHAT IS HAPPENING IN THE MODERN FAMILY?

The modern family is undergoing rapid changes, changes which alter considerably what the family expects the school to do for its children. One way to dramatize these changes and their influence on education is to contrast the modern, changing family with a traditional, unchanging family. Such a contrast is provided by the Amish family, whose traditional ways are passed on almost intact from one generation to the next. Shunning automobiles and modern gadgetry of all kinds, the Amish stick to "horse-and-buggy ways," wear plain clothes, live in undecorated homes, marry within their group, and try to be self-sufficient. They are "in this world but not of it."

Because modern public education is not suited to their ways and needs, the Amish tend to seek residence in states that permit them to operate their own schools or permit their children to leave public schools at an early age. Their position on schooling has frequently brought Amish families into conflict with the public school authorities who are required to enforce compulsory attendance laws. In some states the Amish have operated their own schools with teachers from their own group who are unqualified by state standards. Then state educational authorities find it necessary to invoke teacher certification laws. The following news release grew out of one of these conflicts. It implies much about the educational functions of these traditional families and the kinds of schools they regard as appropriate for their children.[1]

"The gentle Amish people, attempting to cling to their centuries-old traditions, are faced once again with a threat by the state to close their one-room schoolhouse in this quiet farming community.

[1] "Amish Target of Complaint," *The State Journal*, Lansing, Mich., Thursday, January 7, 1965, p. D-5.

"At a hearing Wednesday, the Amish defended their right to use a 20-year-old girl, Ruth Graber, to teach more than 20 children ranging in age from 6 to 16, even though Miss Graber's formal education ended at the eighth grade.

"The hearing was called on the complaint of Walter Holliday, Hillsdale intermediate school district superintendent, that the Amish were being instructed by an uncertified teacher.

" 'We do not feel guilty of the complaint as filed,' said Levi Graber, spokesman for the eight fathers whose children attend the school. Three of the fathers were named in Holliday's affidavit as operators of the school.

" 'This is a church-operated school without any aid from the state,' Graber said. 'In our opinion, Miss Graber is qualified to teach. It is difficult for us to find a teacher that would meet the standards which we have set.'

"One qualification which the Amish have listed in a teacher is fluency in German, since their Bible and some other studies are in that language. The original Amish immigrants to this country were fleeing religious persecution in Germany and Holland. . . .

"Speaking to newsmen after the hearing, Graber said:

" 'We feel our children get a good education. We believe they need no more than an eighth-grade education.

" 'We teach them to cope with our way of life. They learn to cook, to sew, the carpenter trade, to be welders and to be self-sufficient.

" 'If they want to test our schools, they will find our education is superior to the public schools.' "

In these relatively unchanging Amish families the skills which the young must know, sewing, cooking, carpentry, and welding, are known and practiced within the family itself. As Mr. Graber said, the Amish are "self-sufficient," at least as self-sufficient as any group can be in an interdependent world. They do teach their children "to cope with their way of life." The formal school, therefore, as viewed by the Amish, has a simple and direct function: to teach the young to manage the same kind of world as their elders have managed, knowing that for these children the world will never change very much. The elders of the Amish family are the repositories of knowledge and wisdom and the young people depend on them for training and advice.

How different is the modern family. In a rapidly changing society like ours the young are frequently the repositories of knowledge and wisdom, since it is they who frequently learn the latest and most effective ways of doing things. Modern schools are established precisely for the purpose of transmitting the vast accumulation of new

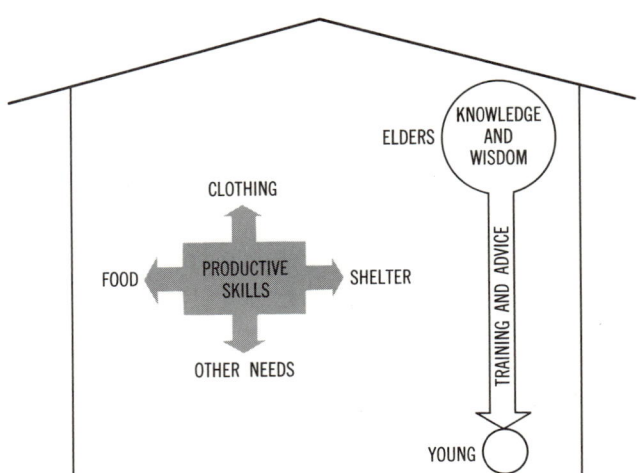

Fig. 6-1   The traditional family was relatively self-sufficient.

knowledge. For this reason children in modern urban schools frequently have more knowledge about certain subjects than their parents. In modern science and mathematics especially there have been extensive discoveries in new knowledge over short periods of time, and children may be far more familiar with these than parents.

In fact, increasingly the schools hold classes for parents to make sure that they understand what their children are learning. In this reversal of roles it is the parents who need to be brought abreast with the children. For example, local newspapers may carry items like this: [2]

"Why can't pop help Johnny with his arithmetic?

"This crisis in family living has faced many parents this year and last night 300 parents met to seek the answer.

"They attended the opening session of a Modern Mathematics seminar at Haslett Junior High School.

"The new concept in mathematics was introduced this year in the Haslett school system. Bernard F. Brown, superintendent of elementary education at Haslett who is conducting the seminar said the new idea is to place emphasis on the child understanding problems and then working out those problems.

"Parents are faced with a foreign language when attempting to

[2] John Ward, "New Math Concept," *The State Journal*, Lansing, Mich., September 30, 1964, p. D-1.

aid children in their new arithmetic studies. Ciphering is a term of the past. Some of the new terms, unheard of 20 years ago, include rational and irrational numbers, integers, natural and whole numbers and numbers of arithmetic. These all represent a definite part of the new number systems. Then there are associative and commutative laws and additive and multiplicative identities.

"Pity poor pop.

"The Haslett seminar will last from four to six weeks, Brown said, with classes being held every Tuesday. Sessions will include an hour of instruction followed by 30 minutes of questions and answers. He said if there is sufficient interest, an additional course will be held for three to four weeks.

"There are no tests, no fees and attendance is not taken.

"The final exam will come when Johnny asks if 55 can equal 35. Then pop can stick out his chest, smile knowingly and answer, 'Sure, Johnny, when you put it in the Base Six system.'"

The Amish child learns what he needs to know from his parents. Today, in modern families, children increasingly learn what they must know from specialists outside the family. And it is the parents who need additional education to "keep up."

Let us look at some of the changes taking place in families which have a major bearing upon schools and the conduct of formal education.

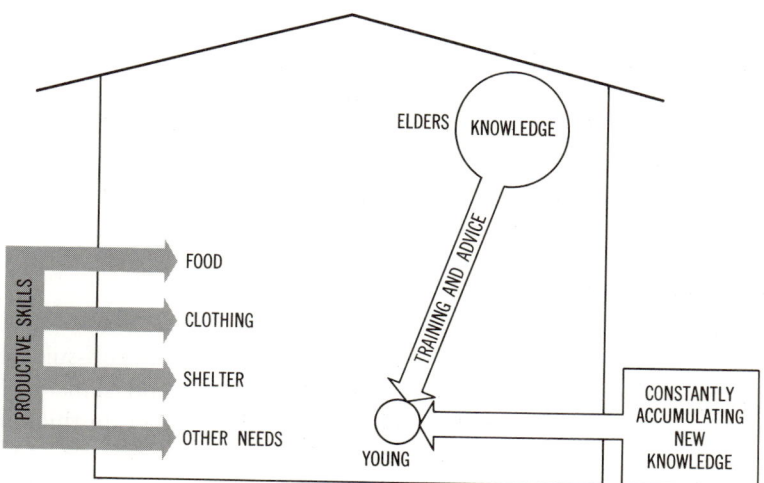

Fig. 6-2 The modern family is a consumer of goods, services, and knowledge.

1. In the section which follows we shall consider the changes which have taken place in the family in recent years. As you read the material, you might keep in mind your own family. What changes have taken place in it over one, two, or possibly three generations? What *educational* changes have taken place in your family during this period?

THE CHANGING FUNCTIONS OF THE MODERN FAMILY

From Economic Production to Economic Consumption

The Amish family of today, like most rural American families of yesterday, is a producing family, an economically self-sufficient group. It produces its own food, makes much of its clothing, builds its houses and farm buildings, raises draft horses for power and trotting horses for transportation, and repairs farm machinery when it breaks down. The Amish family's need for cash is therefore small, for it satisfies many of its own needs. Economically, it is quite self-sufficient.

The modern family is a consumer rather than a producer. Whereas the Amish child is taught to sew, cook, and be a carpenter or welder, the child of the modern family is given an allowance to purchase what he wants. The needs of the family are met by the supermarket, drugstore, and shopping plaza. It is a dependent family, requiring for its economic and social existence the services of literally hundreds of specialists, including producers and processors of food, makers and distributors of clothing, repairmen of a dozen kinds, teachers, doctors, druggists, lawyers, automobile and gasoline manufacturers, entertainers, newspapers, religious counselors, psychologists, and psychiatrists.

The economic and social functions of earlier families have now been taken over by factories, stores, banks, service agencies, schools, churches, clubs, and social-welfare groups. The modern family depends on these for its existence. To survive it must be economically able to purchase goods and services and must know how to earn sufficiently and to consume wisely.

From Authority to Colleague Relationships

If the family is changing as an economic system, it is also changing as a social system. When families were economically self-sufficient groups, parents were the sources of the knowledge and skills which were to be transmitted to the children. As Mr. Graber testified for the Amish: "We teach them to cope with our way of life . . . to be self-sufficient." In this kind of family authority rests easily and naturally in parents.

In the modern dependent family the parents must share the authority that springs from superior knowledge and expertise with dozens of specialists outside the home and with their own children, who are learning new knowledge and ways of doing things. Family relationships have moved from authority to companionship and now, some believe, toward a colleague relationship. In the authority-centered family one or both of the parents dominate decision making. In the companionship family the group is held together by the need for love, security, and continuing personal relationships. In the colleague family the members perform specialist roles in the different areas necessary for family functioning. For example, in a family where the wife works, the father may do the shopping, although traditionally this is not his role, and a daughter may do the cooking. The colleague family defines its various roles according to the functions to be performed and who can best perform them.

Whatever its particular style of relationship, the modern family is moving away from parental authority toward shared decision making among all members of the group.

More Working Wives

Formerly one of the most crucial questions confronting young women was "Marriage or career?" Because women usually gave up work at marriage or shortly thereafter, married women constituted a minority of the female working force.

Today we assume that wives will work and have a career if they choose to do so. Indeed, economic pressures on the consuming family frequently require that wives work if marriage is to take place at all. Purchasing a home and raising a family increase further the pressure on wives to work. As a result, the number of married women at work today far exceeds the number of single women at work.

The effects on schools of the increased employment of mothers are manifold. The impact of a job is to reduce the amount of time the mother spends with her children and to increase her dependency on the school. She now needs the school to perform functions which formerly were performed in the home. The mass employment of women outside the home marks still another step in the changing functions of the modern family and its dependence on outside agencies for vital services.

Accent on the Child

One of the dominant facts of the modern family is its accent on children. We might imagine an Amish family dropping in for a visit on a modern suburban family. The surprises on the part of one would be matched only by the surprises of the other. The Amish family would notice quickly that the suburban children talk to their parents in an easy and spontaneous manner as equals, sometimes asking frank and embarrassing questions. They would observe that children in suburbia have little or only easy work to do, like emptying wastepaper baskets or making their beds, and that they receive an "allowance" for doing it. The Amish would notice that suburban children seem to spend all their time at play; indeed they seem to "work" at play. They are surrounded by the "tools" of play, playthings, toys, and books. They watch television shows and listen to radio programs especially designed for them. Further, their mothers meet in groups to study the latest methods of child care and training. There is great concern about whether this food, that program, or that kind of discipline is good for the child. Not content with sending their children to kindergarten, parents place them in "preschool" to make sure that they get a good start in life. And after the child enters regular school they are pleased when they are told that the curriculum is "child-centered." The Amish family would find all this strange indeed in comparison to their own families, where children are expected to conform to adult standards, be passive and obedient, and perform economically useful work rather than economically wasteful play.

The difference, of course, is that the two families have different goals for their children. The Amish family wishes its children to conform to tradition, or, as Mr. Graber said, "to conform to our way of life." Although we are still concerned that children show deference to tradition, the emphasis has shifted to the interests and needs of the child. In a rapidly changing family the parents' way of life will not be the child's way of life when he grows up. Therefore, the general welfare and education of the child are geared to permit him to cope with an unseen future.

2. "Interview" one of your parents about the attitudes toward children in his or her childhood home. Compare these attitudes with the ones which existed in your own home. How are they alike? How are they different?

The implications for schools of this accent on the child are obvious. The school is given the heavy burden of preparing him for a changing future which neither the family nor the school can clearly discern or understand.

Accent on the School

Implicit in all the changes in the family mentioned thus far is the growing importance of the school. The school must take over and perform functions which were previously performed by the family. Mental and manual skills formerly taught by the traditional family must now be taught in the school. New knowledge which springs up outside the family, and to which the family does not have access, must be taught through the school. The family's shrinking social functions have enlarged the social responsibility of the schools. The child must be prepared to be a specialist in an age of specialization at the very time when the family has given up its specialized functions. These dramatic changes taking place in the family have far-reaching effects in schools upon what is taught and how it is taught.

THE FAMILY AS TEACHER

The Traditional Family

One way to understand better the modern family as the child's teacher is to compare it with the traditional family. Through comparative analysis we can observe what teaching functions the modern family has both lost and gained as it has moved away from tradition. We can see how the school is now attempting to pick up some of those lost teaching functions, and how some of the teaching methods of traditional families that had great merit are frequently incorporated as sound practice in modern schools.

The traditional family we choose for this comparative purpose is a pastoral family which makes its living by raising sheep on the plains of Central Asia, in Pakistan. The family lives in a rural village, is Moslem in its religious faith, and is tribal in its outlook. For generations the tribe has earned its living by running sheep over the almost desolate hills and fertile valleys. The family, village, and tribe are a close-knit social organization bound together by common blood lines resulting from intermarriages and by a deep and proud faith in their tribal way of life. Because their limited horizons do not yet embrace such a faith in their new nation, loyalty to the nation is several generations away. Note the teaching functions of this family.[3]

"This country is not yet industrialized. It is made up primarily of small farmers, herdsmen, artisans, shopkeepers and servants. Formal schooling is not available to the masses. In this situation little boys tend to step quite naturally into their father's or family's occupation, while the little girls assume the retiring domestic role of the mother. They learn the things they need to know by first observing their elders and then taking part along with them in doing at first some of the

---

[3] Cole S. Brembeck, *The Discovery of Teaching*, Englewood Cliffs, N. J., Prentice-Hall, 1962, p. 128.

simpler things and then, as they got more experience, engaging directly in the more complex forms of activity.

"Take as an example, the shepherd boy who is a familiar sight along every road and country lane. One's first reaction is: 'How young to be tending a flock of sheep!' Yet, observe him, and one sees that he knows well what he is about. He shepherds his sheep with great skill along the paths to and from the pasture land. Where fences are unknown he can keep his flock within boundaries, even though greener pastures beckon his sheep beyond. He knows how to protect the sheep from menacing dogs and he can use his stick with great effectiveness. He can recognize poisonous weeds and steer his sheep away from them. At ten years of age he is a good shepherd.

"This boy grew up in his vocation and was probably never aware that he was learning it. When he was very small his father or older brother took him along while they tended the flock. To protect him from the hot sun he was put down in the shade of a bush. From there he watched and listened. As he grew older he ran after the sheep, assisting his father in rounding up the strays. In the spring, at lambing time, he watched his father work with the ewes. He was shown how to teach a new lamb to suckle. At shearing time he was there, assisting first, then later catching, throwing, and holding the sheep for the shearer.

"From his earliest years he knew the value of the flock to his family. From the wool he saw his mother and sisters card yarn from which family clothes were made. The flock provided meat for the table. The wool and sheep which were sold brought the family its meager cash income.

"Here, then, is a learning situation in which the young first observe their elders carry on significant tasks in which they are skilled. Gradually, naturally, they start to take part. Finally, their own skill is developed and they are capable of training others."

Not only did this pastoral and traditional family teach a vocation to its young; it also taught the values of its religion and culture and pride in the family and tribe. In contrast to the modern child who spends large blocks of time away from the family, the shepherd boy, his brothers and sisters, spend almost all their time until they are married with their family. Even after marriage they will likely continue in the family and tribal circle. Through this continual exposure the child quite naturally, and without any conscious effort on the part of the parent, "soaks up" the values of his culture and subculture. There are no competing and alternative ways of life available to the child, as there are for the child of the modern family. The traditional family's isolation within the village and tribe assure that the child will drink deeply and without question of the social and religious values. In contrast, the child of the modern home is barraged daily with crosscurrents of opinions and values which may be quite at odds with those taught by his family.

The Merits of Learning in the Traditional Family

Quite apart from *what* was taught in the traditional family, the *way* in which it was taught had merits worth recording.

First, the learning in a traditional family took place in a completely natural kind of way. There were no tricks or rewards for motivating the child. Learning took place as a part of the functions by which the family lived.

Second, it was easy for the learner, in this case the shepherd boy, to see the relationship between one small aspect of a task and the whole task. For example, he could see the connection between caring for a new lamb and the family's later welfare in terms of food and clothing. He did not need to be motivated by extrinsic means to realize that caring for sheep was important to the family. The motivation was intrinsic.

Third, the parents were associated with the young in carrying on work which was significant to the whole family. In a sense the father and the shepherd boy were co-workers, the father being superior only in experience, knowledge, and skill. The father's roles as teacher and worker blended so harmoniously that it would be difficult to separate them. This father of a traditional family was a great deal like the master artists of the Italian Renaissance who permitted promising apprentices first to observe them at work and then gradually to take part in the painting. Both teaching and learning flourish in this atmosphere.

Finally, this kind of learning had the *readiness* concept built into it. As the shepherd boy demonstrated his readiness he took on new tasks and responsibilities. Readiness was determined simply by what the child was able to do.

In view of the merit of the learning which took place in this traditional family, it is not surprising that by the age of ten this shepherd boy had already learned his life work.

The Modern Family as Teacher

The differences between learning in a pastoral family of Central Asia and learning in a suburban family in America are vast.[4]

[4] *Ibid.,* p. 130.

"First, how many American boys and girls have an intimate knowledge of their father's work? Except in rural areas, few have the opportunity to see their fathers at work, or to gain even a casual understanding of their work. The chances are that the father works far away from home in an environment unknown to the child. The same may be said of the opportunity of young children generally to observe other adults at work.

"Second, the parent's work is such that it is impossible for the child to apprentice in it. The chances are the work is specialized, technical, and beyond the reach of children. It would be cruel to subject a child to it. The shepherd boy's work was within his grasp.

"Third, our industrial and technical society does not make provision for educating children within the production process. We have delegated education to schools and professional teachers. In this act we, in a sense, removed school learning from real life.

"Fourth, modern specialized work permits even the mature worker to see only a piece of the entire operation. The satisfaction which comes in seeing something created and completed is missing. It is incompatible with mass production upon which our economy depends."

This list of differences between learning in the traditional and learning in the modern family would seem, at first glance, to leave the modern family with few vital teaching functions. Actually, such is not the case. Whereas the nature of the teaching functions is altering radically, their importance and significance are not. Let us look at some relevant considerations.

In spite of its shrinking functions the modern family continues to be the dominant educating influence in the learning of children. The popular literature about the "adolescent society" and the "revolt" of youth would lead one to suspect that a wide chasm indeed exists between children and parents, and that the bonds of blood and family are all but broken. It is true, as we shall point out in Chapter 7, that the child stands in a far-different relationship to both his family and his peers than he did in the traditional family. There is some evidence, however, that we have overemphasized the solidarity of the adolescent society and its isolation from the family. In his research on self-concept, Wilbur B. Brookover discovered that almost universally the junior-high-school students in the population sample identified parents as the "significant others" in their lives. "School personnel, other relatives, and peers were named by many in response to each question, but by smaller proportions and usually after parents were named." [5]

[5] Wilbur B. Brookover, Ann Paterson, and Shailer Thomas, *Self-Concept of Ability and School Achievement,* East Lansing, Office of Research and Publications, Michigan State University, 1962, p. 74.

Current popular literature suggests that adolescent values have little in common with parental values. Research, however, makes one cautious about accepting this generalization. For example, H. H. Remmers and Naomi Weltman studied the "attitudes of interrelationships of youth, their parents and their teachers."[6] Using students, parents, and teachers in ten school communities in Indiana and Illinois, these researchers developed an opinion poll designed to answer these questions. (1) How are youths' attitudes related to parental attitudes? (2) How are youths' attitudes related to their teachers' attitudes? After the opinion poll was administered to 207 pupils and their parents, the following conclusions were drawn. (1) There is a strong positive relationship among the attitudes of members of the same family as measured in this study. (2) A fairly accurate measure of adult public opinion is obtainable by measuring the high school population. (3) There is a suggestion that older children (grades 11 and 12) are less like their parents in attitude pattern than are younger children (grades 9 and 10). (4) Patterns of attitude between parents and children are more similar than those between teachers and children or between teachers and parents. (5) So far as this sample is concerned there is a highly integrated pattern of attitudes among children and parents.

The evidence suggests that within the modern family the parents continue to be the "significant others" in the life of the child and that the child's relationship with the family creates a high degree of uniformity in attitudes and opinions among children and parents.

3. Take for this question a family which you know well, either your own or another. Make a list of the things this family teaches. Do you expect the list to be long or short?

To investigate this matter further we can raise this question: Under what circumstances do adolescents conform to the values and behavior of their parents, and under what circumstances do they tend to conform to peer values and behavior? Although the Remmers research suggests that there is a highly integrated pattern of attitudes among children and parents, it is realistic to assume that children are frequently caught in cross-pressures between parents and peer groups. In such a case, what is the basis for the child's decision?

Clay V. Brittain[7] did research to test the hypothesis that adoles-

[6] H. H. Remmers and Naomi Weltman, "Attitude Interrelationships of Youth, Their Parents, and Their Teachers," *Journal of Social Psychology*, Volume 26, 1947, pp. 61–68.

[7] Clay V. Brittain, "Adolescent Choices and Parent-Peer Cross-Pressures," *American Sociological Review*, Volume 28, No. 3, June 1963, pp. 385–391.

cents tend to be peer-conforming in making certain kinds of choices and parental-conforming in making other kinds of choices. For this research Brittain set up hypothetical situations involving conflict between parent-peer expectations. The subjects of the research were girls in grades 9 through 11, and each situation involved an adolescent girl who was trying to choose between two alternatives, one of which was favored by her parents and the other by her friends. The following item illustrates the procedure.[8]

"A large glass in the front door of the high school was broken. Jim broke the glass. But both he and Bill were seen at the school the afternoon the glass was broken and both are suspected. Bill and Jim are friends and they agree to deny that they know anything about the broken glass. As a result, the principal pins the blame on both of them. Nell is the only other person who knows Jim broke the glass. She was working in the typing room that afternoon. She didn't actually see the glass broken, but she heard the noise and saw Jim walking away from the door a few moments later. Nell is very much undecided what to do. The three girls she goes around with most of the time don't think Nell should tell the principal. These girls hate to see an innocent person punished. But they point out to Nell that this is a matter between Jim and Bill and between Jim and his conscience. Nell talks the matter over with her mother and father. They felt that Jim is unfairly using Bill in order to lighten his own punishment. Her parents think Nell should tell the principal who broke the glass.

"Can you guess what Nell did when the principal asked her if she saw who broke the glass?

—She told him that she didn't see it broken.
—She told him who broke the glass."

The conclusions of the study, which were based on the girls' responses to a series of items like these, are:

(1) Adolescents perceive peers and parents as competent guides in different areas of judgment. The responses show that the general orientation of adolescents is of a dual character. The peer society gratifies many identity needs. The adult society gratifies the need for status positions to which one can aspire as an adult. For example, in response to a hypothetical situation involving choice of part-time jobs, preferences commonly were for the parent-favored rather than the peer-favored alternative.

(2) The responses reflect concern to avoid being noticeably different from peers. This concern was expressed in items that showed

[8] *Ibid.*, p. 385.

clear-cut peer-conforming trends involved in the choice of dress for football games or parties.

(3) The responses reflect concern about being separated from friends. For example, in choosing which courses to take in school the girls followed their peers' rather than their parents' choices, especially if the parental choice would have meant some degree of separation from their friends.

(4) The choices reflect perceived similarities and differences between self and peers and between self and parents. For example, when adolescents perceive themselves to be more like peers in regard to taste in clothes and in regard to feelings about school, they find the peer-favored alternative more acceptable. But in other areas they perceive themselves as similar to parents and tend to choose the parent-favored alternative. For example, when faced with the difficult choice whether to report a person who has destroyed property, the children found the parent-favored alternative closer and more acceptable.

4. Interview a high school student. In what areas does he regard parents to be competent guides? In what areas does he regard peers to be competent guides?

Although the teaching functions of the modern family are vastly different from those of a traditional one, they are nevertheless all pervasive in the life of the growing child. The child is born into the family, his first socializing group. His language, his attitudes and values, his ways of behaving are all developed within the social context of the family. Whereas the modern family has given up many of the specialized functions performed in earlier families, especially those connected with skills and vocations, it has gained a freedom for influence unimagined by traditional families. Instead of preparing children simply to perpetuate themselves unchanged, the modern family is free to teach them to create new and enriched family relationships. Instead of preparing children for the known, as was the task of traditional families, the modern family has within its grasp the power to teach for, and therefore help to shape, the unknown.

Let us turn to a consideration of the crucial and vital relationship between the family and the school.

THE FAMILY AND THE SCHOOL

Continuity and Discontinuity

One revealing way to view the relationship between the family and the school is on the basis of the continuities and discontinuities between them. If the values that are taught in the school mirror those taught in the home, we may say there is a continuity between the values of school and home. If, on the other hand, the family teaches one set of values and the school a different or conflicting set of values, we may say there is discontinuity between school and family. One reason the Amish families do not want to send their children to modern public schools is that they correctly surmise these schools teach values that are in conflict with Amish values. In their strong desire to preserve their traditional values from one generation to the next the Amish cannot tolerate the risks such schooling involves.

The continuity-discontinuity factor in school and family relationships is growing more important in the modern world. Many traditional groups, unlike the Amish, are striving to achieve middle-class status—if not for themselves then certainly for their children.

The upward thrust of Negro groups toward full rights as citizens, the mass movements of Southern whites to the big cities of the North, the growing self-assertion of underprivileged groups everywhere signal a new dimension in family and school relationships. For the school stands astride the pathway to upward mobility. Some minority groups view the school with deep suspicion because it teaches values that are discontinuous with their own. The children of these groups feel foreign in the school setting. Many slum children share these feelings. Other minority groups look upon the school as a way for children to

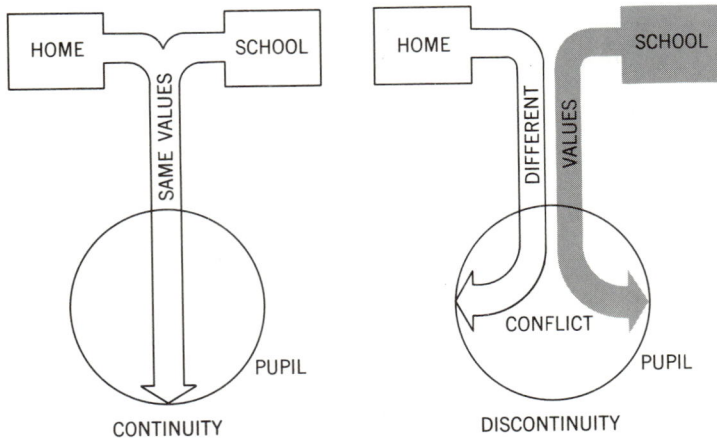

Fig. 6-3 The continuity-discontinuity factor in school and family relationships is becoming ever more important in the modern world.

escape deprivation. They do not understand the school but nevertheless commend their children to it and encourage them to learn in every way they can.

Regardless of the reaction of the particular group to the school, schools are being called on as never before to educate the first generation of families to be educated, or to educate children to a higher level than their parents were educated. There is a strong likelihood, therefore, that discontinuities will exist between families and the schools.

No place demonstrates this phenomenon better than the newly developing countries where children come from traditional and frequently illiterate villages and, vaulting several generations, find themselves in modern schools preparing for lives their village elders never dreamed of. The following story is by a student who came from such a family in New Guinea, went to college, and now writes in his college newspaper of his experiences when he returned home.[9]

"Here is a story that might interest you lecturers and fellow students. I was made a laughing stock by an old man in the village, because I could not speak my mind freely and custom demands that we do not speak so much in front of them or contradict their mature judgments.

"Schooling is an excellent medium whereby our general education and our narrow minds are broadened to see things in their true values. Whether we pass our exams at the end of the year or not, its value to me and the rest of our countrymen who enrolled in this college is incomparable. For here we place ourselves in the hands of cultured men, who set only good literature for our study and by their constant encouragement we are led to treasures of English literature. Through literature then, we know something about European culture and their way of living.

"Although I am a true New Guinean, the little education I get transforms me completely. My ideas and outlook are not in harmony with that of my older people, that is because, as my uncle would say, I strain my eyes too much on those unintelligible marks on the paper and take in all the fantastic lies that the Europeans tell us as a matter of fact, without considering whether I am deceived or not.

"One day, during the last holidays, I saw the old fellows in the village were smoking their pipes contentedly after a good meal, so I decided to leave them to their pipes and got up to go. But an old

[9] S. Hosniel Tade, "The Conflicting Attitude of the Young and Old in New Britain, New Guinea," *Port Moresby Teachers College Newspaper*, November 1964.

man called me and said, 'Son, it is not yet evening, and our friends will not be at home, so stay with us a little longer and tell me something about that frog we saw run along the road this morning.' I asked him in wonderment, 'What frog do you mean?' but soon I remembered that morning we saw a Volkswagen speed past our house. He called it 'frog' because it was shaped like one.

"Before I could tell him everything, he asked at once, 'Who made that frog?' I told him that it was manufactured in Germany, a land which is far away from our own. But he laughed at me and said, 'How do you know?' When I told him that I got the information from magazines and movies, he laughed again, winked at his comrades (to tell them what a fool I was) and then asked me this—'Do you believe in these things that you mentioned?' I admitted that I did. Then he asked, 'How do you know that you are not being deceived?' When I told him that such was not possible, he let loose a prolonged laugh and winked at his companions again, which made me angry, but remembering that I was talking to the venerable old man of the tribe, I managed to control my anger in time and laughed too at his stubborn questions.

"When he had laughed off my ignorance, he gathered his wits and gave me the following instructions:

" 'Son, you have been put over by the cunning whites. No man alive is able to produce a huge frog or a huge bird which is able to put man and cargo inside their bodies and roar along the road or fly in the sky without falling over the cliff or bumping into the tall mountains.'

"When I tried to explain about drivers and pilots, he waved me in silence and proceeded thus: 'Now, when you go back to school dig deeper and find the secret from the whites, then you may bring us the word. For I tell you, the whites have been robbing our cargoes and it is high time that we did something to get our rights. We put our trust in you and your friends who go to school to be the means of getting them, yet the whites have sugared you up, so that you are always on their side. The reason is the whites took advantage of your youthful ignorance, but it will be a different tale if they try it on us.'

"He did not want to hear anything from me and told me to go, so I went.

"I have been digging deep in some sorts of literature, books, and encyclopaedias, to fulfill the old man's desire, but I haven't come across the secret yet. What I have gathered is all opposed to his views."

The conflict created in the student by this discontinuity between school and home is clear. On the one hand, the student wants to "fulfill the old man's desire," but on the other, everything he learns "is all opposed to his views." Nor can we ignore the conflict in the old man himself. The family sent the boy to school, is proud that he is in school, indeed knows that he must be in school. Still it has deep reservations about what he is learning there.

Americans need not go to New Guinea to see the deep impact of discontinuities between family and school. One sees it in its most human terms in slum schools where teachers attempt to bridge the wide chasm between the classroom and the slum family. Notice how this matter pervades the work of a teacher in a slum school in New York City and her truant student.[10]

"Raoul arrived there an unmanageable veteran of seven schools, 17 teachers. Ten years old, his hands stayed protected in his pockets but at times were thrown like small rocks at another child's face. His father had disappeared before he was born. Two years ago his gentle mother, who loves him, moved in with a man who hated Raoul, beat him mercilessly and finally told his mother to get rid of him or he would leave. To her the man was an only hope for the future. So Raoul soon was like a thief in his mother's home, stealing in late at night, darting out at dawn. He slept sometimes at his grandmother's and sometimes rode subways aimlessly through the night.

"But now in this school he found Wendy Lehrman, teacher in the bottom 'junior guidance' class for emotionally shattered children. Some had been given away by mothers to strangers who wanted the relief check a foster child brings. Most were children from homes broken by death or degradation. In Wendy's class the pupils poured out the full torrent of hurts which to some degree trouble so many Negro and Puerto Rican children. Her body sometimes carried bruises from their thoughtless blows. Yet scrambled up with hate was a universal hunger for love. A little boy said, 'I love Miss Lemon.' Another child taunted him, 'She white, man, she white.' Weeping, kicking, the boy swung wildly at the other child and screamed, 'She's no white lady. She's colored . . . just like me . . . colored.'

"At last, in Wendy, Raoul found somebody who loved him simply for himself. He began to be happy. Then Wendy fell sick and was gone from class for three weeks. Raoul ran away, came back, still found no Miss Lemon. 'Why did she leave?' he asked. 'I want only my teacher. Quiero, quiero mucho a mi profesora (I love, I love my teacher very much).'

"Then one afternoon he smashed windows in the new school built

[10] "A Little Boy's Lost Teacher," *Life*, Volume 52, No. 4, January 26, 1962, p. 66.

to replace P.S. 105—hurling stones at the school which seemed to have broken its promise of happiness. Raoul was suspended. His mother could not read the notices to enroll Raoul in another school, so he wandered the streets. He came back again looking for love. The custodian found him at 7:30 a.m. trying to break into the school. The school reported it to the police.

"Finally Wendy was well and Raoul came back, ecstatic that everything was right again. But in the dismal well of the old school stairway Wendy had to tell the little boy he could never return. A prolonged truant, he was consigned by the court to a Children's Shelter. After three days there Raoul vanished."

5. Gather a panel from the class to discuss Raoul's case. Could the school have saved Raoul? What would the members of the panel do if they had a Raoul in class?

Continuities and discontinuities between family and school take many forms, and we shall explore some of these forms in later chapters. They are one of the realities that need to be considered in studying the relationships between families and schools.

The Family and Educational and Occupational Aspirations

Both observation and empirical research show a positive correlation between a youth's educational and occupational aspirations on the one hand, and the social and economic status of the family on the other. It seems quite clear that one's level of aspiration is strongly influenced by the values that grow out of one's social and economic status. Slum children provide an example of the relationship between educational aspiration and social status. Though children like Raoul may be of average intelligence, fewer than 50 percent of them graduate from high school. The main hope of the slum school lies with the better-off slum parents whose children tend to be grouped at the top of each grade. The interest and aspirations of these parents bring a mood of positiveness and exert great pressure on the school and slum to raise standards. The lower-level slum families either exert no such pressure or exert it in the opposite direction.

But it is not only in the slums that one sees the relationship between the status of families and educational aspirations. William H. Sewell, Archie O. Haller, and Murray A. Straus conducted research among more than four thousand Wisconsin high school seniors in all parts of the state to test "the general hypothesis that levels of educational and occupational aspiration of youth of both sexes are associated with the social status of their families, when the effects of intelligence

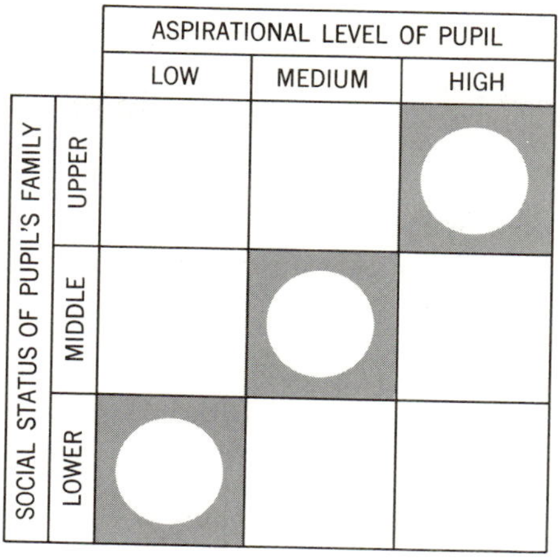

Fig. 6-4 There is a significant association between the level of educational and occupational aspirations of the student and the social status of his family.

are controlled." [11] Their research supports this conclusion: Among both high-school girls and boys there is a significant association between the level of educational and occupational aspiration and the social status of their families.

The educational aspirations of children reflect not only those of their families but also the achievement aspirations which parents hold for their children. Walter Katkovsky, Anne Preston, and Vaughn J. Crandall interviewed mothers and fathers of 40 early grade-school children about their attitudes concerning their children's achievement in four areas: [12] intellectual, physical, artistic, and mechanical. The parents were also interviewed about their own achievement. This study concluded: (1) Both parents hold values for the intellectual achievement of their children similar to those they hold for themselves. (2) Parents do not value highly achievement in physical skills but they value highly achievement in artistic and mechanical areas. (3) Par-

[11] William H. Sewell, Archie O. Haller, and Murray A. Straus, "Social Status and Educational and Occupational Aspiration," *American Sociological Review,* Volume XXII, No. 1, 1957, pp. 67–73.

[12] Walter Katkovsky, Anne Preston, and Vaughn J. Crandall, "Parents' Attitudes Toward Their Personal Achievements and Toward the Achievement Behaviors of Their Children," *Journal of Genetic Psychology,* Volume 104, Part I, March 1964, pp. 67–82.

ents show a strong tendency to apply their own values and expectations to their offspring for success in artistic activities.

Children's educational aspirations, the evidence indicates, are learned to a major extent from the family. This research simply lends further evidence to the sociological claim that values of different social positions are important influences on levels of educational and occupational aspiration.

6. Can you trace your own educational aspirations back into your family? Can you identify the factors in the family which caused you to want to go to college?

7. Let us say that you are the teacher of a child who has the ability to go to college but who receives no encouragement at home. As a teacher, what do you think you should do?

The Family and Educational Attainment

Closely related to educational aspiration is the matter of the actual level of education attained. How do families influence the educational attainment of their children? If there is a positive relationship between educational aspiration and social status, we would suspect a similar relationship to exist between educational attainment and social status. Such is the case.

Using college attendance as a measure of educational attainment Leland L. Medsker studied the forces that bear upon the immediate future of high school graduates.[13] The cooperation of 37 high schools and more than 10,000 graduates in 16 communities in the Middle West and California was enlisted. Data were collected on the graduates while they were still in school, before June graduation, and for comparative purposes the following October. Of the nearly 10,000 graduates, 43 percent entered either a two- or four-year college following graduation in June. Another 7 percent entered some type of special school, including institutions listed as vocational schools and schools of nursing, thus bringing to 50 percent the total continuing their education. A third of the boys in the study entered employment, and 14 percent of the boys went directly into military service. Seven percent of the girls became full-time homemakers, and 6 percent of the total was unemployed.

A number of factors influenced the June graduates in their decision to attend or not to attend college. Of particular interest here are

[13] Leland L. Medsker, "Factors Related to College Attendance and Performance of High School Graduates," presented at the Annual Meeting of the American Educational Research Association, February 13–16, 1963, Chicago. (Mimeographed)

the social and cultural factors. Medsker reports that the father's occupation, the parents' education, and family encouragement were key influential factors in college attendance. The following are his conclusions:

"The percentage of families which sent their children to college declined steadily with the decline in level of the father's occupation. From what was called the 'Professional I' category (medical, dental, legal, etc.) 78 percent of the graduates went on to college. From a 'Professional II' category (teacher, minister, nurse, musician, etc.) and from a category including executives, managers, etc., 73 percent and 72 percent respectively became college students. But at that point the percentages dropped to 55 percent from the homes of small business owners, to 52 percent from the sales and clerical group, to 37 percent from the homes of skilled workers, and to only 28 percent from both the semi-skilled and unskilled workers. It was also found that father's occupation appeared to affect college attendance of sons more than that of daughters.

"Of the graduates going to college, 32 percent of their mothers and 36 percent of their fathers had at least some college. About 12 percent of both parents had finished college. By contrast, these figures were 8 and 11 percent respectively for the group of graduates who did not go on to college. From an analysis of college-going by *father's occupation and mother's education* it appeared that a mother's education is at least as important as the father's occupation in affecting the decision to go to college. In still other analyses it was found that mothers who had not gone beyond high school appeared to exert a more negative college influence on their daughters than upon their sons. On the other hand, it appeared that mothers who had completed college encouraged their sons and daughters about equally, regardless of the father's occupational level.

"When parents strongly encouraged their children to do so, 75 percent went to college. Apparently, strong encouragement is a potent factor, for when the degree of encouragement was reported as mild, only a third entered college. Even when controlled by socio-economic level, the influence of the parents was still apparent."

E. Grant Youmans examined the hypothesis that certain factors in the home, school, and community influenced the formal educational attainments of rural youth. Data were obtained by interviewing 480 mothers and 439 youths, ages sixteen and seventeen, living in the low-income farming areas of Kentucky.[14] By means of a socio-economic

[14] E. Grant Youmans, "Factors in Educational Attainment," *Rural Sociology,* Volume 24, No. 1, March 1959, pp. 21–28.

status scale the 480 families were divided into three social-status groups of approximately equal number. Youmans found that one-half of the youths in the lowest social status group were attending school; seven-tenths of those in the middle-status group were currently going to school; and over eight-tenths of the youths of the highest status group were attending high school.

In this research Youmans discovered that the mother's educational values were influential in their children's educational attainment, especially in the low-status group. Here are Youmans' conclusions:

"The mothers' educational values were related to the school attendance of the youths. Mothers who said 'not finishing high school is a great handicap' were classified as possessing 'favorable' educational values. Mothers who said 'not finishing high school is a moderate or little handicap' were classified as possessing 'unfavorable' educational values. The higher-social-status mothers evidenced favorable educational values more often than did the lower-status mothers. However, the mothers' educational values appeared to influence the school attendance of youth to a significant degree only in the low-social-status group. In this social-status group the mothers who held favorable educational values reported a substantially larger percentage of youths attending school than did the mothers possessing unfavorable educational values. In both the middle and high social-status groups, the educational values of the mother were not associated significantly with the school status of the youth. Apparently other factors associated with higher social status served to motivate the higher-status youth to continue their formal education despite any 'unfavorable' educational values held by their mothers."

Interpreting research like Medsker's and Youmans' might lead one to draw the hasty conclusion that there is a perfect one-to-one relationship between such factors as the family's social status, the father's occupation, and the parents' educational attainments and values on the one hand and the child's educational attainment on the other. We should remember that in American society, and increasingly in others, this is an imperfect relationship, and happily so. If the relationship were a perfect one, where the educational attainment of the child exactly matched the socio-economic status and educational attainment of his parents, children would get no more education than their parents. We know from observation that such is not the case. Taking our whole population, children steadily reach higher educational attainments and achieve higher occupational status than their parents. The schools are means of upward social and occupational mobility. The relationship, then, between family status and educational attainment is a broad one, permitting many children to move educationally beyond the family. Indeed, we believe that society benefits when they do and is penalized when they do not.

Supporting such assertions is Thomas R. O'Donovan's study of "intergenerational educational mobility." [15] O'Donovan tested the hypothesis that because of educational mobility sons moved up the occupational ladder beyond their fathers. Using graduates of a Midwestern university as his sample he found that sons did indeed exceed their fathers in both educational and occupational achievement. He concluded that occupational mobility was due to the sons' higher educational attainment.

8. If you are preparing for teaching, you may be interested in the social and educational backgrounds of teachers. From what educational and social levels do teachers come? Do they tend to have more education than their parents? Interview a group of future teachers to see whether you can find some indicators.

The Family and Achievement in School

Actual school achievement is also related to the socio-economic status of the child's family. James B. Conant's observations on the role of the family in relation to the child's reading ability, for example, illustrate this point. In comparing the reading ability of children in slums and college-oriented suburbs, Conant made this observation: [16]

"In the slum school, the development of reading skill is obviously of first importance. The earlier the slow readers are spotted and remedial measures instituted, the better. Indeed, the same rule applies as well to any school, but in the heavily college-oriented suburb, the number of slow readers is relatively small and teaching children to read by no means looms so large and difficult a problem as it does in the slums. Some commentators have failed to recognize the relation of the reading problem to the socioeconomic and cultural level of the home. Evidence on this point is found in the large cities. Essentially the same methods are used in all the elementary schools in a city, and yet the average grade of reading in the sixth grade, for example, may vary as much as two grades from one school to another. Concern with improving the reading of the pupils, particularly the slow reader, must continue well beyond the elementary school. . . .

[15] Thomas R. O'Donovan, "Intergenerational Educational Mobility," *Sociology and Social Research*, Volume 47, No. 1, October 1962, pp. 57–68.

[16] James B. Conant, *Slums and Suburbs*, New York, McGraw-Hill Book Co., 1961, pp. 23–25.

"In one school I visited, the teachers themselves, mostly Negroes, felt that the only way to improve the reading of the children in the first three or four grades was to do something with their mothers. If the head of the family unit could be located and brought into communication with the school, attempts were made to stimulate an interest in newspapers, magazines, and possibly even books. One of the troubles, the teachers said, is that when the children leave the school they never see anyone read anything—not even newspapers. 'If we could change the family attitude toward reading, we could accomplish much.' With this statement one must heartily agree and likewise agree that even a slight change, which was all that was expected, would probably be reflected in the reading ability of the children."

Family status has a direct bearing on the child's own estimate of his schoolwork ability. Ruth C. Wylie studied "children's estimate of their schoolwork ability, as a function of sex, race, and socio-economic level." [17] For this study 823 junior high school students were asked to make three kinds of estimates of their ability to do schoolwork. Each child was asked to estimate (1) whether he was in the top- or bottom-half of his class, (2) whether he was capable of college work (assuming economic ability), and (3) whether he desired to go to college. These data were then correlated with the previously administered mental abilities tests. Wylie concluded: (1) White girls are more modest in estimating their abilities when compared with white boys. (2) Negro students make more modest estimates of their ability than white students. (3) Children of lower socio-economic levels make more modest estimates of their abilities than children of higher socio-economic levels.

Wylie's research reinforces the point made earlier about the importance of the child's self-concept in learning. This investigation suggests that the student's self-concept of his ability to learn is strongly influenced by family values.

After reviewing a number of research studies on the relationship of the family to underachievement of the child in school W. B. Dockrell summed up the relationship this way: "There are youngsters whose underachievement is a result of general maladjustment or some specific learning block, but the majority of underachievers are drawn from segments of society where aspirations differ from those of the school. The school does not offer them an opportunity to do the things they want to do or to be the person they want to be. Our schools must

[17] Ruth C. Wylie, "Children's Estimate of Their Schoolwork Ability as a Function of Sex, Race, and Socioeconomic Level," *Journal of Personality*, Volume 31, No. 2, June 1963, pp. 203–225.

come to terms with these youngsters or admit the failure of the idea of universal education." [18]

The Family and the Child's Classroom Behavior

Teachers know from experience that the home background of the child greatly influences his behavior in the classroom and speculate, accurately or inaccurately, about the family from simply observing the child in school. A child's classroom behavior is obviously a product of many influences, both in school and out, and we should be wary about asserting too much about the causes of a child's behavior in school.

One hypothesis that seems to be supported by observation and study relates to the continuity-discontinuity patterns between home and school discussed earlier. We said continuity exists when both home and school share common values and hold similar aspirations for the child. Discontinuity exists when the home and school do not have a common set of shared values. Consequently, children tend to behave acceptably in the classroom when the home and school share common ideas about child rearing and hold similar standards for behavior. Conversely, when there is discontinuity the child is likely to exhibit poor behavior in the classroom.

This continuity-discontinuity concept may help to explain why slum children are more likely to present behavior problems in school than middle-class children. The slum children find that the behavior which is expected of them in the classroom is completely discontinuous with their behavior at home. School demands a new kind of behavior which does not make sense in terms of their past. Middle-class children, however, discover in the classroom no particularly new demands regarding behavior. There is continuity of expectation about child conduct between middle-class school and middle-class home.

Another factor in the family which influences the child's behavior in school is the kind of contact which a child has with his parents, especially his mother. Well-motivated and frequent contact between child and parents predisposes the child to adapt more successfully to school. Research from Sweden is relevant to this point.[19] Torsten Husén studied the family relations in 400 families of Swedish school-children. Through interviews, observations, and attitude inventories

[18] W. B. Dockrell, "Society, Home, and Underachievement," *Psychology in Schools*, Volume 1, No. 2, April 1964, p. 177.

[19] Torsten Husén, "Home Background and Behavior in the Classroom Situation," Research Bulletin, No. 5, Stockholm, Institute of Education, University of Stockholm, January 1956.

Husén mapped out actual child-rearing practices of the families. Of special interest to Husén was the "rearing ritual" in the family, the habits they established about a regular time for going to bed, and regularity in doing homework. The amount of contact the child had with his parents and the "contact motivation" were also rated. Husén then got an estimate of the children's behavior at school from the 45 classroom teachers involved in the study.

The data Husén secured by comparing the child's family relationships with his behavior in school support these hypotheses. (1) Children from homes with a consistent and established habit pattern exhibit "better" ratings in their behavior in school. (2) Conversely, children from homes where parents have difficulties in establishing or maintaining a regular habit pattern have "worse" ratings by the teachers. (3) Children from homes with less actual contact with the mother have "worse" ratings. (4) Finally, children from homes where the mother has a low contact motivation adapt less easily to the norms of the school than children from homes where the mother exhibits a higher contact motivation. Husén's findings reinforce what we have said before about the importance of continuity between family and school. The middle-class family will, as in Husén's sample, tend to stress child-rearing matters like habit formation, regularity, and good "contact motivation." These are all values that the schools will tend to approve and reward. Children who come from homes where such matters are a part of the "rearing ritual" come to school prepared to behave in ways acceptable to the school. Children who do not come from homes where such values are taught are not prepared to behave acceptably.

Today's schools are living extensions of the modern family. When the family was traditional and self-sufficient it had little need for the school. Today the family is dependent on others for both its economic requirements and its formal education. And yet its dependence should not be mistaken for impotence. In shaping the early and continuing values, aspirations, achievement, and behavior of the child, the family is without equal.

For this reason the schools must recognize and understand the family as a teaching institution. The purposes of the school are so intertwined with the purposes of the family that one cannot be achieved apart from the other. The school must always set as one of its goals discovery of ways to work with families for the maximum benefit of the object of both, the child.

REFERENCES

Paperbacks

Centuries of Childhood: A Social History of Family Life. Philippe Aries. (V286) Vintage Books, Random House, 457 Madison Ave., New York ($2.45).

Childhood in Contemporary Cultures. Margaret Mead and Martha Wolfenstein, Editors. Phoenix Books, University of Chicago Press, 5750 Ellis Ave., Chicago, Ill. ($2.95).

Children of Sanchez. Oscar Lewis. (V280) Vintage Books, Random House, 457 Madison Ave., New York ($2.95).

Crestwood Heights: A Study of the Culture of Suburban Life. J. R. Seeley, R. A. Sim, and E. W. Loosley. Science Editions Paperbacks, John Wiley and Sons, 605 Third Ave., New York ($2.45).

Educational Issues in a Changing Society. August Kerber and Wilfred Smith, Editors. (Orig.) (2nd Rev. Ed.) (WB3) Wayne State University Press, 5980 Cass, Detroit, Mich. ($3.95).

Family. William J. Goode. (Orig.) Prentice-Hall Spectrum Books, Prentice-Hall, Englewood Cliffs, N. J. ($1.50).

Family in Cross-Cultural Perspective. William N. Stephens. (Orig.) Holt, Rinehart and Winston, 383 Madison Ave., New York ($4.95).

Family in Various Cultures. Stuart Queen, Robert W. Habenstein, and John B. Adams. (Orig.) (P-1) Preceptor Books, J. B. Lippincott Co., East Washington Square, Philadelphia, Pa. ($1.85).

Passing of Traditional Society. David Lerner. (91859) Free Press of Glencoe, Macmillan Co., 60 Fifth Ave., New York ($2.45).

Schools, Scholars and Society. Jean D. Grambs. (Orig.) Prentice-Hall, Englewood Cliffs, N. J. ($2.25).

Summerhill: A Radical Approach to Child Rearing. A. S. Neill. Hart Publishing Co., 74 Fifth Ave., New York ($1.95).

Books

Bell, Norman, and Ezra F. Vogel, Editors, *A Modern Introduction to the Family.* New York: The Free Press of Glencoe, 1960. An anthology which touches on significant issues of family life, with contributions from the fields of sociology, sociopsychology, and anthropology.

Havighurst, Robert J., and Bernice L. Neugarten, *Society and Education.* Boston: Allyn and Bacon, 1962. Chapter 4 discusses school and family values.

Kramer, Judith R., and Seymour Leventman, *Children of the Gilded Ghetto.* New Haven, Conn.: Yale University Press, 1961. A sociological study of intergenerational problems in a Jewish suburb in a Midwestern community.

McGehee, Florence, *Please Excuse Johnny.* New York: Macmillan Co., 1952. An autobiography of a woman who was a truant officer for schools in an area of minority population groups.

Parsons, Talcott, "The Social Class as a Social System: Some of Its Functions in American Society," in *Education, Economy and Society*, A. H. Halsey et al., Editors. New York: The Free Press of Glencoe, 1961, pp. 434–455. Parsons describes how the child is socialized away from the parents and toward the teacher and peer group.

Schelsky, H., "Family and School in Modern Society," in *Education, Economy and Society*, A. H. Halsey et al., Editors. New York: The Free Press of Glencoe, 1961. The stratification of the school system reflects the stratification of society.

Spiro, Melford E., *Children of the Kibbutz*. Cambridge, Mass., Harvard University Press, 1958. In the kibbutz children are raised together under a system in which parents are not present and have little authority over their children.

Periodicals

Bowerman, Charles E., and Elder Glen, Jr., "Variations in Adolescent Perception of Family Power Structure," *American Sociological Review*, Vol. XXIX, No. 4, 1964, pp. 551–567. The effects of different family structural patterns on adolescent motivation and college plans are assessed.

Crescimbeni, Joseph, "Broken Homes Affect Academic Achievement," *Education*, Vol. XXIV, No. 7, March 1964, pp. 437–441. The results of this study indicate that broken homes have a direct effect on the child's academic achievement.

Eron, Leonard D., Leopold O. Walder, Romolo Toigo, and Monroe M. Lepfkowitz, "Social Class, Parental Punishment for Aggression and Child Aggression," *Child Development*, Vol. 34, No. 4, December 1963, pp. 849–867. Increased punishment at home brought increased aggression at school.

Mead, Margaret, "Our Educational Emphases in Primitive Prospective," *The American Journal of Sociology*, Vol. 48, No. 6, May 1943, pp. 633–639. Until racial, national, and class barriers are overcome, it will be difficult to combine the traditional primitive idea of the need to learn with the modern need to teach.

O'Donovan, Thomas R., "Intergenerational Educational Mobility," *Sociology and Social Research*, Vol. 47, No. 1, October 1962, pp. 57–68. This suggests that sons are able to move up the educational ladder and exceed their fathers in educational achievement.

Shaw, Merville, "Note on Parent Attitudes Toward Independence Training and the Academic Achievement of the Children," *Journal of Educational Psychology*, Vol. 55, No. 6, December 1964, pp. 371–374. Parents of achievers want children to make their own decisions, and desire them to be more adult. Parents of underachievers are more concerned with having their children protect their personal rights.

Skillman, Ann G., "Verbal Communication between Mother and Sons in Learning Problem Families," *Smith College Studies in Social Work*, Vol. XXIV, No. 2, 1964, pp. 140–160. Children with learning problems tend to live in families with communication difficulties.

Taylor, Harold, "What the Family Isn't Teaching," *Saturday Review*, Vol. XLVI, No. 20, May 18, 1963, pp. 17–19. The author wonders whether American parents and the schools their children attend are not sacrificing the true goals of education in favor of a "dangerous academic competition."

7

The Student and His Group

"If I were to lose my friends, I'd be lost. I'm afraid of being without friends."
                                                    A HIGH SCHOOL QUEEN BEE

If the family exercises the strongest influence upon the child, his age-mates or peers exert the second strongest. The child's peers become increasingly important to him as he moves away from his parents toward independence. From his peers he learns many of the things he needs to know in order to become an adult. His movement away from parents to peers is not always easy, and indeed is frequently marked by tension and strain for both child and parent. For example, consider the testimony of this father who chaperoned an eighth-grade dance: [1]

"Once again I have chaperoned an eighth-grade dance, and I'm here to tell you the situation has not improved.

"I stood at the door of the gymnasium—and no matter how good the music, it still has that certain gymnasium aroma—and shouted to the man next to me, 'What are they doing?'

"He turned to me with a bewildered expression and bellowed, 'I don't know, but I know my grandmother would have approved. These kids are so far apart I can't tell who's dancing with whom.'

" 'Do they always play the music this loud?' By this time we're pretty much down to sign language. No one can talk over that din.

"He takes me by the arm, and we walk out into the hall, where bedlam reigns only to a minor degree and says, 'I sneaked over and turned down the volume one notch and every kid in the place complained that they couldn't hear the music. I think they get their

[1] Knight D. McKesson, "School Dance," *The State Journal*, Lansing, Mich., March 3, 1963, Section F, p. F1.

rhythm through vibrations in the floor.' . . . I look in from time to time, each time expecting to see a human sacrifice carried in on a golden altar. For this may be dancing, but I strongly suspect it is derived from a Mayan ceremonial ritual.

"There was a twist contest, although I'm told by my kids that the twist is strictly out these days. Just what is 'in' is difficult to say, despite the fact I studied the situation with more than a passing interest. Briefly, it can be best described as six or more youngsters, some eight feet apart, churning the air with their arms and hips while jerking the head and shoulders spasmodically, for all the world as though antibiotic warfare had afflicted each with some manner of seizure. When the music ends, each youngster walks casually away from the group, compounding the difficulty of telling who is dancing with what.

"But there is one mighty advantage to this sort of thing, as compared to when I was in the eighth grade. No one—but no one—expects the chaperons to dance. And there is some comfort in that."

WHAT IS A PEER GROUP?

By definition a peer group comprises persons of roughly the same age. Unlike the family, which has long-range goals in mind for the child, the peer group's interests are short range and temporary. When the peer group does have long-range influence on its members, that influence is unintentional and accidental.

The peer group is not an established institution in the same sense as the family. To be sure the peer group has customs and organization, but the roles of members are less well defined and may change frequently. In some peer groups it may not even be clear who is and who is not a member.

Children change their peer-group memberships as they go through different stages of development. They frequently belong to a number of peer groups simultaneously; at one time the child may belong to peer groups from his neighborhood, youth organization, camp, school, and church. In each group the child has a certain status and in each he is expected to think and behave in a certain way. Because of the expectations of peer groups and the tendency for members to conform to those expectations, the influence on the child is great, both in school and out.

1. Can you describe the peer groups of which you were a member during high school? How many were there? What held them together? Which ones "counted" the most?

WHAT FACTORS GIVE RISE TO PEER GROUPS?

What causes peer groups to be formed among children? First, there is the basic need for all of us to relate to other people. The fear of being alone and cut off from meaningful human contact, of being "a nobody," runs deep within us. As the high-school girl quoted at the head of this chapter said: "I'm afraid of being without friends." Our social needs are among our most persistent and demanding. Solitary confinement, as psychological torture, can be more devastating than physical abuse; humans require human contact.

Second, as the child grows he becomes less dependent on adults for physical and psychological support and more dependent on his peers for security and loyal attachments. This transition is sometimes painful and, to adults, incomprehensible, but it is an important part of maturation. The ritual of the school dance, whether it derives from Mayan ceremony or Tin Pan Alley, does serve its social purpose. It helps the child to live and get along with groups other than his own family.

Finally, there are social and cultural factors which give rise to peer groups. Around the world children group themselves together in some fashion, no matter what the structure of the society. They play and run together, devise various kinds of mischief, and generally enjoy one another's company. But even casual observation tells one that peer groups differ vastly in different societies. For example, it is mainly in the West and particularly in the United States where youth groups are so distinctly separate from adults. Here they are labeled the "adolescent society," and have strong common identification, codes of conduct, and membership. Youth groups in most non-Western societies do not express this degree of solidarity or common identity.

One hypothesis to explain this difference, set forth by S. N. Eisenstadt, is related to the degree of continuity or discontinuity which exists between the family and the larger society around it.[2] If there is continuity between the family and the society, both share common values, responsibilities, and functions. Such a situation is most likely to occur in a traditional society, where the society tends to be simply an extension of the family. On the other hand, if there is discontinuity between the family and larger society, there is little sharing of functions, responsibilities, and ways of doing things. Eisenstadt suggested that when there was great continuity between family and society,

[2] S. N. Eisenstadt, *From Generation to Generation*, Chicago, Free Press, 1956.

what children learned at home was fully adequate for them to get on in the larger society. However, when there was discontinuity between family and society, the values and skills which children learned at home were inadequate to cope with life when they left the family. In such cases the peer group became the bridge between the home and the adult society.

The shepherd boy's family in Pakistan, about whom we spoke in Chapter 5, provides an example of a family which is quite continuous with its tribal society. In the family the shepherd boy learns the skills he needs to know in the tribal society. In that society the family one belongs to determines one's position and to a great extent one's future. *Who* one is is more important than *what* one is. And the family determines who one is. Here there is no great need for a peer group which will help the shepherd boy prepare for adult life. His family status and training are adequate for the task.

The shrinking functions of the modern family do not include training in the vocational or social skills required by a society which is infinitely complex. Living in a small nuclear family does not adequately prepare one to live in a large and bureaucratic society. In our culture, then, peer groups arise as intermediary agents between the family and a mass society. They help youth make the great leap from the small family to the large society.

This explanation of the origin of peer groups suggests that they serve very real functions in our society. Let us look at some of these functions.

THE FUNCTIONS OF PEER GROUPS

First, the peer group provides a way in which children can become independent of authority. If the child, as he grows up, never learns to be independent of the authority of his parents, he never really matures. In our society maturity is equated with independence, with the ability to formulate judgments of one's own, to take independent action, and to live by the consequences of that action. The peer group gives the child a testing ground for his own ideas and feelings.

Second, the peer group provides children with experience in egalitarian relationships not possible in the family. The home may be quite democratic, but the child's relationship with the parent can never be fully egalitarian because the child is too dependent on the adult. If the child is to have experience in groups in which the relationships are roughly equal, he must find that experience outside the home. The peer group does have its own hierarchy of relationships, to be sure. But in the peer group the child is free from the inequalities of home relationships, free to explore with his equals. As he moves into the adult world he will need a highly developed skill in working with his equals.

Third, the peer group gives the child knowledge to which he does not have access in the family. Sometimes this knowledge is about taboo subjects, such as sex, which the family may avoid or at least treat in a formal and unsatisfactory way. In other cases the knowledge may be about adolescent tastes in dress, dances, music, and behavior, things the child must know if he is to remain a member in good standing of the group. These things his parents are not likely to know.

In a rapidly changing society children always need to know a great deal which is unknown to their parents. The bewildered father trying to understand the eighth-grade dance is a symbol of a fast-moving age where the children learn from one another the things they need to know. Frequently they learn these things without even the knowledge of their parents. Contrast this father's bewilderment with the shepherd boy's father who would not be surprised by his son's dance. For it was he who taught his son to dance the tribal dances which are old and honored by long tradition. Passed on from one generation to the next, the wild and exuberant sword dances which express the militant values of the tribe are performed by the fathers before their children. Each dance tells a story of tribal culture, and the stories do not change. In a changing society, however, whether the subject be a new dance or the "new math," we can expect that children must know a great deal which is unknown to their parents. Peer groups help them to know it.

Finally, the peer group helps to lift the child's horizons and to make him a more complex person. In modern society the child's family relationships are confined to a small group of people, normally to two parents and to brothers and sisters. The variety and richness of these relationships are naturally quite different from family to family. At best, the relationships are of limited scope. Through the peer group the child is exposed to values and experiences of dozens, even hundreds, of other families, many of whom are greatly different from his own. Through these contacts the child's horizons are broadened, his perceptions widened. He begins to turn from a family view of things to a society view.

2. Modern literature is rich in studies of the functions of peer groups in our society. Some references are listed at the end of this chapter. Select one reference from this list, or elsewhere, and report its contents to the class.

HOW DOES THE PEER GROUP TEACH?

No one can doubt the effectiveness of the teaching that goes on within the peer group. The speed with which new fads, language, and behavior are learned by children is evidence of a remarkable educational system at work. How does this peer-group educational system operate?

First, there is high interaction among the members of peer groups. The school itself is made to order for them. Its corridors and class-rooms, lounges and gymnasiums provide a natural and convenient place for the young to socialize. Spending as they do a good share of each day together, groups can be in constant touch with one another. The very closeness and the continuing nature of the contact makes learning among the members of peer groups natural and easy.

When we add to the socializing opportunities in school those that are presented through the telephone, the automobile, the corner drug-store, and the teen canteen, we begin to understand why if one adolescent "knows it" they all seem to "know it."

Second, peer groups teach through rewards and punishments. Each peer group has its own system of rewards for members in good standing. Being included in the group is itself frequently the major reward. The approval of the group and a sense of belonging is a strong reward. Sometimes the rewards consist of clothing, pins, or certain styles of hairdos to be worn.

If the peer group teaches through rewards, it also teaches through punishment. For behavior that is against the group's norms a member may be excluded or at least downgraded. Favors may be withheld and intentional slights practiced. The member is forced either to "reform" and agree to conform to the group or to go his own way outside of it.

Third, perhaps the peer group's most effective teaching device is the model. The peer group provides through its leadership be-havior models for all the members. These models "set the pace," as it were, and there is a strong tendency for all members to strive to be like the models. Models differ, of course, from group to group. The behavior models of a street-corner gang, for example, are quite differ-ent types from the models in the cliques of a middle-class suburban high school. Harold Taylor describes the typical model for such a high school.[3]

"There is accordingly a general type of 'American high school

3 Harold Taylor, "The Understood Child," *Saturday Review*, Volume XLIV, No. 20, May 20, 1961, pp. 48–49.

student,' identified by foreign visitors and others who look at our educational system from the outside. He has absorbed the influences of an extroverted community in his hometown, particularly in the urban and suburban areas, and models his conduct to a large extent on a young American type, itself a product of the movies, the magazines, the television, the radio, and phonograph records. The boys and girls have a coeducational attitude to teen-age life and a complicated ritual of dating, pledging, riding in cars, attending sports events, along with a common vocabulary of popular phrases. They provide the material for the concept used by social workers, journalists, and parents —the teen-ager. They also provide the mass market for commercial exploitation by clothing manufacturers, record companies, and television networks. The values are for the most part accepted uncritically. The model for the boy is of a star athlete who has a straight 'A' record, is popular with girls and elected to student office by popular acclaim. The model for the girl is one who is pretty, popular, having a 'B-plus' record so that it will not be a threat to her popularity with boys, likes sports, popular records, movies, has a well-knit social life, and is neither arty nor too brainy nor too intense about anything."

3. Harold Taylor's description is of a peer-group model for the American high school. Is there a peer group model for the American college or university? Does it differ from the high-school model? How? Can you explain the reasons for the difference?

The importance of models in the peer group can hardly be underestimated. Their values tend to be diffused through the group and, in a sense, they are the teachers of the peer group.

PEER GROUPS AT DIFFERENT AGE LEVELS

The Relationship of Peers and Adults

Before we describe peer groups at various age levels let us say a word about the changing position of peers with respect to adults as children move from one age group to another.[4] The relationship can perhaps best be described as a circle upon which peers and parents begin at the same point. The small child has little concern for his age-mates. He identifies almost completely with the adults in his life, usually his parents, as his chief source of security and satisfaction. As

[4] For an informative discussion of this point see David Gottlieb and Charles Ramsey, *The American Adolescent*, Homewood, Ill., The Dorsey Press, 1964, pp. 184–188.

he grows, he starts to move away from the adult point on the circle, reflecting his growing interest in the world of other children. The first feelings of independence stir within him. He may venture down the block alone on his tricycle or visit a little friend. When he enters school, he moves farther out on the circle. His horizons widen, he acquires a "best pal" and a small group of "best friends." His dependence on adults is weakening, his dependence on peers growing.

By the time children reach high school they stand at a point on the opposite side of the circle from adults. Adult values may seem irrelevant or at least remote. What adults teach in high school seems to have no vital relationship to the peers' immediate concerns. The personal-social requirements of adolescence are intense and all absorbing. Anything else seems beside the point.

Yet it is during this period that maximum pressure is exerted by the school and society for academic achievement. For those students who have college ambitions this is the critical period of decision. The record that determines future opportunities for advancement is being compiled during the high school years. Peers are caught in the cross fire of pressures. From their fellows comes the urgent call of allegiance to the group and to peer solidarity and for a strong show of independence from adults. From the adult world comes pressure to achieve in matters not seemingly relevant at the present but supposedly necessary for the future. The student must reconcile what seems to him to be irreconcilable appeals.

4. Experienced teachers sometimes observe: "When children get into junior high school, they suddenly become difficult to teach. Their attention wanders and they couldn't care less about school." Investigate the social psychology of the early adolescent years. Can you help to explain the reasons behind such observations?

From this far-out point on the circle the youth starts his journey back toward identification with adult values. If he enters college, the need for the group begins to wane. He starts to feel independent of it, able now to focus more on his future and its concerns. The need to prepare for a vocation, for marriage and a home, for "making his mark," all adult values, comes more sharply into view. As he proceeds through college and possibly graduate school, or out into marriage and a job, he thinks and behaves more and more like an adult. He has now made the full circle and can say with Saint Paul: "When I was a child I spoke like a child, I thought like a child, I reasoned like a child; when I became a man, I gave up childish ways." [5]

[5] I Cor. 13:11, *The Holy Bible.*

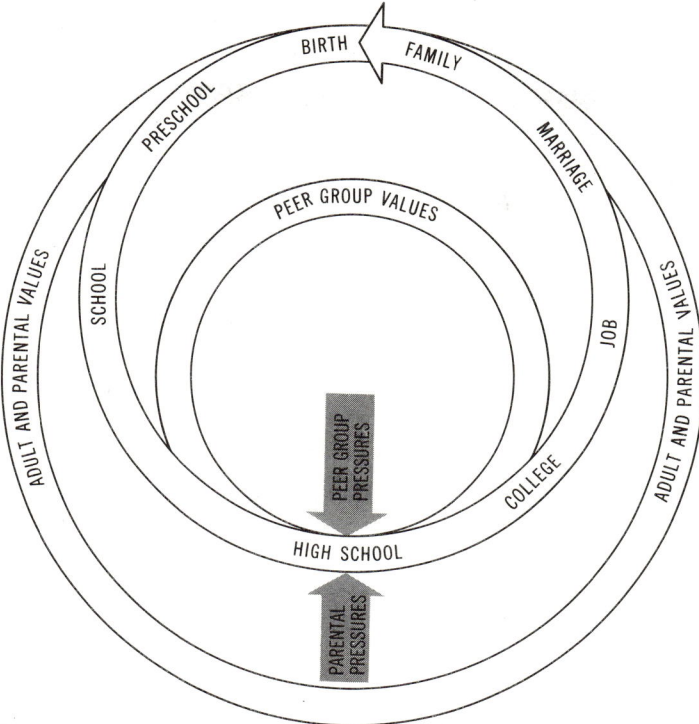

Fig. 7-1 The changing position of peers with respect to adults can be described as three circles which have a common point of beginning and end in adult and parental values.

Let us describe peer groups at three stages in a child's development, the preschool, middle, and adolescent years.

The Preschool Years

Preschool children are deeply concerned with themselves and their parents. They are therefore not greatly interested in developing meaningful relationships with their age-mates. The relationship that children maintain with their peers can, in a sense, be taken as a measure of their social maturity. The preschool child's immaturity is indicated by his individualistic ways and his lack of concern for others. As he matures his interests turn from within, outward. He has a growing awareness of those around him and a growing interest in being involved with them.

Children at play reveal this relationship between inward-outward orientation on the one hand and level of social maturity on the other. Children under three years of age engage largely in solitary play. They like to play beside other children but not with other children and are largely engrossed in their own preoccupations. Or they may simply choose to be onlookers. After three years the child begins to associate himself in play with others. He becomes more cooperative, more eager to get into games where a number of children take part. He is laying the foundation for participating in peer groups in later years.

The Middle Years

The child of five to twelve has reached the stage in which he wants to share his experience. The larger social relationships of the group are now coming within reach. He is no longer content to be alone, without others to play with. During the early years of this period the child is likely to develop a "best pal" relationship. The "best pal" is usually one with whom the child feels at home and to whom he can develop a strong attachment.

At this stage the child usually does not feel a deep need to be associated with a group, but his school life emphasizes the group and soon he has broadened his attachments beyond his "best pal." The early allegiance to the group is not strong. The child tends to stay with one group a short while and then transfer to another. And children under eight years of age prefer small groups of two or three other children. If the group becomes larger, they may exclude the extra members.

By this time the students who are excluded have developed a strong enough group orientation to *feel* excluded. They begin to develop some anxiety about not being in a group. In the preschool years they express anxiety if they are excluded from the family but have little anxiety about being excluded from peer groups. Now they show growing anxiety about being excluded from peer groups and waning anxiety about being excluded from the family. They are now emotionally prepared for membership in the peer groups of the adolescent years.

The Adolescent Years

Adolescence creates in the child an earnest effort to become independent, to reject the symbols of dependence, and to free himself of authority and control. The peer group becomes supreme during this period, and it sometimes wields more control over the child than his family or any other group.

Adolescent behavior bears a special relationship to the child's future as an adult. There is in adolescent behavior a curious mixture of defense against the future on the one hand and a positive orientation toward it on the other. The defense against the future may be observed in the seeming rejection of adult values and practices, in the feverish show of adolescent solidarity, in the drive for conformity. Peer-group members who reflect adult attitudes and values are regarded as "squares," and adolescent models are selected precisely because they express the peer values of the present. By these means the adult world of the future is held at bay.

Yet there is in adolescent behavior a positive orientation toward the future. The very drive for independence which symbolizes adolescent peer-group activity is itself an adult and mature value. The organization of the peer group with its various elite positions is preparation for living in a socially stratified society. The use of conformity to control the behavior of the members reflects an adult society in which social control is exercised by similar means.

This is probably another way of saying that although adults may not like to see themselves reflected in teen-age behavior, the adolescent society mirrors in many respects the adult society, its unconscious model.

Let us now look at other characteristics of the adolescent society and consider first the size of the teen-age population.

CHARACTERISTICS OF THE ADOLESCENT SOCIETY

The Growing Number of Adolescents

A breakdown of the country's population looks something like an hourglass, big at the top and bottom and small in the middle. Because of medical advances and better health care the number of old folks is growing rapidly. At the same time the number of under-18-year-olds is large, a result of the "baby boom" which followed the Second World War. Today nearly one of every twelve Americans is in the 14-to-17 age category. Ten years ago only one in every 18 persons was in this age bracket. Four in every ten Americans are less than 18 years old. In 1955 only one in three was under 18 years of age. In 1965, 3.7 million youths celebrated their eighteenth birthdays, a million more than in 1964.

The following table spells out the impact of this burst of 18-year-olds on the nation's young adult population.[6] It shows the population change in the 13-to-24 age group in recent years.

[6] "Focus on Youth," *Wall Street Journal,* Volume XLV, No. 55, December 31, 1964, p. 1.

	Gain in 18–24 age group
1966	1,062,000
1965	1,401,000
1964	453,000
1963	498,000
1962	589,000

This booming growth in teen-agers has vast implications for education. Nearly 80 percent of today's 17-year-olds are staying in school, compared with 68 percent in 1950. And American teen-agers are staying in school rather than seeking work in greater numbers than are their counterparts in other Western countries. The table below [7] shows the extremely low proportions of 15-to-19-year-old American males in the United States labor force, and it matches this low rate against the comparable percentages in other leading industrial countries.

	15–19 Age group in labor force
United Kingdom	84%
West Germany	77%
France	67%
Italy	63%
United States	45%

Let us now turn to characteristics of the peer groups of this adolescent population.

Status Rating within Peer Groups

We said in Part I that a classroom group organizes itself around the positions held by the students within it. Similarly an informal peer group has a social organization based on the popularity status of its members. Some members have high popularity within the group, some medium popularity, and some marginal popularity. Power within the group and control over it are determined by popularity rating.

Does the popularity rating within adolescent peer groups change over time? We said that the classroom group tended to keep its members in the same social position once the assignments were made by the group. The same tends to be true of informal peer groups, especially over a short period of time. It is less true over a long period of time. Mortimer R. Feinberg studied 298 boys between the ages of 13 and 15 from schools in New York City and the surrounding area.[8]

[7] *Ibid.*

[8] Mortimer R. Feinberg, "Stability of Sociometric Status in Two Adolescent Class Groups," *Journal of Genetic Psychology*, Volume 104, 1964, pp. 83–87.

The study sought to measure the stability of the individual status of group members over a five-month period and in another group over a two-year period. In order to determine the popularity rating Feinberg used a "buddy rating" scale. The pupils in each class were asked to list the four boys they would like to have sit next to them the following term, and who they thought would make the most desirable friends. They were also asked to name the four boys whom they would not wish to sit near and who gave them a feeling of uneasiness in the classroom situation. One group of the boys, 246 of the 298, filled out a similar rating scale at the end of five months, and the remaining 52 boys filled out the same scale at the end of two years. The boys remained together in the same school classes during their period of the study.

A comparison of the results at the end of the two periods showed that during the five-month period some boys did shift their preferences, but most of them did not. There was a high degree of consistency in the boys' choice of best friends over a five-month span. However, over the two-year period shifts in popularity did occur. The results suggest that significant shifts in choice patterns can develop, even with the same group of youngsters doing the selecting. Adolescence is a changing and volatile period, and what is considered important and desirable behavior in a 13-year-old may be rejected by the same child when he is 15.

Evidence suggests that peer groups are organized internally upon the basis of status ratings which are determined by popularity. Over a short period the status ratings within a group tend to remain fixed, but over a longer period preferences do change.

Status Seeking within Peer Groups

The high importance attached to status rating within the peer group requires that the adolescent be a status seeker. He must know the symbols which give him status and how to communicate with these symbols. He must know what is "in" and what is "out." If he possesses or can talk about what is "in," he can usually achieve status within the group. If, however, he possesses and talks about what is "in," when it is actually "out," he runs the risk of being "out" himself. Mary Anne Guitar, in commenting on "status seekers, junior grade," makes clear the importance of symbols in maintaining peer-group acceptance.[9]

"The most fascinating aspect of our status-conscious society may well be the cool way the younger generation accepts the inevitability of status distinctions.

[9] Mary Anne Guitar, "Status Seekers, Junior Grade," *New York Times Magazine*, Volume CXIII, No. 38,921, August 16, 1964, p. 47.

"The status symbol is, above all, a means of communication. One guitar player meeting another guitar player needs no verbal contact. The sight of that peerless symbol serves the same purpose today as the aborigine's peace pipe did in times past. It suggests instantly that these two understand one another and can safely become friends. Or, as one boy put it: 'Without your blanket, you are nothing. You have to carry your status symbol with you or fade.'

"The 'blanket,' however, has become so richly ornamented that it can be described only by those who wear one—the under-20's. Any adult who grew up with such simplistic symbols as dirty saddle shoes and beat-up jalopies is understandably mystified by the complex status system presently in force among the young.

"With a total lack of self-consciousness, a high-school junior explained what is obligatory in his circles:

" 'You have to have long hair, but not Beatle length. The crew cut is out. Your hair should be thick, smoothed down, parted on the side and swept across the forehead.

" 'It's a good thing to own a car. A sports car. Healey Sprites are the best. And if you don't own a car, you should be able to talk about them as if you really knew.

" 'Vespa motor bikes are good and Hondas are even better. They only cost \$400. Nobody has one. It's like the sports car. You have to know enough to talk about them.

" 'It's a good thing to have a summer house on Cape Cod, Fisher's Island, Fire Island. If your parents don't own one, then you should get an interesting job in one of these places.

" 'It's important to travel,' he concluded, 'particularly without your parents.' "

5. The last comment about traveling "without your parents" suggests the adolescent's need to keep his social identity separate from that of adults, especially those adults upon whom he is in some way dependent. Teachers, like parents, are adults upon whom the adolescent is dependent in a particular way. Do you think this adolescent predisposition to stay free of adults influences the teacher-student relationship? Does it suggest anything about teaching methods for adolescents? You might profitably ask an experienced teacher about this matter.

The status symbols of adolescents fall chiefly in the display area. They must be seen to count. The more visible the better. What counts is what you can wear, drive, or play. Such articles communicate strongly the adolescent's desire to maintain and improve his status within the group.

Let us turn from a consideration of status *within* the adolescent peer group to that of status *among* peer groups.

Status among Peer Groups

Peer groups hold given positions in respect to one another. Sometimes competition for supremacy is strong among peer groups. In other instances there is widespread acceptance of the hierarchy of peer groups and of their respective statuses. Note the relative positions of peer groups represented in this description of a high school cafeteria at lunchtime.[10]

"The natives observe a rigid noonday ritual. The social elite—a breezy clique called the Palisades-Brentwood Singing and Drinking Association—hold court at cafeteria tables reserved by custom for them. Nearby, like ladies in waiting, two plain girls snatch at conversational crumbs tossed by a pair of homecoming queens. At another table are the 'social rejects'—girls on the fringes of the elite whose boyfriends are now tired of them. 'They are still allowed to go to parties,' explains a guide, 'but they aren't in on the really big decisions, like who the elite will back in student elections.'

"Toward the rear of the hall sit the service club members and the rah-rah crowd, 'the squares who really believe in student government.' Other tribes are the Saracens, who include a small motorcycling hood element; the clowns, a group of practical jokers who wear Mickey Mouse shirts to signify that all human existence is fraudulent; the intellectuals, who lounge on the steps of the administration building as the rest of the student body speculates over whether the long-haired girls among them are professional virgins or real swingers; and an amorphous crowd that defies classification by declaring unanimously: 'I'm myself.'"

The relative status of peer groups within the school tends to reflect status values of the adult world. High status attends the achievement-minded peer groups who are college bound, groups which have high social approval among adults. High status attends peer groups who can consume lavishly prestige items such as sports cars, or talk knowingly about such symbols of status. This adolescent behavior is a faithful reproduction of our consumption-oriented society. The very division of peer groups along prestige lines mirrors the social-class structure of the adult society. Adults continue to express shock at the social-class biases of peer groups because their own biases are so faithfully exposed.

[10] "Students," *Time,* Volume 85, No. 5, January 29, 1965, p. 57.

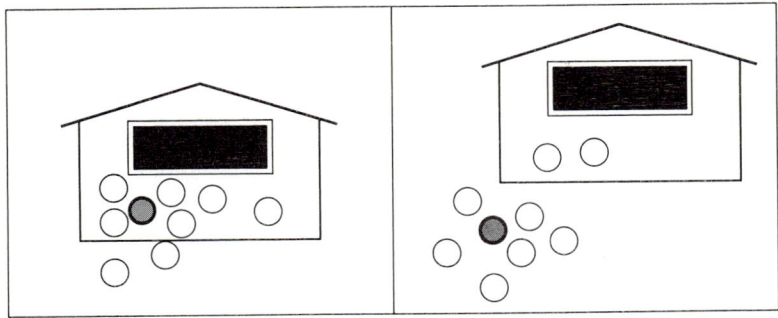

Fig. 7-2   The academically oriented child will have most friends from inside the school; the dropout will have them from outside the school.

6. Comment on status among the peer groups in the high school you attended. Was it different than described here? If so, how?

Peer-Group Conformity

Status seeking either within or among peer groups brings with it strong pressures to conform. As one high-schooler put it: "We have to be like everybody else to be accepted. Aren't most adults that way? We get a lot of stress on being an individual. But, we learn in high school to stay in the middle."

The need to know what is "in" and what is "out," to display the proper symbols, to talk knowingly about the "right" things, creates in adolescents intense conforming behavior. Conversely, it discourages and even punishes nonconformity. "The group," its norms and values, becomes the yardstick by which all is measured.

Even the leaders of the group, its pacesetters, are subject to group censure and must maintain their positions within its rules. Here, for example, is a high school leader of her group, the "queen bee" setting the standards, playing the status game, and yet standing ever in need of "the group." Notice how the group gives her security in exchange for her conformity.[11]

"The real focus of Jill's life is her circle of friends—'the group,' she calls it—who pretty much dictate to the rest of the school what is 'in' and who is 'out.' To anyone outside the group the girls present a solid front of confidence and authority. But within it they maneuver for popularity and approval, in each other's eyes and especially in Jill's.

[11] "The High School," Part II, *Life,* Volume 55, No. 15, October 11, 1963, p. 73.

As a result, the group is in a chronic ferment of girlish intrigue. Jill upset the delicate balance in the group by being elected song leader in her junior year, then going on to other honors. To maintain her own position, Margaret Eldred, who next to Jill is the group's most important member, began dating the president of the student council. Jill countered by quietly adopting a new best pal, Beth Reutter, and snubbing Margaret. Margaret then lined up the group against Jill. At this crisis, Jill had it out face to face with Margaret, who was only too glad to back down, leaving Jill at the top once more.

"Jill needs the group at least as much as it needs her. 'The clique is something you can depend on,' she explains. 'Maybe you can't always depend on any individual friend, but you can on the group. Of course, you put up a front even to your own group—you're hardly ever the real you. There's a certain image you want people to have of you. But in a clique you really learn to handle people.'"

In a peer group one really learns to conform.

PEER GROUPS AND SCHOOL LEARNING

Is there any connection between adolescent peer-group behavior and what is learned in school? In the peer group we see the informal social structure of the school, a structure distinct from the formal program of classes, courses, and teaching. The formal and informal systems exist side by side. Do they have impact upon one another? Does what is learned in formal classrooms influence the values of the peer group? Do the values of the peer group influence what is learned in the classroom?

Some observers feel that the formal and informal aspects of education exist side by side but seldom touch. Harold Taylor, for example, puts the case this way: [12]

"In most cases there is little relation between what the student studies in school and college and what he learned to admire and respect. That is to say, the effect of the formal teaching program is minimal and the effect of social ideas of American success is dominant. The student does his school and college work in order to gain his grades and academic credits. That is what he conceives schoolwork to be. The rest of his life is lived in a social order that has been arranged for him and into which he fits."

7. Do you agree or disagree with this position? Why?

[12] Harold Taylor, "The Understood Child," *Saturday Review*, Volume XLIV, No. 20, May 20, 1961, p. 48.

Although there is good reason to think that the formal and informal social systems of the school do not greatly modify each other, they definitely converge at one critical point. The adolescent's level of educational aspiration seems positively related to his peer-group membership. If his peer group values more education his desire for more is reinforced. If, on the other hand, the values of his peer group work for less education, his desire for less is strengthened. Observe the attitude of a slum group which scoffs at scholastic achievement:

"His gang teaches him to fear being taken in by the teacher, of being a softie with her. To study homework is literally a disgrace. Instead of boasting of good marks in school, one conceals them, if he ever receives any." [13]

Contrast this with the remarks of a middle-class suburban high school boy:

"You would be surprised just how much (schoolwork) counts for boys. I was at a party last year after I came first in the class. I could just stand there and not say a word all evening. Everybody came up to me and all that kind of stuff. Just because I came first in the class, I was the 'brain for the evening.'" [14]

The positive relationship between peer-group membership and educational aspiration is strongly suggested by research. Robert E. Herriott tested 1,489 adolescents in one public high school to determine what social factors influenced educational aspiration.[15] The specific hypothesis which Herriott tested was: The higher the level of expectation perceived from significant others, the higher will be the level of educational aspiration of adolescents. Thus if the adolescent thinks his best friends expect him to have high educational aspirations, he will most likely have such aspirations. Conversely, he is likely to have low educational goals if such goals are valued by his best friends. Herriott's research verified his hypothesis:

"Those concerned with the development of national aspiration of talented adolescents may attach special importance to our finding that significant others in an adolescent's environment can have considerable influence over his educational plans. What should be particularly noted is the finding that the strongest independent relationship with

[13] Allison Davis, *Social Class Influences Upon Learning*, Cambridge, Mass., Harvard University Press, 1948, p. 30.

[14] William A. Westley and Frederick Elkin, "The Protective Environment and Adolescent Socialization," *Social Forces*, Volume 35, 1957, p. 247.

[15] Robert E. Herriott, "Some Social Determinants of Educational Aspiration," *Harvard Educational Review*, Volume 33, No. 2, Spring 1963, pp. 157–177.

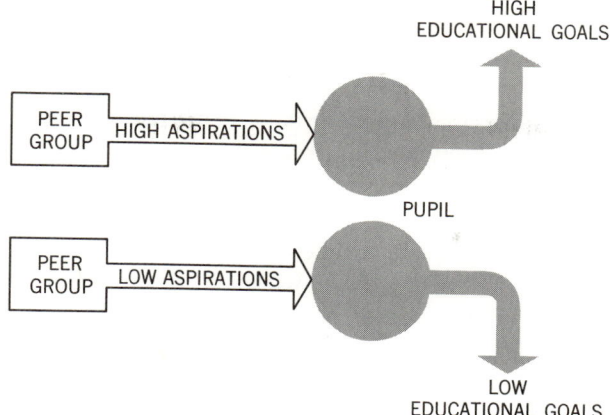

Fig. 7-3 Adolescent level of educational aspiration is positively related to peer-group membership.

level of educational aspiration observed in these data was with the expectation perceived from a friend of the same age." [16]

Other research on educational aspirations within peer groups supports the Herriott findings. C. Norman Alexander, Jr. and Ernest Q. Campbell studied over 1,400 male high-school seniors to determine the importance of peer groups on educational plans.[17] Again the results indicated a significant relationship. Adolescents were more likely to want to attend college, plan to attend, and actually attend if their best friend planned to do the same.

8. The importance of peer associations in determining the child's educational aspirations seems clear. Put yourself in the place of a teacher who has an able youth whose educational aspirations are being pulled down by his peer group. What would you do?

In Chapter 5 we spoke of the cultural predispositions of children to behave in certain ways in classroom groups. We spoke of the passive behavior of Pakistani children, the compulsive behavior of Maori children, and the spontaneous behavior of American middle-class children. We suggested that the good teacher in these different situations

[16] *Ibid.*, p. 171.

[17] C. Norman Alexander, Jr. and Ernest Q. Campbell, "Peer Influence on Adolescent Educational Aspirations and Attainments," *American Sociological Review*, Volume XXIX, No. 4, 1964, pp. 568–575.

works with rather than against these predispositions, using them actually to reinforce learning.

The same approach may wisely be taken toward peer-group behavior in the school. We have seen that there are strong forces in our society which give rise to peer groups. They fulfill both personality and social needs of growing children and youth. They generate powerful emotions and motivations which the school must learn to direct and use.

How peer energies are utilized must be very much the concern of every school and every teacher within it. That concern must relate itself to how these energies are used in terms of the goals of society and the school. For example, when peer groups adversely affect the intellectually able but socially disadvantaged youth, the school cannot be a casual onlooker if it is to take seriously its responsibility to society. If the peer groupings of the school limit the opportunity of some children to widen their social and intellectual horizons, the school cannot be unconcerned. If the school finds that its formal structure of instruction rewards the "have" groups and punishes the "have not" groups, it must seriously examine its program and practices. It must, through new group organization and better counseling, use peer-group energies to promote rather than impede good learning.

In this and previous chapters we were reminded repeatedly that the social-class structure of the larger society around the school plays upon what happens inside the school. Social class influences the learning of the child, the classroom group, the attitudes of the family toward the school and education, and the status of peer groups. Because social class is a pervasive teacher outside the school, in Part III we look in a somewhat more systematic way at its impact upon education.

REFERENCES

Paperbacks

Adolescent Character and Personality. Robert J. Havighurst and Hilda Taba. Science Editions Paperbacks, John Wiley and Sons, 605 Third Ave., New York ($1.65).

Adolescents. Sandor Lorand and Henry I. Schneer, Editors. (0021) Dell Publishing Co., 750 Third Ave., New York ($2.25).

Attitudes of Certain High School Seniors Toward Science and Scientific Careers. Hugh Allen, Jr. (Orig.) (SMP) Teachers College, Teachers College Press, 525 West 120 St., New York ($1.25).

Challenge of Youth. (Orig. title: *Youth, Change and Challenge.*) Erik H. Erikson, Editor. (A438) Anchor Books and Anchor Science Study Series, Doubleday and Co., 277 Park Ave., New York ($1.45).

Elementary School Child. Daniel A. Prescott. (Orig.) Educational Services, 1730 Eye St., N. W., Washington, D. C. ($2.75).

Encounter with Early Teens. Mary Elizabeth Wycoff. (Orig.) (20-0599) The Westminster Press, Witherspoon Building, Philadelphia, Pa. ($1.25).

From Generation to Generation: Age Groups and Social Structures. Samuel N. Eisenstadt. (90928) Free Press of Glencoe, Macmillan Co., 60 Fifth Ave., New York ($2.45).

High School Youth. Daniel A. Prescott. (Orig.) Educational Services, 1730 Eye St., N. W., Washington, D. C. ($2.75).

In Defense of Youth. Earl C. Kelley. (Orig.) (S-30) Spectrum Books, Prentice-Hall, Englewood Cliffs, N. J. ($1.95).

Vanishing Adolescent. Edgar Z. Friedenberg. (9276LE) Dell Publishing Co., 750 Third Ave., New York (50¢).

Books

Blair, Glenn Myers, and R. Stewart Jones, *Psychology of Adolescence for Teachers.* New York: Macmillan Co., 1964, 118 pp. Chapter 5 deals with the adolescent and his peer group.

Coleman, James S., "The Competition for Adolescent Energies," *Teaching in America,* Anthony C. Ricco and Frederick R. Cyphert, Editors. Columbus, Ohio: Charles E. Merrill Books, 1962, pp. 147–159. This article suggests that high schools, even though they differ economically and socially, have a high degree of similarity in adolescent behavior.

Erikson, Erik H., Editor, *Youth: Change and Challenge.* New York: Basic Books, 1963. This collection of articles discusses topics such as: "Youth: Fidelity and Diversity," "The Problem of Generations," "Youth in the Context of American Society," "Social Change and Youth in America."

Gesell, Arnold, Ilg, Frances L., and Louise Bates Ames, *Youth, The Years from Ten to Sixteen.* New York: Harper and Brothers, 1956. Chapter 17 discusses school life during this age span.

Mallery, David, *High-School Students Speak Out.* New York: Harper and Brothers, 1962. The author asked high-school students for their opinions on problems related to school life.

Murphy, Lois Barclay, *The Widening World of Childhood: Paths toward Mastery.* New York: Basic Books, 1962, 399 pp. This book, based on longitudinal study, approaches the child as an organism interacting with his social environment.

Parsons, Talcott, "Age and Sex in the Social Structure of the United States," in *Personality in Nature, Society and Culture,* Clyde Kluckholm and Henry A. Murray, Editors. New York: Alfred A. Knopf, 1949, pp. 269–281. Youth culture tends to be a product of tensions in the relationship of younger people and adults.

Remmeis, Herman H., Editor, *Anti-Democratic Attitudes in American Schools.* Chicago: Northwestern University Press, 1963. The book reports a research study on authoritarian and ethnocentric tendencies which occur among students in high schools and colleges.

Tannenbaum, Abraham J., *Adolescent Attitudes Toward Academic Brilliance.* New York: Teachers College Bureau of Publications, Columbia University, 1962. This survey of adolescent attitudes shows that juniors in high school ascribe more favorable characteristics to athletes than to nonathletes, and more desirable characteristics to nonstudious student types than studious types.

Periodicals

Adams, James F., "Adolescent Personal Problems as a Function of Age and Sex," *Journal of Genetic Psychology*, Vol. 104, Part 2, June 1964, pp. 207–214. Adolescents were asked about their biggest problems. Most frequently mentioned in rank order were school, interpersonal, financial, and family problems.

Gorden, Robert A., James F. Short, Desmond S. Cartwright, and Fred L. Strodtbeck, "Values and Gang Delinquence: A Study of Street Corner Groups," *American Journal of Sociology*, Vol. LXIX, No. 2, September 1963, pp. 109–129. Data gathered indicated no difference between gangs of lower-middle-class and middle-class boys, in their evaluations of behavior representing middle-class norms.

Herriott, Robert E., "Some Social Determinants of Educational Aspiration," *Harvard Educational Review*, Vol. 33, No. 2, Spring 1963, pp. 157–177. The author discovered that self-assessment in terms of significant others and the expectations of others are prime determinants of educational aspirations for adolescents.

LeShan, Eda J., " 'Hard Day's Night' of Today's Students," *New York Times Magazine*, September 27, 1964, pp. 104, 106. The author describes the academic pressures on students during the adolescent years.

Newmann, Fred M., "Adolescents' Acceptance of Authority: A Methodological Study," *Harvard Educational Review*, Vol. 35, No. 3, Summer 1965, pp. 303–325. A clinical study reports the criteria which appear to underscore adolescents' authority.

Pathak, Sumitra, "Environmental Conditions and the Juvenile Delinquent," *Journal of Social Sciences*, Vol. III, No. 2, 1963, pp. 59–73. In the absence of parental control peers become the boys' source of companionship, security, and guidance.

Unger, Sanford, "Relation between Intelligence and Socially Approved Behavior: A Methodological Cautionary Note," *Child Development*, Vol. 35, No. 1, March 1964, pp. 299–301. This study is a brief review of the literature which correlates positively the relationship between approved behavior and above-average I.Q.

Willite, Fern K., and Robert C. Bealer, "The Utility of Residence, for Differentiating Social Conservation in Rural Youth," *Rural Sociology*, Vol. 28, No. 1, March 1963, pp. 70–80. This study examines changes in attitude among rural high-school sophomore students.

III

Social-Class Influences in Learning

8

The Student and His Social Class

"They believe in a 'good' education for their children, but look askance at the educational 'frills' some of their more exuberant and generally more prosperous neighbors constantly propose."
                                                    WILLIAM M. DOBRINER

Growing up is marked by expanding social awareness. The preschool child is individualistic, not greatly interested in joining others in group activities. The child in his middle years develops a "best pal" relationship and becomes interested in gangs. In adolescence peer groups absorb a youth's loyalties, and his behavior is governed by their norms.

With this growing social awareness the child learns to make social distinctions among his age-mates. Some he regards as well or poorly dressed, popular or unpopular, smart or dull. Later he learns to differentiate among the backgrounds of his age-mates. He observes that they live in different kinds of houses in different parts of the community, ride in different kinds of cars, and have fathers who are employed in different occupations.

Almost without knowing it, the child has learned two important factors about social class: (1) Persons who exhibit certain social or economic characteristics are considered "better than" those who do not exhibit these characteristics; (2) every person, including himself, has some position in relation to the "better than" characteristics. That is, some people have more "better than" characteristics than others. In short, the child has been introduced to the social-class structure of his society.

WHAT IS A SOCIAL CLASS?

Almost every community has within it groups which think of themselves as being somewhat alike. The members of these groups may eat similar foods, live in similar houses, dress generally alike, use language in the same way, belong to similar occupational groups, hold similar values, and exhibit similar social behavior. Even though they may have cultural differences, such as belonging to different ethnic or religious groups, when they meet they have common matters to converse about and they tend to feel at ease with one another. Such a group constitutes a social class.

Social class is common to most societies, ancient or contemporary, primitive or modern. The people who occupy high status positions through the possession of power, wealth, or charisma constitute the upper social classes. Other persons are in the middle ranks; they possess some of the qualities of those in the upper classes, but not in commanding amounts. They constitute the middle classes. Still others, who have few or none of those qualities which the society requires of those who hold status positions, are in the lower social classes.

SOCIAL CLASS AS A WAY OF LIFE

One way to view social class is as a way of life. There are many ways of life associated with social class, and there are many ways to divide the population into social classes or ways of life. One can make very fine distinctions and speak of social classes as being "upper-upper," "upper," "upper-middle," "lower-middle," "upper-lower," and "lower-lower."

The *upper-upper* class is that very small and elite group of the population which lives on inherited wealth and divides its time, summer and winter, between great houses in prestigious locations in different parts of the country or world. The *upper class,* just a notch down, is identified by substantial wealth, expensive limousines, listings in the social registry, and a preference for private schools for their children. The *upper-middle* class is a large one in America. People of the upper-middle class live in substantial homes in well-established suburbs and occupy executive, managerial, professional, and lucrative business positions. The *lower-middle* class also occupies a large segment of the American population. Members of the lower-middle class live in homes in the medium and lower price brackets and occupy skilled, semiskilled, technical, clerical, and shopkeeping positions. The *upper-lower* class encompasses those persons who do manual labor and unskilled jobs, many of whom have less than a high school education. For the most part they have regular employment, but are subject to frequent "lay offs." The *lower-lower* class is not a stable working population; it is only periodically employed and is without steady income. It is concentrated in slums and poverty-stricken rural areas.

1. How many of these social classes can you identify in your own community? What is there about them which causes you to place them in one social class or another?

For our purposes we need not make such fine distinctions in the social-class structure. We wish only to say a word about the child's "way of life" in the major social-class groupings. We shall use three social classifications: middle class, working class, and lower class. In using middle class we shall refer to what we described as upper-middle class. The working class embraces both the lower-middle and upper-lower classes. The lower class, as used here, refers to the lower-lower class. Let us turn to the child's way of life in these three social-class groupings.

2. Social classes should not be thought of as airtight compartments in which everyone fits neatly somewhere. There is a lot of "crossing over" of social class lines. For this reason our generalizations about ways of life in the three social classes will not fit all children. You might find it interesting to think of exceptions in your own experience. In what way do these exceptions not fit the general descriptions which follow?

Child of the Middle Class

The child of the middle class, like Beth in Chapter 2, lives in a home in which he has his own bedroom, his own clothes and playthings, and he is never without food, light, or shelter. He is told to keep his room "straightened up," his shoes shined, and his ears clean. In bad weather he is supposed to leave his boots at the door and not drag mud into the house. He is taught to say "please" and "thank you," and he is reminded to "watch your speech." He is accustomed to cleaning women in the house and takes baby-sitters for granted.

His parents follow a "rearing ritual" in which he has regular hours for eating, going to bed, getting up, playing, watching television, and doing homework. He has a spending allowance and he is encouraged by his parents to spend it wisely and possibly to "save some." He has playmates beyond his immediate neighborhood, and he spends time in his friends' homes and they in his.

His parents hold high educational aspirations for him. They inquire frequently about "how are things going at school?" They show interest when he brings home schoolwork to show them and buy the extra things he needs for school. They take interest in such organizations as the Parent-Teacher Association and appear regularly at parent-teacher conferences and special school programs. This child hears his parents talk about college and tell him that someday he will go to college. They might indicate that they would be proud if he were to attend the college they attended, but if he is to get into college, he will have to "work hard and make good grades." He becomes anxious to succeed.

3. Can you identify the residential neighborhoods in your community where middle-class citizens live? What are some of the features of these neighborhoods?

4. Interview a middle-class parent regarding his educational aspirations for his children. How are these aspirations different or like those described here?

Child of the Working Class

The child in the working-class family has a different way of life: He is a "common man's" boy. He lives in a plain but respectable area and his home is owned by his parents who both have high school educations. The values this child holds are in many respects like those of his counterpart in the middle class because his parents are middle class in their outlook, though not in actual status. Working-class parents are apt to stress obedience in the child, whereas middle-class parents are more apt to stress self-control. Working-class parents push the child toward values which are respectable. Middle-class parents, who take respectability for granted, push him toward inner development.

The child of working-class parents often enjoys different recreation, sees different magazines, and watches different television shows. He has more freedom to choose what he watches than the middle-class child. There is evidence that his parents are more permissive generally than middle-class parents.

On the other hand, the parents of the working-class child are more likely to employ ridicule and physical punishment than the middle-class parents who depend more for control on the psychological ties. They will express disappointment in the behavior of the child and appeal to the child's conscience.

The child of the working class does not hear his parents talk about education in the same way as the child of the middle class. His parents believe in education as an ideal but do not regard it with the same urgency as middle-class parents. They *wish* their children could go to college, but they do not *expect* them to.

This child is not driven to achieve, but parents are delighted when he does. The matter of school achievement is left more up to him. Working-class parents want their children to finish high school, but beyond that they are not so sure. A working-class father said: [1]

"College? Well, that is something else. Not for the girl. For the boy, maybe. Might take something in business administration at this Nassau Community College. I don't know. It costs a lot to keep a kid in college these days. These college kids around here don't impress me very much. . . . I never finished high school. The wife did. I guess I should have. She wants me to go to night school. Fat chance. But the boy, he's good. Gets good grades. Maybe it's for him. I don't know. It's up to him."

5. Can you identify the residential neighborhoods in your community where working-class citizens live? What are the main characteristics of these neighborhoods?

6. Interview a working-class parent regarding his educational aspirations for his children. How do his aspirations compare with those of the father quoted above?

Child of the Lower Class

The child of the lower class has a way of life that is different from either that of the working- or the middle-class child. The child of the lower class shares his room, bed, and clothes. Like Julia in Chapter 2, he has known what it is to be hungry and cold. Because cleanliness is not a requirement for him, he is free to go around with dirty hands and face. He can drag mud into the house without being criticized and he is permitted to put his feet on the chairs. His speech tends to be different from that of the working- or middle-class child. He says "yeah," "can I," "ain't," and "me and him." His table manners are undeveloped, for he never sees people at home who practice table etiquette and never eats in good restaurants.

The lower-class child is permitted to express his aggression in physical ways, whereas the middle-class child is taught to control himself. The lower-class child can be loud and rough, can swear and fight. The middle-class child is supposed to fight only in self-defense, is supposed to "let ladies go first," and respect parents, teachers, and others in authority. The lower-class child is esteemed if he fights well, and indeed must fight to maintain the loyalty of his group.

Turn now to the educational aspirations of lower-class parents for their children. Frank Riessman, in his book *Culturally Deprived Child,*

[1] William M. Dobriner, *Class in Suburbia,* Englewood Cliffs, New Jersey, Prentice-Hall, 1963, p. 105.

presents evidence to indicate that lower-class parents are more concerned about educational achievement than they are usually given credit for.[2] One thing does seem clear: education has different meaning for lower-class parents and children than it does for working- or middle-class parents and children. The lower-class child has little interest in knowledge for its own sake. He sees no connection between education and the development of his own self-expression and growth. His is a utilitarian attitude toward education. It must be practical, must open up new opportunities for employment, provide more security, and help cope with modern existence. Said one lower-class student: "I want an education so you can handle the red tape you run into all over nowadays. If you want to buy a TV on time, or get a driver's license, you've got to be able to fill out papers and be able to read; the same thing for a lot of jobs, the unemployment check, getting an apartment in public housing, signing a lease." [3]

If the lower-class child is not without interest in education, why does he encounter difficulty in school? Reissman answers the question this way: [4]

"There are at least three reasons, two of which relate to attitudes and practices of the school, and the third, which concerns the conflicting feelings of the underprivileged individual himself.

"Although the deprived person in many ways desires education, he is inhibited by a number of significant factors. For one thing, he does not think he has a good chance of getting much education. This feeling forces his educational aspirations to remain more at the wish or fantasy level, rather than making of them a definite concrete intention. Then, the mechanics of obtaining higher education are quite vague to him. Getting admitted to college, no less attending classes, is complicated and foreign. He feels threatened by the red tape and his general lack of information concerning the procedures involved. He does not know what he is supposed to say in an interview, or to answer on an application blank in response to the question: 'Why do you want to go to college—what do you expect to get out of college?'

"Most of his friends and relatives do not go to college and he fears he will be out of place. Even more serious, he fears the loss of his familial, community, and peer group ties.

"Apart from these limiting factors that are more internal to him, there is the fact that education has a different meaning to the cul-

[2] Frank Riessman, *Culturally Deprived Child*, New York, Harper and Row, 1962, pp. 10–15.

[3] *Ibid.*, p. 13.

[4] *Ibid.*, pp. 14–15.

turally deprived individual than it does to the educator. The teacher, and most non-deprived students, consider knowledge for its own sake important. It does not have to be useful. Knowledge alone is power, and abstract symbolism need have no practical application. This view of learning is the antithesis of the deprived view. Moreover, self-expression and self-actualization, other aims of education, particularly modern education, are equally alien to the more pragmatic, traditional, underprivileged person. These differences alone might be sufficient to produce a negative attitude toward the school. But this is only part of the story. The school has developed, often unconsciously, various forms of subtle, but pervasive, discrimination against disadvantaged children."

The way of life of children differs from one social class to another. So does their attitudes toward education. The good teacher seeks to understand the social-class background of his children so that he will be better able to understand the child's attitudes toward learning and the school.

7. Visit with a child who represents one of the three social classes which we have described here. Find out what you can about his "way of life" and his attitude toward school.

8. Assume now that you are teaching a class in which children who represent all three of these social classes are present. How do you think their presence in your classroom might influence what you teach and how you teach it? You might wish to consult with an experienced teacher on this question.

THE STUDENT'S SOCIAL CLASS AND EDUCATIONAL OPPORTUNITY

Three classic studies demonstrate the relationships between social class and educational opportunity. Since these three studies have dominated much of the thinking on this subject, we shall look briefly at the main conclusions of each.

Middletown.[5] From 1924 to 1925, Robert S. and Helen Merrill Lynd carried on an anthropological study of a Midwestern industrial city of about 38,000 population. *Middletown* examines many aspects of the life in that city, among them how people in different social classes educate the young. The Lynds discovered that people in all social classes were concerned about the education of the young. There was widespread support for education at the elementary, secondary,

[5] Robert S. Lynd and Helen Merrill Lynd, *Middletown: A Study in American Culture,* New York, Harcourt, Brace and Company, 1929.

and even higher education level evidenced in all social classes. The Lynds stated: "If education is oftentimes taken for granted by the business class, it is no exaggeration to say it works the fervor of a religion, a means of salvation, among a large section of the working class." [6]

In view of the widespread support for education the Lynds became especially interested in those persons who did not share the majority view of education. They inquired into the social influences which kept children from pursuing their education. The Lynds reported two observations: (1) Lower-class parents were less likely than middle-class parents to make education seem important to their children, and (2) lower-class children were penalized within the school because they did not possess the middle-class values and behavior of the dominant group.

Who Shall Be Educated? [7] This book by W. Lloyd Warner, Robert J. Havighurst, and Martin B. Loeb presents the conclusions drawn from earlier studies done by Warner, Havighurst, and others.[8] In the authors' words:

"This book describes how our schools, functioning in a society with basic inequalities, facilitates the rise of a few from lower to higher levels but continue to serve the social system by keeping down many people who try for higher places. The teacher, the school administrator, the school board, as well as the students themselves, play their roles to hold people in their places in our structure." [9]

These investigators pointed out that education was a means by which people moved up the social and economic ladder, but that education did not give the same opportunity to all people. The school selects and sorts those who shall proceed upward. The authors sug-

---

[6] *Ibid.*, p. 187.

[7] W. Lloyd Warner, Robert J. Havighurst, and Martin B. Loeb, *Who Shall Be Educated?*, New York, Harper and Brothers, 1944.

[8] W. Lloyd Warner and Paul S. Lunt, *The Social Life of a Modern Community*, New Haven, Yale University Press, 1941, "Yankee City Series," Vol. I; W. Lloyd Warner and Paul S. Lunt, *The Status System of a Modern Community*, New Haven, Yale University Press, 1948, "Yankee City Series," Vol. II; W. Lloyd Warner and Leo Srole, *The Social Systems of American Ethnic Groups*, New Haven, Yale University Press, 1945, "Yankee City Series," Vol. III; W. Lloyd Warner and J. O. Low, *The Social System of a Modern Factory*, New Haven, Yale University Press, 1947, "Yankee City Series," Vol. IV. Allison Davis, Burleigh B. Gardner, and Mary R. Gardner, *Deep South*, Chicago, University of Chicago Press, 1941. W. Lloyd Warner and Associates, *Democracy in Jonesville*, New York, Harper and Brothers, 1949.

[9] Warner, Havighurst, and Loeb, *op. cit.*, p. 15.

gested that the teachers, administrators, and the curriculum all favored middle-class students. The children who are the "nonreaders," "the first-grade repeaters," the members of the "opportunity class" are moved along "for eight or ten years, then released through a chute to the outside world to become 'hewers of wood and drawers of water.' " [10]

How does the curriculum operate to keep lower-class children "in their place"? The authors explained it this way: [11]

"The evidence is clear that the social class system of Yankee City definitely exercises control over the pupil's choice of curriculum. The children of the two upper and the upper-middle classes, in overwhelming percentages, were learning and being taught a way of life which would fit them into higher statuses. On the other hand, the lower-middle and the lower-class children, in their studies in the high school, were learning a way of life which would help adjust them to the rank in which they were born."

Then the authors turned to the teachers:

"Teachers represent middle-class attitudes and enforce middle-class values and manners. In playing this role teachers do two things. They train or seek to train in middle-class manners and skills. And they select those children from the middle and lower classes who appear to be the best candidates for promotion in the social hierarchy." [12]

In summary, the authors contended that (1) for most people in the community the school might act as a means of social mobility by teaching skills which were essential for occupational advancement; (2) in high school the student's socio-economic status rather than his ability determined the curriculum he enrolled in; (3) among high school students of equal intelligence, those with high socio-economic status had more opportunity to go on to college than those with low socio-economic status; (4) students in high-status curricula, like college preparatory programs, got better instruction than those in low-status curricula like vocational training; and (5) children from lower social classes did not know how to conform to the middle-class values of the school and were therefore penalized.

Elmtown Youth.[13] August Hollingshead's study focuses on the adolescents of *Elmtown* and their relationship to the social structure

[10] *Ibid.*, p. 50.
[11] *Ibid.*, p. 61.
[12] *Ibid.*, p. 107.
[13] August Hollingshead, *Elmtown Youth*, New York, John Wiley and Sons, Inc., 1949.

of this Midwestern community. More specifically, Hollingshead studied the relationships between an adolescent's position in the social structure and his school attendance, participation, educational and occupational aspirations, and his peer-group association. Hollingshead concluded that a youth's opportunities for achievement in *Elmtown* were positively related to his social-class position. Why? Because the lower-class environment did not properly prepare the adolescent for upward educational and occupational achievment and because middle-class adults in the school enforced their own values and "put down" lower-class youth. The middle-class students in the school simply reflected the attitudes and behavior of the citizens in the larger society around the school.

These three studies suggest that there exists a strong positive correlation between a student's social class and his educational opportunity. The higher the student's social class, the higher will be his educational opportunity: The lower his social class, the lower will be his educational opportunity. These studies also argue that the school itself may reinforce this handicapping relationship. Studies like these have helped give impetus to current programs in the schools to equalize educational opportunity for underprivileged children.

9. Perhaps some of the conclusions of these three studies do not "square" with your own experience. With which ones would you argue? Why?

SOCIAL CLASS AND ACHIEVEMENT MOTIVATION

Middle-Class Children Are Urged to Achieve

Members of the lower and middle class differ sharply in their attitudes toward achievement. This difference can be seen in the degrees of pressure which are put on children to achieve in school. The child of middle-class parents is constantly urged to do better in his studies, not to neglect his homework, to "read more books and watch less TV." He may become anxious about his success and fearful of failure. When he does well he is rewarded with family approval and tangible rewards. Parents sometimes have qualms about this pressure, but they also know that they create it. One parent said: [14]

"I feel that during the junior high school years most parents want their children to learn and explore and grow. The marks are quite secondary. But during these final three years, parents get desperate

[14] David Mallery, *High School Students Speak Out*, New York, Harper and Row, 1962, p. 79.

about the 'right college,' and about the things they read about college admissions competition in the papers and magazines. And the whole emphasis on marks and competition suddenly becomes dramatic and loaded with pressure."

This is the voice of the middle-class parent.

To parental pressure for achievement must be added pressure of the school itself. The middle-class school is proud of its record of getting students into college and it wants to keep, and if possible, improve that record. The pressure of the school for achievement can start early. One student recalls: [15]

"I guess it began around the sixth grade in our community. The principal of the high school came over to our school to talk to us about college. I remember going home that night and asking my family if they thought I'd be able to go to college. That kind of thing pretty well conditions you from the sixth grade on. If you get it bad enough, there is really no room for expansion. You sacrifice learning for marks."

10. Do you think that pressure to achieve causes students to "sacrifice learning for marks"? What reasons do you give for your answer?

11. Do you think the principal in this incident did the right thing in talking with the sixth graders about college? Why do you think as you do?

To the achievement pressure of middle-class parents and schools must be added that of peer groups. In the last chapter we learned of the positive relationship between peer-group membership and educational aspiration. College-bound students exert pressure on one another to maintain scholastic records consistent with college admission. Achievement gets built into the fabric of the peer group.

Let us now study the psychological impact of this achievement socialization. Allison Davis suggests that such pressure to achieve causes the middle-class child to be anxious to succeed and that this anxiety itself generates further motivation.[16] Thus, he strives all the more for the goals which are held up as desirable by his parents, his school, and his peers.

And are the goals the middle-class child seeks close at hand or far away? Although the approval of parents, peers, and school is almost immediate, the rewards of education itself are in the future. The real rewards of good learning will come later, with college admission, hopefully a good job, a good marriage, success. In other words, middle-

[15] *Ibid.,* p. 73.

[16] Allison Davis, "Socialization and Adolescent Personality," *Adolescence, Forty-Third Yearbook,* Part I, Chicago, National Society for the Study of Education, 1944, Chapter 11.

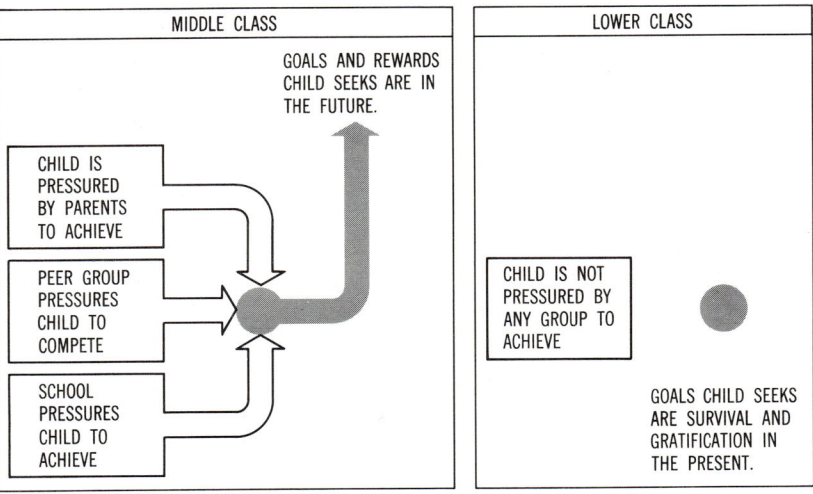

Fig. 8-1 The middle-class child strives for goals which are held up as desirable by his parents, school, and peers. The lower-class child is so occupied with the concerns of the present that he has little time to think about the future.

class motivation is for *deferred gratification.* The child learns not only to achieve but also to achieve now for a future reward. If he works hard now, makes good grades now, uses his time wisely now, avoids trouble now, he will later surely earn his reward. His parents, peers, and school constantly remind him that the future is what really counts, that the present is only preparation for the future.

Lower-Class Children Are Taught to Survive

Contrast the achievement motivation of the middle-class child with that of the lower-class child. The cumulative pressure to achieve from parents, peers, and school is usually absent. The child is so occupied with the concerns of the present that he has little time to think about the future. Survival is his main concern; his satisfactions must be immediate rather than deferred. The pressures for survival are all-absorbing and there is neither energy nor encouragement for higher skills and educational achievement. These represent a kind of luxury which he and his family cannot afford to think about. Not finding support for achievement at home, can the lower-class child find it at school? Sometimes "yes," and sometimes "no." As Davis points out: [17]

"To the underprivileged adolescent, the words and goals of his teacher—those words and goals to which middle-class adolescents react with respect and hard striving—mean very little. For the words of the teacher are not connected with the *acts of training in his home,* with the actual rewards in school, or with actual steps in moving toward a career."

Nor does the lower-class child find support for achievement in the members of his peer group. They, too, are oriented toward the present rather than the future. The values of the school seem remote from their present strivings. The things the teachers talk about and the things the school stands for are frequently inconsistent with their immediate present.

SOCIAL CLASS AND EDUCATIONAL ASPIRATIONS

Considering these social-class differences in motivation to achieve we would expect similar differences in educational aspiration. Education is one of the main ways by which people who aspire to achieve actually do. It follows logically that those who have high aspirations will tend to place high value on education and those who have low aspirations will tend to place low value on education. Thus we would expect that the achievement-oriented middle class would regard education as vital to its welfare. Similarly, we would expect that the present-oriented lower class would see a less vital relationship between education and welfare. Generally speaking, this accurately describes middle- and lower-class aspirations toward achievement in education.

The Educational Choices of Working-Class Children

The working class, the class which we described as falling between the middle and the lower class, shares some of the attitudes and values of each of the other two classes. What is its attitude toward educational achievement?

The working class is a crucial one in respect to educational aspiration, in some ways more crucial than either the middle or lower class. The middle-class commitment to education is clear. Children from middle-class homes are trained to share the values of the school and

[17] Allison Davis, "The Motivation of the Underprivileged Worker," Chapter V in *Industry and Society,* William F. Whyte (Ed.), New York, McGraw-Hill, 1946, p. 99.

the chances are good that they will achieve. In a sense the children of the middle class have limited choice regarding whether to continue their education. The environment has fairly well made that choice for them. Among lower-class children, discontinuities between their environment and the school are quite clear. If these children are to achieve, they will need major help to bridge the wide gulf between their homes and their schools. The children of the lower class, like those in the middle class, have limited choice in deciding whether to further their education. In their case, however, the limited choice argues against rather than for more education. If they do elect to further their education, they will need considerable outside encouragement to accomplish their goal.

The case is somewhat different with working-class students. It is from this group that will come the best candidates for upward achievement in education. In a sense children of this group have wider choice than children from either the lower or middle class. Because their environment is more neutral about education, they may elect to go either way.

What is the level of aspiration in this group? What determines whether the children of working-class parents aspire to something higher than their own class or remain content to stay where they are? To indicate possible answers to these questions we shall examine two significant investigations. The first one tells us something about the level of educational aspiration of working-class boys as compared to middle-class boys in the English grammar schools. The second study deals with the educational aspirations of American "common-man" boys and tells us much about the influences which cause these boys to make the educational choices they do.

In the first study E. Bene studied the difference in attitude toward education between British middle-class and working-class boys in grammar school.[18] In Britain an examination that determines who will go to the grammar schools is taken by students at the age of eleven. The sons of working-class parents who pass the examination are thus thrust into grammar schools which have traditionally held middle-class values. Lower-class boys arrive at these schools from home environments where social striving is not given much importance. They compete with boys from middle-class homes where striving is of great consequence, where status is to be achieved by a person's own efforts. We are not surprised, then, that Bene, in comparing working- and

[18] E. Bene, "Some Differences Between Middle-Class and Working-Class Grammar School Boys in Their Attitude Toward Education," *British Journal of Sociology*, Volume 10, No. 2, June 1959, pp. 148–152.

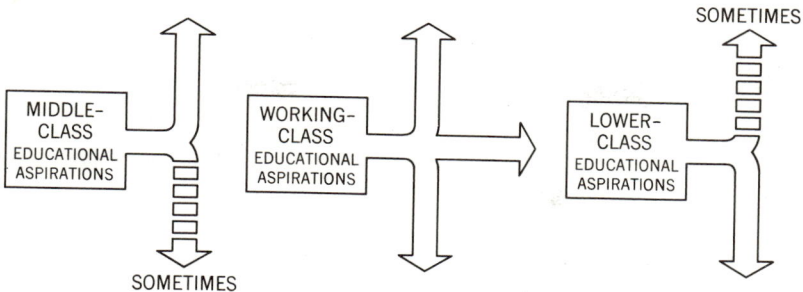

Fig. 8-2 The educational aspirations of students are influenced by social-class values.

middle-class boys, should find the following: Middle-class boys (a) have higher educational aspirations, (b) more frequently feel that work is more important than play, and (c) are more frequently interested in reading.

Bene found further that two-thirds of the middle-class boys and less than one-half of the working-class boys wanted to stay in school after the age sixteen. The study concludes that working-class boys are not as willing as middle-class boys to spend years of their youth in school in order to gain prestige and more social rewards as adults. In other words, working-class boys are not as willing to work hard now to achieve satisfactions later as are middle-class boys.

12. Do you think it would help a teacher in a British grammar school to know the social backgrounds of his boys? How could he use this knowledge to advantage in his teaching?

What Influences Working-Class Children to Make the Educational Choices They Do?

Why aren't working-class boys as willing as middle-class boys to work hard now for satisfactions later? Because the study of "common-man" boys by Joseph A. Kahl helps us to understand the reasons,[19] we shall report the Kahl study in some detail.

The investigation was concerned with the ambitions of 24 high school boys whose parents belonged to the working class. They all had sufficient ability to go to college and thereby improve their

[19] Joseph A. Kahl, "Educational and Occupational Aspirations of 'Common-Man' Boys," *Harvard Educational Review,* Volume XXIII, No. 3, Summer 1953, pp. 186–203.

chances for attaining an occupational status higher than that of their families. Yet 12 of the boys chose not to do so. They preferred to take their chances with the high school education they had and to be satisfied with such employment as might come along when they were ready for a job. The other 12 boys chose to better themselves by getting more education. Kahl conducted intensive interviews with the boys and their parents in order to explore the social influences that helped to explain the choices these two groups made.

The boys and their parents lived in two industrial-residential suburbs of Boston with populations between 50,000 and 200,000. Some of the wage earners in these towns commute to central Boston, but the majority of them work in industries in their own town. The symbol that best represents the communities where these families live is the two-family, wooden-frame house in good condition. These houses cover many square miles of the metropolitan area, are crowded closely together, and have a small yard in the rear. Typically the houses have a living room, dining room, kitchen, a bath, and two or three bedrooms. They are comfortably furnished in the "Sears-Roebuck" tradition, have wallpaper with a flower pattern, and have a linoleum rug on the dining-room floor. There is a small television set in the living room and a secondhand Ford or Chevrolet in the driveway.

About half of the parents completed at least two years of high school. One attended a liberal arts college. A few fathers had gone to a business college or technical-trade school for a year or less after high school. The parents thought of themselves as being ordinary people who were respectable but had little power or importance. They knew that they could not consume conspicuously like the middle class because of their low incomes. They attributed their situation to inadequate education, inadequate understanding of the way things *really* worked, and inadequate social and intellectual skills.

This study reveals that these 24 families all had some view of their position in the social scheme of things. Further, this view made a critical difference in the view that their sons took toward education. The families expressed two views toward the social structure. Members of one group tended to accept their positions in the social order. They thought this position should not only be accepted, it was to be preferred. Their core value was "getting by." The second group of families were not so happy about their position in the social hierarchy. These families felt they had not risen as high as they should, and had as their core value "getting ahead."

The families who were "getting by" were absorbed in balancing the budget, living for the moment, looking neither to the past nor to the future. The children were encouraged to enjoy themselves while they were young, to stay in high school "because a diploma is pretty important in getting a job nowadays," but to pick the curriculum of their choice. A college education was never considered seriously: "We can't afford such things," or "We aren't very bright in school." They expected their sons to be common people, to have a regular job, and to be like their fathers.

The sons of the families who were "getting by" were very sensitive to their family's educational expectations for them and reflected almost perfectly the same "getting by" aspirations. A boy who was not being pushed by his parents took this attitude: [20]

"I'm not definite what I'd like to do. Any kind of job. Anything as long as I get a little cash. . . . My folks tell me to go out and get a job, anything, just as long as it's a job. They say I'm old enough to start turning in board. . . . I haven't got much brain for all that college stuff. . . . You know, nobody would believe me now, but I was an 'A' student in grammar school. I dunno what happened; just started dropping gradually. . . . I guess the work just started getting harder. . . . I could do better work if I wanted to. As long as I pass I don't care. What the hell? I got nothin' to look forward to. . . . I was told to take the college course by the teachers. But I didn't want to. I wanted to take it easy."

13. How would you explain why this student got "A's" in grammar school and then started slipping? Could you trace the factors in his environment which might have led him from being a good student to his "don't care" attitude? (Many students in the working and lower classes go through this cycle, and we shall expand on this matter later in this chapter and again in the next chapter.)

14. This boy was told to take a college course by his teachers. The "telling" apparently had no effect. Do you think the teachers might have *done* something which would have had an effect?

Unlike the parents who were "getting by," the parents who were "getting ahead" thought a lot about their position in the social hierarchy. They used the middle class as a reference group and said frequently that were it not for their poor education, or for the fact that they did not take opportunities when they were young, they would be in the middle class. The fathers in this group frequently pointed to the men immediately above them and commented, "Those fellows are better trained than I and can do things I can't do." They did not complain that the fellows who got ahead did so through "connections."

[20] *Ibid.*, p. 202.

Rather they saw the world of occupations stratified according to the principle of education, where a person who did not get an education when he was young would lose out later on.

Like the sons of the families who were "getting by," the sons of families who were "getting ahead" were sensitive to their family's educational aspiration for them. This boy expresses clearly the relation between his views and those of his parents: [21]

"I'd like to learn to specialize in college. My folks want me to go to college too. My father didn't get through high school, and he wishes he'd gone to college. He has a good job now but he says if he had just a little bit of college he could have gone much higher. He's got a good job but he's gone as high as he can without a college education. . . . My mother and father don't want me to be a hired man. They want me to be in the upper bracket. They want me to learn by going to school and college, to go ahead by getting a higher education."

15. Put side by side for consideration the two boys, one who just wants "to take it easy," the other who wants "to learn to specialize in college." Let us assume that these two boys are in your classroom.

a. Which one would you understand better? Can you explain your answer in terms of your own social-class background?
b. To which boy do you think you would give more attention? Why?
c. Which boy's parents are you more likely to know, either personally or professionally as teacher? Why?

The boys of both parents who were "getting by" and of those who were striving to "get ahead" reflected the values of their subcultural group. This split in values was reflected in the boys' attitudes toward the details of schoolwork, after school recreation, and jobs. The boys who were "getting by" were generally bored with school, wanted to get a common-man type of job, and to be happy with their peers. They tended to be more carefree than the boys who were "getting ahead." They cared less about schoolwork and more about "having fun." They claimed that the "get-ahead" boys "didn't know how to have fun." By contrast, the boys who were "getting ahead" claimed that the "getting-by" boys were "irresponsible," and "didn't know what was good for them."

What shall we conclude about the reasons why working-class boys make the educational decisions they do? The core value of the family is crucial. The working-class family stands socially between the lower class and the middle class. It may choose to stay where it is and so

[21] *Ibid.*, p. 202.

indicate this value to its children. Or it may choose to "get ahead," if not itself then certainly its children. For it is the children who are sensitive to the social-class values which are expressed through the family. Their educational pointers will likely point in the direction set by the subcultural values of the family.

What happens educationally to children who point beyond their own families? Do they face unique kinds of problems? Such children are using the school as an agent of their own social change. The school is the ladder by which they ascend to a new social and occupational status. Let us look now in Chapter 9 at the child who uses education to perform this important task.

REFERENCES

Paperbacks

Class and Society. Kurt B. Mayer. (Orig.) (SS10-RH) Random House, 457 Madison Ave., New York ($1.25).

Class in Suburbia. William Dobriner. (Orig.) (S-50) Spectrum Books, Prentice-Hall, Englewood Cliffs, N. J. ($1.95).

Crucial Issues in Education. Ehlers and Lee. (3rd Ed.) Holt, Rinehart and Winston, 383 Madison Ave., New York ($3.25).

Education and Democratic Ideals. Gordon C. Lee. (Orig.) Harcourt, Brace and World, 757 Third Ave., New York (including Harbrace Books) ($1.95).

Education and Income: Inequalities of Opportunity in Our Public Schools. Patricia Sexton. (C168) Compass Books, The Viking Press, 625 Madison Ave., New York ($1.65).

Educational Issues in a Changing Society. August Kerber and Wilfred Smith, Editors. (2nd Rev. Ed., Orig.) (WB3) Wayne State University Press, 5980 Cass, Detroit, Michigan ($3.95).

Excellence: Can We Be Equal and Excellent Too? John W. Gardner. (CN/3) Harper Colophon Books, 49 E. 33rd St., New York ($1.45).

Growing Up in the City. John Barron Mays. Science Editions Paperbacks, John Wiley and Sons, 605 Third Ave., New York ($1.65).

Middletown. Robert S. and Helen Merrill Lynd. (HB-27) Harvest Books, Harcourt, Brace and World, 757 Third Ave., New York ($2.25).

Middletown in Transition: A Study in Cultural Conflicts. Robert S. and Helen Merrill Lynd. (HB-65) Harvest Books, Harcourt, Brace and World, 757 Third Ave., New York ($2.45).

Slums and Suburbs. James B. Conant. New American Library of World Literature, 1301 Ave. of the Americas, New York (60¢).

Social Class in American Sociology. Milton M. Gordon. (23786) McGraw-Hill Paperback Series, McGraw-Hill Book Co., 330 W. 42nd St., New York ($2.95).

Vital Issues in American Education. Alice and Lester Crow. (Orig.) (QM1008) Bantam Books, 271 Madison Ave., New York ($1.25).

Books

Bagdikian, B. H., *In the Midst of Plenty: The Poor in America*. Boston: Beacon Press, 1964. The author discusses why in the wealthiest nation one-sixth of the people live below minimal standards.

Blair, Glenn Myers, and R. Stewart Jones, *Psychology of Adolescence for Teachers*. New York: Macmillan Co., 1964. Chapter 5 emphasizes the differences between middle-class and lower-class adolescents in terms of attitude toward school, aggression, speech habits, and sexual behavior.

Davis, Allison, "The Structures of Rewards and Punishments in the Middle and Lower Classes," in *Readings for Educational Psychology*, Second Edition, William A. Fullager, H. G. Lewis, and C. F. Cumbee, Editors. New York: Thomas Y. Crowell Co., 1964, pp. 299–305. The author shows how the social-class structure operates in the school and how it works against the lower-class child.

Havighurst, Robert J., "Social-Class Influences on American Education," in *Sixtieth Yearbook of the National Society for the Study of Education*, Part II. Chicago: University of Chicago Press, 1961, pp. 120–143. As our society becomes middle class in standards, there are tendencies toward hardening of the social atmosphere and rigid stratification.

Turner, Ralph H., *The Social Context of Ambition*. San Francisco: Chandler Publishing Co., 1964. This book is a study of the aspirations of high-school seniors in Los Angeles.

Periodicals

Coster, J. K., "Some Characteristics of High School Pupils from Three Income Groups," *Journal of Educational Psychology*, Vol. 50, No. 2, April 1959, pp. 55–62. Coster found a relationship between the economic class of students and their participation in school activities.

Holland, John L., and Robert C. Nichols, "Prediction of Academic and Extra-curricular Achievement in College," *Journal of Educational Psychology*, Vol. LV, No. 1, January 1964, pp. 55–65. Past academic performance indicates future performance.

Long, Howard Hale, "The Inadequacy of Middle Class Education for the Democratic Job: Some Responsibilities of the Teacher," *Journal of Human Relations*, Vol. II, No. 4, Summer 1963, pp. 496–514. The prerequisite to academic achievement is acquisition by the student of desirable attitudes; these are not necessarily based on middle-class values.

Moore, James C., and Paul T. King, "A Comparison of Rural and Urban Pupils on Achievement," *School and Community*, Vol. LI, No. 3, November 1964, pp. 28–29. Intelligence tests tend to favor the urban child and underrate the rural child.

Wilson, A. B., "Residential Segregation of Social Classes and Aspirations of High School Boys," *American Sociological Review*, Vol. 24, No. 6, December 1959, pp. 836–845. The social class of the school affects academic achievement, occupational aspirations, and political preferences of students.

Wylie, Ruth C., "Children's Estimates of Their Schoolwork Ability, as a Function of Sex, Race, and Socioeconomic Level," *Journal of Personality*, Vol. 31, No. 2, June 1963, pp. 203–225. Children of lower socio-economic levels make more modest estimates of their ability than do children of higher socio-economic levels.

9

Students Who Strive to Move Up

"I know a fine and able student who applied for a scholarship and was accepted by a prestige college. Her father, a laborer, was incensed at the whole idea. We were turning his daughter's head. A good girl should get a job, come home, help her mother and get married." SAMUEL TENENBAUM

Education acts in some degree as an agent of social change for practically all classes of society. That it should do so is not surprising in a technological society which requires expert knowledge and specialized skill to succeed. All social classes, middle, working, and lower, use education to achieve the goals they regard as desirable. The goals, especially economic and social, can hardly be achieved now without education. Even the child born into the upper class will find his future difficult if he does not secure an education. His upper-class status alone will not assure his success but must be coupled with a good education. The two together will assure his chances for a good future.

EDUCATION AS AN AGENT OF SOCIAL CHANGE

Whereas all classes use education as an agent of social change, they do not use it in the same way. The middle classes are good consumers of education, and constantly demand more for their children. The working class is a selective consumer of education, depending upon the "getting-along" or "getting-ahead" values of the family. The lower-class family is so occupied with its survival that it can consume education only sparingly. But when any family, middle, working, or lower class, sends its children to school, it usually has some social goal in mind; and achieving that goal through education involves some social change, great or small. The impact of social change on children, especially those of the working and lower classes, is considerable. For them the change is most drastic.

The Impact of Social Change upon Students

If different social classes do not *use* education in the same way, neither are they *used by it* in the same way. The task education places on children of the lower and working classes is different from that placed on the middle-class child and calls for an entirely different kind of adjustment.

At the risk of oversimplifying a complex matter, we may use an analogy of children climbing a ladder. Children from different social classes start to climb the school ladder, not all on the same step but on different rungs. The middle-class child is familiar with the values of the school, having learned them in his family. He starts several steps up the ladder. The working-class child may be indifferent to the values of the school. He starts a step behind the middle-class child. The lower-class child finds the values of the school bewildering and foreign to his way of thinking. He starts on the bottom rung.

In short, if the lower-class child wishes to achieve middle-class status with the help of the school, he has farther to go, more to learn, more changes in behavior and attitudes to internalize than either the working- or middle-class child. The working-class child also has major obstacles to overcome. Let us look at a few of them.

What It Means for Working-Class Children to Strive for a Middle-Class Education

In the first place, the working-class child who is striving for a middle-class education and occupation really lives on the margin of two subcultures and has loyalties to both, but he does not completely belong to either. His life is not easy. As far as his schoolwork is concerned, he is caught in cross pressures. When he receives his first homework assignment, he knows what he ought to do; he should sit down to it straightaway. But his pals are playing baseball, working after school, watching television, anything but doing homework. His friends do not think it is important and do not know why he should. Carrying books home at night "is for the birds."

Other difficulties arise. In the junior high school the time comes to select one of four curricula which will be pursued in high school. The future programs in order of increasing difficulty are: trade, general, commercial, and college preparatory. The striving working-class boy knows he should go into the college preparatory class but practically all of his peer group are taking the trade, general, or commercial curricula. If he wants to aim higher than his friends he must expect some derision or isolation. If he has exceptional social skill he may be able to stick with the old gang; the chances are, however, that he will have to give them up and switch if he can to a college-oriented peer group. All of these pressures combine to make it harder and harder for the working-class child to continue to do good work in school.

1. Interview a student from a working-class family. Find out what you can about the difficulties he encounters in doing his schoolwork.

If the working-class student continues to do good work it is because he has strong reasons for doing so. From where will these reasons come? Joseph A. Kahl's study of the 24 working-class boys discussed in Chapter 8 suggests that such motivation may come from four sources.[1]

1. "If a boy had done well in the early years, and had built up a self-conception in which good school performance was vital, he would work hard to keep up his record. But an idea that school was vital occurred only when that early performance was truly exceptional, or if the importance of his standing to him was reinforced by one or more of the other factors listed below.

2. "A boy would sacrifice other pleasures for homework when they weren't important to him. If a boy was not good at sports, if he did not have close and satisfying peer contacts, or if he had no hobby that was strongly rewarding as well as distracting, then the cost of homework was less and the balance more in its favor. In extreme cases frustrations in these alternative spheres motivated a boy to good school performance as compensation.

3. "If a boy's family rewarded good school performance and punished poor performance, and the boy was not in rebellion against the family for emotional reasons, he was more likely to give up some play for homework.

4. "If a boy had a rational conviction about the importance of schoolwork for his future career, he would strive to keep up his performance. But that conviction never appeared unless the parents emphasized it."

2. You will notice that in Kahl's list of reasons why the working-class boys did well in school little mention is made of the school itself as a reason; there is no mention of teachers, classes, books, or other educational experiences. The strongest reasons for doing well in school, it would seem, are all outside the school. Indeed, if the student cannot do well at certain

[1] *Ibid.*, pp. 200–201.

activities outside the classroom, like sports or socializing, he may then do his homework as compensation. Assuming that Kahl's conclusions are essentially correct, how do you explain this state of affairs?

DOES THE SOCIAL CLIMATE OF THE SCHOOL MAKE A DIFFERENCE IN THE STUDENT'S STRIVING?

Thus far we have looked at the personal problems growing out of the home environment of the working-class boy who strives to improve his social status through education. Let us turn to the school as a factor in his striving. Will the type of school he attends make any difference? That is, will it help or hinder the working-class child if he attends a school which enrolls children who are primarily from the middle class? The question is a crucial one today when lower-class Negro children are being integrated into middle-class white schools, and in some cases where middle-class white children are being transferred to integrated schools to achieve a racial balance. Will the new climate have a salutary impact upon their learning? What we are really asking is: What influence does the immediate environment of the school have on the educational and occupational aspirations of the child?

This question has other practical implications. School districting tends to segregate children from different social and economic strata into different schools. Consequently, school student bodies have different attitudes toward educational achievement and college attendance. They tend to reflect the social-class aspirations of the parents in the community. Will children from lower social classes be influenced positively if they are permitted to attend schools in which the student bodies have higher educational aspirations than their own?

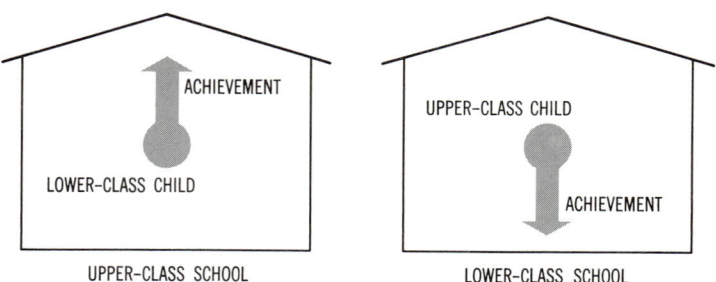

Fig. 9-1   Does the social climate of the school make a difference in students' striving?

Conversely, are the aspirations of children of middle-class families downgraded when they attend a predominantly working-class school?

Alan B. Wilson presents evidence in the affirmative.[2] The data for Wilson's study were provided by a survey of students' interests as related to their success in school and their decisions about educational and occupational specialization. The survey gathered information about students in 13 high schools in and around the San Francisco-Oakland Bay area. Wilson ranked the schools on the basis of the educational and occupational status of the populations from which their student bodies were drawn. Census data were used for this purpose. In addition, impressions of the school "atmospheres" were obtained while observing students in classrooms, halls, and playgrounds. With this data the schools were divided into three categories—Group A: upper-white collar, Group B: lower-white collar, and Group C: industrial. The social-class position of each child in the study was determined by the father's occupation and education and the mother's education. The educational aspirations of the students were determined by a written test.

Wilson discovered that the norms of the schools did indeed make a difference in the aspirations of an individual student. For example, 93 percent of the sons of professional men in the "upper-white collar" schools wanted to go to college. On the other hand, less than two-thirds of the sons of professional men in "industrial" schools wished to do so. In the middle-class schools more than one-half of the sons of working-class parents wished to go to college. On the other hand, in the working-class schools only one-third of the sons of workers wanted to go to college.

Wilson also studied the influence of the school environment upon the high achievers in the different schools. He found that "high achievers are less likely to wish to go to college if they attend a working-class school and conversely, that low achievers are more apt to go to college if they attend a middle-class school."[3]

3. What was the dominant value of the high school you attended in respect to educational achievement? What do you think caused the school to have this dominant value? Do you think this dominant value influenced your own educational choices? How?

Evidence indicates that the school environment indeed influences a child's achievement motivation. The student who is in a school

[2] Alan B. Wilson, "Residential Segregation of Social Classes and Aspirations of High School Boys," *American Sociological Review*, Volume 24, No. 6, December 1959, pp. 836–845.

[3] *Ibid.*, p. 843.

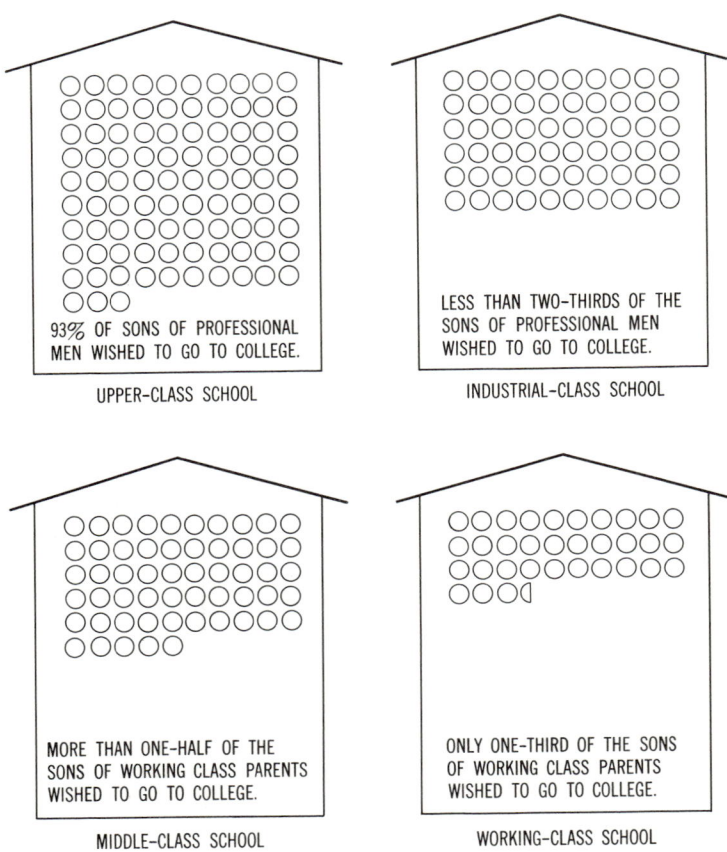

Fig. 9-2 Individual students are drawn toward the achievement norms of the school.

where the dominant values are upward tends himself to have upward motivations. Conversely, the student who is in a school whose dominant values are lower class tends himself to have lower educational aspirations.

HOW DOES ENVIRONMENT INFLUENCE INTELLECTUAL PERFORMANCE?

We indicated earlier that the student's social-class values as conveyed by his parents have a direct bearing upon his educational and occupational aspirations. We now ask: Does the social-class position of the student's parents also influence his mental ability? If so, how?

We would suspect that the student's home environment has strong influence upon his intellectual performance. We can ask, then, what are the conditions in the home which bear upon the child's ability to perform well mentally? B. S. Bloom suggests that the following five conditions, if present in the home environment, can encourage the growth of mental ability.[4] Children tend to perform better intellectually (1) if the parents hold high intellectual aspirations for the child; (2) if the parents furnish reinforcements for different types of intellectual performance; (3) if the parents provide learning opportunities both inside and outside the school; (4) if value is placed on intellectual performance; and (5) if intellectual work habits are emphasized in the home.

It is clear that these conditions are more likely to be found in middle- rather than lower-class homes. Thus, the child in the lower-class home is not exposed to the stimulating conditions which encourage intellectual development. It is not surprising that he tends to score lower in mental aptitude tests than the middle-class child.

4. In what social class are you likely to find homes in which the following occur or are present?

a. A child's desk for doing homework
b. The *National Geographic* magazine
c. The parents do not go inside the child's school
d. The children do not play outside their immediate neighborhood
e. A dictionary or encyclopedia
f. Parents take children to museums
g. Children take private music lessions
h. Children's report cards are not discussed

There have been a number of investigations designed to study the mental abilities of children in different social classes. Most of them show the expected results. Robert J. Havighurst and F. H. Breese studied the relation between ability and social status among 13-year-old children in a Midwestern community.[5] They found significant differences among social-class groups for all the primary mental abilities studied, including ability to handle numbers, verbal comprehension, understanding space relationships, word fluency, reasoning, and memory.

[4] B. S. Bloom, *Stability and Change in Human Characteristics,* New York, John Wiley and Sons, Inc., 1964.

[5] R. J. Havighurst and F. H. Breese, "Relation Between Ability and Social Status in a Midwestern Community. III, Primary Mental Abilities." *Journal of Educational Psychology,* Volume 38, 1947, pp. 241–247.

Gerald S. Lesser, Gordon Fifer, and Donald H. Clark studied the mental abilities of 6-year-old children in different social and cultural groups in New York City.[6] In this investigation first-grade children were studied from both middle- and lower-class families among Puerto Rican, Negro, Chinese, and Jewish cultural groups. The hypothesis tested by the study was: "Significant differences exist among groups of children from different social class and cultural backgrounds in each of four mental ability areas, i.e., space conceptualization, verbal ability, number facility, and reasoning ability."[7] This investigation confirmed the hypothesis. The results were essentially the same as those found by Havighurst and Breese, namely that social class consistently influenced the mental abilities of children. The level of the child's social class is positively related to the level of his performance on mental ability tests.

We should be cautious about interpreting research which finds a positive correlation between mental ability and social class. First, we should keep in mind that mental ability is not a fixed gift which is distributed along social-class lines. The middle-class child does not automatically inherit high mental ability any more than the lower-class child automatically inherits low mental ability. Both may inherit exactly the same biological potential for developing mental ability. What the research does say is this: environment, which is associated with social class, does make a tremendous difference in the development of the inherited capacity for mental growth, be that capacity high or low.

Second, in interpreting such research we should bear in mind that we are talking about mental ability *as we measure it*. We shall point out in Chapter 10 that children of the lower classes are under severe handicap in taking standard mental ability tests based on middle-class values which are frequently foreign to them. Intelligence tests require verbal ability in which lower-class children are usually deficient. When these children are given nonverbal mental tests they frequently do surprisingly well.

Finally, lower-class children who do poorly on mental-ability tests frequently do better on the same tests after they are put in a richer environment which stimulates the growth of mental abilities. The ability to grow mentally is as much a part of a normal child's endow-

[6] Gerald S. Lesser, Gordon Fifer, and Donald H. Clark, "Mental Abilities of Children in Different Social and Cultural Groups," Cooperative Research Project No. 1635, Cooperative Research Program, Office of Education, U. S. Department of Health, Education, and Welfare, 1964.

[7] *Ibid.*, p. 19.

ment as the ability to grow physically. Herein lies the challenge to the teacher and the school. The school is an important part of the child's total environment. How can the school provide the child with the kind of environment which will enable him to reach the full potential of his intellectual growth? How can the school help the child who strives to move up?

5. Each teacher faces the question of what *he* will do in *his* classroom to create the kind of environment which helps students to move up. What would you do?

THE CHILDREN ON THE OPPOSITE SIDE OF THE STREET: A CASE STUDY

We examine now a case study in social-class attitudes toward education. This study summarizes the substance of this and the three previous chapters on the family, peer groups, and social class. The case brings into sharp focus what each teacher needs to understand about social-class differences in education. Most of all, the case illustrates quite dramatically how different social environments influence the strivings of students. To the children on one side of the street moving up is built in and natural, while to those on the other side of the street it is foreign.

In this study Samuel Tenenbaum tells about what happened to his middle-class neighborhood on the West Side of Manhattan when the large hotel across the street from the apartment house in which he lived began to be used by the city to house indigent families.[8] Almost overnight the great hotel began to seethe with life, and the streets were filled with hordes of children, "like milling cattle." They shouted and screamed, ran in packs, and expressed their violence in constant fighting. The streets became cluttered with debris dropped from the windows above. Nobody cared. This comparatively quiet, middle-class neighborhood soon took on all the aspects of a slum block "and some of the aspects of a perpetual carnival." Through it all Tenenbaum's own apartment building remained a bastion of middle-class values. Tenenbaum says: [9]

"What I was witnessing had enormous meaning for me as a student of education and as one who teaches future teachers. I thought I knew the problem of the lower-class student; it is all explained in

[8] Samuel Tenenbaum, "The Teacher, the Middle Class, the Lower Class," *Phi Delta Kappan*, Volume XLV, No. 2, 1963, pp. 82–86.
[9] *Ibid.*, pp. 84–86.

the textbook. Like other instructors, I have discussed the problem in polite, academic terms. But this experience made me see clearly and vividly, as nothing else has, how farfetched and remote is our present school system for these children—in philosophy, methodology, approach, values, and meaning.

"In contrast to the lower-class children, how preciously kept is each child in our house; how carefully clothed; how carefully guarded; how often admonished by parents, grandparents, relatives, and friends. In the elevator, the icy tone of the father to his seven-year-old son: 'Is that hat glued on to your head, John?' How quickly and politely that hat comes off. How often are they shown pride and love. 'My son is the valedictorian of his class. He plans to go to Harvard, get his Ph.D., and teach chemistry.' Even our doorman, hard and brusque and violent with lower-class children, takes on a different tone and manner with the building children; to them he is gentle and tender and protective. The children themselves for the most part are loving and lovable. As they imbibe attention and love, as these qualities are poured into them, they have them to give out. If at times the children become rambunctious, the doorman finds it sufficient to threaten them with parental disclosure and they fall in line. There is no discipline problem. From infancy on, they experience discipline.

"These children have pride and are conscious of family position. Even if you are a stranger, they will inform you that their father, a lawyer, is involved in some famous current trial; or he has been called to Washington on an important mission; or that their father or grandfather owns this well-known establishment or business. And they tell you with equal pride what they themselves plan to be; and they act as if they have already achieved it and have a right to all the honors thereof.

"On school holidays our building takes on a festive air as the children come from out-of-town schools and colleges. You see a little boy with a ramrod figure sporting a magnificent uniform; he attends a military academy. Parents take special pride in introducing children all around. For these holidays parents have a well-planned schedule —theaters, lunches downtown, visiting and inter-visiting, parties that their children give and parties that they go to. The building is full of young people coming and going; it is really more pleasant and exciting.

"Yes, the children in this middle-class building are solicitously nurtured. Just as the parents seem to have purpose and direction for themselves, so the children seem also to have imbibed purpose and direction. Some of them, still in elementary school, speak of college and careers. Coming home in the afternoon, they hold their books tightly and neatly; for it is obvious that for them books represent important and powerful tools for the future."

6. Here are children who are conditioned by the environment to move up. They start well up the ladder. Assume you had these children in your classroom. How would you teach them?

"What a stark contrast are these children on the opposite side of the street! These children seem to have no purpose, no objective; they seem to live for the moment, and the big objective is to make this moment pass away as amusingly and excitingly as possible. And no matter what, they seem a lot more bored and idle than the middle-class children. They hang around, in gangs or small groups, and in boredom they poke at one another or get into mischief; they are ready for any or everything, but mostly nothing happens and there they are, hanging around in idleness.

"Even when playing near the house, the children in our building go to the parks already referred to, and they participate in organized games, or if not, they telephone to a friend or friends to meet and play together. In contrast, the children on the opposite street have many of the characteristics of neglected alley cats, growing up in a fierce, hostile jungle. The children from the two sides of the street never mix. Since the invasion of this new element, the children in our building are more closely supervised than ever; they are so apart in thinking and feeling that functionally they are like two different species.

"As I saw these two groups first-hand, I understood how easily middle-class children fit conventional school systems; how almost from infancy they have been trained for the role of a good, conforming member of this institution; and how easily and naturally their middle-class teachers would respond with understanding and affection.

"Also, I could see how wrong, how incongruous and meaningless this school was for lower-class children; how their very being was an irritant to it, and it to them; how ill-prepared they were for the demands of the school; how what they were and how they lived would elicit from their middle-class teachers scorn, resentment, rejection, hostility, and—worst of all—how these children would create in their teachers fear, a physical, sickening fear, as thirty or forty of them crowded together in one room hour after hour, day after day. This was the most demoralizing feature of all. For once fear sets in, you can no longer understand, appreciate, or help; what you want is distance, separation, safety; or if this is impossible, you want the backing of superior strength or a counter fear; and one cannot educate or help another human being through force of fear."

7. Do you think children on different sides of the street require different school discipline? Would you use force with the lower-class children?

"As I thought of what was happening to my block, I was astonished to realize how in nearly all respects our teachers respond to lower-class children just as my house neighbors do. They cannot understand their idleness, their purposelessness, their lack of ambition. They regard such traits as some congenital evil. Like my neighbors, they are indignant and shocked by their sexual frankness, and are astonished and chagrined by parental indifference to children's progress in school. When parents do come to school they may even side with the child against the teacher. Like my neighbors, teachers remain in a perpetual state of fear of these children, at their acting out, their defiance of discipline, their destructiveness and vandalism. 'Look at what they did!' a teacher will say, pointing to a desk ripped open or shattered panes of glass, speaking as if some holy altar had been violated. Looking at these lower-class children distantly, unapprovingly, and judgmentally, as my neighbors did, many teachers feel trapped, frightened, helpless. Like my neighbors, when a child gets into trouble with the law, they often take a smug satisfaction in the tragedy, as if their original judgment had been vindicated. 'I knew he would come to a bad end.' Middle-class virtue is written all over them.

"A good case can be and has been made that the only purpose of our educational system is to inculcate middle-class values, to create a middle-class person; and its purpose is not at all to transmit knowledge and subject matter. If this is true, and I am beginning to feel that it is, the main task of our schools, to repeat, is to train children in the proprieties, the conventions, the manners, the sexual restraints, the respect for private property of the middle class; and also to promote such middle-class virtues as hard work, sportsmanship, and ambition—especially ambition. The aim becomes to create a gentleman, a person striving for high achievement, so that he can attain the middle-class ideal: money, fame, a lavish house in the suburbs, public honors, etc."

8. Do you agree or disagree with Tenenbaum that this should be the main task of the schools? Why?

"I now perceive more clearly why lower-class children are such problems in school, why they do so poorly, why they are so alien to this institution, why they stand out like sore thumbs. Bluntly put, they don't fit in at all with what the schools and teachers demand, want, and expect.

"I now understand why even bright lower-class children do not do nearly as well in school as middle-class children of equal and even lower ability; why bright lower-class children drop out of school even when intellectually capable of doing the work. They never feel part of the institution, their school is not theirs, their team is not theirs, their classmates are not theirs.

"Just as the children in my building did not mix with the children on the hotel side of the block, so they do not mix in school. But here in school middle-class children are on home ground; it is their school, their teachers, their clubs, their team, their classmates. Parents of lower-class children also feel strange and remote from the institution, frightened by its conventions. Sometimes a lower-class child, through the influence of some good, loving, middle-class person, generally a teacher, begins to aspire to middle-class status. The parents, instead of reinforcing middle-class values, may resent these new feelings in the child and fear that he is being alienated from them; they will try to keep the child in their own class. I know a fine and able student who applied for a scholarship and was accepted by a prestige college. Her father, a laborer, was incensed at the whole idea. We were turning his daughter's head. A good girl should get a job, come home, help her mother, and get married. When he was told that college and marriage are not incompatible, he showed every doubt that the two go together. Then he took another tack. Deep study in college, he said, affects the head, and his daughter had fragile health; he didn't want her to become rattle-brained. Finally, he trotted out his last argument: he wasn't going to have his daughter gallivanting off and mixing with those snobs and good-for-nothings. The father won out."

9. In this case the school acted as an agent of change, placing its own values over those of the parent. Even though it lost the case, do you think the school was justified in urging the girl to move up against the father's wishes? What are your reasons for thinking as you do?

"It also happens, undoubtedly with greater frequency in America than in any other major culture, that a lower-class child does break out of his group to enter the middle class. A play, 'The Corn Is Green,' deals with this theme. It is the true account of a Welsh boy whose teacher, Miss Cooke, out of dedication and devotion, held the youth steadfast in his studies. After many trials, the young man passed his examinations and won an Oxford scholarship. The son of a nursemaid and a seaman, he became an eminent playwright, actor, and director, and, incidentally, the author of 'The Corn Is Green.'

"It sometimes happens that a member of the middle class will flunk out of his class also, although this is quite rare, as a review of your own experience will indicate. Middle-class parents will go to any extreme to save their children for middle-class status. How would an eminent and respected professional person regard his son who worked as a janitor or as a laborer, although the young man might be quite happy with his work and the work right for him? Middle-class parents attempt all kinds of shenanigans to keep their offspring in their class. We all know of the student who fails at a good university, whereupon the parents find a mediocre school where he can obtain the degree. The parents rejoice, for the boy is now a college graduate; he has achieved middle-class status and need not disgrace the family."

10. Let us assume that you are the teacher of a middle-class student who lacks apparent ability to do college work. Yet his parents insist upon his attending college and ask for your assistance in his being admitted to college. How do you think you would react as teacher?

"I am beginning to feel that if we want to help lower-class children we will have to reorient our thinking and philosophy. We will have to adopt fundamental reforms, radical and crucial in nature, so that the school as an institution will be more nearly in conformity with the cultural and behavioral patterns of this class. I am beginning to think that it might be best if we would enlist in this task the more able and brighter lower-class members, with the hope that they will be better able to cope with the lower-class child. Little good can come to any child when a teacher relates to him with fear and condemnation.

"What has been a national fetish, almost religious in fervor, is the effort to shape all children, regardless of their state or condition, in the middle-class mold. It would appear that the chief end of man is to glorify the middle class. When teachers fail at this task, they regard themselves and the school as failures. I believe that until now we have done a remarkable job in converting this 'melting pot' material into a sort of middle-class stew, although frequently of questionable taste and quality."

Tenenbaum's revealing narrative poses questions about the teaching of educationally disadvantaged children which we need to confront. In Chapter 10 we seek answers to these questions: Who are the educationally disadvantaged children? What are they like? How may they be most effectively taught?

REFERENCES

Paperbacks

Education in Depressed Areas. A. Harry Passow, Editor. Teachers College, Teachers College Press, 525 West 120 St., New York ($2.50).

Education in Urban Society. B. J. Chandler, Lindley J. Stiles, and John I. Kitsuse. (Orig.) Dodd, Mead and Co., 432 Park Ave. South, New York ($3.75).

Educational Issues in a Changing Society. (2nd Rev. Ed., Orig.) August Kerber and Wilfred Smith, Editors. (WB3) Wayne State University Press, 5980 Cass, Detroit, Mich. ($3.95).

Excellence: Can We Be Equal and Excellent Too? John W. Gardner. (CN/3) Harper Colophon Books, 49 E. 33rd St., New York ($1.45).

Gang: A Study of 1,313 Gangs in Chicago. Frederic M. Thrasher. Abr. and Intro. by James F. Short, Jr. (Illus. Orig.) (P138) Phoenix Books, University of Chicago Press, 5750 Ellis Ave., Chicago, Ill. ($2.95).

New Perspectives on Poverty. Arthur B. Shostak and William Gomberg, Editors. (Orig.) Prentice-Hall, Englewood Cliffs, N. J. ($1.95).

Poverty in America. Margaret S. Gordon, Editor. (Orig.) Chandler Publishing Co., 124 Spear St., San Francisco, Calif. ($2.50).

Poverty: Its Roots and Its Future. Hyman Lumer. (Orig.) (LNW-2) New World Paperbacks, International Publishers, 381 Park Ave. South, New York (95¢).

Books

Cloward, Richard A., and Lloyd E. Ohlin, *Delinquency and Opportunity: A Theory of Delinquent Groups.* New York: The Free Press of Glencoe, 1963. The authors explain delinquency in terms of differential opportunity systems.

Drophin, Stan, Harold Full, and Ernest Schwarcz, *Contemporary American Education: An Anthology of Issues, Problems, Challenges.* New York: Macmillan Co., 1965. In section III Robert Havighurst discusses social class and education.

Ginzberg, Eli, John L. Herma, et al., *Talent and Performance.* New York: Columbia University Press, 1964. The authors are interested in the processes by which an individual, with his various interests, capacities, and values, tries to shape a career in the real world with its range of opportunities and barriers.

Havemann, Ernest, and Patricia Salter West, *They Went to College.* New York: Harcourt, Brace and Co., 1952. This book is based on a large survey of college graduates in the United States.

Landis, Paul H., *Adolescence and Youth, The Process of Maturing*, Second Edition. New York: McGraw-Hill Book Co., 1952. The last section of the book is concerned with the adolescent in the school.

McClelland, David C., et al., *Talent and Society: New Perspectives in the Identification of Talent.* Princeton, N. J.: D. Van Nostrand Co., 1958. Chapter III, on achievement and social status, presents three case studies. Chapter IV discusses family interaction, values, and achievement.

Periodicals

Ellis, Robert A., and Clayton W. Lane, "Structural Supports for Upward Mobility," *American Sociological Review*, Vol. 28, No. 5, May 1963, pp. 743–756. This study of lower-class youth implies that the push for mobility has its roots in the home and its outside support in the teacher.

Goldrich, Daniel, "Peasants' Sons in City Schools, An Inquiry into the Politics of Urbanization in Panama and Costa Rica," *Human Organization*, Vol. 24, No. 4, Winter 1964, pp. 328–333. This study suggests that only the stable families among the agrarian lower class have the initiative and resources to support the secondary education of their sons in the city.

Goodlad, John I., "Understanding the Self in the School Setting," *Childhood Education*, Vol. XLI, No. 1, 1964, pp. 9–14. The author feels that the school must provide enough alternatives to meet the needs of all children.

Pine, Gerald J., "Occupational and Educational Aspirations and Delinquent Behavior," *Vocational Guidance Quarterly*, Vol. 13, No. 2, Winter 1964–65, pp. 107–112. Students who desired to go to college were less involved in delinquent behavior than those who had only work plans after high school.

Simpson, Richard L., "Parental Influence, Anticipatory Socialization, and Social Mobility," *American Sociological Review*, Vol. 27, No. 4, 1962, pp. 517–522. Lower-class adolescent boys aspire to middle-class norms when encouraged to do so by parents, and when aspirations are reinforced by the peer group association.

Spangen, Berthe, "Impressions of a Volunteer Literacy Worker in Bolivia," *The Student*, Vol. VIII, No. 5, May 1964, pp. 3–10. This article illustrates some of the problems faced by a student worker attempting to change the educational level of an illiterate community.

IO

Teaching Socially
Disadvantaged Students

"The school cannot make the sun rise, but it can let in the light."

CHILDREN WITHOUT

The implication of the preceding three chapters is clear: educational opportunities are not equal for all students. Many children run the education race under severe handicaps owing to circumstances of family, peer group, or social class. These children start school at a disadvantage and, unless something is done to assist them, the disadvantage deepens with time until many of them finally drop out.

In this chapter we refer to these children as "socially disadvantaged." We use the term as a convenient abbreviation to cover a large group of factors which handicap children in school and keep them from fully using their potential capacities. These factors include low income, low social-class status, low educational level of parents, and small "life space." Socially disadvantaged children tend to live in poor housing, come from broken homes, and experience poor health conditions. If they are Negro children, they carry the additional handicap of problems and attitudes related to race. When we use the term "socially disadvantaged," we refer to all those social factors that work against the child's learning in school.

In this chapter we ask: What should and can the school do for these children? What can the school do for children like those in the following narrative in order to keep them from experiencing the ominous future which is predicted for them? [1]

" 'I'm going to be a lawyer,' said Harry, aged six. 'Lawyers make good money. I'm going to keep my money.'

[1] Ben H. Bagdikian, "The Invisible Americans," *Saturday Evening Post*, Volume 236, No. 45, December 21–28, 1963, pp. 27–38.

" 'I'm going to be a doctor,' said his seven-year-old brother firmly, 'and I'm going to take care of my family.'

"Their eight-year-old sister announced serenely, 'I'm going to be a nurse in a big hospital and wear a real uniform and help people.'

"The sweet optimism of youth could have been heard in millions of American homes, but this home was rather special.

"Though it was midafternoon, the tenement was dark. Gray plastic sheeting was tacked to the insides of the windows. Plaster was off part of the ceiling and walls, and strands of hair on laths trembled with the passing wind from outside. Double doors opened onto the kitchen, which was almost invisible. Its windows, too, were sealed with opaque plastic, presumably to preserve heat. But the darkness was thickened by a crisscross of clothes-lines that filled the room with hanging rags of clothes. In one corner of the kitchen was a table with three legs and one chair. In another was a stove bearing a pan of cold soapy water with clothes soaking, next to it a pan of cold beans and beside that a crusted frying pan bearing one single short rib congealed with fat. Through one kitchen door was a bathroom with the toilet boarded over; it had frozen and burst in the winter cold. Through another door was 'the kids' room,' two beds for seven children. Neither bed had a mattress; the children slept on the springs.

" 'Look at this book I got from school,' Harry said. 'Want to hear me read?'

"Harry read about Dick and Jane and their dog, Spot. Dick and Jane were clean-cut, well-dressed Anglo-Saxon children who lived behind a white picket fence in a red-roofed cottage with geraniums in the window. Their mother was a smiling blond with clear, square teeth. Their father wore a snap-brim hat, a conservative suit, and carried a briefcase. And they all lived happily in a schoolbook called *Friends and Neighbors.*

"Little Harry might as well have been reading science fiction. His own family had never in his memory eaten a meal together—there were not enough chairs, dishes or forks. The mother's role or the oldest daughter's at mealtime was to watch as each child took a portion of the pot on the stove to make sure no one took more than his share.

"But Harry was still eager to please. He had not yet learned that other people expected him to be like Dick and his sister to be like Jane, to have parents like Dick and Jane's, to live in a house like Dick and Jane, and that as a Negro slum kid all of this was as remote to him as the canals of Mars. And unless he were uncommonly lucky, this book and the school would soon seem as remote." [2]

What can the school do to lessen the chances that for these children "this book and school" will seem as remote as the "canals of Mars"?

THE GROWING COMMITMENT TO SOCIALLY DISADVANTAGED CHILDREN

One thing becomes increasingly clear in modern America: there is a growing concern for these children. Far as we are from achieving equality of educational opportunity, the social policy of America as embodied in official acts and public conscience makes clear that these children are given high priority. The massive government assault on poverty, widening racial integration in schools, the daily reminders about the build-up of "social dynamite" in the slums, the extensive efforts of private agencies, and the extended efforts of public schools, all speak of a national determination to extend political democracy to include educational democracy. The right to an education is becoming as sacred as the right to vote. Indeed there is a fresh awareness that these two rights are intertwined and interdependent. The right to vote is meaningless without the right to be educated, and vice versa.

1. Current newspapers and magazines feature many stories and articles related to educating socially disadvantaged children. Summarize one of these features for class discussion.

In this chapter, we deal with crucial questions in national policy: How can the nation's will with respect to the disadvantaged child be carried out in the schools? How can educational opportunity be made, if not equal, then more equal than at present? These questions lay upon all who teach, all who administer education, indeed upon all citizens; they reflect heavy responsibilities. For the problem is not only national; it is also local, and it is personal. The teacher who works with a disadvantaged child in the classroom embodies within his effort a national mandate. The local citizen who votes to enable the schools to extend their services to underprivileged children is responding locally to a national concern.

If the problem is both national and local, it is also tough and complex. Behind the disadvantaged child stand disadvantaged families, peer groups, and social classes. The school is but one of many agen-

[2] *Ibid.*, pp. 37–38.

cies whose services are essential in an attack upon the problem. Because of the limitations of space we cannot deal with the many agencies beyond the school which are attacking the problem from community, state, and national levels. Here we focus on the schools and the teachers. What must they understand about educating the socially disadvantaged child? What can they do?

A NEW FRONTIER IN EDUCATION

Educating the socially disadvantaged child is a new frontier in education as exciting as any we have ever undertaken. It may well be regarded as monumental an undertaking as the establishment of free schools along the wide American frontier one hundred and more years ago. From that effort emerged an educated American middle class capable of building the professions, business, and industry. That effort was regarded by many as too revolutionary at the time, but the revolution proved its worth.

Now we are being tested to see whether we can extend that revolution in educational opportunity to the lower classes to make complete what the first revolution started.

How extensive is this new frontier in education? How likely is the teacher in today's classrooms to be touched by it? If we define this new frontier as the effort to teach children to their highest abilities regardless of their social handicaps, the frontier is indeed as wide as our earlier geographic frontier. It is likely that few teachers will be untouched by the problem of educating the disadvantaged child.

The Broad Scope of This Frontier

First, the frontier extends across the South, where Negro children in growing numbers are entering integrated schools. Many of these children are struggling to pull themselves up. They are looking to the schools to help them be what they feel they can be.

Second, it extends through the mountains of the South where many white people are growing restless with their lot and demanding that their children have an education to permit them to compete in the modern world. Here is a voice which is representative of these parents: [3]

" 'Y'know, . . . the things that get me are the little things.' He paused to roll another cigarette with one hand. 'I want the kids to graduate from school. That's the only hope they got to get out and

[3] "This Is Ellis Grigsby's Story," *Newsweek,* Volume LXI, No. 13, April 1, 1963, p. 61.

get jobs. They got to buy clothes and all, and the class ring. I swear, I'll starve to do it. I remember when I was a kid—the things I wanted so fiercely. . . .'

"There was a television set in the corner, plugged into the naked overhead light. 'I bought that secondhand, when I was working,' Grigsby said defensively. 'I know folks wonder why you're on commodities and still have a TV, but it's just a little something to brighten things.'"

Third, this new educational frontier extends into the big cities of the North and West. Demands for the end of *de facto* segregation mean that more and more lower-class Negro children are entering schools where previously only white middle-class children attended. Further, the whites from the Southern mountain region continue to stream into Northern cities where their children are ill-prepared for school and the schools are ill-prepared to teach them. Robert J. Havighurst has estimated that a third of the children now enrolled in Chicago elementary and high schools may be regarded as socially disadvantaged.[4]

In cities of the Eastern seaboard Puerto Rican and Negro children swell the enrollments of slum schools. In cities of the West, Mexican-American children and others from deprived backgrounds create new and perplexing problems for the schools.

Finally, suburban schools do not escape the problem of educating children from lower-class groups. The American urge to "get ahead," to "have a back yard of our own," drives the more fortunate members of the lower and working classes to the suburbs. When they can these people leave the cities, push out into the suburbs, to improve living and education for their children. This upward drive inevitably means that their children are also reaching for the next level of educational achievement. They are not disadvantaged in the sense that slum children are, but they are learning new aspirations and forms of behavior. Frequently they don't "fit" into suburban schools and are at a distinct educational disadvantage.

The new educational frontier is indeed wide and it is the wise teachers and school systems who prepare to master it. For the schools the problem is clear: How can children who are socially disadvantaged be given opportunities to learn which are roughly equal to those of other children? Or, as a more modest goal, how can the gap in educational opportunity be narrowed?

[4] Robert J. Havighurst, *The Public Schools of Chicago*, Chicago, The Board of Education, 1964, p. 60.

2. Visit a teacher who works with socially disadvantaged children. Find out what you can about these children—how they differ from other children, what kind of homes they come from, and how they learn.

THE DISADVANTAGED CHILD'S ATTITUDE TOWARD SCHOOL

Disadvantaged children display a wide range of reactions to the schools. Occasionally they exhibit high motivations to learn. They are more likely to display indifference and boredom and are sometimes openly rebellious in school. Notice the difference in these two students' reactions. The first example is related by a teacher of a Negro child in an integrated Southern school.[5]

"Roberta is the oldest of 11 children. She cooks, irons and scrubs. She helps her mother to rear her brothers and sisters. She even finds time to teach them to read.

" 'They're going to learn,' she says. 'I learned to read before I entered school. They had to move me up a grade I was so far ahead of the others. Then I read everything in the elementary school library and ran out of books before I got to the eighth grade. . . .'

"Roberta waited for more books, as she waited two winters for a warm coat. Since she now has access to a larger library she is seldom seen without an armload of books.

"There are few who notice her insatiable desire for knowledge, but Roberta doesn't appear to mind—not yet, anyway. Her faith in her own potential is deep. It is that beautiful, indomitable faith of youth.

"Therefore, she laughs lustily and goes rushing out of my office with that armload of books, and out the school door, and up the hill to her cabin. Each day, before the sun sets, she will do the work of another woman—a much older woman who has seen hard times and breadless days. When the little ones are bedded down, this 14-year-old girl will return to her borrowed books by lamplight. She must finish them on time; there is no money to pay library fines."

3. If you were to speculate about the positive factors in Roberta's deprived environment which cause her to have high educational aspirations, what would you say?

4. What do you gather from this teacher's story about her own attitude toward Roberta? What words give you the cues? What personal qualities do you think are required of a teacher who works with socially disadvantaged children?

[5] Margaret Anderson, "After Integration—'Higher Horizons,' " *New York Times Magazine,* Volume CXII, No. 38,438, April 21, 1963, p. 10.

Contrast now Roberta's attitude toward the school with that of these New York City slum children.[6]

"No matter what subject was being taught to the churning fourth-grade class in the New York slum school, it was usually the same story. The rhythm band practice broke into bedlam. The math class was stumped by six plus seven. Then it stalled trying to read 'Mew, mew,' said Puff.

" 'What will I do if you don't learn?' railed the frantic teacher. From the back of the classroom a voice yelled, 'Drop dead.' "

Clearly there is a need to understand all we can about the attitude and behavior of socially disadvantaged children. Good teaching must begin with that understanding.

FACTORS THAT SHAPE ATTITUDES TOWARD SCHOOL

The Tragic Cycle

There is in the attitude of the disadvantaged child a kind of tragic cycle of change which moves in the early years from acceptance of, even high interest in, the school, through growing boredom in the middle years, to outright rejection in the adolescent years. It is this cycle that needs to be broken if the disadvantaged child is to be educated. The good teacher will do all he can to help break it.

Harry, the boy who wanted to be a lawyer and "keep my money," his brother who wanted to be a doctor and "take care of my family," or his sister who wanted to be a nurse and "wear a real uniform and help people" represent socially disadvantaged children in the early years of this cycle. Their fascination with the story of Dick, Jane, and their dog, Spot, symbolizes their attitude toward the new horizons of the school. They do not yet see that the lives of Dick and Jane are really "science fiction" when compared to their own miserable circumstances. The narrator of this story anticipates the next stage in the tragic cycle when he predicts that unless they are "uncommonly lucky, this book and the school [will] soon seem as remote," as the "canals on Mars."

The scene from the New York City slum school represents children in the middle years of the tragic cycle. Their boredom and frustration with the school is embodied in their response to the teacher, "drop dead." Here is a portrait of teachers at work with children at this stage of the cycle.[7]

---

[6] "These Children Are at Stake," *Life*, Volume 52, No. 4, January 26, 1962, p. 58.

[7] *Ibid.*, p. 61.

"If the hubbub in her class ever threatens to build toward bedlam, teacher 'Frankie' Leicher looses an ear-splitting blast on her referee's whistle. Frankie is active in community work and popular among the children. But in extreme situations, to get her teaching done, she uses any device at hand to get quiet.

"A good disciplinarian like Frankie really rules by her commanding, affectionate presence. But some teachers fear or dislike their pupils, and the children with devilish intuition spot this. Triggered by any disturbance, they will throw spitballs, drop books, overturn chairs or just wander aimlessly about the room. When the teacher yells at one child, the whole class may snicker. Weaker teachers go to pieces under this and in such schools the problem is especially serious. Every year in this school one out of five experienced teachers leaves because of marriage or moving away—or simply because she cannot cope with the tough job. The replacements are usually barely trained beginners, assigned at random.

"But for even the best teachers the energy-sapping process of staying on top of the class means punctuating sentences with 'You! Cut that out,' 'Quiet down,' 'Stop that.' The extreme cases, pupils who throw tantrums or run from the room, are taken over by the adored assistant principal, Miss Osheroff. She gentles the hysterical child with motherly warmth as she takes the miscreant along on her rounds about the school."

These children are potential candidates for the final scene in the tragic cycle, dropping out.

5. Many school systems have a seniority system which permits those teachers with seniority to select the schools they want to teach in. As a result veteran teachers take the better schools, leaving the difficult ones to beginning teachers. Do you see problems in this procedure? Do you think that school systems would be justified in offering special salary inducements to teachers in lower-class schools?

Let us look now more closely at the factors that create this changing-attitude cycle of the disadvantaged child.

The Key: the Elementary School Years

In many ways the environment in the elementary school gives original shape to the disadvantaged child's attitude toward school. These are the years in which he builds a self-concept of himself as a student. The grades he receives, the support he gets from his teacher and peers, all cause him to think of himself as a student in a certain way.

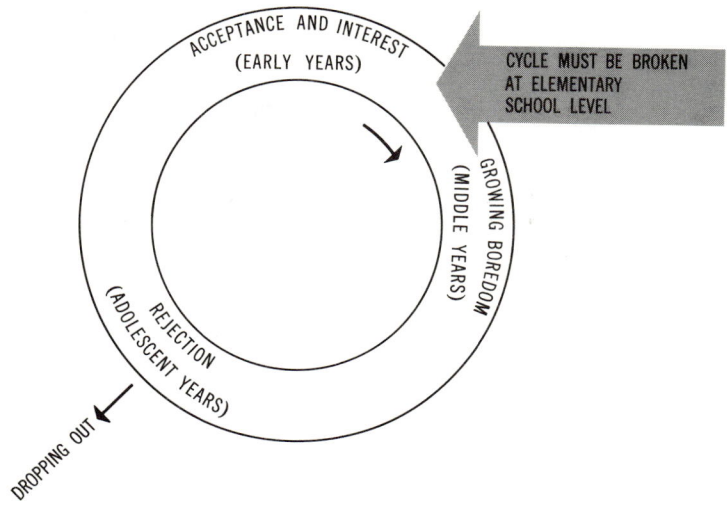

Fig. 10-1 The disadvantaged child's attitude toward school moves through a tragic cycle from high interest during the early years to rejection in the adolescent years.

In the elementary years his parents are also shaping his attitudes toward school. If he does well on his tests his parents are likely to regard him as "smart," if poorly, "dumb." In this way parents "place" their children and thus reinforce the self-concept of the child. The parents of socially disadvantaged children are likely to be tolerant of individual differences, more so than middle-class parents, and they are not surprised if some of their children are "smart," and some "dumb." Because they did not do very well in school themselves, they do not expect a great deal from their children. If their children are good with books, fine; if they are not, qualities such as manual skills can be stressed.

If the child does well, his parents will expect him to continue to do well. If he slips they are likely to blame him for being lazy or "running around with the wrong boys." The expectation is that if the child once demonstrates that he can do good schoolwork, his success is evidence that he can do better. Joseph A. Kahl in his study of "common boys" quotes a father who expresses this view: [8]

" 'John and his sister are the only two that have talent—I think

[8] Joseph A. Kahl, "Educational and Occupational Aspirations of Common Boys," *Harvard Educational Review,* Volume XXIII, No. 3, Summer 1953, p. 199.

those are the only two that are college timber. One of the boys is going to work with his hands—he hasn't said anything about it, but I can watch him. I can see that he wants to do carpentry or mechanical work, machine work of some kind. Couple of the children have been held back in school—none of them are as good as John. You know, I try and keep him from being too much a model for them to follow. I think it's good, but I don't want them to feel that they have to do as well as he can because I know they can't—he's exceptional.'"

6. Do you think a teacher may similarly "type" a student to the student's detriment? Do you think a teacher is more apt to "type" a socially disadvantaged student than one who is not disadvantaged? If so, why?

The elementary years, then, fix the child's attitude toward himself as student. In this process the teacher has a major role to play. If he helps to create in the child a positive attitude, makes it possible for him to experience some rewards in learning, and builds a good self-concept, the child enters the difficult years ahead with a better chance for success.

The Test: the Junior High School Years

By the time the socially disadvantaged child enters junior high school he knows how he ought to act as a student if he is to succeed as one. Knowing and doing are different things, however. For the child is now caught in cross-pressures. For the first time his deprived environment is becoming crucial. Up to this time the bright but socially disadvantaged child can do well in school. Now it becomes harder. The home environment makes it difficult to do homework: it is homework versus the gang, homework versus television, homework versus a part-time job to supplement the meager family income. The parents do not enforce doing homework. The crowded and noisy home itself works against it. The school is asking more of the child at the very time that it becomes difficult for him to produce more.

Other difficulties arise. By the end of junior high school a curriculum must be chosen among those offered by the particular school. Each program carries with it an expectation of the student. Students below the college preparatory curriculum simply are not expected to do as well, and this lower expectation sinks deeply into the attitude of the disadvantaged child. A child who is doing well in his schoolwork might like to try the college preparatory program, but he is uncertain. Where will the money come from? What will his friends think? Perhaps the school counselor himself reinforces the student's self-doubt. Knowing the child's circumstances, he counsels a more "realistic" trade, general, or commercial curriculum. If the student drops his aspiration a notch he also *drops his expectation of himself* a notch.

The selecting and sorting function of the school about which we spoke in Chapter 3 is now becoming apparent to the student. The school, by "placing" him, is shaping his attitude toward what he is able to do in school and toward the school itself. The impact of curriculum choice upon the student is expressed in this statement by one of the "common-man" boys studied by Kahl.[9]

" 'I chose commercial because it was sort of in-between the general and the college course. I didn't want to take the general course, figuring, oh, you know, people would say, "oh, he must be failing." I don't want to go to college; I don't have a brilliant mind.' "

7. What attitudes did the students take toward the several curricular streams in the high school you attended?

8. Did the curricular stream a student chose influence his own expectation of himself?

9. Did teachers hold different expectations of students in different curricular streams?

The Persuaders: the Peer Group

Peer-group pressures also make a constructive attitude toward schoolwork difficult. If the socially disadvantaged student wants to aim higher than his friends he may have to leave them, a difficult matter. He may become an isolate, or he may endeavor to make new friends.

This problem is most acute for the bright boy of the lower class who aspires to higher education. Most of his friends have no use for it and if he is to persist, he will have to "go it alone." The same problem for the bright and aspiring boy from the working class will be less acute, but nevertheless real. Some of his friends may share his position but many may not. The bright and aspiring youth of the middle class with high aspirations has the least difficulty of all. Because he is surrounded by others who are upwardly mobile, all he needs to do is to stay in the stream and ride its current.

Martin Deutsch summarizes the plight of the disadvantaged child in school this way: [10]

"For the lower-class child there is not the same contiguity or continuity, and he does not have the same coping mechanisms for inter-

---

[9] *Ibid.,* p. 199.

[10] Martin Deutsch, "Early Social Environment: Its Influence on School Adaptation," *The School Dropout,* Washington, National Education Association, 1964, pp. 90–91.

nalizing success or psychologically surviving failure in the formal learning setting. If the lower-class child starts to fail, he does not have the same kinds of operationally significant and functionally relevant support from his family or community—or from the school—that his counterpart has. Furthermore, because of the differences in preparation, he is more likely to experience failure. It might even be that both groups are equally motivated, in terms of quantity of motivation, but failure or lack of recognition for the middle-class child might only serve to channel his energies more narrowly, while for the lower-class child it early becomes dysfunctional with the effect of converting the original motivation into a rejection of intellectual striving."

Thus as the disadvantaged child moves through the cycle, intelligence alone is not enough. It may be enough for the middle-class youth but not for the disadvantaged youth. His problems in school increase with the years rather than diminish. The forces in the situation, if left alone to do their work, will pull him down. He will drop out.

10. Interview a student who has dropped out of school. (Better still, bring him to class for the interview.) Trace, if you can, the cycle of events which led to his dropping out. How are they alike and different from the cycle described here?

If this tragic cycle is to be reversed, teachers and schools must provide powerful constructive and counteracting forces. Some teachers and schools are doing precisely that, as we shall observe later in this chapter, but some are not. Note the factual and disturbing conclusion that Kahl drew about the teachers of the 24 "common-man" boys which he studied.[11] "There were no cases in which the boy found in schoolwork sufficient intellectual satisfactions to supply its own motivation. And there were no cases where a sympathetic and encouraging teacher had successfully stimulated a boy to high aspirations."

WHAT DOES EDUCATION MEAN TO THE DISADVANTAGED CHILD?

It is important for teachers to remember that education for the advantaged and disadvantaged child means quite different things. First, *the child from the middle class has developed an interest in learning for its own sake.* A good story carries its own sufficient reason for reading it. The unknown results of a science experiment provide suffi-

---

[11] Kahl, *op. cit.*, p. 201.

cient motivation for doing it. The acquisition of knowledge has become a habitual part of normal life activity and does not have to be connected to external rewards.

For the socially disadvantaged child, learning for its own sake carries no appeal. He must see immediate rewards in sight, preferably rewards of a concrete nature. Education, to be meaningful to this child, must be connected with the here and now in his environment. The teacher therefore seeks to reward his accomplishments immediately in a concrete way.

11. Can you suggest ways by which the teacher might reward accomplishments at once and in a concrete way?

Second, *the middle-class child is interested in his own growth and self-realization.* He looks for new experiences and is excited when he finds them. At home he has been encouraged to venture into new experiences which help to develop him as a person. At school he expects to do the same. The middle-class school, with its emphasis upon progressive methods, growth, and development is created to meet his needs.

The early environment of the disadvantaged child, by contrast, has not encouraged self-realization and expanding experience. Learning at home for this child means rigid rules to be followed. The progressive methods of learning in the school that emphasize creative activity are foreign to his nature. Education for him means a firm adult who holds him in line, prescribes what he should do, and thereby provides continuity with his home environment. It is important that the teacher understand the child's need for firm direction and close supervision.

12. Some children obviously do not need such a firm hand from the teacher. Let us suppose that the teacher has both types in one classroom. Do you see problems in giving differential treatment to children in the same room?

Third, *the disadvantaged student has various motivations for being in school, but most of them are utilitarian in nature.* If he sees a strong and not too distant connection between school and a job, he is more likely to stay in school. He would like to be able to pass the examination to get into military service, to become a fireman, a policeman, or a postal clerk. These are concrete goals which are meaningful to him, and he favors the kind of education that will help him achieve them. The school which demonstrates the connection between learning and job opportunity serves this student well.

Fourth, *closely connected with this youth's interest in utilitarian education is his disinterest in academic subjects.* He sees no future for him in such learning. It does not satisfy his need for immediate goals and rewards. Because he has not learned the middle-class value of deferred gratification, the subjects which are offered in trade and commercial programs are likely to be more attractive to him. Schools that serve these children need strong and attractive programs in the practical arts.

Finally, *education is a means for the disadvantaged child of gaining some control over his environment.* The more immediate the prospects for control, the better. He views the world about him as full of uncertainty and knows that much of it is beyond his comprehension. He is aware that modern science, technology, and ways of doing things are apt to pass him by unless he does something to exercise some measure of control over his environment and his future. He regards education as one means by which he may be able to do so. The good teacher helps the socially disadvantaged child to use education for this purpose.

Closely connected with the disadvantaged child's view of education are the reasons for his difficulty in school.

WHY DO SOCIALLY DISADVANTAGED CHILDREN ENCOUNTER DIFFICULTIES IN SCHOOL?

It is important for teachers to understand why socially disadvantaged children experience difficulty in school learning. It is all too easy to label disadvantaged children as "shiftless," "obstinate," "lazy," or "slow." These moralistic terms do not accurately describe the disadvantaged child, nor are they helpful in working with him. Let us see if we can be somewhat more precise in our diagnosis of the disadvantaged child's learning problems.

Bruno Bettelheim reminds us that a child's determination *not* to learn can often spring from wishes as positive and as strong as those that motivate the good learner.[12] Both the learner and the nonlearner wish to achieve success, but they have vastly different conceptions of what constitutes success. The learner sees success as the achievement of goals prescribed by the school. The nonlearner defines success as the achievement of goals other than those prescribed by the school. The socially disadvantaged child frequently seeks positive

[12] Bruno Bettelheim, "The Decision to Fail," *The School Review,* Volume 69, No. 4, Winter 1961, pp. 377–412.

goals which he can achieve only by rejecting the goals of the school. Let us look at some of these positive motives of the child which are incompatible with learning in school.

The Child May Not Wish to Do Better Than His Parents

For the socially disadvantaged child doing well in school means going beyond the educational level of his parents. This he may not wish to do. Bettelheim explains it this way: [13]

"The child does not wish to do better than his parents because he does not want to make them seem inferior. Typical for this source of learning difficulties is the wish of most children to look up to their parents. Out of the need to rely on them, they anxiously protect the image of their parents as the best of all parents. Because our dominant creed is that every new generation will do better than the last, it often overshadows the fact that many children have reason to wish the opposite. This emotional block to learning has a very strong, positive motivation.

"It is not as simple as if these parents might resent superiority in their children. On the contrary, most of them tell the child he must acquire a better education than they themselves were able to. Nevertheless the parent who, with the very best of intentions, tries to encourage his child in this way may still make him feel guilty about his better opportunities. In order to avoid feeling guilty, he may quit learning at exactly the point where the education of one of his parents stopped. I have observed dropouts, or the sudden appearance of severe learning blocks, in many high-school and college students, terminating a young person's education at exactly the point where that of a parent once ended."

13. Sometimes the teacher who wishes to encourage the child toward higher education levels may unwittingly cause the child to choose between the parents and the school. Such a child, without the teacher's knowledge, may, in his decision to fail, be expressing his deep loyalty to his parents. How do you think a teacher might better handle a problem like this?

The Child May Prefer His Own Set of Values

A second positive reason for not learning is closely akin to the first. The child may prefer his own set of values over those taught in the school. He is not convinced that the exchange is a good one. He is bright enough to know that accepting school values entails a basic

[13] *Ibid.,* p. 389.

change in his way of thinking and behaving. He knows that if he succeeds in school he will be pushed vocationally into new areas previously unknown in his family. He is not prepared to make the change.

Failing Is a Way of Gaining Status

Third, the socially disadvantaged child can gain status by being a poor student. His realistic appraisal of the classroom situation tells him that if he elects to compete as a good student, the competition is severe indeed. His chances of gaining recognition by this route are slim. If his temperament will permit him to accept an "only average" rung on the academic ladder, he may try to compete and settle for a second-best position. If, however, he has a strong need for status and recognition, he may find it satisfied only by being a nonlearner. This is a position in the class he can occupy, and it brings a kind of distinction and recognition which would otherwise be denied him.

Failing Is a Way to Protect Self-respect

The fourth positive reason for failing grows out of the third. Failing may be for the socially disadvantaged child a way of protecting his self-respect. Believing that he will fail even if he makes his best efforts to learn he protects his self-respect by deciding not to try. This is a deliberate act on his part and is calculated to help him find a unique self-identity among his fellow students.

Failing Reconfirms the Ability to Handle Failure

The final positive reason for failure is that it reconfirms for the child his ability to handle failure. Failure for the disadvantaged child has frequently become a way of life. Through repeated experiences in failure he has learned to cope with it, just as the middle-class child, through repeated success, has learned to cope with it. Being no stranger to failure, the disadvantaged child has developed mechanisms for handling it. It does not dismay him, and he has probably forgotten that failure is supposed to make him feel inferior. He is confident, therefore, of his ability to handle one more failure.

What can the teacher do for the child who has positive reasons for not learning? Clearly it does not do much good to urge him to try harder. He has already rejected stringing along with the average group. Urging him to try harder will not quiet his fears that greater effort will bring him only unfavorable comparison. He decided to fail in the first place to avoid that damage to his self-respect.

The teacher must take a different approach, starting at the sources of the original decision to fail. The child's poor self-concept drove him originally to decide against succeeding in school. It is his self-concept as student that must be changed if his nonlearning cycle is to be reversed. First, he must be given credit for his determination. Second, the goals of his determination must be altered. At the same time his determination must be turned to the accomplishment of learning skills. He must eventually learn that the rejection of learning is not the only way to gain personal esteem.

Bettelheim summarizes the matter this way: [14] "We must never forget that many learning inhibitions can come from the child's desire for inner honesty and truth, and from his trying to succeed in terms of his own life experience and of clear-cut desires and values."

Other Reasons for Failure in School

The socially disadvantaged child's trouble in school does not, of course, all spring from positive motivations. Those more negative in character also spring mostly from his deprived home environment.

First, *these children may have the need to defy adults.* They frequently come from authoritarian homes where they have to "knuckle under" to get along. "Good" children are those who "behave themselves and keep quiet." Such treatment is likely to build up in the child a strong wish to defy authority. The school represents authority away from home. One good way for these children to defy authority is not to learn the things that authorities say they must learn.

Second, *socially disadvantaged children may find school difficult because they are ambivalent about it.* Their negative experiences with school make them indifferent. The home environment makes them indifferent. Repeated failure makes them indifferent. This ambivalence is not the same as rejection, though it might eventually lead to rejection. Ambivalence, of course, is not a good foundation for achievement. Achievement requires a determination and a commitment which go beyond ambivalence.

Third, *the socially disadvantaged student is handicapped in school by his lack of know-how.* He doesn't know how to take tests or how to get information. He doesn't know how to apply for college admission. He doesn't understand bureaucratic routines. These matters have no counterparts in his home or out-of-school life. He needs far more help than the middle-class student whose environment makes him more familiar with such matters.

Fourth, *socially disadvantaged children are handicapped in school because of poor reading ability.* Success in school is closely associated

[14] *Ibid.,* p. 393.

with reading skill and reading is closely associated with social-class status. Hubert A. Coleman, in studying the academic performance of junior-high school students, found that "poor readers, as a group, come with surprising consistency from children of the low socioeconomic status."[15]

Socially disadvantaged children have difficulty with reading for many reasons. One pertains to the kind of material these children are required to read in school. These materials tend to be based largely upon vocabulary, experiences, and interests of middle-class rather than lower-class children. William H. Burton puts the matter this way:

"Books used in beginning reading practically never base content upon the experience known to the whole range of children using the books. The experience of the huge majority is, in fact, usually ignored. The very books designed to teach children to read actually cannot be read by some of the children."[16]

Further the view of the world which is presented in readers tends to be foreign to the socially disadvantaged child. His motivation for learning to read is thereby diminished.

Otto Klineberg examined 15 widely used elementary school readers in order to determine "their contribution to the children's picture of American society, the attitudes and modes of thinking which are presumably developed and the desire to read further."[17] Klineberg discovered that the view conveyed in the readers was as follows: The American people are almost exclusively white or Caucasian, and North European in origin and appearance. Americans in these readers are predominantly, almost exclusively, blonds. There are occasional references to dark skin, but these relate to people far away. One reader tells the story of a boy and his father who go "away down South to see Grandmother." But there is no mention made of Negroes in the South. Americans in these readers are quite well to do, or at least in comfortable economic circumstances.

Klineberg suggests that these readers strengthen two attitudes among the children who read them. First they "strengthen the ethnocentric attitudes of those children who share these characteristics, and make all others—of Negro, Puerto Rican, South European, and possibly

---

[15] Hubert A. Coleman, "The Relationship of Socio-Economic Status to the Performance of Junior High School Students," *Journal of Experimental Education,* Volume 9, September 1940, pp. 61–63.

[16] William H. Burton, "Education and Social Class in the United States," *Harvard Educational Review,* Volume 23, No. 4, Fall 1953, p. 250.

[17] Otto Klineberg, "Life Is Fun in a Smiling, Fair-Skinned World," *Saturday Review,* Volume XLVI, No. 7, February 16, 1963, pp. 75–77, 87.

also Jewish origin—feel that they do not quite belong. Since these and other ethnic groups constitute a substantial proportion of the American school population, it would not be surprising if the readers had an alien quality for a great many of the children who come into contact with them." [18] Second, the readers display, in addition to ethnocentrism, "what might rather clumsily be called a socioeconomic-centrism, a concentration on those who are relatively well-to-do. Here the problem is rather more complicated because Americans are in general well-to-do, and the amenities described are within the reach of a substantial proportion of the population. For the remaining 'one-fourth of a nation' it is part of the American dream that a more comfortable life is attainable. Until it is attained, however, the life portrayed in these readers must represent a very frustrating experience for them. Are no other families as poor as ours? Does everybody else live in a pretty white house? Are there no crowded tenements except where we live? Are we the only ones who can't go out and buy the toys we want? On the other side, is it desirable for the well-to-do children to be unaware that there may be poor people living on the other side of the tracks? Surely a more balanced presentation of American life, both from the ethnic and socioeconomic standpoints, would better prepare the children for what they will later encounter and help to correct what would otherwise be a one-sided picture. It may be argued that this will come in time, and that these children are still too young to face that kind of reality. The fact remains that the earliest impressions frequently develop attitudes that persist; it follows that it is never too early to tell children the truth." [19]

14. Select one commonly used school reader, and conduct your own Klineberg-type investigation of the book. Report your findings to the class.

Let us turn now from the reasons these students have difficulty in school to some of the reasons the schools have difficulty in teaching them. The two matters, of course, are closely intertwined.

WHY DO SCHOOLS ENCOUNTER DIFFICULTY IN TEACHING SOCIALLY DISADVANTAGED STUDENTS?

The previous chapters on the family, peers, and social class implied a number of reasons why the schools experience difficulty in educating socially disadvantaged children. Let us make some of these reasons more explicit.

[18] *Ibid.*, p. 77.
[19] *Ibid.*, p. 77.

First, *there may be discrimination in the school, frequently unintentional, which alienates the child from his home.* Children are quick to read the "silent language" of the teacher. If that silent language communicates to the child that he comes from an inferior background, if it communicates a lower expectation on the part of the teacher, the child is quick to sense it. On the other hand, if the behavior of the teacher communicates warmth and support, an honest expectation, a genuine desire to help, that, too, the child is quick to sense. He is likely to respond accordingly.

Frequently, however, teachers do show that they are less favorably inclined to these children. Helen H. Davidson and Gerhard Long report research that suggests that teachers have less favorable attitudes toward these students even when their school achievement is good.[20] These investigators found further that children accurately perceived the teachers' rejection of them. The child's self-concept, this investigation indicated, is lowered by the unfavorable appraisal of the teacher. The teacher's low opinion also adversely affects his academic achievement and classroom behavior.

15. How do you think children are able to sense that teachers hold unfavorable attitudes toward them, even when teachers don't say so or show it overtly? In this connection you will find reading Edward T. Hall's *The Silent Language* a revealing experience.

Second, *the culture of the school frequently downgrades the child's particular skills and way of life.* The background from which he comes has no place in the life of the school, neither in its books and stories nor in its values. The middle-class values of the school tend to be self-contained and peculiarly resistant to influences from the lower classes. The lower-class child knows that he stands on strange soil.

"The modern public school," states a report of the Educational Policies Commission, "often bases its efforts on assumptions which are not valid for all children. The values of the teacher, the content of the program, and the very purposes of schooling may be appropriate for middle-class children but not for disadvantaged children. These children's experiences at home and on the streets do not prepare them for a school established for another kind of child. If the school reinforces a sense of personal insignificance and inadequacy that life may

[20] Helen H. Davidson and Gerhard Long, "Children's Perceptions of Their Teachers' Feelings Toward Them Related to Self-Perception, School Achievement, and Behavior," *Journal of Experimental Education*, Volume XXIX, No. 2, December 1960, pp. 107–118.

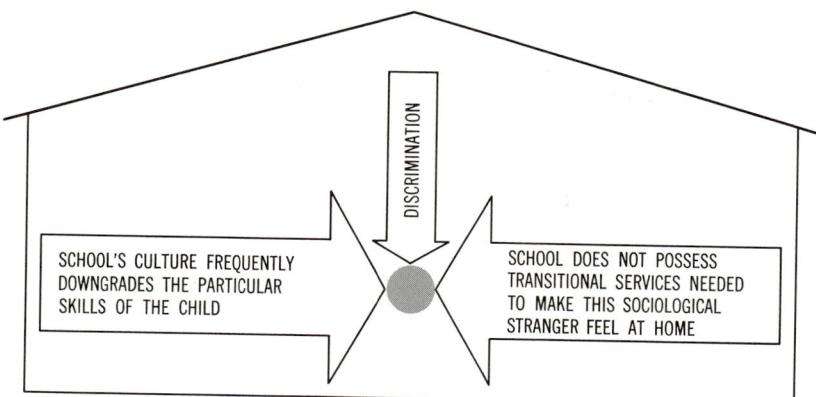

Fig. 10-2 The school may discriminate against the disadvantaged child by insisting on programs and standards which he regards as unrelated to his way of life.

already have imposed on the disadvantaged child, he is likely to benefit little from schooling. If the school insists on programs or standards that he regards as unrelated to his life or that doom him to an unending succession of failures, he is likely to leave at the first opportunity." [21]

16. Do you think the ungraded school system is any better suited to the needs of the disadvantaged student than the graded system? If so, why?

Third, *the school frequently does not possess the transitional services needed to help this sociological stranger feel at home.* The middle-class child doesn't need these services to make him feel at home; he feels at home already. The socially disadvantaged child, however, needs a bridge from home to school over which he may walk.

That bridge is provided in many ways. The teacher who makes it a point to understand the child's background, who attempts to establish a personal and working relationship with the parents, who builds on the child's strengths rather than his weaknesses is helping to provide that bridge. The school systems that provide special academic programs and counseling services for these children, examples of which we discuss later, are providing this bridge. The very recognition that these children need special help, that they have unique needs which are not met in conventional school programs, comes slowly and only with special effort.

[21] *Education and the Disadvantaged American,* Educational Policies Commission, Washington, National Education Association, 1962, pp. 12–13.

Let us turn to what school systems and teachers can do and are doing for the disadvantaged children.

PROGRAMS FOR SOCIALLY DISADVANTAGED CHILDREN

Characteristics of Good Programs

Successful school programs for disadvantaged children usually aim at accomplishing three things. First, they demonstrate a close relationship between the student's life in school and his life outside school. Second, they provide the remedial services these children need. Third, they arouse higher aspirations which constructively can alter young lives.

We have said that frequently the disadvantaged child feels like a stranger in the school because he sees no connection between his in-school and out-of-school life. Programs must help the child to realize that school is important to him. Somehow he must be involved in the work and activities of the school, be brought into the "main stream" of school life. His learning activities must challenge rather than frustrate him. He must be helped to achieve status within the group. Through classroom activities, clubs, field trips, and sports he should be given the opportunity to identify closely with the school and become a part of it. Such a close identification will generate motivation which will lead him to improved academic achievement.

The disadvantaged child, however, needs more than motivation if he is to make use of his potential capacity in school. He needs remedial help in those areas where his deprived background has handicapped him. Reading is one such area. Without the ability to read the child is permanently handicapped in all areas of academic work. Remedial programs for disadvantaged children, therefore, are crucial to all other efforts. Disadvantaged children do not develop at home a sense of what reading is; nor do they develop a motivation to read. These must be supplied by the school before the child grows deeply discouraged by the failures which result from his inability to read.

The speech patterns of disadvantaged children, differing sharply as they do from accepted English, impede learning. Speech therapy should accompany reading instruction. If the child is to get the remedial services he needs, school schedules must be flexible enough for him to keep up his regular classroom work.

Finally, good programs for the disadvantaged raise the educational and occupational aspirations of children. Through planned activities the school must seek to lift the mental and physical horizons of children. Many of these children have never ventured beyond their immediate neighborhoods. Their concept of their world is bounded by their home street, immediate environs, and television. New experiences are not sought out, indeed are frequently feared. These children may feel insecure outside their own neighborhoods. School programs for disadvantaged children seek to get them outside their immediate surroundings and let them start to enjoy new experiences. Visits to museums, zoos, factories, farms, plays, and concerts all help to widen the "life space" of these children.

17. Select one school system for study and find out what you can about what is being done for the socially disadvantaged children enrolled in it.

Let us turn to some specific school programs for disadvantaged children.

Early Enrollment

Socially disadvantaged children, we have said, are behind others the day they start to school and fall further behind the longer they remain in school. To help these children overcome this handicap, many school systems are operating programs of preschool schools. The purpose of these programs is to give disadvantaged children the preparation for learning that middle-class youngsters automatically get at home. The early enrollment idea is supported by current research.

Benjamin Bloom has assembled the results of research which indicates the extent of educational growth experienced by children at various age levels.[22] Bloom finds that at least one-third of the learning which will determine later levels of school achievement has already taken place by age 6, and at least 75 percent by age 13. Based on the estimate that 33 percent of the educational growth takes place before age 6, Bloom suggests that "nursery schools and kindergartens could have far-reaching consequences on the child's general learning pattern." [23]

Children who are admitted to these programs frequently arrive at school without having seen themselves in a mirror. Some do not know their names and can hardly speak. Many have never held a book or seen a telephone. They come from homes that discourage the development of curiosity. Many, with no father at home and with a working mother, spend hours by themselves and have no way of expressing themselves or developing an interest in their surroundings.

[22] Benjamin Bloom, *Stability and Change in Human Characteristics*, New York, John Wiley and Sons, Inc., 1964.
[23] *Ibid.*, p. 110.

18. One school system gives breakfast to the children in the early enrollment program. Can you justify this practice on educational grounds?

Here is a newspaper account of a child in the Pittsburgh school system's early enrollment program. It describes the limitations with which such children come to school, as well as what one school system is doing.[24]

"Tears stain the dirty, small face of 3-year-old Billy Smith. A red welt is rising slowly on the left side of his face.

"Hope has already left his brown eyes.

"Billy is, in the words of one educator, 'a repetitive product of poverty and racial discrimination and will tend to beget more of the same.'

"Used to gestures rather than the spoken word, Billy 'barely has a language.'

"Put him in school at age 6 and you can be sure he will flunk out eventually. He will then be turned loose to look for jobs which aren't there for the uneducated and to roam the streets. . . . Billy will learn how to communicate, listen to stories and take part in plays. But perhaps most important, someone will love him. . . ."

What results may we expect from such programs? A good appraisal of this question is given by Martin Deutsch, one of the pioneers of the early enrollment program in New York City:[25]

"There are no data at the present time to prove that a preschool program could reduce the incidence of later dropout (though such data would not be difficult to collect), so this paper must be considered a speculative discussion. We have some preliminary data on this which indicate that preschool, kindergarten, or day-care experience, or a combination of these, is associated with higher group intelligence test scores. The scores are higher in the first grade, and the differential tends to be accentuated in a fifth-grade population; apparently this differential holds when social class is controlled.

"From present data it cannot be said definitely that there is any direct relationship between the early school experience and the school dropout, but I would hypothesize a very strong relationship between the first school experiences of the child and academic success or failure, and that the more invariant the school experience, the more important the early experience would be to the academic success of the

24 Nicki Wolford, "Children of Poverty Get Special Schooling," United Press International, *The State Journal*, Lansing, Michigan, Volume 110, No. 167, October 11, 1964, p. A-9.

25 Deutsch, *op. cit.*, pp. 94–95.

child. I would also hypothesize that children who have had a pre-school and kindergarten experience are more likely to cope appropri-ately with the kinds of things the school demands intellectually than are children who have not had this experience. This would be particu-larly true for children from lower socioeconomic groups, and would be most true for children who come from the most peripheral groups in our society."

Great Cities Improvement Project

In the summer of 1956 a project was begun at Junior High School No. 43 in New York City that had as its aim the identification and stimulation of able students from low socio-economic homes. The proj-ect was later broadened to include students at all levels, and students in other junior high schools, as well as elementary schools in New York City. Similar projects have arisen in other major cities, including Baltimore, Buffalo, Boston, Chicago, Cleveland, Detroit, Los Angeles, Milwaukee, Philadelphia, Pittsburgh, San Francisco, St. Louis, and Washington. Known as the "Higher Horizons" program in New York City, the expanded program became known as the "Great Cities Im-provement Project."

The programs vary from city to city, but many of them include some or all of the following features:

First, *new instruments are used for assessing the ability of chil-dren*. Most standard IQ tests are inappropriate for measuring the intel-ligence of the disadvantaged child because the test reflects cultural knowledge with which he is not familiar. Further, such tests stress verbal knowledge that the disadvantaged child has not had an oppor-tunity to develop. Many of these children come from homes where English is not the native language. For these reasons many school systems now use nonverbal intelligence tests, and sometimes with sur-prising results. For example, Truda Weil reports that in New York City 5,000 children of non-English-speaking parents were given IQ tests in their native language rather than English. One-fourth came out in the 80th and 90th percentiles. Yet, many of these high-ranking children were being taught in the slowest classes for their grades.[26]

By using a variety of both intelligence and achievement tests schools are better able to assess the true capabilities of the disad-vantaged child.[27]

[26] Jane Whitbread Levin, "Family Business," *New York Times Magazine,* Volume CX, December 8, 1963, p. 100.

[27] See also *Developing a Program for Testing Puerto Rican Pupils in the New York City Public Schools,* New York, 1959.

Second, *the disadvantaged child is given new social models which he can understand and aspire to.* In the New York City program pictures of Negro and Puerto Rican doctors, nuclear physicists, and journalists were displayed in the classrooms to help improve the children's self-concept.

Third, *some cities, notably Detroit, produce "integrated" instructional materials in which pictures of Negroes as well as whites appear, and which contain stories and information about people in lower as well as middle classes.* The effect of such materials is to bring closer together for the child the values of school and home. Following the lead of the cities, some commercial publishing houses are now producing "integrated" readers and textbooks.[28]

Fourth, *special remedial reading classes are established in order to overcome the basic reading deficiency.* All teachers, regardless of the grade they teach, are urged to devote time to the improvement of reading. Further, efforts are made to stimulate reading among all students. Book fairs and circulating libraries of paperbacks are used to stir up interest in reading.

Fifth, *schools have intensified and extended counseling services.* One purpose is to provide better guidance concerning college and career possibilities. A second purpose is to raise career aspirations.

Sixth, *many programs involve parents.* Parents are invited to come to the school, and, where that is impossible, counselors and social caseworkers call on parents in their homes. Active efforts are made to seek parental cooperation and assistance.

Seventh, *these programs seek to give socially disadvantaged children new peer associations.* Earlier we spoke of the impact that peer associations have on educational aspirations. In the case of the disadvantaged child these associations tend to work for lower educational aspirations. These special programs have a tendency to give the disadvantaged student contacts with other students who are likely to have higher educational aspirations. The hope is that these associations will help to upgrade the disadvantaged student's educational sights.

Finally, *efforts are made to broaden the cultural tastes of students.* Through attendance at concerts, plays, and other cultural events, a new social and cultural world is opened to these students.

These features are not the exclusive property of the Great Cities Improvement Project. Many other school systems employ similar means

[28] For a discussion of developments and problems in the commercial publication of integrated books see A. Kent MacDougall, "Integrated Books," *The Wall Street Journal,* Volume XLV, No. 112, March 24, 1965, p. 1.

of assisting disadvantaged children, and many have been creative in developing new programs to serve their local needs.

Throughout this chapter we have stressed what the teacher needs to understand about socially disadvantaged children. We have also suggested what the teacher can do to assist these children. Let us, by way of summary, look at some of the specific things the effective teacher of socially disadvantaged will keep in mind.

THE EFFECTIVE TEACHER OF DISADVANTAGED CHILDREN

How important is the teacher in lifting the educational aspirations of educationally disadvantaged children? Logic would indicate that since such children are not likely to receive strong parental support in advancing their education, they must receive encouragement at school if they receive it at all. There is evidence to indicate that among those students from lower classes who do proceed to higher education, the teachers and counselors have strong influence. David Gottlieb discovered that in a sample of 398 freshmen men the lower-class students were more influenced by teachers and counselors in their decision to go to college than the middle-class students.[29] In the middle- and upper-class families in this investigation it was apparently assumed that children would attend college. The boys from these families did not depend on encouragement from teachers or counselors. In contrast, college attendance was not taken for granted by lower-class families. Thus, the boys in the sample said that support and encouragement for college attendance came not from parents but from teachers and counselors.

It may well be that the teacher and counselor have considerable influence on the disadvantaged child's decision to take the high road to accomplishment or the low road to unskilled oblivion. What can the teacher do to help the child make the right choice? Here are some suggestions from William Moore, a school principal, who speaks from practical experience in dealing with disadvantaged children.[30]

"1. Respect the child's values and if they need changing—mutually evaluate them with him as painlessly as possible. Help him to

[29] David Gottlieb, "Social Class, Achievement, and College-going Experience," *The School Review*, Volume 70, Number 3, Autumn 1962, pp. 273–286.

[30] William Moore, Jr., "Time to Help This Child," *School and Community*, Columbia, Mo., Missouri State Teachers Association, Volume LI, No. 3, November 1964, pp. 14, 78–79.

weigh his values against the predominant ones in the culture to ascertain which would serve him best.

"2. We should not insulate or isolate ourselves from the habits and behavior of the disadvantaged child; rather, we should make ourselves conspicuously available to this child. He needs good models to emulate.

"3. If the child is good in reading and poor in arithmetic, a better part of good judgment might be not to condemn his poor performance in arithmetic but to praise his success in reading.

"4. Go directly to the child's environment. Learn the speech patterns, language idiosyncrasies and slang expressions in order to communicate more effectively with him and to make better positive use of the language skill that he has.

"5. Don't tell this child to try to be somebody—tell him he is somebody.

"6. Children respond almost directly proportional to our expectations of them. If we expect a great deal, they will try hard to live up to our expectations.

"7. We should not pre-judge disadvantaged children. Such statements as, 'They aren't interested in their future' and 'The parents aren't interested either,' are probably not true. Moreover, it is one of the tasks of the school to develop interest.

"It is one of the jobs of the school to guide children toward something of value—or to value something. That something may well be themselves and a positive look at the world. If this is successfully done, the disadvantaged child may view the sun on the horizon—not as evening—but as dawn."[31]

This new frontier in American education, equal educational opportunity for *all* youth, can be won. The mastery of this frontier, like the frontier of space, presents formidable and perplexing problems. They are, however, not beyond solution. Able teachers of good will are demonstrating that every day.

REFERENCES

Paperbacks

Constructive Classroom Control. Irwin O. Addicott. (Orig.) (TGB) Chandler Publishing Co., 124 Spear St., San Francisco, Calif. ($1.25).
Crucial Issues in Education. Ehlers and Lee. (3rd Ed.) Holt, Rinehart and Winston, 383 Madison Ave., New York ($3.25).

[31] *Ibid.,* pp. 78–79.

Dropouts. Terrence A. Sprague. (Orig.) Great Outdoors Publishing Co., 4747 28th St. North, St. Petersburg, Fla. ($1.00).

Educating for Mental Health: A Book of Readings. Jerome M. Seidman. (Orig.) Thomas Y. Crowell Co., 201 Park Ave. South, New York ($4.50).

Education and Income: Inequalities of Opportunity in Our Public Schools. Patricia Sexton. (C168) Compass Books, The Viking Press, 625 Madison Ave., New York ($1.65).

Education in Depressed Areas. A. Harry Passow, Editor. Teachers College, Teachers College Press, 525 West 120 St., New York ($2.50).

Poverty: Social Conscience in the Progressive Era. Robert Hunter. Peter d'A. Junes, Editor. (TB/3065) Harper Torchbooks, Harper College Paperbacks, Harper and Row, Publishers, 49 E. 33rd St., New York ($2.25).

Slums and Suburbs. James B. Conant. New American Library of World Literature, 1301 Ave. of the Americas, New York (60¢).

Books

Clark, Burton R., *Educating the Expert Society.* San Francisco: Chandler Publishing Co., 1962, 301 pp. Chapter 10 discusses education and minorities. When teachers of minority children request transfers to "better" schools, the effect is to retard the education of these children.

Davis, Allison, *Social Class Influences Upon Learning.* Cambridge, Mass.: Harvard University Press, 1952. This classic study points out that the teacher, to be effective, has to know and understand the child's cultural background.

"The Education of Teachers of the Disadvantaged," *American Education and the Search for Equal Opportunity*, Educational Policies Commission of the NEA and the American Association of School Administrators, 1965. Teacher preparation should include observation and practice with the disadvantaged in their community, inside and outside school.

"Educational Planning for Socially Disadvantaged Children and Youth," *The Journal of Negro Education*, Vol. XXXIII, No. 3, 1964. The Yearbook issue includes articles on identifying the culturally deprived and their needs, areas of emphasis for effective planning, evaluation, and research needs. A bibliography is included.

Educational Policies Commission, *Education and the Disadvantaged American.* Washington, D. C.: National Education Association, 1962. The commission believes that schools present one of the best hopes for overcoming children's culturally deprived backgrounds.

A Proposal for the Prevention and Control of Delinquency by Expanding Opportunities. New York: Mobilization for Youth, 1962. Chapter III presents new programs in teacher training, curricula, pre-school activities and guidance services.

Reissman, Frank, *The Culturally Deprived Child.* New York: Harper and Brothers, 1962. The author urges teachers to change their middle-class attitudes and teaching methods in order to help the urban low achiever.

Periodicals

Ausubel, David P., "A Teaching Strategy for Culturally Deprived Pupils: Cognitive and Motivational Considerations," *The School Review*, Vol. 71, No. 4, Winter 1963, pp. 454–463. The best aid for reversing the course of intellectual retardation of culturally deprived students is to provide students with an optimal learning environment as early as possible.

Bettelheim, Bruno, "Teaching the Disadvantaged," *The NEA Journal*, Vol. 54, No. 6, September 1965, pp. 8–12. Negro and white teachers hold similiar attitudes toward their children. Classroom clashes come not from the race factor but from the middle-class attitudes of teachers and the lower-class attitudes of students.

Feldmann, Shirley, "A Preschool Enrichment Program for Disadvantaged Children," *The New Era in Home and School*, Vol. XLV, No. 3, March 1964, pp. 79–82. A description of the experimental nursery school program in progress in New York City.

Finger, John A., and George E. Schlesser, "Non-intellective Predictors of Academic Success in School and College," *The School Review*, Vol. 73, No. 1, Spring 1965, pp. 14–38. The authors feel that underachievement is symptomatic of the possession of attitudes that make it unnecessary to achieve in school.

Harding, Alice Currie, "To be continued . . . the Story of Baltimore Early School Admissions Project," *NEA Journal*, Vol. 53, No. 6, September 1964, pp. 30–32. A description of Baltimore's project in which children from depressed areas enter school at the age of four.

Havighurst, Robert J., "Who Are the Socially Disadvantaged," *The Journal of Negro Education*, Vol. XXXIII, No. 3, 1964, pp. 210–217. The author describes socially disadvantaged children in terms of family, personal, and social-group characteristics.

Kirk, Robert N., "Educating Slum Children in London," *School and Society*, Vol. 93, No. 2258, March 20, 1965, pp. 180–182. An ambitious program, utilizing campus-style building construction, is used in an urban school in a London slum.

Landers, Jacob, "The Responsibilities of Teachers and School Administrators," *The Journal of Negro Education*, Vol. XXXIII, No. 3, 1964, pp. 318–322. The author describes new methods, organizations, and programs to meet the needs of culturally deprived children.

Mizer, Jean E., "'Cipher in the Snow," *NEA Journal*, Vol. LIII, No. 8, April 1964, pp. 8–10. A personal record of what the educational system did to one boy—a nonachiever—who died before completing school.

Rosenfield, Howard, and Alvin Zander, "The Influence of Teachers on Aspirations of Students," *Journal of Educational Psychology*, Vol. 52, No. 1, February 1961, pp. 1–11. This study explored the relationship between the teacher's influence on student aspirations and goal setting by the student.

Stahlecker, Lotar V., "High School Graduation for Slow Learners," *Peabody Journal of Education*, Vol. 42, No. 3, November 1964, pp. 166–172. The article describes the problems encountered by high schools which attempt to provide meaningful education to "slow learners."

Warner, O. Ray, "The Scholastic Ability of School Dropouts," *School Life*, Vol. 47, No. 1, October 1964, pp. 21–22. A statistical study of the scholastic ability of dropouts shows they range widely in individual differences and in levels of intelligence.

IV

The Schools

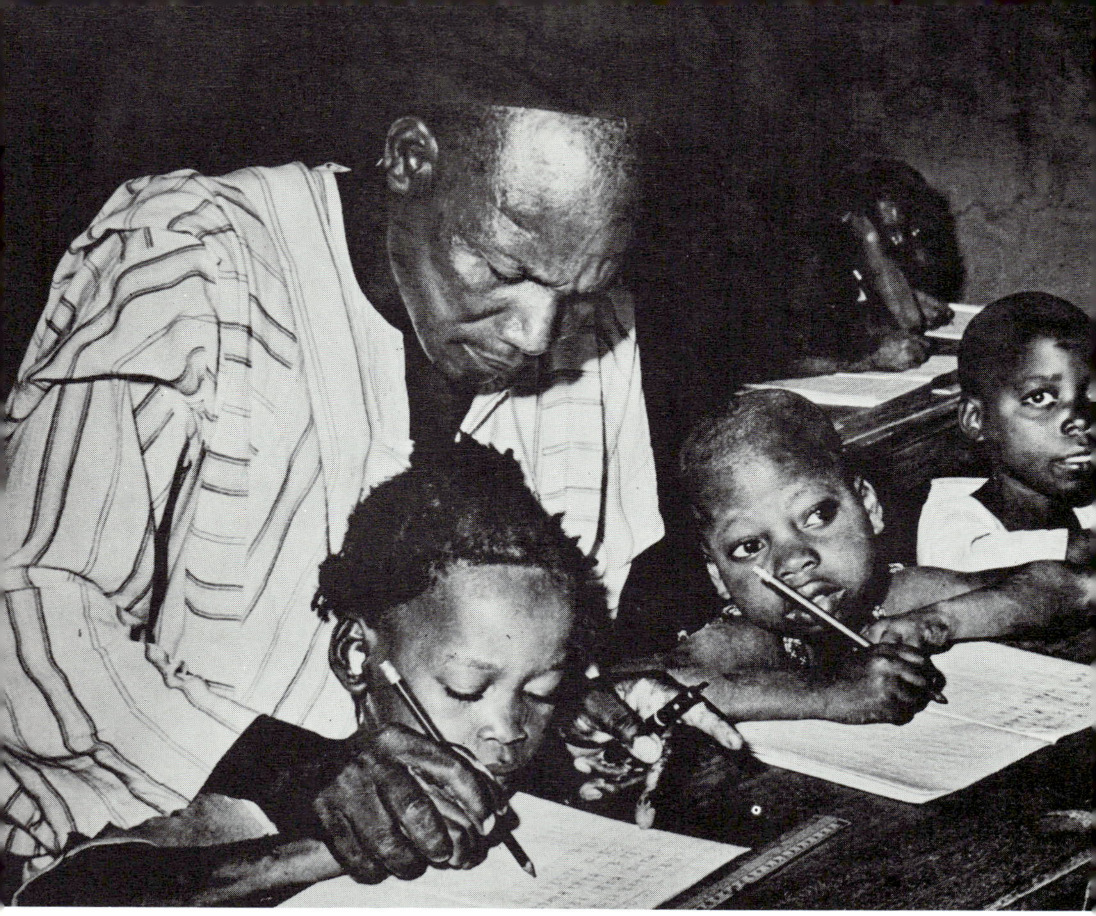

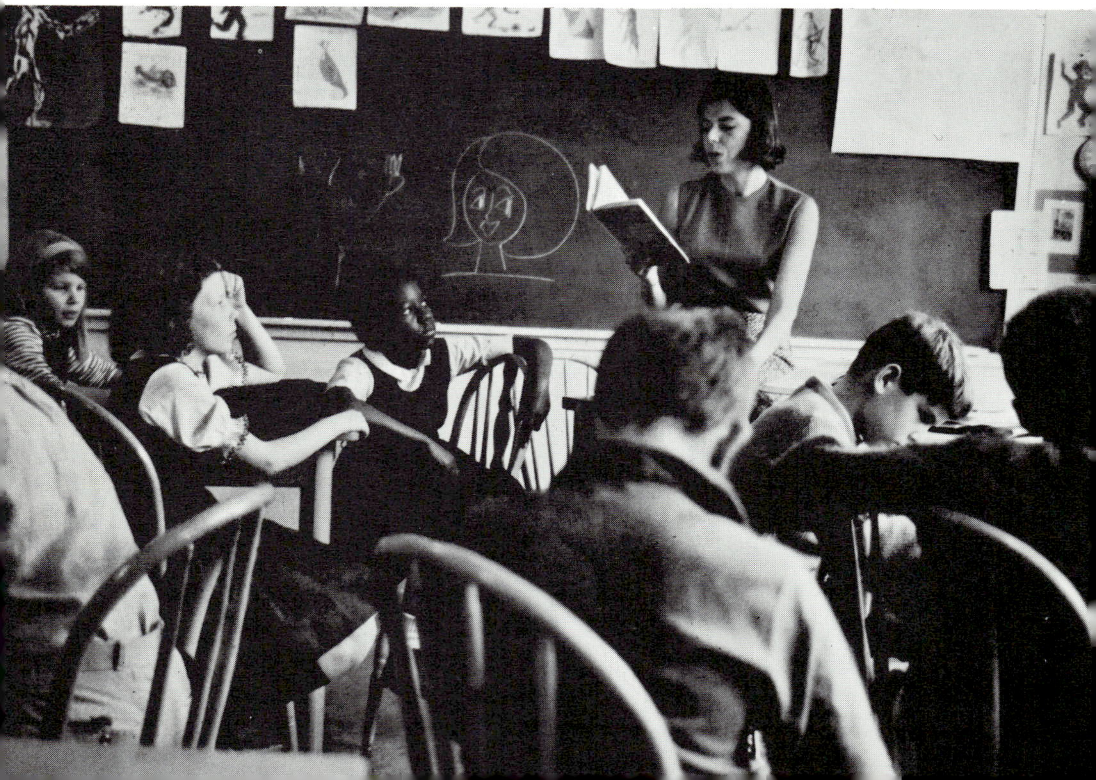

II

The School's Cultural Style

"Yes, you really have to convert yourself into a machine."
"Well, you wouldn't, except for the school's neurotic obsession with college admissions and national tests." DAVID MALLERY

Education itself is old, as old as man's capacity to learn. But schools, as we know them, are quite new on the human scene. They are a relatively recent invention of man, reflecting the complexity of modern society and its need to delegate to a specialized institution the responsibility for educating the young. How do schools discharge this responsibility? Probably in as many different ways as there are numbers of schools. Each school has a character of its own, as we shall see in the course of this chapter.

WHAT IS A SCHOOL?

As a social institution, what is a school? What social needs brought it into being? What social acts does it perform? What are the social consequences of these acts?

In primitive society informal education was quite adequate. The child required no special preparation to learn the things he needed to know. In early societies he learned from his father and other adults the art of hunting and food gathering. In somewhat later societies he learned to cultivate, plant, and harvest. Tasks were unspecialized and were easily transmitted from parent to child. The learning process was quite spontaneous, with both parent and child largely unaware that it was happening.

But most societies do not remain primitive in their outlook and simple in their organization. Endowed with a capacity to learn, man started to control his environment for his own purposes. He developed fire to keep him warm, clothing to shield him from the wind and cold, baskets and kettles to carry more than his hands could, and finally the wheel, to which he transferred burdens from his back.

Some men were better at certain skills than others; they became artisans, making copper pots, weaving baskets, making wheels. Young men came to watch and to learn. They became apprentices, helping and learning at the same time. Probably the first formal schools sprang up around those persons of special skills and knowledge to whom the community had learned to turn in time of special need. Schools sprang from definable social needs growing out of man's increasingly complex way of living.

These new agencies on the social scene separated children from their families for periods of time, called them "students," put them in special places called "schools" in charge of adults called "teachers." Schools became institutions for learning, teaching became a professional activity, and learning became a recognized pursuit of the young. Thus schools may be defined as institutions created by society to perform important social functions associated with the education of the young.

1. Different people define schools differently. Ask six persons to give you their definitions of a school. What elements do they have in common? How do the definitions differ? What social functions do these definitions attribute to schools?

Our purpose in this chapter is first to examine briefly three important social functions of the school and then to see how schools with different cultural styles perform these functions. We shall discover that each school has a unique cultural style for carrying out its social functions, and that this cultural style determines the way the school behaves as an institution.

THREE SOCIAL FUNCTIONS OF THE SCHOOL

The school performs a variety of social functions. We are interested in three: (1) The school socializes the young, helps them to learn the way of life into which they are born; (2) The school transmits its culture; (3) The school selects and sorts students into various educational and vocational streams.

In Chapter 2 we learned that education, in school and out, is a social process. In the examples of Hamid, Raymond, Beth, and Julia we saw how children in the village, town, suburb, and city are socialized to their ways of life. In Chapter 3 we observed teachers transmitting our culture—Mrs. Mullen teaching her first graders the letter "W" and Mrs. Miller challenging her high school students to think critically and independently. Also in Chapter 3 we discussed the selecting and sorting functions of the classroom. Classrooms, we said, allocate youth to particular tasks in our society on the basis of their achievement in school. Since these matters are not new our treatment of them here is brief, with some fresh examples added to help enlarge one's understanding of them.

The new concept in this chapter lies in this question: How are these social functions performed by different schools? Schools in different environmental settings perform these functions in ways peculiar to their settings; each school has a characteristic cultural style through which social purposes are accomplished. Our concern is with the cultural styles of four different schools—Hamid's, Raymond's, Beth's, and Julia's. These four schools symbolize four main types of modern schools, and their cultural styles are interesting to compare and contrast.

Let us turn now to three important social functions of the school.

The School Socializes the Young

Socialization, we said, is the process by which we learn the ways of the society into which we are born. Each society has its own way of conducting its young into the adult world.

Recall the example of the shepherd boy in Asia who learned everything he needed to know within his own family. Or the example of the Amish children whose parents were certain that the one-room school taught by a girl of their own sect was adequate for them. In the case of the shepherd boy there was no need for social experience beyond the family and tribe. By socializing in this group he learned the way of life that he would need all of his life. In the Amish school the child is exposed to no new social experience. The other children are exactly like him, and the teacher is a model of his own way of life. The socialization of the school simply repeats that of the home.

This kind of socialization is not suitable for modern children. The course of their lives takes them far beyond their own families to new values and new ways of doing things. They must be prepared to live in a world where change is the only constant. We said that socialization is the process of learning the ways of society into which we are born. The modern child learns these ways; he also learns that these ways change and that the school itself helps him to change.

2. Schools prepare students for a changing future in many different ways. Can you name four ways in which schools prepare students for change?

Notice in the following example from a kindergarten that the socialization process starts in the earliest days in school. With rare good humor Larry Friedman describes how his five-year-old daughter is learning in kindergarten what is proper in matters of speech, manners, dress, personal hygiene, and conduct.[1]

"What's life like in that wonderful—and sometimes wacky—world of kindergarten?

"We can't be sure, because the only information we receive is from our 5-year-old. And she often takes a flyer into the world of fantasy.

"My wife is anxious to find out what goes on in the little schoolroom with the big doll house. By the bruises on little Arlene's legs, Mommy has discovered the youngsters sometimes toss around blocks. Paint on her hands and clay in her hair are more evidences of kindergarten tools.

"To Mommy's questions of 'How was school today, darling?' comes such no-nonsense answers as: 'Okay,' 'Fine,' or 'The same as yesterday.'

"But Daddy hears all the tales—or at least they sound like tales.

"I was sitting on the sofa one evening reading the paper when Arlene flopped down alongside me. Suddenly she blurted out: 'Daddy, Tommy kissed me in school today.'

" 'Huh. Who kissed you?'

" 'Oh, the teacher didn't see him kiss me,' she said innocently.

" 'Well, what did you do?' I asked anxiously.

" 'I kissed him back. He's a nice boy.'

"After her first day in school, Arlene bounded home breathlessly with this information:

" 'Daddy, the "princess" talked over the "microscope" today and you could hear his voice in all the rooms.'

"Like most youngsters her age, Arlene excels when it comes to fracturing the king's English.

"We finally figured out that the 'princess' was the principal. And the 'microscope,' of course was a microphone and loudspeaker.

"Another day Arlene rushed home excitedly to relate the details of a 'fire grill.'

"Reluctantly, she reported one time about being told to sit in the corner.

[1] Larry Friedman, "What's Life Like in Kindergarten," Lansing, Michigan, *The State Journal* (AP), October 17, 1963, p. A-8.

" 'Well, what did you do to deserve such an honor?'

" 'I was talking after Mrs. Cook told us to keep quiet. Then I started talking low to Vicki. But the teacher said she could hear someone whispering with her special ears.'

" 'Daddy, do teachers have more than two ears like regular people?'

"School has changed Arlene's wardrobe. She has surrendered the blue jeans, polo shirts and sneakers—the uniform of the mud-pie-and-sandbox set—for stiffly starched and ironed dresses and freshly polished saddle shoes.

" 'Mrs. Cook says all the girls should wear dresses and act like young ladies,' she said.

"It sounded like a noble thought. As I watched her combing her hair, washing her hands and face and brushing her teeth without even being told, I began to have gnawing doubts.

"That little boy Tommy has me worried."

3. This is an example of socialization in nonacademic matters. How does the school socialize the student's behavior in regard to academic matters? Can you cite examples?

The school, by enlarging the social experience of the student, becomes an agent of his socialization.

The School Transmits Its Culture

Socialization is the *process* by which we learn the ways of our society. Culture is concerned with the *content and meaning* of those ways, and how this content and meaning is learned and expressed in our behavior. For this reason culture may be defined as *learned* and *shared* behavior.

In five-year-old Arlene, in the kindergarten example, we have an instance of cultural behavior which is being learned and shared. Arlene is learning personal cleanliness—to comb her hair, wash her face, and brush her teeth. Because the value of personal cleanliness is widely learned and shared in our society we may call it a cultural value, and Arlene's school is helping to transmit it.

The school not only provides the setting for the process by which children are socialized to a particular way of life, but also transmits the values embodied in these ways. It transmits the culture.

The school transmits a great range of cultural values which our society learns and shares: our belief in our country, our language and literature, history, traditions, music and art, our ethical beliefs, and our sense of what is proper in personal relations. The school transmits the conflicting values of the culture, for example competition and co-operation. In working on committees and in clubs students are taught to cooperate. In taking examinations and on the athletic field they are taught to compete.

Schools also transmit the learned and shared values of the economic system, and it is from this area that we choose the following example. Notice that in this news story the boys in an industrial arts class are learning the cultural values of free enterprise business.[2]

"A Waverly High School industrial production class has gone into business. The nineteen students have incorporated, selected a name—Wav-Co—and will soon go into production of an unusual note pad called a Pad-L-Roll.

"The class, taught by Dale Hansen, has been working on the design, development and production of the note pad for 27 weeks. Work began last September when students decided upon the product they would manufacture.

"Mark Moore, Jim Christy, and Bill McKnight produced the design, an attractive wood frame which holds a roll of adding machine tape. The tape unrolls across the writing surface under a safety edge which enables the user to cut off the tape at any desired length. A holder keeps pen or pencil handy.

"The class was divided into several groups, each responsible for a single facet of the production. Following actual projection procedures, jigs were made for efficient operation, time studies were made to cut down 'dead' time, and a quality control system was devised.

"Taking advantage of the extensive industrial facilities at the high school, the corporation printed stock certificates, advertising placards and display stands.

"Several area stores have agreed to offer the note pad to the public. Orders for Pad-L-Roll are now being taken at Waverly and the units will be sold for $1 apiece. Profits made will be divided among the 118 stockholders and members of the class.

"Officers of Wav-Co are John Heuchert, president; Steve Hadden and Mike Boog, vice presidents; Jim Christy, secretary, and Mike Boog, treasurer.

" 'The simulated corporation and the mass production methods we have learned and made use of has proven to be an interesting and enjoyable experience for all involved,' says Steve Hadden."

We might add that the experience probably proved to be an effective way for transmitting the values of our economic system.

<hr/>

[2] John Cohoon, "Industrial Class Runs Business," Lansing, Mich., *The State Journal*, Volume 110, No. 349, Sunday, April 11, 1965, p. D-6.

4. Make a list of all the economic values which are implicit in this school project.

5. Do you think that this project is a good way to teach these values? Is it better than teaching them out of a textbook? What are your reasons for thinking as you do?

6. In this project there is no mention made of the role of labor in the production process. The main emphasis is on management. Assume that you were the teacher, and a father of one of the boys in the class, a local labor union leader, asked you about this omission. What would you say or do?

The School Selects and Sorts Students

Not only does the school socialize the young to a particular way of life and transmit the values which inhere in that way of life; it also helps to determine *which* way of life and *which* set of values the student acquires. In short, it helps to determine the life chances of students.

The method by which the school sorts and selects students is based on academic achievement. It is academic achievement which helps to determine the student's curricular program, his scholastic standing, his motivational directions, and his opportunity for further education. Ascriptive factors, the socio-economic status of the student's family, also play a part in selection in school. Notice how in this news item announcing the selection of a high school valedictorian and salutatorian both ascriptive and achievement factors are present.[3] On the one hand, the students have achieved well academically in school. On the other, they come from families of status in the community.

"Mark Swanson, son of the president of Alma College, has been named valedictorian at Alma High School, and Judy Anthony, daughter of the mayor of Alma, is the salutatorian.

"The 17-year-old Swanson had a 4.00 average, is president of the Student Council and a member of the basketball and tennis teams, the Hi-Y Club and National Honor Society.

"Miss Anthony, who is 18, is a member of the National Honor Society, the Tri-Hi-Y Club, and debate team. She had a 3.914 average.

"Swanson is the son of Dr. Robert Swanson, Alma College president, and Miss Anthony is the daughter of Robert Anthony, Alma mayor."

7. In the selection process which do you think is the more important, ascriptive or achievement factors? How does one influence the other?

[3] "Alma High School Names Two for Scholastic Honors," Lansing, Michigan, *The State Journal*, Volume 110, No. 352, April 14, 1965, p. C-8.

By what means does the school select and sort students on the basis of achievement? Most schools have a variety of means, but most rely heavily on standardized tests and classroom examinations. The following is an example of the testing program of one suburban high school.[4] The program is being explained to members of the Board of Education by members of the school staff. Notice the variety of ways in which students can be screened, depending on how well they do on the aptitude or achievement tests. Notice also that the selecting and sorting functions of the tests are never explicitly stated by the staff.

"From pre-kindergarten age to graduation, Okemos students face a battery of tests, all given with one thought in mind—how to help the student realize his potential, members of the School Board were told Monday night.

" 'Human resources have been wasted due to the lack of adequate testing,' said Mrs. Thelma Lamb, high school counselor. She was one of three Okemos staff members reporting to the School Board on testing methods used in the Okemos Schools. The others were Jon Krieder and Mrs. Betty McGowan of the junior high staff.

" 'Testing in the system begins before youngsters enter kindergarten, with a pre-school development examination to determine if they are mature enough to benefit from instruction,' Krieder said.

" 'We think it is better for a child not to start school than to be held back at some later date,' Krieder said. 'More and more we are retaining children to allow more growth and development.'

"Krieder showed Board members a child's incomplete drawing of a man which preschoolers are asked to complete. 'The test indicates positive and negative maturity factors,' he said. The children are also given the Bender Gestalt Test which indicates maturity in visual-motor perception and emotional adjustment.

"Krieder said out of 35 children given the tests this year he recommended six not be allowed to start school. 'After discussion with parents, two of them were accepted,' he said.

" 'It is difficult to explain to some parents that all children are not ready to start school,' he said.

"Krieder said in his job as junior high counselor he sees many students who are just too young and should not have started school so early.

"Mrs. McGowan told Board members that students in the sixth and eighth grades at Okemos are given the Standard Achievement

[4] "Okemos Students Face a Battery of Tests," Okemos, Michigan, *The Meridian News,* Volume 8, No. 13, January 27, 1965, p. 1.

Tests which are designed to measure important skills and knowledges accepted as desirable at the junior high level. 'This test is not completely accurate on an individual basis but is standardized to allow comparison of Okemos with other school systems,' she said.

"In conjunction with these tests the students are given the California Test of Mental Maturity which measures basic abilities such as language skills and allows counselors to compare the student's achievement with his abilities.

"At the high school level students are given the differential Aptitude Test to show strength and weaknesses in such things as numerical ability and verbal reasoning. Used in conjunction with the Kuder Preference Test, this allows counselors to pin-point areas of interest and ability and help the students mold a program which will aid them in career selection.

"Tenth grade students are given the Iowa Test of Educational Development which is standardized to allow comparison of Okemos students with others across the nation.

" 'In the past five years Okemos students have averaged over the 70 percentile,' Mrs. Lamb said. 'Fifty percentile is considered average.'

" 'Weaknesses have appeared in the computational math and reading ability of Okemos students in the past few years,' she said, which indicate the system is only average in these areas. She said a study is underway to determine the causes for the drop in test results.

"Mrs. Lamb stressed that test results are only one means of determining the abilities and accomplishments of students.

" 'Good test scores can overcome a mediocre record on college entrance requirements,' she said.

"But she said that many other factors are taken into consideration and test results are only a small part of the total picture of an individual."

8. We mentioned that the selecting and sorting functions of the testing program were not explicitly mentioned by the staff in its explanation. Instead, what functions and purposes are stressed?

9. In its explanation the staff emphasizes that the testing program is helpful in making comparisons. Okemos students can be compared with those in other school systems and national norms. Student achievement can be compared with student ability. And obviously students can be compared with one another. What does this tell you about the cultural style of the suburban school? Do you think that village and town schools have the same high interest in making such comparisons?

10. Mrs. Lamb indicated that test results "are only one means of determining the abilities and accomplishments of students." Can you name others?

11. We said that the school transmits cultural values. What cultural values are implicit in a testing program like that in Okemos?

Let us turn from the social functions of the school to how the school performs them.

THE SCHOOL'S CULTURAL STYLE

Not all schools socialize the young in the same way. They neither transmit the same cultural values nor select students on the same basis or for the same reason. How the school performs these social functions depends upon its particular cultural style.

When we say "school" an image flashes upon the mind, or perhaps a series of images. These images spring from our own experience in school. We see a particular building, or buildings, the corridors, classrooms, and gymnasium. We recall pictures of classmates, teachers, counselors, and administrators. It brings to mind how they behaved and the values they held. The word "school" brings back memories of basketball and football games, activities, clubs, and ceremonies. It recalls a way of life that was strong enough to etch a vivid set of images. That way of life constitutes the school's style; it describes the *learned* and *shared* behavior of the school, its culture.

12. What were the dominant features of the learned and shared behavior, the cultural style, of the high school you attended?

In spite of the rich diversity among schools it is possible to group them according to their cultural styles for purposes of study. Some schools tend to have a way of life which has much in common with that of other schools. Some teachers present models to their students which are similar to those presented by others. The values that some schools express are expressed by others. This is another way of saying that schools have some common ways by which they socialize the young, transmit the culture, and select and sort students. We turn now to four types of schools which perform these functions in similar ways. In short, we look at schools which represent four cultural styles.[5]

The schools attended by Hamid, Raymond, Beth, and Julia are good examples of four different cultural styles. We can place these schools on a continuum in respect to their styles. At one end is Hamid's village school, with its American counterpart, "the little red school

[5] For a perceptive discussion of three types of schools in American culture see Margaret Mead, *The School in American Culture,* Cambridge, Massachusetts, Harvard University Press, 1951.

house." Next to it is Raymond's school in the town of Midwest. It is neither purely rural nor urban in its cultural style but lies somewhere in between. Farther along the line is Beth's suburban school. Its cultural style is neither that of town nor city. It partakes of both but adds cultural flavors of its own. Finally, at the other end of the line is Julia's city school, with its mixed cultural style that reflects the diversity of the people around it.

Cultural Style of the Village School

There are far more village schools today than most Americans would suspect. They spread in growing numbers over the face of the developing world. They are to be found in the bush and on the veld of Africa, in Asia's barren hills, fertile plains, and valleys, and spread across the length and breadth of South America. They symbolize the growing interest of people everywhere in providing an education for their children.

The American counterpart of the village school, the "little one-room school house," still exists in parts of rural America, but it belongs to a vanishing era. Not so in other parts of the world, where the spread of education is symbolized by an open plot of ground in some remote area where parents have gathered after a hard day in the field to build a school for their children. The land itself is frequently donated by the villagers from their pitifully meager earnings. The materials are gathered together from contributions, and the labor is provided by the parents. After the work is done the proud parents beseech the education officials in the city to send a teacher for their children. This pattern of getting a school and teacher is not unlike the efforts of small American communities to obtain a doctor by first gathering funds to build a clinic and then imploring a doctor to come and use it.

Hamid's is a good example of a school with a village style. It sprang from the very hands of the villagers. They obtained the land and built the high mud wall around the open compound. They nailed together and painted black the crude boards which serve as the portable chalk board. They selected the teacher from among their tribal fellows.

Indeed, Hamid's school was in operation for over a year before the educational officials of the region were even aware of its existence. This is significant for it indicates something about the cultural style of village schools everywhere: They are close to the people. It was no great concern to the villagers that the education officials did not come. In fact, some would probably have preferred that they not come, for they come from the city, a foreign and remote place suspected by the villagers.

They did not want their children to learn city values. Because the school was built to perpetuate village values, education officials from the city threatened the fulfillment of this purpose. The villagers were happy that there was an almost one-to-one relationship between what was taught in school and taught at home. The school behind the high wall was regarded as a simple extension of the homes behind other high walls.

This organic unity was felt by Hamid and his schoolmates. The school imposed no new ideals, opened no strange vistas, spoke rarely about the future and preparing for it. Hamid's future was known, determined within the expectations of the village and family. He was to take no sharp departures from the family's occupation, learn no disturbing new ideologies, perform no acts which lacked time-worn examples. Hamid's school held him close to his past, fixing in him its value, motivating him to follow its precepts. It gave sanction to what was already regarded to be of value. It looked to the past rather than the future and valued stability over change.

Hamid's teacher was selected to teach because he reflected these values. His formal education was good for his surroundings—a high school certificate. The villagers, although they respected him for his learning, did not select him for his learning. Other men had that, too. But other men did not belong to the dominant tribe of the village, did not wear the village dress or speak its dialect. Other men with an education were not orthodox in their religious observance, did not pray toward Mecca five times a day or abstain from eating during the daylight hours of Ramadan, the holy month.

Hamid's teacher did all these things. He was the counterpart of the good father in the home, a secular counterpart of the holy man who sat and taught in the mosque, a reasonable image of "every man" in the village. He held the boys in his school close to their surroundings. In their eyes he represented the stability of the village, the long continuity of their culture, and assurance of its perpetuation.

13. Select one or two of your own teachers whom you have known well and compare them with Hamid's teacher with respect to the matters mentioned above. How were they alike? Different?

We said that the village school has its counterpart in the "little one-room school house" in America. These schools embody many of the values of Hamid's school, with some cultural variations. These schools draw their teachers from the surrounding neighborhood, em-

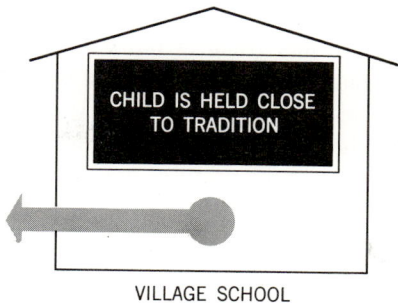

VILLAGE SCHOOL

Fig. 11-1

ploying perhaps the son or daughter of a successful local farmer. The teacher knows the families from which the children come and teaches brothers and sisters of the same family, reminding Mary what Susie did "when she was in my room." This teacher establishes continuity between home and school, helps to hold children close to their past, and assumes that their future will tend to replicate the lives of their parents. He teaches the skills and values which will make this possible.

In spite of the rapid moves toward consolidation in American schools, 10,000 one-room schools still operate, scattered largely across the Middle West. These schools are firmly rooted in the fierce pride of rural residents who, like Hamid's adult fellow villagers, want their own school to resist the corrupting influences of the big cities. Here is the story of one such school and its teacher.[6]

"In Unityville, S. Dak., a twelve-family hamlet 42 miles northwest of Sioux Falls, Mrs. Alice Lundberg, 36, drives her white '59 Mercury eight miles from her farmhouse each morning to reach the white wooden schoolhouse by 7:45 a.m. Alone in the 28-ft. by 25-ft. classroom, she spends 80 minutes plotting the day's 36 separate topics for her 17 pupils, who come from seven nearby farm families. She teaches them on six grade levels, from first to eighth (she has no sixth and seventh graders). The 68-year-old school is surrounded by corn and barley fields; 48 silos filled with Government-owned surplus corn loom near by.

"The school has no running water, which explains one of the 'Ten Commandments' hung on the wall: STOP AND THINK BEFORE YOU DRINK. (Another one says: CHOOSE A DATE WHO WOULD MAKE A GOOD MATE.) Children drink from a canister containing

[6] "Public Schools: Survival of the One-Room," *Time*, Volume 85, No. 15, April 9, 1965, p. 45.

rainwater drained off the schoolhouse roof. Prominent on a bookshelf near the door is a roll of toilet tissue, from which the children unselfconsciously tear off a length as they leave for one of the two privies out back under a couple of evergreens.

"At the 9:05 bell, the patient, methodical Mrs. Lundberg plunges into her multiple chores. For 15 minutes she flashes reading cards to her three first-graders, has them read a story, George and the Cherry Tree. Some of the others stray from their individual assignments to follow the story. Next comes a second-grade language class for Keith Myren, 8, and Becky Koepsell, 7, interrupted by questions from the still-reading first-graders. Then second-graders read aloud, while Mrs. Lundberg checks desk-to-desk on the work of others. An eight-minute science lesson for the fourth and fifth grades centers on such questions as 'Why is water often muddy?' Mrs. Lundberg deftly fields second-grade arithmetic questions while teaching eighth-grade biology, stops to help a boy identify a picture in his reading book. If a pupil cannot get her attention, he amiably asks an older pupil, who is happy to help.

"So it goes throughout Mrs. Lundberg's day. The children remain cooperative and orderly, observing the rule that no more than two can leave their desks at once. Mrs. Lundberg, who has taught for 16 years in one-room schools, has altered her methods little during that time, and doubts the value of such trends as new math and language techniques. 'We prefer the traditional methods,' she says. 'The only technique is good planning.' "

14. Do you think Mrs. Lundberg's approach to teaching would work in suburban or city schools? What are your reasons for answering as you do?

15. Mrs. Lundberg has not changed her teaching methods much over the years. Do you think her students in one-room schools have changed very much over the sixteen years she has taught? Do you think students have influence on the kind of teaching methods which are used?

16. Anthropologist Margaret Mead makes this statement about the one-room American school: "Like so many symbols of the American dream, it stands both for a desirable state never attained, and for a past golden age which has been lost—the school in a world which did not change, a world of rural images, where 'blackberry vines are running' and goodness was literally symbolized by a 'clean slate.'" What do you think Mead means by this statement?

What do this one-room school and Hamid's school symbolize in their unique cultural style? They represent schools in relatively stable social settings, schools which mirror the stability of their surroundings, which hold children close to the family, village, and countryside. We said that education both perpetuates and changes culture. These schools are hard on the side of perpetuation. All schools perpetuate existing culture in some way and to some extent, and in this sense all schools have a village style. But village schools, like the people who own and control them, make the preservation and the perpetuation of values their main concern. They are therefore doing what schools in all times and places have done, expressing their culture.

The village school socializes the young in the exact image of the village. It transmits village culture intact. The village school does not emphasize the selecting and sorting function, for its main purpose is to create children committed and dedicated to the village way of life. Selecting and sorting implies that there are several other routes available to children. In village society choice may exist in theory, but in practice it is extremely limited.

17. In this description of the village school we have emphasized its unique cultural style. Turn for a moment to features it has in common with other schools. Can you name some ways in which the cultural style of the village school is like that of town, suburban, and city schools?

Cultural Style of the Town School

The town school, as we said, has a cultural style which is that of neither the village nor the city. It partakes from each but has distinctive characteristics of its own. For one thing, Raymond's school in Midwest has a more heterogeneous student body than the village school.[7] In it are both "town" and "country" children who represent more than one social and economic class. In the one-room village school the children are pretty much alike in social and economic background. Difference begins to appear in the town school. Social-class differences are not great, however, and the children in Raymond's school do not divide themselves rigidly along class lines, largely because the adults in the town do not. There are no slums, no exclusive shops, no narrow streets, and no mink coats. There is a great amount of contact and communication between social classes. For example, Mrs. Willits, who is in the "upper-lower" class of Midwest, does washing and housework for families in the upper-middle and lower-middle classes. However, she is frequently a guest of the clubs to which the wives of the families for which she works belong. She may be a guest at one meeting and a paid helper at the next. In Midwest there is a great deal of social participation across class lines. The easy mixing of children in the

---

[7] For the following description the author is indebted to Roger G. Barker, Herbert F. Wright, Jack Nall, and Phill Schoggen, "There Is No Class Bias in Our School," *Progressive Education*, Volume XXVII, No. 4, 1950, pp. 106–110.

school, regardless of class lines, is a reflection of the social arrangements in the community.

The cultural style of the town school is reflected in the school board which is responsible for the administration of the school. On the board are the "solid" members of the community who represent the upper- and lower-middle classes. They have a higher class position than either the teachers or the majority of the students. But there is little disagreement among the social classes of Midwest regarding the functions of the school. Parents in the upper classes do not aspire to have a kind of education for their children greatly different from that of parents in the lower classes. Although there is not in Midwest the solid unity about the school as in Hamid's village, there is a consensus about what the school ought to do.

The social position of the teachers of Midwest is also descriptive of the cultural style of town schools. They come predominantly from the lower-middle class, but they are not sociological strangers in Midwest. They have close connections with families both above and below them. They are firmly established in the community and they draw their support more from their status as citizens than as teachers.

Teachers in Midwest are not greatly dependent on professional status for security and satisfactions. Teachers are not highly professionalized members of a close, isolated, or insecure professional group which is set off from the rest of the community. They do not take refresher courses, in part because they are not urged to do so and in part because of family and other obligations.

Three classroom teachers of Midwest are married women; two of them live on farms. Two of the three specialized teachers of music and athletics are men, one of whom has extracurricular farming interests. These teachers are not using the teaching profession as a ladder to reach higher social or professional status. They are solid, middle-aged citizens who are rooted in the community.

Teachers of the town tend to have a wide range of tolerance of individual differences among their pupils, a value they share with village teachers. Not having rigidly fixed professional standards, they exhibit more tolerance than highly professionalized educators. The teacher may be concerned about a youngster's poor reading ability, but he knows there are other important values in life. The child's physical strength, reliability, and initiative will make him a good farmer, an occupation of which he approves. These teachers, who have a wide scale of values and a broad tolerance, reflect the town culture.

Teachers of the town do not regard it as their duty to create anxieties in pupils or to make them upwardly mobile. Rather they regard their function as that of teaching students the values and skills of a wide sector of the community.

Another feature of the cultural style of the town school is that the teachers know the students personally as individuals, and not solely professionally as students. Half of the teachers in Raymond's school have lived in Midwest for many years and know the "cumulative record" of the child far beyond that which exists in the school's files. Through the informal communications network they see the child in the perspective of his parents, his brothers and sisters, his out-of-school playmates, his religious affiliation, his total "life space." The teacher knows the anecdotes about the child, his reputation, his foibles.

18. How important do you think it is for a teacher to know a child as an individual as well as a student?

Perhaps this student-teacher relationship distinguishes the cultural style of the town school from other types of schools better than any other single feature. In city and suburban schools the contact between teacher and student is highly professionalized. In the town it is both professional and personal, with the personal aspect of the relationship being the far more pervasive. Teachers who have only professional acquaintance with children see but one side of the child, his "classroom" side. Teachers of the town bring to the professional relationship a cumulative record which extends far back into family and community. They see more than surface features and deal with him in accordance with deeper behavior characteristics.

The smallness of the town contributes to the school's cultural style. The school's size provides an important deterrent to social-class bias. Its activities include all of the children. If the school were large it would be more selective. Like the community, the school requires wide participation of all its members. Thus, children of widely differing backgrounds are accepted in the school and begin to adjust early to the realities of human difference.

19. Do you think the student activities program of a town school will differ from that of a suburban or city school? If so, how? Why?

What does the town school symbolize in its cultural style? It symbolizes the next step away from the almost complete organic unity of community and school in the village. Diversity is beginning to appear, but that diversity is within an essentially unified community. The community has definable geographic boundaries as identifiable value boundaries. Teachers of the town school are not professionally sophisticated but are broadly tolerant of nonacademic values. Neither

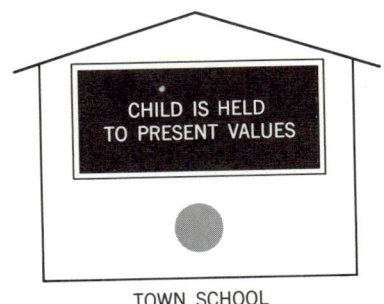

TOWN SCHOOL

Fig. 11-2

they nor parents stir up anxieties in students about school achievement. This school symbolizes education that is ambivalent about change. It teaches students to "take things as they come," neither resisting nor pushing. It holds children close to their past but it does not exclude the future. Its primary orientation is the present.

Thus, the town school socializes the young in terms of town values. It selects and sorts students to some degree, but is relaxed about the process. It does not pressure students to go in directions in which they do not seem to be inclined. Because its broad scale of values permits a kind of natural selection to take place, the town school is not expected to force the child upward.

In this regard the town school's cultural style is in sharp contrast with the suburban school, where the dominant value is achievement for the future.

Cultural Style of the Suburban School

The suburbs that ring our great cities and constantly push out to swallow up more open farm land provide a setting for thousands of relatively new schools on the American scene. These differ sharply from schools of the village, town, and city and have a cultural style distinctly their own.

Many of the people who live in the suburbs were propelled there by the growing congestion of the cities, the deterioration of once elite or middle-class neighborhoods, and the condemnation of land to make expressways and expand commercial and industrial ventures. They come to the suburbs for a variety of personal reasons, "to have a back-yard for the kids to play in," "to get them off the street," "to have a better school," "to live in a place where you can have a say about things."

New suburbanites are prone to change from the beginning. Unlike the citizens of Midwest who had roots deep in the community, the citizens of the suburbs cut their former roots. They are looking for something better both for themselves and their children.

This intentional decision to cut himself off from his former home and take another step up the social ladder expresses the suburbanite's protest and his plans for the future. He knows why he left the city and he knows what he wants in the suburbs. He is vigilant to see that the conditions that caused him to leave the city do not repeat themselves in his new home. He is therefore active in local government and social matters to protect his home against what he regards as evil influences. He is prepared to make claims upon the government and the school in a way which would never occur to the citizens of village or town. His participation is apt to be vigorous and heated. He tells suburban officials what he wants for his neighborhood and tells the teacher what he wants for his child. Suburban governments and schools must, therefore, be prepared to listen and work with citizens who are anxious about their rights and their futures.

20. How do you think parent participation in school affairs might differ in village, town, suburb, and city?

Of course, not all suburbanites come directly from the city. They may move from towns or other suburbs. Mobility, in fact, is another feature of suburban culture. People who are upwardly mobile are likely to be transferred by their employers, take new positions in other cities, or simply move farther out to more exclusive suburbs. Change rather than stability is the dominant feature of the suburb. The future rather than the past or the present is the dominant direction.

Beth's school, which we discussed early in this book, symbolizes this cultural type of school. It is set on a large and landscaped site within the suburb. The architecture of the school is interesting in that it expresses how the community has changed from a village to a suburb with the reaching out of the nearby city. The original building was two-story brown brick with no personality, but it served well when the community was a crossroads village far away from the city. The rural residents regarded the old structure as "their" school, and it had many village features in its cultural style.

Then the new subdivisions began to spring up on all sides. City children began to appear in classrooms where before there were only rural children. First one new wing, then another, finally a third were added to the old brick structure. The new wings are modern one-story buildings with lots of glass and modern facilities. The changing room requirements reflect some of the demands placed upon the school by the new residents—a modern library, music rooms, teacher rooms, cafeteria, gymnasium, and athletic fields. The school which once contained both high school and lower grades soon became inadequate, and a new campus-type high school was built on the rim of the suburb.

The changing program of the school also reflects the changing nature of the community and its educational requirements. When the area was a rural village, few graduates left the brown brick school to attend college; now most of them do. At one time the agricultural program was a main feature; now it is more residual than functional. The stress is on college preparatory programs. Counselors have been added to the program to help students secure college admission, and the "solid" subjects get much stress. The educational look is forward and upward. Whereas the village school orients its students toward the past and the town school toward the present, the suburban school takes its cue from its upwardly mobile public and pushes its students into the future.

21. In Beth's school we have an example of a changing student body owing to a changing community. Do you think these changes in students pose problems for the veteran teachers in the system who came to the school when it was dominated by village values?

The cultural style of the suburban school is nowhere better expressed than in its teachers. We said that teachers in village and town schools symbolized for their children the traditional values of the community. Because they are an integral part of the community, they derive their status and security not as professional teachers but as accepted citizens who are deeply rooted in the community.

This pattern begins to break down in suburbia. A few older teachers who remember the school when the area was a village are a part of its history. They know the "old" families, have wide acquaintances, and are active in church and other organizations. Some of the younger teachers, especially wives, live within the suburb because their husbands hold jobs in the city. But a large number of the teachers are sociological strangers in the community, seeing parents only in a professional capacity at parent-teacher meetings and conferences. They neither own property within the suburb nor are otherwise involved in its problems.

The suburban community takes for granted this relationship with its teachers. It is sufficiently impersonal to grant teachers the right to live their lives as they see fit, short of scandal. It does not place on teachers heavy burdens beyond the school, as do smaller communities, but simply expects the teacher to fulfill his professional role.

22. We are beginning to see now how the cultural style of the school can define the professional role of the teacher. This consideration is important to graduates who are about to enter the teaching profession. In terms of your own concept of the teacher's professional role, where do you think you are most likely to find job satisfaction: in the village, town, suburb, or city?

The impersonality of suburban living is expressed in this expectation of the teacher. If suburban teachers should attempt to become as familiar with the backgrounds of their children as those in Midwest they would likely be told to "stick to your teaching." Because the teacher's role is defined as professional, his status and security must be achieved in the profession rather than in the community. What the teachers of Midwest know almost intuitively about their children from long living among their families, the teachers of suburbia will never know. Their view of the child will be the school view, enlarged perhaps by bits of chance information gathered here and there.

The child is profoundly influenced by the professional role of the teacher in suburbia. He sees the teacher only as "teacher," rather than also as father, mother, community leader, or for that matter as "human being." Thus, the teacher's partial view of the child is matched by the child's partial view of the teacher. One can only speculate whether this partial view of one for the other leads to partial understanding and learning.

Yet the partial view is probably congenial to the main business of the suburban school—academic preparation. The teacher's narrowly defined professional role sharpens the focus upon the academic business at hand in a way that could never happen in village or town schools. The teacher's job is to teach the child to achieve academically. The student's job is to learn academically. Both roles are precisely defined. The broad values of the village and town teacher tend to get screened out in suburbia by the drive for grades and other symbols of academic achievement. Here are suburban students reacting to this aspect of the suburban school's cultural style: [8]

"'We're out for a real drive on marks—the city tests and the national tests, not just the school tests.'

"'Yes, and we work this for all it's worth.'

[8] David Mallery, *High School Students Speak Out*, New York, Harper and Brothers, 1962, p. 25.

" 'And so do the teachers!'

" 'You know, I sometimes wonder if it's really worth it, being in the advanced course and getting all this terrific pressure.'

" 'Yes, you really have to convert yourself into a machine.'

" 'Well, you wouldn't, except for the school's neurotic obsession with college admissions and national tests.'

" 'Who's the school, though? Is it the teachers or is it us?'

" 'It's both, but we're in the fight and they know it, and they know they have us over a barrel.'

" 'The only way you can exist and actually grow as a human being in this set-up is to convert yourself into a machine—no, a super-machine—so that you can knock off all the work, hit the high marks, and have time left over to think and question and explore.' "

23. Can you explain why this student conversation would be less likely to take place in a village or town school, than in a suburban school?

24. What does this conversation tell you about the teacher's professional role in the suburban school?

One final comment should be made about the cultural style of the suburban school. Its student group is homogeneous in social-class background because suburbs tend to attract parents of similar social circumstances. Suburban high school student bodies are apt to be more heterogeneous than those of suburban elementary schools, because high schools draw students from a large area whereas elementary schools serve their immediate neighborhoods. Still, even suburban high schools may be characterized as homogeneous rather than as heterogeneous.

What does the cultural style of the suburban school symbolize? It symbolizes a school geared to the mobile elite of our society. It serves a segment of the population which demands schools that are

SUBURBAN SCHOOL

Fig. 11-3

private in character but public in support. For suburban schools are in many ways similar to private schools. For example, they are exclusive; they draw their students from elite or relatively elite populations. They are academic; their main business is to teach the solid subjects which are required for college admission. They are affluent; they spend more money per pupil than any other type of school. They are educationally stronger; they tend to have the richest curricular programs and attract the best teachers.

The values that suburban schools teach are similar to private school values. The emphasis on history, literature, language, and the arts reminds the student of the past, of the "finer things in life." The selective social setting of the suburban school reminds him of his class position. The emphasis on achievement reminds him that the future must be won.

The cultural style of the suburban school, then, mirrors the values and norms of the middle class. It is in the suburban school that the selection and sorting process becomes feverish, for it is a requirement of upward mobility. The school transmits values connected with achievement, and the socialization process in suburban schools revolves around the acquisition of academic and social status.

Cultural Style of the City School

The cultural style of the city school contrasts sharply with that of village, town, and suburb. Located usually in a crowded quarter of the city, it has an asphalt pavement for a playground, and adjacent, high brick walls for landscape. The milling children on the narrow playgrounds seem like, and frequently are, prisoners of walls and asphalt.

The slum school which Julia attended is representative. Before Julia's time the school served mostly the children of foreign immigrants. It continues to serve immigrants but now the "immigrant" children come from within our own country—Puerto Ricans, Negroes from the South, and whites from worked-out rural areas. The polyglot students speak a babel of dialects, and to most of them standard English is a foreign language. Their food habits are strange to their teachers, their manner of dress sometimes "disgusting," and their behavior "antisocial."

The city school seeks to educate children to a new way of life. It tells them that they must brush their teeth, wash their faces, and speak correctly. It urges them to work hard, compete with their fellow students, achieve. In short, it teaches them to renounce their past and acquire a new way of life.

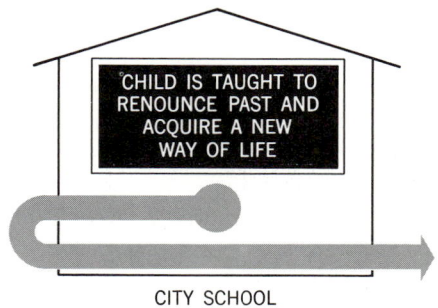

CITY SCHOOL

Fig. 11-4

25. Earlier in this book we spoke of continuity and discontinuity between home and school. How would you compare the four types of schools in respect to continuity and discontinuity with the home?

The village school teaches its children to repeat the way of life of their parents. In so doing it respects and honors that way of life. By contrast the city school teaches children that their immediate environment is worthless and without honor. The suburban school reminds children of their distant past through literature, history, language, and the arts. In preparing them for the future it provides a link with their past. The city school at best can remind children not of their own past but of one with which they have no strong biological or cultural link. As far as the school is concerned, these children are ancestorless.

Thus, the cultural style of the city school is oriented toward the future without the push of the past. The child ventures forth, denying the models in his past and uncertain about those of the future. These children are without the advantage of perspective, and know only that they must move on to something different, something which is apparently more American than the values with which they have been reared.

The conflicts that the city school creates in children were symbolized in Julia. In the arms of an understanding teacher, she found comfort and security which she did not find at home. But ultimately that was not enough. In school "she lived in the reading-book world of Spot, Dick, and Jane, who romp on green lawns under blue skies and eat big meals at grandfather's farm. In that world father is never drunk and mother is always present. 'We try to make school a little bit of heaven for them,' explained Julia's teacher. 'Not for always, but just for now.'" [9] In creating "a little bit of heaven, not for always but

[9] Barbara Cummiskey, *Life*, Volume 52, No. 4, January 26, 1962, p. 65.

just for now" the city school sharpens in the child the conflict between the indefinite future which the school holds forth and the definite present which embraces him. Julia finally had to choose which she would take.

26. Take now the four students, Hamid, Raymond, Beth and Julia, whose schools symbolize four different cultural styles. What "professional styles" do you think these students need in their teachers?

The city school symbolizes education as an agent of change, acting to move children from lower- to middle-class values. It transmits to the students not the cultural values which they have but those to which they should aspire. In terms of the selecting and sorting functions, the city school rewards those students who learn middle-class values and screens out those who do not. It attempts to socialize the student to a new way of life.

SUMMARY

In any discussion of types of schools one can see these four cultural styles: the village school which holds the child, like a parent, close to its own body; the town school which introduces the child to the differences of a heterogeneous community, still holds him close to his past, but not too close, and takes a relaxed attitude toward his future; the suburban school, a modern private school which reflects the upward aspirations of the middle class and urges its students to acquire achievement motivation; and the city school for the in-country immigrants, which teaches children new sets of values and tries to help them to build a bridge between a rejected present and an uncertain future.

Finally, we should add a word of caution about the types of cultural styles described. It is futile to look for ideal types that fit exactly the cultural style of the village, town, suburb, or city school and pointless to force schools into one of these four molds. Such an effort misses the main consideration, that some schools may have in their cultural styles elements of all four types. Some will have many characteristics of one type and few of another. Schools are living, changing institutions and they perform their functions of socializing the young, transmitting the culture, and sorting and selecting students in a variety of ways. As teachers, the important thing is that we learn to see in any school the social functions it performs and the manner in which it performs them. These four classifications become useful when seen as devices for looking at a school to gain a better appreciation of its social functions and its method of executing them.

REFERENCES

Paperbacks

American High School Today. James B. Conant. (Orig.) (12390) McGraw-Hill Paperback Series, McGraw-Hill Book Co., 330 W. 42 St., New York. David McKay Co. ($1.95).

Class in Suburbia. William Dobriner. (Orig.) (S-50) Spectrum Books, Prentice-Hall, Englewood Cliffs, N. J. ($1.95).

Community and Power. The Quest for Community. Robert A. Nisbet. (91) Galaxy Books, Oxford University Press, 417 Fifth Ave., New York ($1.75).

Crestwood Heights: A Study of the Culture of Suburban Life. J. R. Seeley, R. A. Sim, and E. W. Loosley. Science Editions Paperbacks, John Wiley and Sons, 605 Third Ave., New York ($2.45).

Economics and Politics of Public Education, No. 2: Government and the Suburban School. Roscoe C. Martin. (Orig.) Syracuse University Press, University Station, Syracuse, N. Y. ($1.75).

Economics and Politics of Public Education, No. 10: Suburban Power Structures and Public Education. Warner Bloomberg, Jr., and Morris Sunshine. (Orig.) Syracuse University Press, University Station, Syracuse, N. Y. ($1.75).

Economics and Politics of Public Education, No. 11: Social and Economic Factors in Spending for Public Education. Jerry Miner. (Orig.) Syracuse University Press, University Station, Syracuse, N. Y. ($1.75).

Education and the Cult of Efficiency: A Study of the Social Forces that Have Shaped the Administration of the Public School. Raymond E. Callahan. (P149) Phoenix Books, University of Chicago Press, 5750 Ellis Ave., Chicago, Ill. ($2.25).

Education and the Development of Nations. John W. Hanson and Cole S. Brembeck. Holt, Rinehart and Winston, 383 Madison Ave., New York ($4.95).

Education in Culture: Anthropological Approaches. George D. Spindler. (Orig.) Holt, Rinehart and Winston, 383 Madison Ave., New York ($4.95).

Education in Western Culture. Robert Ulich. Harcourt, Brace and World, 757 Third Ave., New York ($1.75).

Educational Anthropology. G. F. Kneller. (Orig.) John Wiley and Sons, 605 Third Ave., New York ($2.45).

Sociology of Teaching. Willard Waller. Science Editions Paperbacks, John Wiley and Sons, 605 Third Ave., New York ($1.95).

Transformation of the School: Progressivism in American Education (1876–1957). Lawrence A. Cremin. Viking Paperbound Portables, The Viking Press, 625 Madison Ave., New York ($2.25).

Books

Brookover, Wilbur B., and David Gottlieb, *A Sociology of Education,* Second Edition. New York: American Book Co., 1964. Chapter 3, "The School as a Social Institution," discusses some of the latent functions of the school: as a retaining force which keeps potential workers out of the labor market, and as a promoter of entertainment via extracurricular activities.

Clark, Burton, *Educating the Expert Society.* San Francisco: Chandler Publishing Co., 1962. Chapter 7 discusses the student culture in the high school, with emphasis on the fun, academic, and delinquent subcultures.

Coleman, James S., *The Adolescent Society*. New York: The Free Press of Glencoe, 1962. Chapter III discusses value climates of various schools, emphasizing grades, leading crowds, ascriptive status, and academic orientation, all within the adolescent culture.

Gross, Neal, "The Sociology of Education," in *Sociology Today, Problems and Prospects*. Robert K. Merton, Leonard Brown, and Leonard S. Cottrell, Jr., Editors. New York: Basic Books, pp. 128–152. Gross's article covers the following topics: social structure and functioning of the school; the classroom as a social system; the external environment of schools; and education as an occupation and a career.

Mallery, David, *High School Students Speak Out*. New York: Harper and Brothers, 1962. Chapter 19, "You're Nothing if You're Not College Prep," although short, gives a strong picture of the noncollege prep student living in the cultural environment of a college-prep high school.

Mead, Margaret, "The School in American Culture," in *Education, Economy and Society*, A. H. Halsey, Jean Flaud and C. Arnold Anderson, Editors. New York: The Free Press of Glencoe, 1962, pp. 421–433. Mead discusses various images of schools in America: the little red school house, the academy, and the city school.

Tyler, Ralph W., "The Impact of Students on Schools and Colleges," in *Social Forces Influencing American Education*, 60th Yearbook of the National Society for the Study of Education, Part II. Chicago: University of Chicago Press, 1961, pp. 171–181. Group attitudes influence what courses students take, and group attitudes and customs set standards which influence the amount, kind of study, and work which students do in school.

Periodicals

Gladwin, Thomas, "The School, Society, and the Child," *Psychology in the Schools*, Vol. 1, No. 2, April 1964, pp. 162–173. An excellent analysis of the many social roles played by the school in the social development of the child.

Henry, Jules, "The Problem of Spontaneity, Initiative, and Creativity in Suburban Classrooms," *American Journal of Orthopsychiatry*, Vol. XXIX, No. 2, 1959, pp. 266–279. The author describes how suburban teachers manage under the pressure of an ideology of permissiveness and spontaneity.

Lagemann, John Kord, "It's Never Too Early to Learn the Economic Facts of Life," *P.T.A. Magazine*, Vol. 59, No. 3, November 1964, pp. 4–7. The article shows how the community and school interact to transmit a cultural value.

Luciano, Orlando Jose, "Primary Education in Brazil," *The Student*, Vol. VIII, No. 10–11, October–November 1964, pp. 10–11. The article illustrates the interaction in the relationships between school and society.

McNeill, I. M., A. E. Howard, and Anthony Chenevix-Trench, "How Our Children Learn About Society," *The Twentieth Century*, Vol. CLXXII, No. 1019, 1963, pp. 78–86. Interviews with three principals on how social responsibility is taught in the secondary schools give a good example of the school's role in cultural transmission.

12

The Educational Climate
of the School

"You don't have to be in a school very long before you *feel* the atmosphere of the place."   ANDREW W. HALPIN

If the school expresses its cultural style through values which are learned and shared it reveals its educational climate through its human relationships. For the school is a web of human interaction, of people who live and work together in particular kinds of ways. Sometimes the way people work together stimulates good relationships and good learning, sometimes bad relationships and poor learning. But good or bad, the school always reveals its human essence by the manner in which the people in it relate to one another. It is this human essence which determines the educational climate of the school.

For example, a teacher has just had a job interview in a school where he thinks he might like to teach. During the course of the interview he talked with the superintendent, a principal, and several teachers who work in the school system. The teachers seemed to enjoy their work. They spoke favorably of the other teachers in the system and commented that the administrators "really back you up." They said that the parents respect the teachers. The superintendent and principal were forthright and forward looking in their educational outlook. When the teacher left he thought to himself: "This *feels* like a good place to teach." His comment is a reflection on the educational climate of the school, on the quality of its human interaction.

THE SCHOOL IS A SOCIAL SYSTEM

The human interaction within a school may be described as a social system. That is, there are defined social positions (students,

270

teachers, principals, etc.) which are distributed, from top to bottom, in an hierarchical order. Persons may interact with others who hold positions different from their own (teachers interacting with principals). When persons who hold defined positions in an organization interact with one another in terms of those positions they constitute a social system. And the way they interact within the social system of the school determines its educational climate.

In this chapter and the two that follow we deal with the educational climate of the school as it is expressed through the school's social system. In this chapter we center attention on the first component of a system, the social positions and the roles which people who hold these positions perform. In the next two chapters we shall turn the social system on, as it were, and observe the interaction among people who hold the positions. When people begin to interact we start to *"feel the atmosphere of the place,"* as Andrew W. Halpin remarks in the quotation at the beginning of this chapter.

What does the school's social system tell us about its educational climate? Why should we be concerned about it? Does it have anything to do with the way teachers teach and students learn? Does it influence what parents think about the school?

We have said repeatedly that learning is a social process. The social system of the school *is* its social process: It determines the nature, quality, and extent of learning in the school. The student who charges that "around here the teachers hate one another's guts and the kids', too," is expressing his feeling about the school as a place to learn. So is the student who exclaims, "Boy, around this place the teachers really go to bat for you. If you don't make it, it's not their fault." Both students are commenting on the social system of the school, on the interaction of people who hold defined positions within it, and both are pronouncing judgments on the school's learning climate.

1. Do you think it possible that two students in the same school might make such contrary statements? If so, can you explain such different perceptions of the same school? What factors might determine a student's perception of the school's climate?

FORMAL AND INFORMAL SOCIAL SYSTEMS

In Chapter 7 we discussed peer groups. Such groups are informal and voluntary. In terms of status, some are "in" and others are "out." These student groups exist largely apart from the organized structure of the school and constitute an *informal* social system among students.

Such a system may encompass anyone in the school whose interaction is not prescribed by the position he holds. The teacher and student who exchange thoughts about mutual interests in trout fishing are a part of the informal social system of the school.

When, however, the same student and teacher confer about a geometry problem they are interacting within the formal social system; they are acting from their respective positions as student and teacher and not as two people who happen to have a common enthusiasm for trout fishing. The formal social system of the school, then, consists of the formal positions, the status relationships among them, and the interactions of the people who occupy them. The informal social system encompasses the relationships which are not prescribed by the formal structure of the organization.

2. Which aspect of the social system of the school, the formal or informal, engages the greater energies of the student? Of the teacher? Does your answer tell you anything about the respective roles which students and teachers play in the school?

In the sense that the school's human relationships constitute its climate it has both an informal and formal atmosphere. We turn first to an examination of the formal climate of the school as it is expressed in the positions that constitute the formal social structure.

The Formal Social System of the School

The formal social structure of the school may be thought of as a hierarchy of positions along which people are assigned different roles. A person's position in the hierarchy is determined by his *authority* and *responsibility*. Those positions that carry the most authority and responsibility are at the top of the hierarchy, those with average authority and responsibility in the middle of the hierarchy, and those with least are at the bottom.

Who, we may ask, determines how much authority and responsibility a position possesses? Frequently the determination is made legally. The state, for example, charges local school boards with maintaining and operating schools and confers upon that body high authority and responsibility in local education. When members of that same board are elected by local voters, as they are in many states, the authority and responsibility of the board is subject to the will of the people. The local citizens cannot change the statutory powers of the board but they can change the membership and therefore the policies of the board if they choose to do so. The voters' authority and responsibility therefore exceeds that of the board of education.

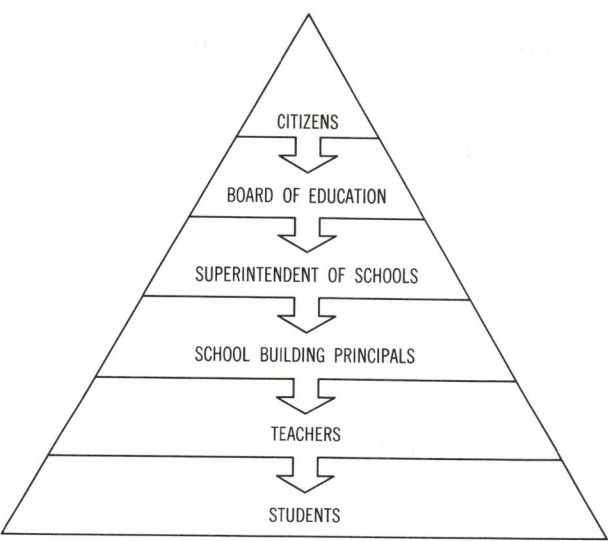

Fig. 12-1 The formal social system of the school consists of the formal positions, the relationships among them, and the interaction of the people who occupy them.

Sometimes the authority and responsibility of a position is determined by the individual who holds it. A "strong" superintendent, principal, or teacher lends power to the position he holds whereas a "weak" person weakens the position he holds. The strong superintendent may increase his power by diminishing that of the board of education, or a strong principal may increase his power at the expense of the superintendent. Thus authority and responsibility may shift within the social system of the school, depending on the personality of those who hold positions in it.

Let us look at these positions and roles as they are usually ordered in the formal hierarchy of the school, according to their authority and responsibility. That order is: citizens, members of the board of education, superintendent of schools, principal, specialists, teachers, service workers, and students.

Citizens. In the American public school system the citizen plays a dominant role. Ours is a long tradition of local control and financial support. All citizens must support education through taxes, even though they may have no children in school. The principle that all citizens benefit equally from education and should therefore pay equally was not easily established in America, but it did prevail. The struggle for free schools, open to all and supported by all, is a fascinating story in American history. Notice, for example, the forceful argument used by Thaddeus Stevens in a fiery speech before an 1834 session of the Pennsylvania legislature. Stevens had sponsored in the legislature a free-school bill which would tax all citizens equally. The bill was under heavy attack by the enemies of free schools, and Stevens rose to defend it.

"Many complain of this tax, not so much on account of its amount, as because it is for the benefit of others and not themselves. This is a mistake; it is for their own benefit, inasmuch as it perpetuates the Government and insures the due administration of the laws under which they live, and by which their lives and property are protected. Why do they not urge the same objection against all other taxes? The industrious, thrifty, rich farmer pays a heavy county tax to support criminal courts, build jails, and pay sheriffs and jail keepers, and yet probably he never has, and never will have, any personal use of either. . . . He cheerfully pays the tax which is necessary to support and punish convicts, but loudly complains of that which goes to prevent his fellow-being from becoming a criminal, and to obviate the necessity of those humiliating institutions." [1]

3. School bond and millage elections sometimes fail in communities where a large proportion of the voters have no children in school. Do you think that the argument which Thaddeus Stevens encountered in 1834 could help explain such failures?
4. Stevens argues that free schools will prevent people from becoming criminals. Can you cite any evidence either for or against his argument?

With local financial support came the local control of schools. Various ways were devised for asserting this control: Sometimes local municipal bodies or officials appointed boards of education. Sometimes members of boards of education were elected directly by the people. In the rural Middle West the township trustee, an elected official, was responsible for the operation of schools. Whatever the means of appointment or type of the controlling body, the control of the school remained close to the local community.

Although all citizens share in the financial support of the school and most in the direct or indirect control of it, not all take an equal interest in its operation. The citizens who are parents of school children are understandably the most interested in the school and are at

---

[1] "A Plea for the Public Schools," in *Report of United States Commissioner of Education,* 1898–99, Volume 1, pp. 519–520, 522–523.

least quasi-members of the school's social system. In this chapter and the next we are more interested in the position of "parent" than simply "citizen."

Members of boards of education. Boards of education symbolize local control of American education. They also symbolize lay citizen control over the professional educators, teachers, and administrators who actually carry on the school's day-to-day business. It is the board of education which is legally responsible to the community and the state, which appoints a chief executive officer, the superintendent, and which sets the policy within which the school operates. Members of boards of education cannot act legally as individuals but only as a body. For example, an individual board member cannot authorize the employment of a superintendent but the board, acting together, can.

Citizens are likely to seek a place on boards of education for a variety of reasons, some in the public interest and some not. A rising politician may see a seat on the board of education as a springboard to larger political power. A citizen from a subdivision with no school may run for the board in order to get a school for his home area. Another may frankly be the candidate of a strong interest group in the community: labor, management, a real estate group, city hall, a service club, or a political party. Citizens may run for the board of education in order to "fire" the superintendent or correct a fault they perceive in the school program. Many members have been elected on a pledge "to keep taxes down."

5. Businessmen who serve on boards of education may, quite naturally, apply business standards to the operation of the schools. They may boast that they "are making things run smoothly," and are "hard men with a dollar." Yet teachers, administrators, and parents like to boast that they are providing constantly better education for children, which costs more money, and frequently change things so that they don't run smoothly. What do these conflicting expectations tell you about the social system of a school? About the responsibilities of teachers and administrators?

School boards are institutions which represent democracy in its finest and most frustrating aspects. On the whole they have brought strength to American schools. Far beyond all selfish reasons for membership has been that of service to education. Public-spirited citizens have probably been attracted to boards of education in larger numbers than to any other local governmental body. To get elected they have usually had to understand something about local education and its problems and convince the voters that they could improve things.

The following statements were prepared by the candidates for the board of education in a suburban school district at the request of the League of Women Voters and were published in the local newspaper prior to the election.[2] Notice how prominently teachers figure in these statements. Notice also the variety of school needs which the candidates see.

Candidate A

Candidate A is a 37-year-old hardware retailer. He grew up in the school district and is secretary-treasurer of the Businessmen's Association. He is the father of six children in the district's schools, in grades 4, 6, 9, 10, 12, and kindergarten.

"One of our greatest problems is communication between the school board and the community. We need to find out what the people want to do about the problem of the schools. What I think isn't important; it is what the majority thinks. I am in a position in my business to hear what people think, and would be available to most people in the community at all times.

"We are losing a lot of good teachers. I don't know the reason, and I would not say the problem is totally pay. We should find out why we are losing them, and do something about it. I believe we ought to have all certified teachers to lend more dignity to the profession.

"One of the problems I hear most about is the classification of students within grades in the elementary schools. I am neither pro nor con the classification, but there are so many complaints from parents of children in all classifications that something has to be worked out to the satisfaction of people in the district.

"The businessmen in town are double taxpayers, and want to know more about school problems. There may be instances where we can get a little more value for the money we are spending.

"I am waiting for the report of the Citizens' Committee study before making any final recommendations about school problems."

6. Candidate A says that one problem he hears most about "is the classification of students within the elementary schools," referring to the ability grouping of students, a matter which we discussed in Chapter 4. Which parents do you think complain—those with children in "slow" or "average" groups, or those with children in "gifted" groups? Does the fact that parents would mention this matter to another parent and hardware merchant tell you anything about the dimensions of the school's social system?

[2] *The Meridian News*, Williamston, Michigan, Volume 6, No. 31, May 29, 1963, pp. 1–6, 7.

Candidate B

Candidate B is the mother of four children in grades 4, 8, 10, and 12, has resided in the district nine years, and is active in Cub Scouts and the PTA.

"Any problems currently facing our school district can be solved only as all parents within the district work together toward a solution. I feel I might be of service to the schools by working to: 1) help provide the best education possible for all children in the school district within the limits of current finances; 2) do all I can as a citizen of the school district to work with other local governing bodies to bring desirable industry to this area to help improve the tax base; 3) help provide a desirable climate for acquiring and maintaining a superior and interested teaching staff, and to encourage parent support of teachers.

"We have a desperate need for more recreational facilities, such as tennis courts, outdoor basketball courts, or shuffleboard. Working together we can provide better recreational activities for our teenagers and also make better use of available facilities, such as making the library available for community use in the evening.

"The increased guidance program is a step toward meeting the emotional needs of our children, but we need to work as a community to broaden the special education program to include children with emotional problems. We need to improve school-community relations. I would encourage the continued use of the school Newsletter, which has been effective in improving communication between the home and school."

Candidate C

Candidate C, a sanitary engineer, is 34. He has a master's degree, is active in church work, has lived in the district eight years, and has three children in school.

"An important need is an adequate program to embrace the educational needs of every student during this technological space age period we find ourselves in today. We must provide a balanced program to meet each facet of education, which would include not only the academic, but social, both organized sports and general recreational needs, the moral training and counseling of our youth today.

"It is imperative that our educational system prepare the student, who will not continue his or her education at the college level, such that each will be well adjusted to enter today's society and have the training and preparation necessary for gainful occupation. It is just as important, if not more important, that our educational program be geared to provide the basic background for the more gifted student who is preparing for study at the college level.

"It is urgent that our curriculum provide these students with college calibre preparatory training in English, language studies, mathematics, physical and social science if he is to endure the transitional change from high school to college training.

"Realization of these goals can be achieved by providing alert and progressive leadership on the Board of Education. Board members must keep well informed of the various school needs such as physical plant, curriculum, accreditation, teacher evaluation, student development and accomplishments to provide a progressive school system for our children."

7. There is great interest among the candidates about communication between the school and community. What does this indicate to you about the public role of the teacher or school administrator?

Candidate D

Candidate D, age 38, is a bacteriologist who works in the Game Division Laboratory of the State Department of Conservation. He belongs to the American Legion, the local Athletic Club, and has a child in kindergarten, third, eighth, and eleventh grades.

"The most important problem facing our school system is the one that has always faced all school systems: providing the best education possible within the means of the people in the school district. To be effective and efficient a school system must have a solid foundation in its faculty; basically, schools are teachers and pupils. I feel our school system should strive to attract and keep good teachers. In general the academic offerings seem adequate. In some instances improved teaching methods and faculty would increase the quality of education offered.

"The Board of Education is continually faced with the problems of expansion, construction and finance. I believe that building construction should be undertaken cautiously, and with restraint. I feel there has been a laxity in building and grounds maintenance. This has recently received some attention, but should not have been allowed to develop as far as it did.

"The physical education program should receive more emphasis, intramural as well as interscholastic. The grounds should be improved and equipment should be provided so that students may participate in physical education and athletics in complete safety.

"In summary, I feel: 1. The faculty should be strengthened. 2. Physical expansion should proceed cautiously. 3. Maintenance should be improved. 4. Physical education facilities should be expanded and improved."

8. You may have noticed that much is said in these statements about the need to keep and employ good teachers. Very little is said about internal classroom matters such as curriculum, teaching methods, or instructional materials. Do you think there may be a reason for this? Does it tell you anything about the respective roles of teachers and board members?

These candidates represent the American citizen's involvement in local education. Taking their authority and responsibility from powers delegated by the state to the local school district, they must rank just below the citizens in the social system of the school.

The superintendent of schools. The superintendent is the executive officer of the board of education, is answerable to the board, and is held responsible by it for the operation of the schools within the school system. The superintendent is a professional educator, in contrast to members of boards of education who in most cases are not. The superintendent usually worked previously as a teacher and principal. He arrived at his position by moving up the educational ladder, either in his present school system or another.

The superintendent makes recommendations to the board of education regarding the employment of principals, specialists, teachers, clerical, custodial, and other personnel. He makes recommendations on curriculum and building programs, prepares budgets, and is in charge of the total operation. The good superintendent is sensitive to the educational needs of the schools in the district and works with both the professional staff of the schools and the board of education to improve education.

Superintendents of schools interpret their roles in a variety of ways. Some may think of themselves as corporation *executives,* hired to direct the school system for the board of directors, the board of education. Some see themselves as *business managers* with teams of education specialists around them whom they hold responsible for the educational program of the school. Some superintendents regard themselves as *educators,* concerned about curriculum, learning, and teaching, with business specialists around them whom they hold responsible for the management side of the schools. Superintendents may see themselves as *public relations experts* who keep the teachers and students happy and give the community what it wants in education. Then there are superintendents who think of themselves as *educational poli-*

ticians seeking consensus among the conflicting power groups which attempt to influence the schools. Finally, there is the superintendent who thinks of himself as a *leader*, encouraging the teachers, students, and community to greater efforts and improved education.

As we shall see in the next chapter, the superintendent's job is likely to require him to play all of these roles.

9. Interview a superintendent of schools in order to discover the various roles which he plays.

The principal. Whereas the superintendent is responsible for the operation of the entire school system the principal is usually responsible for the operation of one building. He has a day-to-day contact with the teachers in the building, represents the needs of his school to the superintendent, works for curriculum and teaching improvement, and endeavors to keep the organization running smoothly. The principal is close to the thinking of parents in the community around his school, for they frequently bring their children's school problems to him. He knows how the teachers think, especially if he is the kind of person who invites their confidence. Like the superintendent, the principal usually has held lower educational positions as classroom teacher or as specialist, or both, prior to being appointed the principal. Access to the higher positions lies through those lower down on the educational hierarchy.

The specialist. The educational specialist represents a relatively new element in the social organization of the school. His work symbolizes the increasing complexity of education, the increase in knowledge about the needs of students, and the increase in financial ability to provide more specialized educational services to students. The specialist's position in the social hierarchy of the school lies usually between that of teacher and principal. However, if the specialist has systemwide responsibility to which high priority is given, his position may be between that of a principal and superintendent. For example, a curriculum consultant who works with all the elementary teachers and principals of a large city system has higher status than the teacher of slow learners, another specialist, who works in a single school. Other specialists' positions include: school psychologist, counselor and guidance workers, audio-visual directors, school nurses, and teachers of children with speech, reading, physical, emotional, or social handicaps.

The specialist, to perform his role, must work closely with classroom teachers and principals. Sometimes the specialist is granted supervisory power over the teachers, but usually he is regarded as a "consultant." The specialist may work directly with teachers and only indirectly with students, or vice versa. If he works directly with students the relationship tends to be different from that of the classroom teacher. The work of the speech therapist is an example. He works with children on a small group or individual basis, whereas the classroom teacher works with children in large groups. The speech therapist is responsible for only one aspect, the classroom teacher for all aspects of the child's educational development.

The classroom teacher. The classroom teacher's key role in working with students is inconsistent with his relatively low status in the social organization of the school. Within the classroom, to be sure, the teacher has high status and autonomy: He is in charge. Within the school hierarchy, however, he is not in charge. Further, he is frequently the object of directives, persuasion, and suggestions coming from all those who outrank him in the social organization—specialists, principals, superintendents, board members, parents, and citizens. Yet good school systems are learning how to enhance the value placed upon the teacher's work and hopefully his status. It is the teacher who mediates among children. He is held responsible for their educational development. If the educational program of the school has an impact on the child, that impact must come through the teacher. Perhaps this is another way of saying that the teacher's function is central in the purposes of the school, but that the importance of this central function is not reflected in the hierarchical organization.

The service workers. Descriptions of the social system of the school frequently neglect to mention the nonprofessional employees. Yet the secretaries, receptionists, dietitians, cooks, custodians, and bus drivers play a vital role in giving the school its climate. They are in continual contact with students, teachers, administrators, parents, and other citizens. They are a part of the web of human relationships. The custodian who opens the school at night for a parent-teacher meeting, has the physical arrangements in good order, and does his job with courtesy and skill, is adding to the positive image of the school. The food workers in the school cafeteria have influence through maintaining health standards and through dealings with the students who go through the cafeteria line. The good secretary or receptionist makes a positive contribution to the educational climate of the school.

The students. The students are the "clients" of the school system and its reason for being. Yet in terms of their responsibility and authority the students must be placed at the bottom of the formal social structure. In some schools students are given considerable responsibility, for example, in areas of classroom planning and student government. In certain instances they may be given actual authority. But student responsibility and authority are always given at the sufferance of adults and they may be withdrawn at any time. Responsibility and authority are not built into the student role as they are into adult roles in the school.

10. We have just described the usual positions in the formal social system of the school and their respective status ratings. This pattern may not fit all schools, indeed probably does not. Think now of the school you attended. Were there positions other than those which we described here? Was the status hierarchy different? If so how?

11. Select one of the roles played by persons in the school's social system —student, teacher, specialist, principal, superintendent, board member, or parent—and learn what you can about what is expected of persons who play that role. Report your findings to the class.

These, then, are the positions in the hierarchy of the school's formal social system. Let us turn to a consideration of the informal social system.

THE INFORMAL SOCIAL SYSTEM OF THE SCHOOL

The formal social system of a school can be diagrammed neatly on an administrative chart, with positions represented by rectangular boxes, top to bottom. Lines connecting the boxes describe the formal relationships among the people who fill the boxes. People holding certain positions may be coordinate with those holding similar positions; they may be superordinate or subordinate to persons occupying other positions. The formal social system correctly assumes that people *tend* to behave according to what is expected of their roles. A teacher, for example, who becomes a principal tends to behave no longer as a teacher but as a principal. The student who becomes a teacher shifts his behavior from that of student to that of teacher. In fact, the main business of teacher education is to train students to behave like teachers. Role behavior lies not only in the individual and his uniqueness; it lies also in what the role *expects* of the individual.

People tend to live up to role expectations. But not entirely. Happily, humans are not exclusively organization people conforming blindly to the formal expectations of their positions. Teachers are both "humans" *and* teachers, though students may find it difficult at times to accept the fact. For example, the little girl who warned her mother: "When you come to school, Mom, be on the lookout for the principal. She goes right into the crowd and disguises herself as a person." [3]

___

[3] Marie G. Kosko, "Laughter, the Best Medicine," *Reader's Digest,* Volume 87, No. 516, May 1965, p. 123.

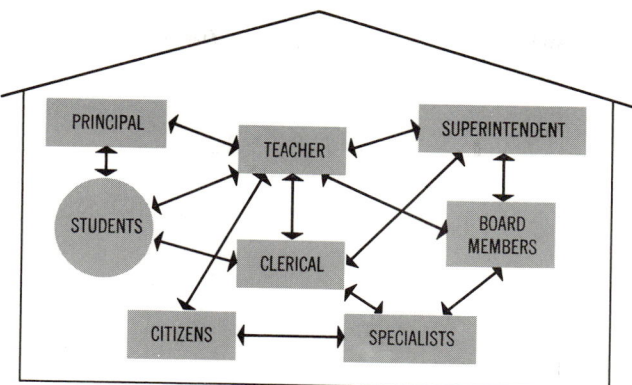

Fig. 12-2 The informal social system of the school encompasses the informal relationships which are not prescribed by the formal structure of the organization.

The informal social system of the school is based upon this ability of people to escape their formal positions and "disguise" themselves in other roles.

Whereas the formal social structure is diagrammatically neat, the informal social system is a scramble of friendship lines which tie people together within and across many boxes and lines. It represents the ability of people to humanize cold bureaucratic structures and to associate with kindred souls. It also represents a way for people to defend themselves against other persons in positions of formal power.

For the informal social system does itself have power. Teachers who do not like a program that they may feel the administration has imposed can quietly agree among themselves to subvert it. Students who do not like a school policy can take measures to have it changed. In these cases the struggle becomes one between the established formal structure of the school and the informal social structure. Notice in the following newspaper account how students used their informal power to change an administrative decision.[4] They did not get the order reversed but they did get it modified. Notice also how in the ensuing struggle the students rallied the support of the parents in their fight with the formal authority of the school.

"About 700 students who walked out of Lincoln Park High School Monday protesting the lack of two senior class functions have been suspended for two days.

[4] "Suspend 700 Pupils for Walkout," *The Detroit News,* Volume 92, No. 231, April 9, 1965, p. 1.

"Principal Thomas M. Cuozzo said the students will not be permitted to attend school on Monday or Tuesday and will be kept an hour longer on Wednesday and Thursday.

"An order that the students would not be permitted to make up any tests or work missed during the two-day suspension was revoked when 70 students and parents protested at a special Board of Education meeting last night.

"The parents and students, while agreeing with the two-day suspension order, said the order barring makeup work was 'too severe.'

"About 200 students had demonstrated in front of the school protesting the lack of a cap and gown day and 'skip' day for seniors, despite an appeal by one of their class leaders to call off the demonstration. . . . A special 12-member citizens' committee, which will study the student grievances, was formed last night."

12. What do these two facts tell you about the authority and responsibility of the positions of principal, board member, and parents?

a. The Board of Education modified an order of the principal under pressure from parents.
b. "A special 12-member *citizens'* committee" was set up to study student grievances.

The informal social system of the students has considerable influence upon academic achievement. In Chapter 7 we examined the impact of the peer group on the adolescent's academic achievement. The formal authority of the school obviously pushes the student to learn. The informal authority of the peer group may push him not to learn. This informal authority of peers may influence academic achievement more than the formal authority of the school. James S. Coleman, in his major study, *The Adolescent Society*,[5] has shown that in ten Midwestern high schools the students' informal social system applies sanctions to support athletics and social activities and discourage scholastic achievement. In these schools the student elites placed less value on academic achievement than on extracurricular activities. In the informal social system of these schools the status of the brilliant student was not valued. He was often regarded as being subservient to adults, and was more sensitive to adults than he was to the standards of his peer group. Coleman's research strongly suggests that in these schools the informal social system of the students was consciously subverting the formal social system of the adults.

[5] James S. Coleman, *The Adolescent Society*, New York, The Free Press of Glencoe, 1961.

Informal personal relationships may exist among and between persons at different levels of the formal social structure. Teachers may be on close personal terms with members of the board of education or with the superintendent of schools. The principal may enjoy the company of the consultants and supervisors, and teachers may develop a relationship with students which goes far beyond the formal relationships of the classroom. Here a teacher in *Crestwood Heights* describes her informal relationships with students.[6]

"I am the female on the staff who has been married and can therefore discuss various problems of sex with the girls. Many of the girls are very friendly towards me, and eight separate girls gave me individual Christmas presents this year. I am pretty proud of that . . . This has been going on for some years now. We often come down to one of these offices or to my room. Or down at the old school with the stagger system I often couldn't get my own room and we would have to meet in the lobby and discuss things with the other students milling around. They (the children) are quite frank about it and will discuss problems in front of one another. Often the boys will hold up the girls and sometimes they will disagree. They seem to be most concerned about saying 'good-night.' Every year before the Prom we have two periods of discussing boy-girl relationships and obligations—during the history classes."

13. Do you think this teacher is a better teacher for having these informal relationships with students?

14. This teacher, "every year before the Prom" extends informal discussions into the formal history class. Would you, as a teacher, like to do this?

The informal social system of the school serves many useful functions. Let us look at a few of them.

Informal relations humanize bureaucratic systems. There are neither enough social positions, nor a large enough variety, in any bureaucracy to accommodate human behavior. A formal social position in a school is far too small a box to contain a living human being. The informal social system should permit humans to express their individuality beyond the role of student, teacher, specialists, principal, or superintendent.

Informal relationships help to get the job done. Frequently in human affairs personal relationships are more compelling than bureaucratic urgings. A friendly discussion over a cup of coffee will fre-

[6] J. R. Seeley, R. A. Sim, and E. W. Loosley, *Crestwood Heights*, New York, John Wiley and Sons, Inc., 1963, p. 272.

quently break loose in a few minutes business which has been jammed in bureaucratic machinery for weeks. Further, subordinates like to work informally with their superiors if they can identify with them on a friendly, face-to-face basis.

Informal social systems provide a means of free expression. School policy is frequently argued within .the formal structure, for example during faculty and board of education meetings. People attend these meetings in their official roles, as "teacher," "consultant," "counselor," "principal," "superintendent," or "board member." In these roles they may feel restricted and unable to say exactly what they would like. In informal discussions which follow people "let down their hair," talk freely, and frequently uncover aspects of the problem which went unexamined before. The principal in a faculty meeting who proposes to the teachers "talk this matter over among yourselves and see what ideas you can come up with" is using the informal social system of the school to arrive at a better decision.

The informal social system of the school is, in some respects, an invisible system. It does not show itself on the administrative chart of the school. It consists of persons who do not hold neatly labeled positions. There are no official titles. Still the informal system is there, and powerfully so. It can work either for or against improved teaching and learning.

FACTORS INFLUENCING THE OPERATION OF THE SCHOOL'S SOCIAL SYSTEM

In Chapter 13 we shall study the social system of the school in action. It seems appropriate, therefore, to conclude this chapter with a discussion of certain conditions that influence the nature of school social systems and how they operate.

Socially Complex Schools Reflect Complex Communities

Mrs. Lundberg, the teacher of the one-room school in Unityville, South Dakota, teaches in a small homogeneous community. It is entirely agricultural and rural. There are no industries, no extremes of wealth and poverty, no culturally mixed population. The social system of the Unityville school consists of one teacher, seventeen students, their parents, and a few others. All the business of this school can be transacted on an informal, face-to-face basis. It is a simple, uncomplicated, social organization.

Contrast Unityville with a modern suburban school system with five hundred teachers, ten thousand students, scores of specialists and administrators, a nine-member board of education, all in a community of fifty thousand people. The web of human relationships within the school becomes fantastically complex.

Complex Social Systems Make for Complex Roles

The roles of students, teachers, specialists, administrators, board members, and parents all become increasingly complex in modern, urban schools. Mrs. Lundberg in Unityville knows well what constitutes her role as teacher. She knows what to expect, because each new day tends to repeat yesterday. She can pursue her traditional ways with a sense of security about what the future will bring. The urban teacher is different: The multiple roles he plays in the space of each day reflect the complexity of his position. He may collect milk money, sell tickets, meet with the PTA, serve on a committee, confer with a parent, counsel a student, supervise a practice teacher, help plan a new school, take courses at a nearby college or university, and, oh yes, teach.

The same complexity characterizes all other social roles performed within the school. They pull people in many different directions and cause them frequently to ask precisely what it is they are supposed to do. Because the definitions of roles which were appropriate before are no longer realistic, these perplexing questions are raised: Who am I? What is my job?

Complex Tasks Lead to the Creation of New Social Roles

The strain put upon school personnel encourages a greater division of labor. New roles are created to meet the need for extended educational services. These new roles find their niche in the social organization and soon are as firmly rooted as the traditional ones.

Counseling and guidance is an example of a field which has witnessed unusually rapid expansion. In schools with a village culture, counseling tends to be handled by the classroom teacher—and frequently also in schools with an urban culture. Indeed, in the larger and more complex schools teachers traditionally performed counseling and guidance functions. However, two factors have worked to make counseling and guidance a specialized function: (1) the increasing use of psychological and achievement tests and (2) the proliferation of jobs in our technological society for which students may prepare. Let us briefly examine each of these.

Chapter 11 cited an example in which the faculty explained one school's testing program to the board of education. The administration of this array of tests alone requires a full-time specialist, to say nothing of their interpretation and use with students. Most schools start to develop a file on each student in the early elementary years. The file contains biographical and anecdotal material as well as test results. As the student moves up through the grades, so does the file, accumulating more material as it goes. This cumulative record becomes increasingly confusing to anyone but a skilled interpreter. The classroom teacher, who is not specialized in test and personnel record interpretation, becomes more and more dependent for this service upon the counseling and psychology experts.

Second, the number of vocational opportunities available to graduates are multiplying rapidly in our technological society. Many of the positions for which students may prepare did not even exist a decade or two ago. The large amount of vocational material and endless vocational opportunities suggest additional need for specialists who can advise students with some degree of expertness.

Although new specialities have sprung up around the classroom teacher, the teacher himself has tended to remain "a teacher," without specialized functions. But this, too, is changing. Burton R. Clark predicts: "It seems likely that a differentiation of teaching positions is on its way in the public schools. Generally speaking, there is now only one official status for teachers in the schools—teachers are 'teachers,' with pay differentiated by years of service and amount of educational preparation (the bachelor's degree, the master's degree). As knowledge becomes more specialized and teaching a more complex task, a dividing of the teaching role enters into consideration. Teachers vary greatly in training and ability, and only some can handle certain demanding tasks. Some school boards and administrators are seeking ways of paying higher salaries to a few teachers without disastrous effects on the morale of the others, in order to attract and retain exceptional persons who otherwise are likely to pursue a career outside of education." [7]

Differentiation among teaching roles is taking place in new innovations such as team teaching in which "master" teachers do the lecturing, while other teachers work with smaller groups or carry on other activities. The use of teacher "aides" to relieve teachers of paper work and menial chores tends further to differentiate types of teacher roles. The practice of having teachers of the "gifted" and "slow learners" pushes specialization within classroom teaching still further. We may now expect to see many new social roles for teachers, just as we have seen new roles for other school personnel.

[7] Burton R. Clark, *Educating the Expert Society,* San Francisco, Chandler Publishing Company, 1962, pp. 181–182.

The New Social Roles Center on the Student

Earlier specialization in the schools centered on subject matter *per se* and the advancement of knowledge about subjects. The new specialization centers on the child and his psychological needs. As the authors of *Crestwood Heights* remind us: "The emphasis is less upon *what* is to be transmitted and more upon *how* it is to be transmitted, with much attention to the consequences of the learning process upon the formation of the child's character."[8]

The whole new emphasis upon psychological and achievement testing and counseling focuses upon the child. The work in the "new" mathematics and science is concerned with developing concepts which can be understood by the child and instructional materials which are geared to his particular requirements. The working assumption is that a child can learn almost anything if we understand how he learns and teach him in harmony with that understanding.

The Greater the Specialization the Greater the Status

Generally speaking, the degree of one's specialization determines one's status in the school's social system. The students who are the least specialized have also the least status. The superintendent of schools, who may be regarded as the most specialized because he directs the work of other specialists, has high status. The specialists mentioned earlier, the psychologists, counseling and guidance workers, and curriculum consultants in reading, mathematics, and science, are more specialized than classroom teachers. They enjoy more status. Salaries are also positively related to the degree of specialization which a position requires; higher salaries tend to be paid to those with greater specialized training, with the usual justification that a longer period of preparation deserves higher compensation. Higher salaries, in turn, tend to give greater status.

Finally, we should note that our generalization about specialization and status does not extend to the board of education, a group of nonspecialists in the field of education. Members of the board might be, and frequently are, specialists in other fields. Their "lay" position in respect to education symbolizes, as we said earlier, the American belief in local and citizen control of education. These nonspecialists delegate the actual operation of the school to specialists in education who carry out their policies.

[8] J. R. Seeley, R. A. Sim, and E. W. Loosley, *Crestwood Heights,* New York, John Wiley & Sons, Inc., 1963, p. 262.

The Greater the Specialization the Greater the Autonomy

Specialization not only tends to give status to social roles, but it also gives autonomy and freedom to act. The teacher, whose degree of specialization is low, enjoys autonomy in the classroom. Yet his work is subject to control and scrutiny by many others in the social system, the principal, specialists, the superintendent, parents, and members of the board of education. His freedom to act is usually hedged in by someone else's freedom to act.

The teacher's autonomy suffers further from the fact that everyone, because he has spent years as a student observing teachers, thinks he knows all about teaching. In a sense the teacher's position suffers from overexposure. Few people, however, have had first-hand experience with the work of a school psychologist, for example, or of specialists in reading or mathematics. Persons holding these positions have advanced training of a type which frequently is little understood by classroom teachers, principals, superintendents, or parents. These people have no direct way to check the work of the specialists, and the absence of such control endows the specialist with freedom and autonomy in his work.

Social Roles May Carry Conflicting Demands

Any social role is likely to have conflicting requirements built into it. The teacher, for example, must be both friend and judge of his students. On the one hand, he needs to understand his students, be sympathetic with their problems, and project the image of one who cares personally about them. On the other, he must "sort and select" his students, evaluate, and grade them. Teachers find these two conflicting requirements difficult to reconcile, and express their concern in such statements as these: "Mary's a cute one, but I hope I didn't let my liking for her influence her grade," and "I detest Johnny's behavior, but I guess he still deserves an 'A' in the course. He topped the class on the final."

Teachers also frequently experience conflict from the different expectations of students and their parents. Parents like to think that the teacher represents their own adult values in the classroom and will maintain high standards of conduct and work. Students, on the other hand, put pressure on the teacher to "give" here and there.

Administrators also experience role conflicts. The principal, for example, stands between the superintendent and the teachers. The superintendent and the teachers play quite different roles in the school system and make different demands upon the principal. Since the principal must work closely with both teachers and the superintendent, he may be described as the "man in the middle." If he listens entirely to the superintendent the teachers may tag him as the administration's "office boy." If he listens exclusively to the teachers he may jeopardize his chances for promotion.

The superintendent also experiences role conflicts, standing as he does between the board of education, a lay body, and the school's faculty, a professional group. The board represents the parents' and taxpayers' points of view, themselves frequently in conflict. The professional educators on the faculty represent the expert's point of view. Because they approach education from different vantage points, citizens and educators frequently have different sets of priorities for the school. It is the job of the superintendent to create sufficient consensus between the board of education and the professional staff to achieve forward motion rather than a stalemate. Frequently he must do this by getting a working consensus between conflicting points of view.

Part of the skill required of all persons who hold educational positions is the ability to mediate between conflicting demands.

Role Conflict Springs from Differing Expectations

A teacher may see his role in one particular way, the principal may see the teacher's role in another way, the superintendent in yet another. The superintendent may hold one view of his own job, the board of education another. The teacher may see his teaching responsibility as stopping at the classroom door. The principal may see it as

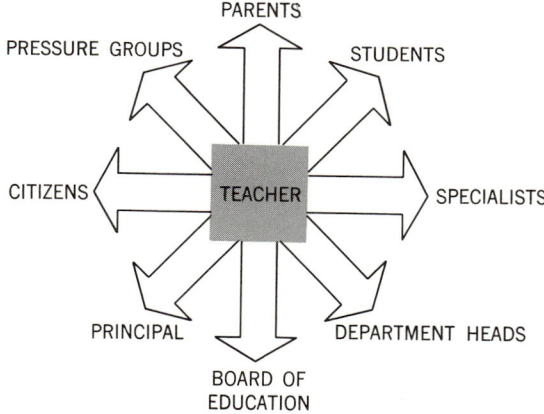

Fig. 12-3 Persons holding educational positions must be able to mediate among conflicting demands.

extending into the corridor, the lunchroom, and the playground. The superintendent may view his position as one to which the board delegates full responsibility for operating the schools. The members of the board may regard it as part of their task to check directly on the operation of the school, the classrooms, the cafeteria kitchens, and the safety of the school buses.

When conflicts such as these arise, teachers and administrators alike should remember that people who play different roles are apt to hold different expectations. Indeed it makes good sense to try to learn the expectations of the relevant persons. The teacher has a right to know what the principal expects of the teachers in the building. Likewise the principal needs to know how teachers view their tasks and what they expect of him. Through full and frank discussion there is a good possibility that the conflicting expectations can be resolved.

Entrance to the Social Hierarchy Is Through the Educational System

Gaining entrance to the social hierarchy of the school requires that the applicant pass successfully through the elementary, high school, and college or university. Most schools now require that teachers have at least a bachelor's degree. Once in the system teachers must do advanced academic work, and many states are now requiring a master's degree or its equivalent for full certification. Thus entry into and permanent status in the system can be assured only by advanced training.

Promotion within the Social System Requires Both Experience and Advanced Training

Moving up through the hierarchy to positions of greater responsibility and authority requires both advanced training and experience. Practically all specialists in the school system have, at one time, been classroom teachers. Classroom teachers would look with great suspicion on the counselor who had not himself taught in a classroom. The same may be said for the teacher's attitudes toward consultants in reading, mathematics, science, or other subjects. It would be inconceivable that a principal could achieve that position without having served at least with moderate distinction as a teacher. The school psychologist may not have come up through the classroom, but his advice will probably be taken more seriously by the teachers if he has.

Advanced training is an important factor in promotion within the system. The reading specialists have taken and successfully passed advanced graduate work in this field. The principal likely has a master's degree in school administration; those who hold the doctor's degree may look for a position as superintendent of schools or as a university professor. Counselors hold at least a master's degree in counseling and guidance, and some hold the doctor's degree.

The size of the school system influences the pattern of promotion. A classroom teacher may move quite easily from a village or town school to a suburban or city school. Such a leap is more difficult for those higher up in the hierarchy. A person who has been a principal or superintendent of a small school may move on to progressively larger schools, until he finally holds a position in a major school system. The odds are against his making the leap in a single jump.

These are some of the conditions which influence the operation of the school's social system and help to determine its educational climate. We are now ready to study the system in motion, to examine the kinds of interaction which take place among the people in the school as they carry out their assigned roles.

15. This may be a good time for you to interview a teacher in depth. Learn all you can about the "life style" of the teacher you have selected to interview: his perception of his role as teacher, his status in the social system of the school, the conflicts he experiences as teacher, the degree of autonomy he enjoys. Find out all you can about the teacher's deepest satisfactions and greatest frustrations.

REFERENCES

Paperbacks

American Secondary Schools. Mawritz Johnson, Jr. Harcourt, Brace and World, 757 Third Ave., New York ($1.75).

Educating the Expert Society. Burton R. Clark. (Orig.) Chandler Publishing Co., 124 Spear St., San Francisco, Calif. ($2.75).

Helping Teachers Understand Principals. Wilbur A. Yauch. (Orig.) Appleton-Century-Crofts, Division of Meredith Publishing Co., 440 Park Ave. South, New York ($1.10).

High School Principal and Staff in the Crowded School. William C. French. (SSA) Teachers College, Teachers College Press, 525 West 120 St., New York ($1.50).

Schools. Martin Mayer. (A331) Anchor Books and Anchor Science Study Series, Doubleday and Co., 277 Park Ave., New York ($1.45).

Schools, Scholars and Society. Jean D. Grambs. (Orig.) Prentice-Hall, Englewood Cliffs, N. J. ($2.25).

Sociology of Teaching. Willard Waller. Science Editions Paperbacks, John Wiley and Sons, 605 Third Ave., New York ($1.95).

Books

The Association for Supervision and Curriculum Development, *Leadership for Improving Instruction.* Washington, D. C.: National Education Association, 1960. Chapter 4 discusses the role of teacher, principal, consultant, guidance worker, and superintendent in instructional improvement.

Brookover, Wilbur B., and David Gottlieb, *A Sociology of Education*, Second Edition. New York: American Book Co., 1964. Chapter 10, "The School as a Social System," is concerned with an analysis of the significant positions in the school society and the relationships that commonly exist between these positions.

Charters, W. W., "An Approach to the Formal Organization of the School," in *Behavioral Science and Educational Administration*, 63rd Yearbook of the National Society for the Study of Education, Part II. Chicago: University of Chicago Press, 1964, pp. 243–261. Charters believes that administrative structure develops from the nature and complexity of the cooperative enterprise.

Coleman, James S., *The Adolescent Society*. New York: The Free Press of Glencoe, 1962. Chapter 8 discusses the psychological effects of the social system and Chapter 9 concentrates on the scholastic effects of the social system.

Gordon, C. Wayne, *The Social System of the High School: A Study in the Sociology of Adolescence*. Glencoe, Ill.: The Free Press, 1957. The general theme of this classic work is: "Dominant orientation to action for adolescents in the school tends toward the fulfillment of expectations of the informal group."

Riesman, David, *The Lonely Crowd*. New Haven, Conn.: Yale University Press, 1950. Riesman demonstrates how cooperative relationships are highly valued in American society. When the teacher asks students to cooperate she is really asking them to be "nice."

Seeley, John R., R. A. Sim, and E. W. Loosley, *Crestwood Heights: A Study of the Culture of Suburban Life*. New York: John Wiley and Sons, 1963. Chapter 8 has an interesting section subtitled "the social system of the school." The classroom, in the authors' opinion, is the most potent unit of interaction in the total social system of the school.

Westby-Gibson, Dorothy, *Social Perspectives in Education*. New York: John Wiley and Sons, 1965. Chapter 14 discusses the school as a social organization, considering both the formal and informal systems.

Periodicals

Katz, Fred E., "The School as a Complex Social Organization," *Harvard Educational Review*, Vol. 34, No. 3, Summer 1964, pp. 428–455. The article studies the whole school as a social system.

McDill, E. L., and J. S. Coleman, "Social System of High School and Academic Aspirations and Orientation," *National Association of Women Deans and Counselors Journal*, Vol. 28, No. 1, Fall 1964, pp. 10–17. Results of a four-year study show that values which shape adolescent academic behavior are to a large extent a function of adolescent social interaction.

Wilhelm, Fred T., "Using the Curriculum to Build Personal Strength," *The Bulletin of the National Association of Secondary School Principals*, Vol. XLVIII, No. 288, 1964, pp. 90–115. The author believes that schools are responsible for teaching both subject matter and personal development of students, and that subject matter can and must be used to achieve personal development.

Wodtke, Kenneth H., and N. E. Wallen, "The Effects of Teacher Control in the Classroom on Pupils' Creativity-Test Gains," *American Educational Research Journal*, Vol. 2, No. 2, March 1965, pp. 75–82. Teachers encourage creativity by showing tolerance for the ideas of their pupils and by allowing the pupils more freedom to follow up their ideas.

13

Board Members,
Administrators,
and Teachers

"Where does the teacher appear in the organizational framework? In this district the classroom teacher finds himself and his pupils in a center position, supported by the superintendent, the principal, consultants, school board, and parents."
ROSEMARY HILLMAN

A school calendar is a remarkable sociological document. It spins out the events in the school's life which are the scene of a thousand human interactions. Those who doubt that the school is a social system will find the calendar's long list of activities and implied relationships convincing evidence to the contrary. Those who think that schools confine themselves to classroom learning may be shocked to see the wide-ranging program of student activities. In the calendar are listed the rituals and rites of the student culture: initiations, fashion and talent shows, banquets, concerts, proms, and activity nights.

The foreign visitor who thinks that schools are strictly confined to the business of masters and pupils must be perplexed to see in the calendar such items as a meeting of the Athletic Boosters Club (composed of fathers), a chicken barbeque for the Parent-Teachers Association, and a rodeo for school bus drivers. If our foreign visitor comes from a country where the control of local schools is vested in the central government he will be curious about the item which states "Regular meeting, Board of Education."

Below is the May Calendar of a suburban school which reveals all these facets of the school's social system. Implied within it are all kinds of relationships: parents and teachers, teachers and students, students and students, superintendents and members of the board of education, and many more. Absent from the calendar, of course, are the many human relationships found in the classroom. These school relationships are the subject of this chapter and the next.

May Calendar

1 "Come Blow Your Horn," Barn Theater, 8 p.m.
3 Honor Society Initiation, High School Cafeteria, 8 p.m.
4 ICEA Banquet, High School Cafeteria, 6:30 p.m.
  Home Economics Fashion Show, 7:30 p.m.
  P.T.A.—Board meeting, at Central, 8 p.m.
7 Fifth Grade Visitation—Central
  Jr. High Report Cards mailed home
10 French Club Banquet—Union Ballroom
  Regular meeting, Board of Education
  Student Teachers' Workshop
11 P.T.A. meeting Central—Gym
13 Spring Concert—Gym, High School, 7:30 p.m.
18 Athletic Booster Club, 7:15 p.m.
21 High School Talent Show, 8:15, Gym.
  Eighth Grade Activity Night
22 Ward P.T.A. Chicken Barbeque
  Bus Drivers' Rodeo
23 Honors Tea, Cafeteria, High School
25 Vision Screening, Ward
  P.T.A.—Cornell
26 Kindergarten Roundup ALL ELEMENTARY SCHOOLS
27 Joint Administrative Council meeting, 2 p.m.
  Orchestra Concert—Central
29 Junior-Senior Prom
30 Memorial Day

1. In Chapter 12 we described the various roles that people perform in the social system of the school. How many of those roles are represented in this calendar of school events?

2. From this calendar what would you infer about the nature and extent of the teacher's out-of-class responsibilities and relationships? The student's out-of-class responsibilities and relationships?

3. Some critics of the schools claim that there are too many "frills" in the schools, and that schools should concentrate more on the "3 R's" and the solid subjects. Could you defend this calendar to such a critic?

4. We said that the school's cultural style consists of the learned and shared values which it transmits. Does this calendar give you any clues about this school's cultural style?

In Chapter 12 we described the positions people hold and the roles they play in the social system of the school. Positions and people alone, however, do not make a social system; they only describe the characters in the play. The play becomes a play when the characters *act* and *react* to one another. Without action and reaction there is only a tableau.

In this chapter and the next we shall catch characters in action. As we watch the interaction among them we shall be interested in such questions as:

(1) *What are the dominant relationships in the school?* We said earlier that the school is a web of human interaction and that it would be almost impossible to diagram the maze of relationships. Certain people, however, relate more to some people than to others, and it is with these dominant relationships that we are concerned. In this chapter we shall discuss the interaction of:

(a) Superintendents and boards of education and
(b) Administrators and teachers.

In Chapter 14 we shall study the interaction of:

(c) Teachers and teachers
(d) Teachers and students
(e) Teachers and parents, and
(f) Students and students.

(2) *How does the behavior expected for each role influence these dominant relationships in the school?* Each social position, we know, carries with it an expectation of behavior. How do these expectations influence the interactions of teachers and students? Principals and teachers? Superintendents and members of the board of education?

(3) *What are the conflicts in role expectations? How do people resolve these conflicts?* Each person who holds a position in the social system of the school is expected to behave in certain ways, but sometimes these expectations are in conflict. In this chapter and the next we shall cite examples of conflicts and observe how they are handled.

(4) *How do human relations influence the learning climate of the school?* We shall discover that human interaction can open or close the climate of the school to good learning. What are the ingredients of the "open" and "closed" climates?

Let us turn to the first of the dominant relationships we shall discuss, that between the superintendent of schools and members of the board of education.

SUPERINTENDENTS AND SCHOOL BOARDS

Begin with the economics of the matter: The board of education hires and fires the superintendent of schools. Tenure does not protect him. He may have a contract, but his only real security is in the skill with which he performs his job. He serves at the discretion of the board, and he is its executive officer.

The board of education may hold for the superintendent an array of expectations, some of them impossible to accomplish, some possible, a few conflicting, and many sensible. Depending upon the nature of the school system, the superintendent may be expected to be, for example, a transportation expert, operating a fleet of buses larger than the city's; a cafeteria manager, feeding more people each day than all the restaurants in town; a highly paid custodian, making sure that the buildings are clean and in good repair; a school construction expert, making sure that the new schools are the latest and finest; an executive, employing hundreds, sometimes thousands, of people; a financial expert, managing a budget of millions of dollars; a labor negotiator, keeping custodians and teachers on the job and satisfied; a public relations expert, promoting education in the community; and above all an educator, strengthening education in the district.

The superintendent's interaction with the board is always conditioned by these expectations, yet these are not the only expectations to which he must be sensitive. The board of education represents the community. Behind it are the citizens, each holding his own expectations of the schools. Although the superintendent works directly with the board of education, the legally responsible body, he must also work with all those who stand behind the board and who voice their opinions through it or directly to him. The board also judges the superintendent's ability to "handle the public."

5. The superintendency is sometimes called an "impossible" job because of the array of expectations and the frequent conflict among expectations. Interview a superintendent or invite one to class in order to find out the various roles which he is expected to perform in his position.

The following newspaper account of a school board meeting lists the items of business upon which the board took action. This rather prosaic account catches the superintendent fulfilling some of the expectations of his job. Notice, for example, how the superintendent is cast in these roles: school financial expert, special pleader for education, labor negotiator with custodians, educator, mediator between the board and the teachers' professional association, businessman collecting bids, paying bills and meeting a payroll, and overburdened executive requesting an administrative assistant.

"Ron Ritter, Center City's high school football and track coach for the past two years, has resigned. His letter of resignation was approved by Center City's School Board at its regular meeting Monday night.

"Although Mr. Ritter's letter did not specify where he would go, it did say that he was resigning to go to a post which offered him an excellent chance for advancement. . . .

"The board also voted to ask residents to approve the levying of 4 mills for five years at the June 15 election. The funds will be used to replace the mills that expired in December. Approval would mean about $75,000 in additional funds to the school district.

" 'Without its approval we're going to have to do some deficit financing,' said School Superintendent Fred Jaffy. 'We work on a tight budget and we have no padding for extra expenses.'

"The board approved hours reductions and a salary hike to custodians in connection with an across-the-board salary increase of about 5 percent for employees other than members of the teaching staff.

"The custodians will work 40 hours a week instead of the usual 44 with the provision that they must accomplish the same amount of work in the 40 hours that they accomplished in the 44 hours. Each custodian also is responsible to inspect the schools on every tenth Saturday and Sunday.

"The increase has already been planned in next year's budget.

"The board approved fees for those interested in Center City's summer educational and recreational program. The program will run from July 5 to August 13. . . ."

6. The extended school year is becoming common in many districts. Does this tell you anything about the cultural style of this particular school? What do you know about the merits and shortcomings of year-round school programs?

"The board also:

"—Accepted a bid of $2,154 from Fox Electric Inc. for installation of three lamps on concrete poles to light up the high school's parking lot.

"The lights will be manually operated and will be placed directly in front of the building.

"—Approved the professional negotiation agreement, effective July 1, which specifies the channels for airing of teachers' grievances and other matters 'of mutual concern.'

"Under the agreement the Center City Education Association through its Professional Negotiations Committee will represent the professional staff for the purpose of meeting with the Board of Education to discuss such things as working conditions, salaries, teacher contracts, dismissals, and other matters of concern.

"The proposal was submitted jointly by both groups. The men responsible for it were John Hanks and Ralph Morrow (board members), and Dean Squires and Mel Dunham (teaching staff)."

7. In this example the Board of Education and the Professional Negotiations Committee of the faculty worked out an agreement regarding discussions on matters vital to the teachers and the Board. The Superintendent was not a member of either group. Does this tell you anything about his relationship with each group in this matter?

"—Heard a request from Superintendent Jaffy for an administrative assistant to help him with the growing chores of his position. The board will discuss the matter further in its July 29 special meeting.

"—Heard a request from high school teacher Dean Squires to increase his position on the teacher salary scale. The board reached no final decision.

"—Approved payment of bills totalling $8,406.24 after Superintendent Jaffy said that the board had 'ample funds to cover payment of salaries and bills through August.'" [1]

This news item illuminates three crucial aspects of superintendent and school board relations. First, there are the wide-ranging responsibilities of the superintendent, as well as those of the board. School operations are many sided, ranging from lights in the parking lot, to tax support, to classroom learning. Second, the wide-ranging responsibilities account for the multiple expectations of the superintendent. Because there are a variety of tasks for which the board is ultimately responsible there are a variety of expectations of the man who is the board's executive officer. Third, much of the interaction between the superintendent and the board takes place in public view. To be sure, the give-and-take is private on many occasions. But the school's business is, and should be, public. Therefore, much of the interaction between superintendents and members of the board is conducted in open meetings where interested citizens and the press are present. Since both parties are aware that many people may hear or read what is said, an understandable strain is put upon the relationship.

These three factors dramatize the large number of test points in the relationship, places where things go wrong, misunderstandings arise, and clashes develop. They also dramatize the need for the superintendent to possess well-developed human relations skills. If the su-

[1] Barry Miller, "Haslett Coach Resigns," *Towne Courier,* Haslett, Michigan, May 11, 1965, Volume 1, No. 6, p. 11.

perintendency were a single-dimension position, if the board were one man, if the community were of one mind, the relationship would be relatively simple. But the position is complex, the expectations multiple, and the publics to be served are many. In short, local school-board operations are public, visible, and open to scrutiny and misunderstanding.

Note, for example, the interaction between the superintendent and members of the board in the following newspaper report. The concern of the members for their public image as reflected in the minutes of the meetings, the intense interest in being sure that the right persons get on the list of election inspectors, the anxiety over the amount of time spent in meetings, are all evident.

"In one of their longest meetings this year, Lanston Board of Education members Thursday night tangled over a host of issues ranging from board minutes to election inspectors.

"Caught in the middle during some of the fray was Dr. William R. Mann, superintendent of schools.

"One of the longtime sore points which came up for review was the practice of board members amending minutes of their regular meetings.

"Harold A. Orr, board member, noted that the board spent about 35 minutes correcting minutes at Thursday night's meeting and said he thought it 'was asinine' to go over the minutes in such detail at each meeting.

"He said he could see no point in the board wasting time correcting commas and inserting semicolons, among other things.

"Orr suggested that board members, if they want to amend minutes, should submit the proposed changes to the superintendent ahead of time to save all the motions and resolutions during regular board meeting time.

"Dr. Mann said he agreed that the amending of minutes in many respects 'is a waste of time.'

" 'I don't think all this amending business is important. What is important is the resolution that the board finally adopts,' he said.

"The superintendent noted that there is a recording secretary present at all formal meetings with a tape recorder but added 'you sometimes tell us that this is what you said but this is not what you meant' and then we have to change the minutes.

"Dr. Mann suggested the possibility of hiring an official recorder with a legal background to take minutes if that is what the board wants. He suggested that the whole matter be reviewed with the administration."

8. Why do you think these board members are so concerned about the way they are quoted in the minutes? Does this concern tell you anything about the nature of the control of our schools?

"Following this, board member Thomas C. Wall complained about informal board meetings which are held during the day about once a week. He said the board often fails to complete its agenda at these sessions and noted that he often is not able to stay until the meeting is completed.

"Douglas M. Aims, board member, commented that if board members would 'quit fooling around with forensics,' these meetings could be handled with more speed.

"He balked at one suggestion that the board consider holding two noon meetings a week and said he also is pressed for time. Aims said if the board considers two meetings a week he might have to consider resignation from the board. He added, 'Don't second that.' "

9. Our American schools are controlled by "lay" citizens who are busy with many other interests besides the schools. Does this fact indicate anything to you about the working relationship between the superintendent and members of the board of education?

10. Some persons claim that local school boards are outdated and that the operation *and* control of the schools should be put entirely in the hands of professional educators. Do you agree or disagree?

"Dr. Mann again entered the picture and said he doubted the value of two meetings a week. He said the administration has an endless list of topics which could be brought up for review but added that he felt it was more important to get through the more vital issues.

"Vernon D. Eber, board member, said he thought the best way to settle the matter would be to have an automatic adjournment of noon meetings at 1:30 p.m., whether the agenda is finished or not.

"Still another argument arose later in the meeting when Dr. Mann presented a list of election inspectors for board approval. The list, made up by the city clerk, involves inspectors who will conduct the December 15 Community College election.

"The list contained 234 names and Dr. Mann said he had only one copy. Wall and Eber objected to the fact that they did not have an opportunity to go over the list.

"Dr. Mann, plainly surprised, said 'you mean you actually would object to some persons on this list?' Both Wall and Eber said it had happened in the past and they wanted to look at the names.

"This issue was put to a vote and the list was adopted 4-0, with Wall and Eber abstaining. Dr. Mann noted that an abstention is a yes vote. Wall shot back 'it is also a protest vote.'

"Earlier in the meeting Wall and Dr. Mann engaged in a prolonged debate over adoption of a policy on the federal free lunch and milk program in the schools. Wall objected to deficit financing aspects of the program and the superintendent made a long and detailed explanation of complications involved in administering the lunch project. Wall moved to have the issue tabled and this was defeated. After a lengthy tangle over parliamentary procedure the policy was finally adopted.

"Wall also objected later to late receipt of administrative staff reports which Dr. Mann puts out once a month. He said he did not have time to review them before the meetings.

"The superintendent indicated that it might be better to have fewer staff reports but other board members said they did not want any change in this policy.

"Dr. Mann indicated he would attempt in the future to break up the printed reports over a period of time rather than submit them all at one meeting." [2]

It would be a mistake to imply that all board meetings display the edgy human relations of this one, or that superintendents and boards are incapable of working together. In the majority of cases the opposite is true. The work gets done efficiently and well, with mutual regard and respect on both sides. One of the classic studies in superintendent-school board relations, conducted by Neal Gross and entitled *Who Runs Our Schools?*,[3] supports this view. Gross interviewed in depth over 100 school superintendents and 500 members of school boards of education in Massachusetts and found most of the conflicts and problems mentioned here. He discovered that on the whole, however, the two groups thought well of each other. Approximately half the superintendents rated the school board members as excellent, and one-third rated them as "good." Similarly, about half of the members of the school boards gave their superintendents a rating of "excellent," and another 40 percent gave them ratings of "good."

TEACHERS AND ADMINISTRATORS

We should first recall the respective positions of the teacher and administrator in the social hierarchy. The teacher is near the bottom and the administrator near the top. The principal of the school, for

[2] Robert Stuart, "Clashes Interrupt Long Board Meeting," *The State Journal,* Lansing, Mich., Volume 110, No. 207, November 20, 1964, p. A-2.

[3] Neal Gross, *Who Runs Our Schools?,* New York, John Wiley and Sons, Inc., 1958.

example, is accepted by most teachers as the supreme authority of the school: "After all, he's the principal, he is the boss, what he says should go, you know what I mean . . . He's the principal and he's the authority, and you have to follow his orders, that's all there is to it." [4] But the teacher is subordinate not only to the principal. He is sometimes subordinate to specialists and always to the superintendent and members of the board of education. In some ways he is subordinate to parents.

One of the first jobs of a teacher, then, is to strike a balance in respect to the power structure of the school. He must be on good terms with the principal, the specialists, the superintendent, parents, and members of the board of education. In accomplishing this diplomatic feat the teacher is in the position of the teacher described in *Crestwood Heights:* "He has to accomplish his end without antagonizing any of the numerous specialists encompassing his path, both within and marginal to the school system. More difficult still, he must attempt to please, without appearing to do so. Like his opposite number, the budding junior executive, if he tries too hard, he runs counter to the prevailing taboo on competition and also to the society's maturity values which call for a high degree of independence and individuality. Yet, if he does not try at all, he runs the risk of being thought apathetic, 'uncooperative,' or lacking in professional interest." [5]

The teacher is not his own boss. In contrast to the successful lawyer, dentist, doctor, or architect, he has restricted freedom of individual action. He does, however, have security of tenure in most places, whereas other professional practitioners do not. Nor does the teacher have any say in the election of his various bosses. The lawyer and doctor, although subject to strict control, do possess some power in electing officers of the professional association which regulates the practice of law and medicine. Thus other professionals are afforded a wider freedom of action than the teacher.

The teacher, of course, is not without power. As indicated in the previous chapter, the informal social system among teachers is powerful and administrators and boards of education are not insensitive to it. Further, teachers have power through professional associations, and in increasing instances are bargaining collectively with boards of education and participating in policy decisions. Parents are also likely to

[4] Howard S. Becker, "The Teacher in the Authority System of the Public Schools," *Journal of Educational Sociology*, Volume 27, November 1953, p. 128.

[5] J. R. Seeley, R. A. Sim, and E. W. Loosley, *Crestwood Heights*, New York, John Wiley and Sons, Inc., 1963, pp. 257–258.

come to the defense of teachers if they think the latter are being unjustly treated by the administration or board of education.

Teachers and Principals

Perhaps the most crucial teacher-administrator relationship is that between teacher and principal. Teaching and learning take place in the local school, and it is here that relationships are most crucial in creating a proper climate for learning.

To what extent do the teachers' and principals' perceptions differ on matters of common interest? One's position in an organizational hierarchy, we know, does influence one's attitude toward it and its activities. One may hypothesize, then, that principals will see things in a different light from teachers. To test this hypothesis Edmund Amidon and Arthur Blumberg compared teachers' perceptions with those of principals on the subject of faculty meetings. Their purpose was to "find out whether or not and to what extent there might be agreement between principal perceptions and those held by teachers." [6]

These investigators asked representative principals and teachers to react to eight questions about faculty meetings. The responses of the two groups were then compared. The questions and the responses were as follows.

How does the principal respond to a teacher's comment? The teachers said that the principal's responses tended to be neutral or non-committal. Principals, on the other hand, perceived that their own responses to teachers were very accepting and encouraging.

How do teachers respond to other teachers' comments? The teachers thought their responses to comments by other teachers were slightly on the critical side of neutral. The principals construed such comments as being on the encouraging end of the scale.

How free do other teachers feel to express themselves? Teachers felt that they had to be "rather careful in what they say." Principals said that teachers could "say whatever they wish."

How free do you feel to express yourself? Teachers indicated a tendency to be rather cautious about their participation. Principals felt free to express whatever they wished.

What is your general reaction to faculty meetings in your school? Teachers' reactions on this question were more extreme than on any other. They viewed faculty meetings somewhere between "fairly satis-

[6] Edmund Amidon and Arthur Blumberg, "A Comparison of Teacher and Principal Perceptions of School Faculty Meetings," paper delivered at the American Educational Research Association Convention, Chicago, 1963 (mimeographed).

factory" and "a waste of time." For the principals faculty meetings were "an effective use of time and energy."

What do you think is the general condition of the faculty? The question concerned the faculty generally, rather than faculty meetings specifically. The average teacher reaction was best described by the phrase, "fairly interested in doing a good job." Yet principals believed these same teachers to be "alert, aware, and interested."

How close do you feel to other members of the faculty? The teachers were neutral, stating that they perceived faculty relations as somewhat casual. The typical response of the principals was that the faculty members were "very close with everyone pulling together."

How easy do you find it talking with teachers (or the principal) about new ideas and suggestions for the school? The typical teacher position was represented by the statement: "rather easy to talk to the principal if my idea is a good one." More positive in their reactions to this question, the principals tended to state that it was "easy for me at any time" to talk to teachers. Although teachers felt limited in the times in which they could comfortably converse with the principal, principals did not feel inhibited about talking with teachers.

Amidon and Blumberg conclude: "Reactions of both teachers and principals are quite consistent on all the items included in the questionnaire, with principals viewing faculty meetings as attractive, free, and productive affairs and teachers being at least rather neutral about these affairs.

"The same attitudes which are evident in answers to items concerning faculty meetings tend to be reflected also in teachers' and principals' attitudes toward interpersonal problems in the school. Responses on this second group of items strongly suggest that faculty meetings are reflections of more general attitudes toward the school."

11. This research suggests that principals feel a closer identification with the school than do teachers. Can you suggest why this may be true? Do you think it has anything to do with the teachers' and principals' relative status positions in the social system of the school?

12. Had this research dealt with discipline problems in the classroom rather than faculty meetings, do you think the results might have been different? If so, how?

13. Sometimes the principal is more sensitive to what parents think than to what teachers think. In one school, a program of ability grouping was established and the teachers agreed that the educational results were good. But the principal discontinued the program because some parents of children who were assigned to slow classes raised a furor. The principal argued: "Any program that the parents aren't for just isn't going to work. You'd be surprised. When the parents are dissatisfied, the dissatisfaction goes into the children, who hear the gripes of the parents at home." Do you think the principal was justified in discontinuing the ability-grouping program? Do you think the teachers should have acted in defense of what they thought was a sound program educationally? If so, how?

The Influence of Principal-Teacher Relations on the Climate of the School

The relationships that teachers and principals develop among themselves determine the organizational climate of the school. Andrew W. Halpin and Don B. Croft have defined six organizational climates which they found in conducting research in 71 schools. The six climates arise from the human interaction among teachers and principals in these schools, and are identified as: *open, autonomous, controlled, familiar, paternal, and closed.*[7]

These six climates demonstrate how sharply different the formal and informal social systems of a school can be. That is, the 71 schools all shared similar formal structures and hierarchies, the kind described in Chapter 12. In each school the principal played the role of "principal," and the teachers played the role of "teachers." Formal administrative patterns were similar, if not the same.

Yet how different were the informal social systems of the schools. At one extreme the informal climate of the school was "open," releasing the creative energies of all persons in the school. At the other extreme the informal climate was "closed." Creativity was frozen out, and esprit among the teachers and between principal and teachers was nonexistent. The difference lay in the informal personal relations which principal and teachers developed among themselves.

Let us turn now to Halpin and Croft's descriptions of the six climates which they identified in the 71 schools.

The open climate. "The open climate depicts a situation in which the members enjoy extremely high esprit. The teachers work well together without bickering and griping. They are not burdened by mountains of busy work or by routine reports; the principal's policies facilitate the teachers' accomplishment of their tasks. On the whole, the group members enjoy friendly relations with each other, but they apparently feel no need for an extremely high degree of intimacy. The teachers obtain considerable job satisfaction, and are sufficiently motivated to overcome difficulties and frustrations. They possess the incen-

[7] Andrew W. Halpin and Don B. Croft, *The Organizational Climates of Schools,* Chicago, Midwest Administration Center, University of Chicago, 1963, pp. 60–66.

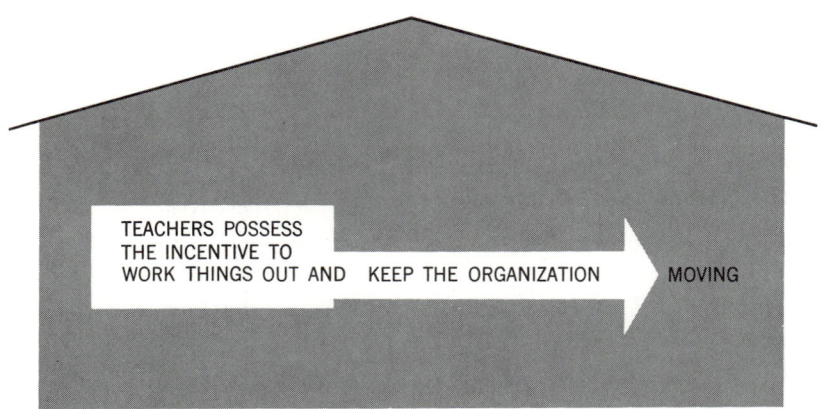

Fig. 13-1   Open school climate.

tive to work things out and to keep the organization 'moving.' Further-more, the teachers are proud to be associated with their school.

"The behavior of the principal represents an appropriate integra-tion between his own personality and the role he is required to play as principal. In this respect his behavior can be viewed as 'genuine.' Not only does he set an example by working hard himself but, depending upon the situation, he can either criticize the actions of teachers or can, on the other hand, go out of his way to help a teacher. He pos-sesses the personal flexibility to be 'genuine' whether he be required to control and direct the activities of others or be required to show compassion in satisfying the social needs of individual teachers. . . ."

14. Do you think that students sense whether the climate of the school is open? How will an open climate show itself to students?

The autonomous climate. "The distinguishing feature of this or-ganizational climate is the almost complete freedom that the principal gives to teachers to provide their own structures-for-interaction as well as to find ways within the group for satisfying their social needs. As one might surmise, the scores lean slightly more toward social-needs satisfaction than toward task achievement.

"When the teachers are together in a task-oriented situation they are 'engaged'; they achieve their goals easily and quickly. There are few minority pressure groups, but whatever stratification does exist among the group members does not prevent the group as a whole from working well together. The essential point is that the teachers do

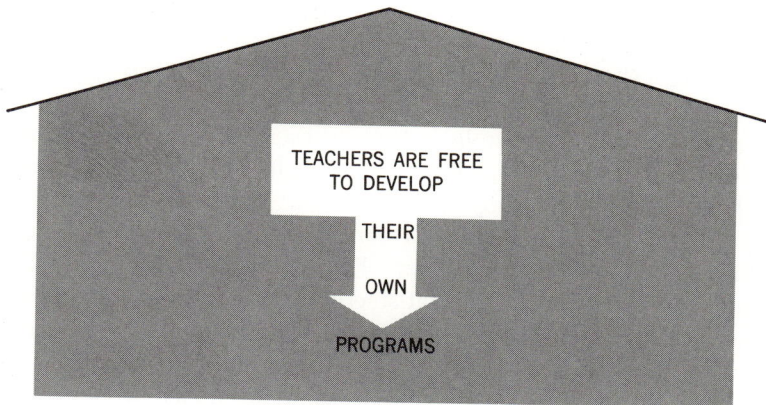

Fig. 13-2 Autonomous school climate.

work well together and do accomplish the tasks of the organization.

"The teachers are not 'hindered' by administrative paper work, and they do not gripe about the reports that they are required to submit. The principal has set up procedures and regulations to facilitate the teachers' task. A teacher does not have to run to the principal every time he needs supplies, books, projectors, etc.; adequate controls have been established to relieve the principal as well as the teachers of these details. The morale of the teachers is high, but not as high as in the open climate. The high morale probably stems largely from the social-needs satisfaction which the teachers receive. (Esprit would probably be higher if greater task accomplishment also occurred within the organization.) . . ."

15. In the autonomous climate the teacher is free to develop his own program. How do you think the new teacher would thrive in the autonomous climate?

The controlled climate. "The controlled climate is marked, above everything else, by a press for achievement at the expense of social-needs satisfaction. Everyone 'works hard' and there is little time for friendly relations with others or for deviation from established controls and directives. This climate is over-weighted toward task-achievement and away from social-needs satisfaction. Nonetheless, since morale is high, this climate can be classified as more 'Opened' than 'Closed.'

"The teachers are completely 'engaged' in the task. They do not bicker, gripe or differ with the principal's directives. They are there to get the job done, and they expect to be told personally just how to do it. There is an excessive amount of paper work, routine reports, busy work, and general hindrance which get in the way of the teachers' task accomplishment. Few procedures have been set up to facilitate their work; in fact, paper work seems to be used to keep them busy. Accordingly, teachers have little time to establish very friendly social relations with each other, and there is little feeling of camaraderie. Teachers ordinarily work by themselves and are impersonal with each other. In fact, social isolation is common; there are few genuinely warm relations among the teachers. Esprit, however, is slightly above average. We infer that the job satisfaction found in this climate results primarily from task-accomplishment, not from social-needs satisfaction.

"The principal is described as dominating and directive; he allows little flexibility within the organization and he insists that everything be done 'his' way. He is somewhat aloof; he prefers to publish directives to indicate how each procedure is to be followed. These directives, of course, are impersonal and are used to standardize the way in which teachers accomplish certain tasks. Essentially, the principal says, 'My way of doing it is best and to hell with the way people feel.' Means and ends have already been determined; the principal becomes dogmatic when members of the group do not conform to the outline he has delineated. He cares little about how people 'feel'; the important thing is to get the job done, and in his way. . . ."

16. Transfer the controlled climate to the classroom. Do you think it would make for an effective or ineffective learning situation?

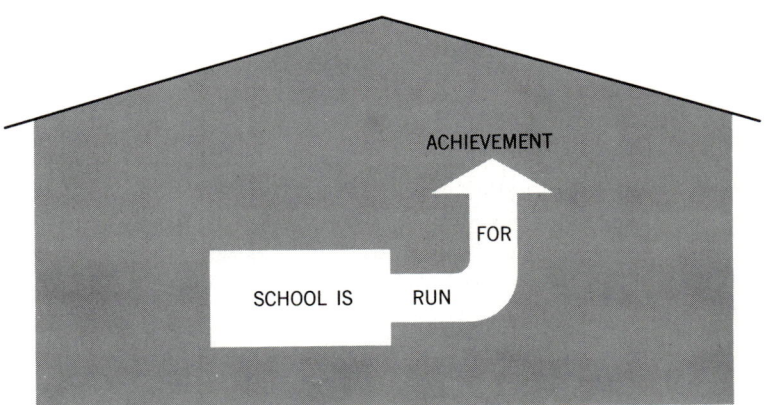

Fig. 13-3   Controlled school climate.

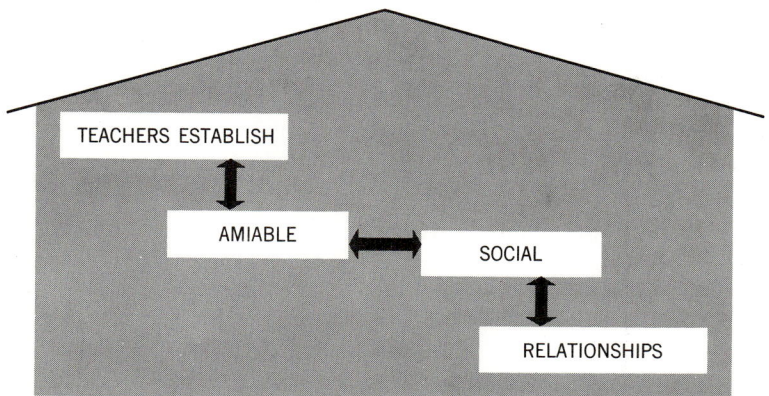

Fig. 13-4 Familiar school climate.

The familiar climate. "The main feature of this climate is the conspicuously friendly manner of both the principal and the teachers. Social-needs satisfaction is extremely high, while, contrariwise, little is done to control or direct the group's activities toward goal achievement.

"The teachers are disengaged and accomplish little in a task-oriented situation, primarily because the principal exerts little control in directing their activities. Also, there are too many people trying to tell others how things should be done. The principal does not burden the teachers with routine reports; in fact, he makes it as easy as possible for them to work. Procedural helps are available. The teachers have established personal friendships among themselves, and socially, at least, everyone is part of a big happy family. 'Morale,' or job satisfaction, is average, but it stems primarily from social-needs satisfaction. In short, the esprit that is found in this climate is one-sided in that it stems almost entirely from social-needs satisfaction.

"The behavioral theme of the principal is essentially, 'let's all be a nice happy family'; he evidently is reluctant to be anything other than considerate, lest he may, in his estimation, injure the 'happy family' feeling. He wants everybody to know that he, too, is one of the group, that he is in no way different from anybody else. Yet his abdication of social control is accompanied, ironically enough, by high disengagement on the part of the group.

"The principal is not aloof and not impersonal and official in his manner. Few rules and regulations are established as guides to suggest to the teachers how things 'should be done.' The principal does not emphasize production; nor does he do much personally to insure that the teachers are performing their tasks correctly. No one works to full capacity, yet no one is ever 'wrong'; nor are the actions of members— at least in respect to task-accomplishment—criticized. In short, little is done either by direct or by indirect means to evaluate or direct the activities of the teachers. However, teachers do attribute thrust to the principal. But in this context, this probably means that they regard him as a 'good guy' who is interested in their welfare and who 'looks out for them.'"

17. Beginning teachers are sometimes warned not to be the "good guy" with their students. Do you think this is good advice?

The paternal climate. "The paternal climate is characterized by the 'ineffective' attempts of the principal to control the teachers as well as to satisfy their social needs. In our judgment, his behavior is 'non-genuine' and is perceived by the teachers as non-motivating. This climate is, of course, a closed one.

"The teachers do not work well together; they are split into factions. Group maintenance has not been established because of the principal's inability to control the activities of the teachers. Few hindrances burden the teachers in the form of routine reports, administrative duties and committee requirements, mainly because the principal does a great deal of this busy work himself. The teachers do not enjoy friendly relationships with each other. Essentially, the

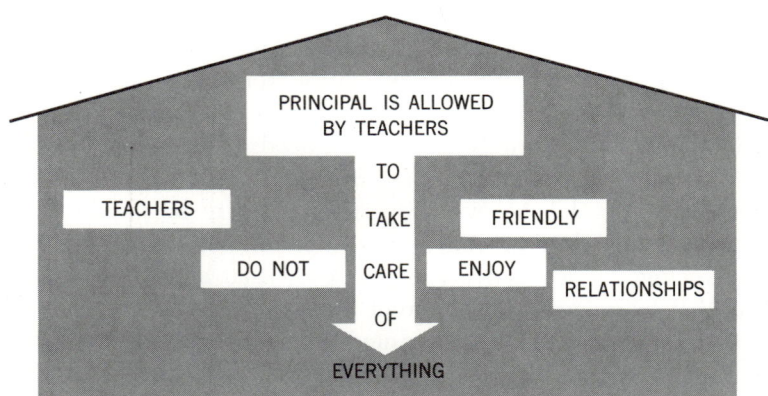

Fig. 13-5   Paternal school climate.

teachers have given up trying; they let the principal take care of things as best he can. Obviously, low esprit results when the teachers obtain inadequate satisfaction in respect to both task-accomplishment and social-needs.

"The principal, on the other hand, is the very opposite of aloof; he is everywhere at once, scurrying here and there, checking, monitoring and telling people how to do things. In fact, he is so non-aloof that he becomes intrusive. He must know everything that is going on. He is always emphasizing all the things that should be done, but somehow nothing does get done. The principal sets up schedules, class changes, etc., personally; he does not let the teachers perform any of these activities. His view is that 'Daddy knows best.' . . ."

18. Do you think the "Daddy knows best" climate might penetrate, through the teacher, into the classroom? What forms of teacher and student behavior might it create? Do you think this climate would restrict freedom and expression in classrooms?

19. At the University of Chicago three sociologists tested a group of women teachers with an average of 10 years' experience. The group showed no drive at all to accomplish demanding tasks, to do things better than other people, to analyze themselves and others, or to show sympathy toward any person in trouble! [8] Do you think a paternalistic climate in the school might contribute to these attitudes on the part of teachers?

The closed climate. "The closed climate marks a situation in which the group members obtain little satisfaction in respect to either task-achievement or social-needs. In short, the principal is ineffective in directing the activities of the teachers, and at the same time, he is not inclined to look out for their personal welfare. This climate is the most closed and the least 'genuine' climate that we have identified.

"The teachers are disengaged and do not work well together; consequently, group achievement is minimal. To secure some sense of achievement, the major outlet for the teachers is to complete a variety of reports and to attend to a host of 'housekeeping' duties. The principal does not facilitate the task-accomplishment of the teachers. Esprit is at a nadir, reflecting low job satisfaction in respect to both job satisfaction and social-needs satisfaction. The salient bright spot that appears to keep the teachers in the school is that they do obtain satisfaction from their friendly relations with other teachers. (We would speculate that the turnover rate for teachers in this climate would be very high unless, of course, the teachers are too old to move

[8] Richard Meryman, "How We Drive Teachers to Quit," *Life*, Volume 53, No. 20, November 16, 1962, p. 112.

readily to another job, or have been 'locked into the system' by the attractions of a retirement system.)

"The principal is highly aloof and impersonal in controlling and directing the activities of the teachers. He emphasizes production and frequently says that 'We should work harder.' He sets up rules and regulations about how things should be done, and these rules are usually arbitrary. But his words are hollow, because he, himself, possesses little thrust and he does not motivate the teachers by setting a good personal example. Essentially, what he says and what he does are two different things. For this reason, he is not 'genuine' in his actions. He is not concerned with the social needs of teachers; in fact, he can be depicted as inconsiderate. His cry of 'Let's work harder' actually means, 'You work harder.' He expects everyone else to take the initiative, yet he does not give them the freedom required to perform whatever leadership acts are necessary. Moreover, he, himself, does not provide adequate leadership for the group. For this reason the teachers view him as not 'genuine'; indeed, they regard him as a 'phony.' This climate characterizes an organization for which the best prescription is radical surgery."

20. From what you know about principal-teacher relations in the high school you attended, how would you describe its organizational climate? Can you be specific in terms of the six climates mentioned here?

It must be clear that of these six climates the one most conducive to learning is the open climate and the least conducive, the closed

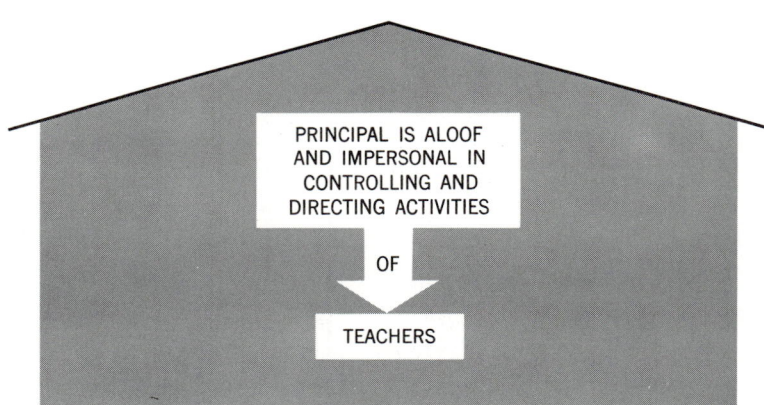

Fig. 13-6   Closed school climate.

climate. More precisely, the open climate will inspire more learning and a different type of learning than the closed climate. The closed climate encourages learning which is grudgingly and mechanically done, because the teachers carry out their tasks in this spirit. On the other hand, the open climate suggests creative teaching and learning carried out in a spirit of mutual regard and satisfaction.

Will the organizational climate of the school stop at the classroom door or will it enter the classroom with the teacher? It is inconceivable that one climate would exist for the principal and teacher and another for teacher and students. The climate of the school is as pervasive as the air. It spreads through the entire school, it is infectious—whether it is of the closed or open type. It profoundly influences how teachers teach and children learn.

To demonstrate the relationship between climate and teaching we close this chapter with a teacher's description of the open climate of her school and how it influenced her attitude toward her work. Rosemary Hillman's testimony shows how the formal social system of the school and its built-in hierarchy need not inhibit teaching. Indeed, the formal system can be turned to place the teacher and the student in the central position of the school, where they rightfully belong.

A TEACHER DESCRIBES THE CLIMATE OF HER SCHOOL

"We are all affected by climate. It dictates and controls our activities in numerous ways. So it is with the educational climate in which a classroom teacher works. The educational climate affects, dictates and controls much of the educational activity of the teacher. It has subtle as well as overt powers that influence attitudes, actions and, most important, strongly affect the view the teacher has of himself.

"I propose to focus on what I think is a unique educational climate, and to describe how it looks from the view of the classroom teacher, and how it affects his actions. Although this is from a personal viewpoint, the relationships and activities described here that comprise the structure of the educational climate, do exist in the district in which I teach.

"What is the district? The district concerned is an elementary school district in a suburban area near a large cosmopolitan city. Each school has its own principal and is under the direct supervision of the district superintendent. The superintendent, in turn, answers to an elected school board. The district superintendent has as his immediate staff, assistant superintendents and consultants.

"Where does the teacher appear in this organizational framework? In this district the classroom teacher finds himself and his pupils in a center position, supported by the superintendent, the principal, consultants, school board, and parents. Does this sound like a team? It is!

"Having taught in good districts, I came to my present assignment unscarred, but wary. When I was told there were consultants available to assist me, I assumed they would fulfill the traditional function of supervisors. When I received my initial orientation at a preschool get-together with an experienced teacher of the district, I expected to be 'told' what procedures to follow. After several days of workshops with consultants, followed by presentations from the superintendent and a school board member, I was aware that what I was feeling was rather unique.

"The total approach was more than warm acceptance. They were saying, 'These are some of the things we do. These are the things we believe in. Perhaps you would like to try them. Perhaps you have better ways. Let us know how we can help you in your exciting task.' Within this framework there comes a release, an opening up within a teacher and what follows is an eagerness to get started.

"The climate is essentially one of academic freedom. The teacher is not distracted with administrative orders, or restricted with a one-way method. He is the creative, artful master of his classroom and he is free to take his pupils as far as he can, knowing he has approval and can call for help along the way. This implicit belief in and respect for the teacher's competency is demonstrated by everyone. Being quite human, the teacher in turn stretches up and views himself in this same light. It is a warm, relaxing, anxiety-free light that allows him to look outside himself, to move about freely and to focus more effectively on his pupils and their needs. Standing in this circle of freedom, he can reach out for tools, materials, and assistance, confident that they will be furnished.

"When the teacher wants help, the district consultants are available and responsive. Generally, the only requirement is that the teacher must sign up or telephone for their services. In other words, the consultant comes on the teacher's terms and fills educational needs as the teacher sees them. They are quick to enrich with an idea, quick to pick up the teacher's enthusiasm for a project and join with him in spirit and assistance.

"The role of the consultant is one of the most unique aspects of this district. It is a helping role that carries no threat to the classroom teacher. Because the teacher-consultant relationship is anxiety free, the teacher is able more fully to utilize the consultant's services. Some of the fruits of this kind of working relationship have been the development of significant depth pilot studies in this district. The consultant's question to the teacher is, 'How are things going?,' rather than, 'What have you done?' What does this do for the teacher? It moves him—in one kind of direction or another. There is no standing still when a teacher is surrounded with this kind of warm assistance.

"How does the principal fit into the climate? Of course, the principal is the evaluator. Viewed from the center of the classroom, however, the principal is another important human being who makes himself available on the teacher's terms. It is his dynamic 'caring about' that prompts the teacher to open the classroom and invite the principal to come in so teacher and pupils can benefit from his perceptions. The joke, the problem, the interesting experiment, are all eagerly shared with the principal in this setting because he has demonstrated a consistent readiness to become involved. He is interested in the teacher as a human being and, because of this, the teacher feels free to turn to him for support and guidance. When the principal opens the door of the classroom he brings with him the breezes that make this refreshing climate possible.

"What is important to note here is that the principal is one of many to whom the teacher can turn. There are no set procedures, no designated channels to go through to enlist aid. The guidance consultant who makes himself available during the lunch hour to soak up the problems, doubts and needs of teachers, the superintendent and other consultants who sit down for coffee after school are demonstrating an openness, a readiness to help, a caring enough to listen. As a result of this, the teacher freely reaches out to everyone. With this kind of openness, all he has to do is figure out who can best help him in a particular situation and go directly to that person." [9]

21. Rosemary Hillman obviously enjoys teaching in a school with an open climate and knows how to make the most of it. But some teachers may not be psychologically suited to this climate. For example, Soloman Rettig, a psychologist, conducted a series of interviews with teachers and concluded: "They are a highly selected kind of person compared with other professional people; a highly intelligent person on one hand, and on the other hand one who doesn't mind being told by rules, parents, supervisors what he or she can and can't do." [10] Do you think the teachers whom Rettig inter-

[9] Rosemary Hillman, "A View from the Center," *Educational Leadership,* Washington, D. C., ASCD, Volume 22, No. 3, December 1964, pp. 155–157, 195.

[10] Richard Meryman, "How We Drive Teachers to Quit," *Life,* Volume 53, No. 20, November 16, 1962, p. 112.

viewed would work well in an open climate? Do you think a closed climate might have been the cause of these teachers' present attitudes?

Having read Rosemary Hillman's description of one teacher's relationship with the administration of her school, we may ask about the teacher's relationships with other teachers, parents, and students. We turn in Chapter 14 to the interaction that takes place among these persons in the social system of the school.

REFERENCES

Paperbacks

American High School Today. James B. Conant. (Orig.) (12390) McGraw-Hill Paperback Series, McGraw-Hill Book Co., 330 W. 42nd St., New York. David McKay Co. ($1.95).

Economics and Politics of Public Education, No. 1: Schoolmen and Politics: A Study of State Aid to Education in the Northeast. Stephen K. Bailey, Robert C. Wood, Richard Frost, and Paul E. March. (Orig.) Syracuse University Press, University Station, Syracuse, N. Y. ($1.75).

Economics and Politics of Public Education, No. 2: Government and the Suburban School. Roscoe C. Martin. (Orig.) Syracuse University Press, University Station, Syracuse, N. Y. ($1.75).

Economics and Politics of Public Education, No. 10: Suburban Power Structures and Public Education. Warner Bloomberg, Jr. and Morris Sunshine. (Orig.) Syracuse University Press, University Station, Syracuse, N. Y. ($1.75).

Education and Democratic Ideals. Gordon C. Lee. (Orig.) Harcourt, Brace and World, Inc., 757 Third Ave., New York (including Harbrace Books) ($1.95).

Education and the Cult of Efficiency: A Study of the Social Forces that Have Shaped the Administration of the Public School. Raymond E. Callahan. (P149) Phoenix Books, University of Chicago Press, 5750 Ellis Ave., Chicago, Ill. ($2.25).

Helping Teachers Understand Principals. Wilbur A. Yauch. (Orig.) Appleton-Century-Crofts, 440 Park Ave. South, New York ($1.10).

High School Principal and Staff in the Crowded School. William C. French. (SSA) Teachers College, Teachers College Press, 525 West 120th St., New York ($1.50).

Books

Clark, Burton R., *Educating the Expert Society.* San Francisco: Chandler Publishing Co., 1962. Chapter 4 discusses the concept of educational authority in relation to pressures from the community.

Clark, Edward, "Rating the Superintendent," in *Social Aspects of Education: a Casebook,* E. T. Ladd and W. C. Sayres, Editors. Englewood Cliffs, N. J.: Prentice-Hall, 1962, pp. 1–20. A case study is presented of a misunderstanding between the administration and the teachers' professional organization.

Fosmire, Fred, and Richard A. Littman, "The Social Psychology of the Superintendency," in *The Social Sciences View School Administration,* Donald E. Tope et al., Editors. Englewood Cliffs, N. J.: Prentice-Hall, 1965, pp. 98–

109. Educational administration, based on sociological perspectives, is discussed as social behavior.

Gross, Neal, Ward S. Mason, and Alexander W. McEachern, *Explorations in Role Analysis: Studies of the School Superintendency Role.* New York: John Wiley and Sons, 1958. This classic work explores the areas of role and role conflict. The book analyzes a series of questions related to school personnel, board members, and citizens interested in public education.

Havighurst, Robert J., *The Public Schools of Chicago.* Chicago: The Board of Education, 1964. Chapter 20 presents a discussion on the administration and organization of the Chicago schools.

Hemphill, John, Daniel Griffiths, and Norman Frederiksen, *Administrative Performance and Personality: A Study of the Principal in a Simulated Elementary School.* New York: Bureau of Publications, Columbia Teachers College, 1962. This research develops concepts for studying administrative behavior, determines some measurable dimensions of performance, and provides materials for the study of school administration.

Rasmussen, Glen R., "Perceived Value Discrepancies of Teachers and Principals— A Threat to Creative Teaching," in *Society and Education,* James D. Raths and J. D. Grambs, Editors. Englewood Cliffs, N. J.: Prentice-Hall, 1965, pp. 213– 224. An empirical study brings to focus the primary functions, often ignored, of the principal—to help faculty members clarify and share mutual goals in education.

Reeder, Ward G., "School Control and Organization," in *Readings in American Education,* William H. Lucio, Editor. Chicago: Scott, Foresman and Co., 1963, pp. 283–294. Reeder presents a description of the structure, functions, and practices found in American School Administration.

Periodicals

Bible, Bond L., and James D. McComas, "Role Consensus and Teacher Effectiveness," *Social Forces,* Vol. 42, No. 2, December 1963, pp. 225–232. An empirical study of the relationship of teacher effectiveness and role definition.

Foster, Richard L., "Poise Under Pressure," *Educational Leadership,* Vol. 22, No. 3, December 1964, pp. 149–154+. A superintendent describes how the type of school organization encourages potentially effective teachers to become effective.

Gullahorn, John T. and Jeanne E., "Role Conflict and Its Resolution," *The Sociological Quarterly,* Vol. 4, No. 2, Winter 1963, pp. 32–49. The article deals with the sociological implication of role conflict and how an individual resolves his problems.

Hechinger, Fred M., "Who Runs Our Big City Schools," *The Saturday Review,* Vol. XLVIII, No. 16, April 17, 1965, pp. 70–71+. Hechinger describes the growing conflicts between lay school boards and professional chief administrators and asks whether these are inevitable and beyond settlement.

Kerr, Norman D., "The School Board as an Agency of Legitimation," *Sociology of Education,* Vol. 38, No. 1, Fall 1964, pp. 34-59. There are a variety of circumstances which convert the school board into an agency which legitimates the goal of the school administration.

Moeller, Gerald H., "Bureaucracy and Teachers' Sense of Power," *Administrator's Notebook,* Vol. XI, No. 3, November 1962, pp. 1–4. The author concludes that the school system sets the general level of sense of power and the teacher varies from this level by his own personal orientation toward power.

Provus, Malcolm M., "NEA Time to Teach Project," *NEA Journal,* Vol. 54, No. 4, April 1965, pp. 8–10. This project is redefining the role of the classroom teacher in bringing about instructional improvement.

Raths, James, "Power in the Classroom," *Educational Leadership,* Vol. 22, No. 3, December 1964, pp. 197–202. This review summarizes some of the research work that has been done on the teacher's power role in the classroom.

14

Teachers, Students, and Parents

"The most joyous moment is when sparks start flying, and something comes clear, a meaning the students hadn't thought of in terms of their own lives."

A HIGH SCHOOL TEACHER

Every teacher is involved in three vital relationships: with other teachers, with students, and with parents. This chapter is devoted to a study of these relationships, and contains, to round out the discussion of the school's social system and the climate it generates, a section on the interactions among students.

INTERACTIONS AMONG TEACHERS

Much of the school's business is conducted among teachers whose interactions may be of either the formal or the informal kind. On the formal level teachers relate to one another in a number of ways: They may work on school committees, jointly supervise student activities and curriculum programs, and teach together as members of a team.

On the informal level teachers are more or less in constant contact with one another, and natural groupings and loyalties arise. In these groupings we best see the informal social system among teachers. Let us look first at some of the factors which stimulate the development of these group relationships.

Conditions Influencing Interactions Among Teachers

Proximity of classrooms and grades taught. Teachers whose classrooms are close to one another and who teach similar grades or subjects tend to see one another frequently, compare notes, and exchange ideas. This year, for example, a fifth-grade teacher may have the same group of children, and of course parents, that the fourth-grade teacher had last year. These teachers have much to talk about and can do so on an informal, confidential basis. Informal groups tend to spring up naturally among lower elementary, upper elementary, junior high, and senior high school teachers because they are likely to teach near one another and have similar professional interests.

Age of teachers. Teachers whose ages are similar tend to group themselves together in the informal social system of the school and are likely to have more in common than might at first be suspected. They probably attended college at about the same time and were exposed to similar educational authorities and philosophies. The older teachers may look askance at modern practices, and the younger teachers may refer to the "old fogies" on the faculty.

Length of service in the school. Closely related to age is length of service in the school. Teachers who joined the faculty at about the same time and have served about the same number of years are likely to feel a close relationship. When a new principal is appointed, for example, they judge his actions in terms of the principal who was on the job when they came to the school. Anything new—schedules, curriculum programs, instructional materials—tends to be evaluated in terms of factors existing when they joined the faculty.

The new children who come in fresh waves each year are likely to be evaluated in the same way. Ten-year teachers are apt to comment that the current crop of children is "harder to teach" than earlier ones. First-year teachers, without perspective, are likelier to accept the current student generation for what it is. They will say, "the kids aren't so bad." Teachers who hold these separate views will naturally find comfort in others who share them.

Length of service and age usually influence a teacher's "traditional" or "progressive" leanings. The older teachers, who are usually dominant in the school's informal social system, generally stress order, firmness, and discipline. They are likely to oppose permissiveness. Younger teachers tend to be more idealistic and liberal in their educational points of view. They incline to be "student centered" in their approach to teaching while older teachers are more "subject centered." Thus, teaching philosophies provide a basis for informal group relations within the school.[1]

1. New innovations in education are taking place at a rapid rate. Some teachers are quick to try new ideas and practices, some are slow, and

[1] See Donald J. Willower and Catherine F. Carr, "The School as a Social Organization," *Educational Leadership,* Washington, D. C., ASCD, Volume 22, No. 4, January 1965, pp. 251, 254–255.

some reject them entirely. In Chapter 13 we discussed six organizational climates of the school, identified by Andrew W. Halpin and Don B. Croft, ranging all the way from "open" to "closed." Which of these six climates is most likely to encourage innovation among teachers? What are your reasons for selecting this climate?

Attitude toward the principal and specialists. The attitudes that teachers hold toward the principal and specialists provide a basis for grouping and interaction in the school. Teachers with similar attitudes toward these status figures in the formal social structure are likely to feel drawn together. If they have common complaints they prefer to exchange them freely and without threat.

Attitude toward parents. Teachers holding similar attitudes toward parents are likely to express their views to one another. Teachers who regard parents as rightful participants in the teaching process tend to communicate these views to one another. Similarly, teachers who regard parents as a "necessary nusiance" are likely to find comfort in those who feel the same way.[2]

These are some factors, then, which influence relationships and loyalties among teachers. We turn now to factors which help to determine status among teachers.

Status Factors Among Teachers

The formal structure of the school provides few status distinctions among teachers; all teachers tend to be considered on about the same level, though we pointed out in Chapter 13 that this is changing. In the informal social system of the school, however, a number of status distinctions are made among teachers.

Social and economic level of the neighborhood. Teaching in an economically well-to-do neighborhood usually carries more prestige than teaching in a marginal one. The status of the affluent community creates special problems for school administrators who recognize the need to staff the schools in poor neighborhoods with the best teachers available. Some city school systems offer special incentives to attract teachers to such schools. Some appeal to teachers to take assignments in poor neighborhoods for a year or two on a rotational basis, with the assurance of transferring later to a school in a good neighborhood.

2. Some colleges and universities have developed special programs for training teachers to work in schools in lower-class neighborhoods. Do you

[2] See Daniel E. Griffiths, David L. Clark, D. Richard Wynn, and Lawrence Iannaccone, *Organizing Schools for Effective Education*, Danville, Illinois, the Interstate Printers and Publishers, 1962, pp. 225–93.

think such programs may help to give status to teaching in such schools? Find out what you can about these special programs and how they differ from other programs in teacher education. Report your findings to the class.

The cultural style of the school. In Chapter 11 we discussed the cultural styles of village, town, suburban, and city schools. Suburban schools, when the suburb is affluent, carry higher prestige than village, town, or city schools. A suburban school in a marginal neighborhood, however, may have a much lower status than a good town or city school.

It is the city schools whose prestige has suffered most with the rise of affluent suburban schools. Before the growth of the suburbs, the better city schools commanded status. However, with the migration of Negroes, Puerto Ricans, and the rural poor into the cities and the exodus of the white middle class to the outlying suburbs, a reversal in status took place. This condition has created special problems in teacher recruitment for city schools. We may now expect to see a similar downgrading of those schools in marginal suburbs as lower economic groups push out from the central cities into the surrounding areas. We may also expect that prestige-conscious teachers will leave these marginal suburban schools and seek employment in the more affluent suburban schools.

3. Matthew J. Pillard states: "Urban teachers are usually transients, often having migrated from rural areas. They may not know or understand the communities they serve and may never come to know two children of the same family or the parents of their pupils. In short, city teachers are likely to be strangers to their communities, the parents of their pupils, and in many respects—since they may teach an individual for an hour a day for one semester and then not see him again—to the pupils themselves. As strangers, urban teachers may be viewed with suspicion or with only neutral reactions; in either case, the total effect is often relatively low esteem." [3] What do you think this statement should indicate to a new teacher looking for a job? Do you think there is a relationship between a teacher's status and his knowledge of the community?

These two status factors, the school's neighborhood and cultural style, are determined primarily by factors outside the schools. Turn now to factors that operate primarily within the school.

Seniority. We have mentioned how teachers with similar ages and length of service are likely to interact positively with one another. A person who has seniority within a school usually has preferred status

[3] Matthew J. Pillard, "Teachers for Urban Schools," in B. J. Chandler, Lindley J. Stiles, and John I. Kitsuse, *Education in Urban Society*, New York, Dodd, Mead, 1962, p. 195.

for a number of reasons. He makes more money because salary schedules reward length of service. His advice is likely sought by administrators, especially new ones who are younger than he is. He may be a rallying point in school disputes, and disputants are likely to vie for his support. Moreover, senior teachers are apt to have greater influence with parents because of their long tenure and wide acquaintance with the school and community.

The subject matter being taught. This is a subtle factor related to the prestige which people accord different types of subject matter. Teaching chemistry usually carries more status than teaching auto mechanics, economics more than physical education. The prestige of the curricular "stream" influences the prestige of the teaching position. Teachers in the college preparatory program are usually given higher social status than those in the "general" or "vocational" divisions.

This transfer of status from the subject to the teacher is an index to the social values of the community. The teachers of subjects that are valued are given status higher than those who teach less valued subjects. For this reason the status attached to a subject may change from community to community, depending on the priority given to certain values. In Hamid's village in Pakistan, for example, the holy man who sits in the mosque and teaches the children to recite the Koran is honored over the teacher in the tree school because religious education is more valued than secular education. In rural American schools like Raymond's in Midwest, the vocational agriculture teacher may be given a higher status than others because agriculture has status there.

4. In a school and community where competitive athletics are prized the coach may enjoy high status, especially if his teams win. Paradoxically, a winning coach may rate high with the community and students but low among other faculty members. Teachers of the academic subjects, particularly, are apt to think of the coach as being outside of the "in" group of the school. Can you explain this seeming paradox?

In Beth's suburban school system the teachers of college preparatory subjects are granted high status because college admission is given high priority. In a large city technical school the teacher of electronics may have status because it is he who prepares students for valued jobs in this field.

The age of the children being taught. One of the paradoxes of our society is the high priority we give to young children and the relatively low priority we give to those who teach them. Generally the prestige of the teaching position rises with the age of the students.

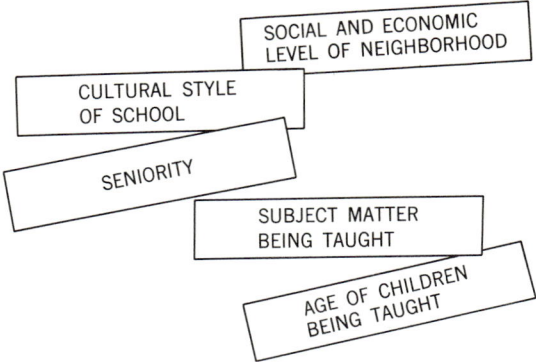

Fig. 14-1 In the informal social system of the school, status distinctions exist among teachers.

In elementary school the teachers of "upper el" hold a slight status edge over the teachers of "lower el." It is from the "upper el" group, for example, that elementary principals are usually chosen. Teachers of senior high school students are granted a status position over that of teachers of junior high school students, and teachers of juniors and seniors over that of teachers of freshmen and sophomores. In colleges and universities, professors who teach graduate students have more status than those who teach undergraduates, and those who teach doctoral degree students more status than those who teach master's degree students.

What we see reflected here in the informal social system of the school are the values of a society which honors those who work with adult affairs, with the "real" business of life. We expect children in time to reach adult status; teachers who help children in that process of growing up are honored in terms of how close the children with whom they work are to adulthood.

That this discrimination against those who teach the young leads to good education may be open to question. Fortunately, there are now signs that this attitude may be changing. For example, most school systems now use single salary schedules which pay the kindergarten teacher the same as the high school teacher, assuming they have similar training and years of experience.

5. In the school you attended which teachers had the greater status? What factors do you think influenced this status?

Let us turn now to a consideration of conflict and cooperation in teacher relationships.

Cooperation and Conflict Among Teachers

Teachers have two needs which are frequently in conflict. On the one hand, they must maintain a solid front before the administration, and on the other, they need to handle conflicts which inevitably arise within the group. We have already mentioned a number of potential sources of conflict among teachers: differences in age and seniority, philosophies of education, attitudes toward administration and parents, assignments to "good" or "bad" schools, and other status factors.

The need for teachers to maintain a solid front before the administration grows out of the teachers' and administrators' roles. For the teachers, the administration is the route to the board of education. Matters relating to salary and working conditions are usually initiated by the professional committee of the teachers' group. Here differences among teachers must be worked out and agreements reached about requests which are to be made. The strength of the requests depends in large measure on solid backing of all teachers; differences must therefore be resolved within the group before the teachers' case is made to the administration and the board of education.

Another source of conflict among teachers is the interaction between classroom teachers and specialists. Specialists in such areas as remedial reading, the "new" mathematics, science, and social studies are frequently regarded as "itinerant" teachers with special training. These itinerant teachers go from school to school and work with classroom teachers. They and the classroom teacher depend on each other, and there is a good basis for cooperation between them. Yet their respective roles are apt to cause them to view matters differently and thus to be a source of conflict. Fred E. Katz, speaking of the itinerant specialist and the classroom teacher, explains:

"The former goes from school to school helping to set up new programs—remedial reading, new mathematics, and so forth. The latter is involved in day-to-day teaching of specific subjects to specific groups of children. Each specialist has a different functional assignment: the itinerant specialist is attuned to his covering weaknesses in the existing programs, introducing improved procedures, and instituting wholly new approaches; the stable teacher (and the administrative staff) is geared to minimizing disruptions, continuing existing programs, and generally preserving the orderly flow of activity in order to produce a fairly predictable product—the pupil who can pass on to the next grade, who can gain admission to college, who can get a job. The teacher's adherence to existing programs is understandable, considering that he will be called upon to carry out the new programs, and, if things go wrong, he will have to pick up the pieces. But, the itinerant specialist requires the collaboration of the teacher—possibly the same teacher whose job he is sharply modifying." [4]

6. Katz's statement presents a good example of conflicts in role expectation and behavior. The classroom teacher's role requires him to keep "an orderly flow of activity" and to preserve existing programs. The specialist's role requires him to "discover weaknesses" and institute "new approaches." Why do you think a school system includes these two conflicting roles in its administrative organization? Can you find a basis for cooperation between the classroom teacher and itinerant specialist?

If opportunities for conflict exist among teachers, so do opportunities for cooperation. In the elementary schools teachers cooperate largely outside the classroom, since most of them work in self-contained classrooms and have little working contact with other teachers. Faculty cooperation is required in sharing responsibilities for hall or lunchroom duty, in playground supervision, and in planning school programs. In ungraded schools the classroom situation itself requires a close working relationship among teachers.

Cooperation among high school teachers has many of the same features as that among elementary teachers, plus some special features. High school teachers "share" students regularly if students are on a "platoon system" and pass from classroom to classroom. This sharing of students provides an additional opportunity for high school teachers to consult with one another on the progress of students and to work out common approaches to common problems.

The interaction among teachers, on the whole, is marked by common points of view growing out of their common experiences in the classroom. Here we have shown, however, that although the formal social structure does not reveal a pronounced hierarchy among teachers, the informal social system does. There are different status positions and expectations which may or may not create sources of conflict. On the other hand, both the elementary and high school teaching positions afford ample opportunities for cooperative endeavors.

THE INTERACTION OF TEACHERS AND STUDENTS

The teacher-student relationship is the focal point of all education. The schools exist to prepare students to take their place socially and vocationally in the adult world. Whether they achieve that purpose

---

[4] Fred E. Katz, "The School as a Complex Social Organization," *Harvard Educational Review,* Volume 34, No. 3, Summer 1964, p. 437.

depends to a great extent upon the quality of the interactions among teachers and students.

The teacher works with the student on a face-to-face basis; there is intensely personal contact. Persons holding administrative, supervisory, or specialist positions rarely know the student in such an intimate way as does the teacher, who sees the student in all of his moods and behaviors. Other people in the school tend to think of students as types; the teacher thinks of them as persons.

The teacher's relationship with the student is sometimes described as a "client" relationship, like that of a doctor with his patient or a lawyer with his client. The analogy is only partly accurate. The relationship *is* a professional one in that the roles of "teacher" and "student" are defined by law and convention. And teachers are trained, like other professionals, to work with students. In this sense the teacher has a client relationship with the student.

The teacher, however, is not granted the freedom to act with his student that a doctor enjoys with his patient or a lawyer with his client. Further, the teacher cannot select his client, as can the doctor or lawyer. Nor does the student client usually have the freedom to choose his teacher. For the teacher, the parent of the student is the indirect client, monitoring, as it were, the professional work of the teacher with the child. This indirect client is also the taxpayer, from whom the teacher ultimately derives a salary rather than a fee for his services.

The teacher's professional relationship with his students is probably closer to that of a social worker and his clients. The social worker acts as a professional agent of the community in a mediating role to counsel, advise, and refer cases to specialists for help. He is not free to make final decisions, but he can recommend. The teacher assumes that final responsibility for the child rests with the home, other specialists, or higher authorities. But the teacher, knowing the child as a good social worker knows his client, makes a valuable contribution in teaching, guiding, and making available to the student the specialized help of others.

Although the relationship of the teacher to the student is prescribed and restricted, we should not forget that the teacher does have freedom to work with the student in the classroom. And the class is the most powerful unit of social interaction in the whole school. Although the teacher may be subordinate to the social hierarchy of the school outside the classroom, within the class he is superordinate. Subject to the ideology of the school, he is free to teach as he wishes, to deal with his students in his own way and on his own terms. No

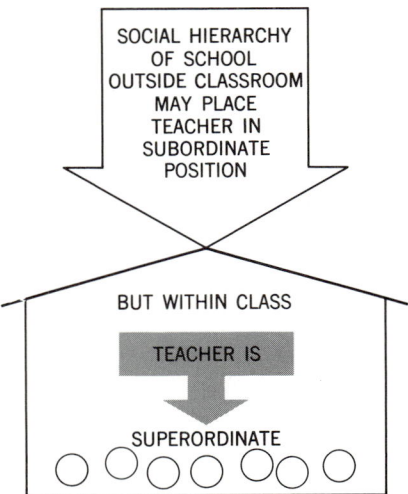

Fig. 14-2 The teaching function rests with the teacher who deals daily with students face-to-face.

matter what orders the superintendent or principal may issue or what advice the specialists may give, the teaching function does not rest with them—it rests with the teacher who deals daily with students face-to-face.

Indeed it is this face-to-face relationship which presents the teacher with one of his greatest problems: that of creating a learning climate which has freedom and self-determination, and yet which has control. In the early grades the problem is not so acute because young children tend to attribute authority and wisdom to the teacher. In the later grades, however, the distinction between the child and adult becomes less clear, especially when the teacher is young. On the one hand, the teacher is in charge and must be responsible for what goes on. On the other hand, the teacher realizes the need for maturing students to assume increasing responsibility for their own behavior and learning. But adolescents, being in the "in-between" years, are neither children nor adults: They vacillate between extremes and over-act. Moving alternately between childish behavior and genuine maturity, they confound the best attempts to establish a proper balance between control and permissiveness.

The teacher's relationship with students brings to him a second major problem: he may be misrepresented by his students. What the teacher says in the classroom is subject to more than the usual number of chances for misunderstanding in communication. First, the teacher frequently deals with subject matter about which there is disagreement in the community and about which strong pros and cons may exist. Second, the students with whom the teacher talks are at an age when discriminating judgments are difficult to make. They tend to see complex matters as black or white. Third, the student may deliberately distort what is said, as a reaction to the teacher's authority or for some other personal purpose. All of these factors condition the teacher's face-to-face relationships with students.

7. The following is an actual incident reported by a teacher: [5] This teacher explained to her "class that Communists, however misguided, act from the premise that what they do is right, not evil. One of her pupils went home and gave a garbled report of her statement. The boy's uncle, who was president of the board of education, heard about it. 'It was discussed at the board meeting,' the teacher said. 'The interpretation was that I was teaching my pupils that Communism is good—me a Roman Catholic educated by Jesuits and a registered Republican! My case was scheduled to come up formally before the Board of Education. While all this was happening, nobody spoke to me. An old friend finally stepped in and settled the situation, but it could have been messy. There was no respect for integrity. I was successfully challenged in my own classroom by a child who misquoted me.' "

Do you think this unfortunate incident might have been avoided? If so, how? Where do you think the fault for it lay? What do you think the principal or administrator should have done in this case?

The teen-ager is also apt to find his relationship with the teacher equally strained. He must submit to the teacher's authority or leave the classroom. There is no question in his mind about who is boss, though he may not admit it. He must adjust to the teacher's particular brand of control, whether it is through friendship with a light touch or through discipline with an iron hand. He must conform if he is to "pass," for it is the teacher who decides that. Even his parents and friends cannot help him here, though they may try.

As the student moves up the grade ladder of the school and matures he is encouraged to think of the teacher as friend and equal. He may spontaneously want to slap a favorite teacher's back and give him a "Hi, there." But it is as hard for the student as it is for the teacher to bring the two images of authority and friend together. Yet there may be positive value in this attempt for the student will frequently face

[5] Richard Meryman, "How We Drive Teachers to Quit," *Life,* Volume 53, No. 20, November 16, 1962, pp. 109–110.

the same conflicts in adult life. As he learns to reconcile informal and formal relationships he will "probably acquire by that very adjustment the training essential to enable them as adults to maintain quasi-intimate relations with people in impersonal situations—such as, for instance, the businessman who feels he must treat all of his customers as 'friends' (and perhaps also his 'friends' as customers)." [6]

THE INTERACTION OF TEACHERS AND PARENTS

Now we turn to the factors that determine the kind of interaction which takes place between teachers and parents. Some of these factors arise simply because teachers are teachers and parents, parents. Because they play different roles in relation to the child, parents and teachers can easily talk past one another without really communicating. Other factors determining the relationship arise in the nature of schoolwork.

Two Adults and One Child

In the parent-teacher relationship two adults are deeply involved in the well-being of one child, with the parent having a prior claim. The child's progress, in a sense, is the progress of the parent. The teacher's professional progress also depends upon his ability to help the child. With two adults so deeply committed to one child the relationship between them is obviously vital to each and capable of either gratifying understanding or tragic misunderstanding.

8. A Chicago suburban elementary teacher said of her charges: "They're just like babies. The parents indulge them, let them talk back, then come to school and say, 'We can't handle them.' But the parents expect *us* to." What does such an incident indicate to you about the relationships of teachers and parents?

Which Adult Is Responsible for What?

At first glance it may seem that the respective roles which parents and teacher play in relation to the child are well defined. Yet each does not know exactly what the other should do. In other words, the role expectations of one for the other may not correspond. A teacher, for example, is educated to take a sincere interest in the child's personal development, but the parent may interpret this interest as an invasion of privacy. For instance: [7]

6 J. R. Seeley, R. A. Sim, and E. W. Loosley, *op. cit.*, p. 271.

7 Ann P. Eliasberg, "Parent Meets Teacher," *New York Times Magazine*, Volume CXIV, No. 38,998, November 1, 1964, p. 112.

"One mother recalled bitterly a teacher who took the trouble to describe some disappointment her child had faced at school and to make suggestions on how she might best approach her daughter to ease her feelings. 'I suppose it was kind of her,' the mother said, 'but in nine years I think I've learned a little about my own child. All I could think of was how she would feel if I told her exactly how I thought she ought to handle Mary in class.'"

9. Do you think the teacher could have avoided this misunderstanding with the parent? If so, how?

Another parent may react in an exactly opposite manner; he or she may want the teacher's suggestions regarding the child's personal problems. Similarly, another teacher may not regard it as his business to point out problems in the child's personal development. He will prefer to concentrate entirely on the positive traits of the child. For example:

" 'When I started teaching,' a woman who has taught for more than 15 years said, 'I greeted parents with long lists of their children's psychological quirks—and every child has some—and what I thought ought to be done about them. Since I've had a child myself, I've realized that parents have the hardest job in the world and that most of them care desperately about doing it well. Lecturing them and pointing out their failures is destructive even though you don't mean it to be. And anyway, that's not my job. My job is to take each child as he comes and try to bring out the best in him.'" [8]

10. The two teachers represented above apparently define their roles quite differently in respect to teaching children and communicating with parents. How do you evaluate the relative merits of these two approaches?

It is probably in the interest of good parent-teacher relations that each discuss freely the expectations he has for the other in order to see if some common understanding can be arrived at.

Focus on the Child's Performance

Most parent-teacher interaction focuses on the child's performance, and no topic is closer to the heart of either. In this case, it is the teacher who is the *judge* of the performance, not the parent. In this most crucial matter of all, it is the teacher who is the dominant figure in the interaction.

This focus of the relationship becomes even more crucial when

[8] *Ibid.,* p. 116.

we remember the importance of school achievement in the student's later success in gaining college admission or in finding employment. Most parents, especially those in the middle class, are quite sure that their child's present school performance will determine his future. The teacher provides both the means of the child's future success and the judgment about it. He understandably feels great pressure from both parent and child.

11. One teacher reported this incident: After giving a student a low grade he got a nasty note from the parents requesting that the grade be reconsidered. The teacher invited the parents to a conference, during which he reviewed the student's work and explained that the grade was both accurate and fair. Unsatisfied, the parents took the problem to the board of education, claiming that the grade was a reflection upon the teaching, not their child. Do you think the teacher handled this problem correctly? What do you think the board of education should do? Does the principal have a responsibility? If so, what?

In order to be successful the student must compete against others. This aspect of school achievement is of high concern to parents. They want to know how their child is doing in respect to other children. Yet it is in the nature of our society to disavow this interest. Note, for example, the comment of these parents: "No one will deny that life is competition, yet life is fullest and best lived in cooperation with those around us. I don't see why they always have to compete, compete, compete!" "I don't expect a teacher to tell me my son's I.Q. or which children in the class are ahead of him in which subject, but I like to know if he has the capacity to do superior work or just average."

Teachers know, however, that the parents' concern for the child's performance is a concern with his performance in relation to other students. The very concepts of "superior" or "just average" work are comparative. Things are "superior" or "average" in relation to other things, and in school the "other things" are other students.

If this is true, what can the teacher say to the parent of the child who is not competing, perhaps cannot compete, successfully in relation to other students? The teacher can attempt to shift the basis of competition from others to the child himself. "The important thing," the teacher may tell the parent, "is that Mary improve on her own past performance. If she can do that she is being successful. We shouldn't worry too much about how she's doing in relation to others. Improving on her own record is the thing that counts."

As another example take this message to parents from a super-

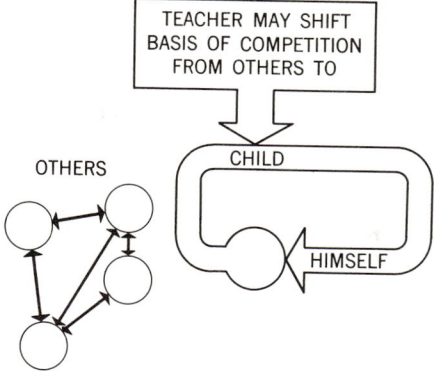

Fig. 14-3

intendent of schools which appears on the cover of the school's report card. Notice how the superintendent shifts the competitive emphasis from others to the individual child.

"To the Parent—Partner in Progress:

"Let us work together in a common interest—that of our children.

"Through this Progress Report we desire to present you with a picture of your child's social habits and capabilities as well as his progress in subject-matter areas.

"We would like to call your attention to the fact that no two individuals are alike in all respects, and we must be conscious of this at all times. Please do not compare your child with other children, but measure him according to his own ability.

"If your child does things successfully, commend him. If his report indicates that he needs additional help, do not reprimand him, but come to the school for a conference where his problems can be discussed with the person who knows most about his schoolwork—his teacher.

"We want you to know that we attempt to develop your child's personality along happy and wholesome channels through every possible means.

"With your interest and understanding, such goals as are outlined above are more adequately achieved."

Superintendent of Schools

12. We have discussed how the school embodies and transmits the cultural values of the society. Make a list of the cultural values which you find either implied or explicitly stated in this communication to parents. Does this statement tell you anything about the cultural style of this school? About its educational climate?

In attempting to play down the competitive emphasis and accentuate individual differences the superintendent and teacher are running counter to popular success values. The school's position must be recognized, however, as an attempt to reconcile conflicting expectations. The community values success as expressed in school performance. Yet children, being different, do not and cannot all achieve success in the same measure. The grading system by definition *grades*. The teacher's attempt to stress other values represents a sensible reconciliation in an area where the school is a battleground of conflicting values.

The Parent's Feeling of Inadequacy

Many parents approach the teacher with a feeling of inadequacy about rearing their children. The parent is barraged by experts who advise him about the "do's and don'ts" of child rearing and who increase the parent's sense of frustration and failure. Now comes the teacher, perhaps in a teacher conference, to remind the parent again how frustrating raising children can be. "I'm always depressed after I talk to Bobby's teacher," commented a parent. "I feel that everything I've done is wrong and that I should consult a child psychologist." [9]

A parent may feel inadequate when he talks with the teacher because he recalls his own unpleasant experiences in school: "You know, I'm scared to death. When I was in school I got called in to see the principal. I knew I'd done something bad. That's just the way I feel now." [10]

The Increasing Reliance of the Parent on the Teacher

These factors in parent-teacher relations, taken together, have increased the reliance of the parent on the teacher. This subtle change is coming over the relationship, but it is unlikely that either parents or teachers would think of it this way. Yet more and more the teacher is a specialist who has knowledge about the child which the parent does not possess. The increasing use of achievement tests, aptitude tests, and personality profiles places the teacher in possession of data

[9] Ann P. Eliasberg, "Parent Meets Teacher," *New York Times Magazine,* Volume CXIV, No. 38,998, November 1, 1964, p. 112.

[10] *Ibid.*, p. 112.

about the child which the parent knows is crucial, but may not understand. Further, most schools are taking more and more responsibility for the socialization of the child beyond formal classroom learning. That sphere of the child's life over which teachers presumably have some control frequently encroaches on that sphere over which the parent has control.

13. Sometimes the parent's feeling of reliance on the teacher is carried to ridiculous lengths. Teachers may be called on the telephone at all hours by parents seeking advice. One elementary teacher reported that a parent called to ask if her child should wear a raincoat to school. If you were a teacher and received such a call, how would you reply to the parent?

Although the increasing reliance of parents upon teachers may give the teacher more power and possibly more status, it simultaneously creates new expectations for which the teacher must be prepared.

INTERACTIONS AMONG STUDENTS

Interactions among students take place, as we would expect, in both the informal and formal social systems of the school. At the informal level students create a network of relationships within and among their peer groups. At the formal level the network revolves around organized student activities, both inside the classroom and out.

In Chapter 7, we studied the student in relation to his informal group. In this section, therefore, we shall focus on the student in the formal social system of the school. It would be well, however, to review the salient features of informal groups because they bear a relationship to the way students interact in the formal social system.

We said that as a student grows he moves away from his parents and other adults toward his age group, his peers. His association with his peers serves a number of useful functions that help him to become an adult. Peer associations let the student test himself outside the home; they give him egalitarian relationships which are hard to achieve within the family; he learns social knowledge and behavior which he usually cannot gain within the family and which he must have if he is to get along with his peers.

The school provides a stage upon which informal peer groups operate. It is here that students organize themselves into an informal social system. Within the system each group has a position and a role to play. Some groups enjoy high status; others are assigned low status. Adolescents spend a great deal of their energy in school trying to meet the expectations of their peers. In this effort some students are successful, others not. Some, having failed in the climb, withdraw from the contest. Students' success in achieving social status has a bearing upon how well they achieve academically.

We said that informal and formal student social systems are closely related. That is, the students who are prominent in the informal friendship and clique groups tend also to dominate the most sought-after formal student organizations. The classic study by C. Wayne Gordon on the social system of "Wabash" high school in a Midwestern suburban community is illuminating here.[11] Gordon devised a social status index based upon three factors: school grades, participation in formal student organizations, and sociometric status, that is, the number of times a student was chosen as "best friend" by other students. By using this composite index Gordon assigned each of the 576 students in the school a place within the social network. When he compared the students' positions in the informal friendship system with that in the formal organization system he found that the two were closely related. Students who ranked high in the informal system also ranked high in the formal system, and vice versa.

The study also indicated that the prestige of different organizations varies widely. Of the fifty organizations in "Wabash" high school students assigned top ranks to Student Government, Varsity Basketball and Football, National Honor Society, Cheer Leaders and Yearbook Queen's Court. The lowest ranks were assigned to the Roller Skating Club, Outdoor Club, Pencil Pushers (creative writing), Riding Club, and Knitting Club.

Offices in the prestige clubs were contested for by students who were prominent in the informal social system of the school, and the campaigns for these offices were a major preoccupation of the majority of the students. As Gordon reported: "The student who belonged to a sufficient number of prestigious organizations and filled a sufficient number of offices warranted the title 'big wheel.' For boys, the sources of this status were primarily athletic achievement, although by extreme effort achievements in other than athletic activities might be combined to produce the 'big wheel.' The label itself denoted a pattern of expected behavior as well as a particular status in the eyes of the group. . . .

"Girls were 'big wheels' too, and the most prized . . . status of all was formalized in the position, Queen of the Yearbook. The queen

[11] C. Wayne Gordon, *The Social System of the High School*, Glencoe, Illinois, The Free Press, 1957.

was crowned in a public ceremony called the Yearbook Coronation, the major social function of the year.

"The social careers of the 12th-grade girls were climaxed with election of the Queen who was selected by a school-wide vote from a slate of nine candidates nominated by senior boys. The eight candidates who were not chosen served as Maids of the Queen's Court."[12]

THE STUDENT ACTIVITY PROGRAM OF THE SCHOOL

Student interaction in the formal social system takes place largely in class sessions or in "co-curricular" (or "extracurricular") programs. We discussed student classroom relationships in earlier chapters; here we focus on out-of-class activities.

Most schools provide extensive activity programs and usually require students to take part in a minimum number of activities. These activity programs are officially approved by the school, and a faculty member usually acts as sponsor for the group.

It is interesting to compare the control aspects of student clubs and classrooms. In the classroom the teacher is the dominant figure. Student initiative and leadership are at a minimum. In the student club the matter is, in theory if not always in practice, reversed. Students are supposed to take the initiative, decide what they want to do, plan programs and carry them out. The teacher role shifts to that of "sponsor," one who helps the students accomplish what they want to do. In the classroom the teacher tries to interest students in accomplishing goals which he or others have devised. In the student club the teacher helps students achieve what they together want to achieve.

14. It has been pointed out that student clubs may be better than classrooms as climates for learning because they place students in a more active role and because the teacher becomes a "resource person" for students. How would you compare student clubs with classrooms as learning environments?

Below is a list of student clubs and activities for a suburban high school of medium size. Notice the wide range of activities which it presents; some are connected quite directly to classroom work, like the Biology Club, some are prevocational, like the Future Teachers of America, some are artistic and cultural, like the Orchestra Club, and some are simply recreational, like the Chess Club.

[12] *Ibid.*, pp. 67–68.

Student Organizations in a Suburban High School

Academic Subject Clubs
    Biology Club
    Business Club
    Spanish Club
    French Club
Pre-Vocational Clubs
    Future Homemakers of America
    Future Farmers of America
    Future Nurses of America
    Future Teachers of America
School Wide Pupil Organization
    Student Parliament
    Forensics
    Assembly Programs
    Student Court
Artistic and Musical Groups
    Art Club
    Band Club
    Orchestra Club
    Chorus Club
Literary and Journalistic Groups
    Library Club
    Dramatic Club
    National Honor Society
    Yearbook
    Newspaper
Other Activity Organizations
    Cheerleading
    Girls Athletic Association
    Varsity Club
    Ski Club
    Chess Club
    Projection (Audio-Visual)
    Intramurals

15. What does this list of student activities tell you about the cultural style of this school?

THE SOCIAL FUNCTIONS SERVED BY STUDENT ACTIVITY PROGRAMS

The formal student activity program of the school serves a number of social functions which are worth noting.

Low control, high responsibility. Student activity programs, we noted, provide a switch in roles from the classroom. The tight control exercised by the teacher in the classroom can be relaxed in the student club. The normally submissive role of the student in class can be shed for one of responsibility in the club. One of the goals of the school is to train students to assume responsibility and conduct their own affairs, to train for adulthood and citizenship. The student club, if properly handled, can become a "halfway house" where under a low control students can assume high responsibilities.

Social-class mixer. We cited Gordon's findings above to indicate how the informal social-class structure of the high school penetrates formal student organizations. The student elites in the informal groups tend to be the elites of the formal groups. What chance is there, then, for the student who is "out" rather than "in"? Can he find anywhere in the modern school a chance to develop his ability to work with groups and possibly take leadership?

His chances are reasonably good if the school manages its student activity program well. Although it is true that elite student groups dominate the leadership of organizations, the large numbers of clubs and the great range of activities which they undertake provide ample opportunity for each interested student to participate in a meaningful way.

More important, the activity program can provide an opportunity for each student to work in an informal way with students from entirely different home environments and economic circumstances. The need continues for the American school to perform its "melting pot" functions, and the end of the need is not in sight.

Counterpoint to peer groups. Not only does the student activity program act as a social-class mixer, it also acts as a counterpoint to peer groups. Informal peer groups, we have noted, have a strong influence upon students, in part because of the irresistible urge of adolescents to join groups. The schools' student clubs impose some structure upon informal peer groups. They present alternatives to students who seek to establish relationships with other students, and they at least modify the influence and power of the informal peer group.

16. Sometimes a peer group may "take over" a student activity and operate it as a private club, excluding from membership those not in the clique. If you were the sponsor of a club in which the "in" group made such an attempt, what do you think you might do?

From student to worker. There is a vocational emphasis in the student activity program cited. Four "future" clubs are listed, for homemakers, farmers, nurses, and teachers. The activity program serves as a first bridge to the world of work and symbolizes the modern comprehensive school's vocational concern.

These are some of the social functions served by the student activity program. Notice how some of these functions are described in the following statement written by a superintendent of schools in a report to parents.

"This is the age of clubs. Consider for a moment the great number of clubs in our community—commercial, professional, social, cultural, recreational, educational, religious, political, service and fraternal, and the large part of the community which the total membership represents. In short, the adult club has become a device that not only educates but also automatically advances the interest represented.

"The school club, while differing somewhat from the adult club in aims, materials, and methods, can nevertheless occupy an equally important place in the lives of the pupils of the school.

"From adolescence onward, pupils seem to have an irresistible urge to get together in groups. Partly to guide the urge in the right direction, and partly to take advantage of the educational opportunity it affords, schools sponsor many kinds of pupil organizations. Some, like the French Club, are immediate outgrowths of the regular instructional program; others, like a dramatics club, are especially created to give instruction not offered in the regular program; and still others, like the Ski Club, are actually outside groups which turn to the school only for adult sponsorship and perhaps a place to meet.

"Most of us will agree that the primary justification for school sponsorship of student clubs lies in their ultimate contribution to the cause of self-government and citizenship. A democracy can succeed only as its people can learn to work towards a common cause and to generate the decisions needed to hold their society together and propel it forward.

"Without question the best opportunity a young person has to practice the art of helping to shape and form a group will be in school-sponsored clubs. This is particularly true when the clubs are led by faculty personnel who have the judgment to set sensible limits and then allow pupils leeway to learn within them.

"School clubs are a vital part of the school program, a training ground for good citizens, a requisite for a democratic society."

Such, then, is the social system of the school in action. It is a system characterized by a subtly balanced relationship of individuals and groups in a vast communication circle. It operates within the school but quickly spills over into the community, involving members of the board of education, parents, and other interested citizens. But its target is always the student, the "direct" client of the school. He is the object of the entire system and it is he who gives it purpose and direction.

REFERENCES

Paperbacks

Adolescent Character and Personality. Robert J. Havighurst and Hilda Taba. Science Editions Paperbacks, John Wiley and Sons, 605 Third Ave., New York ($1.65).

Adolescents. Sandor Lorand and Henry I. Schneer, Editors. (0021) Dell Publishing Co., 750 Third Ave., New York ($2.25).

American Secondary Schools. Marwritz Johnson, Jr. Harcourt, Brace and World, 757 Third Ave., New York ($1.75).

Challenge of Youth (Orig. title: Youth, Change and Challenge). Erik H. Erikson, Editor. (A438) Anchor Books and Anchor Science Study Series, Doubleday and Co., 277 Park Ave., New York ($1.45).

Elementary School Child. Daniel A. Prescott. (Orig.) Educational Services, 1730 Eye St., N. W., Washington, D. C. ($2.75).

High School Youth. Daniel A. Prescott. (Orig.) Educational Services, 1730 Eye St., N. W., Washington, D. C. ($2.75).

Schools. Martin Mayer. (A331) Anchor Books and Anchor Science Study Series, Doubleday and Co., 277 Park Ave., New York ($1.45).

Books

Association for Supervision and Curriculum Development, *Leadership for Improving Instruction,* 1960 Yearbook of the Association. Washington, D. C.: National Education Association, 1960. Chapter 3 explains the role expectancies and conflicts of the curriculum worker, principal, and teacher, and gives various reasons for diversity in expectations.

Bellack, Arno, and Joel R. Davitz, *The Language of the Classroom, Meanings Communicated in High School Teaching.* New York: Institute of Psychological Research, Teachers College, Columbia University, 1963. The objective of this research was to study the teaching process via analysis of the linguistic behavior of the teachers and students in the classroom.

Charter, W. W., and N. L. Gage, Editors, *Readings in Social Psychology of Education.* Boston: Allyn and Bacon, 1963, 350 pp. Section V includes articles on teacher-student interactions.

Jersild, Arthur T., *When Teachers Face Themselves*. New York: Bureau of Publications, Teachers College, Columbia University, 1955. Jersild found that teachers lack adult contacts and adult relationships, outside and inside school.

Waller, Willard, *The Sociology of Teaching*. New York: John Wiley and Sons, 1965. Part IV, "The Teacher-Pupil Relationship," discusses teacher and pupil roles in the classroom situations.

Westby-Gibson, Dorothy, *Social Perspectives on Education*. New York: John Wiley and Sons, 1965. Chapter 15 discusses the social system in the classroom and the school. The roles of administrators, teachers, and students are given consideration.

Periodicals

Amidon, Edmund, and Anita Simon, "Teacher-Pupil Interaction," Chapter IV, *Review of Educational Research*, Vol. 35, No. 2, April 1965, pp. 130–139. The chapter presents a brief description of systems currently used to collect and categorize observational data concerning teacher-pupil interaction.

Carmical, LaVerne, "Five Basic Responsibilities of the Classroom Teacher," *The Clearing House*, Vol. 38, No. 5, January 1964, pp. 307–308. The actions of the teacher strongly influence the learning, attitudes, and behavior of the youngsters under his supervision.

Cautela, Joseph R., "The Phenomenon of Transference in the School Situation," *Psychology in the Schools*, Vol. I, No. 4, October 1964, pp. 432–435. The conflicts that the child has with his parents may be transferred to the teacher.

McConnel, Gaither, "Behavior that Annoys Teachers," *The Elementary School Journal*, Vol. 63, No. 8, May 1963, pp. 448–452. The article is based on a report of urban teachers listing different kinds of annoying behavior of children.

Reinhardt, Emma, "The Teacher Who Helped Me Most," *The Clearing House*, Vol. 38, No. 4, December 1963, pp. 224–226. The ten most frequent reasons for choosing teachers as "most helpful" are given in rank order.

Sprinthall, Norman, "A Comparison of Values Among Teachers, Academic Underachievers, and Achievers," *The Journal of Experimental Education*, Vol. 33, No. 2, Winter 1964, pp. 193–195. An empirical study shows superior achieving high-school students have values markedly similar to their teachers. Underachievers hold values different from their teachers.

Tyler, Louis L., "The Concept of an Ideal Teacher-Student Relationship," *The Journal of Educational Research*, Vol. 58, No. 3, November 1964, pp. 112–117. Professional educators answer the question: What is the ideal teacher-student relationship?

V

The Teachers

15

The Decision to Teach

"There is no more exciting experience in the world than your first teaching job. To switch from student to teacher in one swoop, from passive listener to seer, is rather awe inspiring."   A MOTHER'S LETTER TO HER SON

It is important to know why one teaches. In a sense the real power of teaching lies in this understanding. Teachers who are clear about their motivations for teaching come to the classroom prepared to work with students in ways that are in harmony with their ideals and in a manner which is personally satisfying to them. Why do we teach?

In this chapter we discuss some of the motivations which influence people to teach and the psychological roots of these motivations. We inquire into the time at which the decision is made. We discuss the influence of early teaching experiences in the decision. We look at the career plans of beginning teachers and note how plans differ between young men and young women. We examine the dominant values which new teachers hold. Finally we ask: What are the characteristics of outstanding teachers?

THE MODELS OF CHILDHOOD

One strong motivation for many teachers is their identification with the adult models of their childhood—parents, and especially teachers. As Margaret Mead says: "Those who really want to teach usually have had the good fortune of having encountered a good teacher whose enthusiasm for her subject caught their imagination, and they have stood out against all the other life models provided by relatives and friends." [1]

[1] Margaret Mead, "Where Education Fits In," *Think*, Volume 28, No. 10, November–December 1962, p. 18.

Research suggests that both parents and former teachers are important in a young person's decision to teach, with an edge being given to the influence of former teachers. Among the 1,066 college seniors who participated in the Yale-Fairfield Study,[2] women were influenced by their parents only slightly more than by their teachers in their decision to teach. On the other hand, men were influenced by their teachers more than twice as often as by their parents. The 230 juniors and seniors in Clarence Fielstra's study rated teachers twice as high as parents on a scale of importance in their decision to teach.[3] Forty-one women preparing for elementary school teaching at the University of Chicago were asked who had most influenced them to become teachers. Sixty-four percent named a teacher while only 15 percent named a family member.[4] Isabel Willcox and Hugo Beigel found that among their 152 first semester freshmen the example of a teacher was mentioned more frequently than family influence in their decision to teach.[5] One of these freshmen said: "When I was in school I became very friendly with one of my teachers. She seemed to be the nicest person I had ever met and had all the attributes which I hope that I will someday have. That is why I chose teaching."[6]

Clearly a majority of students who decide to go into teaching are influenced by teachers and parents. At least a quarter, and perhaps as many as two-thirds, of the college students preparing to teach ascribe their choice primarily to a teacher.

1. If you have made the decision to teach, what were the contributing factors? Make a mental list of the people who contributed to your decision. What was there about these people that influenced you?

STUDENT IMAGES OF THE TEACHER

Students who are planning to teach hold quite different images of teachers than those who are not. Mae Seagoe compared a group of 122 California juniors and seniors who were not studying to be teachers

---

[2] "Yale-Fairfield Study of Elementary Teaching," abridged edition for the Report for 1954–1955, by Constance M. Burns et al., New York, 1956, p. 25.

[3] Clarence Fielstra, "Analysis of Factors Influencing the Decision to Become a Teacher," *Journal of Educational Research*, Volume 48, No. 9, May 1955, pp. 659–67.

[4] Benjamin Wright, "News and Comment: Should Children Teach?" *Elementary School Journal*, Chicago, University of Chicago, Volume 60, April 1960, p. 262.

[5] Isabel Willcox and Hugo Beigel, "Motivations in the Choice of Teaching," *Journal of Teacher Education*, Volume IV, No. 2, June 1953, pp. 100–109.

[6] *Ibid.*, p. 107.

with 122 who were.[7] Having matched the two groups by sex, college years, grades, and backgrounds, she asked each student: "Have you ever wished to be just like a teacher?"

Of those who indicated they "wished to be just like a teacher," 75 percent were themselves planning to teach. The prospective teachers also selected a teacher in the elementary school more than twice as often as teachers at other levels. Seagoe concluded that classroom teachers were strong determiners of the teaching personnel of tomorrow.

Do prospective teachers also view teachers generally more favorably than other students? The research of Robert Ritchey and William Fox suggests that they do.[8] They asked a group of Indiana University freshmen to consider all the people they knew in the community and to compare public school teachers as a group with these people. A scale of 24 characteristics was made for the comparison. These investigators then compared the evaluations by the 100 freshmen who definitely planned to teach with the evaluations of the 695 freshmen who definitely did not plan to teach. The prospective teachers evaluated teachers overwhelmingly more favorably than did the students who decided against teaching.

It is interesting to note the differences in the images of teachers which these two groups held. Those who planned to teach held the image of a strong but human teacher, magnetic, a good sport, cultured, a leader. Those who did not plan to teach saw the teacher as busy, mechanical, practical, and industrious.

The image which a college student holds of a teacher is built up over the years of his schooling, his experience with a number of teachers, and the manner in which he was taught. His decision to teach seems to be related to his human view of the teacher more than the mechanical aspects of teaching. On the other hand, the decision *not* to teach seems more related to the mechanical than the human aspects of teaching.

2. Benjamin Wright comments that "a central psychological phenomenon that motivates teachers in their careers is the pleasing of their own former teachers. Of course, the original relationship is long since past. Now the pleasing can take place only in memory. But that is enough."[9] How do you

[7] M. V. Seagoe, "Some Origins of Interest in Teaching," *Journal of Educational Research*, Volume 35, No. 9, May 1942, pp. 673–682.

[8] Robert Ritchey and William Fox, "An Analysis of Various Factors Associated with the Selection of Teaching as a Vocation," *Bulletin of the School of Education*, Indiana University, Volume 24, No. 3, May 1948.

[9] Benjamin Wright, "Identification and Becoming a Teacher," *Elementary School Journal*, Volume 59, No. 7, April 1959, p. 363.

evaluate his psychological explanation in terms of your own decision to teach?

SEEING ONESELF AS A TEACHER

Future teachers, as we said, identify at an early age with the role of teacher.[10] This identification raises two psychological questions: (1) How deep is this identification? (2) To what degree does it work at the subconscious, or covert, level? In other words, are these prospective teachers beginning to see *themselves* as teachers, or is the teacher simply some *other* person, remote and removed from the student's sense of personal identity?

Philip W. Jackson and Fela Moscovici report research designed to shed light on these questions.[11] For this investigation two groups of graduate students were given the Draw-a-Teacher Test. One group was enrolled in a Master of Arts in Teaching program. The other group consisted of graduate students at the same level of graduate training who were not preparing to teach. The performances of the two groups were compared.

In the Draw-a-Teacher Test the student is given a blank sheet of paper with the following instructions at the top: "In the space below draw a teacher with a class. Draw as complete a picture as you can. Avoid the use of stick figures. Don't worry about your artistic ability or lack of it; just draw as well as you can."

The results of this investigation, which are summarized in Table 1, suggest some striking differences between the two groups of students in their covert identification with the teacher's role. First, over one-third of the nonteaching group, the control group, depicted a teacher of the opposite sex in their drawings, or one where sex was not identifiable. On the other hand, only two of the teachers-to-be drew a teacher of the opposite sex, suggesting a much closer identification with the role of the teacher than the control group.

Second, all the students made their drawings while sitting in a college classroom; yet almost all of the prospective teachers pictured elementary or secondary school classrooms in which they would find

[10] For research on how the teacher's conception of his role is built up by the process of identification, see Barbara Shermon, "Teachers' Identification with Childhood Authority Figures," *The School Review*, Volume 71, No. 1, Spring 1963, pp. 66–78.

[11] Philip W. Jackson and Fela Moscovici, "The Teacher-to-Be: A Study of Embryonic Identification with a Professional Role," *The School Review*, Volume 71, No. 1, Spring 1963, pp. 41–65.

TABLE 1

QUALITIES DIFFERENTIATING EXPERIMENTAL AND
CONTROL GROUPS ON THE DRAW-A-TEACHER TEST

Quality	Teachers-to-be ($N = 27$)	Control group ($N = 27$)
Opposite of non-identifiable sex choice for the teacher figure	2	10
Elementary or secondary school setting	23	10
College setting	1	15
Explicit subject matter depicted	15	6

SOURCE: Philip W. Jackson and Fela Moscovici, "The Teacher-to-Be: A Study of Embryonic Identification with a Professional Role," *The School Review*, Volume 71, No. 1, Spring 1963, p. 54.

themselves in the future. The students in the control group, in contrast, showed a marked tendency to draw a college classroom, in which they would find themselves in the future.

Third, the teachers-to-be brought more explicit subject matter into their pictures than did the control group. In this the prospective teachers were probably expressing their concern, felt by many beginning teachers, about having sufficient teaching material to avoid running out.

Summarizing their analysis, Jackson and Moscovici state:

"The results of this study suggest at least two general hypotheses concerning the process by which people become teachers and the psychological qualities that distinguish these people from those who have chosen other careers.

"First, the evidence indicates that the teacher-to-be, even at the beginning of his preparation, has begun to identify on a covert level with his future professional role. Not only does he say he wants to be a teacher, but even when taken off guard he indicates, through his unstructured perceptions, the psychological pervasiveness of his career choice. The stimulus phrase 'teacher with a class' calls forth an image of a person of his own sex working in a setting very much like the one in which he will find himself in the near future. The drawings as well as the word-association material suggest that the teacher-to-be perceives a school as a relatively permanent residence rather than as temporary quarters in which he is forced to live for a brief period.

"Second, the findings give some indication of one of the central psychological problems facing the teacher-to-be: that of knowing how to maintain a pleasant interpersonal environment while performing in that environment as an authority figure. Although he is inclined, on the one hand, to draw classroom settings that are homey and neat, he is careful, on the other hand, to give considerable emphasis to the teacher figure, placing it in a prominent position of authority and control. Although his free associations and work completions contain many references to the homemaker's role and to the act of providing a pleasant and neat environment, they also give some hint of a concern with misbehavior and with the task of being 'absolute' and 'diligent' . . .

"The crucial point is that most writers have identified the authority conflict as a problem facing the beginning or the experienced teacher, while the present data indicate that the teacher-to-be may be experiencing some form of this conflict many months before he has actually faced pupils in the classroom." [12]

3. Willard Waller, in reference to the teacher's role, says: "Conflict is in the role, for the wishes of the teacher and the student are necessarily divergent, and will conflict because the teacher must protect himself from the possible destruction of his authority that might arise from this divergence of motives." [13] Do you agree or disagree with Waller that "the wishes of the teacher and student are *necessarily* divergent"? Can you think of ways in which a teacher protects "himself from the possible destruction of authority"?

WHEN DO STUDENTS MAKE THE DECISION TO TEACH?

We associate career decisions with the late high school and early college years. Vocational counseling in the high school is usually aimed at juniors and seniors who, it is presumed, will soon make decisions about vocational choices. The early years of college usually offer the student a general and liberal program designed to help him "find himself" and select his future vocation wisely. This model does not fit many students who decide to teach. The decision to teach, research indicates, comes earlier for many students, in the early years of high school, and for some in the elementary school. This early choice of teaching is consistent with what we said about the importance of childhood models in the decision.

Authors of the Yale-Fairfield study indicated that among a na-

[12] *Ibid.*, pp. 59–60.

[13] Willard Waller, *The Sociology of Teaching*, New York, John Wiley and Sons, Inc., 1965, p. 383.

tional sample of 1,066 seniors preparing for elementary school teaching, 68 percent reported that their decision was made before leaving high school.[14] Fielstra reported that among 230 California juniors and seniors in an introductory course in education, 50 percent made the decision before graduation from high school.[15]

Other research indicates that the decision to teach may be made even earlier. R. H. Morrison and S. D. Winans reported that 40 percent of a group of 1,423 applicants to New Jersey teachers colleges said that they decided to become teachers before the tenth grade.[16] Among the Yale-Fairfield national sample of students 24 percent made their decision before leaving elementary school.[17] Ritchey and Fox questioned 970 Indiana high school students who had "considered" teaching and discovered that 48 percent had done so before high school. Of the 261 who had "decided" on teaching 35 percent had done so before high school.[18]

Testimony of experienced teachers indicates even more strongly that career decisions are made early. Lawrence Stewart asked a group of 260 summer graduate students, half of whom had been teaching for five years or more, when they had decided to become teachers. Twenty-five percent reported "before high school" and 66 percent "before college." [19] Benjamin Wright summarizes the evidence about the time when career choice in teaching is made: "It seems pretty conclusive that among those who make a decision to become teachers, 20–30 percent make their decision in elementary school, 40–70 percent have made their decision before they leave high school." [20]

Here is the testimony of three students who made early decisions to teach.[21] For the first, interest in teaching started early, even before he realized it:

"The person who influenced me most towards teaching was my fourth-grade teacher. I was not conscious of this at the time. However, when I look back I realize it was my fourth-grade experience which steered me towards teaching. The atmosphere in the room was very

---

[14] "Yale-Fairfield Study of Elementary Teaching," *op. cit.*, p. 26.

[15] Fielstra, *op. cit.*, p. 666.

[16] R. H. Morrison and S. D. Winans, *Choosing Teaching as a Career,* New Jersey State Department of Education, 1949.

[17] "Yale-Fairfield Study of Elementary Teaching," *op. cit.*, p. 24.

[18] Ritchey and Fox, *op. cit.*, pp. 20–21.

[19] Lawrence Stewart, "Certain Factors Related to the Occupational Choice of a Group of Experimental Teachers," *Peabody Journal of Education,* Volume 33, No. 4, January 1956, p. 10.

[20] Wright, *op. cit.*, p. 359.

[21] *Ibid.*, pp. 363–364.

friendly and pleasant, and I really enjoyed going to school. This was due to the teacher's personality. She was a very friendly and outgoing person. There were other teachers along the way who intensified my desire to go into teaching. But it was my fourth-grade teacher who was the first one to do this."

The second student left high school without a conscious intention to become a teacher. Yet his relationship with a teacher was such that it caused him to consider teaching later:

"My high school chemistry teacher was one of only a few of my teachers who were really interested in the children they were working with. A number of us became close friends with him and his family. He was also unusual in seeming to enjoy his work. Although I had no interest in teaching during high school and even had negative feelings on the subject, I feel that this teacher helped make it possible for me later to consider teaching as a profession."

The third student made the decision to teach at the end of high school:

"The person who most influenced me to choose teaching was an English teacher I had in my last year of high school. I had enjoyed and admired other teachers before, but it was she who most reinforced my adult conception of the type of profession teaching was and aroused my interest in teaching as a profession I might enjoy. She was the type of person who was able to convey what she knew without being pompous but rather in a way that created further enthusiasm in you about the topic of which she was speaking. Though the classroom atmosphere was not loose in any way, there was a relaxation that came from being really interested in the topic."

4. We have said that teachers have a close identification with early teachers of their own, and that the decision to teach is made early. Project yourself now into a classroom as teacher, keeping these two factors in mind. What implications do you see for the way you teach and work with students?

The Difference Between an Early and Late Decision to Teach

Do students who decide to teach relatively late hold different attitudes toward teaching than those who decide early? The authors of the Yale-Fairfield study had this to say:

"Those who began early to consider teaching less frequently doubted the wisdom of their choice, and they more frequently reported a social service motivation. They also reported more frequently that they had been influenced to choose teaching by favorable family attitudes and by their teachers.

"Those who began late to consider teaching more frequently reported doubting the wisdom of their choice; they more frequently reported being motivated by the beginning salary and the working conditions. Also more frequently, they reported being influenced by friends, and more thought of teaching as a temporary form of employment." [22]

When Do Students Decide *Against* Teaching?

What about those who decide *not* to become teachers? When do they make their decision? And what causes them to decide against it?

Apparently a child's early negative experiences with teachers and teaching can cause him to decide against teaching. Roderick Langston asked 3,140 Oregon school children what they thought of elementary school teaching as a vocation.[23] Nine hundred and eight sixth-graders said elementary school teaching looked attractive to them but 818 ninth-graders and 581 twelfth-graders strongly disagreed. The authors of this investigation suggested that in this group of children some unfavorable opinion of teaching developed between the sixth and twelfth grades.

The response of the Indiana freshmen studied by Ritchey and Fox adds weight to this suggestion. Among 695 students who had definite intentions never to become teachers 20 percent had come to that conclusion before they entered high school, and 93 percent before they entered college. Most of these students decided against teaching in the ninth and tenth grades.[24]

Early Teaching Experience and the Decision to Teach

The decision to teach is frequently associated with early teaching experiences of some type. A high proportion of prospective teachers report that they had leadership experiences with children in camp, church, community, or school settings. Don Orton asked 405 undergraduates what caused them to want to become teachers and found that 58 percent named experiences in teaching. Orton concluded that "a great many college students are attracted to teaching because they have already had some first-hand experience with it." [25]

Sixty-three of the one hundred Wisconsin seniors in teacher train-

[22] "Yale-Fairfield Study of Elementary Teaching," *op. cit.,* p. 27.

[23] Roderick Langston, "A Study of Attitudes Toward Teaching as a Vocation," *Journal of Teacher Education,* Volume II, No. 2, June 1951, pp. 83–87.

[24] Ritchey and Fox, *op. cit.,* p. 46.

[25] Don Orton, "Why Do They Want to Teach?," *Phi Delta Kappan,* Volume XXX, No. 8, April 1949, p. 343.

ing questioned by Thomas Ringness said that they had early teaching experiences and 58 had actually taught school classes.[26] One senior said:

"Perhaps the greatest single factor in my choosing the physical education field as my major at the University was a direct outgrowth of my days in junior high school. I was on the school basketball team and the coach was having more work than he could possibly handle by himself. So he requested two gym assistants for each of his classes. I was accepted . . . I relished the responsibility . . . shared with the coach the burden of teaching the class. I was proud of this attainment." [27]

Do early informal teaching experiences actually discriminate between those who do and do not make the decision to teach? Mae Seagoe's research suggests that they may.[28] She first asked all the students in her study about their early teaching experiences and then compared the responses of those who were preparing to teach with those who were not. When she counted the number of times a student said he had taught and liked it, the score in favor of the teachers-to-be in informal teaching experiences was: "played school," 80 percent compared with 60 percent; "cared for children outside your immediate family," 61 percent compared with 47 percent; "camp counselor," 29 percent compared with 13 percent.

Seagoe also discovered that teachers-to-be had more experience in *formal* teaching situations. Scores among teachers-to-be as compared with others was: "taking charge of the class when teacher was absent," 65 percent as compared with 45 percent; "tutored a student in a subject," 51 percent as compared with 44 percent; "taught a regular class," 15 percent as against 5 percent.

Ritchey and Fox found that 73 percent of the Indiana freshmen who were intending to teach had early teaching experience as compared with only 46 percent of those who did not intend to teach. They concluded that there was "a substantial relationship between the amount of experience of a teaching nature the students had and the degree to which they were inclined to select teaching. . . . No other items of data in this analysis showed a clearer relationship with the tendency to want to become a teacher. . . . Administrators and teach-

[26] Thomas Ringness, "Relationships Between Certain Attitudes Toward Teaching and Teaching Success," *Journal of Experimental Education,* Volume XXI, No. 1, September 1952, p. 48.

[27] *Ibid.,* p. 44.

[28] Seagoe, *op. cit.,* pp. 673, 682.

ers should make every effort to provide experience of a teaching nature for students in the public schools." [29]

5. Future Teachers of America (FTA) makes it possible for high school students to get actual classroom experience in teaching or in assisting teachers. If you have not had firsthand experience with this organization, you may wish to learn more about it and its contribution to this teaching profession. It might be interesting to interview a former FTA member to find out how experiences provided through the organization influenced that person's attitude toward teaching.

Student Teaching and the Decision to Teach

Student teaching is a systematic teaching experience provided prior to entering the profession on a full-time basis. How does the student-teaching experience influence the decision to teach? This experience comes much later than those we have just been discussing, usually after the intention to teach is clear. Apparently this experience reinforces the desire to teach for most students, yet for a few the student-teaching experience is clear indication that they should not enter teaching.

The writer asked 100 student teachers to evaluate the experience in terms of its influence upon their desire to become full-time teachers.[30] Eighty of the 100 student teachers reported that they looked forward "more eagerly than ever before" to full-time teaching. Ten student teachers were ambivalent and had difficulty in evaluating the experience in terms of their desire to teach; student teaching both encouraged and discouraged this group. Five student teachers believed the experience neither weakened nor strengthened their desire to teach; student teaching did not alter their commitment to teaching. The remaining five found that student teaching weakened their wish to teach on a career basis.

One of the student teachers whose desire to teach was weakened by student-teaching experiences said:

"In education courses teaching is presented generally as an ideal, a bundle of inspiring ideals that will make you a good teacher. In student teaching you climb down from the clouds and get your feet wet. The experience can make the 'natural' for teaching more eager than ever to teach. Or, it can repel one who got several false ideas about the profession during his preparation for teaching. I am in the latter group." [31]

[29] Ritchey and Fox, *op. cit.*, p. 25.

[30] Cole S. Brembeck, *The Discovery of Teaching*, Englewood Cliffs, New Jersey, Prentice-Hall, Inc., 1962, pp. 38–43.

[31] *Ibid.*, p. 39.

A student teacher who thought that student teaching both increased and decreased his desire to teach commented:

"I would say many factors increase my desire to teach. Teenagers and their problems are a challenge. Each day brings a new situation. You must keep well informed in several areas. It's fun to try out ideas and see them in action. On the other hand, several factors decreased my desire to teach: (1) little appreciation is shown for personal time and effort, (2) weak administration, (3) some faculty attitudes which I think are unprofessional." [32]

Two of the 80 student teachers who found that the experience definitely increased their desire to teach commented as follows:

"If you've studied education thinking it would be a snap and an easy way through college, your student teaching experience will open your eyes and show you that teaching is not a snap, and that it involves a great deal of work. This may weaken the desire of some to teach. Among the student teachers I know, however, including myself, it's had the opposite effect." [33]

"Some people believe teaching is an easy life. Actually, this is not true. If a person enters teaching under this false impression, his desire to teach may be weakened. On the whole, though, I think student teaching strengthens your desire to teach. In my own case I like children, and teaching puts you in a position to help them fulfill their objectives in life." [34]

Why Is the Desire to Teach Strengthened by Student Teaching?

When asked why the experience had this influence, the 80 student teachers whose desire to teach was strengthened through teaching gave a variety of reasons. Most of the reasons cluster around two closely related factors: (1) the teaching experience gave a sense of personal fulfillment and growth, and (2) the student teachers genuinely enjoyed working with children. The personal satisfactions that the student teachers found in teaching are summarized in comments like these:

"Now that I'm almost finished with student teaching I feel fully confident to teach on my own."

"I really had a chance to see the product of my efforts. I learned my faults and good points through direct experience and I could profit by them. I got a chance to become a genuine part of the class and learn what it's like to be a teacher."

[32] *Ibid.,* p. 40.
[33] *Ibid.*
[34] *Ibid.*

"I became enriched by the human contacts, and had my knowledge of subject matter deepened. Nothing could be more encouraging or satisfying."

"I can hardly wait to have my own classes. I know there will be many disappointments; yet I feel now that I'm equal to them. I think I can be a good teacher." [35]

The satisfactions almost always had their source in student relationships and the pleasures that derive from working with children and young people. These comments are representative:

"When you see students grow under your guidance, your desire to teach is definitely strengthened."

"Student teaching gives one the satisfaction of seeing how students change, even in a brief period of ten weeks."

"Seeing a student's face light up when he or she understands a point you have been trying to get across is what makes teaching, as far as I'm concerned, the best profession in the world."

"I found how interesting and refreshing students are and how you can do so much with them."

"Students are basically eager to learn. As a teacher I became personally interested in every child and wanted to see each of them develop new learning and attitudes." [36]

Student Comment on the Value of Early Teaching Experiences

How do student teachers feel about the advisability of having early teaching experiences of some type? Apparently the student-teaching experience demonstrates both the worth and the need for such experience. Those who had teaching-like experiences prior to student teaching found them invaluable, and those who did not wished they had.

The writer asked the 100 student teachers what suggestions they would have for other prospective teachers who had not yet reached the point of student teaching. The suggestion made most often by the student teachers was: "Gain as much actual experience as you can in working with children and youth." Here are some representative comments supporting this view:

"Get all the experience you possibly can with children."

"Work a lot with children—baby-sit, teach Sunday School, lead Boy Scouts, be a camp counselor, direct a recreation program—anything to broaden your understanding of children. It will pay off."

"Work with children the same age as you intend to teach. See how

[35] *Ibid.,* p. 41.
[36] *Ibid.,* p. 42.

they think and act and why they do the things they do. See what interests them and why."

"The most important thing is to have experience with children in a supervising capacity. Take opportunities to handle many kinds of children, work with them, talk to them, play with them, use materials with them. Many materials which fascinate adults leave children cold. Much adult vocabulary is meaningless to youngsters. You find these things out when you work with them." [37]

Early Teaching Experiences and Teaching Ability

Are persons who have early teaching experiences more likely to be successful teachers than those who have not? Available research does not permit us to say that there is a causal relationship between early teaching experience and teaching ability. Some research does indicate, however, that the two are associated, though the correlation may not necessarily be positive.

J. C. Gowan studied in depth 20 highly rated women elementary teachers to find clues about the characteristics that appear to be associated with outstanding teachers.[38] Each teacher was interviewed for one and one-half hours, and information was sought about relationships with parents, siblings, and the community. Gowan discovered that all of these 20 outstanding teachers had early teaching experiences:

"There were instances of early teaching experiences on the part of all 20 of the teachers, and, in some cases, the experience appeared to have been surprisingly extensive. One girl taught elementary school when she was seventeen, and another had considerable experience as a substitute teacher while still in high school. A third founded and conducted her own nursery school while still in high school. 'Taking charge of a class in the absence of the regular teacher' while in high school, extensive participation in, and enjoyment of, playing school with peers as children, and similar experiences were reported very frequently." [39]

The Values of Beginning Teachers

One of the major clues to a person's occupational choice is the values which he holds. What important values do people hope to find in the teaching profession? What satisfactions do they seek?

[37] *Ibid.*, p. 43.
[38] David G. Ryans, *Characteristics of Teachers*, Washington, D. C., American Council on Education, 1960, p. 263.
[39] *Ibid.*, p. 363.

6. The mother from whose letter we quoted at the opening of this chapter wrote to her son as follows:

"Dear Son: We've just received your letter telling us you turned down your uncle's offer of a job in his business in order to go to graduate school. I read the letter to your father and when I came to the sentence, 'I think Uncle Bill was surprised that I would choose to be a teacher when I could make all that money,' we looked at each other and laughed. It reminded us of the time right after the war when your father was offered a job on Wall Street. The wartime naval captain who made him the offer was dumfounded when your father said he thought he would prefer to go back to teaching. From the captain's point of view it did not make sense to turn down a good income for the meager salary of a college professor. Maybe it didn't. But we've never regretted not swapping our ivory tower for a penthouse apartment in New York. It's not as smart, but it's right for us. We hope and believe it will be right for you." [40]

This mother is talking about the values which made teaching "right for us." As you think about your own values, do they seem "right" for teaching?

One study of occupational values lists a set of ten values which may be grouped together under four main heads as follows:

People-oriented values
> Give me an opportunity to work with people rather than things
> Give me an opportunity to be helpful to others

Extrinsic rewards
> Provide a chance to earn a good deal of money
> Give me a social status and prestige
> Enable me to look forward to a stable secure future

Self-expression
> Provide an opportunity to use my special abilities and aptitudes
> Permit me to look forward to a stable secure future

Other values
> Leave me relatively free of supervision by others
> Give me a chance to exercise leadership
> Provide me with adventure [41]

Which of these values appeal most to teachers? Ward S. Mason, Robert J. Dressel, and Robert K. Bain asked a group of 7,150 begin-

[40] Marcia M. Mathews, "A Wonderful Profession," *Saturday Evening Post*, Volume 235, No. 4, January 27, 1962, p. 34.

[41] M. Rosenberg, *Occupations and Values*, Glencoe, Illinois, The Free Press, 1957, pp. 10–24.

ning teachers to rate in terms of their own preferences the ten foregoing occupational values, and on the basis of the ratings drew the following conclusions:

"Teaching is clearly an occupation which attracts those with high people-oriented values; the beginning teachers chose both of these items in much higher percentages than did the college students. On the other hand, the percentage placing a high value on earning a great deal of money was lower among the teachers, especially among the men. Of the remaining values, the biggest differences involved the relatively high value placed by teachers on leadership and being creative and original." [42]

When student teachers are asked about the rewards they find in teaching, they commonly express their satisfaction in terms of "people-oriented" values. Notice that in the following classroom incidents reported by student teachers the human values are dominant.[43]

"I tried every method imaginable, every approach I knew to teach Sandra what a fraction is. For two weeks I tried. For two weeks I had little success. Sandra would say she understood, but I could see she didn't. We would start again and eventually end up in the same place —nowhere.

"One day during a class discussion of fractions I hit upon an idea of using a row of twelve children to represent one whole number. Sandra could visualize this. I pushed on. 'Tell one-half of the boys and girls to sit down, Sandra,' I said as I wrote the fraction $\frac{1}{2}$ on the board. Sandra told six of the children to sit down. Her eyes began to light up. In the next ten minutes we used various combinations of children to represent common fractions. Sandra learned what a fraction is.

"A little incident, you say? Sure. Nothing earth shaking. But to me, rewarding beyond measure."

A high school student teacher in history discovered that his most rewarding experience came when his students suddenly grasped the full significance of an historical event.

"Suddenly on the faces you see interest and suspense. The greatest challenge is to awaken such interest.

"As an example I might cite our unit on the rise of European dictatorships in the 1930's. We dealt with the Nazi regime in Germany at some length, working with such concepts as the 'totalitarian state' and

[42] Ward S. Mason, Robert J. Dressel, and Robert K. Bain, "Sex Role and the Career Orientations of Beginning Teachers," *Harvard Educational Review,* Volume 29, No. 4, 1959, p. 380.
[43] Brembeck, *op. cit.,* pp. 5–6.

the 'master race.' When the students began to ask minute questions about life under the Nazis and to draw comparisons between this and the present Russian regime (without any coaching from me), I noted with gratification that they understood the concepts being used. They were seeing the difference between this type of government and the democratic way of life."

A fourth-grade student teacher found her most rewarding experience in teaching a science unit on energy.

"The enthusiasm and response of the children was very encouraging. We divided the class into eight committees, each having a type of energy for its topic. Each committee's assignment was to present a program on its type of energy with each child covering some phase of that type. The programs were excellent. One committee did its program in the form of a TV show. Another presented a science fair. A couple of committees presented plays covering their topics. Another presented a quiz program. The work the children put on the programs was a rewarding experience. Even more rewarding was what they learned about energy. They did excellent work for fourth graders."

A student teacher in English found her most rewarding teaching experience in dramatics.

"Let me illustrate. In dramatics we start with raw material. We first select a cast from inexperienced eighth and ninth graders. We try to develop each individual according to his ability in such things as speaking voice, stage action, and acting ability. The climax of all activity comes in three days of performances before a daily audience of 125 students and parents in the dramatics room. My reward came in watching the audience enjoy a good performance and observing the cast put into practice what they had learned during the year. Probably the most rewarding experience of all is exchanging comments on the performance with the audience immediately following the play and telling the cast they did a good job."

7. Is teaching the first choice career for most teachers? Or do people turn to teaching only as a second choice, after they learn they can't do other things? G. B. Shaw expressed this point of view in his oft-quoted statement that: "Those who can, *do,* and those who *can't, teach.*"

Margaret Mead presents quite a different view: "They (teachers) are not disappointed classical scholars; nor are they aspiring clergymen or clergymen who have lost their faith; nor are they young men who tried to paint and failed, who tried to sing and failed, who tried to be scientists and failed." [44] Which view do you think the research evidence presented thus far in this chapter would tend to support?

[44] Mead, *op. cit.,* p. 18.

The Career Plans of Beginning Teachers

We have examined the motivations that support the decision to teach. Now we shall consider the views that new teachers hold of their careers. How do they regard teaching as a profession? How long do they plan to stay in teaching? What conflicts do they feel about teaching? Do men and women view teaching as a career differently? If so, how?

Teaching is a profession in which large numbers of men and women are employed. In not all occupations are both sexes represented by larger numbers. Some occupations are thought of primarily as "women's occupations," for example, nursing and social work, while others, like engineering, are thought of primarily as "men's occupations." Teaching is sometimes thought of as a "woman's occupation," but in reality at least one-quarter of the public school teachers are men, and men dominate the administrative positions of the public schools.[45]

One would expect that men and women would have different degrees and kinds of involvement in any occupation, considering the major differences in sex roles. Most men engage in an occupation for economic reasons. Most of them have families to support and are compelled for financial reasons to succeed in their chosen work. A minority of women also have strong economic reasons for pursuing an occupation. The majority, however, enter the world of work on a more-or-less temporary basis, perhaps as a short adventure between school and marriage, or later as a means of supplementing family income.

This more tentative professional commitment on the part of women applies to teaching. Of the 7,150 beginning teachers studied by Mason, Dressel, and Bain, fully 70 percent of all the women said they expected to leave teaching at some time in order to become homemakers.[46] The results of this study are recorded in Table 2.

The women who expected to leave teaching were divided into two groups. Fifty-eight percent of those who said they planned to leave teaching expected to return to it later. Twelve percent did not plan to return to teaching. Only 16 percent expected to teach continuously until retirement. If to this 16 percent we add the 58 percent who expected to return to teaching from homemaking, we have 74 percent of this group of beginning teachers who have a partial or contingent commitment to teaching. Nine percent of the women beginning teach-

[45] Mason, Dressel, and Bain, *op. cit.*, p. 373.
[46] *Ibid.*, p. 374.

TABLE 2

PERCENTAGE DISTRIBUTIONS OF THE CAREER PLANS OF MEN AND WOMEN BEGINNING TEACHERS

Career Plan	Men (*N*-2, 602) %	Women (*N*-4, 548) %
Committed to education		
Expect to continue teaching *until retirement*	29	16
Expect to leave teaching in order to devote my time to *homemaking:* would want to return to teaching later	—	58
Expect to continue in the field of education until retirement but hope to move from classroom teaching into some *other area of education* eventually	51	9
Total	80	83
Noneducational plans		
Expect to leave teaching in order to devote my time to *homemaking:* would not want to return to teaching later	—	12
Expect to leave education for *another* occupation	19	6
Total	19	18

SOURCE: Ward S. Mason, Robert J. Dressel, and Robert K. Bain, "Sex Role and Career Orientations of Beginning Teachers," *Harvard Educational Review*, Volume 29, No. 4, p. 374.

ers expected to move to nonteaching educational positions, and 6 percent planned to leave education entirely. The evidence indicates that for most women teaching is a contingent career rather than a dominant one. They will teach *if* they do not marry, *until* they have children, *after* their children are grown, *if* they need the money, and *if* an attractive vacancy appears.

Career plans for young men differed entirely from those of women. Only 29 percent of the men expected to teach continuously until retirement. However, although the remainder expected to leave classroom teaching, the majority did not expect to leave education. The most frequently expressed ambition among the men was to continue in the field of education until retirement, but to move eventually from classroom teaching into some other form of education work. Fifty-one percent of the men made this choice. Nineteen percent expected eventually to leave education for another occupation. Thus most of the men in this survey saw their futures in education, but they regarded the classroom as a stepping-stone to a better position. They would stay in classroom teaching until a better position in education came along.

The Impact of Contingent Career Plans on the Teaching Profession

What is the impact on the teaching profession of the large number of people who apparently have only partial and tentative commitments to it? Does not this situation, many people ask, make it difficult to build up and maintain a professional organization and standards?

To get at this question we should define the nature of a profession. "Its main characteristics are: an area of *exclusive technical competence* requiring long, specialized training, which, in turn, promotes an identification with the professional group and a dedication to professional skills; autonomy, that is, freedom from outside control and substitution of internal control over such practices as training, entry into the profession, and standards of work; and an ideology of *service*, emphasizing the social *responsibilities* of the profession rather than of self-interest." [47]

Keeping in mind the contingent-like commitment of the large number of people in teaching, we ask: To what degree can such persons build technical competence requiring "long specialized training, which, in turn, promotes an identification with the professional group and a dedication to professional skills"? Can people who plan to leave the classroom be expected to build up the "internal control over such practices as training, entry into the profession and standards of work"? Can teachers whose classroom work conflicts with outside interests build an "ideology of service, emphasizing the social responsibilities of the profession rather than of self-interest"?

The widely held view is that tentative professional commitments make it difficult to build up and maintain professional attitudes, organizations, and standards. This view is stated by Myron Lieberman: [48]

[47] John Colombotos, "Sex Role and Professionalism: A Study of High School Teachers," *The School Review*, Volume 71, No. 1, Spring 1963, p. 28.

[48] For a perceptive analysis of professionalism in teaching see Myron Lieberman, *Education as a Profession*, Englewood Cliffs, New Jersey, Prentice-Hall, Inc., 1956, pp. 1–18.

"It should be obvious that the fact that so many women teachers drift in and out of teaching means that it is very difficult for teachers to achieve occupational solidarity. The woman teacher interested chiefly in marriage and a home is not likely to take a strong interest in raising professional standards and in improving the conditions of teaching. Indeed, such women are frequently opposed to raising professional standards; such action runs contrary to their personal long-term interests. The difficulties of building a strong professional teachers' organization should be manifest. The turnover in membership is apt to be so high that teachers' organizations must spend a considerable portion of their resources just to maintain stable membership." [49]

Recent research, however, casts some doubt on Lieberman's generalization and is worth reporting here. An investigation by John Colombotos suggests that the demands which the family role places upon women teachers may only *appear* to be in conflict with professionalism, whereas in fact they may actually *support* professional orientations. The teaching role may actually be an extension of women's dominant roles as mothers and housewives. [50]

Colombotos constructed an "index of professionalism" and asked teachers to score themselves on how important the items in the index were to them. The items that the teachers were asked to check related to the three characteristics of a profession which we mentioned earlier: technical competence, autonomy, and the service ideal. The items that the teachers rated were:

1. "Chance to work with a teaching staff that is highly competent. (Technical Competence)
2. "Doing work my colleagues respect. (Technical Competence)
3. "Autonomy in my work; having enough freedom and responsibility to do my job the way it should be done. (Autonomy)
4. "Chance to help people; to do something worthwhile for society. (Service Ideal)" [51]

Five hundred and forty-five secondary teachers of a Midwestern, suburban public school system rated these items, and their professional scores were computed by adding the importance assigned to each item in the index as follows: 7 points for "necessary," 5 points for "very important," 3 points for "fairly important," and 1 point for "not too important."

There were two findings: (1) Women teachers who are single

[49] *Ibid.*, p. 253.
[50] Colombotos, *op. cit.*, pp. 27–40.
[51] *Ibid.*, p. 33.

are significantly more professional than men, and (2) married women
are more professional than men, but not significantly so. These findings run contrary to the common assumptions about the professional
roles of men and women in teaching. Colombotos offers these expla-
nations:

1. Men in teaching are more upwardly mobile than women. They
tend to use the classroom as a stepping-stone to a better position in
education. Men who plan to "stay in teaching" are more professional
than men who plan "to advance in education." But the "stay in teaching" men are still less professional than women teachers.

2. It is possible that the women's emphasis on service may have
a stronger effect on the total score than men's emphasis on competence
and autonomy. This is not the case, however. Although the difference
between men and women on the service item is the largest difference
between them, women score higher on *each* of the four items.

3. The orientation of women teachers toward their roles as
mothers and housewives actually reinforces the professional role of
teaching. Colombotos concludes:

"Thus, although the demands of the family role appear to conflict
with professionalism, an orientation that values the family role as such,
regardless of objective family status, appears to support a professional
orientation toward teaching. This suggests that the orientations required of women in the teaching role may be an extension of the orientations required by their dominant roles as mothers and housewives,
despite obvious conflicts between these roles in terms of time and energy. Perhaps it is the responsibility common to both roles for socializing and training children, or perhaps it is something else. In any case,
these data suggest a reexamination of the common assumption that
women's family roles inhibit the development of professionalism on
the job—at least among teachers." [52]

The Characteristics of Outstanding Teachers

Teaching is a complex art, and no single answer can ever explain
or describe the qualities of a great teacher. Considerable research has
been done on the characteristics of teachers, and it is appropriate to
close a chapter on the decision to teach with a discussion of the
characteristics that seem to describe outstanding teachers.

8. Make your own list of the qualities which in your view characterize
outstanding teachers. How does your own list compare with those presented
below?

[52] *Ibid.,* pp. 37–38.

What characteristics seem to distinguish highly rated teachers from lowly rated teachers? One of the more recent and thorough studies of teacher characteristics is that of David G. Ryans and colleagues to which we referred earlier in the chapter.[53] Ryans identified three major clusters of observable teacher behaviors which served as criteria for determining the characteristics of teachers rated "high" and "low" by the various means used in his study. The three principal dimensions of teacher classroom behavior were:

1. "understanding, friendly vs. aloof, egocentric, restricted teacher behavior
2. "responsible, business like, systematic vs. evading, unplanned, slipshod teacher behavior
3. "stimulating, imaginative, surgent or enthusiastic vs. dull, routine teacher behavior." [54]

Using these criteria and applying them to the teachers who cooperated in this study, Ryans drew up a list of personal qualities which appear to distinguish teachers selected to be "high" and "low" with respect to over-all classroom behavior. Table 3 compares elementary and secondary school teachers in the "high" group with those of the "low" group.

Concluding this major study of teacher characteristics Ryans makes the following generalizations regarding outstanding teachers.

"A growing body of evidence is accumulating that indicates certain characteristics which may contribute to the model of the teacher. Certain generalizations are suggested, based not only on the results of investigations conducted by the Teacher Characteristics Study, but also on data growing out of various other researches, employing quite different approaches and criteria.

"Superior intellectual abilities, above-average school achievement, good emotional adjustment, attitudes favorable to pupils, enjoyment of pupil relationships, generosity in the appraisal of the behavior and motives of other persons, strong interests in reading and literary matters, interest in music and painting, participation in social and community affairs, early experiences in caring for children and teaching (such as reading to children and taking a class for the teacher), history of teaching in family, family support of teaching as a vocation, strong social service interests . . . appear to apply very generally to teachers judged by various kinds and sets of criteria to be outstanding." [55]

[53] Ryans, *op. cit.*, p. 77.
[54] *Ibid.*
[55] *Ibid.*, p. 366.

TABLE 3

PERSONAL QUALITIES WHICH APPEAR TO DISTINGUISH TEACHERS SELECTED TO BE "HIGH" AND "LOW" WITH RESPECT TO OVER-ALL CLASSROOM BEHAVIOR: CHARACTERISTICS OF "HIGH" GROUP TEACHERS

Elementary Teachers

A. "High" group members more frequently (than "low"):
1. Manifest extreme generosity in appraisals of the behavior and motives of other persons; express friendly feelings for others.
2. Indicate strong interest in reading and in literary matters.
3. Indicate interest in music, painting, and the arts in general.
4. Report participation in high school and college social groups.
5. Manifest prominent social service ideals.
6. Indicate preferences for activities which involve contacts with people.
7. Indicate interest in science and scientific matters.
8. Report liking for outdoor activities.
9. Are young, or middle-aged.
10. Are married.
11. Report that parental homes provided above-average cultural advantages.

B. "High" group (compared with "low" group):
1. Indicates greater enjoyment of pupil relationships (i.e., more favorable pupil opinions).
2. Indicates greater preference for non-directive classroom procedures.
3. Is superior in verbal intelligence (I_{co} scores).
4. Is more satisfactory with regard to emotional adjustment (S_{co} scores).

Secondary Teachers

A. "High" group members more frequently (than "low"):
1. Manifest extreme generosity in appraisals of the behavior and motives of other persons; express friendly feelings for others.
2. Indicate strong interest in reading and in literary matters.
3. Indicate interest in music, painting, and the arts in general.
4. Report participation in high school and college social groups.
5. Judge selves high in ambition and initiative.
6. Report teaching experience of 4–9 years.
7. Report teaching-type activities during childhood and adolescence.
8. Indicate preference for student-centered learning situations.
9. Manifest independence, though not aggressiveness.

B. "High" group (compared with "low" group):
1. Indicates greater enjoyment of pupil relationships (i.e., more favorable pupil opinions).
2. Indicates greater preference for non-directive classroom procedures.
3. Is superior in verbal intelligence (I_{co} scores).
4. Is more satisfactory with regard to emotional adjustment (S_{co} scores).

Elementary-Secondary Teachers Combined

A. "High" group members more frequently (than "low"):
1. Manifest extreme generosity in appraisals of the behavior and motives of other persons; express friendly feelings for others.
2. Indicate strong interest in reading and in literary matters.
3. Indicate interest in music, painting, and the arts in general.
4. Report participation in high school and college social groups.
5. Judge selves high in ambition and initiative.

B. "High" group (compared with "low" group):
1. Indicates greater enjoyment of pupil relationships (i.e., more favorable pupil opinions).
2. Indicates greater preference for non-directive classroom procedures.
3. Is superior in verbal intelligence (I_{co} scores).
4. Is more satisfactory with regard to emotional adjustment (S_{co} scores).

SOURCE: David G. Ryans, *Characteristics of Teachers, Their Description, Comparison, and Appraisal: A Research Study.* Washing-

The decision to teach is closely associated with people-oriented values and is likely to be strongly influenced by the parent and teacher models of childhood and early youth. Young persons who decide to teach start early to identify with the role of the teacher and this early identification is important as preparation for teaching. Early experiences in working with children are important, too, in building a personal commitment as well as a skill in teaching. Those who achieve high skill in teaching have many characteristics associated with mature human beings: intellectual capacity, good emotional adjustment, wide interests, and a genuine concern for children.

Those who decide today to teach will do so in tomorrow's schools, which will be different from those of even a decade ago. What will it be like to teach in the schools of tomorrow?

REFERENCES

Paperbacks

Critical Incidents in Teaching. Raymond J. Corsini, Daniel D. Howard. (Orig.) Prentice-Hall, Englewood Cliffs, N. J. ($4.25).

Education of American Teachers. James Bryant Conant. (12387) McGraw-Hill Paperback Series, McGraw-Hill Book Co., 330 W. 42nd St., New York ($2.95).

Education of Teachers: Consensus and Conflict. G. K. Hodenfield and T. M. Stinnett. (Orig.) (S-17) Spectrum Books, Prentice-Hall, Englewood Cliffs, N. J. ($1.95).

Great Teachers. Houston Peterson, Editor. (V507) Caravelle Editions, Vintage Books, Random House, 457 Madison Ave., New York ($1.95).

How to Plan to Teach the First Year. Carl H. Rich. (Orig.) Fearon Publishers, 2165 Park Blvd., Palo Alto, Calif. ($1.50).

Privilege of Teaching. Dora P. Chaplin. Morehouse-Barlow Co., 14 E. 41st St., New York ($3.00).

Student Teaching: Cases and Comments. Elizabeth Hunter and Edmund J. Amidon. (Orig.) Holt, Rinehart and Winston, 383 Madison Ave., New York ($1.95).

Teacher in America. Jacques Barzun. (A25) Anchor Books and Anchor Science Study Series, Doubleday and Co., 277 Park Ave., New York (95¢).

Your Career Opportunities in Teaching. (Orig.) (CA5) Littlefield, Adams and Co., 128 Oliver St., Paterson, N. J. ($1.00).

Books

Barzun, Jacques, *Teacher in America.* Boston: Little, Brown and Co., 1945. A lively and critical analysis of teaching in school and college.

Koerner, James D., *The Miseducation of American Teachers.* Boston: Houghton Mifflin Co., 1963. This book represents a critical appraisal of educational courses, textbooks, student opinions, and graduate education.

Marson, Philip, *A Teacher Speaks*. New York: David McKay Co., 1960. The author describes his 40 years as a teacher. In the second part of the book he offers a program to solve the deepening crisis facing American education.

Ryans, David G., *Characteristics of Teachers, Their Description, Comparison and Appraisal*. Washington, D. C.: American Council on Education, 1959. Although there are no qualities that are absolutes, certain types of teacher traits are related to teacher success in a wide variety of situations.

Stiles, Lindley J., Editor, *The Teacher's Role in American Society*. New York: Harper and Brothers, 1957. The 14th yearbook of the John Dewey Society is devoted to a study of the American teacher.

Thomas, Lawrence G., et al., *Perspective on Teaching, An Introduction to Public Education*. Englewood Cliffs, N. J.: Prentice-Hall, 1961. Part III examines "Teaching as a Profession."

Wilson, Charles H., *A Teacher Is a Person*. New York: Henry Holt and Co., 1956. This book represents an autobiographical description of a teacher with a keen sense of humor. Wilson uses his own classroom experiences to humanize the teacher's work.

Periodicals

Ahlering, Inez, "I Love to Teach," *Journal of Business Education*, Vol. 39, No. 3, December 1963, pp. 117–118. A teacher reviews her 43 years of teaching.

Briggs, Francis M., "As Five Teachers See Themselves," *The Educational Forum*, Vol. XXVII, No. 4, May 1964, pp. 389–397. The article summarizes the autobiographies of five teachers.

Cartwright, William H., "The Teacher in 2065," *Teacher's College Record*, Vol. 66, No. 4, January 1965, pp. 296–304. A prophetic essay of the teacher a hundred years from now.

Gusfield, Joseph R., "The Meaning of Occupational Prestige: Reconsideration of the NORC Scale," *American Sociological Review*, Vol. 28, No. 2, April 1963, pp. 265–271. A description of the variables used in the National Opinion Research Center Scale and the scale itself. Teachers rank seventh out of 15 selected occupations.

Nelson, Robert H., and Michael L. Thompson, "Why Teachers Quit," *The Clearing House*, Vol. XXXVII, No. 8, April 1963, pp. 467–72. Statistics gathered by the authors indicate that public shools are neither attracting nor holding desirable teachers.

Wright, Benjamin, "Identification and Becoming a Teacher," *Elementary School Journal*, Vol. 59, pp. 361–373. The author discusses psychological types of teachers.

16

The Teacher and the New Designs for Learning

"What we are moving toward is a whole new dimension of learning."

MARGARET MEAD

The rapid pace of change in today's schools causes one to ask: What will the schools of the future be like? What will tomorrow's teachers need to know that today's teachers do not? How will future teachers spend their time, work with students and with one another? How will instruction be carried on? How will students do their work? What about teaching machines and other educational technology?

The innovations that are already adopted in the schools tell us that the teacher of tomorrow will teach in a strikingly different kind of school. He will need new kinds of skills, will work in new kinds of ways, and will be part of a new learning environment. The successful teachers of the future will be those who prepare to work in a changing school where the teaching models of the past have only limited usefulness and where the emphasis will be on creating new ways of teaching for new ways of learning.

In this chapter we shall describe some of the new designs for learning with which teachers of the future should be familiar. Our purpose is to create an understanding of the new frontiers in the schools and how teachers can use them to give new excitement to learning.

New Technology

Figure 16-1 illustrates in graphic form the changing role of the teacher in respect to new educational technology. Before the invention of writing the teacher was the main transmitter of knowledge to the student. He alone had access to knowledge which he conveyed to the student in face-to-face communication. With the advent of writing new avenues to knowledge opened. Teaching took on a new dimension, that of teaching the student to read. With the ability to read the student was no longer absolutely dependent on the teacher for knowledge. Then came printing, which gave students access to more writing, more knowledge, than ever before. With the advent of the twentieth century and the "knowledge explosion" a host of new avenues to knowledge opened to the student. Whereas in earlier times the teacher was almost the sole conveyor of knowledge he is now but one of many; his numbers are multiplied by film, radio, television, and teaching machines.

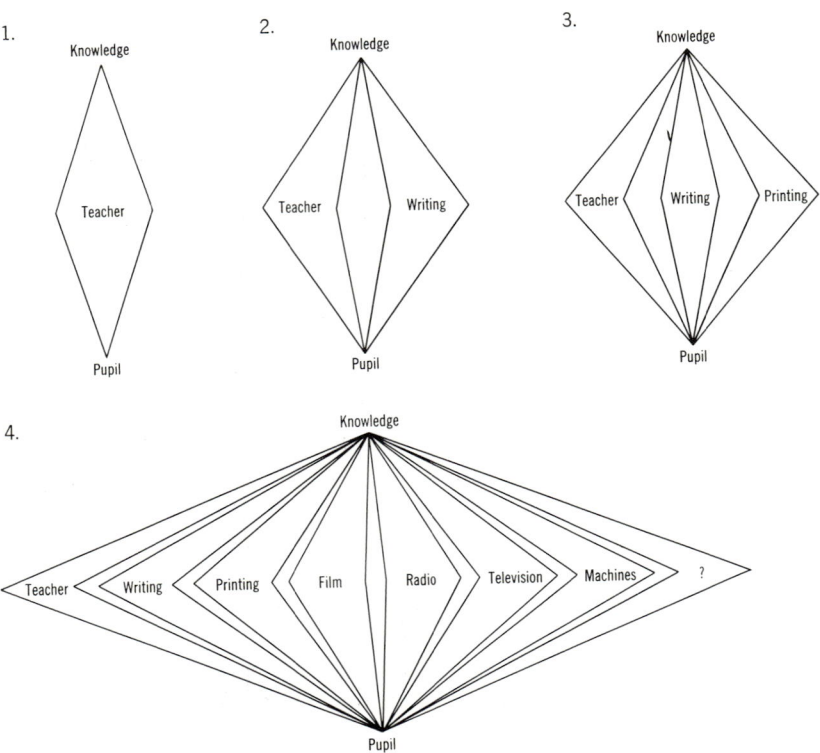

Fig. 16-1 The changing role of the teacher (1) before writing, (2) before printing, (3) until about 1900, (4) the twentieth century. SOURCE: J. Lloyd Trump, *An Exciting Profession—New Horizons for Secondary School Teachers*, Urbana, Illinois: Commission on the Experimental Study of the Utilization of the Staff in the Secondary School, The National Association of Secondary School Principals, Department of the National Education Association (undated), p. 8.

How do the technological changes described in Figure 16-1 alter the way teachers teach and students learn? Two profound changes seem evident. First, the earliest teachers could be masters of the limited and then-known knowledge. They could teach with the reasonable assurance that what they handed down to their students constituted what they needed to know during their life. The teacher was then the source of wisdom. By contrast, today's teachers can themselves know only an infinitesimal fraction of existing knowledge. The emphasis, therefore, shifts to the teacher's skill in motivating students to want to discover knowledge. Second, the earliest students were fully dependent on the teacher for knowledge: Now they are dependent on the teacher for mastery and wise use of the means by which knowledge is acquired. Modern technology provides the student with means of acquiring knowledge undreamed of even a few years ago.

Do these developments in any way diminish the role of the modern teacher? At first glance they might appear to, for the teacher is no longer the sole possessor of knowledge and the sole means of transmitting it. In reality the teacher's role is enhanced by modern technology, which places at his disposal new and more effective means of teaching. The teacher now becomes a strategist in the use of learning tools and can develop in students lifelong learning habits. With the wise use of technology the modern teacher can multiply himself and his influence a hundredfold.

1. Margaret Mead makes a distinction between the *vertical* and *lateral* transmission of knowledge. Of vertical knowledge transmission she says: "We are no longer dealing with the *vertical* transmission of the tried and true by the old, mature and experienced teacher to the young, immature, and inexperienced pupil in the classroom." [1] If the vertical transmission of knowledge is that which is handed down from the old to the young, what do you think the *lateral* transmission of knowledge is?

New Social Roles

Figure 16-1 indicates how infinitely complex is the role of the modern teacher in respect to technology. New social roles of the modern teacher are equally varied and intricate. Children enter modern schools with vast individual differences because they come from a society that is increasingly complex. And the advent of new knowledge and new scientific theories about education have all changed the teacher's role beyond anything that one might have suspected in

[1] Margaret Mead, "A Redefinition of Education," *NEA Journal*, October 1959, p. 15.

earlier and simpler days. William Clark Trow lists some of the social roles the modern teacher is expected to perform:

"Custodian: water plants, care for animals, clean blackboard, take care of books and equipment, and do a bit of dusting, and general housekeeping.

"Clerk: collect money for school events, sell milk, fill out attendance sheets, keep records—academic, health, and other—do mimeographing, and order supplies.

"Foster-parent: suspect and refer health problems, provide first aid; serve as nursemaid for smaller children, giving help with overshoes and other clothing; provide younger children with 'tender loving care' and older children with security, warmth, and affection.

"Disciplinarian: do police duty in the classroom, corridors, lunchroom, and playground, and detective work to discover offenders; serve as judge, jury, and chief executioner in bringing miscreants to justice.

"Examiner: select, construct, administer, and score informal and standardized tests, evaluate achievement and rate character for report cards, decide on the failure or promotion of pupils.

"Audio-visualist and technician: make chart and chalkboard drawings, put up wall decorations and displays, and select, locate, transport, and operate projection equipment.

"Librarian: contribute to the selection of texts, readings, and documents, fetch books from the library, and sometimes maintain a small library in the classroom.

"Student adviser: help students in planning their academic programs.

"Therapist: counsel with students and with their parents and help them with their adjustment problems.

"Recreation leader: sponsor hobby clubs, social and athletic events, and other school activities.

"Responsible citizen: take part in parent-teacher meetings and in local church and social work; be an intelligent voter." [2]

Trow's ample list omits the teacher's most important social role of all: teaching! So to the list must be added the responsibility for instruction.

The Need to Redefine the Teacher's Role

Can any one person reasonably be expected to perform well all of these new roles imposed by technology and changing social con-

---

[2] William Clark Trow, *Teacher and Technology*, New York, Appleton-Century-Crofts, 1963, p. 45.

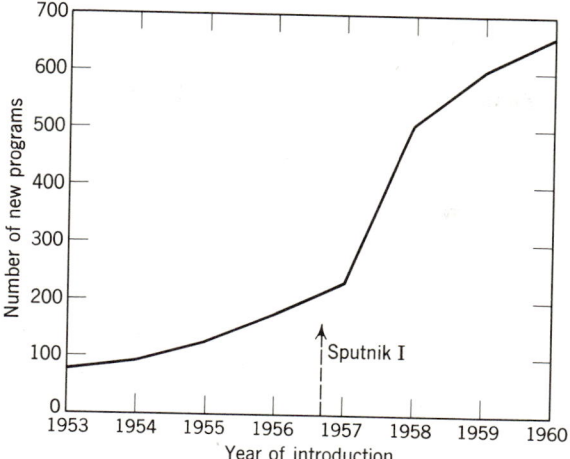

Fig. 16-2 Rate of instructional innovation in New York State public school systems.

ditions? It seems like an impossible assignment, and in many ways it is. Yet schools are presently organized so that all these wide-ranging tasks tend to fall upon the shoulders of individual teachers. It is not a discredit on the profession to say that the tasks are not handled uniformly well: Such an expectation would be unreasonable.

For this reason there is strong support for reconstructing the school organization in such a way that all these demanding roles do not fall at once upon individual teachers. As we shall see the trend is toward using the varied aptitudes, skills, and interests of teachers in such a way as to focus rather than disperse them. In short, the organization should permit the teacher to maximize his strength rather than his weakness.

The Pace and Direction of Change

How quickly are school programs changing and in what direction? One of the most extensive surveys of changing educational practices was conducted in the public and nonpublic elementary and secondary schools of New York State.[3] Four hundred and eighty-four public and 104 nonpublic schools in the state reported data used in the survey.

[3] Henry M. Brickell, *Commissioner's 1961 Catalog of Educational Change,* Albany, New York, State Education Department, October 1961.

For the period from 1953 to 1960, 2,657 new instructional programs were begun by the public, and 249 by the nonpublic schools for a total of 2,906 innovations.

Notice in Figure 16-2 the dramatic shift in the pace of change which took place after the Russian space satellite, Sputnik I, soared into orbit on October 4, 1957. Within 15 months the public schools of New York State had more than doubled their previous rate of educational change. At no other time in the eight-year period from 1953–1960 was there a comparable upward thrust.

2. Harley Earl Allen compared the rate of diffusion of driver-training programs in the schools with the idea of students studying their community. Sixty years were required to reach 90 percent adoption among 168 United States schools of the latter practice while only 18 years were needed for driver training to reach a 90 percent level of adoption. How would you account for this difference? [4]

High-ability Students and the New Programs

On what ability levels have the new programs dwelt? Notice in Table 1 that from 1953 to 1957 the rate of change in programs for students of all ability levels remained quite stable. There was no appreciable alteration in the rates of change. Then in 1958, a year after Sputnik, the pattern was shattered. Attention focused sharply on the higher end of the ability scale. Nineteen hundred and fifty-seven saw the start of three times as many programs for the highly capable as for the handicapped. In 1958, there were five times as many, in 1959 almost six times as many, and in 1960 over seven times as many.

Subject Content of New Programs

Considering the encouragement given to foreign language, mathematics, and science by the National Defense Education Act, one might expect these subjects to lead the others in new programs. The rate of change in science and mathematics almost tripled during 1958, and in foreign language it more than tripled.

Startling is the fact that in *every specific subject listed*, without exception, there was a sharp increase in the number of innovations in 1958. The rate of change in social studies and English more than doubled. In nonacademic programs, too, new instructional programs were introduced at a little more than double the pre-1958 rate. Thus

[4] Harley Earl Allen, *The Diffusion of Education Practices in the School Systems of the Metropolitan School Study Council*, D.Ed. Thesis, N. Y. Teachers College, Columbia University, 1956.

TABLE 1

GROUPING OF PUPILS IN NEW PROGRAMS—1953–1960

Size of Group	Public Schools	Nonpublic Schools
Individual tutoring	184	14
Smaller than before	688	53
Larger than before	94	7
Variable	574	75
Basis for Grouping		
Age	273	20
Mental ability	1148	93
Physical ability	148	3
Emotional stability	390	13
Achievement	1226	93
Interest	804	63
Other	163	15

SOURCE: Henry M. Brickell, A survey of changing instructional approaches and descriptions of new programs in the public and nonpublic elementary and secondary schools of New York State, Commissioner's 1961 Catalog of Education Change, Albany, The University of the State of New York, The State Education Department, October 1961, p. 21.

active attention to the introduction of new instructional approaches is apparently increasing as rapidly in nonacademic as academic areas. "The effect of Sputnik seems to have been pervasive indeed and was virtually without focus among the various subjects."[5]

Grouping of Students

Many of the new programs group students differently than before. Table 1 reveals that most programs involve either smaller groups or groups variable in size. It is interesting to note that in the new approaches in both public and nonpublic schools the use of individual tutoring is more frequent than the use of large instructional groups.

The bases for grouping students for new instructional approaches are primarily subject-matter achievement and mental ability. Interest in the subject is used as a basis for grouping, but less frequently than achievement or mental ability.

[5] Brickell, *op. cit.*, p. 18.

Assignment of Teachers

Table 2 indicates the extensive way in which the teacher's duties are being rearranged in the new programs. For example, one teacher may lecture to large groups while another teaches small seminar groups. Or one elementary teacher may instruct two classes in reading while another elementary teacher instructs the same two groups in arithmetic.

Resource people are apparently being used extensively by these schools to supplement the talents of the regular staff. In 108 of the programs listed the public schools used outside personnel to teach students independently, as, for example, in classes taught by local scientists on Saturday mornings.

TABLE 2

ASSIGNMENT OF PERSONNEL IN NEW PROGRAMS—
1953–1960

Responsibility	Public Schools	Nonpublic Schools
Regular duties divided differently (e.g., departmentalized elem.)	496	51
Regular duties combined in new ways (e.g., two teachers combine groups)	223	23
Leadership positions created in faculty (e.g., team leader appointed)	217	26
Personnel		
Nonprofessionals perform nonteaching services	68	12
Resource people assist with instruction	388	20
Semi-professionals perform instructional services	37	2
Outside personnel teach students independently	108	8

SOURCE: Henry M. Brickell, A survey of changing instructional approaches and descriptions of new programs in the public and nonpublic elementary and secondary schools of New York State, Commissioner's 1961 Catalog of Education Change, Albany, The University of the State of New York, The State Education Department, October 1961, p. 22.

The pattern of change presented in the following pages emerges from this comprehensive survey of the public and nonpublic school systems in New York State. The dramatic shift in the pace of change came in the 15-month period following the launching of Sputnik I, but its momentum continues. These programs have concentrated in largest numbers on the "highly capable" and "above average" students. In every specific subject listed there has been a sharp jump in new instructional approaches, bringing activity up to an entirely new level.

Practices of grouping pupils and assigning teaching personnel have especially felt the impact of new programs. The standard classroom practice of having groups of similar size is giving way to either smaller groups or groups of variable size; individual tutoring also figures prominently in the changes. New arrangements for using staff is popular in all programs. The effect is to divide the teacher's time and responsibilities differently, permitting teachers to specialize and do those teaching assignments in which they feel most comfortable and qualified.

THREE NEW FRONTIERS

In what respects are the schools changing most rapidly? In what areas is the impact of change most keenly felt? The pioneering work in the schools comes mainly in these areas: (1) educational technology, (2) teaching, and (3) learning. Let us take a closer look at the new practices in these three areas.[6]

Educational Technology

In an historical sense the schools are pioneers in the use of educational technology, for the book and the blackboard are among the earliest of its forms. However, schools have been slow to apply the new technology to education. Now the breakthrough has come: The technology that is commonplace in home, office, and factory is entering the schools. Recognizing that learning depends upon good communication, modern schools are using television, audio tapes, new kinds of projectors, programed textbooks, and teaching machines to extend the work of the teacher.

3. How do teachers feel about the new technology in education? Some research indicates that they have unfavorable attitudes about it. Sigmund Fobias found that teachers have the most favorable feelings toward terms

[6] For a perceptive discussion of developments in these three areas see Ronald Gross and Judith Murphy, *The Revolution in the Schools*, New York, Harcourt, Brace and World, Inc., 1964, pp. 1–6.

describing traditional educational devices, such as *flash cards,* and less favorable attitudes toward terms stressing programing, such as *programed instruction,* and the least favorable feelings concerning devices described by technological language, such as *automated instruction.*[7] Can you explain these attitudes on the part of teachers? What do you think research like this implies for those who wish to encourage the use of new technologies in the schools?

Let us turn to some actual examples of the use of the new educational technology in the schools. The following reports from schools, selected from Brickell's survey, illustrate the use of television, tapes, and programed textbooks in the elementary schools.[8]

"TELEVISION—Educational television is being used to interest 5th and 6th graders in a foreign language. Spanish is taught to a group of 25 for an hour a week. Before the class views the telecast it is prepared for what it will see. Afterwards there are follow-up sessions making use of charts, puppet shows, and stories. Outside people with something to offer in Spanish language, music or general culture are sometimes called in to add interest. Children pay close attention during the telecasts and are developing the ability for simple conversation and songs in Spanish. The original suggestion for use of television came from the State Education Department."[9]

"TAPED SCIENCE—Fourth, fifth and sixth graders are deep in the mysteries of weather and what makes it act as it does in this experiment with taped lessons. Twenty pupils in each class, with average or better ability, are taking part in small groups or as individuals.

"The unit on weather consists of six tapes, an introduction and five lessons. Also included are study guides, vocabulary cards, directions for experiences and experiments, reference lists, films and filmstrips, and inexpensive materials. The amount of time spent varies with the individual pupils, who are said to be interested in and stimulated by the approach. More taped units on other science topics are to be prepared."[10]

"PROGRAMED SPELLING—All spelling instruction in the 5th grade is being given by means of 'automated' or 'programed' instruction, the building up of concepts through progress in small sequential steps. Special programed spelling materials are used, permitting the pupil to teach himself and providing immediate reinforcement of what

[7] Sigmund Fobias, "Teachers Attitudes Toward Programed Instructional Terms," *Journal of Programed Instruction,* Volume 2, No. 3, 1963, pp. 25–29.

[8] Brickell, *op. cit.,* p. 81.

[9] *Ibid.*

[10] *Ibid.,* p. 93.

is learned. The interest of the plan is to see whether teacher time can be saved for more creative work in improving vocabulary, comprehension and critical thinking. Two hundred pupils of average ability are involved. No specific results are available yet." [11]

The following examples drawn from secondary schools illustrate the use of the language laboratory, programed textbooks, and films.

"LANGUAGE LABORATORY—A language laboratory with 30 listening stations has been set up for the use of pupils in grades 7–12. Three teachers and 250 pupils are affected. The average pupil is spending about five hours a week in the laboratory, listening to tapes and making his own tapes. With its four tape heads, four separate languages may be transmitted at one time. Students listen to the questions asked by tape and speak their own responses which are also recorded on tape. Later they can compare their own pronunciation with that of the master tape. The laboratory has proven effective in the year it has been in operation." [12]

"PROGRAMED GRAMMAR—English grammar is being taught by means of a programed text. The programed text is used alone in one average 7th grade class and two 8th grade classes (one above average and the other below average). The same text supplements regular instruction for 10 remedial 9th graders and 60 average 10th graders. Each pupil works through it at his own pace without assistance from the teacher, teaching himself the material in small sequential steps and receiving immediate reinforcement for right answers. The principle is the same as that used in teaching machines. A close evaluation, with controls, is being carried on." [13]

4. Programed textbooks are now available in such diverse subjects as how to write a memo, logarithm, the sacraments of the Catholic Church, second-year German, boiler inspection, and no-trump bid in bridge.[14] If you have not already used a programed textbook you may find it of interest to obtain one and (1) discover how it works, and (2) investigate the principles of learning on which it is constructed.

"TYPING FILMS—Films have replaced the conventional workbooks used to teach typewriting. The chief benefit gained from the substitution is that pupils find it nearly impossible to look at their keyboards while they are following the films. When books are used, the

[11] *Ibid.*, p. 44.
[12] *Ibid.*, p. 82.
[13] *Ibid.*, p. 51.
[14] See Eric Bender, "The Other Kind of Teaching," *Harper's Magazine*, Volume 230, No. 1376, January 1965, pp. 48–55.

school points out, the pupils' eyes inevitably shift back and forth from book to keys, thus slowing down the development of typing by touch alone. Time tests show a definite improvement, and pupils seem to like the system as indicated by greater interest and an eagerness to improve." [15]

New Designs for Teaching

The way teachers employ their time and work with students is undergoing radical change.

"The egg-crate school, composed of identical, self-enclosed classrooms, is giving way to a more flexible, functional arrangement. Teaching is frequently done in teams rather than solo, with each team member concentrating on his strongest technique or specialty. The system of grades has begun to disintegrate, with students permitted to progress at their individual rates in each subject. Our teachers are beginning to assume a new look, too, owing to programs of training which stress broad liberal education, meaningful practice teaching, sophisticated professional courses, and training in the use of technology." [16]

The schools of the future will be organized along more flexible lines to permit students to move at their own rate rather than remain in fixed groups. In today's schools, students tend to get locked into homogeneous groups along some dimension, for example, age, intelligence, or ability. Students are now being permitted to break out of these groups and to think of themselves not as numbers in a class but as colleagues of other students, working together to learn more about specific subjects.

Changes in the way the students work in schools are being accompanied by changes in the way teachers work with students. Instead of one teacher spending all his time with a standard class of 25 students, the flexible school will permit the teacher to work alternately with large and small groups and in new relationships with his colleagues on the faculty. The following descriptions of school programs illustrate new ways of organizing instruction in the schools. Consider first some examples drawn from elementary schools, which illustrate the use of the nongraded, primary classes, large-group instruction, team teaching, and achievement grouping.

"NONGRADED PRIMARY CLASSES—To provide continuous learning for each child at his own speed, the kindergarten and first

[15] Bricknell, *op. cit.*, p. 64.
[16] Gross and Murphy, *op. cit.*, p. 4.

three grades in this school system were ungraded three years ago. Many levels have been substituted. The child moves from level to level just as rapidly as he masters the skills and content at each one. There is no failure and there is no boredom as is often found in the graded system. The arrangement has special advantages at an age when children often progress in spurts, and it virtually assures a successful experience in the early school years that will shape a wholesome attitude toward school in the future. Parents, teachers and pupils have all approved." [17]

"LARGE-GROUP INSTRUCTION—Overhead projectors and other equipment are being used to give instruction in handwriting, phonics, science, social studies, and study skills to classes of 100 pupils in grades 2–6. Follow-up and testing takes place back in the normal classroom. Some of the large group sessions present basic material; others are used chiefly for enrichment. Time spent varies on different grade levels but all pupils are involved to some extent.

"One benefit of the system is that a uniform approach to instruction is achieved. Testing and assessment by teachers show that results are promising." [18]

"TEAM INSTRUCTION—In order to obtain greater teaching effectiveness without losing the advantages of the self-contained classroom, pupils in grades 1–6 have been grouped in three levels: grades 1–2, 3–4, and 5–6. A team of two teachers is responsible for each two-grade class.

"At Level II (grades 3–4) and Level III (grades 5–6) the five-hour day is divided into two 2½ hour periods. One teacher gives the language-citizenship core to both grades during one period, and the other does the same in science, mathematics, and health. Both teach reading. There are special teachers for art, music, and physical education. Enthusiasm for the plan is high." [19]

"ACHIEVEMENT GROUPING—In an effort to offer more opportunities to bright pupils and more help to those who are slower to learn, this school has divided its 4th, 5th, and 6th grade classes in reading and arithmetic by achievement levels.

"One teacher takes a slow class, another takes an average class, and a third takes a fast class. The program has been in effect for three years. Last year 614 pupils and 21 teachers were involved. Evaluation, by Stanford Achievement Tests, Iowa Reading Tests and

---

[17] Brickell, *op. cit.*, p. 34.
[18] *Ibid.*, p. 39.
[19] *Ibid.*

teacher observation, indicates that the system has been especially good for the fast group." [20]

The secondary schools also present good examples of new ways to teach. The following descriptions illustrate the "schools within a school" (here called a House Plan), team teaching, the use of teacher aides, flexible grouping, and the use of large- and small-group instruction.

"HOUSE PLAN—A school with 1,000 pupils and 45 teachers in grades 6–8 has been divided into three complete 'houses.' Each has its own permanent staff and is assigned pupils spanning all three grades. Each house also offers a complete program except for physical education, shop, homemaking, instrumental music and library skills. The object of the arrangement is to retain the advantages of the small school in the midst of a large one and to improve guidance and instruction. This plan, interestingly enough, was invented by a local faculty committee. The building was planned to carry out the house system of organization. Results have been very successful." [21]

"TEAM TEACHING—Team teaching is being used in the 7th grade for instruction in English, citizenship education, science, and mathematics. A total of 250 pupils of average ability are under the guidance of 10 classroom teachers. Each group of 75 is the responsibility of a team of teachers who plan the schedule cooperatively and follow the progress of individual pupils. Both teachers and the Board of Education are enthusiastic about the arrangement, which allows teachers to deal with groups of varying sizes on topics in which they are most interested and best prepared. Achievement tests and pupil attitude inventories will be used in evaluation." [22]

5. Selected research indicates that students achieve better in team teaching situations than they do in traditional classrooms.[23] Considering the various differences between team teaching and traditional teaching, how might you explain the difference in achievement?

"THEME READERS—Theme readers are used to let pupils do more writing, and have it corrected, without imposing an intolerable burden on the classroom teacher.

[20] *Ibid.*, p. 43.
[21] *Ibid.*, p. 46.
[22] *Ibid.*, p. 48.
[23] See John R. Ginther and William A. Shroyer, "Team Teaching in English and History at the Eleventh-Grade Level," *The School Review*, Volume 70, No. 3, Autumn 1962, pp. 303–313; and Joseph Jackson, "Analysis of Team Teaching and of a Self Contained Homeroom Experiment in Grades 5 and 6," *Journal of Experimental Education*, Volume 32, No. 4, 1964, pp. 317–331.

"College graduates with strong backgrounds in English correct and grade weekly compositions, using a standardized procedure, under the direction of the teacher. There is a preliminary orientation for the graders and weekly teacher-reader conferences. Teachers review all compositions." [24]

"FLEXIBLE GROUPING—A system has been devised to provide both homogeneous and heterogeneous grouping where each is most desirable. Pupils are organized into *basic* groups of 80. Within each basic group are five *component* groups, ranged by ability from 'academically talented' to 'basic skills,' for work in science and mathematics.

"Also within each basic group are standard groups—balanced to include all ability levels and all variations of personality, attitude, and motivation—for the study of all other subjects. An unusual feature is an intensive core program in English and social studies taught by a team of 8 teachers." [25]

"LARGE LECTURES–SMALL LABS—Larger lecture sections have made it possible to have smaller laboratory sections in science teaching, where close individual instruction can be given. A lecture section of 80 pupils was set up in biology and one of 40 in chemistry. The resulting saving in staff lecture time resulted in small laboratory sections.

"In the large lectures each teacher had the support of a second teacher or of a teacher-aide. The large lecture sessions made good use of audio-visual projectors—filmstrip, overhead, and opaque.

"Results are to be evaluated by a variety of test instruments, local, state, and national." [26]

New Designs for Learning

New knowledge and understanding of how students learn is changing the patterns for learning in the modern school. We are coming to understand, for example, that human ability takes many varieties and forms unmeasured by IQ tests. We are learning that students should not be forced into learning molds not suited to their individual needs and abilities. We are taking steps to motivate students from within rather than by outside rewards and punishments. We are coming to view the school not as a place where students are taught a fixed body of knowledge, but as a place where the desire to learn is enhanced, hopefully for life, and where competence to learn is brought to a high peak. More of the responsibility for actual learning is being

---

[24] Bricknell, *op. cit.*, p. 48. [25] *Ibid.*, p. 49. [26] *Ibid.*, p. 58.

shifted to the student himself in a rich environment of materials and resources.

Here are some examples from elementary schools in which new designs for student learning are evident. The descriptions have three common elements: (1) the student is an active participant in his own learning; (2) the emphasis is on individualized instruction; (3) a richer learning environment is provided. The following examples are drawn from elementary schools:

"STRUCTURAL-DISCOVERY—MATHEMATICS—Instead of telling children that two and two are four, this school helps them find it out for themselves through the use of concrete materials, usually colored rods or cubes. Pupils see how these materials fit together, how several can be brought together so that they are the same as various other groupings. Number symbols to signify the concrete materials are employed later as a sort of shorthand description of what has been done physically. The primary purpose is to develop in the pupil an awareness of the structure of mathematics. Five thousand pupils from kindergarten through grade 3 are involved. Tests have shown achievement to be above grade level." [27]

"INDIVIDUALIZED READING—Reading is being taught on an individual basis from trade books rather than from a basal reading series. Each pupil has complete freedom of choice of the books and the order in which he reads them. Teachers work individually with each youngster. About 900 pupils in kindergarten through the third grade are participating in the project, which is designed to test the effects of better motivation on reading development. The approach was first used by one or two teachers in the school twenty years ago; many others have adopted it in the past three years. Test results so far have been good. A formal evaluation is to be made." [28]

"ENRICHMENT GROUPS—Two 45-minute periods a week are being devoted to special enrichment work for 900 pupils in grades 4–6. Pupils are grouped across grade lines to explore and work in areas of their individual abilities and interests with teachers of similar interests. The 60 'teachers' taking part include 18 lay persons from the community who have unusual backgrounds or competencies. They are paid a nominal sum for participating. The areas in which work is being done include advanced academic work, remedial instruction, art, crafts, sewing, cooking, and manual arts. An elaborate evaluation pattern is used to make certain the program is producing good results year after year." [29]

[27] *Ibid.*, p. 34. [28] *Ibid.*, p. 34. [29] *Ibid.*, p. 42.

The following descriptions are drawn from secondary school practice. In these programs the emphasis is on independent work.

"INDEPENDENT SCIENCE—Twelve to fourteen ninth graders of superior ability are chosen each year for a 'creative experimental science course.' After a short period of instruction in the scientific method, they spend five periods a week on original research projects they have selected for themselves.

"The purpose of the course is to lead the pupils to understand the methods of scientific inquiry by requiring them to find out for themselves that these methods actually work. Resulting projects have been good, valuable experiences. In the 12th grade there will be an objective evaluation of the work done by this group and a comparison control group." [30]

"ENRICHMENT SEMINAR—Ninety-two sophomores, juniors and seniors are taking part in an enrichment seminar that meets two hours a week, either on Tuesday or Saturday evenings. A guest lecturer from a college faculty speaks for at least an hour and then responds to questions. In addition to the seminar there are related field trips, usually after a lecture. A lecture on astronomy, for instance, was followed by a trip to the Reynolds Planetarium and one on nuclear radiation was followed by a trip to a nuclear laboratory. The lectures cover the fields of English, social studies, science, and mathematics. Students are enthusiastic." [31]

"AFTERNOON HONORS GROUP—Students have shown tremendous enthusiasm for this honors group which cuts across all fields. Top pupils in the 11th and 12th grades make up the group, which arranges meetings with men and women known for their great capabilities in specific fields. The group meets together with the invited guest to discuss a topic chosen by the group leader. Meetings run 1½ hours after school and are usually held in a student's home.

"The purpose of the seminar is to raise the sights of its members in intellectual fields and to give them familiarity with an intellectual approach. No objective evaluation has been made, but students rarely miss meetings for any but major reasons." [32]

Learning Gains in the New Programs

These examples of new school programs illustrate a number of different practices associated with recent changes in the schools. In

[30] *Ibid.*, p. 53.
[31] *Ibid.*, p. 61.
[32] *Ibid.*, p. 65.

order to round out our understanding of these practices let us look briefly at some of the advantages of each.[33]

Large-group instruction. Large-group instruction commonly brings together from 100 to 200 students to hear a presentation by a teacher, view a film, or watch a television program. Usually the large group is taught by a member of a teaching team, working with two or more other teachers who help plan the program and evaluate the results.

The advantage of large-group instruction is that it encourages efficient and economic use of technological equipment. Schools that cannot afford to provide all classrooms with the latest equipment can afford to equip one. Large-group instruction permits teachers to specialize and to work in areas in which they feel most competent, rather than forcing each teacher to carry all the duties and responsibilities carried by every other teacher. For the student, large-group instruction exposes him to the best teachers and best resources, and gives him experiences which will be valuable in college or university, such as taking notes and developing responsibility for his own learning.

Small-group discussion. Small-group discussions provide four opportunities not found in large groups. They (1) permit the teacher to give students individual attention and to measure their growth, (2) help students learn to function as members of a group, (3) permit the exploration of the significance of subject matter and its application to real-life situations, and (4) give students an opportunity to get to know the teacher well, on a personal, individual basis. Small-group discussions provide the setting for direct interaction between student and student and between teacher and students.

Teacher assistants. Teacher assistants usually serve to relieve the teacher of nonprofessional chores which keep him from the main business of working with students in learning situations. Teaching assistants create new staffing patterns in the schools, in which more adults, relatively few of whom are professional teachers, are employed to work with students. These new staff specialists supplement rather than duplicate the work of the teacher.

Team teaching. Team teaching is one means of recognizing and using individual differences among teachers. Patterns for team teaching are various. Some schools team teachers within a given subject area, whereas other schools create teams across related learning areas.

[33] For an informative discussion of these practices, see J. Lloyd Trump and Dorsey Baynhorn, *Guide to Better Schools,* Chicago, Rand McNally and Company, 1963, pp. 73–99.

Teams may be as small as two or as large as six or eight. Cooperatively they plan, instruct students, and evaluate the results.

Schedule modification. The bell rings every 50 or 55 minutes in most of today's schools. Whatever is happening in the classroom stops and students burst into the corridor, headed for another 50 or 55 minute session. The underlying assumption is that learning takes place by the clock rather than by student interests and teacher plan. Flexible scheduling, on the other hand, places learning ahead, rather than behind, the rigidity of the bell. Flexible scheduling permits teachers and counselors to arrange schedules as they see fit. Because the student's schedule is not the same each day, he is permitted to follow through on absorbing interests and special projects.[33a]

6. In flexible scheduling programs students are sometimes given choices in course selection. No attention is paid to the grade of the individual, but only his interests, desires, needs, past achievements, and abilities. If a second-year student, for example, wishes to study chemistry and physics and he has the interest and desire to do so, he is scheduled this way. What do you think is the psychological impact on the student of permitting him to select the areas in which he will study?

New educational facilities. The increasing use of new technology in education has caused some persons to worry about making teaching too impersonal. Studies of schools in which technology has been widely used indicate, however, that student achievement is satisfactory. Yet teachers frequently express reservations.[34] Today the wide range of technological equipment available adds to the variety and effectiveness of teaching in both small and large schools. These new devices open up avenues to knowledge that have been unavailable in the past. They can help motivate students and transmit knowledge. Like all changes in education their use must be carefully studied and planned to secure the best results.

Individual responsibility for learning. Most of the new approaches which we have been discussing place upon the student new responsibilities for his own learning. The purpose of learning is to help the student develop the ability to work alone and to learn by doing. The assumption of greater responsibility creates in many students an increased motivation and sense of inquiry. Studies indicate that students who assume more individual responsibility for their learning

[33a] The hour-long movie, "And No Bells Ring," is an excellent presentation of the educational values of flexible scheduling.

[34] Trump and Baynhorn, *op. cit.*, p. 91.

develop better independent study habits and concern for their work.[35] When students assume more responsibility, teachers are freed to perform other professional tasks.

The Process of Curriculum Change

Let us turn our attention from specific changes taking place in the schools to the process by which changes are brought about in the curriculum. Who are the participants in the change process? What are the sources of power and methods of influence? What are the phases by which a change emerges? Who are the actual determiners of change?

Gordon N. Mackenzie obtained from graduate students 30 descriptions of recent curricular changes in elementary and secondary schools.[36] These case studies were based on direct observation or on interviews with those who had participated in the changes. Figure 16-3 summarizes Mackenzie's analysis of the elements involved in the change process. At the extreme left of the chart are listed the participants involved in curricular change. They are the persons or agencies who in any way take part in the change. These participants have control of certain sources of power and methods of influence which are listed in column two. The participants exert this power and influence through various phases which are listed in column three. Finally, the targets in the process of curricular change are listed in the extreme right column. These are persons and agents who actually determine change, the objects toward which all other change elements are directed. Let us examine briefly the four categories in the change process which the chart describes.

Participants in change. Mackenzie classifies participants in change as *internal* or *external.* "Internal participants are those who have direct connection with the legal or social system from which a particular description is taken. . . . External participants are those outside the immediate social or legal system under consideration." [37] Our interest here is primarily on the internal participants in change. Let us look briefly at these.

Students in these case studies were participants in curriculum change in many ways. The abilities, backgrounds, and aspirations of students both limit and increase the actual changes which can be

35 *Ibid.,* p. 97.

36 Gordon N. Mackenzie, "Curricular Change: Participants, Power, and Processes," in Matthew B. Miles (Ed.), *Innovation in Education,* New York, Teachers College, Teachers College Press, 1964, pp. 399–424.

37 *Ibid.,* p. 409.

CULTURAL CONTEXT

Participants in Curricular Change →	Having control of certain sources of power and methods of influence →	Proceed through various phases in a process →	To influence the determiners of the curriculum
Internal participants: Students Teachers Principals Supervisors Superintendents Boards of education Citizens in local communities State legislatures State departments of education State and federal courts External participants: Non-educationists Foundations Academicians Business and industry Educationists National Government	Advocacy and communication Prestige Competence Money or goods Legal authority Policy, precedent, custom Cooperation and collaboration	Initiated by internal or external participants: Criticism Proposal of changes Development and clarification of proposals for change Evaluation, review and reformulation of proposals Comparison of proposals Initiated by internal participants: Action on proposals . Implementation of action decisions	Teachers Students Subject matter Methods Materials and facilities Time

SOURCE: Gordon N. Mackenzie, "Curricular Change: Participants, Power and Processes," *Innovation in Education*, Matthew B. Miles (Ed.), New York, Bureau of Publications, Teachers College, Columbia University, 1964, p. 401.

Fig. 16-3 Participants in curricular change, sources of their power, and phases in the process of change of the determiners of the curriculum.

made. In some cases students have a direct influence on change by helping to plan content, methods, materials, and time allotments. Students indirectly influence change by expressing their opinions to parents, teachers, and principals on subject matter, methods, and time allocations.

Teachers, as participants in change, influence in their own classrooms the five remaining *determiners of change*, listed in the right-hand column of Figure 16-3: (1) students, (2) subject matter, (3) methods, (4) materials and facilities, and (5) time.

Principals in these case studies were influential participants in changing the determiners of change. "For example, some principals had the authority to control the assignment of teachers to grade or ability groupings. Also, some principals controlled, with broad limits, decisions on the student composition of class groups, the human and nonhuman resources to be introduced into classrooms, and the time allotments to be followed. They also had much to do with the extent to which parental pressures were brought to bear directly on teachers, and with the provision of in-service educational opportunities for teachers." [38]

Supervisors, although they have less authority than principals, nevertheless had considerable influence on the determiners of change. Through their visits to classrooms and by their encouragement to teachers they stimulate the use of new approaches.

Superintendents were frequently the most powerful single participants in change. Situations were found in which superintendents intervened directly to influence determiners of change. Sometimes they also worked to build up community support for change.

7. John H. Fischer relates this incident: "Not long ago I talked with a town official in an Eastern state who was convinced that his town should not have as superintendent of schools a man who wanted to experiment. The official wanted nothing introduced into his schools that had not been thoroughly tested and proved elsewhere. To the query whether he favored a backward looking superintendent and a stagnant staff, he replied that all he asked for was a sensible, well managed and economical school system." [39]

Boards of education figured prominently as participants in change. In some instances they ordered changes over the objections of the professional staff, for example, in the use of television in classrooms, the introduction of foreign languages into elementary schools, and

[38] *Ibid.*, pp. 410–411.
[39] John H. Fischer, "Some Thoughts on Teaching in Tomorrow's Schools," a paper delivered at the annual meeting of the American Association of Colleges of Teacher Education, Chicago, Illinois, February 16, 1963.

the purchase of language laboratories. Further, the financial control which the boards exercise strongly influences the determiners of change.

Citizens in local communities in some instances were very powerful participants in change, operating through citizens' groups, parent-teacher associations, and school board elections.

State legislatures are the primary legal bodies responsible for the curriculum. They sometimes establish a pattern for change through law, but in most instances they delegate much of their authority to state boards of education, state departments of education, and local school boards.

State departments of education are often able to require certain kinds of curriculum changes. They may influence content and method through state testing systems, where such systems are used. Through the allocation of funds they stimulate numerous changes, which vary from the way pupils are served to content which they are taught.

State and federal courts may influence curriculum change through rulings and interpretations of laws. Rules in regard to racial integration are cases in point.

Sources of power and methods used by participants. Various kinds of power and methods are used by participants to secure change. All participants engage in some kind of advocacy of change. People confer with associates and seek to persuade others to accept their way of thinking. They make an effort to get people to feel an involvement in and an identification with the proposed change.

What are the sources of power of those who seek change? Mackenzie identified these sources in the case studies: prestige, competence, money and goods, legal authority, policy, and cooperation. The prestige of individuals or groups advocating change causes people to give special deference to their recommendations. The recognized competence of the advocates in skills like writing, speaking, conferring, and knowledge of a problem is an influential factor. The control of money or goods is one of the most significant sources of power mentioned in these case studies; the ability to either give or withhold money is a genuine source of power. The legal authority of local boards of education, state boards of education, and state departments of education is a strong source of power for change. Where the responsibility to administer policy has been delegated by the local board of education to a professional staff person, for example, to the superintendent of schools, that delegation confers power. Cooperation among individuals may greatly strengthen their influence and power.

Phases in the process of change. Participants use their power in certain ways to achieve change. In some cases there is an orderly sequence of steps, whereas in others the order of events seems to be unimportant.

Criticism of existing practices usually figures prominently in curriculum change. For example, the public criticism of reading practices in the schools encouraged changes in practices in the teaching of reading. Criticisms of current practices are frequently combined with proposals for change and suggestions for specific courses of action. In the criticism of reading programs, for example, the use of phonics was advocated to improve the teaching of reading.

The making of proposals is usually followed by the development and clarification of them. Proposals are expanded, and illustrations are set forth to explain how they might work. Sometimes outside expert opinion is sought to give support and reinforcement to proposals. Evaluation and review frequently follow the development and clarification of proposals. The proposal may then be reformulated or it may be initiated on a "pilot" basis to test its feasibility.

Comparison of one proposal with another is a common practice in the change process. In a local school system, for example, a study group may be charged with the responsibility of examining alternative "new" mathematics programs, or team teaching arrangements, and be asked to make recommendations to the faculty and administration.

The determinants of curriculum. Mackenzie identified six focal points or determinants of change: (1) teachers, (2) students, (3) subject matter, (4) methods, (5) materials and facilities, and (6) time.

Most curricular changes involve teachers. New language teachers may be employed to develop the teaching of French in the elementary school. Present teachers may be given additional training to handle new programs in mathematics or other subjects. Workshops may be organized to foster discussions of new proposals or to plan experimental programs.

8. What are the characteristics of people who initiate change? Everett Rogers points out that one characteristic is that "innovators are young. Since the young are less likely to be conditioned by traditional practices within the established culture, there are theoretical grounds for expecting them to be more innovative. Research studies on farmers provide actual evidence that innovators are younger than their peers who are later adopters." [40] Do you think that this finding, which holds true for farmers, would also hold true for teachers?

[40] Everett Rogers, "What Are Innovators Like?," Paper presented at the Seminar on Change in Public Schools, Portland, Oregon, October 14–16, 1964, p. 5.

Most curriculum changes cited earlier in this chapter involve drastic changes in the way students are grouped and the way they spend their time. Thus regrouping of students is a means of changing the interactions of teachers and students. "Some of the more common approaches to altering the composition of class groups were modification of school district boundaries, and shifts in the bases of grouping (homogeneous, heterogeneous, or inter-age). Changes in class size, and the removal of problem children of various types to special classes or schools, were used as means of modifying the classroom interactions." [41]

Subject matter, methods, materials, and facilities are closely interrelated in the change process. Changes in subject matter, for example, are established by the introduction of new materials, methods, and facilities. The introduction of French in the elementary school, for example, may bring with it new printed materials, language tapes, and laboratory facilities. Yet these elements, although interrelated, are also independent. Curriculum change usually begins with changes in subject matter, and other changes follow. Changes in curriculum are most frequently referred to as changes in subject matter.

Many changes focus on method, the manner or means by which something is taught. Illustrations are the introduction of large-group or small-group instruction, or the method of teaching mathematics by discovery. Materials and facilities may strongly influence methods because they are a significant part of the school environment. Their presence or absence can substantially determine what happens in the learning situation.

Time is an important determinant of curricular change. A number of the examples of change cited earlier in the chapter involved changes in the allotment of time for both students and teachers. An increase or a decrease in the amount of time given a subject may strongly influence what is learned.

Of the six determinants of curriculum change, does any one, or any combination of them, hold more potential for change than the others? We would expect, for example, that the teacher, who figures prominently in all six, might be the key to change.

"Yet, many change efforts in the cases which focused solely on teachers did not appear to bring about change; many changes appear to have occurred through a major emphasis on students, materials, methods, facilities, or time allocations. It may be that where the focus was on determiners other than teachers, there were changes and ad-

[41] Mackenzie, *op. cit.*, p. 403.

justments required of teachers which they were able to handle individually. Undoubtedly, the six determiners vary in their significance from one instance to another. Yet, there may be many situations in which the neglect of one or more of the determiners may lead to failure to bring about desired changes.

"What is the optimum or necessary interrelationship among determiners? It appeared from the cases that they were often interrelated, and that changes in one were accompanied by or made necessary changes in another." [42]

The Cultural Context of Change

It is easy to omit one crucial factor in all change that occurs in the schools, that of the cultural context. The line running across the top of Figure 16-3 is labeled "cultural context." From it, arrows point down to the participants, the sources of power and methods of influence, the phases of the process, and the determinants of change. The culture in which the school is set modifies all of these factors and determines the *cultural style* of the school in respect to change.

Most of the changes examined in the chapter have had their roots in local community and national concerns with education. The concerns for the gifted, the socially disadvantaged, college entrance, reading ability, teaching by television, team teaching, teaching machines, and advance placement, all find support from certain segments of the society which urge changes upon the schools.

The mass media, the large, educationally minded foundations, and nationally prominent individuals strengthen this social support and give practical direction to new programs. These national influences explain in part the similarity among schools in their programs of change. They exist within a common cultural context.

A reminder of the cultural influences on changes in the schools sets the stage for the next part of this book. Social forces in our changing society converge in such a way that they make certain problems in education critical. We shall select five of these crucial problems for examination in Part 6.

REFERENCES

Paperbacks

Change and Innovation in Elementary School Organization. Maurie Hillison and Ramona Karlson. Holt, Rinehart and Winston, 383 Madison Ave., New York ($3.95).

[42] *Ibid.,* pp. 405–406.

Education Automation: Freeing the Scholar to Return to His Studies. R. Buckminster Fuller. (AB-11) Southern Illinois University Press, Carbondale, Ill. ($1.95).

Educational Technology: Readings in Programmed Instruction. John P. De Cecco. (Orig.) Holt, Rinehart and Winston, 383 Madison Ave., New York ($4.25).

Explaining "Teaching Machines" and Programming. David Cram. (Prog. Bk. Orig.) Fearon Publishers, 2165 Park Blvd., Palo Alto, Calif. ($2.00).

Focus on Change: Guide to Better Schools. J. Lloyd Trump and Dorsey Baynhorn. (Orig.) (6201) Rand McNally and Co., P. O. Box 7600, Chicago, Ill. ($1.25).

Frontiers of Elementary Education—Vols. I, II, III, IV, V, VI, VII. Vincent J. Glennon, Editor. (4-1130-4-1530) Syracuse University Press, University Station, Syracuse, N. Y. ($1.75 each).

Programs, Teachers, and Machines. Alfred de Grazia and David Sohn, Editors. (Orig.) (NM1007) Bantam Books, 271 Madison Ave., New York (95¢).

Revolution in Teaching. Alfred de Grazia and David Sohn, Editors. (Orig.) (NM1006) Bantam Books, 271 Madison Ave., New York (95¢).

Revolution in the Schools. Ronald Gross and Judith Murphy, Editors. (Orig.) (H040) Harbinger Books, Harcourt, Brace and World, 757 Third Ave., New York ($2.95).

Schools for the Sixties. National Education Association. (46120) McGraw-Hill Paperback Series, McGraw-Hill Book Co., 330 W. 42nd St., New York ($2.45).

Schools of Tomorrow—Today! Arthur D. Morse. (Orig.) Doubleday and Co., 277 Park Ave., New York ($1.50).

Schools within Schools: A Study of High School Organization. Karl R. Plath. (Orig.) (SSA) Teachers College, Teachers College Press, 525 West 120 St., New York ($1.50).

Teacher and Technology: New Designs for Learning. William Clark Trow. (Orig.) Appleton-Century-Crofts, Division of Meredith Publishing Co., 440 Park Ave. South, New York ($1.95).

Television and the Teaching of English. Neil Postman. (Orig.) Appleton-Century-Crofts, Division of Meredith Publishing Co., 440 Park Ave. South, New York ($1.25).

Books

Association for Supervision and Curriculum Development, *Using Current Curriculum Development.* Washington, D. C.: National Education Association, 1963. The book includes descriptions of current curriculum projects and reports of studies and references to source materials.

Beggs, David W., *Decatur-Lakeview High School: A Practical Application of the Trump Plan.* Englewood Cliffs, N. J.: Prentice-Hall, 1964. This school employs team teaching, small- and large-group instruction, multimedia teaching aids, and flexible scheduling.

Brown, B. Frank, *The Non-Graded High School.* Englewood Cliffs, N. J.: Prentice-Hall, 1963. The nongraded school lets the student achieve without regard either to grade level or sequence.

Conant, James Bryant, *Recommendations for Education in the Junior High School Years.* Princeton, N. J.: Educational Testing Service, 1960. Conant feels that the program provided for adolescent youth in junior high school is more important than organizational structure.

Education in a Changing Society. Washington, D. C.: National Education Association, 1963. Social forces and educational values compose the setting in which change takes place.

Gross, Ronald, and Judith Murphy, *The Revolution in the Schools.* New York: Harcourt, Brace and World, 1964. The book's purpose is to present pioneering articles which challenge theory and practice in today's education.

Plath, Karl R., *Schools Within Schools: A Study of High School Organization,* Secondary School Administration Series. New York: Bureau of Publications, Teachers College, Columbia University, 1965. Plath presents a promising approach to the large school and its internal organization. Chapter 4 presents job descriptions for school personnel, including teachers.

Shaplin, Judson T., "Team Teaching," in *American Education Today,* Paul Woodring and John Scanlon, Editors. New York: McGraw-Hill Book Co., 1963. Team teaching is seen as an effort to improve instruction by the reorganization of the teaching personnel.

Thelen, Herbert A., *Education and the Human Quest.* New York: Harper and Row, 1960. Chapter 5 presents four models for teaching: personal inquiry, group investigation, reflective action, and skill development.

Wiles, Kimball, *Teaching and Learning the Democratic Way.* Englewood Cliffs, N. J.: Prentice-Hall, 1963. Chapter 13 discusses "The High School of the Future."

Periodicals

Cavanagh, Peter, "The Autotutor and Classroom Instruction: Three Comparative Studies," *Occupational Psychology,* Vol. 37, No. 1, January 1963, pp. 44–84. This particular teaching machine has the advantage of being applicable to a wide variety of training situations.

"Focus on Change," *NEA Journal,* Vol. 51, No. 3, March 1962, pp. 43–58. A special feature suggests what the schools of the future may be like.

Ginther, John R., and William A. Shroyer, "Team Teaching in English and History at the Eleventh Grade Level," *The School Review,* Vol. 70, No. 3, Autumn 1962, pp. 303–313. Enthusiasm of teachers and interest of students were increased by team teaching.

Goodlad, John L., "Meeting Children Where They Are," *Saturday Review,* Vol. XLVIII, No. 12, March 20, 1965, pp. 57–59. Goodlad defines nongrading as both a concept and a plan within a larger view of education embracing a few simple compelling principles of child development, learning, and school function.

Lee, J. Murray, "Elementary Education: 1985," *Educational Leadership,* Vol. XVII, No. 8, May 1960, pp. 475–479. An article summarizing the best practices of selected schools.

Shumsky, Abraham, and Rose Mukerji, "From Research Idea to Classroom Practice," *The Elementary School Journal,* Vol. 63, No. 2, November 1962, pp. 83–86. The authors discovered that some teachers who accepted the validity of research for improving instruction resisted putting into practice the new ideas that emerged from that research.

"Team Teaching: a Special Issue," *School and Society,* Vol. 91, No. 2234, December 14, 1963. An issue devoted to the topic of the antecedents of team teaching and to the question: Is team teaching the answer?

VI

Educational Problems in Our Changing Society

17

The Struggle for Control of the Schools

"The schools today are deeply involved and controversially embroiled in all the great issues of social change."   FRED M. HECHINGER

The superintendent of schools was at home and ready to sit down to dinner when the telephone rang. It was the principal of the Fairlawn elementary school in a new area of a suburban city. He had just heard that some parents were organizing a march on the school to protest the Board of Education's decision to bus children to the Urbandale school while Fairlawn's new wing was being built.

"What do you think we should do?" the superintendent asked.

"Can you meet me at the school in fifteen minutes?" the principal requested, as he hung up.

While driving to the Fairlawn school, the superintendent had a moment to reflect on the circumstances leading up to the principal's urgent call. Fairlawn was a new subdivision of white, middle-class families, with homes in the $25,000 to $30,000 price range. Fathers in the area held good, white collar and managerial positions in Metropolis not far away. The Urbandale community, in contrast, was one of the old sections of the city, located near a race course which depressed surrounding home values and gave the section a bad name. Houses in Urbandale were old and small. As white parents left the area, Negroes from Metropolis moved in and now constituted about three-quarters of the Urbandale population. The school was old, but substantial and in good repair. In terms of status, however, it was considered to be the "worst" of the 15 elementary schools in the city.

The Fairlawn school was new and, because the subdivision was attractive as a place to live, quickly became overcrowded. The Board of Education was constructing a new wing on the school, but it had to provide for the extra children while the new classrooms were being built. The Urbandale school, which had extra space, was less than a mile away. In fact, the only physical landmark which separated Fairlawn from Urbandale was the main line of a railroad which ran on a high embankment through the city. To Fairlawn residents Urbandale was "across the tracks." To Urbandale residents Fairlawn was where the "rich, white folks" lived.

In making its decision to send the overflow of Fairlawn children to Urbandale during the construction period, the Board of Education was well aware of the attitude of Fairlawn parents toward Urbandale. They reasoned, however, that the parents would understand, since the situation was only temporary. The children would be brought back as soon as the new wing was completed. If what the principal reported about the protest march were true, however, the parents apparently did not "understand."

As the superintendent neared the school, he thought of the irony in the situation. He was scheduled to meet in the morning with a parents' civil rights group from Urbandale which wanted to protest the *de facto* segregation in their school and propose that it be closed and the students be transferred to Fairlawn. Tonight he would confront white parents who were violently opposed to having their children go to school with Negro children in Urbandale. Tomorrow he would confront Negro parents who were insisting that their children were getting a second-rate education in Urbandale and should go to school with white children in Fairlawn.

The multipurpose room of the school was already filling up with people when the superintendent and principal arrived. From the animated conversation it was clear that feeling was running high. The superintendent invited the parents to be seated so that the discussion could proceed in an orderly fashion. When things had quieted down, he described the problem of the Board of Education in having to find a place for Fairlawn children until the new wing to the school was completed.

"As you came into the building," he reminded the parents, "you noticed that construction on the new addition is proceeding well. We should be able to bring your children back from Urbandale in six months." He assured the parents that the Board of Education was sensitive to the wishes of the parents, but that the members thought that it was better to have the Fairlawn children in the Urbandale school on full-day sessions, rather than in the Fairlawn school on half-day sessions. He then invited the parents to express their views.

"We know the Board of Education has its problems," one of the spokesmen began, "but we have ours, too, and we think you ought to know about them. Most of us here tonight moved out to Fairlawn to get out of Metropolis and the mess in the schools there. Every time a Negro family moved into our neighborhood in Metropolis our school went down another notch. Finally our kids started to behave like the Negro kids. That's why we got out. Now it looks to us that the same thing is starting to happen here. It's bad enough if our kids have to go to Urbandale for six months. We're *really* sunk if the Urbandale kids start coming to Fairlawn, like the rumors say they're going to."

Another spokesman added: "In Metropolis we were in the minority and nobody in the schools would listen to us. So we came to Fairlawn where we could exercise some control over what happens in the schools and that's what we propose to do tonight. And, if we can't do that, we're prepared to have our children boycott the school."

The next morning the superintendent sat in his office with the parents' civil rights group from Urbandale and heard the other side of this story of conflict.

"We don't object to Fairlawn children coming to Urbandale," one Negro parent in the group said. "In fact we think that if they come they should stay. Then maybe you'd build a new school for us, too; then all the children would benefit. As it is, our school is the slum school of this city, and our children deserve something better. After all, we pay taxes to the schools just like everybody else. Yet the children in Fairlawn have a school that's three times as good as ours, teachers that are three times better, and besides Fairlawn children don't have an inferiority complex from going to a slum school like our children do. We think you should either bring Fairlawn children to Urbandale for good and build us a new school, or close our old one and send all our children to Fairlawn. Sentiments in Urbandale are running high. I've heard lots of talk about it. In fact some parents say they'll boycott the school unless something is done, and soon."

1. How do you think the Board of Education of this suburban city should resolve this conflict? Do you think the case of one group is stronger than the other? Should either group have more "say" in the final decision than the other? If so, why?

2. Do you think that parents should boycott the schools in order to enforce their demands? What are your reasons for answering as you do?

This incident, drawn from the life of one school system and illustrative of the problems of many others, suggests the problem with which we are concerned in this chapter, the struggle for control of the schools. The parents' group from Fairlawn and the civil rights group from Urbandale were on opposite sides of the issue, but they were engaging in the same process. They were attempting to control the policies of the school by exercising their powers as citizens in a democracy. In this chapter we shall define the concept and types of control and examine the social forces which determine the nature of the control exerted upon the school. In Chapter 18 we shall turn to the politics of education and ask: Who does control the schools, and how? From this question follows another: Who *should* control the schools? Our emphasis shall be on the former question but we shall not sidestep the latter.

Schools as Institutions "in the Middle"

The Fairlawn versus Urbandale incident points up the crucial nature of the question of control of the schools. As Fred Hechinger, the education editor of *The New York Times,* points out in the sentence at the head of this chapter: "The schools today are deeply involved and controversially embroiled" in the great social issues of our times. The school, for example, is the storm center of the racial integration conflict in both the South and the North. In the political and economic arena, forces to the right and left seek to control what is taught in the schools. In the educational arena the conservatives battle the liberals over "fundamental" and "progressive" education. The school is the institution "in the middle."

That contending forces should seek to control the schools is entirely understandable. In any society the schools offer a rich prize to those who seek to shape the future. No dictator would dare to permit schools to be controlled by his opposition; the first move of most dictators is, therefore, to make sure that the schools educate the young in the "proper" manner.

In a democratic society we say that "the people" should control the schools. But the people are many and their persuasions diverse. In a democracy the people are divided in loyalties, interests, and goals. In order to express their loyalties, further their interests, and achieve their goals, they organize themselves in special interest groups. The people who run the schools are those who are most interested and best organized and equipped to make their voices heard and to exert pressure where they think it will do the most "good." Sometimes, as in the case of Urbandale versus Fairlawn, these groups are in direct, head-on contention. The school stands in the middle as the battleground. Upon it is placed the awful responsibility of trying to reconcile seemingly irreconcilable forces.

The contest for the control of the schools is not confined to the higher levels of the school's administration, to the principal, superintendent, and board of education. It moves into the classroom, and every teacher has experienced it. It takes many forms, some obvious, some subtle, some trivial, some crucial. Parents who demand that a child be moved from one room to another because "that class is smaller and the teacher is better," who complain to the teacher that he is assigning too much homework or too little, and who suggest that "Mary will do better in mathematics if you give her more personal help," are all exercising a measure of control over teaching and learning in the classroom.

Many teachers experience harassments of a more critical nature that cut deeply into the freedom to teach. Rightist groups who demand that the teacher use no materials from the United Nations, who attempt to censor textbooks, who instruct children to spy on teachers and report what they do and say, pose threats of a serious nature to education itself.

3. In Chapter 11 we discussed the cultural styles of schools in the village, town, suburb, and city. In which type of school do you think the teacher is most likely to experience attempts to influence his classroom work? Why? Do you think the types of control may differ from one school to another? If so, how?

School Personnel Also Exercise Control

We should not assume that all the forces which seek control are outside the school. The school is a bureaucracy with power of its own: The administrators, teachers, and students constitute an organization of full-time school personnel who have definite ideas about how the school should be run, what it should teach, and how. Even the members of the board of education, who are legally responsible for the school, give only part of their time to its operation. Besides, they are "lay" citizens rather than professional educators. The full-time, professional members of the school establishment, therefore, are in a privileged position to exercise control. In Chapter 18 we shall observe how teachers exercise control in school affairs.

What Do We Mean by Democratic Control?

Before we continue we should explain more fully what we mean when we speak of the democratic control of the schools. The word "control" may seem to have a negative connotation and to be in conflict with our deep beliefs in individual freedom and action. We use the term here simply as a way to describe the means by which society gives shape and direction to an institution which it created and from which it expects a great deal.

Social control, in this sense, is indispensable in human society. The schools are a product of society, a means of educating the young. We would not expect society to establish schools and then cut them off without some means of guidance and control. The schools can only serve when they are a part of the influences and counterinfluences of their society. There must be some way to make the school continuously sensitive and aware of the needs of the society. In our society this is achieved by democratic control, in which citizens have a voice in the operation of the schools.

We do not imply that control may not be "bad." Persons may indeed judge certain kinds of control of the school to be harmful, especially when they are contrary to their own interests. As we saw in the case of Urbandale versus Fairlawn, when contrary interests attempt to control the schools conflicts surely result. In fact, the continuing debate about the schools can be better understood in terms of the conflicting expectations which various groups in our democracy have of the schools.

4. Can you cite instances, perhaps from your own home community, in which you think efforts to control the school were either "good" or "bad"? Upon what basis do you judge these examples to be "good" or "bad"?

What we are saying is that the schools are not a privileged sanctuary isolated from and above the turmoil of events swirling beneath them. Rather, whether they be public and tax-financed or parochial and privately supported, schools are at the confluence of social forces, both acting and reacting, subject to pressures, and capable of exerting pressure. The control of the schools is created by the accommodation and reconciliation of forces that impinge upon the school and by the school's reaction to them.

It is important for teachers to understand this concept of democratic control because it has much to say about the teacher's role. The teacher who views the classroom as a privileged sanctuary with a sign over the door, *Teachers and Children Only,* is a candidate for disillusionment. The teacher who knows that his position is truly public, that all kinds of unexpected influences flow through the classroom door with the students and with all others who come and go, is in a better position to render public service with poise and confidence. To the teacher's classroom art must be added the skill of diplomacy in understanding and handling social forces and people in constant contention.

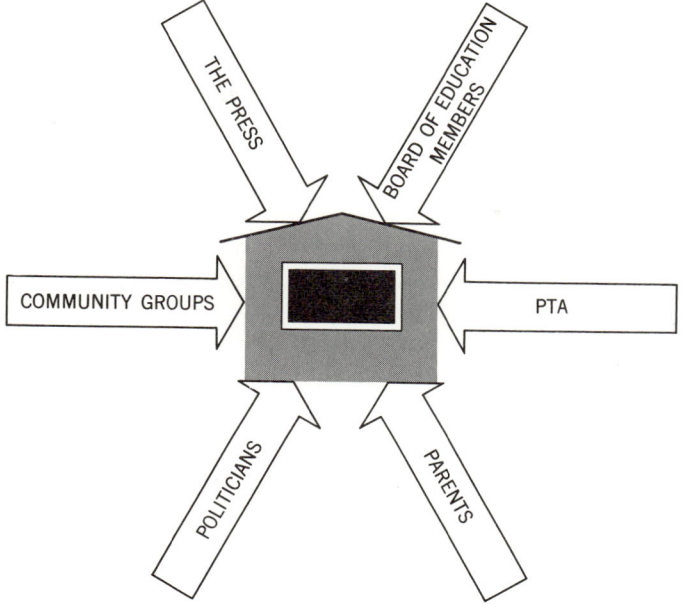

COMMUNITY GROUPS

PTA

THE PRESS

BOARD OF EDUCATION MEMBERS

POLITICIANS

PARENTS

Fig. 17-1 To the teacher's classroom art must be added the skill of diplomacy.

5. One teacher quit the classroom because "I can't take the constant squabbling about the schools. It's always interfering with my teaching." Another teacher who stayed in teaching commented: "I like the give and take with children and parents. When I can help smooth over some conflict, I feel real good." Do these comments suggest anything to you about the personality requirements for a teacher?

Formal and Informal Control of the Schools

The control of the schools may be either *formal* or *informal*. Formal means of control are those provided by law. Informal means rest upon personal relations.

The parents of Fairlawn and Urbandale were using informal means of influencing the school, one through a protest meeting to give visibility to their cause, the other through an informal session in the superintendent's office. Had these groups decided to nominate and elect school board candidates who were sympathetic to their respective causes they would have been using formal and legal means to control the policy and actions of the school. The parent who asks the principal to transfer his child from one room to another is exerting his informal influence on the school. A national group which censors textbooks and distributes lists of censored texts to teachers and school board members is using informal means to exert control. On the other hand, citizens who attend a regular meeting of the school board to oppose a proposed bond issue for building new schools are using the formal means available to them to influence the school program.

Informal means are frequently used by citizens as a way to influence formal control. The protesting parents of Fairlawn, for example, used an informal method as a way of getting the Board of Education to take formal action favorable to their position. Similarly, the parents' civil rights group from Urbandale used their informal meeting with the superintendent for the same purpose.

Variations in the Nature of Control

Variations in the community inevitably influence the nature of control exerted on the school. People who live in different regions of the country, hold different social and economic positions, live in conservative or progressive communities, and have different levels of education are likely to have different views of education. They will therefore exert different kinds of influence in order to make the schools conform to their particular points of view.

Lawrence W. Downey reported that various kinds of subpublics in our society perceive the task of public education in different ways.[1] Downey questioned people who lived in different regions, held different social-economic positions and occupations, had different amounts of education, were educators and noneducators, and were of different ages, religions, and races about the tasks of public education.

Downey asked representatives of these various groups to give their priorities among four aspects of education: intellectual, social, personal, and productive. The *intellectual* aspects of education were defined as including such matters as the possession, communication, and creation of knowledge. The *social* aspect of education was defined to include such matters as man's day-to-day relationships, his civic rights and duties, loyalty to his country, and relationships among nations and peoples. The *personal* aspects of education included such matters as physical and mental health, moral integrity, and aesthetic pursuits. The *productive* aspects of education included items related to the preparation for and selection of a vocation, home and family living, and consumer education in buying, selling, and investment.

Let us now see how people from various groups in Downey's investigation rated these four aspects of education.

[1] Lawrence W. Downey, *The Task of Public Education*, Chicago, The University of Chicago, Midwest Administration Center, 1960.

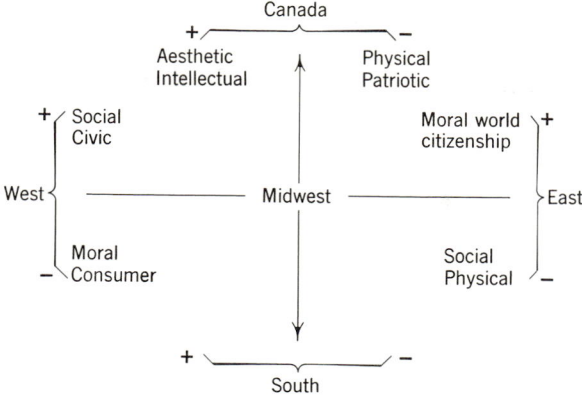

Fig. 17-2 Regional differences in perception of the public school's task. SOURCE: Lawrence W. Downey, *The Task of Public Education,* Midwest Administration Center, University of Chicago, Chicago, Illinois, 1960, p. 38.

Regional differences. As Figure 17-2 shows, responses were obtained from residents of four geographic regions in the United States and Canada. The respondents from these five regions differed considerably from one another in their perceptions of the task of the public school. Downey summarized the regional differences this way: "The Midwest assumed what might be called a middle-of-the-road position; the West deviated in the direction of socialization; the South emphasized personal development, particularly physical; and Canada, the greatest deviant, favored intellectual, world citizenship, and aesthetic development, but minimized the physical and patriotic aspects of education." [2] The East gave strong support to the moral and world citizenship aspects of education, while minimizing its social and physical aspects.

Within these five large geographical regions Downey discovered tendencies for the (1) residential suburb to emphasize the aesthetic and the intellectual tasks of education, (2) industrial center to emphasize homemaking and fix-it-yourself training, and (3) rural community to attach greater than average importance to physical and consumer training.

6. Reflect a moment about your own community in relation to the regional and local differences which Downey discovered in perceptions of the tasks of public education. Does he accurately or inaccurately describe these perceptions in your community as you understand them?

[2] *Ibid.,* p. 37.

Socio-economic differences. Surprisingly, the respondent's income level did not appear to influence his perception of the school's task. Occupation, however, did prove to be a rather strong and consistent predictor of educational viewpoint. As Downey stated: "Priorities assigned to knowledge, creativity, desire to learn, world citizenship, emotional stability and aesthetic appreciation decreased systematically *down* the occupation scale, that is from professional to laborer. Social skill, physical training, morality, job training, and consumer education, on the other hand, decreased systematically *up* the occupational scale . . . one can assume from these observations that the mere acquisition of wealth does not alter those values on which perception of the task of the public school are based. The achievement of a station of life, however, as represented by occupation, does appear to coincide with educational point of view." [3]

Educator-noneducator differences. How does the teacher's view of his own task differ from that of the public? Today's clamor for more attention to academic matters in the schools has caused many teachers to see their task in terms of giving increasing attention to the intellectual development of students. According to this investigation, however, the lay public saw things differently. Without exception the tasks perceived to be most important by the public were nonintellectual. Noneducators considered vocational guidance and home and family living to be more important than did educators.

Age differences. For the elementary school, older respondents gave higher priority to physical education, moral training, and vocational training than did younger respondents. Concerning high school, older respondents gave higher priority to patriotism, physical education, and moral training than did younger respondents. Older respondents also assigned lower priority to world citizenship and vocational guidance in the high schools than did younger respondents.

Religious differences. The number of significant differences between Catholic and Protestant respondents was greater at the elementary school than at the high school level. Downey stated: "The differences which persisted in perceptions of the tasks of both schools included: favor for moral training by Catholic educators; favor for physical training by Protestant educators; and favor for the desire for knowledge by Protestant non-educators." [4]

Race differences. Whites and Negroes expressed several differences in their perceptions of the tasks of public education. Negroes consistently regarded physical training and home and family skills as

[3] *Ibid.*, p. 47.   [4] *Ibid.*, p. 52.

more important school tasks than did whites. On the other hand, whites regarded creativity, desire for knowledge, and world citizenship to be more important than did Negroes.

The significant point in the Downey investigation is that people's perceptions of the job of the school depend on a number of factors, including the region and type of communities in which they live, their occupations, ages, religious affiliations, and race. It seems logical to assume that these people will attempt to influence public education in different ways and directions. With various and frequently conflicting forces bearing upon them, those who operate the schools must find a working consensus among divergent groups in order to proceed. The Fairlawn versus Urbandale conflict is consistent with Downey's findings. These two groups, while living practically side by side and while not divided by regional differences, were sharply divided by other differences, especially those of race, socio-economic status, and occupation. Each, therefore, sought to influence the school in the direction of their special interests and social positions.

7. What groups can you name in your own community which seek to influence the schools? In what directions do they seek to influence the schools?

Control and the Cultural Style of the School

Another way to illustrate how patterns of control differ is to examine them in schools with different cultural styles. The schools attended by Hamid in the village, Raymond in the town, Beth in the suburb, and Julia in the city present quite different types of control.

Control of village schools. Hamid's school serves only the few favored boys of his village, most of whom are the sons of landowners. Because the school is not open to all the boys, in a sense it is a closed corporation run for the benefit of those fortunate boys whose families largely manage and dominate the affairs of the village. The elders of these families feel a paternal responsibility toward the school and the boys who are in it. They are all in agreement about what the school should do because they are a close-knit and closed group. There are no other factions in this village which might challenge their control of the school. When the village starts to change under the impact of modernization new groups will likely rise up and challenge the old. But not yet. The control of Hamid's school resembles a family's control of its own affairs: Differences of opinion are resolved within the family and not in public.

The American rural school, as the counterpart to Hamid's village school, bears both resemblances and differences in its pattern of control. The parents who live on farms around the one-room school share an occupation and a style of life. They, therefore, tend to hold similar views of education. Like the elders of Hamid's village, they feel possessive about their school and fight attempts to close it. The school may have served the neighborhood for a century, and parents and a few grandparents might have sat in the same seats where today's children sit. There is high consensus about the school, built up over many years, a consensus rooted in a homogeneous community. The control of the school is entrusted to a respected group of citizens, preferably from the "old" families in the neighborhood, who hire teachers with a rural background because "they understand our children and have a wholesome influence on them." This kind of control "fits" the rural community as long as it remains unchanged by urban influences.

Control of town schools. Raymond's Midwest represents the stable, established community which is often run by a small conservative group of city fathers who quietly exercise control over school affairs. When a vacancy appears on the board of education this small group quietly selects a man, persuades him to run, and gets him elected, frequently without opposition. In commenting on this type of town, Burton R. Clark writes: "Power in the hands of a few is coupled with apathy on the part of the vast majority, and the apathy is reinforced by lack of interest and lack of influence. In towns with an oligarchy of city fathers, successful school superintendents are those who learn to consult informally with the few who count, securing their nod before making an important move. Such towns are located from coast to coast, but are more heavily concentrated in the long-settled states of the Eastern seaboard. Many such towns have been broken out of this pattern by industrial and population movement, such as the flight to the suburbs, which brings new blood willing and able to challenge the old leadership." [5] With the new blood will come democratic discussion and debate, some unsettling experiences for the "old-timers," and ultimately a new control over the schools.

Control of suburban schools. As Clark indicates, the flight to the suburbs "brings new blood willing and able to challenge the old leadership." The control of suburban schools like Beth's rests in the hands of newer residents who tend to take a more active interest in the operation of the schools than their counterparts in the town. In fact, it is in the suburbs where the attacks on the schools have been sharp-

[5] Burton R. Clark, *Educating the Expert Society,* San Francisco, Chandler Publishing Company, 1962, p. 132.

est. Yet it is also in the suburbs where most educational experimentation is going on and where new practices are taking root.

Suburban boards of education as a rule do not represent a wide spectrum of society, because the suburbs themselves do not. Members tend to come from the same socio-economic and occupational rank. They may bring to the board sharply divergent points of view about school operation, but usually they find themselves in agreement on the goals of the school. The school, in their view, must give sound academic training, prepare students for college entrance, and broaden them esthetically and socially. These members are expressing the essential unity toward education characteristic of persons in their economic and social position.

Whereas the power centers of the town are readily identifiable and held by a few, power in the suburb is scattered and loosely held. Each open position on the school board is, therefore, likely to be contested for by several candidates, and the winner is he who can muster a coalition of different interest groups. In a sense the suburb is not a community at all in the way that a town is. Even the geographical boundaries of the suburb fade away into the next suburb. Power constantly shifts in suburbia from one coalition to another. Board of education membership is likely to shift as new groups come into positions of influence.

Control of city schools. It is in the city that schools are thrust most forcibly into the arena of political conflict. The homogeneity of the village and town is lost in the welter of hundreds of homogeneous groups each attempting to raise its voice and be heard. The consensus about educational goals, present in the suburb, is hard to find among diverse and heterogeneous groups of the metropolis. In the city the special interest group is best organized, best financed, and commands the best means of communication.

Members of city boards of education most likely did not "make it on their own." They achieved board membership as spokesmen for some geographic section of the city, a racial group, a taxpayers' association, or other special interest organization. In some cities where mayors or other government bodies appoint board members, special care is given to keep "balance" on the board, that is, to give proper representation to each of the political power groups within the city. Thus members do not sit upon the board as individuals but as representatives of their groups. Control of city schools frequently rests in the compromise and reconciliation of special interests within an atmosphere of charged political debate.

8. The nature of the control of the school is likely to influence considerably the working conditions of teachers. Find out what you can about the control and working conditions in different types of schools. You will find the reading references at the end of this chapter helpful.

Changing Social Structures and Control of the Schools

School board members, whether in village, town, suburbia, or city, act as links between the school and the social structure of the total school district.[6] More specifically, they link specific *parts* of the social structure. Board members may represent one or more subgroups within the community: business or professional groups, labor organizations, parent-teacher associations, taxpayers' leagues, service clubs, the "old guard," and the "young turks." If one observes the actions of board members during meetings, one sees the sentiments of these subgroups of the community converge upon the board. In a sense board members are "spokesmen" for those individuals and groups who share their position in the socio-economic structure of the school district.

One would therefore expect that as the social structure of the community changes so will school board actions and decisions. Such is the case. Changes in school board membership and policy are interdependent with changes in the social structure of the school district. As groups gain or lose power and influence, that gain or loss is reflected in the school board and in the kind of decisions it makes.

If the generalization about the interdependence of community social structures and school board actions is sound, four corollary assertions may be made:

(1) Changes within the social structure of the community result in changes in school board membership. That is, as social changes take place, new members are elected who more nearly reflect the new social arrangements of the community and the resulting shifts in power.

(2) Changes in the composition of school boards result in changes in interactions among the members.

(3) Changes in interactions among school board members lead to changes in school board policy.

(4) Changes in school board policy result in changes in the educational program of the school.

---

[6] A contrasting view is that board members act not as links to the community but as legitimizers of the goals of the school administration. For a perceptive discussion of this point of view see Norman D. Kerr, "The School Board as an Agency of Legitimation," *Sociology of Education*, Volume 38, No. 1, Fall 1964, pp. 34–59.

Frank W. Lutz presents a case study of a board of education which tends to support these four assertions.[7] What makes Lutz's study unique is that he was himself a member of the board of education that he studied. Because of the "insider" view presented in this investigation, we shall quote directly from Lutz's account of his observations as a participant-observer on a school board in a community in which changes in the social structure were reflected in school board interaction and policy making.

Several points in Lutz's case study are worth noting. (1) Robertsdale is changing from a town to a suburban community; (2) New power groups are arising as a result of this change and are challenging the older "as is" groups; (3) Divisions within the community are reflected in the divisions within the board of education; (4) Prentice, the name which Lutz uses for himself in his study, owes his election to new power groups; (5) Prentice mobilizes these new groups in the social structure to get other sympathetic board members elected, which results in his own election as president of the board; (6) The superintendent of schools, as much as board members, is involved in the struggle for control.

Let us turn now to Lutz's own account:

"On April 5, 1960, I was elected to a school board. This provided an opportunity for a participant-observer field study of the mobilization of social power affecting school board policy and decision making. My code name in this study is Mr. Prentice, thirty-one years of age, public school teacher and resident of the new community of Bluffview which is located in the Robertsdale School District in Mid West County, U.S.A. . . .

"I was an active member of the community, and an elected member of the school board. My role as a researcher was completely hidden from all members of the community, the school board and the school staff. In other words, I was a hidden participant-observer in the strictest sense. While such a role offers the disadvantage of prohibiting usual methods of data collection such as the questionnaire and formal interview, it opens to the researcher areas of information which are guarded from the 'outsider's' view since the researcher is a member of the 'inner-circle.' Examples of this type of information appear in the excerpts from my diary. . . .

[7] Frank W. Lutz, "Power Systems in School Districts: A Study of Interactions and Sentiments in a School Board's Policy Making," Presented at the Annual Meeting of the American Educational Research Association, Chicago, February 14, 1963. (Mimeographed)

"The Robertsdale School District. The Robertsdale School District was an old district which was originally divided into separate rural districts. Through a series of annexations and reorganizations it had become one of the largest districts in Mid West County. At the time of the study, the superintendent had held office for more than twenty years. About 1950, the suburban trend began in the school district, reaching a peak between 1955 and 1960. Most of the developments were superior to the majority of the housing in the Robertsdale district and quickly changed the percentage of first class housing in the district. As one might expect, the people moving into the new areas had different expectations of public education than did the old residents of Robertsdale. The new residents began to show some dissatisfaction with the level of education in the schools. Prentice was elected largely because of this dissatisfaction. . . .

"Data from the Diary. Before presenting some excerpts from my diary, it would be well to have in mind the general composition of the school board and the top administrative staff. Figure 17-3 shows the school board divided into two informal groups. The two groups were apparent throughout the study. Mr. Joyce, the superintendent, was considered as a member of the 'As Is' group.

'As Is' Group	'Show Me' Group
Mr. Dyke—secretary	Mr. Prentice—member
Mr. Scott—member	Mr. Clubb—vice-president
Mr. Mahan—president	Mr. Wilke—treasurer

Fig. 17-3 General group division of Robertsdale school board as noted in Prentice's diary.

"The following are quotes from my diary of personal interactions concerning school district business. These are characteristic of the interactions reported in the diary and are selected as such. Remember that my code name in the diary is Prentice. . . .

"June 1, 1960

As the meeting adjourned, all board members still in attendance and Joyce walked out of the Board Room (which was in the Superintendent's office) and turned left down the corridor toward the main exit of the high school. The 1960 graduating class picture, which had recently been placed on the wall, caught Wilke's eye and he stood looking at it. Prentice walked up and a few complimentary remarks were passed about the picture. Joyce had also stopped and was in conversation. Meanwhile Mahan, Scott, and Dyke passed the three looking at the picture, went by the exit and into the high school principal's office which was then vacant. As they passed, Mahan said, 'Good-night,' to Wilke and Prentice. Joyce turned away from the picture, leaving Wilke and Prentice. Dyke stopped momentarily as Joyce, Mahan and Scott entered the principal's office. Mahan returned to the corridor, looked at Dyke and again said, 'Good-night,' to Wilke and Prentice. Dyke left the picture and entered the office saying, 'Good-night,' and leaving Wilke and Prentice alone in the hall.

"As the two left the building, Wilke commented to Prentice, 'I guess you see they're having an after-the-board meeting to decide what to do. That's probably where they decided to name the junior high.' (This comment refers to a sharp controversy during which none of the 'Show Me' group remembered voting to name a new junior high in honor of the Superintendent, but all of the 'As Is' remembered the decision. There was no record in the minutes, but the name was already on the building.)

"Prentice continued to seek information from residents of long standing about the School District which would better enable him to understand the present School Board and the School District. . . . He had a conversation with Mrs. Franz, one of the people who had the meeting which had initiated Prentice's candidacy for the School Board. Prentice mentioned to Mrs. Franz that he understood that Joyce was a member of the Baptist Church in the community. Mrs. Franz replied, 'Goes to the church!' Mrs. Franz said that Joyce was a deacon and had a good deal to say about the running of the church. She recalled that Joyce had replaced the former superintendent after the former superintendent had an auto accident which indicated he had been drinking. Mrs. Franz verified Troy's statement that Robert Little was on the School Board when Joyce was first hired and that the two were close friends.

"Special Meeting, July 14, 1961

Clubb, as of his telephone conversation with Prentice, brought up Chris' employment during the routine business of approving the inclusion of the names of teachers already employed according to the minutes. Joyce claimed that not only had the Board voted to hire Chris, but had seen his credentials. Prentice broke in, 'I didn't see any credentials or vote to employ anybody. I think Mr. Chris is a good man and we should take the correct formal action.' Immediately Dyke, Mahan and Scott agreed with Joyce that they remembered the entire proceeding, while Clubb, Wilke and Prentice claimed they knew nothing before Chris was presented as employed. Prentice said to Dyke, 'If we acted on his employment, find it in the minutes, I can't.' Dyke started to look back. Joyce told him not to look but just to make another motion.

"Dyke insisted that he could find it. Finally he admitted, 'I can't find it, but I know it's there!' Clubb replied, 'Why isn't it in the minutes then?' With no further comment, Scott moved the Board hire Chris, and Clubb seconded the motion. The motion passed unanimously. (An examination of the official minutes proved that no action had been taken to hire Chris prior to this meeting.)

"The formal minutes . . . make this item look like an instance of full agreement among Board members. The minutes officially state:

" 'Motion made by Mr. Scott and seconded by Mr. Clubb that Mr. Chris' employment be made a matter of record, his salary. . . . Ayes; Mahan, Clubb, Dyke, Wilke, Scott, and Prentice.'

"Regular Meeting, September 8, 1960

Prentice made the following motion:

" '. . . that the Board request the teachers' association to form a salary study committee composed of three elementary teachers, three secondary teachers and one principal to develop a schedule and that they submit same to Board for their consideration no later than the regular November meeting. Further, that our educational plan be submitted to this Board by the Superintendent after consultation with his principals no later than our regular December meeting. That this plan include any additional curriculum or teaching aids which the group feels sound. Further, that the principals be present to present their reasons why any additions should be implemented.'

"There was considerable discussion regarding the motion without anyone seconding it. Clubb finally asked if there was a second, saying he couldn't second it as he didn't understand it, and Dyke said he wouldn't second it as he didn't believe there was a necessity for a teachers' association salary study committee because the teachers had in fact approved the salary schedule when they signed their contracts in the spring. He stated that anyone who didn't like the schedule could have gone somewhere else.

"At this point Prentice angrily replied to Dyke, 'You wouldn't have the nerve to stand before the teachers' association or the PTA and say what you just said, "That if teachers didn't like our salary schedule they could get out!" ' Dyke said, 'I didn't say that and if you say I did I'll sue you for libel.' Prentice replied, 'I know exactly what you said . . . and I'll repeat it any place I please. I'm not the one who's known for misquoting other members of this board.' The discussion was abruptly dropped here and the minutes recorded. . . .

" 'The motion lost for want of a second. . . .'

"Prentice said he would continue to make these motions . . . until they passed. . . . He also noted privately that he felt they (the 'As Is' group) could not afford to continue to oppose them in the light of public sentiment, particularly if visitors were to increase in number at Board meetings.

"On September 19th, Prentice received a call from Mr. Lindzey, president of Elm Grove PTA. He had heard of Prentice's lack of backing for his motions. . . . He asked what he could do to help. Prentice said that he felt increased attendance at Board meetings by members of the PTA would be a great help. Lindzey agreed to do what he could.

"Regular Board Meeting, October 13, 1960

All members were present and the meeting was held in the library instead of the regular room, due to the large number of visitors present. This was the first meeting held here owing to an overflow of visitors so far as Prentice was aware.

"Two questions came up regarding finances and in both areas Wilke defended Joyce. Prentice felt this was because Wilke was Board treasurer and thought he was attacked when some question arose.

"Just before adjournment two motions were presented by Prentice, one regarding the submission of an educational plan by the Superintendent, the other regarding the distribution of a summary of Board minutes to building principals. Both of these motions had been made at the September meeting and both failed for lack of a second. (This time both passed unanimously before the visitors at the open meeting. The minutes do not indicate this, however. The motion regarding the educational plan appears in the minutes of the executive session which followed, and there is no record of the motion regarding the summary of Board minutes.) Prentice then asked to be allowed to make a motion regarding salary schedule, but the chairman ruled that it should be discussed in the executive session to follow.

"Executive Session, October 13, 1960

Prentice stated that he felt he had made a mistake by not making his motion regarding the committee before the open session as he had planned. There was a good deal of discussion and Prentice made a motion that the teachers' association be asked to form a salary study committee and report to the Board at the December meeting.

"During the discussion it was apparent that Prentice had at least three votes for the motion. Dyke then indicated that he would vote for the motion. He said that regardless of what the teachers asked for he would go along with their request. He added that he felt their request would be a ridiculously high salary schedule which would require a tax higher than the District would support. He stated that, regardless of this, he would support their request and the District would have to operate without a tax levy, for the people would never vote the levy necessary to implement what the teachers would request. At this point Dyke seemed very bitter and resentful.

"The motion carried with Prentice, Clubb and Wilke voting for; Scott voting against; and Mahan, who said nothing was wrong with the motion as he saw it but nothing good about it, abstaining. In spite of Dyke's proclamation that he would vote for it, he also chose to abstain."

Lutz's account is further illuminated in a description of the way the community divided itself in support of the "As Is" and "Show Me" groups. Figure 17-4 shows that in 1960 the division within the community was already apparent. Notice that some groups were at that time divided in their loyalties, for example, the PTA and the principals.

Lutz's evidence indicates a constant increase in power of those elements in the social structure which supported the "Show Me" group and education in general. In April 1961, Prentice was elected president of the board, after only two years, indicating the rapidity with which the new groups mobilized and exerted their power. In the 1962 election the PTA members organized a quasiformal organization which worked with Prentice to elect two new men to the board who

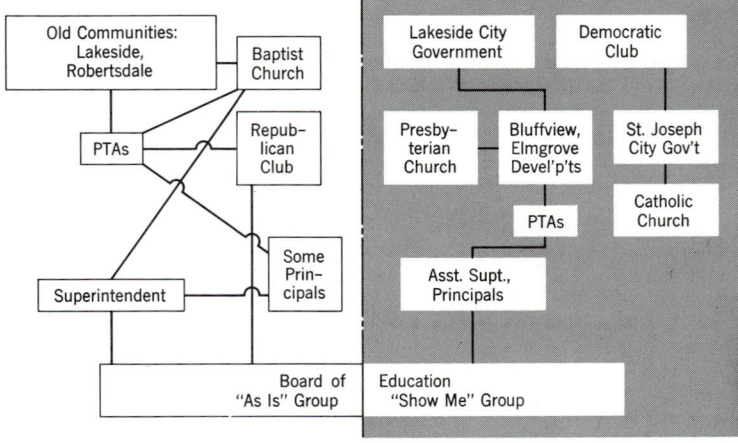

Fig. 17-4

were specifically selected by leaders and supporters of the "Show Me" point of view. In addition, those parents who supported the "Show Me" subgroup on the board continued to support, without exception, every tax levy and bond issue in the school district.

9. Do you think Robertsdale may have been a better place to teach after Prentice and his group gained control of the board of education? Why do you answer as you do?

10. Assume that you are interested in teaching in a particular school district and want to know about the nature of the controls under which the school operates. What kinds of information would you seek, and from whom?

11. What effect do you think the struggle for control of the Robertsdale board had on the classroom teachers? How do you think they may have reacted to the struggle? How do you think they *should* have reacted?

In this chapter we examined the nature of control in school districts and saw how this control expresses itself in different types of communities and under changing social conditions. The exercise of such control over educational decision making leads us to a consideration of the politics of education in Chapter 18.

REFERENCES

Paperbacks

American Education—A National Failure. Hyman G. Rickover. (Orig.) (D122) Dutton Paperbacks, E. P. Dutton and Co., 201 Park Ave. South, New York ($1.95).

Can America Loose Her Free Public Schools? Virgil M. Rogers. (Orig.) Syracuse University Press, University Station, Syracuse, N. Y. ($1.00).

Community and Power. The Quest for Community. Robert A. Nisbet. (91) Galaxy Books, Oxford University Press, 417 Fifth Ave., New York ($1.75).

Crucial Issues in Education. Ehlers and Lee. (3rd Ed.) Holt, Rinehart and Winston, 383 Madison Ave., New York ($3.25).

Educating the Expert Society. Burton R. Clark. (Orig.) Chandler Publishing Co., 124 Spear St., San Francisco, Calif. ($2.75).

Education and Democratic Ideals. Gordon C. Lee. (Orig.) Harcourt, Brace and World, 757 Third Ave., New York (including Harbrace Books) ($1.95).

Education and Liberty. James Bryant Conant. (V506) Random House, 457 Madison Ave., New York ($1.45).

Education and the Cult of Efficiency: A Study of the Social Forces That Have Shaped the Administration of the Public School. Raymond E. Callahan. (P149) Phoenix Books, University of Chicago Press, 5750 Ellis Ave., Chicago, Ill. ($2.25).

Education as Power. Theodore Brameld. Holt, Rinehart and Winston, 383 Madison Ave., New York ($1.75).

Educational Issues in a Changing Society (2nd Rev. Ed., Orig.) August Kerber and Wilfred Smith, Editors. (WB3) Wayne State University Press, 5980 Cass, Detroit, Mich. ($3.95).

Future of Public Education. Myron Lieberman. (P94) Phoenix Books, University of Chicago Press, 5750 Ellis Ave., Chicago, Ill. ($1.50).

Sociology of Teaching. Willard Waller. Science Editions Paperbacks, John Wiley and Sons, 605 Third Ave., New York ($1.95).

Vital Issues in American Education. Alice and Lester Crow. (Orig.) (QM1008) Bantam Books, 271 Madison Ave., New York ($1.25).

Books

Brookover, Wilbur B., and David Gottlieb, *A Sociology of Education,* Second Edition. New York: American Book Co., 1964, pp. 99–127. Chapter 5, "The Social Control of Education," suggests that schools at all levels of society are integral parts of the total social system and are subject to some form of control.

Burkhead, Jesse, *Public School Finance, Economics and Policies.* Syracuse, N. Y.: Syracuse University Press, 1964. Educational decisions are influenced by societal attitudes and values.

Campbell, Ronald F., and John A. Ramseyer, *School-Community Relationships.* Boston: Allyn and Bacon, 1955. The authors examine the meaning of citizen participation in school affairs.

Gross, Neal, *Who Runs Our Schools?* New York: John Wiley and Sons, 1958. A provocative study investigating the pressures that operate on school boards and the schools.

Martin, Roscoe C., *Government and the Suburban School.* Syracuse, N. Y.: Syracuse University Press, 1962. The book describes the environment of suburban education, its school, and government. Chapter IV contrasts the suburban and city school.

Periodicals

Bunzel, John H., "Pressure Groups in Politics and Education," *The National Elementary Principal,* Vol. 43, No. 3, January 1964, pp. 12–16. The author feels that our society is pluralistic and that the community's educational program is not just a reflection of the electoral vote.

Charters, W. W., Jr., "Social Class Analysis and the Control of Public Education," *Harvard Educational Review,* Vol. XXIII, No. 4, Fall 1953, pp. 268–283. Charters analyzes the evidence for the dominant class control of the school.

Lowe, William T., "Who Joins Which Teachers' Group?," *Teachers College Record,* Vol. 66, No. 7, April 1965, pp. 614–619. A sample survey of the members of three teacher groups showed no difference in educational level and values.

Lutz, Frank W., "Power Structure Theory and the School Board Decision Making Process," *Educational Theory,* Vol. XV, No. 1, January 1965, pp. 19–25. Lutz discusses the multidimensional character of school board decision making.

Steffensen, James P., "Board-Staff Negotiations," *School Life,* Vol. 47, No. 1, October 1964, pp. 6–8. An appraisal of areas of conflict between school board and teaching staff.

Wilson, Charles H., "The Superintendent's Many Publics," *Saturday Review,* Vol. XLIV, No. 42, October 21, 1961, pp. 49–51. Wilson thinks the superintendent is basically a politician. His public includes the professional staff, the board, and the many diverse elements that compose the community.

18

The Politics
of Education

"Education is one of the most thoroughly political enterprises in American life—or for that matter in the life of any society."

JESSE BURKHEAD

What does education have to do with politics? Or politics with education? The very thought of considering the two together is repulsive to some people. The word "politics" is considered by many to be "bad" whereas "education" is regarded as "good." If politics and education are mixed, it is education which suffers, not politics. It is better, therefore, the argument runs, to "keep education out of politics." Yet the struggle for the control of the schools which we discussed in Chapter 17 is a highly political struggle, and the conduct of public education is a political enterprise. In this chapter, then, we shall examine the politics of education and the problems which arise from education's political nature.

Let us see how education and politics are intertwined. As Vincent Ostrom pointed out, "education is an enterprise in learning; politics [is] an enterprise in decision-making and social control."[1] It follows, then, that persons who are directly or indirectly engaged in educational decision making are involved in political activity; they are exercising social control by means of education. To be sure, educational decision makers do not carry political party labels, but the education process is frequently most political when it is called "nonpartisan" and "nonpolitical."[2]

[1] Vincent Ostrom, "Education and Politics," Nelson B. Henry (Ed.), *Social Forces Influencing American Education*, Part II, Chicago, University of Chicago Press, 1961, p. 8.

[2] For a series of excellent papers see *The Politics of Education in the Local Community*, Robert S. Cahill and Stephen P. Hencley (Eds.), Danville, Illinois, The Interstate Printers and Publishers, Inc., 1964.

Politics and education are intertwined in other ways. Public education is a governmental function, a part of national, state, and local government. It is governed by formal laws, and its monies are derived from the power of the state to tax, borrow, and spend.

Further, school board members are usually elected officials, and teachers are public employees. Although school board elections are usually nonpartisan in the sense that candidates shun political party labels, we shall see presently that school board elections are deeply political. As Howard Dean points out, when school boards "assemble to do business, they function as political institutions, serving as the legislative bodies to establish the basic policies for their districts." [3] Nor are students exempt from the political aspects of education. Attendance at school is not a matter of free choice but is a duty imposed by the state exercising its power to make decisions in the area of education. [4]

In this chapter we are particularly interested in the decision-making and control aspects of the politics of education and the problems that arise therein. Who actually makes decisions in public education? How are they made? And who attempts to influence these decisions and how?

Major Political Forces in Education

The persons and groups who figure prominently in the politics of education are: citizens, teachers, boards of education, state agencies, special interest groups, and national agencies.

Citizen participation in the politics of the schools. Citizen control of the schools may be of either the formal or informal type. The citizens of the Fairlawn and Urbandale communities were exercising informal control over the schools in the integration dispute. In this section our interest is in the formal political means available to citizens to influence the operations of the schools.

Citizens of most school districts exercise two crucial controls: (1) they elect members of the board of education, and (2) they vote on money propositions for the schools. The citizens' opportunity to influence school financing usually takes two forms. First, each year the superintendent of schools must prepare and recommend to the board

[3] Howard Dean, "The Political Setting of American Education," Dan Cooper (Ed.), *The Social Sciences View School Administration*, Englewood Cliffs, New Jersey, Prentice-Hall, Inc., 1965, p. 217.

[4] Citizenship training in the schools is another important aspect of the politics of education. Although the school's role in civic training does not fall within the purposes of this chapter, an informative discussion of it will be found in Robert D. Hess and David Easton, "The Role of the Elementary School in Political Socialization," *The School Review*, Volume 70, No. 3, Autumn 1962, pp. 257–265.

of education an annual operating budget. The operating budget covers all operating expenses such as salaries, supplies, and maintenance. Some boards of education hold public hearings on the school budget, at which time citizens may express their views. Even though the board may not schedule public hearings, the budget is discussed at regular meetings of the board where citizens may make their opinions known. Citizens exercise the second type of financial control over the schools through the ballot. Appropriations for the schools beyond those of operations, for example, for building, *or* those for operating funds beyond those provided by regular school tax sources, must be approved by a vote of the people.

The following official notice of a school election appeared in a local newspaper. Boards of education are required by law to publish such notices prior to each school election. Note that this advertisement informs citizens of the two opportunities to influence the schools. The voters will select one of three candidates to fill a vacancy on the board of education and will vote on a proposition to increase their taxes by five-tenths of 1 percent of assessed valuation "for the purpose of providing additional funds for operating expenses."

ANNUAL SCHOOL ELECTION [5]

Notice of Annual Election of the Qualified Electors of

Williamston Community Schools School District

Ingham County

To Be Held June 14, 1965

To The Qualified Electors Of Said School District: Please Take Notice that the Annual Election of the qualified electors of said School District will be held in the Junior High School Building, 201 School Street, in the City of Williamston, on Monday, June 14, 1965.

The Polls Of Election Will Open At 7:00 O'Clock A.M., And Close At 8:00 O'Clock P.M., Eastern Standard Time.

At said annual election there will be elected one (1) member to the Board of Education of said district for full term of four (4) years, ending in 1969.

The Following Persons Have Been Nominated To Fill Such Vacancy:

Oliver Light
Harold Lowell
George Strother

Take Further Notice That the following proposition will be submitted to the vote of the electors qualified to vote thereon at said annual election:

[5] Adapted from *The Meridian News*, Williamston, Michigan, June 9, 1965, p. 14.

Shall the limitation on the total amount of taxes which may be assessed against all property in Williamston Community Schools School District be increased by five-tenths of one per cent (0.5%) (5 mills) of the assessed valuation, as equalized, of all property in said school district for a period of five (5) years, from 1965 to 1969, both inclusive, for the purpose of providing additional funds for operating expenses? Each person voting to elect a member to the Board of Education and on the above proposition must be a citizen of the United States, have attained the age of 21 years, and have resided in the State six months and in the School District 30 days next preceding the election.

Only persons registered as electors in the city or township in which they reside are eligible to vote.

This Notice is given by order of the Board of Education of Williamston Community Schools School District, Ingham County.

Wendell H. Darrow
Secretary, Board of Education

In the election of school board members and the approval of financial support American citizens exercise their most direct, formal control over the schools.

1. Opinion seems to be divided among teachers about how active they should be in school board elections. Some teachers feel it is wrong for them to campaign actively either for or against their own potential "employers." Others disagree, saying that both as citizens and teachers who want board members who are sympathetic to their cause, they must be politically active in school board elections. Find out what you can about the pros and cons of teacher participation in school board campaigns.

Teachers and the politics of education. "We struck because the school board wouldn't listen to us," explained a teacher. "The issue involved everything from how many kids are put in a classroom and how we spend money in shop training to what hours varsity athletes go for practice. We feel we are more qualified than the school board to say what schools need because we teach there every school day."

This teacher is expressing the new and growing militancy of American teachers and their increasing demands for a greater voice in the management of schools.[6] Everywhere there is a rising feeling among teachers that because they do work in the schools "every school day," they are "more qualified than board members to say what the school needs." What we are witnessing is the growing political power of teachers and their use of that power to demand greater participation

[6] For two case studies of "teachers on the march" in New York and Utah, see John Scanlon, "Strikes, Sanctions, and the Schools," *Saturday Review,* Volume 46, No. 42, October 1963, pp. 51–55, 70–74.

in school decisions. This indicates a shift in the historic control of schools from lay to professional leadership.

Teachers have long wielded informal influence over school policy. We now are seeing the teachers' influence formalized as part of the regular policy-making process of the schools. As Myron Lieberman comments: "No aspect of education is changing more rapidly than that of employer-employee relations. Here we are witnessing a veritable revolution whose consequences are only dimly understood even by those chiefly involved in it." [7]

No longer content to negotiate their salary and working conditions on an individual basis, teachers are swiftly banding together and making strong organized efforts to back up their demands. It is estimated that 25 percent of the nation's teachers now have their contracts negotiated by teachers' organizations. Five years ago only 5 percent of the teachers were represented by organizations in their negotiations with school boards. This aggressive drive of teachers for control over the conditions under which they teach will most likely accelerate in the future.

What effect on school boards does this new militancy have? The results are clearly favorable to the teachers. Teachers' salaries and fringe benefits are climbing at unprecedented rates, and in many cases the improvements in contracts can be traced directly to the united front presented by teachers. In a Western school district the board of education agreed to teachers' demands after a threat of a boycott of teaching jobs in its district.[8] The settlement provided salary increases ranging up to 15 percent of current pay. In a Midwestern metropolis teachers won a salary raise of up to 10 percent. This raise followed an average 10 percent increase won the previous year after teachers boycotted classes at the beginning of the year to back up their demands.

Teachers' demands have not been confined to salary increases; they have also pushed for fringe benefits. In a Midwest industrial city teachers received a fully paid family medical and hospital insurance policy plus a $3,000 life-insurance policy. In a Southern school district teachers with a master's degree recently won a half-pay study leave after three years in the system. California teachers, under a provision won through united efforts, can take accumulated sick leave with them when they transfer to other schools in the state.

[7] Myron Lieberman, "Who Speaks for the Teachers," *Saturday Review,* Volume XLVIII, No. 25, June 19, 1965, p. 64.

[8] For this and the following examples the author is indebted to Richard R. Leger, "Militant Educators," *The Wall Street Journal,* Volume XLV, No. 169, Monday, June 14, 1965, pp. 1, 13.

The teachers' increasing control in the school is expressed in their ability to improve salaries, fringe benefits, and working conditions. Their power is seen even better in the major bids which teachers are making for a larger voice in school policy. One of the nation's ten largest school systems has agreed to a once-a-month "professional consultation" period with teacher groups in each school. Under this agreement teachers are guaranteed an audience with their school principal to discuss such matters as the quality of teacher supplies, the library hours, and how teachers are backed up by the principal in student discipline cases. It would be reasonable to assume that examples such as this will lead rapidly to other formal agreements for giving teachers direct participation in school policy making.

In spite of the growing militancy of teachers, there is sharply divided opinion among them about how this militancy should be expressed. A great many of the nation's teachers abhor the idea of a strike. Most of these teachers belong to the largest teachers' organization, the 950,000 member National Education Association, which looks upon strikes as "unprofessional." [9] The NEA, which considers itself a professional society rather than a union, prefers to bring pressure on school systems by applying "sanctions." The ultimate sanction is that all members refuse to sign a contract with the school district in question. For example, the NEA placed a sanction against the whole state of Oklahoma, in which the NEA charged that "sub-minimal" working conditions existed in the state and offered to find jobs elsewhere for Oklahoma's 22,000 teachers.[10]

In contrast, the American Federation of Teachers, a small union which has demonstrated its effectiveness in several major cities, advocates the strike as the ultimate weapon, claiming that the strike leaves the school system more intact and gets results more quickly than the sanction.[11]

Not only are teachers strengthening their power in the control of the schools through sanctions and strikes; state legislation is also reinforcing them. As of this writing the Washington, Oregon, New Jer-

[9] For the NEA's position, see "Professional Negotiation," *NEA Journal*, Volume 51, No. 8, November 1962, pp. 28–30.

[10] See *Oklahoma, A State-Wide Study of Conditions Detrimental to an Effective Public Education Program*, Washington, D. C., National Education Association, 1965.

[11] Lindley Stiles describes the differences between the NEA and the AFT, and compares both of them to a foreign teachers' organization, the Egyptian Teacher Syndicate, in "Ideas from Abroad: For Winning Teacher Loyalty," *Phi Delta Kappan*, Volume 45, No. 6, March 1964, pp. 278–282. For a survey of "Who Joins Which Teachers Group," see the article by William T. Lowe in *Teachers College Record*, Volume 66, No. 7, April 1965, pp. 614–619.

sey, and Minnesota legislatures have passed bills, the first of their kind, requiring school boards to negotiate with associations representing the majority of teachers. The Michigan State Board of Education has recommended that teachers be given the right to strike. Clearly teachers are increasing their control and, as we indicated above, the schools of the future will surely feel greater professional control than in the past.

2. Myron Lieberman comments: "The present freedom of school boards to refuse to recognize or to negotiate with a majority organization of teachers is indefensible from almost any standpoint, except perhaps that of employers who prefer to deal with weak employee organizations or none at all." [12] Do you agree or disagree with this comment? Why?

School board control of the schools. Ninety-five percent of the school districts in America are operated by school boards whose members are elected by a direct vote of citizens of the district. Boards usually consist of five to nine members. Large city boards may have eleven or more members. Most members are elected on a nonpartisan ballot at an election held at a time other than that of political elections.

Although school board elections do not usually stir up as much voter interest as political elections, they can have the features associated with political campaigns: promotion and advertising, behind the scenes organizing by the candidate's friends, the declaration of "issues," and a "get-out-the-vote" drive. Here, for example, is the advertisement of a candidate for a local school board.

VOTERS OF MERIDIAN [13]

Do you want to:

Lighten your tax burden?

Take greater advantage of Federal and State Funds?

Develop a better curriculum for Meridian's college-bound students?

Reduce teacher turnover?

VOTE FOR

JOHN WALTON

University Graduate

5 years chief accountant—Liberal Arts College

Presently comptroller Education Association state headquarters

MERIDIAN BETTER SCHOOLS COMMITTEE

[12] Myron Lieberman, *op. cit.*, p. 65.

[13] Adapted from *The Meridian News*, Williamston, Michigan, Volume 8, No. 11, June 9, 1965, p. 6.

What does this advertisement tell us about the legal control of American public education? A perceptive foreign visitor who knew nothing at all about the history of our schools would find this piece of campaign promotion very informative. It would tell him, for example, that the control of our schools is local. The candidate is appealing for the support of the voters of a single community. It would indicate to him that financial support from the schools comes from local taxes, with other support available from state and federal governments. This ad indicates that school board members must be sensitive to the wants of local parents and citizens. For example, the candidate has defined issues which he thinks will appeal to local residents: taxes, better education for college-bound students, and teacher turnover. The advertisement implies that candidates should be able to demonstrate special qualifications to serve by indicating educational achievements and connections. Finally, the advertisement suggests that school board members may be indebted for their election to special interest groups, in this case the "Meridian Better Schools Committee."

What happens after school board members are elected? How they conduct their business and arrive at decisions is a matter of crucial concern both to teachers and administrators. Little systematic study has been directed toward an examination of the dynamics of school board decision-making processes and the impact of these processes on the role of the teacher and administrator. However, Donald J. McCarty has reported a helpful investigation of school board decision making in seven communities in Illinois and Wisconsin.[14] The seven communities included a single-industry, attractive village of 500 homes, an economically diversified city with a population of approximately 700,000, a heavily industrialized city of 60,000 residents, a residential suburb catering to young mobile executives, a "Gold-Coast" suburb serving an elite clientele, a mature residential suburb with a sprinkling of lower-class ethnic groups, and a farm village which becomes a tourist attraction in the summer.

All 52 of the board members interviewed represented an advantaged economic position. Thirty had yearly incomes in excess of $10,-000; 16 earned over $15,000 annually. Their educational level was also high. Thirty-four had attended college and 17 had taken some graduate or professional training. Thirty-nine of the board members were technicians, proprietors, executives, or professionals. McCarty asked board

---

[14] Donald J. McCarty, "Board Types and Their Effect on the Role of the Administrator," A paper prepared for the annual meeting of the American Educational Research Association held at Chicago, February 13–15, 1963. (Mimeographed)

members this question: "If you have difficulty in reaching agreement on issues, how are these differences ironed out?" From the resulting descriptions the investigator identified three discernible types of boards: the "rationale," the "factional," and the "dominated" board.

The *rationale* board solves its problems by considering a wide range of alternatives and selecting the most appropriate one to meet the purposes of the school board. Disagreements that arise are mediated by endless discussion which ultimately terminates in group acceptance of the result. The rationale board is composed of individuals who resemble one another both socially and economically. The members enjoy their association; they act as a committee of peers. Members are usually asked to run for the board by a community caucus; the "office seeks the man" concept prevails.

3. Above we described briefly the seven communities in which this investigation took place. In which of the communities do you think "rationale" boards would be found? Why?

The *factional* board uses the power of the majority vote to solve its complex issues. The coalition which can muster the necessary votes makes the decision. Voting is more important than discussion in board meetings and the majority faction always wins. The differences within the board arise from various sources: religious and ethnic differences, rural-urban conflicts, labor-management ideologies, and social-class cleavages. The factional board is socially heterogeneous. Members get on the board with the aid of special interest groups to whom they feel an obligation after being elected.

4. Which of the seven communities are likely to have "factional" boards of education?

The *dominated* board displays a clear hierarchy of superordinate and subordinate relationships. Either one member or an elite group that has economic and social power controls the board's decisions. The subordinate members usually take the advice of the elite group. Relationships within the board are harmonious, since there are clearly defined "leaders" and "followers." New members are usually asked to serve by present members, and the citizens usually ratify at the polls those "nominated" by the leadership group.

5. Which of the seven communities are likeliest to have "dominated" boards of education?
6. Under which type of board would you prefer to teach? Why?

The control of American schools rests legally with local boards of education whose composition reflects the power structure of the school district. These boards are ultimately as good as the citizens of the community want them to be and demand that they be. In this sense communities, generally speaking, get the kinds of boards and schools they deserve.

State politics and the public schools. The Federal Constitution is silent on the subject of education. It does indicate, however, that all powers not specifically assigned to the Federal government by the Constitution are delegated to the states. Education in America is thus a state, rather than a Federal, responsibility. No public school in America exists without state legislative sanction. Most of the individual states, in turn, delegate the responsibility for local education to school boards.

Decision making and control in education at the state level center mostly around the financing of the schools. Fortunately there are two studies which shed light on the state control of education, particularly as it relates to the allocation of resources, in two groups of states in different parts of the country. Jesse Burkhead and his colleagues studied the politics of state aid to education in eight Northeastern states: Maine, New Hampshire, Vermont, Massachusetts, Connecticut, Rhode Island, New York, and New Jersey.[15] Nicholas A. Masters, Robert H. Salisbury, and Thomas H. Eliot studied state politics and the public schools in Missouri, Illinois, and Michigan.[16]

Burkhead found that the politics of state aid to education is surrounded by four historic tensions in the eight Northeastern states: (1) religion, (2) control of the state educational apparatus, (3) localism, and (4) urban-rural rivalries.

In the colonial days, Burkhead points out, religion in education was not an issue, since schools were primarily for religious instruction. However, in the nineteenth century internal Protestant controversies and the influx of Catholic immigrants into the Northeast brought latent tensions to a boiling point. Protestants were split between those who desired and those who feared public support for religious schools. Catholics were unhappy about sending their children to ostensibly nondenominational public schools which actually gave Protestant religious instruction. In 1842 New York passed a law prohibiting the awarding of state school monies to any school in which "any religious sectarian doctrine was being taught, inculcated, or practiced." But the

---

[15] Jesse Burkhead, *Public School Finance*, Syracuse, New York, Syracuse University Press, 1964, pp. 93–128.

[16] Nicholas A. Masters, Robert H. Salisbury, and Thomas H. Eliot, *State Politics and the Public Schools*, New York, Alfred A. Knopf, 1964.

struggle continues. The present attempts of the parochial school interests to devolve some of their costs upon the state are the latest manifestations of a conflict that is more than four generations old and is yet unresolved.

How should the state educational apparatus be set up and who should control it? Should it be in the hands of the governor? A separate board or boards of education? A legislature? A commissioner of education? Or a combination of all of these? New York finds its answer in the Board of Regents, whose members are elected for overlapping terms, which acts as a fourth branch of government. In the other seven northeastern states the state boards of education are appointed by the governor, and the independence of the boards from political pressure is a matter of long-standing tradition.[17]

The struggle between state and local education bodies is common in Northeastern states, as it is almost everywhere in the nation. There is no question about where the ultimate power and authority rests: It rests with the states and not with the local bodies. "This doctrine, however, has been in constant tension with a widely shared and strongly held view that education was in essence a local responsibility, and that educational policy should be determined locally." [18]

Because urban and rural interests frequently see the needs of education differently, much educational history is written around the conflicting concerns of small, reasonably homogeneous communities and larger, highly diversified communities. Widening industrialization and improved transportation are now bringing rural and urban centers together, but the rise of the suburbs brings a new educational power onto the scene.

Friends of education in state officialdom. Burkhead discovered that pro-education interests at the state level can be divided broadly in four groups: the educational academics, usually university professors, fashion in the first instance plans for school aid and form the intellectual core of the movement. Second come the officials in the state government, sometimes leaders in state departments of education, sometimes officials with other responsibilities, who adopt the school course. The third group consists of the professional educators—teachers, superintendents, principals—and their lay supporters, school board members, PTA's and school betterment groups, and the formal coalitions which those interests form. Fourth, there are the "surprise" actors, individuals and associations engaged in pursuits not normally aligned

[17] Burkhead, *op. cit.,* p. 99.
[18] *Ibid.,* p. 100.

with public schools but who for numerous and often subtle reasons make common cause with the school men.[19]

7. If education has its supporters it also has its opposition. In his article, "The Politics of Education," [20] Wallace S. Sayre lists these as forces opposing the schools: tax sensitive business groups, the spokesmen for rural localism, and conservative leaders in the legislative and executive branches of state government. Sayre also asserts that educators are ill-equipped to participate effectively in the political process that is necessary to resolve the extraordinarily intricate conflicts of interests between the supporters and opponents of education. Do you tend to agree or disagree?

State education politics is not restricted to the inner group of academics, state education officials, and professional politicians. Another set of actors performs the role of uniting the education professionals in the capital with teachers and administrators at the local level and with the public at large. The professional education associations of teachers, superintendents, principals, and other education specialists have staffs which lobby in the capitols and keep the membership alerted to legislative action and how that action will influence their interests. As Burkhead points out, for the Northeastern states "the more professionally oriented associations claim by far the majority of teachers as members, around 90 percent. They have professional staffs, at least an executive director and a research (figure gathering) person, and are active at their respective state houses. Minimum salary laws, teacher retirement plans, and teacher dismissal laws occupy the attention of professional associations year in and year out. So does the publication of journals, the holding of conventions, and workshops, and the organization of committees." [21]

8. State educational associations are a major force in the politics of education. For an account of how the members of one state association helped to defeat a governor whom they regarded as unfriendly to education, read Mitchell Davis' article, "How Kentucky Teachers Won at Politics." [22] Active participation of the Kentucky education association and local teachers who informed the public about the issues helped to determine the outcome. As you read this article ask yourself this question: What does this account indicate about the changing political role and power of teachers?

[19] *Ibid.,* pp. 103–104.
[20] Wallace S. Sayre, "The Politics of Education," *The Teachers College Record,* Volume 65, No. 2, November 1963, pp. 178–183.
[21] Burkhead, *op. cit.,* p. 110.
[22] *Phi Delta Kappan,* Volume XCV, No. 1, October 1963, pp. 25–30.

9. Find out what you can about the state education associations which are active in your state. How do they work in the capital to influence legislative action favorable to the schools?

All of these groups help to determine how and by whom power in education is exercised in the states. One thing seems very clear from the two studies cited: Education is very much a part of the political fabric of the states and its welfare must be won within the give and take of these political forces. As Masters, Salisbury, and Eliot conclude in their study, *State Politics and the Public Schools*, in Missouri, Illinois, and Michigan: "Our experience with three Midwestern states reveals that the political issues which questions of public school policy generate become entangled in varying degrees with the many processes and patterns of conflict and resolution in the total state political system." [23]

Special interest groups and the control of the schools. We indicated how the public has a direct say in the control of the schools through electing school board members and through voting on financial propositions. We saw, too, in the examples of Fairlawn and Urbandale, how citizens can exert informal though direct pressure on schools.

Citizens also exert *indirect* pressure on the schools through special interest groups. Consider, for example, the education director of the local chamber of commerce who calls on the superintendent of schools to discuss the "wonderful educational materials developed by the United States Chamber of Commerce for economics and social studies teachers." The education director points out that "with so much loose thinking these days about our free enterprise system the Chamber thought it would be a good idea to make sure that the students in the school get the facts about our American economic system." He has samples of the materials with him. They are attractively prepared and reflect considerable research and expenditure. "What I'd like to do," the visitor explains, "is to put these materials in the hands of the high school social studies teachers and if they think they can use them I can get enough copies for all their students."

This visitor is representative of the many special interest groups which have "free and inexpensive" materials for the schools or who seek by other means to exert some control over the schools.

Who precisely are the special interest groups who exert pressure on the schools? In this study of *Who Runs the Schools?*, Neal Gross reported 19 individuals or groups which exerted pressure of some

[23] Masters, Salisbury, and Eliot, *op. cit.*, pp. 278–279.

type on superintendents and school board members in schools in the State of Massachusetts.[24] Gross' list follows:

PERCENTAGE OF SUPERINTENDENTS AND SCHOOL BOARD MEMBERS WHO SAID THEY WERE EXPOSED TO PRESSURES FROM THE SPECIFIED INDIVIDUALS AND GROUPS

	Superin- tendents ($N = 105$)	School Board Members ($N = 508$)
1. Parents or PTA	92	74
2. Individual school board members	75	51
3. Teachers	65	44
4. Taxpayers' association	49	31
5. Town finance committee or city council	48	38
6. Politicians	46	29
7. Business or commercial organizations	45	19
8. Individuals influential for economic reasons	44	25
9. Personal friends	37	37
10. The press	36	19
11. Old-line families	30	26
12. Church or religious groups	28	18
13. Veterans organizations	27	10
14. Labor unions	27	5
15. Chamber of commerce	23	5
16. Service clubs	20	11
17. Fraternal organizations	13	9
18. Farm organizations	12	4
19. Welfare organizations	3	1

Do you think that some of the pressures exerted by these individuals or groups might be "good," while others might be "bad"? Which pressures would you rate as "good"? Which as "bad"? Why do you classify them as you do?

Notice the individuals and organizations which put most frequent pressure on the schools. Since schools function to educate children it is probably not surprising that parents and the PTA constitute the most frequent source of pressure on the schools—in fact, more frequent than individual school board members who are second on the list. It may be surprising to some to see that teachers are listed as the third most frequent source of pressure on superintendents and school board members. Yet this finding is not startling in view of the growing in-

[24] Neal Gross, *Who Runs the Schools?*, New York, John Wiley and Sons, Inc., 1958, p. 50.

fluence of teachers in school operations and decisions. Taxpayers' associations exert the fourth most frequent pressure, reflecting the burden which schools place on local taxpayers and their response to this burden. The next two sources of pressure, the town finance committee or city council, and the politicians, probably reflect the closeness of boards of education to other local governmental bodies and their competition for the taxpayer's dollar.

10. Select an organization which falls within one of the categories in Gross' list and find out what you can about its interest in education, and how it attempts to influence the schools.

Of special concern to teachers, administrators, and board members has been the mounting criticism of the schools by extremist groups both from the political right and left.[25] These critics most commonly allege some sort of subversion in the schools. They direct their fire at teachers, administrators, and school boards, teaching and testing methods, textbooks, and the general content of school courses. Outside the schools the pressure is applied most heavily through parent-teacher organizations, the newspapers, and civic and political organizations.

Some of these critics openly advocate high pressure tactics, including harassing telephone calls to public officials and school personnel. There is a documented case in which a pupil, acting at the request of his parents who belonged to an extremist organization, "spied" on a teacher by hiding a tape recorder in his desk.[26] In other cases school custodians have been employed to report what was said by teachers and principals.

11. Teachers are especially concerned with the way community conflicts over the schools affect children in daily school activities. For a case study of one community struggle over the schools and its impact on children, see Ramon Ross' account, "Uproar in Valley City," [27] a new community in Southern California in which liberal and conservative factions battled each other over psychological testing and state adopted textbooks.

Edwin W. Davis of the National Education Association, who constantly studies criticisms of the schools, has estimated that 150 of the 1,800 or more rightwing organizations in the nation are at one time

---

[25] For a summary of political extremist activities in the schools of four communities see Mary Anne Raywid, "Political Extremism and Public Schools," *The National Elementary Principal*, Washington, D. C., National Education Association, Volume 43, No. 3, January 1964, pp. 27–31.

[26] "Hell Breaks Loose in Paradise," *Life*, Volume 54, No. 17, April 26, 1963, pp. 73–82.

[27] Ramon Ross, "Uproar in Valley City," *National Elementary Principal*, Washington, D. C., National Education Association, Volume 43, No. 3, January 1964, pp. 23–31.

or another involved in attacks on the schools.[28] Many of these criticisms can be simply ignored. But, as Davis suggests, when critics reach the point of trying to get a good teacher fired, or censor a textbook, or alter the whole course of education in school, then educators and citizens must act to protect what they consider to be a good school system.

12. In their book, *The Censors and the Schools,* Jack Nelson and Gene Roberts, Jr. identify and describe five special interest groups who censor textbooks. The authors also suggest that teachers and administrators sometimes aid and abet censorship by their reluctance to speak up or take a stand. Also suggested are ways teachers and administrators can combat censorship. Read *The Censors and the Schools,* and then determine what you would do if, as a teacher, you discovered you were using, or were considering using, a book which appears on some organization's censored list.

13. Donald L. Ayres, a California teacher of English, proposes this method for handling the censorship problem: [29] "The teacher needs to consider the emotional climate of the community. The obvious way for him to gain community acceptance for his program is to consult parents before introducing his students to any questionable literary work.

"For convenience, he might ask students to bring signed releases from home before presenting a controversial literary piece. These releases should not be thought of as a means for shifting the responsibility to parents for selecting appropriate instructional material; rather they should be regarded as invitations to share in the process of determining which books best enrich the lives of youngsters."

What do you think of Ayres' suggestion regarding consulting parents before introducing questionable literary works? Do you foresee problems in this approach?

National Agencies and the Control of the Schools

The local control of American education is historically rooted and popularly accepted. Yet the growing tendency of Americans to think in terms of solving national problems *nationally* is introducing a new force into the control of local schools. The image of local school boards making independent decisions without regard to national agencies and influences is now regarded by some observers simply as folklore. New voices of national influence are arising in the schools, these observers claim, and the real influence of local authorities is diminishing.

[28] Bruce Biossat, "Pressure Groups Attack Schools," *The State Journal,* Lansing, Michigan, September 20, 1964, p. 3.

[29] Donald L. Ayres, "What Can the Teacher Do?," Washington, D. C., *NEA Journal,* May 1963, p. 24.

In order to investigate these new influences on the schools, Roald F. Campbell and Robert A. Bunnell studied the *Nationalizing Influences on Secondary Education.*[30] These investigators and their colleagues, after interviewing school officials and teachers in seven Chicago area high schools, decided that there were four national agencies which were having particular influence on the schools:

The National Science Foundation
The National Merit Scholarship Program
The National Defense Education Act of 1958
The College Entrance Examination Board

The investigators, having identified these four forces, then studied their impact on secondary schools by means of a questionnaire administered to the chief school officers of 240 Illinois high schools.

Before examining the impact of these agencies upon the schools, we should say a descriptive word about them. All of them are national in character. All of their programs have tended to ignore the local-state approach to educational problems, long the dominant pattern in our country. All the programs are voluntary; no local school district or state legislature must participate in them. But most states and many schools are meeting the requirements of and following the practices advocated by these new national forces. Local school boards are confronted by nationwide programs characterized by scholarly insight, prestige, and money; the boards apparently have little choice but to conform to them. Although we retain the forms of local and state control of the schools, in reality we are moving rapidly toward national influence and control.

The National Science Foundation. The National Science Foundation was established in 1950 as an independent agency in the executive branch of Federal government. The organization was given a broad mandate to strengthen basic research and education in the sciences. Endowed with considerable autonomy, the National Science Foundation has used its resources to strengthen the teaching of science and mathematics throughout the nation, especially in secondary education.

Campbell and Bunnell sought several kinds of information from the schools in order to determine the impact of the National Science Foundation: (1) Had any present staff members attended one or more NSF Regular Term or Summer Institutes? (2) Were changes made in the content of courses in science and mathematics as the result of par-

[30] Roald F. Campbell and Robert A. Bunnell, *Nationalizing Influences on Secondary Education*, Chicago, University of Chicago, Midwest Administration Center, 1963.

ticipation of staff in NSF Institutes? (3) Were courses added as the result of such participation by staff members? It was discovered that schools in the higher socio-economic areas had the greatest staff participation in National Science Foundation Institutes and made the greatest number of changes in course content and course additions. Among all the schools 50 percent participated in science institutes and 32 percent in mathematics institutes. Suburban schools, however, had 90 percent participation in science and 85 percent in math, while urban schools had 84 percent in science and 47 percent in math. Chicago schools participated at the rate of 59 percent in science and 45 percent in math.

The suburban schools were again highest in content changes in curriculum, with 75 percent change in math and 60 percent in science. For urban schools 46 percent reported content changes in math and 48 percent in science. About a third of the Chicago schools reported changes in both science and math resulting from NSF participation. In the rural group, changes were reported by less than 30 percent of the schools.

When asked to judge the over-all effect of NSF programs on their schools the highest "great effect" response came from suburban schools, while the highest "little or no effect" response came from the Chicago schools.

The National Merit Scholarship Program. The National Merit Scholarship Program, a private organization, was started in 1955 in recognition of the national need for scholarships and for an organization which would assume the financial burden of providing scholarships. The program employs external examinations to award scholarships to outstanding students throughout the nation. The program is financed by grants from the Ford Foundation, the Carnegie Corporation, and other donors, and has granted thousands of scholarships having a value of many millions of dollars.

Regarding the impact of the National Merit School Program, a very high percentage of the schools reported participation. The questionnaire also asked schools if they offer some form of special preparation for students writing National Merit examinations. In the Chicago school system 69 percent of the schools reported that they offered students special preparation for the examinations. About 30 percent of the suburban and urban schools offered such preparation to students.

The comments made by school officials about the National Merit Scholarship Program carry a negative tone, but this very tone seems to indicate the impact of the program on the schools.[31] Two suburban respondents wrote: "The National Merit Scholarships are too greatly overrated by parents as a measure of the quality of the school program." Another school administrator reported: "We think the National Merit plan is harmful. It is geared too much toward math and science. Persons win over better students because of where their parents are employed. The public gains a false impression of the overall caliber of the school. We have experienced these reactions." A Chicago respondent commented: "When we place seventeen students above the 98th percentile but earn no scholarships the word gets around that it is rather hopeless. We receive 40 to 60 other scholarships annually, and though the amount may be small (in money) it is very encouraging."

The National Defense Education Act. The National Defense Education Act was passed by the Congress and signed into law on September 2, 1958. The act has a single stated purpose—"to provide substantial assistance in various forms to individuals and to states and their subdivisions, in order to insure trained manpower of sufficient quality and quantity to meet the national defense needs of the United States." Among its ten titles the National Defense Education Act includes provisions for loans to students in institutions of higher learning, financial assistance for science, mathematics, and modern foreign language teaching, financial assistance for the improvement of guidance, counseling and testing in the schools, and area vocational programs.

In assessing the impact of the National Defense Education Act the investigators sought information regarding (1) the present staff members who had attended one or more NDEA summer or Regular Term Institutes in foreign language or in guidance, (2) equipment which had been purchased or remodeled with NDEA funds, (3) course changes and additions made as a result of increased staff, additional equipment, or remodeling available through NDEA assistance.

It was discovered that there was unusually high participation, about three-fourths, of all the schools in all socio-economic settings. As a general rule the greatest participation in all aspects of the NDEA program came from schools in the higher socio-economic areas.

The impact of NDEA upon the schools is best seen in responses such as these. A suburban school reported: [32] "We have been able to enrich the courses we were already teaching and have been able to add botany and zoology to the curriculum. Science has been the major field helped by NDEA. We are adding a sophomore chemistry course and moving toward an advanced placement program due to the possibility of financing additional equipment and labs." Another

---

[31] *Ibid.,* pp. 101–102.   [32] *Ibid.,* p. 96.

respondent in a middle-sized urban school said that the school increased the counselor's time from nine to ten months as a result of NDEA assistance.

The College Entrance Examination Board. The College Entrance Examination Board, a private organization which had its beginning more than sixty years ago, has risen to a place of prominence and influence in American secondary education. It is regarded by many as the leader in the field of college admissions testing. The basic testing programs include the Scholastic Aptitude and Preliminary Scholastic Aptitude tests. Of special interest today are the Advanced Placement Programs sponsored by the College Board. The main purpose of the College Entrance Examination Board has changed little since Nicholas Murray Butler, the first secretary of the Board, gave his first report in 1901: "To ascertain whether a pupil is well enough equipped for more advanced study in college or a scientific school."

To determine the impact of the College Entrance Examination Board, the investigators sought to discover if some kind of special preparation was given to students who were preparing for the College Board examinations in addition to routine announcements and record keeping. It involved such matters as special classes, orientation, or coaching.

Again the schools in higher socio-economic surroundings showed the highest participation in College Board activities: applications for membership, attendance at meetings, and advanced placement programs. The clearly evident leadership lay with the suburban schools, with 75 percent applying for membership, 75 percent reporting staff members in attendance at meetings, and 65 percent with one or more Advanced Placement Programs. Chicago, however, reported the highest percentage of schools (48) giving some form of special preparation for the examinations.

Fifty percent of the suburban schools reported that the College Entrance Examination Board had a noticeable influence on the school's curriculum. Other schools reported that the CEEB had "some" influence or "little or no" influence on the school's curriculum.

14. Did your own high school participate in the programs of any of the four agencies we discussed here? Have you personally participated in any of these programs? What kind of influence did these programs have on your high school?

Regarding the general influence of these four agencies upon local schools the investigators concluded: [33]

[33] *Ibid.*, p. 103.

"In general terms it would appear that these four influences have had a considerable impact on the high schools studied. They have brought about changes in course content, addition of new courses, increased academic training of teachers, additions to facilities and equipment, and introduction of special forms of preparation for the various testing programs employed. These kinds of influence, moreover, are not uniformly felt among the schools. In a number of instances it appeared that the wealthier, larger, nonrural schools were the ones that were most frequently influenced by these programs through their participation in the many opportunities offered. This differential utilization of programs, combined with the recurring discrepancy between reported influence and degree of participation can only suggest that educators, school boards, and citizens must become more aware of these influences in order to make informed decisions about participation. However, these decisions will have to be based not only on adequate information, but will have to be consistent with the philosophy that each local district is empowered, in fact required, to develop."

The struggle for control of the schools is a democratic struggle carried on within a society where people are free to organize politically in order to promote their particular interests. The schools, since they educate the young and thus influence the future, are subject in a democracy to all kinds of pressures from groups who see in the schools a means of advancing their beliefs and goals. The consensus regarding what the schools should do expresses, therefore, both the social and political power structure of the community, state, and nation. Sometimes certain groups hold dominant and undisputed power in the community and can wield absolute control over the schools.

This situation is most likely to occur, when it does, in the homogeneous village and town. Sometimes power is about equally divided among contending groups, as in the heterogeneous suburb or city. Here the control of the school hangs in delicate balance and may shift from time to time.

In a sense the future of the school is being determined every day by the persons and groups who feel they have a stake in it. It is in the democratic faith to believe that out of the great and continuing debate will come schools equal to the needs of our future. There is no assurance in the democratic process, however, that this will happen, for the possession of power to influence the schools alone does not guarantee responsible action. Power must be coupled with a strong awareness of the kinds of schools required in a democratic society.

REFERENCES

Paperbacks

Can America Loose Her Free Public Schools? Virgil M. Rogers. (Orig.) Syracuse University Press, University Station, Syracuse, N. Y. ($1.00).

Church, State, and Education. Sir Ernest Barker. (10) Ann Arbor Paperbacks, University of Michigan Press, 615 East University, Ann Arbor, Mich. ($1.35).

Crucial Issues in Education. Ehlers and Lee. (3rd Ed.) Holt, Rinehart and Winston, 383 Madison Ave., New York ($3.25).

Economics and Politics of Public Education, No. 1: Schoolmen and Politics: A Study of State Aid to Education in the Northeast. Stephen K. Bailey, Robert C. Wood, Richard Frost and Paul E. Marsh. (Orig.) Syracuse University Press, University Station, Syracuse, N. Y. ($1.75).

Economics and Politics of Public Education, No. 2: Government and the Suburban School. Roscoe C. Martin. (Orig.) Syracuse University Press, University Station, Syracuse, N. Y. ($1.75).

Economics and Politics of Public Education, No. 3: National Politics in Federal Aid to Education. Frank J. Munger and Richard Fenno. (Orig.) Syracuse University Press, University Station, Syracuse, N. Y. ($1.75).

Economics and Politics of Public Education, No. 4: Issues in Federal Aid to Education. Sidney C. Sufrin. (Orig.) Syracuse University Press, University Station, Syracuse, N. Y. ($1.75).

Economics and Politics of Public Education, No. 5: Cost and Quality in Public Education. Harold F. Clark. (Orig.) Syracuse University Press, University Station, Syracuse, N. Y. ($1.75).

Economics and Politics of Public Education, No. 6: Federal Aid to Science Education: Two Programs. Paul E. Marsh and Ross A. Gortner. (Orig.) Syracuse University Press, University Station, Syracuse, N. Y. ($1.75).

Economics and Politics of Public Education, No. 7: State and Local Taxes for Public Education. Jesse Burkhead. (Orig.) Syracuse University Press, University Station, Syracuse, N. Y. ($1.75).

Economics and Politics of Public Education, No. 10: Suburban Power Structures and Public Education. Warner Bloomberg, Jr. and Morris Sunshine. (Orig.) Syracuse University Press, University Station, Syracuse, N. Y. ($1.75).

Economics and Politics of Public Education, No. 11: Social and Economic Factors in Spending for Public Education. Jerry Miner. (Orig.) Syracuse University Press, University Station, Syracuse, N. Y. ($1.75).

Education and Democratic Ideals. Gordon C. Lee. (Orig.) Harcourt, Brace and World, 757 Third Ave., New York ($1.95).

Education and Freedom. Hyman G. Rickover. (D47) Dutton Paperbacks, E. P. Dutton and Co., 201 Park Ave. South, New York ($1.45).

Education and Liberty. James Bryant Conant. Random House, 457 Madison Ave., New York ($1.45).

Education as Power. Theodore Brameld. Holt, Rinehart and Winston, 383 Madison Ave., New York ($1.75).

Educational Issues in a Changing Society. August Kerber and Wilfred Smith, Editors. (2nd Rev. Ed., Orig.) (WB3) Wayne State University Press, 5980 Cass, Detroit, Mich. ($3.95).

Future of Public Education. Myron Lieberman. (P94) Phoenix Books, University of Chicago Press, 5750 Ellis Ave., Chicago, Ill. ($1.50).

The Politics of Education. Frank MacKinnon. University of Toronto Press, Front Campus, Toronto 5, Canada ($1.95).

Books

Cahill, Robert S., *The Politics of Education in the Local Community.* Danville, Ill.: The Interstate Printers and Publishers, 1963. This book discusses education from the viewpoint of political science, sociology, and educational administration.

Campbell, Ronald F., Lavern L. Cunningham, and Roderick F. McPhee, *The Organization and Control of American Schools.* Columbus, Ohio: Charles E. Merrill Books, 1963. The authors utilize an interdisciplinary approach to explain the pressures and forces at work in school-society relationships.

Dean, Howard, "The Political Setting of American Education," in *The Social Sciences View School Administration* by Donald E. Tape et al. Englewood Cliffs, N. J.: Prentice-Hall, 1965, pp. 213–236. Education as a formal agency for making citizens is related directly to the political system.

Kimnbrough, Ralph B., *Political Power and Educational Decision Making.* Chicago: Rand McNally, 1964. The author explains how schools are involved in politics.

MacKinnon, Frank, *The Politics of Education: A Study of the Political Administration of the Public Schools.* Toronto, Canada: University of Toronto, 1962. A Canadian educator discusses the roles of the decision makers inside and outside of education.

Masters, Nicholas A., Robert H. Salisbury, and Thomas H. Eliot, *State Politics and the Public Schools.* New York: Alfred A. Knopf, 1964. A Study of three states suggests that educators must understand the political realities of education.

Ostrom, Vincent, "Politics and Education," in *Social Forces Influencing American Education, The Sixtieth Yearbook of the National Society for the Study of Education,* Part II, Nelson B. Henry, Editor. Chicago: University of Chicago Press, 1961, pp. 8–45. Education is an undertaking in learning, politics an enterprise in decision making. The author discusses the proper relation between the two.

Wiggin, Gladys A., *Education and Nationalism; An Historical Interpretation of American Education.* New York: McGraw-Hill Book Co., 1962. Chapters 3 and 4 deal with the political, social, and economic influences on American education.

Winick, Charles, "When Teachers Strike," in *Society and Education,* James D. Raths and J. D. Grambs, Editors. Englewood Cliffs, N. J.: Prentice-Hall, 1964, pp. 224–241. A discussion of the factors which go into a strike and its effects on teachers, parents, and students.

Periodicals

Bailey, Stephen K., "Education Is a Political Enterprise," *NEA Journal,* Vol. LIII, No. 8, November 1964, p. 13. The author strongly urges educators to take a long, hard look at the political facts of life.

Braden, Tom, "I Was the Target of a Hate Campaign," *Look,* Vol. 27, No. 21, October 22, 1963, pp. 54–60. An appointed member of the State Board of

Education in California describes his ordeal with far-right groups who unsuccessfully tried to block his appointment.

"Hell Breaks Loose in Paradise," *Life,* Vol. 54, No. 17, April 26, 1963, pp. 73–84. A pictorial essay of a student's tape recording of his teacher's class, the uproar in the community, and the ultimate vindication of the teacher.

Orlich, Donald C., "The Schools, the Public and Politics," *The American School Board Journal,* Vol. 149, No. 2, August 1964, pp. 8–10. Educators should be encouraged to lobby and form their own pressure groups, the author feels.

Ostrom, Vincent, "The Interrelationships of Politics and Education," *National Elementary Principal,* Vol. 43, No. 3, January 1964, pp. 6–11. Just as long as new ideas create new potential for action, problems of stress and tension are bound to persist in the interrelationships between the domains of politics and education.

Ross, Ramon, "Uproar in 'Valley City,' " *National Elementary Principal,* Vol. 43, No. 3, January 1964, pp. 23–31. Liberal and conservative factors battle over psychological testing and state-appointed texts.

Sayre, Wallace S., "The Politics of Education," *Teachers College Record,* Vol. 65, No. 2, November 1963, pp. 178–183. The author suggests that educators are ill-equipped to participate effectively in the political process necessary to resolve extraordinarily intricate conflicts of interests and forces.

Scanlon, John, "Strikes, Sanctions and the Schools," *Saturday Review,* Vol. 46, No. 42, October 19, 1963, pp. 51–55. A pertinent discussion on the power, or lack of it, of the public school teacher.

Stiles, Lindley J., "Ideas from Abroad: For Winning Teacher Loyalty," *Phi Delta Kappan,* Vol. 45, No. 6, March 1964, pp. 278–282. The teachers' organization of the United Arab Republic has a unique way of securing and keeping teacher loyalty.

19

The Crisis in Urban Schools

"What happens to cities happens to schools. For no school system exists in a vacuum. Can we reverse the trend of urban deterioration and make our cities good places for children to live and learn?" ROBERT C. WEAVER

The growth of our towns into cities and cities into sprawling urban complexes has tremendous impact upon education. The modern megalopolis, the extended city, is now the dominant fact on the American landscape, and places upon education new and heavy responsibilities.

The public schools emerged in an America that was predominantly rural in fact and outlook. The schools were sensitive to rural and agrarian views and needs, and they operated in ways appropriate to a rural society. Their cultural style was that of village and town.

Now we are an urban nation, living in clusters of great cities strung together by new industrial and residential developments. According to census reports in 1960, more than half the population of the United States was living in metropolitan areas. These metropolitan areas are growing at a much faster rate than the remainder of the country, and it is estimated that by 1980 they will accommodate between 70 and 75 percent of the population. In the East extended cities now stretch from Boston to New York, to Philadelphia, Baltimore, and Washington. In the Middle West they run from Milwaukee, south to Chicago, and east to Detroit, Toledo, Cleveland, and Pittsburgh. In the West a chain of urban-industrial communities links Los Angeles and San Diego. In the South great cities now ring the Gulf of Mexico.

The impact on schools of urban growth is so tremendous that it is difficult even to assess the implications. In this chapter we shall inquire into three aspects of the subject. (1) What population changes are taking place in urban areas? (2) What impact are these changes having upon the social structure and styles of life? (3) What is the impact of these social changes upon the schools?

1. As you study the problems of urban education with which this chapter deals you may quite naturally wonder what schools are doing about them. A review of Chapter 10 on "Teaching Socially Disadvantaged Students" will give you added perspective on this chapter. You may find the three sections on *The Disadvantaged Child's Attitude Toward School, Why Do Socially Disadvantaged Children Encounter Difficulties in School?* and *Programs for Socially Disadvantaged Children* of special interest.[1]

Patterns of Urban Growth

How do metropolitan areas grow? An early explanation of population patterns in urban areas was developed by E. W. Burgess, in which he suggested that high-status residents lived on the edge of the settled area, whereas the central portions contained the new immigrants and those whose low earning power condemned them to inexpensive or run-down residences.[2]

The Burgess model of urban growth was a static model, however, and did not explain the movement of people within the metropolitan area. L. F. Schnore has more recently rephrased the Burgess model to explain shifts in population. Schnore states: "With the growth and expansion of the center and with radical improvements in transportation and communication technology, the upper strata have shifted from central to peripheral residence, and the lower classes have increasingly taken up occupancy in the central areas abandoned by the elite." [3]

Actual population movement within urban areas confirms the Schnore model. Lower-class people in the areas of poorest housing usually live in the oldest parts of the city, near the center, now abandoned by the more affluent citizens. Working-class people with steady incomes take up residence a little farther from the center of the city, frequently in areas midway between the inner city and the suburbs. Middle- and upper-class people flee to the suburbs far from the inner

[1] For an informative discussion of the special needs of urban teachers see Harry N. Rivlin, "Urban Schools and Their Teachers," *The New Era in Home and School,* Volume XLV, No. 8, 1964, pp. 228–233.

[2] R. E. Park, E. W. Burgess, and R. D. McKenzie, *The City,* Chicago, University of Chicago Press, 1925, p. 55.

[3] L. F. Schnore, "The Socio-Economic Status of Cities and Suburbs," *American Sociological Review,* Volume 28, February 1963, p. 84.

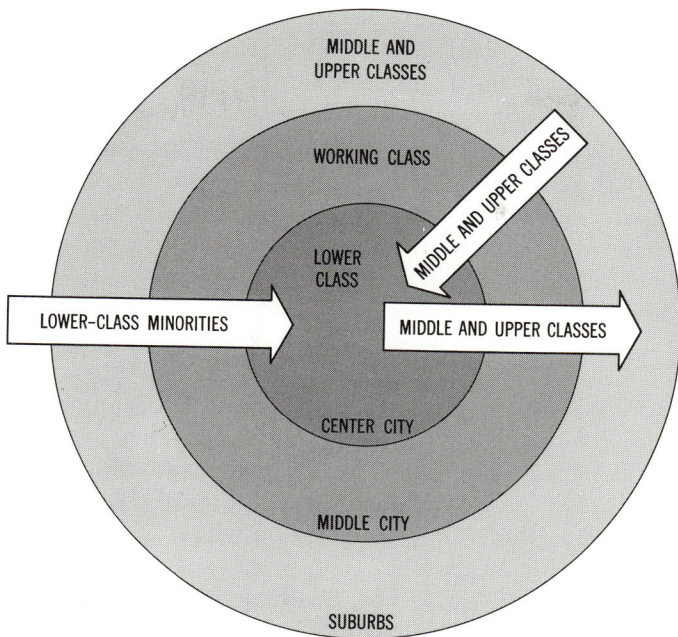

Fig. 19-1 Residential movements in the city may be thought of as a series of concentric rings with the lower social classes at the center.

city. Thus residential movements in the city may be thought of as a series of concentric rings with the lower-class conglomerate at the center, and successively higher socio-economic groups in population rings radiating out to the suburbs.

2. There is a countertrend to the movement of the financially able citizens to the distant suburbs. Luxury apartments in downtown areas are now attracting a considerable number of people back into the cities. Can you account for this countertrend? Do you think it will have any impact upon schools in the central city?

With most of the affluent citizens constantly moving out from the center we should ask: Who takes their place in the inner city and from where do these replacements come?

New Minorities in the Cities

One of the striking changes in the composition of urban population is the waning significance of European ethnic groups and the rising dominance of new minorities who migrate into the inner cities, not from abroad, but from within our country. During the last century over 37 million immigrants entered the United States, mostly from Europe. For the past century the country's minority population has been comprised of foreign-born immigrants. However, "this is no longer true." The children born in the coming decades will be the first in the history of the United States to be reared amidst a population that is over 95 percent native-born.[4]

The new minorities consist primarily of three groups, the Puerto Ricans, Southern whites, and Negroes. Puerto Ricans are not legally immigrants since they can pass freely from the island to the mainland without a passport. Sociologically, they are voluntary immigrants who leave the culture in which they grew up and move to a new land. Puerto Ricans are concentrated in a few large cities, mostly in New York City where over 600,000 reside, and where they are marked off from the dominant population by language and religion. Racially Puerto Ricans are ambiguous: Some have physical characteristics that are considered in the United States to be white; others are classified on the mainland as Negroes.

In contrast to Puerto Ricans, Southern whites are both English-speaking and native-born. They are, however, an ethnic minority in the city, for they are unprepared by their upbringing, values, and behavior to live in cities and to be assimilated into the life of the metropolis. Their means of making a livelihood in the mines and on the farms of the Southern mountains broke down, and they came to the Northern industrial cities to seek economic opportunity. There they are frequently regarded as "hillbillies" or "okies," inferior and undesirable.

The third minority, the Negroes, are by far the largest. In many ways they come to the city with all the handicaps of the Southern white, plus one more: they are more visible. Throughout their history in the United States Negroes have lived in the rural areas of the South. Now the pattern has changed. In 1900, 90 percent of the Negroes lived in the South, and 80 percent of all Negroes in the United States lived in rural areas. In 1960, 73 percent of the Negroes lived in urban areas and, outside the South, 90 percent lived in cities.[5]

We may summarize the changing composition of urban minorities

---

[4] For this discussion of minorities the author is indebted to Raymond W. Mack, "The Changing Ethnic Fabric of Metropolis," in *Education in Urban Society*, B. J. Chandler, Lindley J. Stiles, and John I. Kitsuse (Editors), New York, Dodd, Mead and Company, 1962, pp. 54–69.

[5] U. S. Department of Commerce, Bureau of Census, *Statistical Abstract of the United States*, Washington, D. C., U. S. Department of Commerce, 1961, p. 30.

by saying that, although for 150 years European immigrants were the dominant group, now our minority population in the cities is composed of citizens of the United States. These immigrants into the cities must adjust to urban life and must exchange rural values and behaviors for urban ones. All three minorities face the burden of being assimilated into a new environment. The largest group of the three, the Negroes, face an added block to assimilation, their color. We reserve for Chapter 20 a discussion of the Negro's assimilation into the schools.

What about the educational level of the new minorities in the cities? In recent years our newspapers and magazines have carried features and editorials expressing alarm about the low level of education which the new immigrants bring to the cities and the problems which they pose. However, the facts run contrary to popular belief. The new minorities migrating into the cities have a higher level of education than the resident urban minorities who are already there. Mack cites this evidence:

"Of the resident population of the Chicago metropolitan area in 1950, for example, less than 15 percent had attended college. Of the in-migrant population to the Chicago area that year, over 30 percent— more than twice as many—had attended college. In-migrants present this favorable contrast with the resident population whether the data are considered as a total or broken down by race. That is, the Negroes who are arriving in the city have a higher level of educational attainment than the Negroes already there; the whites arriving have a higher level of educational attainment than the whites already there; all migrants arriving average more formal education than the present residents." [6]

3. Can you explain why in-migrant minorities in the cities have a higher level of education than those already there?

City Loss—Suburban Gain

The flow of more affluent citizens to the suburbs and of the less affluent into the cities has had the net effect of enriching the suburbs and impoverishing the cities. Karl E. and Alma F. Taeuber made an analysis of migration patterns between 1955 and 1960 for twelve large metropolitan areas and discovered that "cities have been contributing more high-status migrants than they receive to the flow of population within and between metropolitan areas, while suburban rings have been receiving more high-status migrants than they lose. This inter- and intra-metropolitan circulation of persons of higher levels of edu-

---

[6] Mack, *op. cit.*, p. 62.

cational attainment and occupational status has the net effect of diminishing the socio-economic level of the population in central cities and augmenting the socio-economic level of suburban populations." [7]

A study of Detroit illustrates this pattern of socio-economic gain of the suburbs at the expense of the city.[8] The Detroit pattern applies to many, though probably not all, major cities. According to this investigation the median family income of Detroit families bore a positive correlation to the distance the family lived from the center of the city. That is, the closer families lived to the center of the city, the lower the median income, while the farther they lived from the inner city the higher their income. In fact, during the period of the study, 1951 to 1959, the people in the central part of the city grew poorer while the people in the suburbs grew richer. For example, the median income of families living within six miles of the central business district rose 3 percent from 1951 to 1959, while the cost of living rose 12 percent; thus these families lost real income. Families living between the six-mile radius and the city limits gained 5 percent in median income. They, too, lost real income. Meanwhile, families in the Detroit suburban area gained 37 percent in median income. Thus during the period of this survey the city became more socio-economically stratified, with the central part of the city becoming more lower class in composition and the suburbs becoming more middle class.

4. What impact do you think these socio-economic changes had on Detroit city schools? On suburban schools around Detroit?

The Social Impact of Urban Change

Increased socio-economic segregation. One of the major changes which accompanies urbanization is suggested by the Detroit study: the population becomes more socially and economically stratified. Small towns, like Raymond's Midwest, are relatively homogeneous in their social organization. There are no extremes of wealth and poverty. The rich and the poor maintain contact in both community and school. Raymond, the son of a hardware employee, went to school with children representing all the socio-economic classes of Midwest. Social and economic distinctions among them were slight. The children of Midwest played and worked together and developed an appreciation for one another as individuals, rather than simply as representatives of dif-

[7] Karl E. and Alma F. Taeuber, "White Migration and Socio-economic Difference Between Cities and Suburbs," *American Sociological Review*, Volume XXIX, No. 5, 1964, p. 728.

[8] Detroit Area Study, "Family Income in Greater Detroit: 1951–1959," Ann Arbor, Michigan, University of Michigan, Survey Research Center, 1960.

ferent social classes. The income and social class position of Raymond's parents did not isolate him from others either above or below.

Contrast now Raymond's situation with that of Beth of suburbia and Julia of the slums. Both of these girls experience the economic and social stratification of the metropolitan area. Beth, as far as she can recall, has never seen a child from the slums, much less gone to school and had close association with one. Julia has never gone to school or associated with a child from middle-class suburbia. Beth's waking hours are spent with white, upper middle-class children; and as far as she is aware, these are the only kind of children there are. From her books and travels she may be vaguely aware that children in different circumstances do exist, but they have not touched her life in any meaningful way.

Similarly, Julia's life is circumscribed by the high walls of her slum. From her schoolbooks and experiences she is probably aware of the existence of middle-class children, but they are picture-book children rather than real ones.

Further, this stratification of the cities is increasing at a rapid rate. Robert J. Havighurst cites the case of Chicago. "To a child growing up in Chicago today this trend of population means that he is more segregated by family socio-economic status than he would have been if he had grown up in the Chicago area about 1940. At the earlier time, a child in a Chicago school was more likely to have in his school or class children of quite different family backgrounds. At present, there are slum areas so large that a child living there never sees children from middle-class homes. The middle-class children for the most part live in the suburbs or on the edges of the city." [9]

5. How do you think this social class separation of children in schools influences the development of their attitudes toward persons who are culturally different?

Increased racial and ethnic segregation. Urban growth not only leads to increased socio-economic stratification, but also fosters increased racial and ethnic segregation. As working- and middle-class whites leave the inner city, the new minorities move in. For example, in Chicago in 1940 only three of the 44 working-class communities had 50 percent or more Negroes. In 1960, 14 of the 41 working-class communities had 50 percent or more Negroes, and eight of these 14 had 90 percent or more Negroes.[10] Thus Chicago is losing its white population while it is rapidly gaining a Negro population. Table 1 shows

[9] R. J. Havighurst, *The Public Schools of Chicago*, Chicago, The Board of Education of the City of Chicago, 1964, p. 25.
[10] *Ibid.*

TABLE 1

POPULATION OF CHICAGO AND SUBURBAN AREA

	City of Chicago		Suburban ring	
	White	Nonwhite	White	Nonwhite
1940	3,115,000	282,000	1,148,000	25,000
1950	3,112,000	509,000	1,512,000	45,000
1960	2,713,000	838,000	2,588,000	82,000
1965	2,579,000	980,000	2,980,000	113,000
1970 (est.)	2,427,000	1,173,000	3,525,000	175,000
1980 (est.)	2,234,000	1,540,000	4,499,000	347,000

SOURCE: U. S. Census and Population Projections for the Chicago Standard Metropolitan Statistical Area and City of Chicago. Population Research and Training Center, University of Chicago. Robert J. Havighurst, *The Public Schools of Chicago,* Chicago, The Board of Education of the City of Chicago, 1964, p. 24.

recent population trends and white-nonwhite changes. It also projects the future racial mixture of the population if present trends continue.

Two items are of special interest in Table 1. First, the central city of Chicago will probably not grow much. Second, the proportion of Negroes will continue to increase both in the central city and the suburbs.

These changes in the racial and ethnic composition of cities are understandably reflected in school populations. Take New York City as an example. In a five-year period the schools of New York City showed a net loss to the suburbs of fifteen thousand white students.[11] This movement of white children out of the city and the parallel inward movement of Negroes and Puerto Ricans increased the segregation in the schools. In 1958, among 704 New York City public schools, 455 had enrollments in which 90 percent or more of the pupils were of similar racial and ethnic origins: Negro, Puerto Ricans, or other whites. Thus about two-thirds of the schools were segregated in that 90 percent or more of the students belong to the majority group while fewer than 10 percent did not.[12]

[11] *Sixtieth Annual Report of the Superintendent of Schools,* New York, Board of Education of the City of New York, 1959.

[12] J. Cayce Morrison, *The Puerto Rican Study,* New York, Board of Education of the City of New York, 1958.

6. This situation in which Northern schools are segregated *in fact* is known as *de facto* segregation, in contrast to legal segregation supported by law which exists in some areas of the deep South. For an illuminating discussion of the educational problems surrounding *de facto* segregation read James Conant's *Slums and Suburbs*.

Stratification among the suburbs. Whereas the suburbs have gained in socio-economic status at the expense of the cities, they have not gained equally. Stratification also exists among the suburbs. The city dweller who decides to find a house in the suburbs looks for one that he can afford to buy. What he can pay determines the type of suburb he can live in. If he is employed as a worker on an automobile assembly line, he may buy a small home in a vast real estate development where most homes look alike, are set along checkerboard streets, with tiny lawns in front and back. If he is a professional man he will be interested in a more spacious house on a large wooded lot in a development with winding streets, a flowing stream, and preferably not far from a golf course and country club. The skilled technician will probably look for a home in the suburbs that falls in price between that of the auto worker and professional man, a modest ranch home in a respectable, though not affluent, development. Thus the suburbs themselves become stratified into communities that are predominantly lower, middle, and upper class.

In contrast to the city which is rapidly changing its socio-economic characteristics, particular suburbs tend to retain their particular socio-economic characteristics over longer periods of time, and even rapid population growth does not produce substantial changes. In other words, the upper classes continue to move into upper-class suburbs, the middle classes into middle-class suburbs, and the lower classes into lower-class suburbs. Reynolds Ferley studied socio-economic census data in 137 suburbs of 24 central cities between 1920 and 1960 and discovered that "a sound prediction of the 1960 socio-economic characteristics of a particular suburb could be made merely by knowing that suburb's characteristics in 1920. When the shorter time span—1940 to 1960—is used there is even greater evidence for persistence of suburban characteristics." [13]

The Impact of Urban Social Changes Upon the Schools

Social and economic changes within metropolitan areas place severe limitations upon the ability of city schools to cope with them.

[13] Reynolds Ferley, "Suburban Persistence," *American Sociological Review,* Volume XXIX, No. 1, 1964, p. 39.

A conference called by the U. S. Office of Education to consider "The Impact of Urbanization on Education" identified crucial problems which confront city schools.[14]

Disappearing taxable property. The ability of any school district to finance a good educational program depends upon a good tax base in the community. Schools located in communities with valuable taxable property can spend more on education than schools located in communities with little taxable property. The financial position of a school district may be judged by the amount of property valuation available for each pupil. The "per-pupil valuation" may be easily determined by dividing the number of pupils in the school district into the number of dollars of tax valuation. As an example, if there are 100 pupils in a small district with $100,000 tax valuation there is $1,000 valuation for each pupil.

The per-pupil valuation varies greatly from district to district, depending on taxable wealth. For example, a poor district may have as little as $5,000 assessed property valuation "behind" each child, whereas a wealthy district may have as much as $40,000. The quality of educational programs which two such schools can offer obviously will differ sharply.

One of the crucial problems of city schools is the diminishing amount of taxable property supporting each pupil. Paradoxically, urban renewal projects which are designed to improve cities are a major factor in taking property from the tax rolls and thus reducing tax dollars available for schools. The activities of the Federal government in building freeways and public housing pose special problems for city school districts. When property is condemned for freeways and traffic arteries, the lost revenue cannot be recovered. In case of Federal housing projects, an annual payment for the school is agreed upon in lieu of taxes, but the school district may have to wait a considerable amount of time to receive its money. Furthermore, the amount paid is frequently lower than the amount of tax which would be paid by an owner of a private apartment development. Yet the increased numbers of children who live in Federal housing developments require the school district to make large capital investments in new schools. Thus while the need for educational services increases the amount of taxable property per pupil decreases.

Deterioration and decline of real property. The people who can afford to maintain their property in the cities are the same ones who

[14] Washington, D. C., *U. S. Department of Health, Education and Welfare,* 1962.

move to the suburbs. Tenants replace these homeowners and the value of the real property goes down. Further, city property tends to be old property and unless constant efforts are made to replace and repair it deterioration is rapid. The cumulative effect of these conditions is an ever-decreasing property valuation per pupil.

Displacement of people. All urban renewal programs in one part of the city compound the school's problem in other parts. Heavy impact in one area is felt throughout the school system. Displaced people crowd into other areas in numbers and ways that are hard to predict. Sometimes existing residents resist and resent the intrusions from the "outsiders." For a school system to prepare and plan for these changes requires a great deal of money and time. The need for new school facilities in a given area is almost bound to be acute before these facilities can be made available.

High mobility and physical change. People who live in the congested areas of cities are transients, living in one place only a short time before they move on. City schools reflect this mobility in their high rates of pupil turnover. In Manhattan in a recent year, the mean mobility rate was 51 percent. In three schools that were almost completely Negro, the turnover was 100 percent.[15]

This mobility, combined with that caused by urban renewal, makes long-range school planning in large cities very complex. Such planning depends on a good understanding of the demographic structure of the city and the way it affects and is affected by the physical change within the city.

Replacement of school facilities. City school buildings are frequently condemned to make way for urban renewal, highway construction, and other public purposes. The process of condemning school property for public purposes is usually easier and cheaper than condemning property in control of private home, business, or industrial owners. Yet it is the school system, not the condemners, which must replace these schools, and for the most part school districts receive little aid or interest from the agency that took the property and caused the displacement.

Relationship of Income to School Facilities and Programs

Because the center of the city is old and the suburbs are new, one would expect that the ages of school buildings and facilities would vary accordingly. Such, of course, is the case. Inner city schools tend

---

[15] Frederick Shaw, "Educating Culturally Deprived Youth in Urban Centers," *Phi Delta Kappan*, Volume LXIV, No. 2, November 1963, p. 93.

TABLE 2

PERCENTAGE OF SCHOOLS WITH NO FACILITIES OR
SUBSTANDARD FACILITIES

	Major Income Groups				Income Halves	
Facilities	Group I $3000—	Group II $5000—	Group III $7000—	Group IV $9000—	A Below $7000	B Above $7000
Science	50%	46%	3%	0%	47%	2%
Conservatory	67	50	6	6	54	6
Art room	11	11	4	0	11	6
Library	11	16	15	11	15	14
Instrumental Music & speech	78	95	59	39	91	56
Speech	83	88	84	89	86	85
Store room	6	18	6	6	15	6
Men's & women's rest rooms	61	68	40	16	66	30
Auditorium	5	16	2	6	14	3
Auditorium Activities room (backstage)	78	95	52	39	91	50
Office	0	11	2	0	8	2
Clinic	17	21	11	11	20	11
Kitchen	44	55	31	17	53	28
Air raid shelter	67	61	25	6	62	21

SOURCE: Patricia Cayo Sexton, *Education and Income*, New York, The Viking Press, 1961, p. 125.

to be old; suburban schools tend to be new because the families with the lowest incomes are in the inner city where the old schools are and those with the highest incomes live in the suburbs where the new schools are located.

Patricia Sexton brings these two facts together to discover precisely how the age of the school, its facilities and programs are related to the income of the people served by the school. She obtained the average income of the families living in various school districts in the city of Detroit and related the income to the type of school found there and the educational program offered.[16]

[16] Patricia Cayo Sexton, *Education and Income*, New York, The Viking Press, 1961.

Sexton found an almost parallel relationship between family income and school facilities and programs. As Table 2 indicates, with few exceptions all facilities listed are more adequate in the school districts with upper-income families.

Sexton concludes: "Except for library and speech, all facilities listed are much more adequate in upper-income schools. Perhaps the most unfortunate deficiency is found in science facilities. In the lower-income half, 47 percent of all schools do not have proper facilities for scientific studies while only 2 percent of schools in the upper-income half have inadequate facilities." [17]

7. An ideal of American education is to provide equal educational opportunity for all children, regardless of social-class position, race, or place of residence. Facts such as those which Sexton presents indicate how far we are from that ideal. Some persons suggest that artificial school district boundaries which give high tax support to certain schools and meager tax support to others are at the root of the problem. They recommend that larger tax units be formed for the support of the schools, thus eliminating the inequalities between the rich and the poor schools. How do you react to this proposal?

8. Sexton comments that science facilities in the low-income schools are conspicuously poorer than in high-income schools. Can you suggest some things a science teacher in a low-income school might do to overcome the lack of facilities? For an account of what one science teacher did see Cole S. Brembeck, *The Discovery of Teaching*, Englewood Cliffs, New Jersey, Prentice-Hall, 1962, pp. 136–137.

The Impact of Urbanization Upon Students

Having examined the impact of urbanization upon schools, their facilities, and programs, let us now turn to students. The problems of urban schools quickly become the problems of urban students. The decreasing tax base, the aging school facilities, the loss of middle-class and the gain of lower-class parents, all create intensely human student problems.

The first and perhaps the most pervasive influence of urbanization upon students is caused by segregation along both economic and racial lines.

Urban stratification and student segregation. Among parents who are able to move out of the city, the schools are of prime importance in selecting a new neighborhood in which to live. The parents of Fairlawn, mentioned in Chapter 17, were representative of those middle-

[17] *Ibid.,* p. 125.

class, white parents who selected that neighborhood because the school promised to be the kind they wanted for their children. The schools they left in Metropolis had reached a critical point as far as the parents were concerned. Two developments were taking place which alarmed them: (1) The socio-economic composition of the neighborhood was changing from middle to lower class, and (2) the racial composition of the schools was changing from predominantly white to predominantly Negro. These two factors combined to lower the status of the school to the critical point where parents began to look for a new neighborhood in which to live.[18]

These parents seek schools in keeping with their aspirations for their children. Will the school make it possible for them to be admitted to college? Does it have good teachers and a sound academic program? Are there large playground areas and adequate recreational facilities? Does the school provide social contacts with children of their own social class? Does the school have "status"?

These are the questions which the parents of Fairlawn had answered to their satisfaction. Now they saw their school threatened by the Urbandale intrusion in the way that their former school had been threatened by changes in Metropolis. They did not want to repeat the experience. The motivations of these parents are understandable in terms of the dominant middle-class values which they share. Further, many lower-class parents make the same decision to escape the slums with their children when and if they are financially able to do so. The aspiration to move up is basic to both our social and economic way of life.

Yet rising aspirations, as they express themselves in socio-economic stratification, create deep-running social and educational problems which we know all too little how to handle. The schools which middle-class parents and students leave behind in their flight to the suburbs suffer a loss of status as lower-class parents move in. The quality of educational programs goes down at the very time that quality education is most needed by the new students who already tend to be disadvantaged.

Thus students like Julia are denied two experiences which are vital if education is to help her to raise her sights and grow away from her slum existence: (1) a rich educational program, and (2) other children from the middle class who may act as models for her. Not

---

[18] For quantitative indicators of the critical point at which parents may withdraw their children from a particular school because of status and race see Robert J. Havighurst, "Metropolitan Development and the Educational System," *The School Review,* Volume 69, No. 8, Autumn 1961, pp. 251–259.

least among the forces that conspire to downgrade the urban school is the absence of middle-class parents and children whose achievement aspirations give the school its cultural style and set an educational standard for all.

The concept of the school as a "melting pot" in American history is more than platitude: It has a substantive base.[19] This historical function of the school took place in a heterogeneous setting where all social classes were represented. The "melting pot" schools were "consolidated" in terms of the social composition of their student bodies.

The student in the contemporary urban school, whether it is located in the inner city or outer suburb, is likely to get to know well only students of his own social class and racial and ethnic background. To the degree that this is true his education is ethnocentric rather than cosmopolitan. No place does socio-economic stratification express itself more sharply than in variations in educational achievement among students who live in different localities in urban areas.

Variations in Educational Achievement

How is the socio-economic and racial stratification of metropolitan areas reflected in the educational achievement of students? In this book we have discussed a number of factors which influence educational achievement: (1) inherited biological potential for learning, (2) family background and training, (3) classroom and school experiences, and (4) the self-concept. All of these factors, with the exception of the first, are socially determined by the child's total environment. The evidence indicates that children of metropolitan areas live in sharply different environments. We would therefore expect them to have sharply different achievement records in school. This is true. The socio-economic differences among school districts found in a metropolitan area reflect almost perfectly the differences in school achievement. Because of stratification, individual school districts in metropolitan areas consist of people who are greatly similar to one another in educational level, occupation, and income. These factors tend to provide similar climates for learning and achieving among children.

This close parallel between socio-economic status of the school district and school achievement can be observed in a striking way in Figures 19-2 and 19-3, which show maps of the school districts of the city of Chicago. The legend in Figure 19-2 shows the socio-economic status of the school districts, based upon the educational and income

[19] See Henry Steele Commager, "Our Schools Have Kept Us Free," *Life*, Volume 29, No. 16, October 16, 1950, pp. 46–47.

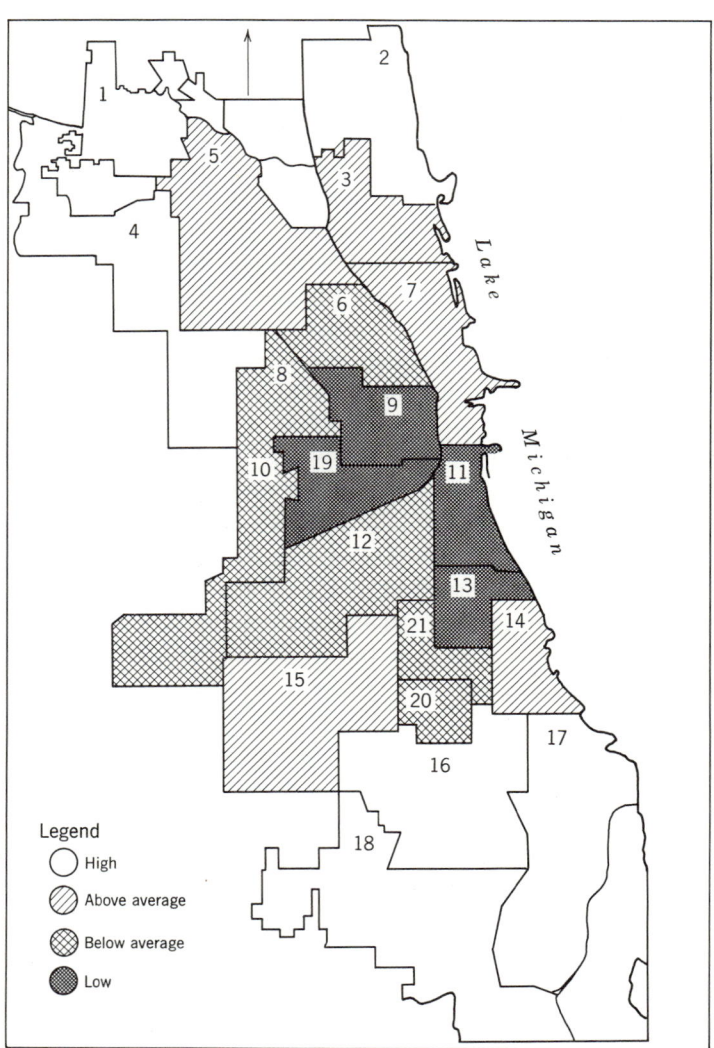

Fig. 19-2   School districts according to socio-economic status: based on educational level plus mean income of adults. SOURCE: Robert J. Havighurst, *The Public Schools of Chicago,* The Board of Education of the City of Chicago, 1964, p. 36.

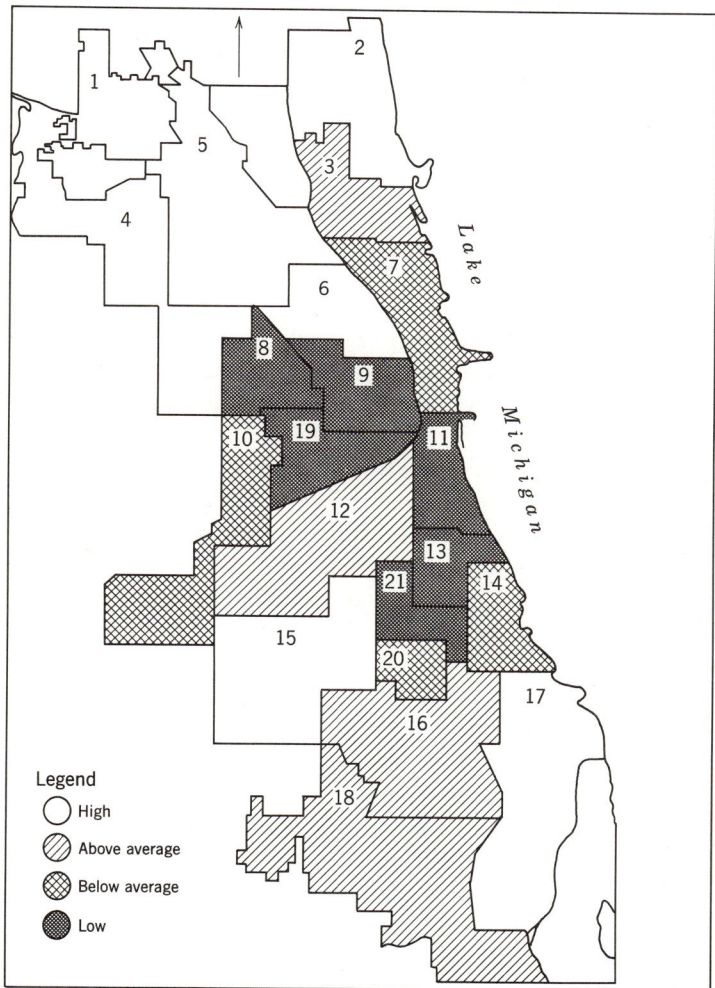

Fig. 19-3 School districts according to achievement of elementary school pupils: sixth-grade reading and arithmetic; first-grade reading readiness. SOURCE: Robert J. Havighurst, *The Public Schools of Chicago,* The Board of Education of the City of Chicago, 1964, p. 37.

level of adults. Figure 19-3 shows the educational achievement of pupils in sixth-grade reading and arithmetic, and first-grade reading readiness in these same districts.

In Figure 19-2 the black areas, representing the low socio-economic areas, are near the center of the city. Next to these areas are the "below average" areas, which in turn are bordered by the "above average" areas farther out. Farthest from the center are the high socio-economic areas. In Figure 19-3 we discover the striking similarities between educational achievement and socio-economic status. The parallel is not perfect, but it is close. In certain transitional districts, educational achievement exceeds socio-economic status. District 12, for example, is "below average" in socio-economic status and "above average" in educational achievement. District 18 has "high" socio-economic status and only "above average" educational achievement. Four districts have a higher level of educational achievement than socio-economic status and six have a lower level of educational achievement than economic status. However, the majority of the districts, eleven, have the same level of educational achievement as socio-economic status.

Two high schools: two levels of achievement. While Figures 19-2 and 19-3 reflect variations between socio-economic status and selected aspects of elementary school achievement, similar variations are found in high school achievement. Havighurst describes achievement in two Chicago high schools, one located in a district with the highest socio-economic rating, and one located in a district with the lowest socio-economic rating.

"School B is in a section of the city with the highest socio-economic ratings on occupation, income, and education of adults. School A is in the lowest section of the city. . . . School B has more than half of its students just at the 'normal' age, and about 25 percent over-age.[20] But School A has 61 percent of its ninth graders over-age, and 55 percent of its 12th graders. School A has only a fourth as many 12th graders as it has ninth graders. At least half of its entering ninth graders drop out of school within the first two years. School B has very few drop-outs. . . .

"The two schools show a great contrast in the proportion of pupils in the various 'tracks' of the program. School A has 4 tracks or ability groupings, called Basic, Essential, Regular, and Honors. School B does not have the lowest, or Basic, track.

[20] Normal age refers to a child's being in the school grade which is "expected" for his age. For instance, a child who entered first grade at six would normally be 13 or 14 when he enters the 9th grade, if he did not skip or fail a grade.

"The two schools contrast sharply in their offerings of Basic, Essential and Honors courses. Students with reading or arithmetic scores below a grade level of 5.9 are placed in 'basic' courses. These pupils are three years retarded or more, since they are in the ninth grade or above. Furthermore, many of them are average, and therefore even further retarded. Those with a reading or arithmetic score between grade level 5.9 and 7.9 are placed in 'essential' courses. They are from one to two years retarded if they are in the ninth grade.

"School A has 65 percent of its ninth graders in Basic or Essential English, and 75 percent in Basic or Essential Mathematics. By the sophomore year there have been many drop-outs, but Basic and Essential English still enroll 59 percent of the students. An Essential Mathematics course continues with 44 percent of second year students. Essential English is continued throughout the four years, with 31 percent of the seniors in it.

"In contrast, School B has nobody in Basic English or Mathematics, but has 12 and 14 percent of ninth graders in Essential English and Mathematics, respectively. After the ninth grade there are no Essential or Basic courses.

"Honors courses enroll 12 percent of ninth graders in School B, in English and in mathematics, and they continue through all four years. But School A has only one percent of ninth graders in English Honors, and 2 percent in Mathematics Honors. Mathematics Honors does not continue, but English Honors continues, getting up to 7 percent of the senior class.

"School A has 15 classes in foreign language, while School B (with a lower enrollment) has 41. School A has a one-semester course in trigonometry for 11th grade students, and nothing beyond that, while School B has honors courses in advanced mathematics, analytical geometry, and calculus for 11th and 12th graders.

"There are, in School A, about 4 percent of 11th and 12th graders who are in the top quarter of all students in the city in ability and achievement test scores. In School B, 63 percent are in the top quarter. Such a vast difference in the abilities and achievement of pupils means that the program of School B is probably better and richer for bright students. One might argue that the program of School A can be expected to be better for slow students. At least, it offers that possibility.

"Both of these schools have unusually good faculties in terms of experience and interest in their work. The principal of School A has energy and insight and determination. Though this is his first year at this school, he has developed a plan for intensified teaching of Basic

English which appears to be working well. He has also established biweekly meetings with new teachers to help them learn to teach in this kind of school.

"Young people in Chicago are a very diverse group. By the time they get to high school, their abilities, their scholastic knowledge, and their expectations in life are so widely different that those who go to one school may have to be taught in ways that would not work in another school." [21]

9. Havighurst states: "One might argue that the program of School A can be expected to be better for slow students. At least, it offers that possibility." How do you react to this possibility?

Cumulative Deficit in School Achievement

The parallel between low socio-economic status and low educational achievement can be better understood through the concept of cumulative deficit. Children from the low socio-economic areas of the city not only start school with the handicap which their environment imposes; they also fall farther and farther behind their more favored peers in achievement as they advance through the grades. The deficit with which they begin becomes cumulative with the passing years. In one large school district of New York the average child was retarded one year in reading in the third grade, almost two years in the sixth grade, and two and one-half in the eighth. [22]

Benjamin S. Bloom, Allison Davis, and Robert Hess described the cumulative deficit phenomenon in achievement among disadvantaged children this way:

"The children begin school with certain inadequacies in language development, perceptual skills, attentional skills, and motivation. Under the usual school curriculum, the achievement pattern of deprived children is such that they fall increasingly behind their non-deprived peers in school subjects. On the average, by eighth grade these children are about three years behind grade norms in reading and arithmetic as well as in other subjects. These effects are most marked in deprived children of average and low ability. One of the consequences of this cumulative deficit is that dropping out of school is much more frequent and this in turn leads to less mobility and opportunity in the occupational sphere.

"The fact that the achievement deficit of these children is cumulative and increases over time seems to reflect some basic weaknesses

---

[21] Havighurst, *op. cit.*, pp. 41, 43, 44.
[22] Shaw, *op. cit.*, p. 92.

in both curriculum and school practices for these children. It would appear from the research that it is easier to overcome these deficits in the earlier years of school than later." [23]

Project Head Start

Bloom, Davis, and Hess indicate that "it would appear from the research that it is easier to overcome these deficits in the earlier years of school than later." Project Head Start, in which culturally deprived children are enrolled for preschool training, is based upon this assumption. It symbolizes the new consensus that preschool education for socially disadvantaged children is a high priority educational need. Begun in the summer of 1965, Project Head Start is designed to reach 560,000 children and their parents and involves 500,000 volunteers and 37,000 teachers.[24] The project places children of four, five, and six into "child development centers" where they are given educational experiences designed to help them avoid cumulative deficits and acquire cumulative credits. In addition, the children are given physical examinations, dental care, and free meals.

More than half of the communities cooperating in Project Head Start are in Southern and border states. A high proportion of the children are Negro, and in conformity with the Civil Rights Act, the project is integrated in both North and South.

Martin Deutsch gives research support to early school enrollment programs.[25] Deutsch's thesis is that lower-class children enter school so poorly prepared to produce the kind of work the school demands that early failure is almost inevitable. These initial failures become negatively reinforced with time and it becomes almost impossible for the child to do other than fail and eventually drop out.

Deutsch believes that the main factors which affect the child's lack of readiness for school include the lack of stimulation in the home. This includes visual, tactile, and auditory stimulation. At home the child sees few objects that help to develop his visual discrimination skills. The lack of playthings curbs the child's tactile development. High noise levels cause him to learn to be inattentive in order to drown

[23] Benjamin S. Bloom, Allison Davis, and Robert Hess, *Compensatory Education for Cultural Deprivation*, New York, Holt, Rinehart and Winston, pp. 73–74.

[24] *Time*, July 2, 1965, p. 64.

[25] See Martin Deutsch, "The Disadvantaged Child in the Learning Process" in A. H. Passow (Ed.), *Education in Depressed Areas*, New York, 1963 Teachers College, Teachers College Press, pp. 163–180; and "Early Social Environment: Its Influence on School Adaptation," in D. Schreiber (Ed.), *The School Dropout*, Washington, D. C., National Education Association, 1964, pp. 89–100.

out noise. Meager communication in the slum home thwarts his development in language. Deutsch's data indicate that as the child grows he can overcome his deficit in visual, tactile, and auditory experience, but his deficit in language increases with time rather than decreases. Since language is the key to much of the child's schoolwork in concept formation and in problem solving, this deficit has a tremendous impact on his learning at all levels.

Following the lead of research which indicates the tremendous importance of the early years in a child's learning, Deutsch studied slum children who were exposed to preschool, kindergarten, or day-care experience, or a combination of these which were designed to overcome deficits. He found that children who had these experiences achieved higher group intelligence scores than those who did not. Further, they maintained their superiority and even widened the gap between themselves and other culturally deprived children as they advanced through the grades. Their scores were higher than others in the first grade, and the difference was accentuated in the fifth grade.

The Head Start Program, which is part of the Federal government's war on poverty, has its rationale in this kind of research. By taking underprivileged children from their constricting environments during the preschool years, it attempts to provide them with enriching experiences to overcome the deficits imposed by their deprived surroundings.

10. One of the features of the Head Start Program is the use of persons from slum areas, frequently mothers, who assist the professional teachers in the project. Why do you think persons from slum homes are used? Can you explain the social meaning of the position in terms of our discussion in Chapter 6 of continuity and discontinuity between home and school?

Changing School Requirements in Suburbia

Urbanization has as much impact upon suburban education as it does on education in the city, though it is of a different nature. The kind of impact which urbanization has depends in part on the type of suburban school district. We indicated earlier that suburbs tend to be socially and economically stratified, just like large cities. It is not easy, therefore, to classify suburban school districts into meaningful groups. For our purposes here we shall use the threefold classification suggested by Alfred W. Beattie,[26] recognizing that these are types

[26] Alfred W. Beattie, "Changing School Needs in Suburban Areas," in *The Schools in the Urban Crisis,* August Kerber and Barbara Bommarito (Eds.), New York, Holt, Rinehart and Winston, 1965, pp. 80–83.

rather than real school districts. Beattie divides suburban school districts into three types: "one-time queen communities," "growing municipalities," and "underdeveloped communities."

The one-time queen communities are those that were formally town centers of business, culture, recreation, and education for neighboring smaller towns. These communities provided secondary schooling for children of the surrounding area, and money and students flowed in, enabling boards of education to build up educational facilities and programs which enjoyed a good reputation.

At the same time other forces started to destroy these communities. Houses and business buildings grew old. Streets became choked with cars when there was no place to park. Industry was shabby in these communities, especially in contrast to the newer industries which were springing up in the surrounding area. It was in these new areas that young professional people decided to build their homes and to commute to work in the one-time queen community or in the urban center. The populations of the new communities increased and built their own high schools, drawing money and students away from the older communities and causing them to retrench in their educational programs. The young people who left the one-time queen communities for the new areas were replaced by older citizens from the outlying rural areas and by culturally deprived families from urban centers. As the tax base of the community went down, the educational program deteriorated, and the same depressing cycle found in many large cities started to repeat itself in one-time queen communities.

The second group of suburbs are those where growth is taking place through the development of new subdivisions. These are the communities where the builders of mass homes are operating. These new communities require in a short space of time all the services of an established community—water, streets, sewers, churches, and schools. For every 1,600 families there must be a 12-room elementary school. Every 6,000 families need a 750-pupil junior high school. And every 12,000 families require a 1,200-pupil senior high school.[27] Thus the district's need for money for education grows at a rapid pace, forcing school boards either to ask citizens to raise taxes or to cut back on other operating expenses such as teachers' salaries, textbooks, libraries, visual aids, and other requirements for an excellent education program. The citizens may or may not respond favorably to the board of education's request to raise taxes; these people are heavily committed to purchasing homes, paving streets, and providing other serv-

[27] *Ibid.,* p. 81.

ices required of a new city. More than likely, however, they will vote for higher school taxes because they moved to the suburbs to get a better education for their children and because they have high educational aspirations.

The third group of suburbs are the unattractive areas that do not appeal to residential developers or buyers. They are frequently not easily accessible to expressways. City water is not available. Cheap housing in these suburbs gives them the reputation for being depressed areas. Hence they attract only persons with low socio-economic status who set the general character for the community. The future will not likely change that basic character very much.

The schools in these depressed suburban areas are usually old, having served the area for some time. There is no tax base and no strong public demand for building new schools or improving existing ones. The deprived educational program simply reinforces the unattractive condition of these undeveloped suburbs.

11. Do you know a suburban community which fits into one of the three groups we have described here? Do the schools tend to reflect the type of community? Can you be specific in terms of the quality of teaching, the curriculum, school buildings, and educational services?

Regardless of the type of suburban area, the rapid transition from the city to suburbia creates changes in the political, economic, and cultural fabric of the community, all of which influence the schools. Here are a few of the difficult problems confronting suburban schools: (1) changing community leadership, (2) changing faculty leadership, (3) the acute need for teachers and the need for adequate financing.[28]

Changing community leadership. The growth of a suburban community with its influx of new families has a disorganizing effect on the power structure. The old residents may regard the new as "intruders," largely because they have different backgrounds, interests, status, and cultural orientation. The old residents find it difficult to face the problems created by rapid growth, especially the need for new schools. They blame their higher taxes on the presence of the new residents.

Mr. Prentice's community of Robertsdale discussed in Chapter 17 was a community in transition in which power was being shifted from the old "As Is" group to the new "Show Me" group whose spokesman on the board of education was Prentice. As in Robertsdale the schools in transitional communities are frequently caught in the power shifts

[28] For a discussion of these and other problems of education in suburbia see Paul Zintgroff, "Bedroom Communities and the School," *Educational Leadership,* February 1960, pp. 292–297.

which, until they are settled, can leave the school without strong lay leadership. Worse still, the school itself becomes the battleground for contending power factions in the community.

Changing faculty leadership. Building a school faculty requires far more than simply employing the required number of teachers and administrators. The faculty develops as people learn to organize themselves for effective action, work together, solve problems, and develop common programs and goals. Teachers and administrators employed for a new school in a short period of time come with diverse social backgrounds, training, and philosophies of education. Until they have had an opportunity to form a common base for action their efforts are likely to be diffuse and uncoordinated.

If the school district is an established one which is experiencing sudden and rapid growth, a power struggle may ensue between the "old" and the "new" teachers. Veteran teachers in the system may find the progressive educational ideas of the newcomers disquieting, and the new teachers will think the existing programs of the school are not equal to the broadened requirements of the growing community.

The acute need for teachers. The demands put upon a new and growing school district are frequently greater than those put upon a fully developed community whose schools have their full complement of students and teachers. It is during the growing years that resources in money and people are shortest and demands upon these resources are the heaviest. In the period of rapid growth the district must acquire land for future school sites, plan and build buildings, sell bond issues, go to the taxpayers for increased revenues, constantly integrate new families and children into the school program, develop a transportation system, build libraries and curriculum materials, and develop special services in such areas as counseling and guidance, mental retardation, and physical handicap. All of these goals must be accomplished in a relatively short time.

These are large orders to accomplish for even an established school system. In the new and growing school system they are constant reminders of the need to employ more teachers and administrators at the very time when money is not available.

Adequate financing. Suburban areas tend to be predominantly residential rather than industrial. Indeed the appeal of a suburb to homeowners is that it is far from the sight, sound, and smell of industry. Yet industry has high tax valuation and residences have low tax valuation. Most children, however, are in the residential rather than industrial areas.

Suburban schools must educate their many children on a relatively modest tax base. Even the high-priced homes of affluent suburbs do not produce adequate revenue to maintain a program of education that meets the demands of the citizens. Suburban boards of education find themselves constantly in need of more adequate financing and must usually appeal to the citizenry to raise its taxes.

This crisis in urban schools springs from the crisis in urban development generally. As Robert C. Weaver states in the sentence at the head of this chapter: "What happens in cities happens to schools. For no school system exists in a vacuum." The schools, however, do more than reflect urban change. Through strong efforts to upgrade educational programs for urban youth they can have a constructive influence on urban change.

Closely knit with education problems resulting from urban change are those springing from the Negroes' rising demand for full citizenship and equal educational opportunity for their children. We shall turn next to this important educational development in our changing society.

REFERENCES

Paperbacks

Changing Metropolis. Frederick I. Tietze and James E. McKeown. (Orig.) Houghton Mifflin Co., 2 Park St., Boston, Mass. Educational Div.: 110 Tremont St., Boston, Mass. ($2.25).

Class and Society. Kurt B. Mayer. (Orig.) (SS10-RH) Random House, 457 Madison Ave., New York ($1.25).

Crestwood Heights: A Study of the Culture of Suburban Life. J. R. Seeley, R. A. Sim and E. W. Loosley. Science Editions Paperbacks, John Wiley and Sons, 605 Third Ave., New York ($2.45).

Economics and Politics of Public Education, No. 2: Government and the Suburban School. Roscoe C. Martin. (Orig.) Syracuse University Press, University Station, Syracuse, N. Y. ($1.75).

Economics and Politics of Public Education, No. 5: Cost and Quality in Public Education. Harold F. Clark. (Orig.) Syracuse University Press, University Station, Syracuse, N. Y. ($1.75).

Economics and Politics of Public Education, No. 10: Suburban Power Structures and Public Education. Warner Bloomberg, Jr. and Morris Sunshine. (Orig.) Syracuse University Press, University Station, Syracuse, N. Y. ($1.75).

Education and Income: Inequalities of Opportunity in Our Public Schools. Patricia Sexton. (C168) Compass Books, The Viking Press, 625 Madison Ave., New York ($1.65).

Education in Depressed Areas. A. Harry Passow, Editor. Teachers College, Teachers College Press, 525 West 120 St., New York ($2.50).

Education in Urban Society. B. J. Chandler, Lindley J. Stiles, and John I. Kitsuse. (Orig.) Dodd, Mead and Co., 432 Park Ave. South, New York ($3.75).

Growing Up in the City. John Barron Mays. Science Editions Paperbacks, John Wiley and Sons, 605 Third Ave., New York ($1.65).

Integrating the Urban School. Gordon J. Klopf and Israel A. Laster. (Orig.) Teachers College, Teachers College Press, 525 West 120 St., New York ($1.95).

Learning to Teach in Urban Schools. Dorothy M. McGeoch, et al. Teachers College, Teachers College Press, 525 West 120 St., New York ($1.95).

Metropolis 1985. Raymond Vernon. (A341) Anchor Books and Anchor Science Study Series, Doubleday and Co., 277 Park Ave., New York ($1.45).

Metropolitan Area as a Racial Problem. Morton Grodzins. (Orig.) (58-59695) University of Pittsburgh Press, 3309 Cathedral of Learning, Pittsburgh, Pa. (50¢).

Poverty in America. Margaret S. Gordon, Editor. (Orig.) Chandler Publishing Co., 124 Spear St., San Francisco, Calif. ($2.50).

Poverty: Its Roots and Its Future. Hyman Lumer. (Orig.) (LNW-2) New World Paperbacks, International Publishers, 381 Park Ave. South, New York (95¢).

Poverty: Social Conscience in the Progressive Era. Robert Hunter. Peter d'A. Jones, Editor. (TB/3065) Harper Torchbooks, Harper College Paperbacks, Harper and Row, 49 E. 33rd St., New York ($2.25).

Schools and the Urban Crisis: A Book of Readings. August F. Kerber and Barbara T. Bommarito. (Orig.) (t) Holt, Rinehart and Winston, 383 Madison Ave., New York ($3.95).

School's Role in Metropolitan Area Development. Richard C. Lonsdale. (Orig.) Syracuse University Press, University Station, Syracuse, N. Y. ($1.00).

Slums and Suburbs. James B. Conant. New American Library of World Literature, 1301 Ave. of the Americas, New York (60¢).

Squeeze: Cities without Space. Edward Higbee. (A43) Apollo Editions, 425 Park Ave. South, New York (Imprint of T. Y. Crowell, Dodd Mead, William Morrow, and The Dial Press) ($1.85).

Books

Editors of Fortune, *The Exploding Metropolis.* Garden City, N. Y.: Doubleday and Co., 1958. This book presents a study of a metropolitan area and its rapid growth. Chapter 4 is entitled "The Enduring Slums."

Hoover, E. M., and R. Vernon, *Anatomy of a Metropolis.* Cambridge, Mass.: Harvard University Press, 1959. Occupational groups tend to live near their jobs, except the upper white-collar workers who choose low-density communities, the suburbs, even if these communities are a great distance away.

Glazer, Nathan, and Daniel Patrick Moynihan, *Beyond the Melting Pot: The Negroes, Puerto Ricans, Jews, Italians, and Irish of New York City.* Cambridge, Mass.: M.I.T. Press and Harvard University Press, 1964. As a minority social class is integrated into the American middle class, changes within the minority group take place. In several groups the move to the suburbs and the growth of interest in parochial education are documented.

Handlin, Oscar, *The Newcomers; Negroes and Puerto Ricans in a Changing Metropolis.* Cambridge, Mass.: Harvard University Press, 1959. This book discusses education as a means of opportunity for Negroes and Puerto Ricans.

Hunter, Evan, *Blackboard Jungle.* New York: Simon and Schuster, 1954. A novel describing the uphill battle of a new teacher in an urban school attended by juvenile delinquents.

Whyte, William Foote, *Street Corner Society.* Chicago: University of Chicago Press, 1955. A description of a slum environment within a large city.

Periodicals

Cunningham, William J., "Stirrings in the Big Cities: Boston," *NEA Journal,* Vol. 51, No. 7, October 1962, pp. 48–50. This article discusses the educational changes that are taking place in the schools of Boston. Included in the changes are the addition of summer reading laboratories, English as a second language, Operation Second Chance, and a pre-apprentice program.

Goldstein, Sidney, and Kurt Mayer, "Population Decline and the Social and Demographic Structure of an American City," *American Sociological Review,* Vol. XXIX, No. 1, January 1964, pp. 48–54. An analysis of changes in class structure in one city during a two-decade population decline.

Green, Myrtle, and H. Bailey Gardner, "Stirrings in the Big City Schools: Kansas City," *NEA Journal,* Vol. 51, No. 9, December 1962, pp. 34–36. Three examples of changes are given: teacher centers, teacher retraining workshops, and scholarships for disadvantaged children.

Havighurst, Robert J., "How Big City and Suburban Schools Can Get Together," *The Nation's Schools,* Vol. LXXIV, No. 3, September 1964, pp. 60–61. The author suggests that city and suburban school districts should be consolidated into an administrative unit.

Mayer, Martin, "Close to Midnight for the New York Schools," *New York Times Magazine,* Vol. CXIV, No. 39,180, May 2, 1965, pp. 34–35. The New York public school system is losing its middle-class students, and the minority problems it faces become more and more acute.

Tyler, Ralph W., and Richard I. Miller, "Social Forces and Trends," *NEA Journal,* Vol. 51, No. 6, 1962, pp. 26–28. The tendency toward class stratification in metropolitan areas poses a serious problem to the American concept of the school as an important laboratory of democracy, enrolling all the children of all the people.

Ward, Barbara, "The City May Be as Lethal as the Bomb," *New York Times Magazine,* Vol. CXIII, No. 38,802, April 19, 1964, pp. 22–23. Miss Ward believes cities should be communities in which human beings are civilized and enriched, but she wonders if we are not heading toward an urban world that will not be worth living in.

20

The Negro Child
and the Schools

"My grandmother says I'm the first of her grandchildren to come through high school. You see how important this is to me?" A NEGRO GIRL

In Chapter 17 we described the struggle of parents in two neighborhoods, Fairlawn and Urbandale, to influence the policy of the schools. This incident illustrates equally well three key issues in the continuing conflict over racial integration.

First, there is reflected in the conflict the social and economic stratification of urban areas, a topic examined in Chapter 19. The parents in both Fairlawn and Urbandale had left Metropolis and settled in "their kind" of neighborhood with people of similar social, economic, and racial characteristics. The result was distinct segregation between the upper middle-class whites of Fairlawn and the lower middle-class Negroes of Urbandale.

Second, there is the emotional base of the conflict. The white parents of Fairlawn left Metropolis because the Negroes were beginning to move into their neighborhood. Property values and the quality of the school's program were falling. They came to Fairlawn to have what they regarded as a good place to live, and to have a school suited to the high educational aspirations which they held for their children. In the proposed temporary move of their children to Urbandale and the possibility of the later transfer of Urbandale children to Fairlawn, they saw repetition of the conditions that they escaped in Metropolis. With strong protest they indicated they were not about to have this happen.

Emotional feelings ran high among Negro parents, too. They were convinced that the *de facto* segregation in their school resulted in inferior education for their children. They wanted something better.

This emotional tone of the racial conflict cannot be resolved by a Supreme Court decision making segregated schools illegal; nor is logic of much avail. Because the emotions in the conflict are strong, they infuse all considerations of law and logic.

Third, there is in the Urbandale and Fairlawn conflict the question of the proper role of the neighborhood school, an almost sacred institution in American community life. If the Urbandale and Fairlawn schools were to serve only ther own neighborhoods, they would probably remain segregated as long as their respective neighborhoods were segregated. School attendance lines were drawn to enclose the neighborhoods. The Negro parents of Urbandale wished to apply a new principle to the drawing of attendance lines. Instead of using neighborhood boundaries for determining attendance areas they wished to use racial mixture as the determining principle. This was precisely what Fairlawn parents opposed.

This issue pervades much of the current debate on school desegregation. Those who favor the neighborhood school principle for determining attendance areas argue that each child is entitled to go to school close to his home and that parents are entitled to be near their school so they can develop a sense of ownership and pride. This point of view is expressed in comments like this: "Now don't get me wrong. I ain't got nothing against colored people. If they want good schools, they ought to have good schools, but they ought to go to schools in *their* neighborhood—just like white kids ought to go to school in *their* neighborhood." [1]

1. Do you think that "good" schools in Negro neighborhoods are as good as "good" schools in white neighborhoods?

More important, those who favor neighborhood schools argue that segregated residential patterns are not the fault of the schools. Residential segregation is determined by forces over which the schools have no control. The school should not, therefore, be made responsible for correcting social conditions which the community itself seems to accept.

Persons who argue for racial balance in the schools argue that even though the schools did not create segregated residential patterns they can do something to soften the impact of this segregation upon children. They point to the low quality of segregated Negro schools and they claim that as a part of good education children should be permitted to grow up with those of different racial and socio-economic

[1] Peggy Streit, "Why They Fight for the P.T.A.," *New York Times Magazine,* Volume CXIV, No. 38,956, September 20, 1964, p. 20.

backgrounds. The school, they say, must develop cosmopolitan values rather than narrow, ethnocentric attitudes. Segregated schools can only promote biased views toward others, whereas the integrated school develops a broader appreciation of cultural differences. They state that this cosmopolitan appreciation for and tolerance of others is basic to our democratic society.

2. Sometimes it is said that teachers and school administrators should be color-blind, taking no account of the racial, social, or national backgrounds of their students. This argument seems to be the epitome of nondiscrimination and democracy. Do you think it is?

These three factors, segregated residential patterns, the deep emotions of the conflict, and the neighborhood school, all pervade the school integration issue. They underlie the consideration of the Negro child and the schools in this chapter. We shall not deal with the historical and legal aspects of integration. Our main concern is with the human aspects: how the issue influences what happens to and in schools. We are interested especially in seeing how the problem influences the way students learn, teachers teach, and schools organize to meet the new challenge of extending equal educational opportunity to all children.

The Search for Guiding Principles

Desegregation is no longer a legal issue. Legal challenges to the Supreme Court decision outlawing segregated schools continue, but there is little doubt as to their eventual outcome. These may serve to delay integration and gain time for those school districts that are quite honestly searching for workable ways to desegregate. For the "hard core" hold-out districts that "never intend to integrate" legal action is an effective stalling device. Yet the law is clear: "Separate educational facilities are inherently unequal," and public education "must be made available to all on equal terms." [2]

The dominant emphasis now shifts to a search for principles which can guide the crucial transition from segregation to integration. How can integration be accomplished with reverence and regard for the rights of all children? The Advisory Commission on Human Relations and Community Tensions of the New York State Department of Education proposed six principles as guides in dealing with *de facto* segregation, racial imbalance, and similar questions. These principles place in perspective the human aspects of the transition from segregated to desegregated schools.

[2] Brown versus Topeka Board of Education, 347 U. S. 483.

1. "The common school has long been viewed as a basic social instrument in attaining our traditional American goals of equal opportunity and personal fulfillment. The presence in a single school of children from varied racial, cultural, socio-economic, and religious backgrounds is an important element in the preparation of young people for active participation in the social and political affairs of our democracy.

2. "In forming school policies, every educationally sound action should be taken to assure not only passive tolerance but active acceptance of, and genuine respect for, children from every segment of the community, with particular attention given to those from minority groups that may have been the objects of discriminatory treatment.

3. "No action, direct or indirect, overt or covert, should be taken by any public agency to exclude any child or group of children from a public school because of ethnic, racial, religious, or other educationally irrelevant reasons. Wherever such action has occurred it is the obligation of the school authorities to correct it as quickly as possible.

4. "No action should be taken which implies that any school or any group of pupils is socially inferior or superior to another, or which suggests that schoolmates of one group are to be preferred to schoolmates of another. In establishing school attendance areas, one of the objectives should be to create in each school a student body that will represent as nearly as possible a cross section of the population of the entire school district. At the same time due consideration should be given to other important educational criteria, including such practical matters as the distance children must travel from home to school.

5. "A 'neighborhood school' offers important educational values that should not be overlooked. The relation between a school and a definable community with which it is identified can, in many cases, lead to more effective participation by parents and other citizens in the support and guidance of the school. It can stimulate sound concern for the welfare of the school and its pupils and can lead to beneficial communication between the school staff and the community that staff serves.

6. "When a 'neighborhood school' becomes improperly exclusive in fact or in spirit, when it is viewed as being reserved for certain community groups, or when its effect is to create or continue a ghetto-type situation, it does not serve the purposes of democratic education." [3]

[3] Reported by John H. Fischer, "Desegregating City Schools," *P.T.A. Magazine,* Volume 59, No. 4, December 1964, pp. 11–12.

This statement of principles argues strongly for (1) the educational values of culturally mixed classrooms as preparation for active participation in our democracy, (2) positive acceptance in schools of children from every segment of the community, especially minority groups, (3) positive action on the part of the school to correct public actions which discriminate, for any reason, against children, and (4) the neighborhood school, except when it becomes "improperly exclusive," or results in racially ghetto-type situations.

A Search for Plans

The search for principles to guide integration has been accompanied by a search for integration plans. A number of plans have been proposed for applying the above principles to the desegregation of schools.[4] No one plan is suitable to all communities and none offers the perfect solution anywhere. Here are some of the plans, however, which are being proposed and used.

Open enrollment. Under this plan schools with available space are authorized to receive pupils from other schools which are crowded and otherwise less desirable. The sending school is usually a heavily segregated school and the receiving one usually has a better "racial

[4] For this discussion the author is indebted to John H. Fischer, *op. cit.*, pp. 12–13.

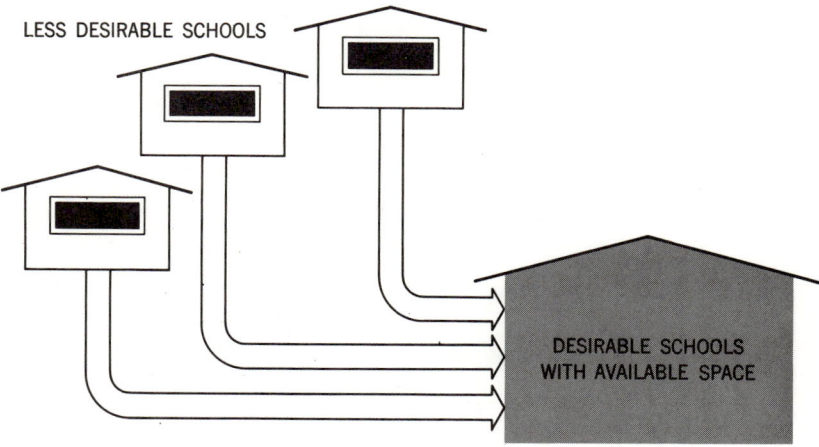

Fig. 20-1 Open enrollment.

balance." Commonly Negro children are transferred by bus to a predominantly white school, though it is not uncommon for white children to be "bussed" to predominantly Negro schools. The plan, however, is more likely to correct racial imbalance in the receiving school than in the sending school, because the heaviest flow of students is from the congested slum schools to more middle-class white schools.

There is evidence to indicate that the open-enrollment plan is unpopular both with white and Negro parents.[5]

Pairing. This plan, sometimes called the "Princeton Plan" after the New Jersey town where it was first used, is best suited to situations where adjacent schools enroll predominantly white pupils in one and Negro pupils in the other. The two schools are brought together and treated as a single attendance area. For example, the first three grades may attend School A, and the second three grades, School B.

In this manner both schools enroll both racial groups and can concentrate on a narrower span of grades. The disadvantages are that because some children must travel longer distances, the needs for transportation are increased. Further, the established neighborhood pattern for the school is disrupted.

[5] See "Reading, Writing and Racial Unrest," *Wall Street Journal,* Volume XLIV, No. 232, September 4, 1964, p. 20.

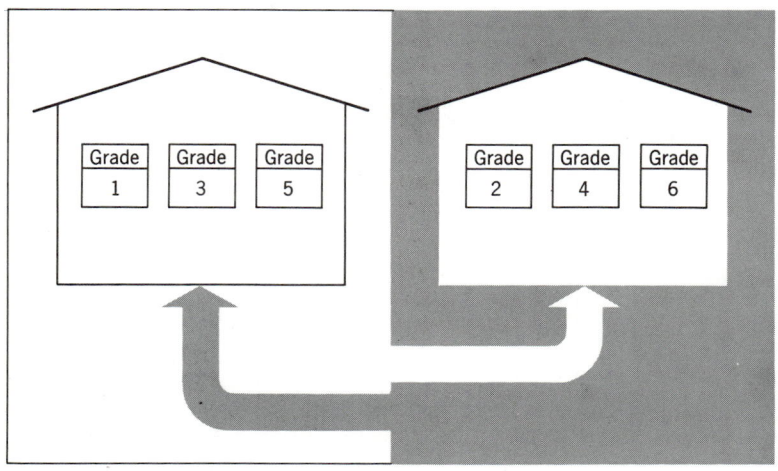

AVERAGE NEIGHBORHOOD   SEGREGATED NEIGHBORHOOD

Fig. 20-2   Pairing.

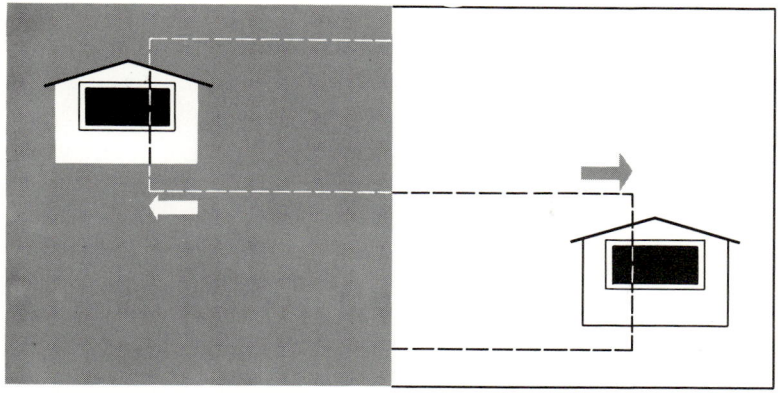

SEGREGATED NEIGHBORHOOD   AVERAGE NEIGHBORHOOD

Fig. 20-3 Zoning changes.

3. A New York City taxicab driver said: "You buy a house because you want your kid to go to school nearby and the church is just around the corner. And then here comes the government or school board and what do they say? They say, 'Mister, you can't send your kid to school near you. You got to bus him to school in a Negro neighborhood, 20 blocks away, that's been—what do they call it—paired with a white school because of racial imbalance.' Now I ask you, is that right?" [6] If the taxi driver were to ask you, what would you say?

Zoning changes. In this plan school attendance lines are redrawn to take into account the racial composition of neighborhoods. Generally school attendance lines demark neighborhood lines, which tend also to demark racial lines. In making zoning changes, lines are deliberately redrawn to include children in all districts of different racial and cultural backgrounds. This plan is best suited to the inner city where attendance areas are compact, but is least suited to outlying areas where distances are greater. In outlying areas it is difficult to achieve a reasonable balance of racial population by rezoning, and if it is accomplished the travel time for students may be great.

Educational complexes. Under this plan a group of adjacent schools, perhaps a junior high school and its elementary feeder schools, are brought together as a small school system within a larger one.

[6] Streit, *op. cit.*, p. 20.

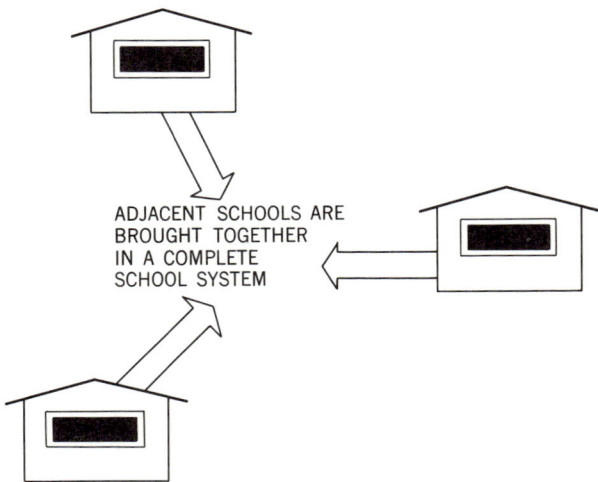

Fig. 20-4   Educational complexes.

The boundaries of the small system are drawn in order to include areas of different racial composition. Within this cluster several types of arrangements are possible. Children can be assigned and reassigned among the schools to achieve a better racial balance. Special activities and educational services which cannot be carried on in each of the buildings can be conducted in one or two, and students can be transferred among buildings for these special purposes. The educational complex combines the advantages of the neighborhood school with the benefits of membership in a larger community and wider choices of personal associations and program offerings.

Educational parks. The educational park is one of the newest and boldest plans offered for coping with segregation problems in the urban community.[7] The educational park is a plan for bringing all the schools of a large section of the city, or even the whole city, onto

[7] For discussion of this plan see James E. Mauch, "The Education Park," *The American School Board Journal,* Volume 150, No. 3, March 1965, pp. 9–11.

a single campus. The plan applies the rural consolidated school idea, in which children from a large attendance area are brought to a single school site, to the urban setting. Thus in urban districts where pupils cannot be furnished adequate education in existing schools they would be transported to a central "consolidated" school and there be assigned to classes with students from other parts of the city. Some advocates of this plan would like to see all elementary, junior, and senior high schools, concentrated on one site. Others would prefer that separate campuses be designed to accommodate different level schools.

On a central campus some economies might be effected in the operation of the schools, but these would probably be offset by increased cost in transportation. Against these increased outlays must be set the possibility for better education than can be provided under existing circumstances.

4. As you review these various plans for accomplishing integration, which do you think comes closest to embodying the guiding principles discussed earlier? Why?

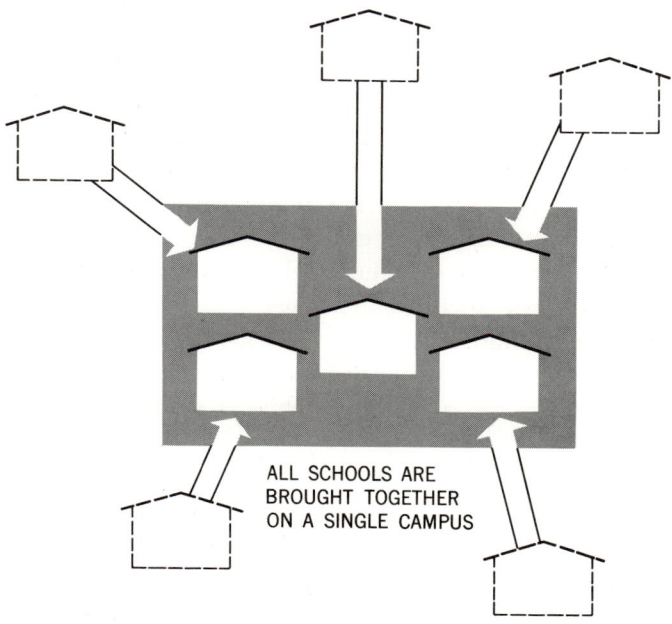

ALL SCHOOLS ARE
BROUGHT TOGETHER
ON A SINGLE CAMPUS

Fig. 20-5 Educational parks.

The search for principles to guide integration and for plans to accomplish it must always take into consideration the child, Negro or white. It is his educational opportunities which are at stake, and it is the Negro child to whom we now turn.

The Lower-Class Negro Child

Negroes of all social classes are deeply involved in and concerned about achieving equal educational opportunity. It is in the lower-class Negro child, however, that we see the problem in its sharpest human outlines. His constricted environment and its impact upon him make clear the size of the challenge to education. What is the lower-class Negro child like? [8]

His social world. What is the Negro slum child's social world like? Does it differ from that of the white child in the slum? If so, how? Suzanne Keller studied selected aspects of after-school and home activities of poor Negro and Caucasian children attending the first and fifth grades in New York City public schools.[9] Taking for her study 46 first- and fifth-grade Negro and white students, Keller gave the children intelligence tests, gave the parents questionnaires, and interviewed one-fifth of the families in their homes.

Keller found that Negro children came from larger families than white children, and that fewer of these children were supported by their father's earnings. Unemployment was three times more prevalent in Negro than white families. The fathers of white children had on an average one more year of schooling than Negro fathers, and in both groups mothers were better educated than fathers. Negro parents were more mobile geographically but less mobile occupationally.

Fifth-grade Negro children had more negative self-concepts than did white children. Eighty percent of the Negro children compared themselves unfavorably with others, whereas only 30 percent of the white children made such comparisons. The teachers judged over half of the Negro children to have little motivation, to be sad, preoccupied, or to be working below capacity in school. Negro parents expressed more concern about their children's schoolwork than did

[8] For an investigation of the differential influences of rejection on lower- and higher-income Negro children see R. M. Goff, "Some Educational Implications of the Influence of Rejection on Aspiration Levels of Minority Group Children," *Journal of Experimental Education*, Volume 23, No. 2, December 1954, pp. 179–183.

[9] Suzanne Keller, "The Social World of the Urban Slum Child: Some Early Findings," *American Journal of Orthopsychiatry*, Volume 33, No. 5, October 1963, pp. 823–831.

white parents who were, on the whole, satisfied with their children's school performance.

Keller reports other findings of interest about both Negro and white children. Although the children came from large families living in crowded areas of the slums, they had little sustained contact with adults. In both Negro and white homes there was little shared family activity. Keller believes that this constricted experience may account for the below normal I.Q. scores which the children achieved. The mean score for the first-grade children was 97, and for the fifth grade, 89.

5. What does I.Q. measure? Anthropologist S. L. Washburn states: "It is exceedingly difficult to see why anyone ever thought that the I.Q. measured innate intelligence, and not the genetic constitution as modified in the family, in the schools, and by the general intellectual environment." [10] What do you think this statement should mean for a teacher of socially disadvantaged children?

His self-concept. Keller reports, as noted, more negative self-concepts among fifth-grade Negro children than white children. What, we might ask, are the sources of the Negro child's feelings of inferiority? Apparently his negative feelings spring from two sources, (1) the reality of his immediate experience, in which he is made constantly aware that he does not measure up to the performance of others, especially white children, and (2) his emotional accommodation to the demeaning role which segregation imposes upon him. The Group for the Advancement of Psychiatry summarizes the observations of numerous investigators of Negro personality this way: "Wherever segregation occurs, one group, in this instance the Negroes, always suffers from inferior social status. The damaging effects of this are reflected in unrealistic inferiority feelings, a sense of humiliation and constriction of potentialities for self-development. This often results in a pattern of self-hatred and rejection of one's own group, sometimes expressed by antisocial behavior toward one's own group or the dominant group. These attitudes seriously affect the levels of aspiration, the capacity to learn, and the capacity to relate to interpersonal situations." [11]

D. P. and Pearl Ausubel, in "Ego Development Among Segregated Negro Children," gave this description of the development of self-identity.

[10] S. L. Washburn, "The Study of Race," *American Anthropologist,* Volume 65, No. 3, Part 1, June 1963, p. 529.

[11] "Psychiatric Aspects of School Segregation," New York, Group for the Advancement of Psychiatry, 1947, p. 10.

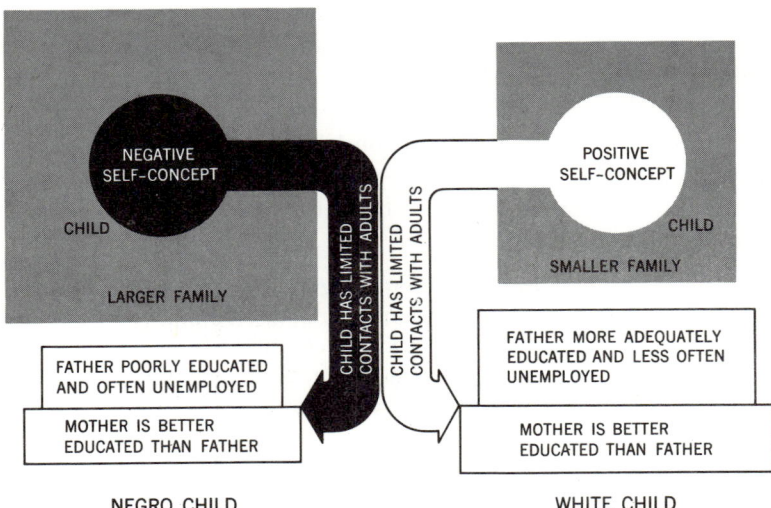

Fig. 20-6 Social world of the Negro and white underprivileged child.

"Beginning in the pre-school period, the Negro child gradually learns to appreciate the negative implications of dark skin color for social status and personal worth. Hence he resists identifying with his own racial group and shows definite preference for white dolls and playmates. This reluctance to acknowledge his racial membership not only results in ego deflation, but also makes it difficult to identify with his parents and to obtain from such identification the derived status that universally constitutes the principal basis for self-esteem during childhood. Much of the derived status that white children obtain from their parents is made available to the Negro child by virtue of his membership in an unsupervised peer group, which accordingly performs many of the socializing functions of the white middle-class home. This is especially true for the Negro boy who often has no adult male with whom to identify in the frequently fatherless Negro family, and who finds maleness deprecated in his matriarchal and authoritarian home. Early experience in fending for himself results in precocious social maturity, independence, and emancipation from the home.

"During pre-adolescence and adolescence, segregated Negro children characteristically develop low aspirations for academic and vocational achievement. These low aspirations reflect existing social class and ethnic values, the absence of suitable emulatory modes, marked educational retardation, restricted vocational opportunities, lack of parental and peer group support, and the cultural impoverishment of the Negro home. Because of loyalty to parents and rejection by the dominant white group, Negro adolescents develop ambivalent feelings toward middle-class achievement values and the personality traits necessary for their implementation. Girls tend to develop a more mature ego structure than boys probably because of their favored position in the home." [12]

His self-fulfilling prophecy. One of the critical aspects of the Negro child's negative self-concept is that it is self-perpetuating and self-fulfilling. A poor self-concept tends to reinforce rather than correct itself.

It is interesting to note the manner in which this reinforcement takes place. The Negro child in a segregated society is defined as inferior by that society. This very definition tends to produce in the child, regardless of its truth or untruth, inferior behavior in keeping with society's expectations. If society characterizes him as mentally inferior, incompetent, and irresponsible, he will tend to confirm this in his behavior by being mentally inferior, incompetent, and irresponsible.

This confirmation does not come about automatically, however. In the first place, society "institutionalizes" the Negro child's inferior role through segregated schools, lower expectations on the part of teachers, and other acts of discrimination. Then the society rewards the child's behavior when he fits docilely into the pattern and punishes him when he does not. Thus the child's behavior is "correct" when he fulfills society's expectations and incorrect when he does not. His negative self-concept is thus continuously self-perpetuating. [13]

Efforts to improve the Negro child's education must be aimed at breaking this self-fulfilling prophecy, of creating an awareness that new, more positive behavior is both possible and rewarding. One of the strong arguments for integration is that it helps to break the constantly reinforced inferiority implicit in segregated schools. As we shall see later in this chapter, integration alone cannot guarantee this result; but it can be the first all-important step. It can set up the necessary conditions in which the Negro student can build a new self-concept,

[12] D. P. and Pearl Ausubel, "Ego Development Among Segregated Negro Children," in A. H. Passow (Ed.), *Education in Depressed Areas,* New York, Teachers College, Columbia University, 1963, pp. 109–141.

[13] For further discussion of this topic see Ralph H. Hones, "Social Expectations and Cultural Deprivation," *The Journal of Negro Education,* Volume XXXIII, No. 2, 1964, pp. 136–142; and R. K. Merten, "The Self-fulfilling Prophecy," *Antioch Review,* Volume 8, No. 2, Summer 1948, pp. 193–210.

especially if he discovers he is able to compete successfully with his white peers. Here is the comment of a Negro student who made that discovery in Atlanta's Henry Grady High School: "Before I went to a white high school, I didn't know how I'd compare with white students. When I found out I could do well, it gave me great self-confidence." [14] This student is not only conquering the negative, self-fulfilling prophecy; he is substituting a positive one in its place.

6. What specific things can a classroom teacher do to help a minority-group child reverse the self-fulfilling prophecy?

The social world of the lower-class Negro child tends to consist of a large fatherless family in which there is little genuine communication between children and adults. Frequently it consists of a segregated school where discrimination engenders a negative self-concept, where low aspirations are the rule, and where low estate is perpetuated through a self-fulfilling prophecy. What do we know about the level of achievement in segregated schools?

His segregated school. There is abundant research evidence to indicate that the education that Negro children receive in segregated schools is inferior to that received by white children. R. L. Plaut summarized the over-all situation this way:

"Negroes have long been aware that most of their schools in the South, and often the *de facto* segregated schools in the North, are rundown, poorly staffed, and shorthanded. Second and third-rate schooling for Negroes leaves them without the ability to compete with white students and robs them of the initiative to compete." [15]

To support Plaut's general conclusion we cite several specific research studies. In testing for achievement in Atlanta schools W. G. Findley found that from 40 percent to 60 percent of white pupils met the standards set by the top 50 percent of a national sample on different tests; but only 2 percent to 10 percent of Negro students met this standard on the various tests. [16] In Tennessee, according to E. Wyatt, Negro students average one and one-half to two years behind grade level when transferred to biracial schools in the upper grades. [17] In the

[14] "Integration Has Its Quiet Side," *New York Times*, Volume CXII, No. 38,431, April 7, 1963, p. 60.

[15] R. L. Plaut, *Blueprint for Talent Searching*, New York, National Scholarship Service and Fund for Negro Students, 1957, p. 5.

[16] W. G. Findley, *Learning and Teaching in Atlanta Public Schools*, Princeton, N. J., Educational Testing Service, 1956.

[17] E. Wyatt, United States Commission on Civil Rights, *Civil Rights U.S.A.— Public Schools, Southern States*, Washington, D. C., United States Government Printing Office, 1962, pp. 105–130.

earlier grades Negro students performed satisfactorily. Wyatt's report also describes the status of the Negro and white teachers in the Tennessee urban area. Among the white teachers more than 97 percent of the 783 passed the National Teachers Examination. Only 49 percent of 901 academically qualified Negro teachers passed the test. This same report indicates that the academic retardation of segregated Negro elementary school students gets progressively worse as they move through the grades.

Other data indicate that the racial gap in academic achievement continues to widen through high school and college. S. O. Roberts found that less than 3 percent of the students from segregated high schools would meet the standards of nonsegregated colleges.[18] Roberts estimated that not more than 10 to 15 percent of Negro American college youth were capable of exceeding the minimum level score on the American Council on Education test that is recommended for college admission.

The poor quality of segregated Negro education is not confined to the South. It is evident in the North as well, where many schools, although legally integrated, are in fact segregated.[19] Martin Deutsch took time samples of classroom activity and found that from 50 to 80 percent of all time in elementary schools with predominantly Negro, lower-class children was "devoted to disciplining and various essentially non-academic tasks. By comparison, only thirty percent of classroom time in elementary schools attended by white children was given over to such activities."[20]

It is clear from the evidence that the Negro child suffers academically in segregated schools. Does he fare better in integrated schools? As we shall see, the question is a complex one. How the Negro child succeeds in integrated schools depends on many factors.

Effects of Integration on the Achievement of Negro Students

When a Negro child transfers from a segregated to a desegregated school, what is likely to be the impact upon his intellectual performance? Almost invariably he is confronted with two new sets of

---

[18] S. O. Roberts, "Test Performance in Relation to Ethnic Group and Social Class," Report, 1963, Fisk University, Nashville, Tenn. (Mimeographed)

[19] For a study of *de facto* segregation in a Northern city see Max Wolff, "Segregation in the Schools in Gary, Indiana," *The Journal of Educational Sociology,* Volume 36, No. 6, February 1963, pp. 251–261.

[20] Martin Deutsch, "Minority Group and Class Status as Related to Social and Personality Factors in Scholastic Achievement," *Social and Applied Anthropology,* Monograph, 1960, No. 2, p. 8.

environmental conditions: (1) He enters a new racial environment. There is a substantial increase in the proportion of white peers and in white teachers; (2) He is exposed to relatively high academic standards. Higher educational standards generally prevail in the schools into which he is integrated than in the school he left.[21]

On the basis of these two new environmental conditions Irwin Katz postulates that four determinants will have important influences on the Negro student's scholastic achievement in the integrated school.[22] He lists these determinants as (1) social threat, (2) social facilitation, (3) probability of success, and (4) failure threat. Any one or all of these factors may influence the Negro child's performance in integrated situations.

Social threat. Negro children enter integrated schools under some social threat, the amount of which depends on two conditions: (1) the extent to which there is white hostility in the integrated school, and (2) the power possessed by whites in their numerical predominance and control of authority positions. Indifference on the part of white students may itself be a source of social threat: It may lower the Negro student's self-esteem and make him desire to escape the situation. Or indifference may cause the Negro to fight back with aggressive behavior. Thus actual or implied threats may deter the Negro child from achieving scholastically.

Another way in which social threat may impair academic performance is by causing Negro children to abandon their efforts to excel in order not to arouse resentment and hostility from white competitors. In the competitive situation of the school, academic success on the part of the Negro may arouse white reprisals. In this case any stimulus which encourages Negro students to achieve will be compounded with anxiety.[23]

Finally, social threat may emanate from a white teacher, who represents power over the Negro child. The teacher may patronize, punish, or devalue the Negro child and thus have unfavorable effects upon his performance.

[21] See United States Commission on Civil Rights, *Civil Rights U.S.A.—Public Schools, Cities in the North and West,* Washington, D. C., United States Government Printing Office, 1962; and United States Commission on Civil Rights, *Civil Rights U.S.A.—Public Schools, Southern States.*

[22] Irwin Katz, "Review of Evidence Relating to Effects of Desegregation on the Intellectual Performance of Negroes," *American Psychologist,* Volume 19, No. 16, June 1964, pp. 381–399.

[23] See the discussion of "Coercive Power" in J. R. P. French and B. Raven, "The Bases of Social Power," in D. Cartwright and A. Zander (Eds.), *Group Dynamics* (2nd Ed.), Evanston, Illinois, Row Peterson, 1960, pp. 607–623.

7. A white teacher in a newly integrated school asks a Negro child to play the part of a Negro "mammy" in a pre-Civil War play which the class is doing. The role calls for the subservient Negro behavior and speech of plantation life. Do you think this was a good decision on the part of the teacher?

Social facilitation. If the social conditions in the integrated school are favorable to the Negro child, his scholastic achievement may be facilitated. White children, we know, are responsive to the standards of those with whom they desire to associate.[24] There is evidence that Negro children want friendship with white age-mates.[25] Negro children in a racially mixed classroom accept white prestige, but if rejected by the whites they increasingly withdraw to their own group.[26] Thus if the Negro child's desire for acceptance is not inhibited or frustrated by unfriendliness and rejection he will likely adopt the scholastic norms of his white peers.

Social facilitation in the direction of rising achievement may also be enhanced by white teachers, especially if the white teacher has more prestige for the Negro student than the Negro teacher. The prospect of winning the approval of the white teacher may be attractive and thus academically motivating for the Negro student.

Probability of success. The Negro child enters an integrated school that has higher standards than those to which he has been accustomed, and he may be uncertain about his chances for success. If he experiences initial failures, he may become discouraged and not try to succeed. Thus if the Negro student perceives that the standards of the desegregated school are substantially higher than those he encountered before and that his chances of success are slim, his academic motivation will most likely decline.

8. A high school English teacher states: "A good teacher, aware that students thrive on success, finds ways in which they can succeed. No matter how limited his ability every student has some contribution to make. The Pied Piper [teacher] applauds any degree of success. He lets his students taste that heady wine, even if only a drop of it." [27] Do you think this advice is founded on good psychology? If you do, why?

[24] See B. M. Bass, "Conformity, Deviation, and a General Theory of Interpersonal Behavior," in I. A. Berg and B. M. Bass (Eds.), *Conformity and Deviation,* New York, Harper, 1961, pp. 38–100.

[25] See Marion R. Yarrow (Issue Ed.), "Interpersonal Dynamics in a Desegregation Process," *Journal of Social Issues,* Volume 14, No. 1, 1958.

[26] See Joan H. Criswell, "A Sociometric Study of Race Cleavage in the Classroom," *Archives of Psychology,* No. 235, New York, 1939.

[27] Ruth Agnew, "Discipline? Follow the Yellow Brick Road," *NEA Journal,* Volume 53, No. 8, October 1964, pp. 52–53.

Failure threat. Closely associated with the Negro student's calculation of his probability of success is the threat of failure. The threat of failure itself may elicit anxious expectations of harm or pain as a consequence of failure. These reactions may cause the Negro student to indulge in self-blame or to strike out in hostility at those around him who he perceives to be associated with his failure. S. B. Sarason and his associates suggest that a high expectancy of failure arouses strong unconscious hostility against the adults from whom the negative evaluation comes.[28] Or the hostility may be turned inward on the self and take the form of self-derogatory attitudes, which strengthen the expectation of failure and the desire to accept the situation. Psychological distraction of this kind can certainly create emotional conflicts which may cause the Negro student's performance to decline.

To What Extent Are Negroes Rejected by White Classmates?

Two examples of desegregation that were highly stressful for Negro students are described by R. Coles[29] and C. Trillin.[30]

Coles said of the first Negroes to enter white schools in Atlanta and New Orleans: "When they are in school they may experience rejection, isolation, or insult. They live under highly stressful circumstances."[31] And "during a school year one can see among these children all of the medical and psychiatric responses to fear and anxiety. One child may lose his appetite, another may become sarcastic and have nightmares. Lethargy may develop or excessive studying may mark the apprehension common to both. At the same time one sees responses of earnest and effective work. . . . Each child's case history would describe a balance of defense against emotional pain, and some exhaustion under it, as well as behavior which shows an attempt to challenge and surmount it."[32] Among the 60 students who were studied by Coles "only one child really succumbed to emotional illness." Coles suggests that the Negro children's worries about schoolwork were of less importance than their reactions to the prejudice of the white children.

[28] S. B. Sarason, K. S. Davidson, F. F. Lighthall, R. R. Waite, and B. K. Ruebush, *Anxiety in Elementary School Children,* New York, John Wiley and Sons, Inc., 1960.

[29] R. Coles, "The Desegregation of Southern Schools: A Psychiatric Study," New York, Anti-Defamation League, 1963.

[30] C. Trillin, *An Education in Georgia,* New York, Viking Press, 1964.

[31] Coles, *op. cit.,* p. 4.

[32] *Ibid.,* p. 5.

Trillin studied two Negro students who initiated integration at the University of Georgia and reported that both experienced rejection and isolation during the entire two-year period of enrollment: "As Hamilton (Holmes) began his final ten-week quarter at Georgia, he had never eaten in a University dining hall, studied in the library, used the gymnasium, or entered the snack bar. No white student had ever visited him and he had never visited one of them." [33]

The other student, Charlayne Hunter, was somewhat more successful in establishing friendly relations with white students. She interacted with white classmates and was generally in the company of white students when walking to and from classes. In her dormitory, however, she experienced social rejection and lived in a room by herself. Both Negro students graduated from the University, Holmes with a distinguished academic record.

A generally favorable picture of race relations in school integration in the South is presented by a journalist, James C. Farmer: "On the social side, younger white and Negro children attending segregated classes seemed to accept each other better than the older ones. Negro and white youngsters can be seen playing together on the slides and swings of almost any desegregated Southern elementary school's playground. At Nashville's Buena Vista Elementary School Negro boys have won two of the three positions of captain on the school's safety patrol. And in Birmingham, often called the most segregated U.S. city, a Negro boy was chosen vice president of a sixth-grade class that was desegregated last fall.

"Even in segregated high schools, some Negroes win quick social acceptance. When a lone Negro was admitted to the 10th grade of one high school in a small Texas town, he was elected vice president of his class the first day. A Negro has also become president of Oklahoma City's integrated Central High School Student Council." [34]

It seems clear that the social acceptance or rejection of Negroes in integrated schools varies from community to community.[35] Let us now turn to a related matter, the actual academic achievement of Negroes in integrated schools.

[33] Trillin, *op. cit.,* p. 83.

[34] "Integration in Action," *Wall Street Journal,* Volume 64, No. 97, January 26, 1964, p. 1.

[35] For an encouraging and analytical report of race relations of Negro and white children from Southern and border states in a camp setting see Marion R. Yarrow (Issue Ed.), "Interpersonal Dynamics in a Desegregation Process," *Journal of Social Issues,* Volume 14, No. 1, 1958 (Entire Issue).

Reports of Academic Achievement of Negroes
in Integrated Schools

Regrettably there is a dearth of research data about the performance of Negro students in integrated schools. Katz suggests that this may be true for three reasons.[36] First, many integrated school systems have a policy of not classifying children according to race, and separate data on Negro and white children are therefore not available. Second, when total integration occurs in a previously segregated system, it is usually accompanied by vigorous efforts to raise the educational performance of *all* children in *all* schools; hence it is difficult to isolate the effects which integration has on the achievement of either individuals or groups of children. Third, in several Southern states only small numbers of highly selected Negro pupils have been admitted to previously all-white schools, and since before and after comparisons of achievement are not usually presented, reports of "satisfactory" adjustment by these Negro children shed little light on the question of relative performance.

Taking these limitations into consideration the reports we do have present a favorable picture of Negro academic adjustment to integrated schools. Two reports from the school districts of Louisville and Washington, D. C., are worthy of attention. F. H. Stallings reported on the results of achievement testing in the Louisville school system during the year prior to total elimination of legal segregation and again two years later.[37] Stallings found that the median scores for *all* the students went up during the period, with Negro students showing greater improvement than white students. This report does not claim that the gains made by Negro students were due to the actual change in the racial composition of the schools. In fact, Stallings states that "the gains were greater where Negro pupils remained by choice with Negro teachers." [38]

In Washington, D. C., where legal segregation was abolished in 1954, the United States Commission on Civil Rights "found some evidence that the scholastic achievement of Negroes in such schools has improved, and no evidence of a resultant reduction in the achievement of white students." [39] C. F. Hanson gives us a detailed account

[36] Katz, *op. cit.*, p. 383.

[37] F. H. Stallings, "A Study of the Immediate Effects of Integration on Scholastic Achievement in the Louisville Public Schools," *Journal of Negro Education*, Volume 28, No. 4, 1959, pp. 439–444.

[38] *Ibid.*, p. 443.

[39] *Southern School News*, Untitled, August 7, 1960, p. 6, Columns 1, 2.

of academic progress of Negro and white students in the Washington, D. C., schools since 1954. His account rests upon the following three hypotheses:

1. "That both white and Negro pupils in the District of Columbia public schools have, on the whole, enjoyed educational conditions and opportunities during the past five years which are superior to those available under the previous policy of racial segregation in the schools.
2. "That Negro pupils in our schools have, on the whole, performed somewhat better during the past five years, in terms of objectively measured scholastic achievement, than did such pupils during a similar period immediately preceding the abolition of racial segregation in the schools.
3. "That white pupils in our schools have, on the whole, performed at least as well during the past five years, in terms of objectively measured achievement, as did such pupils during the years immediately preceding the abolition of racial segregation in the schools." [40]

Hanson's data, which is not broken down by race, indicates year-to-year gains in achievement on every academic subject tested at every level where tests were given.

As in the Louisville study it seems reasonable to attribute the achievement gains made in Washington to an ambitious program of educational improvement rather than desegregation *per se*. At the same time these two studies offer reassurance to white parents who fear that school integration will automatically lower achievement levels for white students. The Louisville and Washington, D. C., experience indicates that factors other than integration determine academic achievement and that schools are well-advised to concentrate their efforts on total improvement if they wish to raise the scholastic achievement of students.

Improving Achievement in Integrated Schools

From what we have said it is clear that integration in and of itself contains no special magic to raise the Negro child's level of academic achievement. Although it is an essential first condition, it does not itself guarantee results. However, if good planning takes place prior to

[40] C. F. Hanson, "The Scholastic Performances of Negro and White Pupils in the Integrated Public Schools of the District of Columbia," *Harvard Educational Review,* Volume 30, No. 3, Summer 1960, pp. 216–217.

integration and if the suggestions implied in the research are followed, the prospects are good for raising the academic achievement of both Negro and white students. Let us turn to some implications for educational practice which seem indicated by both experience and research.[41]

Preparing students for integration. Research indicates that segregated schools, generally speaking, have lower academic standards than integrated schools. For this reason the transfer for the Negro student to an integrated school is frequently difficult. The standards of Negro schools need to be raised so that minority children who are transferred to previously all-white schools will have a reasonable chance to succeed.

Preparing parents for integration. The cooperation of parents is crucial in the process of integration. Efforts need to be made to establish contact with parents and secure their assistance and understanding, especially during the transitional phase. Parents must know what they can do to prepare children for school and to foster achievement once the children are in school. In the case study that closes this chapter parents were vitally involved in the school during the difficult period of change from segregation to integration.

Preparing teachers for integration. Integrated schools impose new problems on teachers and open new dimensions for teaching which may be only dimly seen at first. The emotional needs of children in integrated schools may differ from those in segregated schools. There is a new kind of need for children to get acquainted with one another. In such situations it is important for schools to provide in-service training for both white and Negro teachers to develop an awareness of their new responsibilities and opportunities in integrated schools.[42]

Preparing the curriculum for integration. Accepted curriculum practices need to be reexamined in integrated schools to determine their impact upon both Negro and white children. For example, the practice of assigning children to homogeneous ability groups may

[41] For an insightful discussion of this matter see G. J. Klopf and I. A. Laster (Eds.), *Integrating the Urban School,* New York, Teachers College, Columbia University, Bureau of Publications, 1963.

[42] For research on the similarity and differences between Negro and white teachers and their views of students see David Gottlieb, "Teaching and Students: the Views of Negro and White Teachers," *Sociology of Education,* Volume 37, No. 4, Summer 1964, pp. 345–353. Also, for research on the differences in behavioral expectations of Negro and white teachers see Nebraska Mays, "Behavioral Expectations of Negro and White Teachers in Recently Desegregated Public School Faculties," *Journal of Negro Education,* Volume 32, No. 3, Summer 1963, pp. 218–226.

"freeze" Negro children into lower groups and actually segregate them as completely as if they were in a segregated school. This practice may further reinforce the Negro child's negative self-image as well as the white child's negative image of him. It may also reinforce the teacher's low expectation of the Negro child. These forces will combine to impair the child's intellectual development, especially in the early grades.

Preparing the integration plan. Negro children have the smallest educational handicap in the lowest grades. Because of the cumulative deficit phenomenon which operates on the school achievement of lower-class children the handicap is greater in later grades. Therefore, where grade-a-year plans of desegregation are adopted, the process should begin at the lowest grades where Negro children have the smallest educational handicap and where unfavorable racial attitudes are least strong.

In this chapter we have considered in sociological perspective the Negro child and the schools. This view takes into account the human and educational problems that are encountered in the transition from segregated to integrated education. It is in the schools that the social issues which we have been discussing get translated into student and teacher behavior. For this reason we shall conclude this chapter with a firsthand account of how one school is successfully making the transition from segregation to integration and is enhancing human values in the experience.

CHANGING PUPILS IN A CHANGING SCHOOL [43]

" 'Once nine hundred children went to school here.' The retiring custodian of West School was speaking 16 years ago when, as neophyte principal, I first came to work in the community. 'That was when the neighborhood was young.'

"But 'young' neighborhoods grow up. At the time he spoke, only 400 children were attending. Later, in 1954, numbers had dwindled to less than 300, and West's 'grandchildren'—offspring of parents who had attended the school—frequently enrolled. Meanwhile, small changes were taking place in the area as urbanization forces crept slowly out from the center of the city. The neighborhood kept neatly manicured lawns, proud and gracious homes. Yet, here and there on the edges were evidences of a creeping blight—hedges left untrimmed, or worn through by careless feet, a crumbling porch, homes converted into small business enterprises.

[43] Fern H. Jacobi, "Changing Pupils in a Changing School," *Educational Leadership*, Volume 17, No. 5, February 1960, pp. 283–287.

Our Community Changes

"Most of the parents were still 'salt of the earth,' stable, friendly people providing a background of cultural experiences for their children and cooperating with their school and community. Almost half were Jewish people, ambitious for their children and generous with time and money. As time went on changes were noted in the occupation of the fathers. The percentage of professionals dropped, and more children from lower middle class homes attended. Differences began to be noted in the background of the children. The span of intelligence level widened. Mothers went to work outside of the homes—some because of economic necessity, others to provide for their children the luxuries of life, or a college education. Soon there appeared in the windows a dark face or two. In the back yards little Negro children played quietly together. Slowly, conducting themselves with decorum and dignity, upper class Negroes moved into some of the homes on quiet streets. We had Negro neighbors.

"Later, after integration, we were to know these people better as kind and loving parents and as cooperative patrons of the school. Now, however, we learned little about them except through an occasional confidence from the earlier residents, 'I used to step out to get the milk in the morning in my robe, but our new neighbors never do that, so I have stopped doing it now.'

"In September 1954 West opened as an integrated school. The enrollment soared. Three classes were opened the first year, and two each succeeding year. Now children from parents in all occupational classes came. The widest disparities were noted in cultural background. We had become in truth a small 'melting pot' from which, with other similar schools, the liberties of future generations of Americans of all races must be forged.

Our Children Differ

"Our children's range in intelligence was tremendous—at one time from 68 to 167 IQ! In many cases there was an educational lag of one to six years in reading achievement. 'Sixth grade' children tested in reading from grade 1.4 to 9.0. For many years past our children testing high average in intelligence had ranked far above the national norm in reading. Now our reading achievements dropped down far below national norms. Faculty morale slipped to a low ebb. Our Negro teachers were eager to learn new methods and willing to share with us their understanding of Negro children. But even they grew discouraged with achievements.

"The problem of discipline reared its ugly head. Freedom in classroom and corridor sometimes became license. Indirect methods of control were of no avail. Hall and playground duty became difficult tasks for experienced teachers and thwarting for the inexperienced.

"White and Negro teachers were working together—many with the pride of long years of successful experience, working harder than any of us had worked in all our lives before. Were we failing in our duty to these children and so to our country?

We Accept the Challenge

"The words of Abraham Lincoln in his Address to Congress in 1863 leaped to new life within our minds: 'The dogmas of the quiet past are inadequate to the stormy present. The occasion is piled high with difficulty, and we must rise to the occasion. As our case is new so we must think anew and act anew. We must disenthrall ourselves and then we shall save our country.'

"We decided to 'think anew and act anew.' The methods by which we had established a good school in other days with outstanding character development and achievement in our children were unequal to the stormy present. We began to 'disenthrall ourselves,' and it wasn't easy.

"We resolved to hold fast to our high standards, to learn more about our present pupils, and to experiment with different methods of work.

We Seek New Dimensions

"It was not easy to gain clear understandings about our children. We were plagued by oversized classes and high rate of mobility.

"We studied our children in class, on the playground, in their homes, and in the community. We invited parents for long conferences which revealed family values, mores, and methods of home discipline. We learned that in some homes beating was the form of punishment accepted by both parent and child. In school, without fear of physical reprisal, children often worked out their aggressions and thwartings with results not at all conducive to pupil progress.

"We learned, too, from these conferences that the insistent demand for more and more homework from homes, cultured and uncultured, was tied to ambition for the children, to a lack in many instances of sound recreational patterns, and not infrequently to a desire to use the homework to substitute for family discipline.

"We learned that false and too sweeping generalizations on the part of Negroes about whites, and on the part of whites about Negroes, created tensions. Sometimes rejection was experienced by young children. A young mother wrote to explain a sudden rebellious attitude of her daughter to her kind and capable white teacher: 'In January we moved here from a block in which Phylicia was one of the most popular children in the area. She had almost too many friends, if such is possible. Never a dull moment. Then abruptly we bought a home, moved to a block where not one little girl has been allowed to play with Phylicia although at first all have attempted friendliness. Reared in an atmosphere where only behavior has counted, the rejections of the past months have been a great shock to Phylicia and she is still confused. She could not understand the "sudden" color distinctions, especially since her own complexion is fair and people have always "made a lot over her." After our talk this morning, Phylicia went to school probably feeling quite rebellious toward an image of Susan's (a rejecting playmate's) mother. As a result, she associated Susan's mother with you probably (through no fault whatever of yours).'

"We studied pupil records. We saw broken homes, children living insecurely, in many instances with neither parent. We saw frequent changes of schools as economic necessity forced families to move from one school area to another.

"As a faculty we shared our knowledge and understanding of the children. We asked for, and gave advice and help to each other. Sometimes the teachers served as my consultants. We used our master teachers, white and Negro, as group leaders, policy planners, helpers to new teachers.

"As we learned more about our children we saw changes in their reactions to us. Faces of children in trouble lost the 'dead-pan' look and came alive with changing emotions as they sought with us a solution to their problems. Children in trouble trusted us. Rude, negative answers to questions diminished in number and violence. Often the truth, even though damaging, was told at the start of a conference, and a healthy emotional tone was established for the improvement of the situation and of the child.

We "Act Anew"

"Coincident with our deepened understanding of our children came changes in methods of teaching. Frequent evaluation meetings were held. In these, our faculty took an honest look at our methods and their effect on the learning of our children.

"Both our experience with the children and the low test scores in paragraph meaning showed us that our children needed consistent and sequential development of concepts. Through trips and other firsthand experiences as well as with books and visual aids we developed concepts in science, in social studies, in math, and the arts. 'Milk really does come from a cow!' said a sixth grade girl aide helping a second grade group on their trip to a farm, 'and a cow is so big!'

"We worked constantly for improvement in pronunciation and enunciation. In our oral English work, in spelling and in phonetics related both to reading and to spelling, we worked to improve speech habits.

"Each teacher learned to make an informal reading inventory and used this technique to group her children for instruction in reading.

"We made assignments on the level of each group—very simple factual ones for slow groups and, for those more highly endowed, assignments involving fine discrimination, critical thinking, and interpretation.

"It was early evident that some form of ability grouping was necessary. It was completely unrealistic, for instance, to give a sixth grade teacher a class of sometimes 40 children, ranging in IQ from 73 to 167, and in reading level from 1.4 to 9.3.

"We wanted, however, to avoid the undemocratic complications of the old XYZ ability groupings—with consequent parental pressure to put each child, no matter how limited, in the highest group. Rather we developed a policy which we called Overlapping Ability Grouping. We used reading level as our main criterion, but also considered mental age and social maturity. Miss A, who had the fastest learners, had also a few high average ones. Miss B had a high average to low average range. Miss C had the slowest ones with some low average children. Not a perfect system, of course, but under it grouping for reading instruction could be done on three levels usually, and so each child could read at his instructional level. Yet since there was no hard and fast delineation between groups, parents seldom asked for changes of placement. A truly democratic grouping is one where each child's needs, social and intellectual, can most nearly be met.

"We gave our children the kind of discipline they needed—firm and kind—with external controls established first and leading to internal controls. We found something in every child that we could honestly praise. We feel that a child needs *something to live up to, not to live down.*

"We provided many opportunities for pupil leadership through Patrols, Girl Aides, and school and classroom committee work. We made every opportunity to overcome the handicaps under which some of our children live—social, moral, intellectual, and economic—and to make school a happy place for them to live and to work in.

Our Children Achieve

"We had worked prodigiously. We had studied, planned, evaluated as a faculty. Early in the year 1958–59 there were some evidences that a degree of success was crowning our efforts. We knew that many of our children had achieved a high level of self-control in halls, in classrooms and on the playground. Some of them had developed outstanding leadership. But what about reading and understanding? There were evidences throughout the year in books read, in teachers' tests and in semi-standardized commercial tests that our children were achieving very well. By now we were almost afraid to believe it.

"At the start of the year the fifth grade tests (Standard KM) disappointed us. We felt that in one class they did not reveal the children's true ability. So two months later we gave 30 children the Stanford M, a comparable test. Increments ranged from −.1 year to 3.6 years with the mode from one to two years (instead of the expected .2 increment). These results to some extent increased our confidence in the job we were doing. Our Superintendent and our Department of Pupil Appraisal were much interested in the results of our second test.

"In March 1959, our sixth grade pupils were tested with the Stanford Reading Test, Intermediate Form. Results indicated that in all subjects West sixth graders averaging 100 in IQ were well above national norms. Concerning our reading achievements Dr. Carl Hansen, our Superintendent, said in his 'Summary of the Desegregation Experiences in the Public Schools of the District of Columbia for the Notre Dame Conference (May 8, 1958)':

'An illustration of superior growth is found in the summary of achievement gains (in reading) made by three classes of sixth grade students in the West Elementary School, March 1959, over their fifth grade placement in the fall of 1957.'

"The West School, formerly all white, has an enrollment of 572 Negro and 84 white pupils, a faculty of 12 white and 8 Negro persons.

Class A	Fifth grade median	6.3
	Sixth grade median	8.7
	Mental maturity	7.7
Class B	Fifth grade median	4.5
	Sixth grade median	7.2
	Mental maturity	6.5
Class C	Fifth grade median	4.5
	Sixth grade median	6.4
	Mental maturity	6.2

"How well have we succeeded in educating these youngsters? Improvement in achievement tests is only one index. It is difficult to evaluate the major factors—the growth in poise, in self-discipline, the development of cultural background and interests, the growing desire of the children to learn, to understand, the constant use of the public library, and the increase in pleasure and pride in their school.

"Over and over again in their letters evaluating their school the children refer to it as a respected school or as a school with a good reputation. They recognize that the program involves more than the skills. 'The teachers teach us right from wrong.' Pamela, a sixth grader in Class B, writes: 'I think that West is a wonderful school. I like it because I know that I can be well educated. I also like it because I have such a nice teacher. Another reason why I like West is because I not only learn to read, write and do arithmetic, but I have learned how to make friends and keep them. I have learned that when someone picks a fight with me, to walk away. I have learned all that from West School's teachers and my principal.'

"Through the years, our community has changed, and the children entering our school have reflected these changes. Our faculty has accepted the challenge of a changing school, has reached out to new dimensions in understanding children, has held to high standards while adapting methods of work to the learners' needs."

REFERENCES

Paperbacks

A Profile of the Negro American. Thomas F. Pettigrew. D. Van Nostrand Co., 120 Alexander St., Princeton, N. J. ($2.75).

Children of Bondage: The Personality Development of Negro Youth in the Urban South. Allison Davis and John Dollard. (TB/3049) Harper Torchbooks, Harper College Paperbacks, Harper and Row, Publishers, 49 E. 33rd St., New York ($1.85).

Crucial Issues in Education. Ehlers and Lee. (3rd Ed.) Holt, Rinehart and Winston, 383 Madison Ave., New York ($3.25).

Education and Democratic Ideals. Gordon C. Lee. (Orig.) Harcourt, Brace and World, 757 Third Ave., New York ($1.95).

Education and Income: Inequalities of Opportunity in Our Public Schools. Patricia Sexton. (C168) Compass Books, The Viking Press, 625 Madison Ave., New York ($1.65).

Education and Liberty. James Bryant Conant. Random House, 457 Madison Ave., New York ($1.45).

Education in Depressed Areas. A. Harry Passow, Editor. Teachers College, Teachers College Press, 525 West 120 St., New York ($2.50).

Excellence: Can We Be Equal and Excellent Too? John W. Gardner. (CN/3) Harper Colophon Books, Harper and Row, Publishers. 49 E. 33rd St., New York ($1.45).

Integrating the Urban School. Gordon J. Klopf and Israel A. Laster. (Orig.) Teachers College, Teachers College Press, 525 West 120 St., New York ($1.95).

Learning to Teach in Urban Schools. Dorothy M. McGeoch et al. Teachers College, Teachers College Press, 525 West 120 St., New York ($1.95).

Mental Health and Segregation. Martin M. Grossack. (Reissue, Orig.) Springer Publishing Co., 200 Park Ave. South, New York ($4.00).

Negro and the Schools. Harry S. Ashmore. (Rev. Ed., Orig.) University of North Carolina, Chapel Hill, N. C. ($1.50).

Negro in America: The Condensed Version of Gunnar Myrdal's "An American Dilemma." Arnold Rose. New intro. by Author. Frwd. by Gunnar Myrdal. (TB/3048) Harper Torchbooks, Harper College Paperbacks, Harper and Row, Publishers, 49 E. 33rd St., New York ($1.95).

Negro Self-Concept. William C. Kvaraceus. (Orig.) (35716) McGraw-Hill Paperback Series, McGraw-Hill Book Co., 330 W. 42nd St., New York ($2.45).

On Being Negro in America. J. Saunders Redding. (H2806) Bantam Books, 271 Madison Ave., New York (60¢).

Prejudice and Your Child. Kenneth Clark. (BP150) Beacon Press, 25 Beacon St., Boston, Mass. ($1.75).

Race Awareness in Young Children. Mary Ellen Goodman. Intro. by Dr. Kenneth B. Clark. (Illus.) (09582) Collier Books, 60 Fifth Ave., New York ($1.50).

Race Relations in Transition: The Segregation Crisis in the South. James W. Vander Zanden. (Orig.) (SS25) Random House, 457 Madison Ave., New York ($1.65).

School Desegregation: Documents and Commentaries. Vice President Hubert H. Humphrey. (Orig.) Thomas Y. Crowell Co., 201 Park Ave. South, New York ($2.50).

Story of the American Negro. Ina Corinne Brown. (Orig.) Friendship Press, 475 Riverside Drive, New York ($1.50).

Books

Charter, W., Jr., and N. L. Gage, *Readings in Social Psychology of Education.* Boston: Allyn and Bacon, 1963. Section II presents articles on school desegregation.

Clark, Burton R., *Educating the Expert Society.* San Francisco: Chandler Publishing Co., 1962. Chapter 3 discusses education and minorities. Clark believes that "in the metropolis, those who live apart are likely to go to school apart."

Group for the Advancement of Psychiatry, *Emotional Aspects of School Desegregation.* New York: The Group, 1960. A study of Negro behavior in newly integrated situations.

Harlem Youth Opportunities Unlimited, *Youth in the Ghetto: A Study of the Consequences of Powerlessness and a Blueprint for Change.* New York: HARYOU, 1964. In summary, the author says: "The basic story of academic achievement in central Harlem is one of inefficiency, inferiority and massive deterioration."

Havighurst, Robert J., *The East Orange Education Plaza, A New Plan for a Modern Community*. Chicago: University of Chicago Press, 1964. A community in an urban renewal area explores the concept of an educational park for its 10,000 children.

Periodicals

Anderson, Margaret, "The Negro Child Asks: 'Why?,'" *New York Times Magazine*, Vol. CXIII, No. 38,662, December 1, 1963, p. 32. Negro youth suffer the anguish of the times as they strive to pull themselves out of an old culture and into a new one. A teacher finds they have oustanding courage and hope for a new day.

Fischer, John H., "The Inclusive School," *Teachers College Record*, Vol. LXVI, No. 1, October 1964, pp. 1–6. The author challenges the position that equality will occur when teachers are color-blind and beneficently neutral toward all the antecedent differences of students.

Foster, G. W., "The North and West Have Problems, Too," *The Saturday Review*, Vol. XLVI, No. 16, April 20, 1963, pp. 69–72. Problems raised by *de facto* segregation are sophisticated and subtle, and they stem from complex causes.

Josey, E. J., "An Intellectual Confrontation," *The Quarterly Review of Higher Education Among Negroes*, Vol. 32, No. 1, February 1964, pp. 15–20. A Negro educator deals with the relative disadvantage of the Negro student compared with the white.

Knoll, Erwin, "Ten Years of Deliberate Speed," *American Education*, Vol. 1, January 1965, pp. 1–3. An analysis of "deliberate speed" in integration in Southern and border states.

Larrick, Nancy, "The All-White World of Children's Books," *The Saturday Review*, Vol. XLVIII, No. 37, September 11, 1965, pp. 63–65. Six million non-white children learn to read and understand the American way of life in books which either omit them entirely or scarcely mention them.

Lieberman, Myron, "Equality of Educational Opportunity," *Harvard Educational Review*, Vol. 29, No. 3, Summer 1959, pp. 167–183. The author explores this question: "What is or what should be regarded as equality of educational opportunity?"

21

The Dropout:
No Room at the Bottom

"Machines are taking over the unskilled jobs. These are the jobs which, up to this time, absorbed the casualties of the educational system."

W. WILLARD WIRTZ

The social forces that cause students to drop out of school are, for the most part, the same ones that influence education generally. For more fortunate students these social forces work to promote educational achievement and future well-being. In the case of the dropout they conspire to cut short his schooling and his life opportunities.

Consider briefly the dual nature of some of the social forces that influence education. We learned in Part I that the classroom is a small society in which a good mental health climate can lift the achievement of all students. A poor classroom climate, on the other hand, can isolate and reject students and contribute to the development of poor self-concepts. In an almost literal sense students begin either to succeed or to fail in the early grades; their success or failure depends greatly on the quality of the classroom's social climate.

The family and peer group as social influences in learning were examined in Part II. They may either discourage or stimulate achievement in school. Fortunate is the student whose family and peer group value school achievement: Unfortunate is he whose family and peer group downgrade it. The dropout is usually in this latter group.

The whole apparatus of social class which we studied in Part III may work for or against motivation to learn. The social-class position of people conditions their attitudes toward education and achievement, and their economic circumstances condition their ability to take advantage of educational opportunities. The cultural style of the school, its system of values and learned behavior, may stimulate high achievement or discourage it. The social climate of the school and its system of human interaction may similarly inspire students either to lift their sights or to lower them.

The study of the dropout is, in a sense, the study of all students and all social forces that influence their education. In the case of the dropout, unfortunately, the forces operate negatively in relation to school achievement and educational aspiration.

The one strong social force in education we have not yet discussed is the subject of this chapter. Like the other forces just mentioned, it operates differentially in respect to educational achievement. It rewards high educational achievement and penalizes low achievement. The dropout is its victim, whereas the graduate is in a position to ride its tide and benefit from it. We refer to the social force of technological change. This is the force that is making it possible for the educated to find room at the top and almost impossible for the uneducated to find room at the bottom.

To gain an appreciation of how technological change deepens the plight of the dropout we should first consider some facts about dropouts.

What Is the Dropout Rate?

The number of students who drop out of school varies considerably from state to state as Table 1 indicates. The number of high school graduates in 1962, as a percentage of the eighth-grade enrollment in 1957–58, varied from 92.3 percent in Wisconsin to 51.8 percent in Georgia. Among all states, an average of 70.6 percent of students graduated in 1962. In other words, the average dropout rate between the eighth grade and high school graduation is approximately 30 percent.

When do students drop out? At what age do most dropouts leave school? The greatest percentage of students withdraw from school when attendance is no longer compulsory, which in most states is age 16. The Bureau of the Census reports that in October of 1959, 929,000 or 17.1 percent of youths aged 16 and 17 were not enrolled in school.[1]

The greatest single dropout rate occurs between the ninth and tenth grades, when students normally move from junior to senior high school. Another significant drop occurs between the tenth and eleventh grades among students who have tried high school and have apparently discovered that they do not like it.[2]

[1] U. S. Department of Commerce, Bureau of the Census. *School Enrollment, October 1959.* Current Population Reports, Population Characteristics, Series P-20, No. 101. Washington, D. C., Government Printing Office, 1960, p. 8.

[2] See National Education Association, Research Division and Department of Classroom Teachers, *High-School Dropouts,* Discussion Pamphlet No. 3, Washington, D. C., 1959, p. 6.

TABLE 1

1962 HIGH SCHOOL GRADUATES AS PERCENT OF 1957–58
EIGHTH GRADE ENROLLMENT

1.	92.3%	Wisconsin		26.	72.4%	Ohio
2.	88.2	Minnesota		27.	72.0	Delaware
3.	86.4	California		28.	71.1	Arizona
4.	84.8	Nebraska		29.	70.1	Alaska
5.	84.5	Illinois		30.	69.3	New Hampshire
6.	84.2	Washington		31.	68.2	Massachusetts
7.	80.6	Hawaii		32.	67.9	Oklahoma
8.	78.8	New Jersey		33.	67.5	Maryland
9.	78.6	Iowa		34.	63.7	Nevada
10.	78.4	Michigan		35.	62.9	Florida
11.	78.1	Kansas		36.	62.2	New Mexico
12.	78.1	South Dakota		37.	61.0	Maine
13.	78.0	Pennsylvania		38.	60.6	Texas
14.	77.9	Oregon		39.	57.8	Arkansas
15.	77.2	Utah		40.	57.8	Louisiana
16.	76.8	North Dakota		41.	57.8	Mississippi
17.	74.1	Indiana		42.	57.4	North Carolina
18.	74.1	New York		43.	56.4	Vermont
19.	73.3	Montana		44.	55.5	West Virginia
20.	73.3	Rhode Island		45.	55.1	Tennessee
21.	73.1	Connecticut		46.	55.0	Alabama
22.	73.1	Wyoming		47.	54.2	South Carolina
23.	73.0	Missouri		48.	52.6	Kentucky
24.	72.9	Colorado		49.	51.9	Virginia
25.	72.5	Idaho		50.	51.8	Georgia
					70.6	50 states and D. C.

SOURCE: National Education Association, Research Division. *Rankings of the States, 1963*. Research Report 1963-R1, Table 47. Washington, D. C. As cited by John K. Norton, *Changing Demands on Education and Their Fiscal Implications*, Washington, D. C., National Committee for Support of the Public Schools, 1963, p. 55.

CHARACTERISTICS OF SCHOOL DROPOUTS

A number of studies are adding to our knowledge of the school dropout and are also dispelling some myths about him. It is frequently assumed, for example, that the dropout is incapable of doing school-work. Most dropouts are fully capable of achieving in school, however, and their withdrawal from school stems from reasons other than lack of ability. Poor achievement among dropouts is sometimes regarded as a result of "laziness" or "obstinateness." Yet evidence indicates that the dropout lacks certain basic skills required for school achievement, for example, reading. It is commonly said that dropouts could achieve in school if they "wanted to." Yet information about dropouts shows that most of them come from social environments which conspire against academic achievement; "wanting to" achieve is infinitely more difficult for the dropout than for the student who comes from a more congenial environment.[3]

John K. Norton summarizes some of the major research findings which characterize the dropouts:

1. "The average dropout is not uneducable. He does tend to score lower on IQ tests than his in-school counterpart, but a nationwide study conducted by the U. S. Department of Labor showed that 70 percent of the dropouts surveyed had registered IQ scores above 90, clearly in the educable group. An intensive six-year study in the State of New York revealed that 13 percent of the dropouts had IQ scores above 110. This rating should permit high school graduation and some post-high school training.

2. "The average dropout is at least two years retarded in reading ability by the time he quits school. Reading remains the fundamental education skill; without it no student can perform adequately in school. The consequences of retardation in reading are obvious: dropouts fail three times as many courses as 'stay-ins,' and 9 of every 10 dropouts have been retained in some grade at least one extra year.

3. "The majority of dropouts are from lower socio-economic families. They often come from families where the father is missing, where cultural backgrounds and horizons are limited, where education is viewed with indifference, distrust, or open resentment. Any redemptive or preventive effort of the school will have to take account of the student's total environment and will depend heavily on the school's staff of guidance counselors and school-community coordinators.

4. "There is a high percentage of dropouts among minority groups. This fact was detailed as follows at the 1961 *Conference on Unemployed, Out-of-School Youth in Urban Areas:*

'Estimates of the number of Mexican-American youth who leave school before getting to high school range as high as 50 percent in

---

[3] See Daniel Schreiber (Ed.), *The School Dropout,* Washington, D. C., Project: School Dropouts, National Education Association, 1964; and National Committee for Children and Youth, *Social Dynamite,* Report of the Conference on Unemployed, Out-of-School Youth in Urban Areas, Washington, D. C., 1961.

the major cities. Today, two-thirds of all Negroes live in urban areas, one-third in urban areas outside the South.

'In a slum section composed almost entirely of Negroes in one of our largest cities the following situation was found. A total of 59 percent of the male youth between the ages of 16 and 21 were out of school and unemployed. They were roaming the streets. Of the boys who graduated from high school, 48 percent were unemployed in contrast to 63 percent of the boys who had dropped out of school.

'An even worse state of affairs was found in another special study in a different city. In a slum area of 125,000 people, mostly Negro, a sampling of youth population shows that roughly 70 percent of the boys and girls ages 16–21 are out-of-school and unemployed.

'The problem of unemployed youth in the large cities is in no small part a Negro problem. We do not facilitate its solution by trying to find phrases to hide this fact.'

5. "Dropouts are not entirely from minority groups. Of the four special surveys made for the *Conference on Unemployed, Out-of-School Youth in Urban Areas,* two dealt with racially mixed urban school districts where the majority of the dropouts interviewed were white. Like the minority group dropouts, however, most of these white boys and girls belonged to lower income families who had recently arrived in the city. Theirs were families who had left subsistence farms, families said to be among the nation's least educated, with a lack of motivation no less deadening than that of darker skinned families from depressed areas. But the problem of school dropouts is not confined to the big cities. It exists in small towns. It is particularly acute in rural areas, and the problems of the rural areas and the big cities are closely related." [4]

1. One way to get a first-hand impression of the characteristics of a dropout is to talk to one. Make arrangements to interview a youth who has dropped out of school within the last several years. Find out all you can about why he dropped out, his attitude toward the school then, his attitude toward it now, and his experiences in finding employment. How do these specific characteristics which you discover through the interview compare with those general ones listed above?

One of the dropout's biggest problems is to find and hold a job. The high rate of unemployment among dropouts can best be under-

---

[4] John K. Norton, *Changing Demands on Education and Their Fiscal Implications,* Washington, D. C., National Committee for Support of the Public Schools, 1963, pp. 57–58.

stood by examining the occupational distribution of workers in the United States as a result of technological changes.

RECENT OCCUPATIONAL TRENDS

The occupational distribution of workers in the United States is undergoing rapid change. One of the most persistent changes is the growing demand for workers with higher levels of education and the decreasing demand for workers with lower levels of education. The demand is for persons with more general education and advanced technical and professional training. "A college degree is required even for admission to training for a mounting number of callings. Many business concerns look upon a college degree as the minimum requirement for employment in positions that lead to the more attractive types of work. The fastest growing occupations are those that require larger amounts of general education and advanced technical and professional training." [5]

Figure 21-1 indicates the percentage of change among occupational groups during this decade. The most dramatic growth is taking place in the professional and technical group, with an increase of 40 percent from 1960 to 1970. The next five groups down the scale are changing at a rate which clusters around 20 percent. These groups include professional and technical personnel, proprietors and managers, and clerical, sales, skilled, semiskilled, and service workers. No change at all will take place in the size of the unskilled labor group. The size of the farm labor group actually will shrink by close to 20 percent. [6]

2. Not many years ago a man who acquired a specific skill as a boy had learned what he needed to know for the rest of his life. A skilled man was one who had learned a traditional craft, for example tailoring or blacksmithing. Today craft skills, as such, are becoming meaningless, because the need for them disappears with changing technology. This condition may force us to change our very idea of what a "skill" is. Can you redefine the concept of a skill in such a way that it is adequate for a technological society in which a man may hold many different jobs during a lifetime?

3. Walter Buchinghan points out that because of technological changes about 200,000 production jobs have been eliminated in recent years in the aircraft industry, 267,700 in the soft coal industry, 540,000 in the steel industry. At the same time productivity has gone up dramatically in each of these fields due to automation. As these hundreds of jobs were being wiped out, new ones were being created whose titles defy easy understand-

[5] *Ibid.*, p. 3.

[6] U. S. Department of Labor, *Manpower, Challenge of the 1960's*, Washington, D. C., U. S. Government Printing Office, 1960, p. 11.

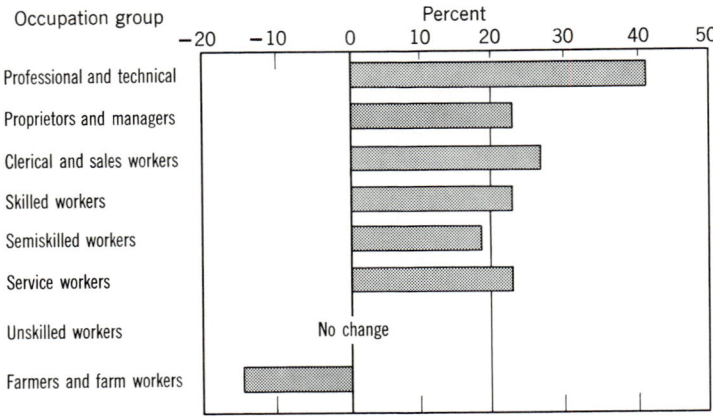

Fig. 21-1 Percent change in employment, 1960–1970. SOURCE: U. S. Department of Labor, *Manpower, Challenge of the 1960's,* Washington, D. C., U. S. Government Printing Office, 1960, p. 11.

ing and even pronunciation: data telemetry, gyrodynamics, microminiativization, transistor circuitry, and ferret reconnaissance.[7] Many of these jobs must be filled. What do you think are the implications of this situation for teachers and for the school curriculum?

Why Are Occupational Patterns Changing?

Changes in employment trends are resulting from a number of causes. The United States Department of Labor summarizes the major causes as follows:

1. The continuing shift from an agricultural economy to one that is predominantly industrial.
2. The rapid expansion in research and development activities.
3. The tremendously rapid increase in the application of technological improvements.
4. The increasing size and complexity of business organizations.
5. The widespread growth of record keeping among all types of enterprises.
6. The growing need for educational and medical services.[8]

[7] Walter Buchinghan, "The Impending Revolution in Education," Washington, D. C., Educational Implications of Automation Project, Occasional Paper No. 1, National Education Association, October 1961, pp. 2–3.
[8] *Manpower, Challenge of the 1960's, op. cit.,* p. 11.

Occupational Status and Education

Occupational status is becoming increasingly important, because factors that influence occupational status help to determine one's social and economic position in our society. As Wilbur B. Brookover and Sigmund Nosow point out, "The individual has few other statuses which are capable of offering him a respected position in the community." [9] In our technological society a man's occupation is his most significant single status-conferring role. A job status, whether high or low, gives the individual a secure place in society and permits him to form a stable conception of himself.

In our society occupational status is linked closely with one's level of education. The higher the occupational status the higher the median years of schooling. Table 2 indicates the number of years of schooling held by persons in major occupational groups. White-collar workers have the most education, with professional and technical groups averaging more than four years beyond high school. Blue-collar workers, with less than a high school diploma, are next in amounts of schooling.

4. In a society that constantly requires more and more education the largest employee group is likely to be the one that transmits knowledge: the teachers. Teachers are already the largest employee group in the American economy, and are the one that will have to grow the fastest. What do you think are the implications of this fact for the future of teaching as a profession?

The educational level of persons within an occupation tells the same story as that among the different occupations. For example, in the professional and technical group fewer than 6 percent of the workers have less than a high school diploma. Nineteen percent have a high school diploma only and 75 percent have some college education. Among skilled workers 59 percent have less than a high school diploma. Thirty-three percent have a high school diploma only, and 8 percent have some college education. Among unskilled workers, by contrast, 80 percent have less than a high school diploma. Seventeen percent have a high school diploma, and 3 percent have some college education. [10]

These figures have other interesting implications. They indicate

[9] Wilbur B. Brookover and Sigmund Nosow, "A Sociological Analysis of Vocational Education in the United States," *Education for a Changing World of Work: Report of the Panel of Consultants on Vocational Education*, Appendix III, Washington, D. C., U. S. Government Printing Office, 1963, p. 26.

[10] *Manpower, Challenge of the 1960's, op. cit.*, p. 17.

TABLE 2

MEDIAN YEARS OF SCHOOL COMPLETED AS OF MARCH 1962, BY MAJOR OCCUPATIONAL GROUPS

Occupational Group	Median Years of Schooling
White-collar workers	
Professional and technical	16.2
Managers and proprietors	12.5
Clerical workers	12.5
Sales personnel	12.5
Blue-collar workers	
Craftsmen and foremen	11.2
Semi-skilled operatives	10.1
Laborers (exclusive of farm and mine)	8.9
Others	
Service workers	10.8
Farm workers	8.6

SOURCE: *Manpower Report of the President* and *A Report on Manpower Requirements, Resources, Utilization, and Training by the United States Department of Labor,* Transmitted to the Congress, March 1963, p. 13.

the level of education which is required today both to enter an occupational group and to advance in it. The entry requirements are constantly rising, as are the requirements for promotion. As Grant Venn points out:

"A high school diploma is a minimum requisite for most production workers, and a bachelor's degree, often in engineering, may be a requisite for the foreman or supervisor. A college education is the only ticket for entry into the professions, with graduate study often a necessity for advancement. The technical, skilled, and semi-professional occupations all demand substantial amounts of post-secondary education for entrance. In the accelerating job-upgrading process of technology there is a steady increase of higher education and skills needed for entry and retention. Education has become the crucial ladder to the reward positions in society." [11]

5. Peter Drucker predicts that "twenty years hence, the child who has not gone to college will increasingly be a dropout problem. For, in an

[11] Grant Venn, *Man, Education and Work,* Washington, D. C., American Council on Education, 1964, p. 16.

educated society the jobs to be done do not only tend to call for people with higher education; the opportunities tend to be restricted to people who can produce the formal evidence of higher education: the college degree, if not an advanced degree." [12] Can you find any evidence that Drucker might be right in his prediction?

Education and Income

Still another way of viewing the relationship between education and occupational status is to examine the parallel between education and income levels. There is generally a positive correlation between education and income. We are not indicating that more education *causes* the individual to earn more income, but are simply pointing to facts which do at least *associate* additional education with additional income.

Comprehensive figures on this relationship are presented by Herman P. Miller, whose findings show that the average earnings for males 25 years of age and over are associated with varying amounts of schooling as follows:

Less than eight years	$2,551
Eight years	3,769
High school, one to three years	4,618
High school, four years	5,567
College, one to three years	6,966
College, four years and more	9,206

SOURCE: Herman P. Miller, "Annual and Lifetime Income in Relation to Education," *American Economic Review*, Volume 50, No. 5, December 1960, p. 4.

Miller notes the regularity which marks the correlation between education and higher earnings. He finds "that in every year for which data are presented, the completion of an additional level of schooling was associated with higher average incomes for men. This finding parallels that obtained in numerous other studies of the relationship between education and income dating back to the early part of this century. Although the income levels have changed considerably during the past 20 years, the basic relationship between the extent of schooling and income appears to have remained the same." [13]

[12] Peter Drucker, "Education in the New Technology," *Think*, Volume 28, No. 6, June 1962, p. 5.

[13] Herman P. Miller, "Annual and Lifetime Income in Relation to Education," *American Economic Review*, Volume 50, No. 5, December 1960, p. 965.

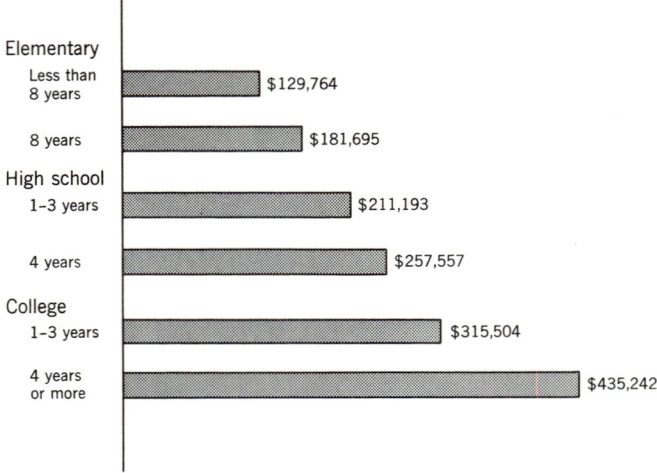

Elementary
Less than 8 years — $129,764
8 years — $181,695
High school
1–3 years — $211,193
4 years — $257,557
College
1–3 years — $315,504
4 years or more — $435,242

Fig. 21-2   Estimated earnings from age 18 to death, and years of schooling completed. Note: the data are based on arithmetic mean for males, 1958. SOURCE: Herman P. Miller, "Annual and Lifetime Income in Relation to Education," *American Economic Review*, 50, 21, December 1960.

Education and Lifetime Earnings

Increased earnings associated with increased education are not limited to a single year, but occur over the period of one's working lifetime. Miller, by using complex computations, arrives at "derived figures" for lifetime earnings from age 18 to death of individuals in the United States in different educational groups. Figure 21-2 is based on calculations from Miller's study.[14]

Miller, commenting on his estimates, states:

"Additional schooling is associated with a very substantial increase in lifetime income. On the basis of conditions in 1958, an elementary school graduate could expect to receive during his lifetime about $52,000 (or two-fifths) more income, on the average, than the person who had no schooling or who terminated his formal education before completing the eighth grade. The difference between the expected lifetime income of the average elementary school and high school graduate was equally striking. In 1958, the average elementary school graduate could expect a lifetime income of about $182,000, as compared to about $258,000 for the average high school graduate. The ex-

[14] Norton, *op. cit.*, p. 21.

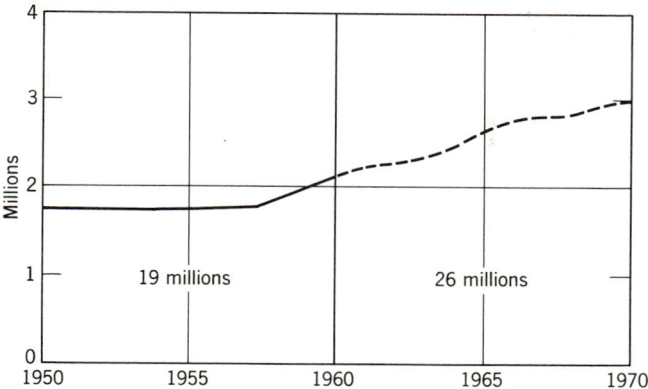

Fig. 21-3 New young workers entering the labor force annually, 1950 to 1970. SOURCE: U. S. Department of Labor, *Manpower, Challenge of the 1960's,* Washington, D. C., U. S. Government Printing Office, 1960, p. 14.

pected income differential associated with the four years of high school education therefore amounts to about $76,000, or 42 percent." [15]

As we indicated, Miller does not claim that a direct causal relation exists between lifetime income and education. There are many complex factors other than education which can increase or decrease the lifetime earnings of persons with higher levels of education.

The Employment Problems of Youth

One of the critical problems that confronts the dropout is that of employment. Finding a job is an acute problem for him in part because competition for jobs among all youth is keen, and the dropout is poorly prepared to compete. Let us consider first the employment problems of all youth in order to see the dropout's problem in clearer perspective.

Competition for jobs among young workers in the 1960's increased sharply over that of the 1950's. And, considering the rapidly increasing numbers of young people now entering the job market, the competition for jobs among new workers will grow sharper in the 1970's. Figure 21-3 shows that during the decade of the 1950's less than two million young men and women entered the labor force. In 1960 the figure exceeded the two million mark, and by 1965 there were 2.5 million new young workers in the labor force. It is expected that by 1970 there

[15] Miller, *op. cit.,* p. 982.

TABLE 3

CHANGES IN THE WORKING POPULATION DURING THE 1960's

| | Change 1960 to 70 | | |
| | 1960 | 1970 | Numbers | |
THERE WILL BE:	(Millions)	(Millions)	(Millions)	Percent
Many More Young Workers	13.8	20.2	6.4	46
Workers under 25 will account for nearly half of the labor force growth during the 1960's, even though they will stay in school longer.				
A Relatively Small Increase Among Workers 25–34	15.3	17.1	1.8	12
Actually Fewer Workers Age 35–44	16.6	16.4	−.2	−1
Many of these persons were born during the depression of the 1930's when birth rates were low.				
Larger Numbers of Older Workers	27.9	33.4	5.5	20
More workers will be 45 years and over in 1970 than in 1960, despite earlier retirements.				

SOURCE: U. S. Department of Labor, *Manpower, Challenge of the 1960's,* Washington, D. C., U. S. Government Printing Office, 1960, p. 6.

will be three million. Figure 21-3 indicates that during the 1960's 26 million youths will seek jobs, an increase of 40 percent over the 1950's, when 19 million sought employment.

Another way to see the impact of the growing numbers of young people entering the work force is to compare their numbers with other age groups. Table 3 shows that young people account for a major share of the changes taking place in the working population between 1960 and 1970.[16] Workers under 25 are responsible for 46

[16] *Manpower, Challenge of the 1960's, op. cit.,* p. 6.

percent of the labor force growth during this decade, even though this group is staying in school longer.

Workers between the ages of 25 and 34 are accounting for only a small increase of 12 percent in the labor force. There are actually fewer workers in the 35–44 age group, by 1 percent, than there were in the decade of the 1950's. The second largest increase in labor force growth is accounted for by workers of 45 and older, who increased their numbers by 20 percent. The figures describe quite graphically the increasing competition among youth for available jobs.

What Are the Job Prospects of Youth?

Unemployment data reflect the difficulties confronted by youth in finding employment.[17] In 1962 there were 4.5 million workers unemployed in the United States, of whom 751,000 were workers between the ages of 14 and 19 years, representing about one-sixth of the total unemployment. Whereas the national unemployment rate for February 1962 was 6.5 percent of the labor force, almost 20 percent of all workers 14–19 years of age were unemployed. More recently the unemployment rate among young workers has been two to three times the rate of the nation as a whole.

Young men are finding it more difficult than young women to obtain employment. In February 1963, the rate of unemployment for young men was 15.8 percent and for young women 12.6 percent in the 14–19 year age group.

How Do Graduates and Dropouts Compare?

How do the high school graduates and dropouts compare in their efforts to find employment? It is here that we see most graphically the plight of the dropout. The evidence indicates that school dropouts compared with high school graduates suffer greater unemployment, take longer to find jobs, get less desirable jobs, and earn less money.

First, look at the rate of unemployment for high school graduates and dropouts. In recent years the unemployment rate of school dropouts has consistently been higher than that of high school graduates. On an average, one out of every four school dropouts is unemployed, in contrast to only one in every eight high school graduates. Further, the duration of unemployment is longer for dropouts than for high school graduates.[18] In the years 1959 and 1960, 48.9 percent of high

[17] For the following unemployment figures the author is indebted to Daniel H. Kruger, "School Dropouts—A Tragic Manpower Problem." (Mimeographed)

[18] U. S. Department of Labor, *Monthly Labor Review,* May 1961, p. 468.

school graduates looked for work less than five weeks, in contrast to 41.1 percent of the dropouts. Only 5.3 percent of the high school graduates looked for work 27 weeks or more; in contrast 15.5 percent of the dropouts looked for work 27 weeks or more.

The younger the dropout the greater difficulty he has in finding employment. Young workers 16 and 17 years old who were not enrolled in school had an unemployment rate of 20.9 percent, whereas 18- and 19-year-olds had an unemployment rate of 14.9 percent.

What Kinds of Jobs Are Available to Dropouts?

The U. S. Department of Labor cites evidence to indicate that the better jobs are given to high school graduates while the more menial tasks go to the dropouts.[19] Almost 50 percent of the 1960 high school graduates were in good clerical and sales jobs compared to 12 percent of school dropouts. By contrast one-third of the school dropouts held service and nonfarm labor jobs as against only 17 percent of the school graduates. Almost one-fourth of the school dropouts, but only one-sixth of the graduates, were "operatives and kindred workers," which are typical factory jobs.

There are dramatic contrasts between the kinds of jobs for which young women graduates and dropouts are hired.[20] In 1960, 70 percent of the female graduates 16–19 years of age held clerical jobs. Only 16 percent of the female dropouts held such jobs. Over one-fifth of the female dropouts were operatives and kindred workers. Another 20 percent were service workers, as compared with about 10 percent of the girl graduates.

There is also a sharp difference between the occupational status of male high school graduates and male school dropouts. Almost one-fourth of the male graduates had clerical and sales jobs as compared with less than 5 percent of the dropouts. Fifteen percent of the graduates held laborers' jobs, whereas 27 percent of the dropouts were so employed.

The foregoing evidence indicates that there is indeed a significant relationship between education and unemployment. The completion of at least a high school education is becoming a requisite for employment. Generally speaking, the more years of formal education workers have, the less is their rate of unemployment, and the higher is their occupational status.

[19] *Ibid.,* p. 466.
[20] See U. S. Department of Labor, Washington, D. C., Special Labor Force Reports, No. 5, 1960.

From data like that just considered we can formulate a picture of the occupational prospects of the dropout. They are anything but bright.

What Happens to School Dropouts?

1. A large percentage of them are unemployed, and they are unemployed for longer periods of time than their counterparts who graduate from high school. This high rate of unemployment among youth creates a social condition which James B. Conant describes as "social dynamite." [21]

2. Most school dropouts work at unskilled and menial tasks. They find themselves unprepared in a labor market which is constantly demanding higher levels of education. The jobs the dropouts can find frequently offer only irregular employment and are least open for advancement. Even if opportunities for advancement do present themselves dropouts cannot compete with others who have better educational credentials to offer.

3. The competition which dropouts face grows continuously keener. Because of the rapid rise in birthrates in the 1940's and 1950's the youth population is increasing especially fast, from 2.6 million in 1960 to 3.8 million in 1965, up nearly 50 percent in five years. The 1965 rate will continue through 1970.

At the very time when the number of unskilled occupations is declining and the number of youths competing for them is increasing, the dropout seeks employment. It is estimated that 7.5 million youths will drop out of school during the decade of the 1960's.[22] They will enter a labor market already overcrowded with unskilled workers at a time when fewer than ever before are being employed.

4. The life earnings of the dropout are low. During his lifetime the dropout will earn much less than the high school graduate.

The plight of the dropout presents the school and the teacher with a crucial problem and an unusual opportunity.

A New Task for the School

The high status that is given college attendance today exerts an understandable pressure on the schools to gear their programs to the needs of the college-bound students. Schools naturally take pride in

[21] James B. Conant, National Committee for Children and Youth, "Social Dynamite in Our Cities," *Social Dynamite*, Report of the Conference on Unemployed, Out-of-School Youth in Urban Areas, Washington, D. C., 1961.

[22] Norton, *op. cit.*, p. 61.

the number of graduates who have been accepted in colleges and universities, and especially in prestige institutions of higher learning. The winners of National Merit Scholarships are applauded in the school and community, and comfort is extended to the student who is turned down by the college or university of his first choice and has to accept his second or third choice. Today college attendance is viewed as virtually a prerequisite for success and as the only passport to happiness.

In this chapter we are considering another large group of students, those who do not even graduate from high school and whose highest aspirations frequently are to escape the daily frustrations which the school inflicts; to get a job, earn some money, and be independent.

6. James Bryant Conant has stated that "it is worse for a boy to remain in school and become frustrated than to leave school and get a satisfying job." [23] Do you agree or disagree?

The evidence in this chapter strongly indicates that the dropout's first aspiration, that of leaving the school, is more easily achieved than the others. He enters the world of work as an "education casualty," as W. Willard Wirtz points out in the lead sentence to this chapter, having added no skill to the strength in his arms and back.

The dropout challenges the schools with a series of dilemmas not unlike his own. At the very time when students who have college admission as their goal place greater and greater demands upon the schools, the problems of the dropout are becoming most acute. The two factors are related; as a school gives increasing attention and resources to its college-bound youth, the potential dropout's feelings of alienation from the school are intensified. As Goodwin Watson states: "One factor which complicates the problem is pressure from middle class and upper class spokesmen for higher academic standards in public schools. College subject matter has been introduced in the high school, and the mathematics and language once taught in high school is now being required of elementary school pupils. This may have a salutary effect on some of the pupils who are high in aptitude for this kind of study, but it has probably widened the gap between the existing motives of most lower class families and the goals schoolteachers pursue in their classrooms." [24] The already sharp distinction be-

[23] James B. Conant, "Public Concerns for All American Youth," *Ladies Home Journal,* Volume 77, No. 30, May 1960, pp. 30, 184.

[24] Goodwin Watson, *No Room at the Bottom,* Washington, D. C., Project on the Educational Implications of Automation, National Education Association, 1963, pp. 4–5.

tween the dropout's aspirations and those of other students can only become sharper in his mind. If he already has doubts about the relevance of school to his own future, the school's emphasis upon academic, college-oriented programs will hardly dispel them.

7. Edward W. Chase says: "The biggest failure of American education is . . . the way in which it is turning millions of young people into unemployables. . . . This menacing situation is a direct consequence of the gross imbalance of our educational system. Its attention has been overwhelmingly concentrated on the 20 percent of students who go through college. The vocational future of the other 80 percent has been either ignored or sabotaged by an archaic system of job training. It is a system that produces unneeded farmers, cabinetmakers, and weavers, while the demand is rising for business machine repairmen, chefs, auto mechanics, and electrical servicemen, to mention only a few of the skills in short supply." [25] Find out what you can from some representative high school vocational programs to determine if Chase's charge is justified.

Clearly the dropout presents a new challenge to the schools. What can the schools do about them? John W. Gardner suggests some ways in which schools can meet this challenge, and they are worthy of consideration here.[26]

Giving status to alternatives to college. The student who is not academically inclined frequently feels rejected in a school where the dominant emphasis is on college admission. He regards himself as a second-class citizen, shunted into low-prestige vocational streams, and given the leftovers from the academic table.

The school can do much to give status and meaning to noncollege programs. College admission programs need not and should not be regarded as the sole means of establishing one's human worth. It is *not* the goal of democracy that every citizen should be a brain surgeon or a top executive. It *is* the goal of democracy that every individual fulfill his own potentialities and live a meaningful and satisfying life within the limits of his abilities. The school, through the worth it attaches to *all* programs serving *all* students, can help give dignity to programs designed to help youth find employment after high school graduation.

The school's ability to give importance to programs for employment-bound youth depends in part upon how well it is equipped to ease the transition from school to job.

[25] E. W. Chase, "Learning to Be Unemployable," *Harper's Magazine,* Volume 226, No. 1355, April 1962, p. 33.
[26] The Carnegie Corporation, New York, *Annual Report,* 1960.

Easing the transition from high school to job. The transition from high school to job is too frequently an unceremonious rejection: If the student does poorly in school he seeks employment. Some schools are now devising means to make this transition a carefully planned transfer to a new setting for personal growth. Instead of feeling that he has been dropped from the scrap heap, the student needs to feel that he is being moved into new and significant experiences.

Basic to this approach is the recognition that preparation for this transition must begin early. The abilities to read and write, to handle basic mathematics, to know something about himself and the world around him, are essential to every young person's eventual transfer to the world of work. The nonintellectual lessons that the school provides are important in the transition, too. Learning good habits of work, of self-discipline, and of working with others are all basic to employment.

In addition, vocational programs of high quality must be available for those young people who do not want to go on to college but whose abilities fit them for skilled work.[27] Another means of providing an effective transition between school and community is the work-study program, in which the student spends part of his day, or week, on the job and part in school. Such programs deserve to be enriched in quality and should be adopted on wider scales than they have been to date.

Arrangements that make it easy for a young dropout to resume his education can soften the transition from school to employment. Many dropouts do not realize until a year or two later that their lack of education is a grievous handicap. The common answer to this problem is the night school. In existing night classes will be found a high proportion of youth who ended their formal schooling and have returned for further education.

Finally, all transitional experiences which the school provides will be more effective if they are backed up by first-class counseling services. The good counselor helps the potential dropout to see attractive alternatives to dropping out, and to see how he can better achieve his goals through other courses of action.

The successful transition of young people from school to job becomes easier as the artificial walls between the schools and the community break down. Fortunately these walls are crumbling. The development of educational programs in industry, the military, and business is striking evidence of the growing community of interest be-

---

[27] For a good description of such programs see Grant Venn, *Man, Work, and Education,* Washington, D. C., American Council on Education, 1964.

tween the formal system of schooling and programs outside. These programs are impressing upon all the fact that learning in our technological society must be a continuing enterprise. We are coming to recognize that education should be lifelong, that it may be interrupted at times, and that it may take place in many settings. Perhaps the finest contribution that the school can make to a potential dropout, or to any other student, is to develop in him a wholesome attitude toward lifelong learning.

The teacher and the potential dropout. The school's programs are embodied in teachers. Students do not see the school as a series of curricula or guidance programs. Instead, they regard the school in more human terms, as a group of personalities such as students, teachers, counselors, supervisors, and principals.

Any discussion of school dropouts must end where the school program expresses itself in terms of human interaction between teachers and students. What is the teacher's responsibility to the potential dropout? How can a teacher increase the possibility that students in his classroom will not drop out? If he can do that, his classroom will probably be a more attractive place to learn for all students.

Herbert Thelen indicates that there are two ways to approach the problem of the dropout:

"One way assumes that our schools are fine the way they are and that the cause of dropping out must therefore be sought in personality and in social conditions outside the school. A person with this orientation tends to seek procedures for rehabilitating or recapturing the student after he has dropped out. The other approach assumes that students drop out because school is less attractive, more punishing, or less useful than life outside of school. A person with this orientation is less prone to ask what to do with dropouts and more prone to ask how to keep people in. Both approaches are necessary." [28]

In the course of this book we have examined the social conditions that influence learning *both inside and outside* the school. The good teacher remembers how the child's environment *everywhere* conditions his ability to learn. The teacher is frequently unable to affect the child's out-of-school environment. But if he knows how that environment profoundly influences the child's attitudes toward school and achievement, he will know better how to teach the child in school.

School is for most children a series of challenges. It is important that the teacher learn ways to fit the challenge to the child. A series

[28] Watson, *op. cit.*, p. 34.

of challenges successfully met leads on to more success. A series of challenges unsuccessfully met leads to repeated failures. Most dropouts have repeated their failures to the point where they are humiliated, confused, and resentful. Dropping out is a way to avoid these painful encounters. The good teacher makes it possible for the potential dropout to have experiences which resemble those of students who succeed in school. For the dropout success rather than failure needs to become habitual.

The problem, then, is to permit the student to find an area of challenge where he can learn to operate with success rather than failure. Goodwin Watson puts the matter succinctly this way: [29]

"Psychological study can identify for any learner an area of challenge that is hard enough that its mastery will bring a sense of accomplishment and easy enough that the individual feels he has a fair chance to succeed. A good illustration is a dart game. If the player stands too close to the target, he can make a perfect score, but it is no fun. If he stands too far away, his lack of success becomes discouraging. At the right distance, the zest of the game is at its peak. The player thinks he may well succeed, but it is not a foregone conclusion. He cannot be sure, but it is fun to try and elation to succeed.

"It is important to note that the learner can estimate his own area of challenge better than a teacher can. It would be a hopelessly complicated job for a teacher to devise every assignment so it would fall in the area of challenge for every pupil. It is not too difficult, however, for a teacher to create a classroom climate within which each pupil enjoys the excitement of setting goals which provide satisfactory challenges to him."

If the teacher can create a classroom climate in which "each pupil enjoys the excitement of setting goals," the teacher, too, will enjoy the true excitement of teaching.

REFERENCES

Paperbacks

Automation: Implications for the Future. Morris Philipson, Editor. (Orig.) (V46) Vintage Books, Random House, 457 Madison Ave., New York ($1.95).

Automation. William Francois. (Orig.) (AS525) Collier Books, 60 Fifth Ave., New York (95¢).

Challenge of Youth. (Orig. title: *Youth, Change and Challenge.*) Erik H. Erikson, Editor. (A438) Anchor Books and Anchor Science Study Series, Doubleday and Co., 277 Park Ave., New York ($1.45).

[29] *Ibid.,* p. 12.

Dropouts. Terrence A. Sprague. (Orig.) Great Outdoors Publishing Co., 4747 28th St. North, St. Petersburg, Fla. ($1.00).

Education and Democratic Ideals. Gordon C. Lee. (Orig.) Harcourt, Brace and World, 757 Third Ave., New York ($1.95).

Education and Income: Inequalities of Opportunity in Our Public Schools. Patricia Sexton. (C168) Compass Books, The Viking Press, 625 Madison Ave., New York ($1.65).

Education in Depressed Areas. A. Harry Passow, Editor. Teachers College, Teachers College Press, 525 West 120th St., New York ($2.50).

How Much Is a College Degree Worth to You? William V. Levy. (Orig.) (60-S-505) Macfadden Book, Macfadden-Bartell Corp., 205 East 42nd St., New York (60¢).

Human Problems in Technological Change. Edward H. Spicer. (Illus.) Science Editions Paperbacks, John Wiley and Sons, 605 Third Ave., New York ($1.65).

In Defense of Youth. Earl C. Kelley. (Orig.) (S-30) Spectrum Books, Prentice-Hall, Englewood Cliffs, N. J. ($1.95).

Of Men and Machines. Arthur O. Lewis, Jr., Editor. (Orig.) (D-130) Dutton Paperbacks, E. P. Dutton and Co., 201 Park Ave. South, New York ($1.95).

Slums and Suburbs. James B. Conant. New American Library of World Literature, 1301 Ave. of the Americas, New York (60¢).

Books

Borow, Henry, Editor, *Man in a World of Work.* Boston: Houghton Mifflin Co., 1964. Part II discusses occupations in relation to youth. Part IV deals with the professional practice of vocational guidance.

Burchill, George W., *Work-Study Programs for Alienated Youth; A Case Book.* Chicago: Science Research Associates, 1962. Nine case studies convey policy suggestions and practical guidelines.

Gottlieb, David, and Charles Romsey, *The American Adolescent.* Homewood, Ill.: The Dorsey Press, 1964. Chapter 8 discusses occupational choice from three points of reference: the social system, the structure of the labor force, and the adolescent himself.

Lichter, Solomon O., et al., *The Drop-Outs.* New York: The Free Press of Glencoe, 1962. The authors investigate the interrelationships between emotional and familial problems at home and underachievement and behavioral problems at school.

Project on the Educational Implications of Automation, *Automation and the Challenge to Education,* Luther H. Evans and George E. Arnstein, Editors. Washington, D. C.: National Education Association, January 1962. The economic worth of education and structural changes in employment are among the topics discussed.

Schreiber, Daniel, Editor, *Guidance and the School Dropout.* Washington, D. C.: National Education Association, 1964. The main focus of the book is on the potential school dropout and the implications for the school counselor.

Schreiber, Daniel, Editor, *The School Dropout.* Washington, D. C.: National Education Association, 1964. Papers in this symposium deal with the societal factors influencing the school dropout and the implications for school programs.

Periodicals

Arnold, Walter M., "An All-Age, All-Job Program," *American Education,* Vol. 1, No. 1, January 1965, pp. 8–11. The author describes a variety of vocational education projects that are attempting to solve problems related to the dropout and automation.

"Automation's Challenge to Education and Human Values; A Special Issue," *School and Society,* Vol. 92, No. 2248, October 31, 1964. A series of articles by leading authors makes up this issue devoted to the problems created by automation and the human need to do something about them.

Clague, Ewan, "The Occupational Outlook," *The Bulletin of the National Association of Secondary School Principals,* Vol. XLVIII, No. 295, 1964, pp. 37–44. The analysis points out that the most rapidly growing occupations are generally those that require the most education and training.

Evans, Luther H., "The Challenge of Automation to Education," *The American Behavioral Scientist,* Vol. VI, No. 3, November 1962. Evans describes the impact of technology upon education. He sees a lifelong formal learning process in store for the general population.

Hechinger, Fred M., "Technology's Challenge to Education," *Saturday Review,* Vol. XLVII, No. 50, December 12, 1964, pp. 21–22. The author sees priorities for education in an age of technology.

Heckscher, August, "Reflections on the Manpower Revolution," *The American Scholar,* No. 4, 1964, pp. 568–578. This article discusses the changing work force and the depth of the problems of the unemployed.

Hepfinger, Charles J., "The Dropout—Who Didn't Drop Out," *Industrial Arts and Vocational Education,* Vol. 53, No. 1, January 1964, pp. 19–21. What a counselor did to help a potential dropout complete high school.

Honn, Floyd R., "A Pilot Program to Aid Returning School Dropouts," *Journal of Secondary Education,* Vol. 40, No. 4, April 1965, pp. 177–183. Two hundred seventy students dropped out; 105 agreed to come back; 35 completed the school year.

Index